MW01120944

WILLEM VAN AARDT

COVID-19 LAWLESSNESS

How the vaccine mandates, mask mandates,
and the perpetual state of emergency
are unethical and unlawful in terms
of natural law, the social contract,
and modern international human rights law

Mallard Publications-Chicago

Copyright Notice
Copyright © 2022 by Willem van Aardt. All rights reserved. Printed in the United States of America. No portion of this book may be reproduced, stored in a retrieval system, or transmitted in any form or by any means electronic, mechanical, photocopying, recording, scanning, or other – except for brief quotations in critical reviews or articles – without the prior written permission of the publisher.

Paperback ISBN: 979-8-9870465-1-7 | E-book ISBN: 979-8-9870465-0-0
Hardcover ISBN: 979-8-9870465-2-4

First edition.

Legal Disclaimer
The legal research and independent peer-reviewed studies set out in this book are provided for informational and educational purposes only and are believed to be current and accurate at the time of publication. It is not intended as, and should not be construed to be, legal advice or legal guidance. The information is not intended to substitute professional legal advice or consultations with licensed domestic legal professionals. Before taking any actions based on the research or general information provided in this book, the counsel of a local licensed attorney or other legal professional, within the jurisdiction that you are domiciled should be sought, to ensure that you fully understand your individual legal risks and legal obligations.

Medical Disclaimer
The author is not a medical professional and nothing in this publication constitutes medical advice. The medical research and independent peer-reviewed studies in this book are provided for information purposes only and are believed to be current and accurate at the time of publication. It is not medical advice and should in no way be relied upon for any diagnostic or treatment purposes. The information is not intended to substitute professional medical advice or consultations with licensed healthcare professionals. Before taking any actions based on the research or general information provided in this book, the services of a licensed doctor or other medical professional with knowledge of your personal circumstances should be sought.

Limits of Liability and Disclaimer of Warranty
The author and publisher shall not be liable for the use or misuse of any of the information contained in this publication. The book is strictly for informational and educational purposes only.

Acknowledgments

Cover Designer:	Vanessa Mendozzi (London, United Kingdom)
Developmental Editor:	Brian Spindler (New York, NY, United States)
Interior Designer:	Vanessa Mendozzi (London, United Kingdom)
Proofreaders:	Ben Bredenkamp (Pretoria, South Africa)
	James Ryan (Laugharne Township, United Kingdom)
Language Practitioner:	Tinus Kühn (Pretoria, South-Africa)
Publicist:	Dalyn Miller (Chicago, IL, United States)
Typographer:	Vanessa Mendozzi (London, United Kingdom)

The author and publisher gratefully acknowledge permission to reference and reproduce copyright material in this book. Every effort has been made to trace copyright holders and give recognition, but if any copyright infringements have been made the author and publisher would be grateful for information that would enable any omissions or errors to be corrected in subsequent impressions and online versions. The publisher can be contacted at covid19lawlessness@mallardpublications.com.

Willem van Aardt

is an International Human Rights and Constitutional Law specialist who resides in Barrington, Illinois, a northwestern suburb of the Chicago area. He obtained B.Proc. (*Cum Laude*) and LL.M. degrees from the University of Pretoria (South Africa) in 1994 and 1996 and finalized his *Doctor Legum* degree in Public Law through the North-West University (South Africa) in 2005. After completing his articles and being admitted as an Attorney of the High Court of South Africa in 1996, Willem was also admitted as a Solicitor of the Supreme Court of England and Wales during 2005. In 2017 he relocated to the United States of America. In 2020 he was appointed as an Extraordinary Research Fellow North-West University, Research Unit: Law, Justice, and Sustainability. Willem is the author of numerous peer-reviewed articles relating to the violation of fundamental human rights during the COVID-19 pandemic. Over the past two years Willem's articles have been downloaded and read by thousands of researchers in more than 120 countries globally.

CONTENTS

EPIGRAPH

For two years now we have been witnessing a global *coup d'état*, in which a financial and ideological elite has succeeded in seizing control of part of national governments, public and private institutions, the media, the judiciary, politicians and religious leaders. All of these, without distinction, have become enslaved to these new masters who ensure power, money and social affirmation to their accomplices. Fundamental rights, which up until yesterday were presented as inviolable, have been trampled underfoot in the name of an emergency: today a health emergency, tomorrow an ecological emergency...

This global *coup d'état* deprives citizens of any possibility of defense, since the legislative, executive, and judicial powers are complicit in the violation of law, justice, and the purpose for which they exist. It is a global *coup d'état* because this criminal attack against citizens extends to the whole world, with very rare exceptions. It is a world war, where the enemies are all of us, even those who unwittingly have not yet understood the significance of what is happening. It is a war fought not with weapons but with illegitimate rules, wicked economic policies, and intolerable limitations of natural rights.

Supranational organizations, financed in large measure by the conspirators of this *coup d'état,* are interfering in the government of individual nations and in the lives, relationships, and health of billions of people. They are doing it for money, certainly, but even more so in order to centralize power...

Archbishop Carlo Maria Viganò
November, 16 2021

Lawlessness:

*"A state of disorder due to
a disregard of the rule of law"*

PREFACE

"Knowledge makes a man unfit to be a slave."

— Frederick Douglass

To what extent can a State legitimately enact a state of emergency and restrict the human rights of its citizens in order to serve the common good? Moreover, to what extent has the protection of the nation's health been a pretense for States to illicitly limit and erode basic human rights? These questions enlivened by a deep-rooted skepticism of self-serving big business-big government partnerships and ensuing totalitarianism that has historically led to barbarism and immeasurable human suffering form the foundation of this book.

The main reasons for this book are:

1. To provide an *ex post facto* independent objective international legal analysis of the human rights and bioethical normative rules and standards in relation to vaccine mandates and other COVID-19 restrictions.
2. To educate ordinary citizens with the relevant legal, moral, and ethical laws regarding their innate God-given fundamental human rights that no man can take away from them.
3. To clearly set out those peremptory fundamental human rights, in terms of international human rights law (IHRL), that no government may ever violate, not even during a public health emergency.
4. To expose the dishonesty and central fiction of the perpetual state of emergency that is the "arch of power" and anti-juridical governmental technique to expand authoritarian power.
5. To lay bare the illegality of COVID-19 emergency measures such as lockdowns, mask mandates, isolation mandates, and vaccine mandates in terms of the social contract and contemporary IHRL.

6. To distill a set of conceptual, analogical, and legal perspectives that might help interpret the significance of the present rise of government lawlessness.

7. To provide the general public with the truth and expose the mainstream misinformation propaganda and scientific fraud propagated during the pandemic.

8. To reveal the dramatic similarities between pharmacratic controls in Nazi Germany and COVID-19 public health measures instituted in the West.

9. To show that the effort to replace constitutional democracy with global biomedical fascism in light of the World Economic Forum's (WEF's) "Great Reset" model of public private partnerships (PPPs) between "Big Business" and "Big State" is not only ill-conceived but historically proven to be doomed to lead to misery, death, and destruction.

10. To encourage COVID-19 marginalized, dispossessed, and injured with the knowledge that history and the rule of law is on their side!

11. To provide an abstract legal framework to hold to account those responsible and liable who have committed, planned, ordered, executed, and profited from the COVID-19 human rights abuses, and to compensate victims.

12. To highlight the dysfunctional condition of the United Nations' specialized agencies and international juridical order that no longer maintains, guards, or enforces IHRL and *jus cogens* norms and what should be done to restore it.

Disregard and contempt for human rights in Hitler's Third Reich resulted in barbarous acts that outraged the conscience of humanity and led to the implementation of IHRL safeguards to prevent a recurrence following the Second World War. The era of modern human rights law commenced in 1945 with the drafting of the Charter of the United Nations and the convening of the International Military Tribunal at Nuremberg.[1] Individuals once considered mere objects of the sovereign were now deemed subjects of international law with positive legal claims to protection, not only from State tyranny and oppression, but also to protection by the State from human rights abuses by non-State actors.[1]

International law acknowledges and permits governments to govern and implement public policy to protect their citizens against external and internal threats. History teaches that rule by mandate during declared states of emergency is often correlated with decreased respect for human rights.[1] International law mitigates this risk by subjecting States to several legal frameworks protective of fundamental human rights, such as IHRL and international law's regime for regulating emergencies. Within this legal framework, some norms, such as the prohibitions on torture, slavery, arbitrary detention, and medical experimentation without free and informed consent, are regarded as peremptory or *jus cogens* and are of a kind from which no limitation or derogation is permitted – not even during a declared *justitium* (state of emergency)![1]

In 2020, power-hungry plutocrats and government officials abruptly and unlawfully seized power from the world's citizens by gutting sacred fundamental human rights and freedoms in the name of combating a disease with a global infection fatality rate of less than 0.15% in violation of international law and international covenant obligations![2] Numerous non-sensical and arbitrary public health dictates were implemented, violating citizens' rights to freedom of speech, freedom of movement, freedom of assembly, freedom of religion, and freedom from medical experimentation. Ordinary citizens were treated as "raw material to be experimented on, processed, and wasted at will."[3] Shocking eyewitness accounts of human rights abuses in countries such as Austria, Australia, Belgium, Canada, France, Germany, Italy, the Netherlands, New Zealand, Spain, the United Kingdom, and the United States under COVID-19 passport rules reveal medical police States gone completely mad. It is not overstating things to describe the COVID-19 biomedical pseudo-juridical order as a madhouse in which the lunatics are running the asylum and the inmates are being punished for their sanity.

These arbitrary public health mandates were an illegitimate exercise of unchecked power not authorized by IHRL, natural law, or the social contract. COVID-19 vaccine mandates, mask mandates, and isolation mandates are illegal, unethical, and immoral. Bought and paid-for biomedical despots are fallaciously proclaiming that these mandates are perfectly lawful and in the interest of public health and the greater good while contravening key international legal and bioethical principles and norms. History has proven that "For the greater good [is] the phrase that always precedes the greatest evil."[4]

Pre-pandemic, an estimated two billion people worldwide were struggling to put food on their tables. Worldwide about nine million people die each year of hunger, 690 million people globally are undernourished, and an estimated 14 million children under the age of five suffer from severe acute malnutrition. This was and is not considered an emergency, but for a virus with a survival rate of 99.85%, it is considered necessary to change the world. We have seen a worldwide collaborative effort to vaccinate every human being on the planet, but never a global attempt to feed every human being! The COVID-19 response has never been about health nor the greater good![5]

Throughout the COVID-19 pandemic, many government leaders and public health officials breached their fiduciary duties to the public by violating inviolable fundamental human rights. What should have been a fight against the pandemic to protect the people became a fight against the people to preserve and increase the power and profits of the global political and corporate aristocracy. Since the onset of the COVID-19 pandemic, the world witnessed a creeping replacement of democratic States with fascist pharmacratic forms of government imposing pseudo-medical political solutions in the form of various public health mandates monitored and censored by dominant transnational technology companies that increasingly and inexorably erodes fundamental human rights and freedoms. Under the guise of a global pandemic, the dominant political ideology has been transformed from liberal constitutional democracy legitimized by the rule of law to illiberal unconstitutional managed democracy legitimized by pseudo-science and biomedical collectivism.

Fascism, which in essence represents a disguised corrupt collaboration between the political and corporate elite, constantly contorts and corrupts law and science to legitimize its violation of fundamental human rights and freedoms. Opinions and facts become interchangeable. Truth is no longer based on factual data and verifiable proof; it is based on ideology and sentiment. Lies become true. Fascism is a semantic social strategy designed to manipulate, mislead, subvert and control to mask the lawless pursuit of money and power.[6,7,8]

The biomedical fascist State utilizing a continual state of emergency as a mechanism and technique of government to obtain and sustain fascist totalitarian rule (subsequent to collusion between the political elite and the ultra-wealthy corporate elite) is not new. Hitler's Third Reich with its obsession with public health and genetics is a prime example.[9] What is unique in the COVID-19 era is the worldwide implementation of pharmacratic principles in nearly all United Nations Member States, newfound conjectural gene-editing biotechnology, and advanced technology to enforce and monitor mandatory biomedical procedures that could have dire ramifications for humanity. When we study the birth of the gruesome fascist regimes in Germany and Italy in the previous century, it is important to note that the technique of government utilized to transform sophisticated democratic societies into totalitarian States was the groundless declaration of an enduring state of emergency with an extra-juridical character. Similarly, the defining feature of the current transformation that operates "through the introduction of a sanitation terror and a religion of health", is that the mechanism that renders it formally possible "is not a new body of laws", but the state of emergency, in other words, not an affirmation of but a suspension of constitutional guarantees.[8,10] In fact, under the paradigm of a perpetual near-global COVID-19 state of emergency, the entire political-juridical life of Western societies assumed a new totalitarian form of government that conflates political-biomedical and economic crises and objectives.[11] In the words of Italian philosopher Giorgio Agamben, "From the real state of exception in which we live it is not possible to return to a state of law, for at issue now are the very concepts of 'State' and 'law'. But it is possible to attempt to halt the machine, to show its central fiction…."[11]

While the versions of totalitarianism represented by 1930's German and Italian fascism consolidated power by ousting the established democratic governance system and structures through revolution, unrestrained COVID-19 era power represents a drive towards totality that draws power from a *modus operandi* that corrupts; subverts; and then manipulates, manages and controls established democratic governance structures to defeat the original purpose. It is Nazism turned upside-down, "inverted totalitarianism."[12]

With the victory of the United States and its allies in the Cold War and the collapse of the Soviet Union in 1989, the balance of power that led to the post-Second World War juridical order ended. The United States bestrides the world like no other power since the Roman Empire. Because politics entails exercising power and influence, American hegemony presents a problem. Whichever forces, ideology, or value system rules the polity of the United States and its allies, rules the world. When the United States became amoral, pharmacratic, lawless, and fascist, the world followed suit. The globalization of the world economy and waves of deregulation and privatization have facilitated the emergence and increased the power of large transnational corporations that have acquired great influence on both the global economic and political systems, including the perversion and corruption of the world hegemon the United States and its Western allies. Through the undue corporate influence on the United Nations and its various specialized agencies such as the World Health Organization (WHO) and the Office of the United Nations High Commissioner for Human Rights (OHCHR) globally and constitutional democratic principles nationally, States are managed and controlled by the global elite, and citizens are oblivious to those who exercise real power.

Characterized by obscurity, the global elite professed to pay fealty to the rule of law, human rights, and liberal democracy, but secretly had seized all the levers of power nationally and internationally to render the citizen impotent. The *dispositif* (that is, not based upon a monist conception of sovereignty) as an apparatus to control humanity manifested itself and is employed with perfection to coerce, fool, and rule the public. "The general population doesn't know what's happening, and it doesn't even know that it doesn't know."[13]

The citizen's attention is consumed by the contemporary equivalent of the Roman arena. Non-stop mainstream media propaganda and cliché-ridden "greater good" slogans assuring the public that the freedoms we cherish remain inviolable and that the State is protecting "the health of the nation," dominate the international and national discourse as these very freedoms are taken from us by medical mandate. The propaganda and slogans are a stupendous scam to keep the *populus* enslaved to a system of thinking that keeps them mentally ignorant and dependent. As Noem Chomsky stated:

> As long as the general population is passive, apathetic, diverted to consumerism or hatred of the vulnerable, then the powerful can do as they please, and those who survive will be left to contemplate the outcome.[14]

Through this *dispositif*, the individual is transformed into both a subject and an object of power relations.[15] This network of relations responded to the COVID-19 emergency and organized, oriented, and fixed outcomes in favor of the global elite and impeded any opposition.[16,17] Despite these *dispositifs* having a creative force in that they are responsible for the ordering of society, the nature of biopolitics means that those very same *dispositifs* also have a destructive dimension. They control and order which lives are worth preserving and which are not. Biopower (or the techniques of government that translate life into an element of the financial system) focuses on punitive and controlling mechanisms designed to transform and influence human life, improve health and extend the life of the elect. Videlicet, biopower endeavors to sustain life, even with horrendous misery and death.[18] This deadly combination of biopower and sovereign power, exemplified in Nazi Germany, was on full display during the COVID-19 pandemic as a key condition of Western politics.[17] What COVID-19 biopolitical practices and strategies entailed was not just the ability to act lawlessly under the pretense of protecting life (in the name of the common good) but also regulating death. This meant that the demise of any particular individual was insignificant, as life continued at the population level. Indeed, a form of *thanatopolitics*.[19]

You cannot use the word "freedom" when your government mandates you to take an experimental mRNA gene therapy with deadly side-effects while withholding lifesaving affordable alternative medications from yourself and your family! You cannot use the word "freedom" when your government issues arbitrary discriminatory lockdowns destroying private businesses, while declaring big businesses to be essential services. You cannot use the word "freedom" when government agencies conspire with pharmaceutical companies to conduct biosurveillance and quarantine healthy citizens. You cannot use the word "freedom" when it is not possible to vote against the activities of Apple, Blackrock, Google, IBM, Meta (Facebook), Moderna, Microsoft, Pfizer, Twitter Vanguard, and other WEF partners. You cannot use the word "freedom" when all those with a different opinion are censored, canceled, and declared enemies of the State. You cannot use the word "freedom" when our lives have been reduced to a purely biological state. You cannot use the word "freedom" when society is in a constant illicit state of emergency, when we are tracked, biosurveilled, monitored, controlled, and told what we can and cannot do, say and cannot say, think and cannot think. You cannot use the word "freedom" when the State and their transnational corporate handlers put profit before people, ignore IHRL and violate any of your fundamental human rights at will. For this type of governance, you would use the words "master" and "bondservant".

People seem to be under the illusion that because the United Nations, the WHO, and the dominant Western States sidelined universal and inalienable human rights during the COVID-19 pandemic, that these no longer apply; nothing could be further from the truth! Universal human rights are codified in IHRL. All States that are members of the United Nations and signed the Vienna Convention on the Law of Treaties and the core international human rights treaties such as the International Covenant on Civil and Political Rights depicted in dark grey below are legally bound to respect and protect fundamental human rights.[20]

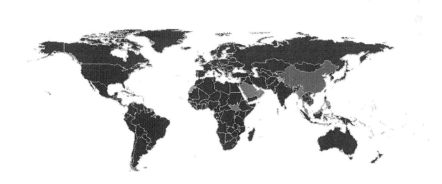

Figure 0.1: Status of Ratification Interactive
Dashboard: International Covenant on Civil and Political Rights
Source: Office of the United Nations High Commissioner
for Human Rights https://indicators.ohchr.org/

States are the primary duty bearers under IHRL. States are obligated to respect, protect, ensure and fulfill human rights to all within their territory. To protect and fulfill core human rights, *jus cogens* and obligations *erga omnes*, States are legally bound to also protect citizens from human rights abuses by non-State actors, such as transnational corporations.[21] Corporate lobbying, corrupt corporate practices, neoliberal ideology, deregulation, privatization, and criminal tax avoidance schemes adorned as billionaire "philanthropic foundations" have weakened the State. Concurrently these policies have enabled increased "market concentration and the accumulation of wealth and economic power in the hands of a relatively small number of corporations" and über-rich global plutocrats with disproportionate control over the global economy.[22] The principles espoused in IHRL, and the *weltanschauung* held by these plutocrats reflect two fundamentally different views of the role of the State. IHRL regulates States as primary duty-bearer, particularly with respect to ensuring respect for human rights and as central providers of public goods and services. In contrast, the plutocrats view States as moderators and facilitators of actions to ensure the increased profitability of various public and private "partnerships".[22] In other words, States are pawns in the hands of the global elite to exploit the citizenry for maximum profit and zero repercussions – quintessentially, global institutionalized organized crime.

A revealing illustration of the biomedical collectivist worldview is the "Global Redesign Initiative" report of the WEF.[22] The report posits that "a globalized world is best 'managed' by a coalition" of transnational corporations, States, the UN system, and select civil society organizations.[22] It contends that States are no longer the "dominant actors on the world stage" and that "the time has come for a new stakeholder paradigm of international governance."[25] The WEF vision incorporates a "public-private" United Nations, in which specialized agencies would work under joint State and non-State control. This model also presumes that specific topics would be taken off the agenda of the United Nations to be addressed by "plurilateral, often multi-stakeholder, coalitions of the willing and able."[22]

Between 2020 and 2022, the world witnessed firsthand the devastating effect of the WEF globalist PPP model that ruthlessly exploits the citizens of the world and led to human rights abuses on a scale unseen hitherto. Under the leadership of Professor Klaus Schwab, the WEF has played a considerable role in coordinating the globalized hegemony of transnational capital over Western democracies during the past three decades. C. Wright Mills in "The Power Elite," one of the finest studies of the pathologies of the plutocrats in previous eras, wrote:

They exploited national resources, waged economic wars among themselves, entered into combinations, made private capital out of the public domain, and used any and every method to achieve their ends. They made agreements with railroads for rebates; they purchased newspapers and bought editors; they killed off competing and independent businesses and employed lawyers of skill and Statesmen of repute to sustain their rights and secure their privileges. There is something demonic about these lords of creation; it is not merely rhetoric to call them robber barons.[23]

Curiously, in October 2019, the WEF and Johns Hopkins University held a training exercise simulating the global response to a worldwide zoonotic coronavirus pandemic. The exercise was sponsored by the Bill and Melinda Gates Foundation and GAVI, the vaccine alliance. The exercise published its findings and recommendations in November 2019 as a "call to action". One month later China recorded its first COVID-19 case and massive profits followed for most major WEF members.[24]

Biomedical fascism, which has, in essence, destroyed our Western constitutional democracies, has given unchecked power to the global plutocratic elite and their political puppets. The international and State apparatus they control now entirely serve their interests. They empower those national and global organizations that keep the *populus* oppressed and debase those organizations that expose their duplicity, corruption, and lies.[25]

Transnational corporations have an essential role in realizing sustainable development goals that will require large-scale changes in corporate practices. Nevertheless, recognizing big businesses' role should not mean advocating the accretion and concentration of wealth and economic power, resulting in an inordinate and amoral corporate influence on global and national policy while disregarding corporate powers' detrimental impact on fundamental human rights.[22] Instead of further promoting the misleading discourse of WEF "multi-stakeholderism" and PPPs that serve only the interest of the global elite, a fundamental change, of course, is necessary.[26-28] To achieve the vision of a better world for all, States have to reclaim their rightful place on the international stage as the primary actors and duty bearers. States should take bold measures to strengthen national public finance, root out corruption, dismantle corporate power and weaken the grip of transnational corporate power.[29] Adherence to and enforcement of international legal covenant obligations that are premised on State loyalty to citizens and not to global corporations is all that will ensure a return to a world where fundamental human rights and freedoms are respected and protected. To re-establish fundamental trust and accountability in society, there is a need to publicly acknowledge the widespread human rights abuses that took place during the COVID-19 pandemic and hold to account those responsible who have planned, ordered, and committed atrocious violations, and to compensate victims or their families.[30]

Across the continuum of risks to public healthcare, innate tensions between the collective good and the individual exist.[8] Recent events have unfortunately shown that, once a "perceived" threat to individual health is in place, the vast majority of people are willing to accept limitations on their fundamental human rights and freedoms they would never before have considered enduring.[10] The public support for draconian COVID-19 policies confirms that most people in the West indeed prefer "health" – or at least what they think is "health" – over fundamental human rights and freedom, disregarding Benjamin Franklin's warning that "they that can give up essential liberty to obtain a little temporary safety, deserve neither liberty nor safety." People fail to recognize that by giving up freedom to attain the delusion of "protection" against COVID-19, they lose both. To acknowledge this is not to preordain the response to the question "How far can the State go?"; instead, it is to be resolute that public health is always subject to IHRL and its peremptory norms that are the supreme law of the international juridical order which all policy determinations should adhere to. Public health is neither above the law nor exempt from the rule of law!

If we want our children to experience the freedoms, liberties, and opportunities that we experienced in the post-Second World War pre-COVID-19 era, we need to challenge the biomedical fascists and expose their inherently lawless and anti-humanity agenda.

The freedoms we surrender today are freedoms that our children will not be able to enjoy and that our grandchildren will never know existed. The righteousness of the law is on our side, but if we want to see justice, "we the people" will have to insist that our governments start acting in line with IHRL. The only way to end the illegitimate exercise of lawless COVID-19 powers and prevent future recurrence by the corporate and political elite is by "we the people" raising our voices that this lawlessness will not be tolerated and demanding a return to the "rule of law" through legitimate political action and civil disobedience.

Dr. Willem van Aardt
September 23, 2022 – Chicago IL USA

ACRONYMS

AAICJ	American Association for the International Commission of Jurists
AE	Adverse Event
BLA	Biologics License Application
BMJ	British Medical Journal
BMGF	The Bill & Melinda Gates Foundation
CIDRAP	University of Minnesota's Institute for Infections Disease and Research Policy
COVID-19	Coronavirus Disease 2019
CRC	Convention on the Rights of the Child
CDC	United States Centers for Disease Control and Prevention
CEPI	Coalition for Epidemic Preparedness Innovations
CFR	Case Fatality Ratio
DWTP	Dealing with The Past
ECDC	European Centers for Disease Prevention and Control
ECtHR	European Court of Human Rights
EMA	European Medicines Agency
EUA	Emergency Use Authorization
FCCCA	Frontline COVID-19 Critical Care Alliance
FDA	United States Federal Drug Administration
FOIA	Freedom of Information Act
GAVI	Global Alliance for Vaccines and Immunization (the Vaccine Alliance)
GISAID	Global Initiative on Sharing Avian Influenza Data
HHS	US Department of Health and Human Services
HCQ	Hydroxychloroquine
JAMA	Journal of the American Medical Association
ICCPR	International Covenant on Civil and Political Rights
ICESCR	International Covenant on Economic Social and Cultural Rights
IFI	International Financial Institution
ICJ	International Court of Justice
ICU	Intensive Care Unit
IFS	International Financial Institution
IFR	Infection Fatality Ratio
IHL	International Humanitarian Law

IHRL	International Human Rights Law
IHR	International Human Rights
ILC	International Law Commission
ILA	International Law Association
IVM	Ivermectin
mRNA	Messenger RNA (a type of single-stranded RNA involved in protein synthesis)
MIES	Mask Induced Exhaustion Syndrome
MFP	Mass Formation Psychosis
MIT	Massachusetts Institute of Technology
NEJM	New England Journal of Medicine
NIAID	United States National Institute of Allergy and Infectious Diseases
NIH	United States National Institutes of Health
NHS	United Kingdom National Health Service
NPI	Nonpharmaceutical Interventions
OHCHR	Office of the High Commissioner of Human Rights
ONS	United Kingdom Office for National Statistics
OVIEDO	The Convention for the Protection of Human Rights and Dignity of the Human Being with regard to the Application of Biology and Medicine
PCR	The Reverse-Transcriptase Polymerase Chain Reaction test
RCT	Randomized Controlled Clinical Trial
RNA	Ribonucleic acid (a polymeric molecule essential in various biological roles in coding, decoding, regulation and expression of genes)
SARS-CoV-2	The coronavirus (of the genus) that is the causative agent of COVID-19
SDG	Sustainable Development Goals
TNC	Transnational Corporation
TNI	Trusted News Initiative
UNESCO	The United Nations Educational, Scientific and Cultural Organization
UNHCR	United Nations Human Rights Committee
UDBHR	The Universal Declaration on Bioethics and Human Rights
UDHR	Universal Declaration of Human Rights
UN	United Nations
UNICEF	United Nations International Children's Emergency Fund
VAERS	Vaccine Adverse Event Reporting System
VIS	Vaccine Information Statement
WEF	World Economic Forum
WMA	World Medical Association
WHO	World Health Organization

1. INTRODUCTION

"'For the greater good':
the phrase that always precedes the greatest evil."

— Jakub Bożydar Wiśniewski

Since the onset of the COVID-19 pandemic, a considerable amount of political argument revolved around justifying government actions taken in the name of the "common good" or the "greater good". Lockdowns, mask mandates, social distancing mandates, and vaccine mandates have all focused on safeguarding public health for the "greater good" regardless of consequences.

Clearly, many in the West today believe that the coercive medical control of most freedoms is justified and appropriate because those freedoms are potentially the causes of diseases. When individuals protest over the harm caused by COVID-19 public health measures, the arbitrary nature of these measures, or the erosion of fundamental human rights there are seldom any understanding or good faith reactions. The general thinking is that since the State action was executed in the name of "public health" and the "greater good", this indicates that those opposed to such benevolent government action are selfish and immoral because they do not care about the "greater good" and such self-evidently good causes as the health and safety of the nation!

There are some people who, having examined and evaluated the contradictory research and evidence, have concluded that the iron-fisted COVID-19 public health measures were essential, but they are few and far between. They are vastly outnumbered by individuals who thoughtlessly support any government action performed in the name of public health. "Public health is a good thing" is an incontrovertible statement. The healthier citizens are, the better. But it does not follow that if public health is a good thing, then any State action taken in the name of public health is necessarily also a good thing. The numerous atrocities perpetrated in the name of "the nation's health" and "the common good" in Germany during the 1930s and 1940s are testament to that. Something done in the name of the "greater good" is not automatically good. Purporting to promote the public good and actually promoting the public good are altogether different concepts. Recent State claims to promote the "common good" were "linguistically mediated strategic action" rather than communicative action genuinely orientated towards the eradication of disease. Society applauds, not reviles, the heroes of the past who battled against the atrocities committed by the Nazis in the name of "public health" and the "greater good." Surely, then, people should be able to comprehend how anything that is done in the name of the "greater good" or simply labeled "for the greater good" is not necessarily good. Automatic dismissal of informed criticism of the COVID-19 public health measures is a trait of the most malevolent and ignorant in society.

Aristotle (384–322 BC) utilized the notion of government in "the common interest" (*polity*) as the foundation for his differentiation between "right" constitutions, which are in the common interest, and "wrong" constitutions, which are in the self-interest of corrupt leaders.[1] Thomas Aquinas (1225 -1274) held "the common good" (*bonum commune*) to be the objective of law and just governance.[2] He explains that:

> …all who are included in a community, stand in relation to that community as parts to a whole; while a part, as such, belongs to a whole, so that whatever is the good of a part can be directed to 'the good of the whole.'[2]

In his "Discourses on Livy", Machiavelli (1469-1527) notes that the "common good" (*commune utilità*) is drawn from "a free way of life" (*vivere libero*) and that freedom, safety, dignity, security, enjoyment, and good life are key elements of the common good.[3] James Madison (1751-1836) wrote of the "common good" as being tightly bound with justice and proclaimed that justice is the ultimate goal of the State, while George Mason (1725-1792) argued that any government that is no longer directed to the sole end of "the general good, happiness and safety of the community" and that governs "by laws to which [the people] have not given their consent is no longer government, but tyranny."[4]

According to its primary and broadly accepted sense, the common good indicates "the sum total of social conditions which allow people, either as groups or as individuals, to reach their fulfilment more fully and more easily".[5] Belonging to everyone and to each person, it is and remains "common", because it is indivisible and because only together is it possible to attain it, and safeguard its effectiveness, with regard also to the future.[5] A society that wishes and intends to remain at the service of the human being at every level is a society that has the common good – "the good of all people and of the whole person as its primary goal".[5] The "common good" principle in essence entails the government's duty to protect the fundamental human rights of the individual and the people as a whole. Whenever individual rights are arbitrarily violated the rights of the people as a whole or the common good are automatically jeopardized.[5] Over the course of the past two and a half years we have witnessed a paradoxical phenomenon where States claim to act for "the common good" while destroying the common good through a perpetual state of emergency as paradigm of government that annuls fundamental human rights and the rule of law. It is a paradoxical articulation as it is impossible to obtain the common good (that is, the end of law) without law.[6] As espoused in Dante Alighieri's "*De Monarchia*" (1312-1313):

> ...who-ever intend to achieve the end of law, must proceed with the law [*quicunque finem iuris intendit cum iure gratitur*][6]

The nebulous nature of the "common good" standard will necessarily lead to the imposition by the executive of its own political and social views. The idea that the suspension of law or violation of the juridical order may be necessary for the common good is incompatible with the primordial sources of law.[6] As many States around the globe announced either the relaxation or lifting of COVID-19 restrictions that grossly violated fundamental human rights and freedoms for more than two and a half years, it is essential to reflect on some pertinent questions: Can governments annul peremptory norms or make them conditional to the adherence of medical mandates? Does public health trump fundamental human rights? Is the tyrannical rule by medical mandate a legitimate government phenomenon? Did States adhere to the post-Second World War safeguards to prevent a recurrence of the Nazi biomedical atrocities? Did the State action comply with international human rights law (IHRL)?

COVID-19 has presented many scientific, medical, legal, bioethical, economic, epidemiologic, etiologic, and public health policy challenges. It has brought the tension between individual rights and public health to the forefront of the international discourse.

There are many different perspectives to consider in determining the appropriateness and legitimacy of State action during the COVID-19 pandemic. However, ultimately, the final arbiter on right and wrong, legitimate, and illegitimate is the "rule of law" developed over thousands of years and expressed in the social contract, natural law, and IHRL. The entire legal concept and construct of inalienable fundamental human rights are that the State's power cannot supersede them.

Public Health Über Alles?

Since the beginning of the COVID-19 pandemic, Western States have been powerfully asserting the primacy of public health over individual human rights and civil liberties and used pseudo-medical arguments to justify the expansion of unbridled and intemperate State power.[7] In March 2020, when there was little known about the novel coronavirus, many citizens agreed with the extreme measure of lockdowns to flatten the curve, prepare the health system and protect citizens against a virus that many experts suggested would have a mortality rate of between 3% and 7%. But with the benefit of hindsight (more than 24 months' worth of worldwide granular data, 435,626,514 confirmed cumulative infections;[8] known results of different approaches by different countries) and numerous expert studies around the globe concluding that the crude mortality rate of COVID-19 is approximately 0.0003% to 0.3% (more or less the same as the seasonal flu), it has been evident since the middle of 2020 that the draconian public health measures and restrictions have never been statistically justifiable.

Despite this evidence, fundamental human rights to freedom of speech, freedom of movement, freedom from medical experimentation, freedom of thought, freedom of assembly, and freedom of religion guaranteed by the Universal Declaration of Human Rights (UDHR) and the International Covenant on Civil and Political Rights (ICCPR) were illegitimately violated on a global scale unseen in living memory.[9,10] Many public health measures were comprised of non-sensical arbitrary rules that have no basis or justification in law, medical science, or epidemiology.

In stark contradiction with John F. Kennedy's declaration in 1961 that "the rights of man come not from the generosity of the State but from the hand of God", Western governments are advocating the false narrative that fundamental human rights and freedoms are privileges bestowed upon citizens by their government, if and only if citizens comply with the public health dictates of the State.[11,12] The contention is thus that freedom is earned by absolute subservience to the State's arbitrary public health emergency dictates, adhering to all mandates, and having an up-to-date "vaccine passport." However, did the adherence to the COVID-19 mandates really give individuals freedom? The answer is assuredly and unarguably NO! By adhering to the COVID-19 vaccine, mask, and isolation mandates, citizens were not granted freedom but privileges! To be granted a privilege is very different from freedom. Freedom is not something that you receive from anyone! Freedom is innate in every human being and the God-given birthright of every human being. Freedom is self-determined! Freedom allows the individual to decide what is in his or her best interest. On the other hand, privileges are granted to an individual as a reward for subservience and capitulation to corrupt authority figures! However, the reality is that anyone who extends a privilege to an individual can retract the privilege at any time! They can randomly and arbitrarily change the rules to suit their agendas. By adhering to COVID-19 mask mandates, vaccine mandates, and isolation mandates, citizens were not gaining freedom, but agreeing to the random, whimsical discretion of tyrants, which is the exact opposite of freedom!

COVID-19: When Public Health Trumps Freedom

When public health trumps fundamental human rights, freedom, as a constitutional concept, fades and the illicit is rendered as licit. The global political and corporate fervor to develop and deliver a vaccine to "protect" people against COVID-19 (that did not pose a risk of death to 99.85% of the world population), were extraordinary. Following the Emergency Use Authorization (EUA) of several experimental COVID-19 mRNA vaccines during December 2020 (less than a year after the COVID-19 genetic sequence was published on January 11, 2020), rapid mass vaccination deployment efforts commenced in earnest. By October 1, 2021, a total of 6,143,369,655 vaccine doses had been administered globally. By January 28, 2022, more than 10 billion doses had been administered across 184 countries – a rate of roughly 30.3 million doses a day.[13] In the United States, by the end of January 2022, approximately 64% of the population were fully vaccinated, with more than 537,171,553 vaccine doses having been administered.[14]

In 2021, objective data from across the globe irrefutably proved that the COVID-19 vaccines neither prevent the contraction nor transmission of

COVID-19 nor prevent mortality.[15] Numerous peer-reviewed studies also irrefutably prove that naturally acquired immunity is superior to vaccine-induced immunity.[16,17] In addition, it was established that the COVID-19 vaccines have also caused more deaths and adverse events in less than one year than all other prior vaccines combined over a period of 20 years.[18,19] In January 2022, Israel, one of the most COVID-19 vaccinated and boosted countries in the world with 65% of its population fully vaccinated, became the world leader in daily COVID-19 cases, while in South Africa, with only 26% of its population vaccinated, infections were amongst the lowest in the world.[20,21]

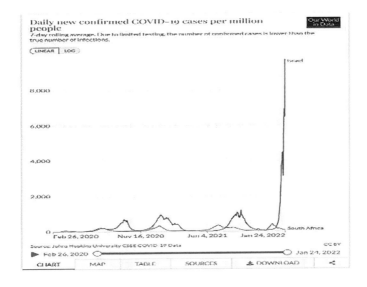

Figure 1.1: Daily new confirmed COVID-19 cases per million: South Africa vs. Israel
Source: Our World in Data, University of Oxford

Numerous countries such as Israel, the United Kingdom, Malaysia, Indonesia, Qatar, Tunisia, Uruguay, and Brazil experienced a significant increase in infection, hospitalization, and excess death rates following the mass vaccination campaigns.[22] In simple terms, the experimental COVID-19 vaccines did not work and posed significant health risks to many people across the globe.

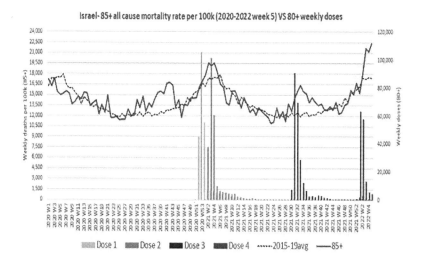

Figure 1.2: Israel 85 + all-cause mortality rate per 100k (2020–2022) week 5
Source: Israel Government Databases https//data.gov.il/dataset/covid-19/resource
and Human Mortality Data Base, Max Planck Institute for Demographic Research
https://mpidr.shinyapps.io/stmortality/

Major public health regulators such as the US Centers for Disease Control and Prevention (CDC), National Institute of Health (NIH), and Federal Drug Administration (FDA) are fraught with conflicts of interest and profits directly from the sale and distribution of COVID-19 vaccines.[23,24] Safe and effective early treatment options and lifesaving medications were completely ignored or suppressed by the World Health Organization (WHO), the US FDA and CDC, the European Centre for Disease Prevention and Control (ECDC), the Africa Centre for Disease Control and Prevention (Africa CDC) and others despite overwhelming scientific evidence that FDA-approved drugs such as Ivermectin and hydroxychloroquine (HCQ) are effective as both a prophylactic and cure against COVID-19, reducing infections, hospitalizations, and death by 86%.[25,26] According to the Yale School of Public Health's Dr. Harvey Risch, HCQ could have saved hundreds of thousands of lives. Hundreds of peer-reviewed studies show a strong correlation between death rates and government suppression of life-saving early treatment drugs.[31]

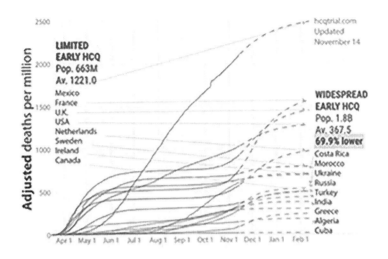

Figure 1.3: Correlation between death rates
and government suppression of early treatment drugs
Source: HCQ for COVID-19: real-time meta-analysis of 352 studies

For the first time in history a president, governors, mayors, hospital administrators, and bureaucrats "were determining medical treatments based not on accurate scientifically based or even experience based information, but rather to force the acceptance of special forms of care and "prevention" – including remdesivir, use of respirators and ultimately a series of essentially untested messenger RNA vaccines."[32] For the first time in history, medical treatment protocols were not being formulated based on the experience of the medical practitioners treating the largest number of patients successfully, "but rather individuals and bureaucracies that have never treated a single patient – including Anthony Fauci, Bill Gates, EcoHealth Alliance, the CDC, WHO, State public health officers and hospital administrators."[32]

Ignoring the science and the data strongly indicating that the COVID-19 vaccine was ineffective and unsafe, the push to get a needle into every arm at any cost has led to numerous States making a COVID-19 vaccine compulsory and implementing vaccine passports.[33,34] Mandatory COVID-19 vaccinations of adults and children (that faced a zero risk of severe illness or death from COVID-19) were implemented by both State and non-State actors such as government agencies, schools, colleges, private employers, airlines, cruise ships, sports stadiums, concert venues, shopping malls, and others.[35] In flagrant disregard of the ICCPR and Nuremberg Code's principal tenet that the voluntary consent of the human subject, without any element of force, duress, overreaching, or coercion, is essential, many Western governments absurdly claimed that obligatory COVID-19 vaccination could be justified and implemented penalties and the loss of freedoms and civil liberties for non-compliance.[36] For the first time in history, numerous States were nonsensically insisting that perfectly healthy people who are not at risk of disease should be vaccinated against their will with a vaccine that is neither safe nor effective.

Protests erupted in cities across the globe in response to illegitimate government efforts to impose COVID-19 vaccine passports. At the end of September 2021, hundreds of thousands of people of all political persuasions commenced mass protests in American, European, and Australian cities to protest government overreach and defend civil liberties. The protests did not have the intended effect of reversing State policies and practices but highlighted the fact that the West is thoroughly divided on the issue of mandatory COVID-19 vaccines.[37]

An important question in the *ex post facto* analysis is whether mandatory COVID-19 vaccination policies not requiring prior free and informed consent are ethical and legal in terms of IHRL and bioethical norms and standards.[38] Oppressive COVID-19 public health policies raise crucial questions regarding the legitimacy, efficacy, necessity, and proportionality of public health guidelines and practices that need to be answered if we value fundamental human rights and freedoms.[39] In pursuing public health policy, it is essential to strike an appropriate balance between the public interest and individual human rights guaranteed by numerous international human rights conventions.[40] If a disease with a crude mortality rate similar to that of the common cold can be used to justify gross violations of fundamental human rights, then governments *de facto* and *de jure* have carte blanche to completely disregard all international human rights obligations with impunity. Sadly, this is precisely what happened. The COVID-19 crisis has been widely abused as illegitimate justification for widespread human rights violations that have no grounding in the rule of law and the post-Second World War international juridical order. In the words of Ayn Rand: "We are fast approaching the stage where the government is free to do anything it pleases while the citizens may act only by permission, which is the stage of the darkest periods of human history, the stage of rule by brute force."[41]

The denial of certain international human rights fundamental to human dignities, such as the right to free and informed consent to medical experimentation, can never legitimately be violated in any conceivable emergency. As asserted by German MEP Christine Anderson in her October 21, 2021, address to the European parliament:

But it is not the goal that renders a system oppressive, it is always the methods by which the goal is pursued. Whenever government claims to have the people's interest at heart you need to think again. In the entire history of mankind there has never been a political elite sincerely concerned about the wellbeing of regular people. What makes any of us think that it is different now? If the age of enlightenment has brought forward anything, then certainly this: Never take anything that any government tells you at face value. Always question everything any government does or does not do. Always look for ulterior motives and always ask, *qui bono*, who benefits. Whenever a political elite pushes an agenda this hard and resort to extortion and manipulation to get their way you can almost always be sure that your benefit is not what they had at heart. As far as I am concerned, I will not be vaccinated with anything that has not been properly vetted or tested and has shown no sound scientific evidence that the benefits outweigh the disease itself in possible long term side-effects, which to this day we don't know anything about. I will not be reduced to a mere guinea pig by getting vaccinated with an experimental drug and I will most assuredly not get vaccinated because my government tells me to and promises in return, I will be granted freedom. Let's be clear about one thing. No one grants me freedom! For I am a free person![42]

Etiology 101 – Safety is Paramount in Mass Preventative Measures

There are essentially two public health approaches to etiology and infectious disease prevention: population-based and individual-centered. The "population strategy" seeks to control the causes of disease incidence in the population. In contrast, the individual-centered approach seeks to identify high-risk susceptible individuals and offer them some individual protection.[43,44]

Generally, it can be said that the protection strategy that focuses on high-risk individuals may be appropriate for those individuals, as well as being a prudent and cost-effective use of limited medical resources; but its capability to reduce the burden of disease in the whole population tends to be modest.[43,44] Because a large number of people exposed to a small risk might yield more cases in the community than a small number exposed to a big risk, the mass approach is inherently the ultimate answer to the problem of a mass disease that objectively represents a serious health risk to the population to alter the whole populace's dispersal of the risk variable.[43,44] Here, however, the number one concern and priority of public health officials must be that prior to undertaking any population-based measures, it must be absolutely sure that the advice is safe. Intervention for prevention where the risk is low, and the disease does not objectively represent a serious health risk to the vast majority of the population, such as COVID-19, is different and requires an extremely conservative approach. According to eminent epidemiologist and author of 1985 seminal article "Sick Individuals and Sick Populations", Geoffrey Rose:

> If a preventive measure exposes many people to a small risk, then the harm it does may readily outweigh the benefits, since these are received by relatively few.... Consequently, we cannot accept mass preventive medication [without long-term safety data].[43]

According to Rose, public health officials may usefully differentiate two types of preventive measures to serve as an early indicator of safety for population-based preventative actions.

> The first consists of the removal of an unnatural factor and the restoration of "biological normality" - that is, of the conditions to which presumably we are genetically adapted.[43]

For the treatment of COVID-19, such measures would consist of an increase in physical activity, reduction in the intake of saturated fat, maintaining a healthy weight and avoiding obesity, quitting smoking, drinking alcohol in moderation, washing your hands frequently, boosting the natural immune system with the increase in the consumption of Vitamin A, Vitamin C, Vitamin D, Zinc, and Selenium and perhaps the social distancing and voluntary isolation of high-risk individuals to avoid infection. Such normalizing measures may be presumed to be safe, and therefore public health officials should be prepared to advocate them based on a reasonable presumption of benefit. According to Rose,

> The second type of mass preventive measure is quite different. It consists not in removing a supposed cause of disease but in adding some other unnatural factor, in the hope of conferring protection. The end result is to increase biological abnormality by an even further removal from those conditions to which we are genetically adapted...

For such measures as these the required level of evidence, both of benefit and (particularly) of safety, must be far more stringent.[43]

For the treatment of COVID-19, such measures include mandatory medication such as the Pfizer-BioNTech or Moderna COVID-19 vaccines, which is brand-new biotechnology with no long-term safety data. If public health officials cannot assure safety based on long-term safety data, then it should be reasonably assumed that the harm may outweigh the benefit, and the mass prevention action should not be implemented.[43,44]

According to Pfizer-BioNTech F-1 Form filings, their novel "mRNA Therapeutics" formulations of messenger ribonucleic acid, or mRNA, that deliver genetic information to cells, where it is used to express proteins for therapeutic effect "may not work as intended, may cause undesirable side-effects or result in significant negative consequences following marketing approval."[45]

The COVID-19 vaccines that increase biological abnormality should never have been utilized in a population-based prevention strategy by the most rudimentary etiological and epidemiological principles and standards.[43,44]

Public Health versus Private Health

In the case of disease, determining the boundary between the private and public spheres requires a careful understanding of various disciplines. As a first guesstimate, we may say that we have a "right to be sick" and whether to be treated or not. The right to privacy and to be left alone supports this reasoning, provided that your disease does not directly cause harm to others. We have a "right" to be sick with the flu because it does not endanger the lives of 99.5% of the people we interact with. However, we do not have a right to be sick with the deadly Ebola virus because it does endanger others and poses a risk of death to 65% of people that get infected.[46,47] Yet, even such a seemingly uncontroversial example as flu oversimplifies the matter. To relieve symptoms, the person suffering from flu may consume medication that, in turn, may leave him just as impaired to drive a vehicle as would inebriation with alcohol. Merely being an adolescent or advanced in years makes the person, statistically, an unsafe driver. The advocates of mandatory health mandates threaten freedom because they obscure or even deny the differences between the kinds of risks posed by COVID-19 and the risks posed by a private lifestyle and other diseases such as cardiovascular disease, cancer, and other respiratory diseases with significantly higher mortality rates than COVID-19.[48,49]

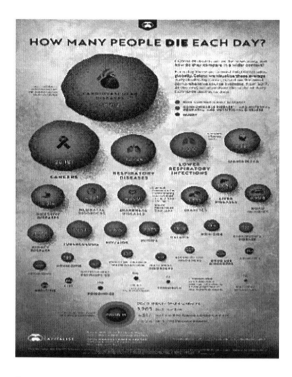

Figure 1.4: How many people die each day?
Source: The Visual Capitalist using data from Our World in Data and the EU CDC[48]

Absurdly, individuals cannot by an act of will protect themselves against COVID-19, but they can somehow by an act of will protect themselves from cancer, heart attack, and seasonal flu. What makes forced public health measures unjustified is not so much that they do not protect everyone equally, but that they do so by means that illegitimately violate fundamental human rights and freedoms and replace personal medical autonomy with State coercion and control through pseudo-medical mandates and legal sanctions.[49]

From a public perception perspective, what represents a health threat to the public depends in part on what people perceive as a risk, a perception (as again demonstrated by the COVID-19 pandemic) shaped mainly by mainstream media propaganda and subjective judgment rather than by statistical probability.[49]

To complicate matters, the ill health of persons and populations represent vastly different challenges for individuals, doctors, and policymakers. In assessing the benefits of preventive action from an etiological perspective, an individual high-risk approach that benefits the individual may offer little benefit to the community. In contrast, a population strategy that benefits the community may not benefit the individual. The conflict between private health and public health is an integral part of the tension between the individual and the State.[49] Rose coined this tension the "prevention paradox" and notes that "a measure that brings large benefits to the community offers little to each participating individual."[43,44]

Dealing with health care and mass prevention strategies as a public good raises certain questions, such as:

- To what extent can the State restrict the liberty of its citizens to serve the common good?
- Are all government actions taken in the name of public health legitimate, irrespective of rationality or reasonability?
- What are the legal requirements to declare a state of emergency?
- Did politicians act illegally during the COVID-19 pandemic?
- What are the limitations to government power during a declared state of emergency?
- Who are the objective arbiters of "the science" or are the State bureaucrats the ultimate authority?
- Does the State have the right to mandate experimental medical procedures on the population?
- Do governments have the right to force medicine on healthy people that pose no risk to any person around them?

These are essential questions that most people and nearly all politicians prefer to avoid. Instead, politicians pander to the public with "greater good" slogans, welfare payments, and rule by medical mandate, and most people like that pandering. However, with the increasing realization that public COVID-19 health measures were abhorrently abused for political and financial gain and the mounting dissatisfaction, we ought to confront rather than shirk from these questions.[49]

If the wellbeing of the individual and the wellbeing of the collective are deemed to overlap, then the ill conduct or ill health of the one imperils that of the other.[49] The issue ultimately comes down to whether the individual is viewed as a private person or as public property. The former aligns with the social contract, natural law, IHRL, juridical order, and peremptory norms while the latter does not. In the absence of a clear partition between the private and political, the personal and the public, there can be no separation between private health and public health. What should be private then becomes political and the political becomes inherently pseudo-medical. Explicitly moral criteria are substituted with ostensibly medical criteria to judge personal conduct and to expand State power.[49]

World War COVID-19

On March 16, 2020, World Economic Forum (WEF) "Young Global Leader" alumnus and French President Emmanuel Macron ordered the French people to stay at home and warned people to "severely restrict movements for the next 15 days at least," limiting social interactions, and said any violation of the new rules would be "punished". He also called for a "general mobilization" of anti-virus workers and postponed the second round of French local elections. Macron said, "the country was at war with an invisible, elusive enemy, and [although] the measures were unprecedented, circumstances demanded them."[50] On January 22, 2022, after almost two years of "war," Macron described those opposed to the COVID-19 vaccinations as "irresponsible," adding that "they undermined the strength of a nation." "When my freedom threatens that of others, I become irresponsible," he said. "An irresponsible person is no longer a citizen."[51]

Macron was not alone in declaring war on COVID-19. The war-cry chorus resounded throughout the Western world. "We are at war with a virus that threatens to tear us apart," World Health Organization Director-General Tedros Adhanom Ghebreyesus told world leaders on March 26, 2020, in a special virtual summit on the COVID-19 pandemic. The deadly coronavirus, Tedros said, "is the defining health crisis of our time." A year later the war cry was still being echoed by United Nations Secretary-General Antonio Guterres who again on May 24, 2021, urged recognition of the fact that "we are at war with a virus."[52,53]

The practice of medicine and the allegory of war is nothing new. The disease first understood and subjugated by biomedical science was the infectious virus. Because the immune system's response to viruses is readily analogized to a country resisting an attacking army, the war metaphor has become amiable in thinking about disease and treatment. When society speaks about germs "attacking" the body, anti-bacterial agents as magic "bullets," doctors as "fighting" diseases, and COVID-19 vaccinations as the "best weapon available," we use symbols to communicate the notion that the medical doctor is like the soldier who protects the motherland from foreign aggressors.[49,56] However, when Western politicians speak about the war on COVID-19, they use metaphors to convey the idea that the State is like a doctor when it uses public health edicts and public health officials as soldiers to protect people from themselves and others. In the first instance, doctors are helping patients to overcome diseases. In the second instance, the State prevents citizens from making their own informed medical choices.[49]

In the case of dangerous infectious diseases with high rates of crude mortality, the war allegory of the microbe as an alien pathogen threatening the host (patient's body) helps us understand the mechanism of the illness and justifies the mandatary isolation of sick and contagious individuals. What is concerning is that in the case of COVID-19 (a disease with a low crude mortality rate), government leaders cast the "unvaccinated" and those individuals with an opposing view to the COVID-19 pseudo-science in the role of the alien pathogen threatening the host (the nation) and the "greater good".[49,56] Those holding a different point of view are thus maliciously misidentified as a "disease" in order to convince society that the "unvaccinated" and any person holding an opposing view is like a dangerous pathogen, justifying the mandatory, cruel, punitive treatment and segregation of and discrimination against these individuals given their "danger to themselves and others."[44]

Failure to understand the semantic manipulation of the war metaphor in the COVID-19 mainstream propaganda precludes perceiving unlawful medical coercion as an issue.[44] Unfortunately, as esteemed psychiatrist and social critic Professor Thomas S. Szasz (1920-2012) eloquently articulated, "the first casualty of all wars is clear thinking and personal independence, replaced by collective stupidity and timidity of a people united by fear and hatred against a common enemy, while absurdly viewing the sacrifice of liberty as liberation."[49]

The persistent rhetoric from political and corporate leaders of categorizing certain groups of people such as "the unvaccinated" and "those who hold an opposing view" as "a public health risk" implies that the persons in question lack reasonable judgment and therefore need the assistance of the State to protect others from them. The idea that the State must protect people from themselves is an integral part of an authoritarian, paternalistic outlook on life, now favored by many Western governments.[49,54-56]

Differences of view on how to manage personal health risk choices is intrinsic to human existence but regulating disagreements as if those who hold an antagonistic view were carriers of deadly diseases despite being perfectly healthy is a recipe for forgoing fundamental human rights and freedoms in pursuit of an illusory and unattainable (by design) zero-COVID-19 utopia that only benefits the ultra-rich global elite and the powerful politicians.[49]

State of Emergency as a Paradigm of Government

World War COVID-19 coincided with an unjustifiable enduring state of emergency or state of exception in the vast majority of "warring" countries. Democratic regimes were transformed to totalitarian States by the rapid expansion of the executive's power, with the state of emergency becoming the rule and not the exception to the rule. Through the use, abuse, and perversion of the state of emergency, the entire politico-constitutional life of Western societies assumed a new form of government akin to Nazi-era biomedical fascism.

It is a well-known historical fact that the systematic and perpetual implementation of a state of emergency leads to the "liquidation of democracy". As soon as Hitler assumed power, he declared a state of emergency through the proclamation of the "Decree for the Protection of the People and the State", which effectively suspended the articles of the Weimar Constitution that guaranteed fundamental human rights and freedoms. The decree was never repealed. The dubiety between the rule (norm) and the exception to the rule (norm) was precisely what led to the creation of the Third Reich and what enabled Hitler and his corporate allies to implement their agenda.[57] From a juridical standpoint, the entire Nazi Third Reich was conducted under a state of emergency that lasted 12 years. Nazi jurists spoke openly about a "willed state of exception" (*gewollte ausnahmeszustand*) or "state of necessity" (*Notstand*), for the sake of establishing the Nationalist Socialist State.[57]

In his seminal work "State of Exception", Giorgio Agamben correctly postulates that:

> In this sense, modern totalitarianism as the establishment, by means of the state of exception, of a legal civil war that allows for the physical elimination not only of political adversaries but entire categories of citizens who for some reason cannot be integrated into the political system...

> [T]he state of exception in which we live.... [is the] *arcanum imperi* (secret power) par excellence of our time. What the "ark" of power contains at its center is the state of exception- but this is essentially an empty space, in which human action with no relation to law stands before a norm with no relation to life...[57]

This does not mean that the lawless governmental machine, with its empty center, is not effective. On the contrary, the state of emergency has been effectively used by despots without exception prior to the First World War through Nazi Fascism and National Socialism, and up to our own time.[57] Indeed, the state of emergency as a "technique of government" has reached its maximum worldwide deployment during the COVID-19 era.[52] Ignoring and contravening IHRL and peremptory norms, numerous Western nations essentially suspended the entire juridical order and, through the state of emergency, illicitly attempted to subtract the State from any consideration of national or international law.

Agamben further correctly posits that:

> It is a paradoxical articulation, for what must be inscribed within the law is something that is essentially exterior to it, that is nothing less than the suspension of the juridical order itself...

> The normative aspect of law can thus be obliterated and contradicted with impunity by a governmental violence that while ignoring international law externally and producing a permanent state of exception internally- nevertheless still claims to be applying the law...

> The modern state of exception is instead an attempt to include the exception itself within the juridical order creating a zone of distinction in which fact and law coincide....

> Indeed, from this perspective the state of exception appears as a threshold of indeterminacy between democracy and absolutism.[57]

During the COVID-19 era, so-called Western democracies incongruently created an enduring state of emergency with an extra-juridical character and utilized it as an essential practice and the dominant paradigm of government to achieve political ends. This transformation of an exceptional measure into a technique of government threatens to radically alter – in fact has already palpably altered – the structure and meaning of the international political and juridical order.[57]

The state of emergency as implemented during the COVID-19 pandemic by numerous State Parties is not a "state of law" but a "space without law", that presented itself as an anomie that resulted from the suspension law.[57] Despite having the appearance of law, the various COVID-19 edicts and mandates neither made nor preserved law but in reality, "deactivated and deposed law" and thus inaugurated a new historical epoch.[57] Law has suffered an ephemeral eclipse because it has been contaminated by corrupt globalist politics and international monopoly capital.

The COVID-19 emergency measures and instruments of government depicted originally as short term "crisis" arrangements have in almost all Western nations become lasting practices of government conflicting with the fundamental hierarchy of law specifically relating to IHRL and *jus cogens* norms. The aporia of inscribing an unjustifiable state of emergency within the law has led to a global juridical void and widespread State lawlessness with various peremptory IHRL norms *de facto* being annulled in the name of public health.

The Creeping Medicalization of Global Law and Order

We are in the process of profound global biomedical, technological, and societal transformation. Following the Second World War, where "disregard and contempt for human rights have resulted in barbarous acts which have outraged the conscience of mankind," the IHRL order was established that principally rested on the notion that the "recognition of the inherent dignity and of the equal and inalienable rights of all members of the human family is the foundation of freedom, justice, and peace in the world" and was enforced by a judicial apparatus based on the rule of law.[9] As the world became ever more globalized, politicized, "legitimized" and enforced by a self-selected coalition of multinational corporations, government bureaucrats and "charitable" foundations that comingle the principles and practices of totalitarianism, paternalistic "biomedical therapy", and socialist public health, the rule of law became ever more perverted and distorted.

Throughout the COVID-19 pandemic, public health and the practice of medicine have become increasingly politicized, and global politics has become increasingly medicalized. Medicalization can be defined as "a process or movement whereby the phenomena, which had belonged to another field such as education, law, religion, and so on, have been redefined as medical phenomena that are subject to medical judgment."[56] In today's world, the forces of medicalization rule virtually unopposed and indeed unrecognized for the monetary, immoral, corrupt, and political interests they represent.[54] Western democracies deprived people of freedom by relieving them of responsibility for their own decisions relating to health, religious gatherings, travel, education, and social interaction and called the interventions "medical treatment" in the interest of the "greater good."

We are witnessing the global monopolization of public health and a bid to medicalize the rule of law and peremptory fundamental human rights norms by the global political elite and their ultra-wealthy colluders. The attempted medicalization of fundamental human rights and freedoms entails the process by which State public health authorities asserted authority over a sphere of life previously overseen by national and international human rights law. Public health authorities substituted ostensibly medical criteria for explicitly legal criteria for judging personal conduct and used pseudo-medical arguments to justify the illegitimate expansion and exercise of State power.[49,54-56]

In the words of Dr. Anthony Fauci, the chief medical advisor to US President Joe Biden and the director of the National Institute of Allergy and Infectious Diseases: "There is a misplaced perception about people's individual right to make a decision that supersedes the societal safety net…as a member of society…particularly in the context of a pandemic…you have a responsibility to society…you have got to look at it and say, there comes a time when you do have to give up what you consider your individual rights…for the greater good of society."[58,59] That is an extremely dangerous opinion, the more so because ever fewer people realize its danger.

The modern-day COVID-19 public health penchant for transforming treatable flu-like viruses into "deadly diseases" and judicial mandates into "vaccine therapies," replacing the rule of law with the rule of arbitrary medical discretion, is the result of a type of government Thomas Szasz coined a "therapeutic State" or "pharmacracy" in 1963 and 1974 respectively.[56] Szasz explains:

> Inasmuch as we have words to describe medicine as a healing art but have none to describe it as a method of social control or political rule, we must first give it a name. I propose that we call it pharmacracy, from the Greek roots pharmakon, for "medicine" or "drug," and kratein, for "to rule" or "to control." . . . As theocracy is rule by God or priests, and democracy is rule by the people or the majority, so pharmacracy is rule by medicine or physicians." In a theocracy, people perceive all manner of human problems as religious in nature, susceptible to religious remedies; similarly, in a pharmacracy people perceive all manner of human problems as medical in nature, susceptible to medical remedies.[56]

> I propose the term therapeutic State to identify the transformation of our dominant political ideology from a democratic welfare State legitimized by the rule of law to an autocratic therapeutic State legitimized by … medicine.[49]

The late professor Szasz (former professor of psychiatry at the State University of New York Upstate Medical University in Syracuse, New York and distinguished lifetime fellow of the American Psychiatric Association) is the academic who has most comprehensively and thoroughly considered, analyzed, and described the now worldwide phenomenon of the "Therapeutic State."[49,56] The therapeutic State or biomedical State as a type of totalitarian State with a sacred and therefore unopposable mission is not a brand-new historical phenomenon. The theological State, the communist State, and the fascist States of Hitler and Mussolini may be viewed as former incarnations of it.[49] Given Nazi Germany's eugenics programs and "biomedical" panaceas as final solutions to solve societal problems, Hitler's Third Reich practices are comparable to the current global phenomenon.

From the beginning of his political career, Hitler couched his struggle against "enemies of the State" in biomedical rhetoric. Hitler compared the Jews to germs and stated that diseases cannot be controlled unless you destroy their causes.[60] The declared task of the 1930's German police was "to root out all symptoms of disease and germs of destruction that threatened the political health of the nation." An ever-expanding number of behaviors were defined as "dangerous diseases" and mandatory medical treatment was added to the armamentarium of the German public health authority. Examples of medicalization included such diverse conditions as feeblemindedness, schizophrenia, manic-depressive disorder, epilepsy, dementia, physical deformity, and alcoholism. Coercion was used not merely to treat those with contagious diseases but to force medical "treatments" on perfectly healthy individuals deemed to be a threat to the "greater good" and the "health of the nation," which included all those who held opposing views to the government-approved public health narrative. Through mass corporate and State-funded mainstream media propaganda, academics, the medical establishment, students, and the vast majority of the German nation viewed "biotechnology" public health solutions as the only solution to Germany's problems, leading to the eventual biomedical sterilization, euthanasia, and extermination of millions of German citizens, including many Jews.

The more medical re-classifications invade more social categories in more States, the greater the potential for creating a global order corresponding to a totalitarian ideology that closely resembles Nazi Germany and its biomedical reign of terror in the 1930s and 1940s. We should view the Nazi experience with medicalized politics resulting from Germany's ultra-wealthy colluding with Hitler to bring the Nazis to power in 1933 as a cautionary tale illuminating the dangers lurking in the alliance between medicine, the State, and the ultra-wealthy global elite.

The world's future freedom, and health, may depend on whether we dismiss the analogy between pharmacracy in Nazi Germany birthed from the collaboration between the German political and corporate elite and global pharmacracy realized during the COVID-19 pandemic following public-private-partnerships (PPPs) between the global political and corporate elite as marginal. Or whether we view it as terrifyingly relevant and treat it with utmost seriousness.[49]

Mandates as Treatment: Justifying the Biomedical State

Deception and self-deception by biomedical rhetoric and coercion impersonating medical therapy is the bedrock of the political practice of medical tyranny. One of Professor Szasz's most significant insights is his depiction of the method whereby State coercion is transmuted into biomedical treatment:

1. The subject's "condition" is diagnosed as a "disease" threatening the nation's life.
2. The mandatory medical intervention imposed is defined as a "treatment."
3. Legislators and judges ratify these categorizations as "diseases" and "treatments" by therapeutic pseudo-jurisprudence.[49,56]

Simply put, the biomedical State's stock-in-trade is rejecting the distinctions between the medical care that individuals ask for and the "biomedical treatments" imposed on them against their will. In short, it characterizes violent government behavior as benevolence.[49] According to the fascist pharmacratic ideology, with body ownership vested in the government, it is acceptable that the State should classify and define "disease" and "treatment." Both "the proper treatment" and "recognized disease" are determined not by medical doctors treating patients at the coalface but by the government bureaucrats of the therapeutic State and their corporate masters who self-servingly define "diseases" in need of mandatory government "treatment" for the "greater good."[49]

The concept of defining disease in terms of treatability is also not a new phenomenon. The prescientific physician and his clients often perceived illness that way.[49,61,62] Even though there were groundbreaking inventions being made throughout the 17th century, predominant medical procedures were still centered on the Hippocratic hypothesis of the Four Humors. The concept was that the human body was regulated by four humors, or fluids: blood, yellow bile, black bile and phlegm. Each humor matched to the elements (water, fire, earth, and air, correspondingly) and temperaments (sanguine, choleric, melancholy, phlegmatic).[61] Thus, if an individual was sick, it was believed that their humors were out of balance, likely due to an excess of one humor. A 1947 Time magazine article revealed that:

> The 17th century was the Golden Age of the enema, or clyster, as it was then called. The crude instruments of yesteryear—tubes of bone or wood attached to animal bladders or silk bags—were replaced by a formidable piston-&-cylinder device. An apothecary or doctor's assistant, marching through the streets with a clyster tube on his shoulder, became a common sight, as a mania for enemas swept France. Fashionable Parisians, convinced that inner lavements purified the complexion and produced good health, took as many as three or four enemas a day. The craze was often burlesqued on the stage, notably by Molière, and it was a lively topic of elegant discourse in the salons. Louis XIV had over 2,000 enemas during his reign, sometimes holding court while the ceremony progressed. Aristocratic enemas were delicately tinted and scented. They were also so widely used as a means of poisoning that Louis XIV set up a special detective agency to combat the wave of enema-murders among his nobility.[62]

The principal difference between the old-fashioned medical quackery relating to the treatment of Hippocrates' "theory of the four humors," that included restoring balance and health through practices like blood-letting, purging, and enemas, that led to the 17th-century golden age of the enema, and the newfangled COVID-19 vaccine quackery of Dr. Antony Fauci and his snake oil pushing global corporate collaborators, is that 15th to 18th-century quack "medical treatments" were never imposed on individuals against their will through State mandate, whereas the experimental "medical treatments" endorsed by Dr. Fauci, the CDC, and the WHO are.

From a medical, scientific point of view, a medical intervention counts as a *bona fide* treatment only if it aims to remedy an actual disease where the actual safety data and risk factors of the disease and the remedy are known and transparently communicated.[49,56] Withholding safety data to present a more favorable risk profile of the remedy amounts to scientific fraud.[63] From a legal point of view, a medical intervention counts as *bona fide* treatment only if it is performed by a doctor licensed to practice medicine, with the informed consent of the patient or his guardian. Consensual treatment is treatment only if the patient has an actual disease or the risk of contracting such a disease, and the consent provided was not fraudulently obtained through material misrepresentation of the risk relating to the treatment. Nonconsensual "treatment" is assault, even if it cures the patient of his disease.[49]

People do not have to be told that leukemia and melanoma are life-threatening diseases. They know they are. But people were told repeatedly, for more than two years, that COVID-19 is a dangerous disease. Why? Because the government knew that COVID-19 did not pose a risk of death to more than 99.5% of the population, that COVID-19 is not "like other deadly illnesses," that CDC prescribed COVID-19 treatment protocols deviated from the norm and that the medicalized political COVID-19 objectives are State coercion and control, not a medical cure and care.[49,54] Accordingly, the biomedical State engaged in a never-ending task of "educating" citizens through government-sponsored mainstream media propaganda campaigns that non-life-threatening diseases such as COVID-19 are extremely dangerous diseases threatening the nation's future existence. Formerly, people who had no symptoms of a disease were healthy, productive members of society. Since 2020, such people who refuse to be vaccinated are potential "symptomless carriers" of a "deadly disease". Formerly, an individual who died of a heart attack and had the flu officially died of a heart attack. However, during the COVID-19 era, definitions were changed, obfuscating the lines between dying "of COVID-19" to dying "with COVID-19". Since 2020, an individual who died of a heart attack or gunshot wound to the head and had COVID-19 officially died of COVID-19. Formerly, some people died of natural causes due to old age, cancer, heart disease, accidents, cerebrovascular diseases, chronic lower respiratory diseases, Alzheimer's disease, diabetes, influenza, pneumonia, and nephritis, but since 2020 (virtually), everyone who died is said to have died "with COVID-19". In short, COVID-19 political medicalization is neither about medicine nor science; it is a dishonest semantic-social strategy that benefits the political elite and their international corporate conspirators and harms the average citizen.[54]

The global biomedical fascist's agenda, based on the coercive mandatory therapeutic concept of disease, differs entirely from the medical scientist's agenda, based on the ethical non-coercive-clinical concept of informed consent prior to the treatment of disease. To advance their agenda, the biomedical State shifts the focus – their own and society's – from actual experience to tactic, from empirically demonstrable disease to dramatically propagated prevention and treatment strategies for the "greater good."[63] The true medical doctor treats COVID-19 by assessing the patient's condition and prescribing effective multi-drug medications such as doxycycline, azithromycin, Ivermectin, hydroxychloroquine, and corticosteroids to prevent exponential viral replication to save the patient's life.[64] The political puppet doctor treats COVID-19 strictly in line with CDC recommendations, irrespective of the irrationality or imminent death of the patient. Sanctimoniousness, pretense, and hypocrisy replace honesty and objective medical science. COVID-19 political doctors preach that children are the nation's future and in need of protection yet inject them with an experimental mRNA gene-therapy that increases the risk for myocarditis in children by 13,000%.[49,65]

Global Public Health Fascism

The West's newfound love affair with global pharmacracy now transcends traditional distinctions between Nation States left and right, liberal and conservative. Even major global human rights NGOs and the Human Rights Commission are indifferent to the dangers posed by the global therapeutic State provided the WEF, WHO, and the US CDC endorse it.[66-68] As in Nazi Germany, medical doctors, who ought to know better but for the most part do not, are conceivably the most naive and at the same time the most passionate advocates of medical interventions for all types of societal challenges.[49] After two and a half years of non-stop State and corporate propaganda, many people seem to be accepting a new global order based on the erroneous assertion that if "X" is labeled a "dangerous disease" by government bureaucrats, then "X" is a public-health problem whose prevention and therapy justify massive infringements on personal freedom and other fundamental human rights.[49]

The State commands vast funds to deploy towards propaganda, misinformation, and economic compulsion and has the sole power to create laws and bylaws. During the COVID-19 crisis, the global political and transnational corporate elite self-servingly and opportunistically marshalled State resources, fueled the flames of global medicalization, and transformed a lingering fire into an all-consuming global inferno with catastrophic ramifications for the protection of fundamental human rights and freedoms.

International human rights norms are explicitly founded on the principle that States should respect and protect certain inalienable fundamental human rights and in the inevitable contest between individual rights and State power; the former should be superior to the latter. There is a balance of power between State power and immutable fundamental human rights. This balance of power demarcates the line between the State-controlled and owned and the immutable private rights freedoms. If a thing is State-controlled and owned, it is subject to State authority; if it is private, it is not.[49] The COVID-19 biomedical global, collectivist agenda intends to abolish the private realm altogether since it is the private sphere that is problematic for public health pharmacratic control, given that the private sphere does not fall within the legal authority of State and public health.[49]

People have more freedom as more aspects of their lives are private. During COVID-19, the West and much of the globe invited the globalist elite to take over the management of their personal health. Now they have less control not only over the healthcare they receive but also over other aspects of their personal lives, such as the ability to travel, earn a living, study, and attend social events. Nor is that loss of control and fundamental human rights and freedoms the end of the medical fascist's mischief. The more money the global corporate elite make, and the more tax monies are spent on emergency health care provision and mainstream media propaganda; the more firmly entrenched becomes the idea in nearly everyone's mind that caring for people's health requires not informed individual consent but politicized total medical control – that is, control by deceit, seduction, compulsion, and mandate.[49,54-56]

Speaking Law to Power

Long before the sway of COVID-19 pseudo-medical global totalitarianism, the social contract, natural law, and *jus cogens* international human rights norms and principles were established as the sovereign law of the world that cannot legitimately be medicalized or subverted by medical statism or global biomedical plutocracy. IHRL should re-claim its rightful position as the supreme law of the international legal order and play an increasingly important role globally. Unbridled State power is always rationalized by fear of collective morality and accompanied by a justifying mission – to defeat the communist, to win the war on terror, to eradicate COVID-19 infections – that requires anti-juridical emergency measures against an "enemy" whose powers are dynamic but whose exact location is indeterminate. Untrammeled government power liquidates democracy. Multinational corporations and States should not be allowed to do as they like, as they did throughout the COVID-19 pandemic, but should be bound by international law and their international legal obligations.[69] All human rights are universal, indivisible, interdependent, and interrelated. Human beings cannot enjoy any of their human rights unless they can enjoy all of them. The argument that the right to health supersedes all other fundamental human rights is an extra-juridical fallacy, especially when dealing with a disease with a global infection fatality rate of 0.15%.[70]

Collectively, human rights are inviolable, codified, universally shared, measurable, and enforceable. They provide the framework within which public health, democracy, and human security can be realized. The UDHR and the ICCPR call upon all States to promote respect for these rights and freedoms and to ensure their observance in order to limit the harm that the powerful can inflict on the vulnerable.[71-73] Legal outcomes should be determined by identifying claims of right, not by measuring assertion of political and corporate power. Once the legal rules are set, outcomes should not depend on politics or the relative power of disputants. Laws "prescribe the means by which power and its proper limits and improper uses is legitimated, accountable and constrained."[74] When political power determines legal outcomes, it means that the system has been corrupted, and drastic reform must be pursued if the values of the rule of law are to be maintained.[75,76]

Over the past two and a half years, the balance between power and law tilted dramatically in favor of power – meaning the unrestrained capability to advance State and monopoly capital's ends independently of the norms and procedures of IHRL. Today, we face the unique situation that almost all the world's so-called Western democracies are acting lawlessly. Law and power are different – they promote different values, evaluate the national interest differently, and express different commitments. Law is associated with multilateralism, diplomacy, and respect for fundamental human rights; power, on the other hand, with unilateralism, force, and political and financial self-interest.[75,76] Law expresses long-term rather than short-term interests and attends more faithfully to the protection of fundamental human rights. In contrast, political and corporate power attends to short-term advantages and profits and has no respect for fundamental human rights. Unfortunately, COVID-19 clearly demonstrated that today's international affairs are predominantly a world of power and politics – law is marginal.[75,76] It speaks but does not do.[76] But when power no longer subjects itself to law (*nomos*), it becomes lawless (*anomos*)! To be lawless is to be contrary to the law and to act without regard to the law. When law itself is ignored and dismantled by those who are in power, lawlessness is the result, and chaos, iniquity and knavery ensue. Lawlessness inevitably leads to human suffering and degradation and eventually to the collapse of the system.

In the COVID-19 era, numerous Western governments across the globe that style themselves as champions of the rule of law are breaching their international legal obligations and illicitly abusing emergency declarations to enact a near permanent *justitium*. Bedrock human rights principles have been displaced by legally meaningless terms such as the "Great Reset," "for the greater good," "Build Back Better," the "Fourth Industrial Revolution", "Agenda 21", and "Agenda 2030." Fundamentally, human rights norms and standards have not changed, but the political atmosphere has palpably altered. The human rights regime is menaced by dramatic disrespect and non-adherence to the rule of law. States and their corporate allies run roughshod over and trample on fundamental human rights. It is vital for the human rights regime of law and order to recover its balance through mass civil disobedience and grass roots political action as the current global fascist control techniques are unsustainable. At stake is the preservation of the international law concept of human rights and the post-Second World War juridical political order.

Although much has been written about the US legal position on vaccine mandates and the ruthless exploitation of the COVID-19 pandemic by out-of-control politicians, tech giants, big pharma, medical malpractitioners, large multinational corporations, and a cabal of global health and economic elites under the guise of a global pandemic to bring about a "Great Reset," there is an evident void regarding the flagrant breach of international human rights norms and the rule of law by world governments' imposition of COVID-19 emergency public health measures that created an extra-juridical zone of anomie in which lawless biomedical fascism without any legitimate juridical form acts.[24,26,57]

Thomas Jefferson asserted that "A well-informed citizenry is the best defense against tyranny." The primary purpose of this book is to equip and educate ordinary citizens across the globe with the relevant legal principles and laws developed over centuries in order for them to stand their ground in the face of current and future corporate and State biomedical despotism, lies, and deception!

Following this introductory chapter, the chapters of the book will unfold as follows:

- In Chapter 2, the theories of natural rights and the social contract will be scrutinized. The historical context and development of these safeguards are elucidated in order to be understood and correctly employed. From this historical overview, it will be apparent that fundamental human rights are inalienable rights from God not imparted by the good graces of governments nor conditional on adherence to pseudo-medical dictates. These natural rights are not subject to politics or public health but are inherent in the individual. The first and most basic duty of the State is to protect the fundamental human rights of its citizens. Everyone in society has a right to be protected by the State in the unhindered enjoyment of his or her life, liberty, and property in the pursuit of happiness. Citizens owe no duty of obedience to a government that violates natural law and breaches the social contract.

- Chapter 3 will be devoted to analyzing IHRL concerning the immutable nature of fundamental human rights as contained in the various binding international treaties that hold States legally accountable for their actions. IHRL, unlike classic international law, sees individuals as the main subjects of international law. It is not based on reciprocity but rather on a network of objective obligations. Readers will learn that the ethical and human rights standards that States need to adhere to are unambiguous. Human rights law is the supreme law of the international juridical order to which all States must adhere. The COVID-19 practice where countries such as Austria, Australia, France, Germany, Italy, New Zealand, Netherlands, Belgium, the United States, and the United Kingdom, to name a few, actively violated citizens' most basic fundamental human rights is irreconcilable with this legal order.

- Chapter 4 will consider the facts, medical science, and arguments for and against mandatory COVID-19 vaccination and conclusively refute the false mainstream narratives. The arguments for mandatory COVID-19 vaccination were not supported by objective science and data and did not align with democratic constitutional values rooted in respect for fundamental human rights and freedoms. The COVID-19 era phenomenon of State-sponsored and generated misinformation and disinformation by ignoring, suppressing, and censoring all objective scientific and medical data that do not align with the mainstream narrative will also be scrutinized and explicated. History teaches that the COVID-19 misinformation that insidiously determines prevailing norms that are deemed unassailable and sacrosanct by the biomedical-political establishment will ultimately be defeated by the truth.

- Chapter 5 will explore the legal requirements for the legitimate limitation of fundamental human rights in terms of IHRL. To determine the legality of emergency measures and vaccine mandates, the Siracusa Principles and Paris Minimum Standards are analyzed, and both a "respect for the essence test" and a "proportionality analysis" are applied. The limitation of fundamental human rights is legitimate only if it respects the essence and if it is proportional. Proportionality is the mainstay of the protection of human rights in Western democracies and the most critical standard that must be met to restrict human rights and freedoms lawfully. It is a substantive requirement, defining how far States may go in limiting fundamental human rights. It will be apparent to readers that vaccine mandates and other emergency measures are illegal in terms of prevailing international human rights norms and standards.

- Chapter 6 will analyze the state of emergency as a the "dominant paradigmatic form of government" in contemporary politics subject to a vicious cycle in which the emergency measures the State seek to justify in the name of defending the democratic constitutions are the same ones that lead to its ultimate ruin.[3] During a state of emergency "law is suspended and obliterated in fact". It will further be investigated whether COVID-19 represents an emergency "threatening the life of a nation." The threat to the life of a nation is a rudimentary legal prerequisite for declaring a state of emergency and implementing numerous COVID-19 human rights-violating public health measures, including vaccine mandates. Human rights derogation can only be justified as a temporary mechanism for empowering States to protect human rights rather than as an iniquitous government mechanism enabling national authorities and multinational corporations to advance their own interests in a manner that compromises human rights protection. It will be shown that the COVID-19 state of emergency, as paradigm government, rather than an exceptional temporary measure, *de facto* creates a juridical void, resulting in lawlessness and the abuse of power.

- Chapter 7 will highlight that the human right to freedom from torture, cruel, inhumane treatment, and medical experimentation without free and informed consent can never be legitimately violated in terms of IHRL. It will become evident to readers that COVID-19 vaccine mandates represent an illegal derogation of non-derogable fundamental human rights that should not be tolerated or accepted. Because of their normative specificity and status, non-derogable rights are core human rights *jus cogens* and obligations *erga omnes*. Under case law and legal doctrine, *jus cogens* comprises super norms or superior constitutional rules that every State is obligated to follow. Compelling law does not give a government the right to opt-out or renegotiate as is the case with other international norms deriving from custom or treaty. Peremptory norms limit the ability of the State to create public policy, which would contradict *jus cogens*. Any act, or health policy of the State contrary to *jus cogens* that were abundantly enacted during the COVID-19 pandemic, represents a breach of the international legal order.

- In Chapter 8, the four main biomedical ethical principles, beneficence, non-maleficence, autonomy, and justice, are defined and explained to provide a universal, moral analytical framework to make morally and ethically sound decisions. The principles provide the most universal and complete norms intended to guide medical ethical actions. If any one of the principles is violated by medical intervention, it would be deemed unethical and immoral. The four main ethical principles are then applied to the policy and practice to coerce people to get the COVID-19 vaccine in order to attend school, clearly showing that during the past two and a half years, private and public medical practitioners violated the four medical ethical principles on a grand scale.

- Chapter 9 explicates the rudiments relating to the mainstream narrative that mask mandates are legitimate and that masks effectively prevent the spread of the SARS-CoV-2 virus. But has the "science" regarding mask effectiveness and the legality regarding mask mandates been settled as decisively as we have been directed to believe?[13,16] Despite public health authorities consistently and insistently proclaiming that they are merely following "the science", numerous arbitrary, irrational public health policies have been implemented during 2020, 2021, and 2022. Though scientific evidence can be a sound justification for State action, the correlation between politics, society, and science is considerably more intricate than purported. What exactly is "the science" that was followed over the past two and a half years? An analysis of the contemporary COVID-19 epistemological philosophy of "the science" subscribed to by the West provides some clarification. Orthodox science, according to the Western democratic States in the COVID-19 era, is science narrowly tailored and packaged to achieve a predestined ideological outcome. This epistemological view of science was the same world view held by tyrants such as Hitler, Stalin, Mussolini, and others.

- Chapter 10 will be dedicated to investigating COVID-19 legal paternalism and the limitation of fundamental human rights. The biomedical paternalistic State has grown in reach and power since

2020, with its pseudo-scientific biological theories and gene therapy mandatory vaccinations having led to the exploitation, suppression, coercion, and antagonization of the global population. The chapter examines critical issues related to the appropriateness of paternalistic public health measures during the COVID-19 pandemic, including the essential indicators to determine the legal voluntariness of a decision: 1.) Freedom from Coercion and Pressure, 2.) Informed and Educated Consent, and 3.) Healthy Psychological State. Legal paternalism implies that the State knows the interests of individual citizens better than the citizens themselves. But do governments have the right to influence citizens' behavior through biomedical mandates, or does this create an authoritarian State, leading to serious violations in individual autonomy and liberty? It will be clear that where governments interfere in individuals' autonomy, it is imperative that paternalistic policies should be subjected to rigorous scrutiny to determine their legitimacy, efficacy, necessity, and proportionality prior to implementation. The thesis of "implied limitations" is a consequence of the inviolability and interdependence of fundamental human rights. Fundamental rights are constitutively inalienable; they exist necessarily, inhere in every person, and cannot be limited for a reason other than their overall protection. If a fundamental right could be restricted for reasons other than their overall protection – for instance, for a general social benefit – they would no longer be inviolable.

- Chapter 11 juxtaposes the rule of law and tyranny with historical perspectives from Plato, Aristotle, and Thomas Aquinas. Modern perspectives are gained from Professor Lon Fuller's Morality of Law theory and Professor E. J. Criddle and Professor E. Fox-Decent's "prohibition on unilateralism principle" and "fiduciary criterion of legitimacy". The State is always subject to the rule of law concerning what type of mandates it may issue. Any human laws or mandates are nothing more than the expression of the natural order of justice, which limits the State's authority. A distinction is also drawn between laws that possess the "efficacy of the law" – which entail valid legislative acts – and inferior COVID-19 mandates that have the "force of law" but in essence lack the value of law. The limit case is the Nazi regime in which Adolf Eichmann never tired of repeating "the words of the Fuhrer have the 'force of law.'" It will be manifest that "an unjust law is no law at all", but rather a form of violence. The State cannot lawfully act erratically, irrationally, or arbitrarily. There is a "fiduciary principle" within international law analogous to the power-conferring rule *pacta sunt servanda* that transmutes international accords into binding treaties. The fiduciary principle permits States to retain and utilize public powers, but on the condition that those powers are used in the name of or in the best interest of their citizens. All juridical benchmarks applied confirm that the COVID-19 practices by Western States are illicit and lack the efficacy of law.

- Chapter 12 focuses attention on contemporary global biomedical fascism as a form of inverted totalitarianism pointing to the frightening similarities between Nazi Germany's public health (*Volksgesundheit*) policy in the 1930s and the *modus operandi* followed by Western democracies during the COVID-19 pandemic. Global public health was appropriated by the world's political and corporate elite and trans-formed from a personified state of individual choice into an abstract classification made subject to global capital's exploitative interests that pits the interests of ordinary citizens against those of the emergent global public health fascist. In the newfangled public health fascist State, the "rule of medical discretion" and "therapy" replaced "the rule of law". The United States as the world's only superpower played a key role in the globalization of inverted totalitarianism culminat-ing in the lockstep worldwide comportment and subservience of numerous States to implement COVID-19 policies. In modern-day biomedical fascism, transnational corporate control, surveillance, coercion, seduction, and mass manipulation, which far surpass those employed in Nazi Germany, are effectively masked by concentrated global mainstream media propaganda, political play acting, tech-nocratic censorship, technology addiction, sensationalism, sham wokeness, and superfluous consumerism that pacify and manipulate the public to relinquish their individual human rights and freedoms. The similarities between Nazi Germany's "greater good" biomedical practices and the COVID-19 "greater good" public health policies are striking and cannot be dismissed as irrelevant given the incremental death and destruction that such, in principle, totalitarian policies would continue to cause if tolerated and sustained.

- Chapter 13 observes how citizens should respond to the widespread violation of human rights and peremptory norms, and what should be done to counter the current global state of lawlessness. Roman poet Decimus Junius Juvenalis posed the classic question: *Quis custodiet ipsos custodes?* (Who shall guard the guardians?) When the guardians of society succumb to the temptation to exploit and harm the people that they are supposed to protect, by becoming anti-juridical and abusing emergency provisions, it is up to the citizenry to guard and defend the constitutional order *in extremis* to ensure a restoration to law and order. Historically, the most horrendous crimes against humanity – such as the holocaust, genocide, enforced sterilization, mass disappearances, torture, and other cruel inhumane acts – have resulted not from disobedience to government but from inappropriate subservient obedience to unjust, arbitrary pseudo-medical mandates. Civil disobedience and vocal opposition become a sacred duty when the State has become lawless. Dealing with a culture of human rights abuses is one of the most complex tasks facing citizens in transitioning from inherently fascist forms of government to true democratic forms of administration that protect and respect fundamental human rights. To restore confidence and accountability in the world, it is necessary to admit publicly the gross abuses that have taken place during the COVID-19 pandemic and to hold to account those responsible and liable who have committed, planned, ordered, executed, and profited from such abuses and to compensate victims. The "Joinet/Orentlicher" principles relating to impunity provide a helpful framework, from both a juridical and normative point of view, to deal with the insidious human rights violations that occurred during the COVID-19 pandemic.

- The postscript ends with seven measures to be taken at national and international level to counter the current global state of lawlessness. Instead of further accepting the disingenuous solution of "multi-stakeholderism" and PPPs between partners with fundamentally different fiduciary duties and legal obligations, a radical change of direction is necessary to restore the rule of law globally. The seven measures are crucial to thwarting the increasing, non-monitored, non-democratic, extra-judicial undue influence of a small corporate elite on the execution of the global agenda that since 2020 has led to an egregious violation of the post-Second World War juridical order and IHRL.

2. THEORIES OF NATURAL RIGHTS AND THE SOCIAL CONTRACT

"You have Rights antecedent to all earthly governments: Rights, that cannot be repealed or restrained by human laws; Rights, derived from the Great Legislator of the universe."

— John Adams

When one is analyzing fundamental human rights, the protective shield safeguarding citizens' most sacred rights from illicit government incursion, Oliver Wendell Holmes's famous statement that "a page of history is worth a volume of logic" is especially appropriate and important.[1] Consequently, it is paramount that the historical context and development of these safeguards be thoroughly understood and correctly employed, or their protective value inevitably will be corroded.

The development of the State's obligation to protect and respect the fundamental human rights of those within its jurisdiction as its first responsibility and duty is essentially a historical process. This historical process unfolded not only through the history of the formation of various States, but also in the history of the political ideas and instruments that have prompted their development.[2] The dictum *Salus populi suprema lex* ("The welfare [happiness, good fortune, salvation, felicity] of the people is the supreme law") is at once ancient and very new; it is as old as Roman antiquity and as new as the twentieth-century international human rights treaties and conventions.

In the context of the COVID-19 emergency measures, it is vital to reflect on where human rights originate. Does the government grant them? Or are they innate to every human being made in the image of God? If the former, then government can take away these rights. If the latter, then no government has the authority to take them away.

Fundamental Human Rights Come from God Through Natural Law

In Christianity and, more specifically, in the Bible, we find the original source of universal human rights. All humans are created in the image of God and therefore are deserving of life, liberty, and freedom.[3]

The Bible begins with the history of Creation, where God the Almighty Creator speaks the universe into existence. Within that history is the account of the creation of humanity. According to Genesis 1:26-27, above and beyond everything else God made, human beings are extraordinary, his crowning achievement![3]

> 26 Then God said, "Let us make mankind in our image, in our likeness, so that they may rule over the fish in the sea and the birds in the sky, over the livestock and all the wild animals, and over all the creatures that move along the ground.
>
> 27 So God created mankind in his own image, in the image of God he created them; male and female he created them.[4]

Humans are unique because, unlike all the other creatures on planet earth, we are created in God's image (*imago Dei*). For this reason, men and women have infinite worth and have value more than anything else in creation.[3] Freedom, equality, and human dignity are bestowed on all human beings by virtue of being the image-bearers of God Almighty. In Galatians 5:13-14, the Apostle Paul reminds us that these rights are not earned but divinely ordained. This is what makes our worth and our dignity innate and inseparable from who we are. Humans do not have fundamental human rights because we deserve them or earned them by adhering to government health mandates! We do not have human rights because we are black or white, female or male, vaccinated or unvaccinated. We have fundamental rights because each of us is created in the image of God (*imago Dei*) and therefore have inherent worth and dignity.

According to the catechism of the Catholic Church:

...the foundational principles upon which human rights derive come from natural law. Natural law is defined as "nothing other than the light of understanding placed in us by God; through it, we know what we must do and what we must avoid." God has given this light or law at the creation.[5]

Cicero (106 BC–43 BC) confirmed that the natural law, present in each man's heart and determined by reason, is universal in its principles and its authority extends to all human beings; it expresses the dignity of the person and determines the basis for their fundamental human rights:

> For there is a true law: right reason. It is in conformity with nature, is diffused among all men, and is immutable and eternal; its orders summon to duty; its prohibitions turn away from offense .... To replace it with a contrary law is a sacrilege; failure to apply even one of its provisions is forbidden; no one can abrogate it entirely.[6]

All power is from God, and therefore the law always has a sacred character.[7] Thomas Aquinas (1225-1274) bases this notion on the Biblical texts, *quæ autem sunt, a Deo ordinatæ sunt* (All things that are, are set in order by God), and *omnis enim potestas a Domino Deo est* (For all power is from the Lord God).[7,8,9] Natural law (the law of God), provides the foundation on which all governments should structure just juridical rules; it provides the necessary moral foundation for regulating the human society and provides the needed basis for civil law with which it is connected.[10] Therefore, all fundamental human rights come from God through natural law, which is absolute and unalterable. Natural law is the foundation of all just human laws, and any mandate that violates the natural law principles is an unjust or "contrary law" and "a sacrilege."[10] Aquinas categorically postulated that:

> Human law is law only by virtue of its accordance with right reason; and thus, it is manifest that it flows from the eternal law. And in so far as it deviates from right reason, it is called an unjust law; in such case, it is no law at all, but rather a species of violence.[11]

It is the duty of the government to protect and improve the rights of its citizens. It acts against its natural function, the function for which it exists, if it harms rather than helps its citizens.[7] The rule of law requires State institutions to act in accordance with the natural law. The purpose of the rule of law is to protect basic individual rights by requiring the State to act in accordance with the law. If the State acts without legal authority, it is acting lawlessly, which is against the notion of a constitutional democracy and represents a perversion of government that is no longer just.[7]

The role of government is to foster and protect human rights, not to endow them. Unfortunately, in 2022 this truth is no longer self-evident, and many Western democracies turned modern tyrannies are propagating the false narrative that human rights are privileges granted by governments and corrupt and conflicted public health agencies, subject to adherence to capricious and arbitrary health mandates.[7,12]

The English Common Law Tradition

In the Great Charter of the *Magna Carta* (1215), one finds clear rules that afforded protection to citizens' fundamental rights. King John, obsessed with regaining possession of French lands, abused the strong central government and system of taxation. Out of the rebellion that ensued, the *Magna Carta* emerged which restrained the crown's power and articulated political and civil rights. All through the *Magna Carta*, King John agrees to correct his injustices and remedy his abuses of authority. The *Magna Carta* places the sovereign ruler firmly under the rule of law, not above it. Some articles in the Canadian Charter of Rights and the American Constitution bear great resemblance to various articles in the *Magna Carta*.[2] The clause in the *Magna Carta* that provides that a free man shall be punished only "by the lawful judgement of his peers or by the law of the land" became a central tenet of the rule of law.[2,13] Although some say that it is only the ill-informed that regard the *Magna Carta* as important, it cannot be contested that the charter of the *Magna Carta* bestowed certain rights and liberties on the people that protected them from both government abuses and private abuses.[2] Even if one argues that all that happened in 1215 at Runnymede was that some nobles stood up to King John, broke his autarchy, and exacted some concessions for themselves; even that was a clear limitation on monarchy and a seed of constitutionalism and for the rights of the individual.[2] Rights that the nobles obtained for themselves later slowly spread to others. Unknowingly, the nobles laid the foundations for representative government.

Under the traditional English doctrine, every loyal subject was entitled to the king's protection.[2,14] This traditional doctrine received its classical expressions in the works of Sir Edward Coke (1552-1634), who defined the relationship between sovereign and subject in terms of a "mutual bond and obligation."[2,15] Under this arrangement, the subject owed "allegiance or obedience" while the king was bound to the duty of "government and protection" of his subjects. For Coke, these reciprocal obligations were best defined by the maxim *protectio trahit subjectionem, et subjectio protectionem: protection implies subjection and subjection protection.*[2] These reciprocal obligations and duties were inherent in the very nature of the relationship between the sovereign and the subject. Coke made it clear that the sovereign's duty of protection included the duty to respect and protect subjects' fundamental human rights to life, human dignity, and freedom from bodily harm by asserting that "The subject's right to protection entails the safety of his person, from violence, unlawful molestation or wrong."[2]

For Coke, the relationship between sovereign and subject arose from the law of nature and was immutable and unchangeable. Over the next 150 years, the basis of Coke's doctrine was transformed into the *"original contract doctrine"* between sovereign and subject under which the subject owed obedience in return for the ruler's protection.[2,16-18] Under this constitutional conception, the subjects had no duty to obey if the sovereign failed in his duty to protect and respect their basic human rights.

The Social Contract Theory

The theoretical foundations of modern constitutionalism were laid down through the doctrine of natural rights and the social contract by numerous eminent philosophers during the 17th and 18th centuries such as Thomas Hobbes, John Locke, Jean Jacques Rousseau, Francis Hutcheson, Jean Jacques Burlamaqui, William Blackstone, and Immanuel Kant.

Thomas Hobbes (1586-1679)

One of the earliest and most famous exponents of the social contract theory was Thomas Hobbes.[2] In his book "The Leviathan" (1651), he postulated that the state of nature was intolerably bad and that it was not a very convenient condition due to the lack of "established, settled and known law," the lack of "known and impartial judges," and the absence of an executive to enforce judgments. In this state of nature, a man's fundamental rights to life, liberty, and property were very insecure. Accordingly, for the purpose of self-preservation by unanimous consent, men abandoned the state of nature and entered a "social contract" that created a government designed to protect their natural rights.[2,19]

Hobbes's main contribution to constitutionalism lies in his radical rationalism and makes it abundantly clear that there are certain rights that an individual can never transfer or forfeit:

> Whensoever a man transferreth his right, or renounceth it, it is either in consideration of some right reciprocally transferred to himself, or for some other good he hopeth for thereby. For it is a voluntary act: and of the voluntary acts of every man, the object is some good to himself. And therefore, there be some rights which no man can be understood by any words, or other signs, to have abandoned or transferred. As first a man cannot lay down the right of resisting them that assault him by force to take away his life, because he cannot be understood to aim thereby at any good to himself. The same may be said of wounds, and chains, and imprisonment, both because there is no benefit consequent to such patience, as there is to the patience of suffering another to be wounded or imprisoned, as also because a man cannot tell when he seeth men proceed against him by violence whether they intend his death or not. And lastly the motive and end for which this renouncing and transferring of right is introduced is nothing else but the security of a man's person, in his life, and in the means of so preserving life as not to be weary of it.[19]

John Locke (1632–1704)

John Locke was another major proponent of the theory of natural rights and social contract, which were based upon the individual's consent to form a society that existed and had a government for the purpose of preserving the individual's natural (human) rights.[2,20] According to Locke's theory, man is not naturally subject to a sovereign. In a state of nature, which is "a state of perfect freedom," each human being is free to do as he sees fit, without being subject to or depending on the will of others. In his famous work "Two Treatises of Government" (1690), Locke declares that:

To understand political power right, and derive it from its original, we must consider what State all men are naturally in, and that is, a state of perfect freedom to order their actions, and dispose of their possessions and persons, as they think fit, within the bounds of the law of nature, without asking leave, or depending upon the will of any other man.[20]

The natural state of humankind is a state of equality in which free men and women live out their lives without any subordination or subjection to a ruler. In a state of nature, men are not subject to positive laws but only to the law of nature.[2,20] The law of nature is a law that can be associated with and shares the same characteristics as the law of reason. The law of nature teaches "That being all equal and independent none ought to harm another in his life, health, liberty, and possession."[2,20] In this state of nature, every person has the right to enforce the law of nature by acts of retribution, punishment, or restraint against a potential or actual violator of his natural human rights. In a state of nature, however, an individual often lacks the capability and capacity to defend himself against invasions or attacks by others rendering the actual enjoyment of his rights to life, liberty, security, and property very insecure and subject to violation. Due to this "very insecure" status of rights, an individual agrees to give up his natural power to a community or society "for the mutual preservation of their lives, liberties, and estates."[2,20]

The individual's association with the State or community was entirely voluntary, resulting from the individual's inability to provide protection for himself. Consequently, the individual agrees to be regulated by the just, rational laws made by society to preserve himself and the rest of that society, in exchange for the "protection from its whole strength."[2]

According to Locke, the main aim of a government was to be the force of all the members of a society to preserve and protect the members of that society from injury and violence. Because a government is established to protect the individual members, it is obliged and owes a duty to secure every individual's right to life, liberty, and freedom. In the event of the State acting contrary to this trust, the State must be dissolved, and the community has the right to establish a new government. Such dissolution will occur either when the government itself invades and violates the rights of its subjects or where a government fails or omits to use its power to secure human rights.[2,20]

Jean Jacques Rousseau (1712-1778)

In his "Social Contract" (1762), Rousseau argued that if a man was born for freedom and yet was everywhere in chains, the only means of rendering the slavery legitimate lay in the retention of the sovereign power in the hands of the people who had made the contract, which turned a multitude of individuals into a society.[21,22]

Rousseau's doctrine determines that liberty results from the nature of man and that the social contract secured the preservation of man's natural rights. "[Man's] first law is to provide for his own preservation, his first cares are those which he owes to himself; and, as soon as he reaches years of discretion, he is the sole judge of the proper means of preserving himself, and consequently becomes his own master."[22] In this state of nature where man is his own master, he inevitably reaches the point where the obstacles and resistance facing him in his challenge to preserve his own rights are greater than the resources one man has at his disposal. To protect himself and to preserve the enjoyment of his natural human rights to life, health, and security, a man enters into a social compact and forms a society where the sum of forces is great enough to overcome the threat of violation of natural rights. As Rousseau asserts:

> This sum of forces can arise only where several persons come together: but, as the force and liberty of each man are the chief instruments of his self-preservation, how can he pledge them without harming his own interests and neglecting the care he owes to himself? This difficulty, in its bearing on my present subject, may be stated in the following terms: The problem is to find a form of association which will defend and protect with the whole common force the person and goods of each associate, and in which each, while uniting himself with all, may still obey himself alone, and remain as free as before. This is the fundamental problem of which the Social Contract provides the solution.[2,22]

It is clear that according to Rousseau, the main object of the State was to protect individuals from actual or potential violations of their fundamental rights.[1] Any government that harms an individual's self-interest and self-preservation through arbitrary unjust laws obliterates natural rights and violates the social contract.

Francis Hutcheson (1694 -1746)

The writings of Francis Hutcheson, a key figure in the Scottish Enlightenment that were widely read in the American colonies, also supported the doctrine that the main aim of government was the protection of the individual's basic human rights.[2] In his book, "A Short Introduction to Moral Philosophy", Hutcheson wrote that:

> [A]s the end of all civil power is acknowledged by all to be the safety and happiness of the whole body, any power not naturally conducive to this end is unjust, which the people, who rashly granted it under an error may, justly abolish again when they find it necessary to their safety to do so.[23]

This proposition regarding the main aim and duty of government is, in turn, premised upon Hutcheson's view of the nature of men – that men are "necessarily determined to pursue their own happiness."[2,23] When Hutcheson wrote that the end of civil power is the "safety and happiness of the whole body," it is clear that the State should refrain from committing abuses. It is the duty of the State to ensure that the members of society are protected and safe in order for them to pursue their own happiness in a secure environment.

A government that declares that citizens that do not comply with arbitrary mandates lose certain fundamental freedoms and the ability to pursue happiness becomes an unjust, illegitimate form of government that no longer fulfills the aim for which it was created.

Jean Jacques Burlamaqui (1694–1748)

Writing at about the same time as Hutcheson, and along the same lines, was the Swiss philosopher Jean Jacques Burlamaqui.[1] Burlamaqui was also an advocate of the social contract theory. He saw man as a social creature for whom society and government are necessary for the development of his *faculta* or mental and physical abilities. Foremost among those faculties is the desire of man for happiness, which according to Burlamaqui, is "as essential to man and as inseparable from his nature as reason itself."[24]

Since man is designed to pursue happiness, it is the function of society and the duty of the government to assist him in attaining it. When a person has a natural right, other people ought not to employ their strength and liberty in resisting him in this point. They should respect his right and assist him in the exercise of it.[2,24] A "just society," in Burlamaqui's view, was a society where the State's main aim was to protect the people's rights so that the people could pursue their own happiness in a safe and secure society.

Burlamaqui emphasized that the nature of human beings placed certain affirmative obligations upon the State by including an obligation to increase the happiness of its citizens. Man has a duty to pursue happiness and he posits an extension of that duty upon the State. The State has a positive obligation to create an environment where individuals can pursue their dreams and ideals. For a man to be happy or to pursue happiness, his basic rights to life, liberty, security, and property must be protected and respected by the State and other members of society.[2]

Burlamaqui's works were widely read in America during the 18th century, and his ideas are traceable in the writings of many American patriots. In 1774, James Wilson, basing many of his views on Burlamaqui's, wrote an essay called "Considerations on the Nature and Extent of the Legislative Authority of the British Parliament", in which he stated:

> The happiness of the society is the first law of every government. This rule is founded on the law of nature: it must control every political maxim: it must regulate the legislature itself. The people have a right to insist that this rule be observed; and are entitled to demand a moral security that the legislature will observe it.[2,25]

Wilson also commented that in a state of nature, man has a natural right to property, character, and liberty and, importantly, to the safety and security of the person that must be protected by the government at all times and as its chief aim. Happiness and safety implied more than physical safety. It meant a state of wholeness and complete wellbeing.[2,25]

The arbitrary COVID-19 edicts led to the extreme unhappiness of vast sections of the population, leading to dramatically increased suicides, substance abuse, and domestic violence.[26-31] The State has a positive obligation to create an environment where individuals can pursue their dreams and ideals. For a man to be happy or to pursue happiness, his basic rights to life, liberty, security, and property must be protected and respected by the State and other members of society. It follows that a government that imposes vaccine mandates, mask mandates, and self-isolation mandates resulting in millions of citizens losing their ability to live, work, and socialize significantly decreases the happiness of its citizens.

Sir William Blackstone (1723–1780)

Sir William Blackstone, in the eighteenth century in his publications "Commentaries on the Laws of England" (1765-1769), combined Coke's common law doctrine of allegiance and protection and Locke's theory of natural rights and the social contract theory into the mainstream of English constitutional theory.[32] Blackstone contended that "it was a maxim of law that protection and subjection are reciprocal."[32]

Blackstone's doctrine of reciprocal allegiance and protection was set in a broad framework of the social contract that provided that: "the whole should protect all its parts, and that every part should pay obedience to the will of the whole," or, in modern terms, the State should guard the basic human rights such as the right to life, the right to freedom of movement, and the right to be free from medical experimentation of each member and in return for this protection, each individual will submit to the just laws of the State.[2,32]

Blackstone revealed the structure of the positive and negative character of individual rights and duties, expounding Coke and Locke's theories. In a state of nature, an individual has a right to be free from interference by others; thus, in a sense, natural liberty is negative. On the other hand, in terms of the social contract theory, when a society is formed to obtain the advantages of association with others, the benefits are positive in nature.[2,32] One of the most important benefits was the protection of one's fundamental human rights by the community. Blackstone writes the following on the rights of persons:

> For the principal aim of society is to protect individuals in the enjoyment of those absolute rights, which were vested in them by the immutable laws of nature; but which could not be preserved in peace without that mutual assistance and intercourse, which is gained by the institution of friendly and social communities.[32]

Protection is a positive right claim on the society to provide something to which the individual is entitled. This encompassed a positive legal duty of protection not only from governmental oppression and tyranny but also from private acts of aggression and exploitation. In return for the benefits of protection by society, the individual also assumes certain positive duties. These duties require that the individual contributes to the subsistence and peace of society. The citizen is *inter alia* obliged through the obligation of allegiance to pay taxes, aid in enforcing laws, and defend the society against invasion. The obligation of protection is, therefore, a reciprocal obligation.[2,32] The individual not only has a right to protection from society but also has a duty to protect society and its citizens. Under the classical view, a society that is an aggregate of people living together in an ordered community is also an association of mutual protection. Society fulfills its duty of protection through the making of various just, reasonable, rational laws, regulating society, and by respecting and protecting fundamental human rights effectively.[2]

The classical legal tradition also distinguished between two sorts of substantive rights, namely "absolute rights" and "relative rights." Absolute rights were rights that belong to individuals in a state of nature. Relative rights were rights that were incidental to persons as members of society and standing in several relations to each other. According to Blackstone, the primary end of all human laws was to protect individuals in the full enjoyment of their absolute rights. The protection of relative rights was a secondary aim of human laws. Absolute rights of individuals were defined as "the rights of personal security, personal liberty, and private property."[2,32] Personal security was seen as "a person's legal and uninterrupted enjoyment of his life, his limbs, his body, his health, and his reputation."[2,32] When Blackstone discussed the ways in which the law protected absolute rights, he reviewed not only the barriers against governmental oppression contained in the Magna Carta and the American colonies Bills of Rights, but also the protection against private aggression afforded by civil and criminal law. Absolute rights were not merely natural rights, but legal rights protected by the law. Personal security was defined not merely as a negative right against invasion of one's life and person, but as a positive right to legal protection. Absolute rights were rights to the security of person and property, and this security was provided by law, whose end was the protection of rights.[2,32]

Mandatory pseudo-medical mandates that violate a broad array of fundamental human rights and have known life-threatening side-effects, brutally interrupt the enjoyment by an individual of "his life, his limbs, his body, his health" and as such violates the social contract.[2,32]

Immanuel Kant (1724–1804)

German philosopher and one of the most important Enlightenment thinkers, Immanuel Kant, argued that the supreme principle of morality is a standard of rationality that he dubbed the "Categorical Imperative" (CI). Kant described the CI as an empirical, rationally necessary, and unconditional principle that we should always follow in the face of any natural yearnings or proclivities we may have to the contrary.[33] All moral requirements, according to Kant, are justified by this important principle, which implies that all immoral acts are irrational because they disregard the CI.[33]

According to Kant, there is only one innate right, "Freedom (independence from being constrained by another's choice), insofar as it can coexist with the freedom of every other in accordance with a universal law."[33] Kant rejects any other foundation for the State, specifically reasoning that the wellbeing of citizens cannot be the foundation of State authority. Kant contends that a State cannot lawfully enforce any "particular conception of happiness upon its citizens."[33] To do so would be for the sovereign to treat citizens as children, presuming that they are not capable to comprehend what is truly beneficial or harmful to themselves.[33]

The COVID-19 legal paternalism that has swept the globe since 2020 is irreconcilable with Kant's philosophy. He was resolutely opposed to authoritarian governments. A government that views subjects as a father views his children as immature beings who are incompetent to decide for themselves what is good or bad for them and dictates instead "how they ought to be happy" is "the worst despotism we can think of" that "subverts all the freedom of the subjects, who would have no freedom whatsoever." The sovereign who "wants to make people happy in accord with his own concept of happiness…becomes a despot."[34,35]

According to Kant, justice, or the protection and enforcement of individual rights (especially the *"innate"* right to individual freedom), is at once the proper purpose of an ideal government and the standard by which a government should determine proper legislation.[36]

The American Revolution

During the American Revolutionary era, all the above theories of Coke, Locke, Rousseau, Hutcheson, Burlamaqui, and Blackstone on State responsibility for the effective protection of its citizens were expressed into a coherent world view for Americans in the Whig ideology.[2,37] In terms of the American Whig ideology, protection was a primary purpose of government.

The concept of "protection" encompassed three elements under the Whig ideology:

- To be under the protection of the law meant to have the status of a free man.
- Protection further meant that the law recognized and secured an

individual's rights to life, liberty, and property.

- Protection referred to the specific ways the government prevented violations of human rights or redressed and punished such violations.[2]

Coke's doctrine of "reciprocal obligations" was at the forefront of American constitutional thought during the American Revolutionary period. Americans, however, rejected the tenet that the bond between king and subject was natural and, therefore, immutable.[2] Instead, they classified this relationship between sovereign and subject in terms of the original contract that determined that the sovereign was bound to protect the various rights of his subjects in turn for their allegiance and obedience.[2] As noted by Phillip B. Scot in the "West Virginia Law Review":

> The American Revolution was rooted in the belief that the people are the ultimate sovereign, that government is, and must be, only an institution of enumerated powers, limited in scope, and instituted and sustained by the public will. Thus, government as envisioned by our forefathers is a means to an end - the preservation and protection of the individual and collective rights of the citizenry. This provision in our constitution protects the people from government, reaffirming the truism that no government can impose its rule on an unwilling people.[38]

One of the most influential documents of revolutionary America was the Virginia Declaration of Rights. It was the first constitutional confirmation by a North American government that citizens have certain inalienable rights that the government can never infringe upon or take away. Authored by George Mason, who was a proponent of Locke's conceptions about the state of nature, the social contract, and the innate rights of man, it was adopted by the Virginia Constitutional Convention on June 12, 1776.[38] The root of the Virginia Declaration of Rights is that men, in establishing a government, surrender only a part of their relative rights and not their absolute fundamental human rights. In other words, the people "have certain inherent natural rights, of which they cannot, by any compact deprive or divest their posterity."[39] The Virginia Declaration further determines that all government power is derived from the people, and in Article III specifies that:

> Government is, or ought to be, instituted for the common benefit, protection, and security of the people, nation, or community; of all the various modes and forms of government, that is best which is

capable of producing the greatest degree of happiness and safety and is most effectually secured against the danger of maladministration. And that, when any government shall be found inadequate or contrary to these purposes, a majority of the community has an indubitable, inalienable, and indefeasible right to reform, alter, or abolish it, in such manner as shall be judged most conducive to the public weal.[40]

The "common benefit" section was meant to articulate the democratic principle that the State exists to help the community as a whole. Whenever State officials take more power than needed to accomplish these objectives, "government has gone too far and when government is being used to exploit the people, they have the right to change it."[38]

When the American Revolutionaries decided to break from Great Britain, they justified their revolutionary acts in terms of the fact that the king had abdicated government as a result of breaking the original contract between sovereign and subject.[2] The American Declaration of Independence of 1776, after naming a number of grievances that the king of Great Britain failed to redress, alleged that the king "has abdicated government... by declaring us out of his protection and waging war against us."[41] Therefore, by not protecting his subjects as he ought to have, the king broke the original contract, and his subjects owed no allegiance or obedience to him.[2]

The American War of Independence subsequently broke out and ended in the establishment of a new political entity known as the United States of America, which was founded upon a constitution promulgated in 1787, which came into operation in 1789 and is still in existence today.[2] This was the true beginning of modern constitutionalism and the protection of civil liberties and fundamental human rights. This Constitution embodies the principles enunciated in the Declaration of Independence (1776), which categorically pronounced that:

>...all men are created equal; that they are endowed by their Creator with certain unalienable rights.... That to secure these rights, governments are instituted among men, deriving their just powers from the consent of the governed, that, whenever any form of government becomes destructive of these ends, it is the right of the people to alter or abolish it, and to institute a new government, laying its foundations on such principles, and organizing its powers in such form, as to them shall seem most likely to affect their safety and happiness.[42]

Professor Carl Becker, the late, eminent Cornell University historian, in his 1922 book "The Declaration of Independence", argued that the famous second paragraph of the Declaration is "a frank assertion of the right of revolution, whenever the people are convinced that the existing government has become destructive of the end of which all governments are instituted among men."[43] This of course is an accurate depiction of the legal philosophy of the founding fathers, but a nuisance and inconvenient truth when preservation of the corrupt *status quo* is sought.[43] The Anglo-American legal tradition has endorsed the legal right that under certain circumstances the people, rather than the government, may best represent the constitution and the rule of law.[44] The founding fathers' legal doctrine of resistance developed from the notion that when the State seeks to subvert the terms of the social contract, then it becomes an aggressor against the people, who then have a right to revolution.[44] A distinction is drawn between "law-making violence" (*rechtsetzende Gewalt*) through a proliferation of unjust mandates and "law preserving violence" (*rechtserhaltende Gewalt*) through a just revolution.[45] A revolution that aims to preserve or reinstate the law is a form of pure or divine violence.[46] When elected officials break their oath to uphold the rule of law, it is not the patriotic citizen who is abrogating the constitution, but the governing officials![44] A revolution that *de facto* seeks to establish or re-establish constitutional norms that align with the natural law is, therefore, lawful irrespective of the pseudo-laws by a corrupt power elite that may "outlaw" such civil action.[46]

It is noteworthy that the American Revolution was itself not a democratic movement. About 20% of the colonists were loyalist to the British crown and a further 33% were averse to war and "lukewarm to Engand". According to John Adams only about 33% of Americans at the time supported the revolution and the consensus is that only 3% actively participated in the war at any one time.[47,48] The British had lost legitimacy, and Thomas Paine's booklet "Common Sense" in January 1776, concisely provided American legitimacy to revolt based on natural law.[49]

In the COVID-19 era, many Western democracies "have abdicated government" by "declaring" the unvaccinated and those with opposing views "out of their protection" and "waging war" against the unvaccinated by not protecting their fundamental human rights and violating their fundamental human rights.

The French Legacy

The final article of the Declaration of the Rights of Man and the Citizen *"Declaration de l'Homme et du Citoyen"* was approved on August 26, 1789 by the National Constituent Assembly, during the period of the French Revolution, as the first step toward composing a constitution for France.[2,20,40] The Declaration preamble describes the fundamental characteristics of the rights that are listed as being "natural, unalienable and sacred" and embracing "simple and incontestable principles" on which ordinary citizens are legally entitled to base their demands.[2,20,40] The document is saturated with the dogmas of the contractual origin of the State, of popular sovereignty and of individual rights, as is clearly shown by the following phrases:

1. Men are born and remain free and equal in rights. Social distinctions may be founded only upon the general good.
2. The aim of all political association is the preservation of the natural and imprescriptible rights of man. These rights are liberty, property, security, and resistance to oppression.
3. The principle of all sovereignty resides essentially in the nation. No body nor individual may exercise any authority which does not proceed directly from the nation.
4. Liberty consists in the freedom to do everything which injures no one else; hence the exercise of the natural rights of each man has no limits except those which assure to the other members of the society the enjoyment of the same rights. These limits can only be determined by law.
5. Law can only prohibit such actions as are hurtful to society. Nothing may be prevented which is not forbidden by law, and no one may be forced to do anything not provided for by law.
6. Law is the expression of the general will. Every citizen has a right to participate personally, or through his representative, in its foundation. It must be the same for all, whether it protects or punishes. All citizens, being equal in the eyes of the law, are equally eligible to all dignities and to all public positions and occupations, according to their abilities, and without distinction except that of their virtues and talents.
7. No person shall be accused, arrested, or imprisoned except in the cases and according to the forms prescribed by law. Anyone soliciting, transmitting, executing, or causing to be executed, any arbitrary order, shall be punished.

8. The law shall provide for such punishments only as are strictly and obviously necessary, and no one shall suffer punishment except it be legally inflicted in virtue of a law passed and promulgated before the commission of the offense.

9. No one shall be disquieted on account of his opinions, including his religious views, provided their manifestation does not disturb the public order established by law.

10. The free communication of ideas and opinions is one of the most precious of the rights of man. Every citizen may, accordingly, speak, write, and print with freedom, but shall be responsible for such abuses of this freedom as shall be defined by law.

11. Society has the right to require of every public agent an account of his administration.

12. A society in which the observance of the law is not assured, nor the separation of powers defined, has no constitution at all.

The French Revolution and Declaration in the opinion of some were even more influential than the American Revolution in spreading fundamental human rights and freedom principles to many parts of the world.[2] The French Declaration, moreover, articulated some ideas that were at best implicit in the American Constitution. It also propagated ideas more advanced than the American Constitution, some of which took a long time to reach and take root in the United States. Importantly the final French Constitution, which followed in 1791, and to which the Declaration was prefixed, in Article 6, *force de loi* designates the supremacy of "the rule of law," which even the sovereign himself can neither abrogate nor modify by decree.

After the American Revolution, this was the second great stage in the development of modern constitutionalism and the recognition of certain inalienable fundamental human rights and freedoms. The French Revolution lighted a fire of political liberty that was never again to be permanently smothered.[2]

Chapter Conclusion

We are all created in the image of God (*imago Dei*). This is what makes our dignity and our worth innate and inextricable from who we are as human beings. We do not have human rights because we earn them; we do not have human rights because we deserve them; we do not have human rights because we are black or white, female or male, vaccinated or unvaccinated. We have inalienable fundamental rights because each of us is made in the image of the Creator and therefore has innate dignity and worth. Therefore, all fundamental human rights come from God through natural law, which is absolute and unalterable.

Natural law provides the foundation on which all governments should structure just juridical rules and provides the necessary moral foundation for regulating society. Natural law is the foundation of all just human laws, and any mandate that violates the natural law principles is an unjust law. The rule of law requires State institutions to act in accordance with the natural law. If the State violates the natural law, it is acting lawlessly, which is against the notion of a constitutional democracy and represents a perversion of government that is no longer just.

Absolute rights are rights that belong to individuals in a state of nature while relative rights are rights that are incidental to persons as members of society and standing in numerous relations to each other. In terms of the social contract, individuals agree to give up some of their relative rights but never give up their absolute rights such as the right to life, the right to bodily integrity and the right to freedom from medical experimentation. In other words, the people "have certain inherent natural rights, of which they cannot, by any compact deprive or divest their posterity." The primary end of all human laws should be to protect individuals in the full and unfettered enjoyment of their absolute fundamental human rights. The State should guard the absolute human rights of each member of society and in return for this protection, each individual will give up some relative rights and submit to the just laws of the State. The principle is that protection and subjection are reciprocal. Protection implies subjection and subjection protection. Citizens have no duty to obey if the State fails in its duty to protect and respect their absolute rights. As advocated by Alexander Hamilton in 1775:

> The origin of all civil government, justly established, must be a voluntary compact, between the rulers and the ruled; and must be liable to such limitations, as are necessary for the security of the absolute rights of the latter; for what original title can any man or set of men have, to govern others, except their own consent? To usurp dominion over a people, in their own despite, or to grasp at a more extensive power than they are willing to entrust, is to violate that law of nature, which gives every man a right to his personal liberty; and can, therefore, confer no obligation to obedience.[50]

States do not have the right to decide when people are entitled to enjoy their absolute fundamental human rights. These natural rights are not subject to politics or vaccination status but are inherent in the individual. The first and most basic duty of government in terms of the social compact, is to protect the absolute fundamental human rights of its citizens. The government derives its power to govern from the people. The purpose of the State is to serve the people and not the converse.

Human law is law only by virtue of its harmony with right reason. Insofar as human law deviates from rationality and right reason, it is an unjust law and therefore no law at all, but rather a kind of violence towards the public. Many of the irrational pseudo-medical emergency measures enacted to combat COVID-19 infringed absolute natural rights in contravention of natural law, the social contract, and constitutional legal norms developed over the past 1,000 years. To mandate a COVID-19 genetic vaccine with side-effects that include death, injury, or disability equates to "by force to take away life" and instituting health passports that violate freedom of movement equates to causing "wounds, chains and imprisonment" that defy the very essence of the social contract theory by infringing rights that were never and could never be transferred to the State.[2,32]

Governments do not have the moral high ground as they claim, but have become lawless, illegitimate, and tyrannical by breaching the social contract. A government that does not protect its citizen's fundamental human rights has abdicated government by declaring citizens out of their protection and "waging war" against them by violating their fundamental human rights. History has proven repeatedly, that when governments violate the social contact, ordinary citizens will eventually take the necessary action to restore the natural legal order.

3. MODERN INTERNATIONAL HUMAN RIGHTS LAW AND BIOETHICAL NORMS

"Respect for human life, liberty, and wellbeing must be enshrined as rights beyond the power of any force to diminish."

— Nelson Mandela

The era of modern human rights law commenced in 1945 with the birth of the United Nations and a transformative vision of human beings as ends in themselves. Individuals once considered mere objects of the sovereign were now deemed subjects of international law with positive legal claims to protection, not only from State tyranny and oppression but also from human rights abuses by non-State actors.[1,3]

Prior to the Second World War, the relationship between the ruler and the citizens of a particular country was treated as a completely "internal" matter, beyond the purview of the international community. This conception of sovereignty was changed with the ratification of international conventions and treaties that governments are legally obligated to adhere to. The modern international human rights regime redefined the meaning of international law by substituting the understanding of law as defined in terms of State borders with a transformed construction where human rights are the supreme law of the world.[1,2] After the Second World War and the atrocities committed during it, there have been enormous advances in the development of human rights law, normative bioethical standards, and the legal instruments to implement them. States are no longer "free" to do as they will in the domestic sphere;

instead, they are bound by provisions in international law that are aimed at protecting individuals from government tyranny.[4]

IHRL, unlike classic international law, sees individuals as the main subjects of international law. It is not based on reciprocity, but rather on a network of objective obligations, the enforcement of which is: a) not primarily in the interest of other States, and b) sometimes accomplished through international bodies.[2,4]

The State is the entity primarily responsible for upholding human rights on the international level as well as in the national sphere. To conceptualize this responsibility fully, it must be made clear who is responsible and to what degree, where that responsibility arises from, towards whom such responsibility exists, and how such responsibility is asserted. The constitutive relation between human rights law and politics in the international sphere is complex and dynamic. It makes use of a prodigious body of customary human rights norms and the legal norms contained in the various international treaties to hold States legally accountable for their actions and omissions under international law.[4] This framework includes various principles bearing on the interpretation of treaties and the *grundnorm* of treaty law, *pacta sunt servanda*.[3]

IHRL is based on the concept that every nation has an obligation to respect the human rights of its citizens and that individuals and the international community at large and the *populus* have a right and responsibility to protest and intervene if States do not adhere to this obligation *erga omnes*.[2,6] Kofi Atta Annan, who served as the seventh Secretary-General of the United Nations (UN) from 1997 to 2006 and was one of the co-recipients of the 2001 Nobel Peace Prize, on September 30, 2003 opined that:

> .... human rights by their very nature, do sway with the distinction traditionally drawn between the internal order and the international order. Human rights give rise to a new legal permeability...the State should be the best guarantor of human rights. It is the State that the international community should principally entrust with ensuring the protection of individuals. However, the issue of international action must be raised when States prove unworthy of this task, when they violate the fundamental principles laid down in the Charter of the United Nations, and when – far from being protectors of individuals – they become tormentors.[2]

The Universal Declaration of Human Rights

The process of the universalizing of human rights through the codification of "natural law" started with the adoption of the UDHR as a common standard of achievement for all peoples and nations in 1948.[3] This was the first action in the promulgation of an International Bill of Human Rights and a major step forward in the promotion of the rule of law and respect for human rights and freedoms at international and national levels. The Declaration comprises in one consolidated text nearly the entire range of what today is recognized as human rights and fundamental freedoms. The UDHR is an impressive set of legal norms and one of the greatest single milestones in human history. Never has an international forum committed itself to human rights as a precondition to justice and peace, nor has an organization of governments set forth human rights as a normative goal.[2,5]

Any deprivation of fundamental human rights, as we are currently witnessing on a grand scale across the globe in the name of COVID-19 public health, should not be tolerated since the UDHR requires that dignity and equality shall be the inalienable rights of all men and women.[5]

In the preamble of the UDHR, all Member States declare that "the inherent dignity and the equal and inalienable rights of all members of the human family are the foundation of freedom, justice, and peace in the world" and commit themselves to "the promotion of universal respect for and observance of human rights and fundamental freedoms."[5]

Member States further proclaimed and accepted the UDHR as "a common standard of achievement for all peoples and all nations, to the end that every individual and every organ of society, keeping this Declaration constantly in mind, shall respect fundamental human rights and freedoms."[2,5] Under international human rights normative standards as set out in the UDHR, governments have a responsibility to respect, protect and fulfill the human rights of all people in their territory. If a government fails in this obligation, it shares responsibility with those who commit the abuse, whether it is a big tech company illegitimately silencing a government critic or a large corporation coercing individuals to take a vaccine against their will. When governments breach their duty to safeguard those in their territory from human rights abuses through arbitrary health mandates, they violate their international obligations *erga omnes* and should be held accountable.[2,6]

There are a number of articles in the UDHR that place specific positive duties on States to protect fundamental human rights and that are worth highlighting:

Article 3
Everyone has the right to life, liberty and security of person.

Article 5
No one shall be subjected to torture or to cruel, inhuman or degrading treatment or punishment.

Article 6
Everyone has the right to recognition everywhere as a person before the law.

Article 12
No one shall be subjected to arbitrary interference with his privacy, family, home or correspondence, nor to attacks upon his honour and reputation. Everyone has the right to the protection of the law against such interference or attacks.

Article 28
Everyone is entitled to a social and international order in which the rights and freedoms set forth in this Declaration can be fully realized.

Article 30
Nothing in this Declaration may be interpreted as implying for any State, group, or person any right to engage in any activity or to perform any act aimed at the destruction of any of the rights and freedoms set forth herein.

The UDHR meets a worldwide demand for adequate personal freedom through the universally accepted human rights norms reflected therein and the respect for the dignity of human beings. It communicates the demands that men and women of all nations have held about freedom throughout human history. The Declaration and the various binding treaties that followed moved the world community from a system where States have sovereignty over all that occurs within their territories to a system where human rights law is the supreme law of the new international legal order to which all States must adhere.[1] The COVID-19 practice whereby countries such as the United States, the United Kingdom, France, Germany, Austria, Australia, Italy, Netherlands, New Zealand, and Latvia, to name a few, are actively violating citizens' most fundamental human rights in order to combat a disease that poses a risk of death to 0.15% of the infected population is irreconcilable with this legal order.

As outlined in the UDHR, respect and protection for human rights are needed to ensure minimum world public legal order. Non-adherence and disregard for human rights lead to the current government lawlessness and insecurity that some refer to as the "new normal". Only with the firm foundation of a minimum global legal order, where governments honor their international legal obligations, can the world be shaped to achieve security and full enjoyment of human rights for all. The full enjoyment of all human rights in a secure environment is a precondition for men and women to exist with dignity and honor in society. Their primary goal is to foster the growth and protection of the individual. As President Kennedy asked in his June 10, 1963 speech, "Is not peace, in the final analysis, basically a matter of human rights?"[7]

In the 73 years since the General Assembly of the United Nations adopted the UDHR, it is difficult to find a period in the history of the world when the question of human rights has had a greater and more general significance in theory and practice than in the COVID-19 era. There have been times when the matter held capital importance in a given State or region, but never has the question of human rights violations been the object of such broad global general attention as in the aftermath of declaring COVID-19 a pandemic.

The Vienna Declaration and Program of Action

On June 15, 1993, 171 Member States adopted the Vienna Declaration and Programme of Action.[6] On adoption of the Declaration, Member States of the United Nations solemnly pledged to respect human rights and fundamental freedoms and undertook individually and collectively to actions and programs to make the enjoyment of human rights a reality for every human being that lives within their various jurisdictions.[2]

Through the Declaration, all 171 Member States rededicated themselves to the global task of promoting and protecting all human rights and fundamental freedoms to "secure full and universal enjoyment of these rights." The Vienna Declaration again placed several very specific duties on Member States to comply with the human rights standards as set out in the Vienna Declaration of rights and other IHRL instruments to ensure that the citizens within their territories are satisfactorily protected to enjoy all their human rights in a secure environment.[8] The most important are:

Section 1
The World Conference on Human Rights reaffirms the solemn commitment of all States to fulfil their obligations to promote universal respect for and observance and protection of all human rights and fundamental freedoms for all in accordance with the Charter of the United Nations, other instruments relating to human rights and international law.

Section 4
The promotion and protection of all human rights and fundamental freedoms must be considered as a priority objective of the United Nations in accordance with its purpose and principles, in particular the purpose of international cooperation. In the framework of these purposes and principles, the promotion and protection of all human rights is a legitimate concern of the international community.

Section 5
It is the duty of States, regardless of their political, economic and cultural systems, to promote and protect all human rights and fundamental freedoms.

Section 15
Respect for human rights and for fundamental freedoms without distinction of any kind is a fundamental rule of international human rights law.

Section 27
Every State should provide an effective framework of remedies to redress human rights grievances or violations. The administration of justice, including law enforcement and prosecutorial agencies and especially an independent judiciary and legal profession in full conformity with application standards contained in international human rights instruments, are essential to the full enjoyment of human rights.

The Conference reaffirmed the universal nature of all human rights, and that human rights and fundamental freedoms are the birthright of all human beings, and equally that it was the solemn commitment of all States everywhere to fulfil their obligations to promote and respect human rights.[8]

The notion in the COVID-19 era that human rights are privileges granted by governments subject to adherence to public health directives is contrary to long-established international human rights norms and principles.

State Responsibility for Human Rights Abuses Committed by non-State Actors under International Human Rights Law

There are many reasons why human rights violations by non-State actors are on the increase and in certain countries are more numerous than those committed by State actors. The globalization process driven by neo-liberalist forces led to a decreasing importance of the traditional Nation State compared to other global actors, that range from the self-serving "philanthropic foundations" of the ultra-wealthy and trans-national corporations to independent organizations such as the WEF and global networks of organized crime. The policies of deregulation and privatization that serve the interest of the ultra-wealthy global elite have led to an erosion of State power and responsibilities and the taking over of essential governmental functions (specifically in the fields of public health, public communication and national security) by non-State actors.[9] Another reason for the increase of human rights abuses by non-State actors is the fact that more and more of these abuses take place in the context of the ruthless exploitation of the population by powerful transnational corporations that with the aid of their political puppets mask the pursuit of super profits in a "public health" or "national security" cloak.

Under the Doctrine of State Responsibility, States are responsible and liable for breaching their international legal obligations. Such obligations can be positive or negative and can give rise to direct and indirect responsibilities. International legal obligations are derived from conventions, where States expressly consent to retain legal obligations by ratifying the treaty or from international customary law where it is necessary to show a widespread practice by States conforming to the rule, together with evidence that States follow the practice due to the belief that they have the normative obligation to comply with the rule.[2]

As the central actors of international law, and primary duty bearers of positive legal obligations, States remain, in the first instance, responsible for protecting and ensuring the basic human rights of all who live within their jurisdiction, in line with the universally accepted norms reflected in international custom and convention. If States fail in their obligations to respect and protect human rights, they are responsible and liable for the violations that occur within their jurisdiction.[2]

A UN Secretary-General report on minimum human rights standards affirms that:

> …the development of international human rights law as a means of holding Governments accountable to a common standard has been one of the major achievements of the United Nations. The challenge is to sustain that achievement and at the same time ensure that our conception of human rights remains relevant to the world around us.[10,11]

Under IHRL, States have a positive legal duty to respect, protect and fulfill the human rights of all the people who live within their territory. If a government fails in this obligation to protect citizens against public health mandates that violate citizens' fundamental human rights to free and informed consent, freedom of movement, and freedom of religion, and from corporations that force employees to get vaccinated and from big tech companies such as Google, Facebook, and Twitter that stifle freedom of speech, then the State is responsible and liable because it neglected to fulfill its positive obligation of protection. The United Nations Human Rights Committee (UNHRC) in 2004 specifically determined that:

> However, the positive obligations on State Parties to ensure Covenant rights will only be fully discharged if individuals are protected by the State, not just against violations of Covenant rights by its agents, but also against acts committed by private persons or entities that would impair the enjoyment of Covenant rights in so far as they are amenable to application between private persons or entities. There may be circumstances in which a failure to ensure Covenant rights as required by Article 2 would give rise to violations by State Parties of those rights, as a result of State Parties' permitting or failing to take appropriate measures or to exercise due diligence to prevent, punish, investigate or redress the harm caused by such acts by private persons or entities.[12]

The actions of the non-State actors are not considered as an act of State. However, the State is responsible because it failed to carry out a legal obligation to act to prevent or control the abusive actions of private actors.[2]

The Vienna Convention on the Law of Treaties and *Jus Cogens* Norms*

The definition of the concept of *jus cogens* emerged in international practice from the work of the International Law Commission (ILC) devoted to the codification and development of the legal regime of international agreements, which resulted in the signing of the 1961 Vienna Convention on the Law of Treaties.[6]

International human rights conventions are legally binding treaties between States that create legal obligations both positive and negative on the part of States to ensure the effective implementation of the commitments spelled out in the various conventions.[2,13] Only States can be held accountable for human rights violations under the various international conventions whether they are committed by government agents or by private actors.

The Vienna Convention on the Law of Treaties in Article 26 codifies the brocard and fundamental principle of law that "agreements must be kept" (*pacta sunt servanda*) by determining that: "Every treaty in force is binding upon the parties and must be performed by them in good faith." Article 27 specifically determines that a State Party "may not invoke the provisions of its internal law as justification for its failure to perform a treaty" while Article 31 stipulates that: "a treaty shall be interpreted in good faith in accordance with the ordinary meaning given to the terms of the treaty in their context and in the light of its object and purpose."[13] Treaty wording must be interpreted in line with the intention of the treaty. *Non oportet ius civile culumniari neque verba captari, sed qua mente quid diceritur animadvert covenit* (the law should not be used to effect misrepresentation, nor should words be twisted, but it is proper to consider with what intention each statement was made). The presumption of good faith justifies the conclusion that State Parties intend treaties to be effective. The failure of a State to enforce treaty provisions adequately would constitute a violation of the treaty.[2,13]

Protection of certain groups and their human rights and *jus cogens* (peremptory) norms that evolved from customary law such as the abolition

* Portions of this chapter are republications of the content of two peer-reviewed articles by the author Dr. Willem van Aardt, "Jus Cogens Norms, Public Policy and the Fiduciary Criterion of Morality" published in the De Rebus Attorneys Journal in July 2022; and "The Mandatory COVID-19 Vaccination of School Children: A Bioethical and Human Rights Assessment" published in the Journal of Vaccines and Vaccination in 2021.

of slavery existed before the modern-day international human rights system. *Jus cogens* norms developed as a natural law concept and was incorporated into legal positive and modern international law by Article 53 of the Vienna Convention on the Law of Treaties. From Latin *iūs* ("law") and *cogēns*, from *cōgere* ("compel"), *jus cogens* or "compelling law", is the technical term given to those norms of international law that are hierarchically superior.[6] It designates peremptory norms from which no derogation is permitted and stems from Roman law legal principles that certain legal rules cannot be contracted out, given the fundamental values they uphold.[6] Even though the legal term "*jus cogens*" did not take root in international law until the 20th century, the notion that several fundamental norms warrant peremptory authority within international law has a much older lineage. Both human rights and "*jus cogens*" are deemed to have the same origin: natural law. These two bodies of international law are etiologically correlated.[14,15] Professors Criddle and Fox-Decent in their article "A fiduciary theory of jus cogens" published in the "Yale Journal of International Law" posit that:

> Classical publicists such as Hugo Grotius, Emer de Vattel, and Christian Wolff drew upon the Roman law distinction between *jus dispositivum* (voluntary law) and *jus scriptum* (obligatory law) to differentiate consensual agreements between States from the "necessary" principles of international law that bind all States as a point of conscience regardless of consent. In contrast to ordinary legal obligations derived from treaty or custom, *jus scriptum* norms would not permit derogation…. because they derived from a higher source - the natural law of reason itself.[16]

The antonym of *jus cogens* is *jus dispositivum* or law adopted by consent. It is the category of international law that consists of norms derived from the consent of States. *Jus dispositivum* binds only those States consenting to be governed by it.[6,17] *Jus cogens*, antagonistic to *jus dispositivum*, is "compelling law."

Article 53 of the Vienna Convention on the Law of Treaties expressly declares void any existing or future treaty, which, at the time of its conclusion, conflicts with a peremptory norm of general international law:

> A treaty is void if, at the time of its conclusion, it conflicts with a peremptory norm of General International Law. For the purposes of the present Convention, a peremptory norm of General International Law is a norm accepted and recognized by the international

community of States as a whole as a norm from which no derogation is permitted and which can be modified only by a subsequent norm of General International Law having the same character.[18]

This signifies that a government cannot discharge itself from the obligations imposed by the norm of *jus cogens*, even by a new treaty.[6] Therefore, it is a prohibitive norm constituting a crucial limitation to governments' autonomy.[19] The unique function of these peremptory norms is to render void any treaty obligation or State action that conflicts with such a peremptory norm.[6] A 2012 peer-reviewed research paper by Predrag Zenovic on the legal effects of *jus cogens* encapsulates the essence well:

> *Jus cogens*, as stipulated in the Vienna Convention, makes all treaties annulled if those are contrary to a norm considered to be *jus cogens*. The power of a State to make treaties, its contractual right that derives from its equal sovereignty, is restrained when it confronts the super-customary norm of *jus cogens*. That is the first and paradigmatic effect of *jus cogens* – it disables the State (both de *jure imperii* and *de jure gestionis*) to get into contractual relations which might be detrimental to human rights recognized as *jus cogens*.[15]

The peremptory norm acts as a kind of "super-norm" to render any conflicting treaty or State action illegitimate. The *jus cogens* norm, therefore, acts as a check on unbridled and unlawful State power. It is further critical to note that "*jus cogens*" principles apply not only to treaties but also to "any other act or action of States."[6,20-23]

The ILC highlighted certain fundamental human rights as norms that can be distinguished as peremptory in character.[22] There is an almost intrinsic correlation between *jus cogens* and human rights. Under an objective approach, *jus cogens* can be defined as "a concept embodying the community interest and reinforced by its link with public morality (existing) in modern international law as a matter of necessity."[24] As prognostications of the individual and collective conscience, it materializes as both identity values for society and ordering factors of social practices.[6,24] Customary *jus cogens* norms include prohibition of slavery, piracy, and genocide. Following the Second World War, *jus cogens* norms developed to include crimes against humanity, murder, torture, cruel, inhuman, or degrading treatment or punishment, and medical or scientific experimentation without free consent.[6] All the *jus cogens* norms diachronically listed here are either innately or implicitly related to human rights.[15]

Jus cogens norms reflect the interests of the international community as a whole, not the narrow interests of a particular State and safeguard fundamental values. That brings a substantial normative impact of *jus cogens*: legal duties in this case are owed by States, not only to their own citizens, but to the international community at large. The prevention of genocide, torture, slavery, medical experimentation without consent, and crimes against humanity reflect core values of international society that can never be violated under any circumstances.[15] Any new treaties, such as the Convention on Pandemic Preparedness and Response proposed by the WHO, will be void if they conflict with these peremptory norms.

Major Human Rights Treaties

Since the adoption of the UDHR, eight major human rights treaties have been adopted under the auspices of the United Nations that converted the declarations of the Universal Declaration into binding legal obligations.[2] The first, adopted in 1965, was the International Convention on the Elimination of All Forms of Racial Discrimination (CERD). Soon thereafter, in 1966, it was followed by the ICCPR and the International Covenant on Economic, Social and Cultural Rights (ICESCR). In 1979, the international human rights regime was further supplemented by the Convention on the Elimination of All Forms of Discrimination against Women (CEDAW), and in 1984 by the Convention against Torture and Other Cruel, Inhuman or Degrading Treatment or Punishment (CAT) and in 1989, by the Convention on the Rights of the Child (CRC). In 1999, the International Convention on the Protection of the Rights of All Migrant Workers and Members of Their Families was adopted, while the Convention on the Rights of Persons with Disabilities was implemented in 2006.[2]

In international treaty law, there is a traditional distinction between obligations of means and obligations of ends, that is: between obligations to take specified steps toward aspirational goals and obligations to achieve certain results. Under the six major international conventions State Parties have agreed to "ensure" by all necessary steps and all appropriate means, the various fundamental human rights set out in the conventions.[2] This translates to an international legal obligation of means and of results.[7] The obligation of result requires State Parties to respect and ensure practically to all within their jurisdiction the rights enumerated in the conventions and the obligation of means requires State Parties to take all the necessary steps as may be necessary to give full effective practical realization to fundamental human rights.[7] Because the object of human rights treaties is to ensure the effective protection of human rights, due weight must be given to the principle of effectiveness. State Parties to conventions accept a duty to act to achieve the stated objectives effectively in accordance with international standards of performance.[2]

In the COVID-19 era of gross violation of fundamental human rights by prominent UN members, the covenant most egregiously violated by both State and non-State actors is the ICCPR and therefore it is necessary to set out in more detail what rights the ICCPR guarantees to individuals across the globe.

The International Covenant on Civil and Political Rights

The ICCPR, which is a legally binding international treaty that was ratified by 173 governments worldwide, in its preamble recognizes that, "the inherent dignity and of the equal and inalienable rights of all members of the human family is the foundation of freedom, justice and peace in the world", and that "these rights derive from the inherent dignity of the human person".[25]

Article 2(1) of the ICCPR determines that "each State Party to the present Covenant undertakes to respect and to ensure to all individuals within its territory and subject to its jurisdiction the rights recognized in the present Covenant, without distinction of any kind, such as race, color, sex, language, religion, political or other opinion, or other status" such as the status of being "unvaccinated".[25] The principal obligation of result reflected in Article 2(1) is to take steps "with a view to achieving progressively the full realization of the rights recognized" in the Covenant. The obligations of the Covenant in general and Article 2(1) to 2(3) are binding on every State Party as a whole. It applies to all branches of government (executive, legislative and judicial), and other public or governmental authorities including public health authorities.[24] Importantly Article 2(3) requires that State Parties make reparation by way of financial compensation to individuals whose Covenant rights have been violated. The UNHRC's General Comment No. 31 of 2004 specifically directs that:

> Without reparation to individuals whose Covenant rights have been violated, the obligation to provide an effective remedy, which is central to the efficacy of Article 2, paragraph 3, is not discharged. In addition to the explicit reparation required... the Committee considers that the Covenant generally entails appropriate compensation.[12]

Article 5 of the ICCPR prohibits States, groups, and persons to engage in any activity or perform any act aimed at the destruction of any of the rights and freedoms recognized in the ICCPR. The rampant destruction of fundamental rights and freedoms through COVID-19 public health measures specifically breached this ICCPR covenant obligation.[25]

The beneficiaries of the rights recognized by the Covenant are individuals. The ICCPR guarantees to all citizens that reside in the Member States that ratified the Convention civil and political rights that were grossly violated by arbitrary COVID-19 policies and *inter alia* include that:

Article 6
Every human being has the inherent right to life. This right shall be protected by law. No one shall be arbitrarily deprived of his life.

Article 7
No one shall be subjected to torture or to cruel, inhuman or degrading treatment or punishment, in particular, no one shall be subjected without his free consent to medical or scientific experimentation.

Article 9
Everyone has the right to liberty and security of person. No one shall be subjected to arbitrary arrest or detention. No one shall be deprived of his liberty except on such grounds and in accordance with such procedure as are established by law.

Article 12
Everyone lawfully within the territory of a State shall, within that territory, have the right to liberty of movement and freedom to choose his residence. Everyone shall be free to leave any country, including his own.

Article 17
No one shall be subjected to arbitrary or unlawful interference with his privacy, family, home or correspondence, nor to unlawful attacks on his honor and reputation.

Article 18
Everyone shall have the right to freedom of thought, conscience and religion.

Article 19

Everyone shall have the right to hold opinions without interference. Everyone shall have the right to freedom of expression; this right shall include freedom to seek, receive and impart information and ideas of all kinds, regardless of frontiers, either orally, in writing or in print, in the form of art, or through any other media of his choice.

Article 26

All persons are equal before the law and are entitled without any discrimination to the equal protection of the law. In this respect, the law shall prohibit any discrimination and guarantee to all persons equal and effective protection against discrimination on any ground such as race, colour, sex, language, religion, political or other opinion, national, or social origin, property, birth or other status.

The positive legal obligation to respect and ensure includes the duty of States to make adequate provision in the law for the effective protection of fundamental human rights.[26] This duty includes the effective enforcement of the law and taking reasonable steps of prevention by providing an effective judicial system and by conducting proper investigations, prosecuting offenders, as well as providing for adequate remedies for victims in the event of the rights being violated by private acts of violence or government abuses. Article 50 of the ICCPR also establishes that the provisions of the Covenant extend to all parts of federal States such as the United States of America without any limitations or exceptions.[2]

State responsibility for human rights abuses in the COVID-19 era are to be approached with reference to the specific ICCPR treaty provisions. The specific undertakings regarding *inter alia* the right to life, the right to live free from torture, inhumane treatment and medical experimentation, the right to freedom of thought and opinion, the right to freedom of movement, and the right to security of the person are also to be read in context of the general undertakings to "respect and ensure" human rights by all appropriate means. A State complies with the general duty "to respect" a right by not interfering with its exercise or violating the right, but the obligation "to ensure" a right is substantially broader. Rights under the Covenants are "negative", in that States must not obstruct individuals' exercise of them, but also "positive", in that States must take affirmative measures to prevent violation of the human rights, also from private actors.[2]

The UNHRC's General Comments 3 and 31 emphasize that the obligation under the ICCPR is not confined to the respect of human rights, but State Parties have also undertaken "to ensure the full enjoyment of these human rights to all individuals under their jurisdiction".[12,27] The Committee has also linked the right not to be subjected to torture or ill-treatment under Article 7 of the ICCPR to an obligation to provide protection, through "legislative and other measures" against torture or ill treatment inflicted by large corporations. The Committee held that:

> The aim of the provisions of Article 7 of the International Covenant on Civil and Political Rights is to protect both the dignity and the physical and mental integrity of the individuals. It is the duty of the State Party to afford everyone protection through legislative and other measures as may be necessary against the acts prohibited by Article 7, whether inflicted by people acting in their official capacity, outside their official capacity or in a private capacity.[2]

The Committee further held that States need to ensure that those responsible for human rights violations are brought to justice:

> As with failure to investigate, failure to bring to justice perpetrators of such violations could in and of itself give rise to a separate breach of the Covenant. These obligations arise notably in respect of those violations recognized as criminal under either domestic or international law, such as torture and similar cruel, inhuman and degrading treatment [and medical experimentation without free and informed consent] (Article 7), summary and arbitrary killing (Article 6) and enforced disappearance (Articles 7 and 9 and, frequently, 6)......When committed as part of a widespread or systematic attack on a civilian population, these violations of the Covenant are crimes against humanity (see Rome Statute of the International Criminal Court, Article 7).[12]

It is also implicit in Article 7 that State Parties have to take positive measures to ensure that private persons or entities do not inflict torture or cruel, inhuman, or degrading treatment or punishment on others within their power.[12] A State Party internationally, may also not juridically point to the fact that an action incompatible with the provisions of the Covenant was carried out by a non-State actor such as a transnational corporation as a means of seeking to relieve the State Party from responsibility and liability for the human rights violation.

Bioethical Norms and Standards

Bioethics can be defined as "the study of the ethical dimensions of medicine and the biological sciences" or "the application of ethics to the biological sciences, medicine, nursing, and healthcare."[28,29]

Bioethics deals with practical ethical questions raised in everyday healthcare. International bioethical norms and human rights standards with regard to informed consent for all medical interventions logically apply to COVID-19 vaccines, an invasive medical procedure that carries both known and unknown risks and benefits.[4]

Over the past 80 years there have been numerous international instruments setting out acceptable bioethical standards and practices, many of which have tragically been totally disregarded during the COVID-19 pandemic. The issue is not that there were no bioethical rules to follow or that the rules were ambiguous but rather that numerous governments, public health agencies, and conflicted multinational pharmaceutical companies, vaccine manufacturers, non-governmental organizations, and "philanthropic foundations" maliciously contravened clear bioethical rules, guidelines, and norms for political and financial gain.

The Nuremberg Code

The Nuremberg Code has served as a foundation for ethical biomedical practice and research since its publication. This historic document, developed in response to the atrocities of human experimentation at the hands of Nazi physicians and public health officials, focused crucial attention on the fundamental rights of medical research participants. The trials of the Nazi physicians and public health officials were held at the Palace of Justice in the city of Nuremberg, Bavaria, Germany, in 1945 to 1946.

The Nuremberg Code determines that:

1. The voluntary consent of the human subject is absolutely essential. This means that the person involved should have legal capacity to give consent; should be situated as to be able to exercise free power of choice, without the intervention of any element of force, fraud, deceit, duress, over-reaching, or other ulterior form of constraint or

coercion, and should have sufficient knowledge and comprehension of the elements of the subject matter involved as to enable him to make an understanding and enlightened decision. This latter element requires that before the acceptance of an affirmative decision by the experimental subject there should be made known to him the nature, duration, and purpose of the experiment; the method and means by which it is to be conducted; all inconveniences and hazards reasonably to be expected; and the effects upon his health or person which may possibly come from his participation in the experiment.

2. The experiment should be such as to yield fruitful results for the good of society, unprocurable by other methods or means of study, and not random and unnecessary in nature.

3. The experiment should be so designed and based on the results of animal experimentation and a knowledge of the natural history of the disease or other problem under study that the anticipated results justify the performance of the experiment.

4. The experiment should be so conducted as to avoid all unnecessary physical and mental suffering and injury.

5. No experiment should be conducted where there is an *a priori* reason to believe that death or disabling injury will occur; except, perhaps, in those experiments where the experimental physicians also serve as subjects.

6. The degree of risk to be taken should never exceed that determined by the humanitarian importance of the problem to be solved by the experiment.

7. Proper preparations should be made and adequate facilities provided to protect the experimental subject against even remote possibilities of injury, disability, or death.

8. The experiment should be conducted only by scientifically qualified persons. The highest degree of skill and care should be required through all stages of the experiment of those who conduct or engage in the experiment.

9. During the course of the experiment the human subject should be at liberty to bring the experiment to an end if he has reached the physical or mental state where continuation of the experiment seems to him to be impossible.

10. During the course of the experiment, the scientist in charge must be prepared to terminate the experiment at any stage, if he has probable cause to believe, in the exercise of the good faith, superior skill,

and careful judgment required by him that a continuation of the experiment is likely to result in injury, disability, or death to the experimental subject.[30]

The primary principle in the Nuremberg Code is that "the voluntary consent of the human subject is absolutely essential." Under the Nuremberg Code, no one may be coerced to participate in a medical experiment.[4] The COVID-19 era practices to ostracize, spurn, pressure, mandate, pay, fraudulently induce, and shame people into getting vaccinated against their will is a clear violation of the Nuremberg Code!

While this right to choose relating to medical experimentation in international law sprang from the Nuremberg Code, the international right to informed consent now encompasses the right to free and informed consent for all medical decision-making.[4]

Article 7 of the International Covenant on Civil and Political Rights

The ICCPR, a legally binding treaty dealt with earlier in the chapter, clearly dictates in Article 7 that "no one shall be subjected without his free consent to medical or scientific experimentation." Importantly, Article 7 is specifically listed as an article from which no derogation may be made even in times of a public emergency that threatens the life of the nation![25]

The public health and corporate policies mandating COVID-19 vaccines violate the ICCPR and are, therefore, illegitimate.

The Universal Declaration on Bioethics and Human Rights

The Universal Declaration on Bioethics and Human Rights (UDBHR) was adopted by UNESCO in 2005 after two years of development.[31] Utilizing a human rights framework, the UDBHR established bioethical normative standards in 15 areas, including fundamental human rights, justice, equality, dignity, equity, and safeguarding future generations.[31]

The UDBHR is an important international document in setting global minimum ethical standards in biomedical research and clinical practice.[31]

The UDBHR specifically determines that:

Article 3
Human dignity, human rights and fundamental freedoms are to be fully respected. The interests and welfare of the individual should have priority over the sole interest of science or society.

Article 4
In applying and advancing scientific knowledge, medical practice and associated technologies, direct and indirect benefits to patients, research participants and other affected individuals should be maximized and any possible harm to such individuals should be minimized.

Article 5
The autonomy of persons to make decisions, while taking responsibility for those decisions and respecting the autonomy of others, is to be respected. For persons who are not capable of exercising autonomy, special measures are to be taken to protect their rights and interests.

Article 6
Any preventive, diagnostic and therapeutic medical intervention is only to be carried out with the prior, free and informed consent of the person concerned, based on adequate information. The consent should, where appropriate, be express and may be withdrawn by the person concerned at any time and for any reason without disadvantage or prejudice.

Article 11
No individual or group should be discriminated against or stigmatized on any grounds, in violation of human dignity, human rights, and fundamental freedoms.

While the UNESCO Declaration does not establish enforceable rights, it is convincing regarding what the global standard for bioethical norms should be and is a scathing indictment of current COVID-19 public health practices.[4]

While mounting the proverbial moral high-horse, public health officials across the West were breaching their fiduciary duties to the public by blatantly disregarding international bioethical norms and standards.

The Oviedo Convention

The Convention for the Protection of Human Rights and Dignity of the Human Being with regard to the Application of Biology and Medicine: Convention on Human Rights and Biomedicine (Oviedo Convention) is the best current example of how to promote the protection of human rights in the biomedical field at a transnational level.[32,33] The importance of this instrument lies in the fact that it is the first comprehensive legally binding multilateral treaty intended to protect human dignity, basic human rights, and freedoms, through a series of rules and prohibitions against the abuse of biological and medical innovations.[4,32,33]

The Treaty's starting point is that the dignity and identity of all human beings must be protected and the interests and welfare of human beings rank above the interests of society or science. It sets out a series of standards and proscriptions relating to medical research, bioethics, consent, rights to privacy and information, and public debate.[32,33]

The Oviedo Convention specifically determines that:

Article 1
Parties to this Convention shall protect the dignity and identity of all human beings and guarantee everyone, without discrimination, respect for their integrity and other rights and fundamental freedoms with regard to the application of biology and medicine.

Article 2
The interest and welfare of the human being shall prevail over the sole interest of society or science.

Article 5
An intervention in the health field may only be carried out after the person concerned has given free and informed consent to it. This person shall beforehand be given appropriate information as to the purpose and nature of the intervention as well as on its consequences and risks. The person concerned may freely withdraw consent at any time.

Article 8
When because of an emergency situation the appropriate consent cannot be obtained, any medically necessary intervention may be carried out

immediately for the benefit of the health of the individual concerned.

Article 10
Everyone has the right to respect for private life in relation to information about his or her health.

Although the Oviedo Convention is only legally binding on the 29 European Union Member States that signed the Convention, it clearly sets an authoritative moral standard with regards to the protection of human rights in the biomedical field.

The World Medical Association (WMA) Declarations

Since it was founded in 1947, a central objective of the WMA, "an international and independent confederation of free professional medical associations representing more than 10 million physicians worldwide, has been to establish and promote the highest possible standards of ethical behavior and care by physicians."[4,34] According to the WMA, "In pursuit of this goal, the WMA has adopted global policy statements on a range of ethical issues related to medical professionalism, patient care, research on human subjects, and public health."[34]

In the WMA's Declaration of Geneva (sometimes referred to as the modern Hippocratic Oath), physicians pledge to "respect the autonomy and dignity of patients," while the WMA's Declaration of Helsinki Ethical Principles for Medical Research Involving Human Subjects further confirms that "Participation by individuals capable of giving informed consent as subjects in medical research must be voluntary."[35,36] The Declaration of Helsinki section dealing with Risks, Burdens, and Benefits further determines that:

> In medical practice and in medical research, most interventions involve risks and burdens. Medical research involving human subjects may only be conducted if the importance of the objective outweighs the risks and burdens to the research subjects.

> All medical research involving human subjects must be preceded by careful assessment of predictable risks and burdens to the individuals and groups involved in the research in comparison with foreseeable benefits to them and to other individuals or groups affected by the condition under investigation. Measures to minimize the risks must be implemented.

The risks must be continuously monitored, assessed, and documented by the researcher. Physicians may not be involved in a research study involving human subjects unless they are confident that the risks have been adequately assessed and can be satisfactorily managed. When the risks are found to outweigh the potential benefits or when there is conclusive proof of definitive outcomes, physicians must assess whether to continue, modify or immediately stop the study.[37]

Almost none of the above norms were being complied with in the COVID-19 responses despite the WHO's data showing almost 2.5 million adverse events from the COVID-19 vaccine by November 12, 2021, as mandatory vaccinations continued unabated in numerous countries across the globe.[38,39]

World Health Organization

VigiAccess was launched by the World Health Organization (WHO) in 2015 to provide public access to information in VigiBase, the WHO global database of reported potential side effects of medicinal products.

Vaccine or Drug Name	Total ADRs	Years
Mumps vaccine	711	1972-2021
Rubella vaccine	2,621	1971-2021
Ivermectin	5,705	1992-2021
Measles vaccine	5,827	1968-2021
Penicillin nos	6,684	1968-2021
smallpox vaccine	6,891	1968-2021
chloroquine	7,139	1968-2021
tetanus vaccine	15,085	1968-2021
Hydroxychloroquine	32,641	1968-2021
Hepatitis A vaccine	46,773	1989-2021
Benzylpenicillin	51,327	1968-2021
Rotavirus vaccine	68,327	2000-2021
Accutane	70,719	1983-2021
Vancomycin	71,159	1974-2021
Hepatitis B vaccine	104,619	1984-2021
Polio vaccine	121,988	1968-2021
Meningococcal vaccine	126,412	1976-2021
Ibuprofen	166,209	1969-2021
tylenol	169,359	1968-2021
Aspirin	184,481	1968-2021
Pneumococcal vaccine	234,783	1980-2021
Influenza vaccine	272,202	1968-2021
Covid-19 vaccine	2,457,386	2020-2021

www.vigiaccess.org
Updated Nov. 12th 2021

Figure 3.1: Vaccine adverse events as at November 12, 2021
Source: WHO https://vigiaccess.org/

World Health Organization Guidance for Managing Ethical Issues

Despite being one of the central actors whose declarations and advisories led to widespread violation of fundamental human rights during the COVID-19 pandemic, according to the WHO's own "Guidance for Managing Ethical Issues in Infectious Disease Outbreaks 2016," the only bioethical basis for the justification of emergency use medical interventions emphasizes "the ethical principle of respect for patient autonomy – i.e., the right of individuals to make their own risk–benefit assessments in light of their personal values, goals and health conditions."[4,40]

The WHO Guidance is also explicit that:

> The ultimate choice of whether to receive the unproven intervention must rest with the patient if the patient is in a condition to make the choice. If the patient is unconscious, cognitively impaired, or too sick to understand the information, proxy consent should be obtained from a family member or other authorized decision-maker.[40]

The WHO's Guidance for Managing Ethical Issues is a further authoritative indication of the global ethical standard and requirements regarding the use of emergency medical interventions.

COVID-19 vaccines are experimental, with no medium- and long-term safety and efficacy data, and all individuals have the right to refuse such a vaccine for themselves and their children.[4] The right of refusal stems from the fact that COVID-19 vaccination products are experimental in nature, given the unknown medium to long-term side-effects, and under the Nuremberg Code and other relevant international human rights conventions, prior informed consent is an essential prerequisite.[4]

Chapter Conclusion

International commitment to human rights protection is in the process of undergoing a paradigm shift towards lawlessness and non-adherence to IHRL that will have significant adverse ramifications for the international legal and political arena if allowed to proceed unchallenged.

Over the past 30 months, there has been a major expansion of illegitimate covenant-breaching COVID-19 policies and processes such as lockdowns, mask mandates, and vaccine mandates occurring across the globe that should immediately be halted where still in place and prohibited from recuring! In the 2020 to 2022 COVID-19 era, fundamental human rights obligations *erga omnes* were breached and violated on a scale unseen in living memory under the guise of public health. The idea that human rights are privileges granted by the State subject to adherence to pseudo-medical diktats is simply irreconcilable with the peremptory norms embraced in the Universal Declaration. Now more than ever, the international community of citizens should be insisting on adherence to the universally accepted set of legal norms by all States. Disregard and contempt for human rights during the COVID-19 pandemic have again resulted in cruel, inhumane policies and practices which have outraged the conscience of mankind. The re-emergence of a world in which human beings shall enjoy freedom from medical tyranny, freedom of thought, and freedom of movement should be the highest aspiration of all people.

Individuals, once considered mere objects of the sovereign will, are subjects of international law with positive legal claims to protection, not only from State tyranny and oppression but also to protection by the State from human rights abuses at the hands of multinational corporations and corrupt philanthropic foundations. Any deprivation of fundamental human rights should not be tolerated since the Universal Declaration requires that dignity and equality shall be the inalienable rights of all men and women. If States fail in their obligations to respect and protect human rights, they are responsible for the violations that occur within their jurisdiction.

Human rights norms do not exist for the benefit of States, but the benefit of human beings subject to their power.[6] Several international treaties spell out the specific obligations of governments to respect the human rights of their citizens.[6] The major assumptions behind the internationally recognized human rights are that these rights are:

- immutable, not able to be altered by any State Party,
- universal, always applying to all persons; and
- interdependent and indissoluble, requiring respect for specific individual rights as mutual reinforcement for respect of all rights.[6,25]

The view that unvaccinated people do not have certain key human rights or that human rights are privileges granted by government subject to adherence to draconian health mandates is simply incompatible with the norms espoused in the UDHR.

In terms of IHRL, certain fundamental rights can never be derogated from under any circumstances, even in times of a public health emergency.[42] Because of their normative specificity and status, non-derogable rights are core human rights *jus cogens* and obligations *erga omnes*. Under case law and legal doctrine, *jus cogens* comprise a particular form of constitutional rule that every government is obligated to follow. Being compelling law, it does not give a government the right to opt-out, as is the case with other international norms deriving from custom or treaty.[6] Peremptory norms limit the ability of the global polity and States to create public policy that would contradict *jus cogens*.[6] Any new treaty, or global health policy or agenda such as "Agenda 21" or the "Great Reset" of the State contrary to *jus cogens*, would be illicit.[42]

Article 4 of the ICCPR specifies a list of fundamental human rights from which no derogation is allowed.[6] This list *inter alia* includes:

- The right not to be arbitrarily deprived of life.
- The right not to be subjected to torture.
- The right not to be subjected to cruel, inhuman, or degrading treatment or punishment.
- The rights not to be subjected to medical or scientific experimentation without free consent.[6]

Other *jus cogens* norms include prohibitions on crimes against humanity, war crimes, genocide, and slavery.[6] *Jus cogens* norms have significant contemporary relevance considering the Fourth Industrial Revolution and the advent of "cyber-physical systems" characterized by a range of new technologies that are fusing the physical, digital, and biological worlds.[43] Genome editing, COVID-19 mRNA gene therapy, under-the-skin biometric surveillance, the internet of bodies, inorganic biochemistry, and transhumanism are all 21st century forms of "medical and scientific experimentation" that can only be legitimate if conducted with the prior, informed consent of the citizenry.

The interests and welfare of the individual should have priority over the interest of science or society.[4] Any justification for emergency use medical interventions must accord with the bioethical principle of respect for patient autonomy, which is the right of individuals to make their own risk-benefit assessments considering their personal values, goals, and health conditions.

Human rights and fundamental freedoms are the birthrights of all human beings; their protection and promotion are the first responsibility of governments. Human rights are not privileges granted by public health officials subject to obedience and compliance! The COVID-19 public health argument that arbitrarily determined societal health diktats supersede all fundamental human rights and freedoms is juridically fundamentally flawed! States do not have the right to decide when people can enjoy their fundamental human rights. The government's first duty is to protect these rights. In the words of Kofi Annan: "States prove unworthy of this task, when they violate the fundamental principles laid down in the Charter of the United Nations, and when – far from being protectors of individuals – they become tormentors."[44]

4. COVID-19 FACTS, MISINFORMATION, AND DISINFORMATION

"Of all tyrannies a tyranny exercised for the good of its victims may be the most oppressive. It may be better to live under robber barons than under omnipotent moral busybodies. The robber baron's cruelty may sometimes sleep, his cupidity may at some point be satiated; but those who torment us for our own good will torment us without end for they do so with the approval of their own conscience."

— C.S. Lewis

In 2021, France introduced strict COVID-19 vaccine mandates, including making vaccination compulsory for all health workers and introducing a vaccine passport to enter public spaces, including cafes, bars, theater venues, and hospitals. The controls have encountered a considerable amount of criticism, leading to many French people taking part in demonstrations. On October 3, 2021, the Social Affairs Committee of the French Senate presented a bill making the COVID-19 vaccine mandatory for all French citizens.[1] In the United States of America, President Joe Biden issued "executive orders mandating vaccines for federal workers and contractors and announced new requirements for large employers" and healthcare providers that he said "would affect around 100 million workers, more than two-thirds of the US workforce."[2] "We've been patient, but our patience is wearing thin," Biden said, on September 9, 2021, directly appealing to the 80 million people he said were still unvaccinated at that time.[2]

Globally there has been a great deal of talk and action to subject people who are not vaccinated to restrictions involving their access to public places, flights, hotels, and continued employment, thereby indirectly making vaccination compulsory. During 2021, New York City Mayor Bill de Blasio implemented a plan to permanently discriminate and segregate the unvaccinated from society. In New York, the unvaccinated were being condemned as a new sub-class of humans – in a society now rooted in medical discrimination, hatred, and bigotry. According to De Blasio, "If you're vaccinated, you'll have the key, you can open the door…. But if you're un-vaccinated, unfortunately, you won't be able to participate in most things. It's time people see vaccination as literally necessary to living a good, and full, and healthy life."[3,4]

Any opposing views are promptly silenced by State Parties, Google, Facebook, Twitter, and other major technology companies while the mainstream media continue to relentlessly spin official public health propaganda, which has been refuted as falsehoods by all independent objective data sets.[5-11] In 2020, 2021, and 2022 the only acceptable narrative was the official government propaganda, and no scientific debate was tolerated. Disciplinary procedures were launched against academics, professionals, and other experts who publicly expressed their opposition to compulsory vaccination.[12]

Viral vaccine safety and efficacy misinformation by government experts, the mainstream media, conflicted technocrats, vaccine manufacturers, and transnational corporations, combined with distrust in government institutions and politicized vaccine development and distribution processes, have left many people skeptical of COVID-19 vaccines.

In the COVID-19 period, more than ever, vaccination evokes strong opinions and emotions. Many are grateful and relieved to get COVID-19 vaccines and see it as a pathway to normality. In contrast, many others are indignant and exasperated at the prospect of COVID-19 vaccination mandates, specifically in light of fatal side-effects and the absence of long-term safety data. A Quinnipiac University Poll conducted in September 2021 showed that Americans were thoroughly divided on the issue of mandatory vaccinations.[14] A majority of Americans (51%) disapproved of Joe Biden's COVID-19 vaccine mandates. Interestingly, according to a paper by researchers from Carnegie Mellon University and the University of Pittsburgh that analyzed more than five million survey responses, hesitancy and education level follow a U-shaped curvature with the greatest hesitancy among those least and most educated. The ultimate hesitancy was amongst those holding a Ph.D.[13]

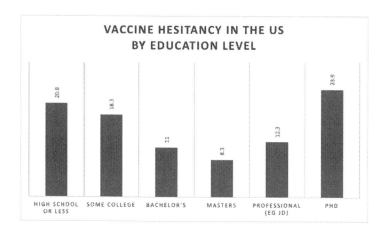

Figure 4.1: Vaccine hesitancy in the US by education level
Source: Researchers from Carnegie Mellon University and the University of Pittsburgh[13]

What is more, the research paper observed that in the first five months of 2021, the most significant reduction in hesitancy was among the least educated. Meanwhile, hesitancy held constant in the most highly educated class. By May 2021, those with Ph.D. degrees were the most hesitant group.[13] Consequently, not only are the most educated people most distrustful of taking the COVID-19 vaccines, but they are also the least likely to change their minds.

Irrespective of one's point of view, the critical question is: Do the COVID-19 vaccines work? Was there evidence to support the government and mainstream media narrative that once 80% of the population had been vaccinated, infection rates and death rates would significantly reduce? By October 2021, Singapore was credited as being the most vaccinated country on earth, with 80% of its population fully vaccinated. At the same time, Vermont was the most vaccinated State in the United States, with 99.9% of the population over the age of 64 fully vaccinated and 75% between the ages of 18 and 64 fully vaccinated.[15,16] As can be seen from the relevant WHO graph below, after fully vaccinating more than 80% of its population, Singapore's infection rates and death rates were at an all-time high.[17]

In Singapore, from 3 January 2020 to 5:45pm CEST, 22 October 2021, there have been 162,026 confirmed cases of COVID-19 with 280 deaths, reported to WHO. As of 14 October 2021, a total of 9,563,625 vaccine doses have been administered.

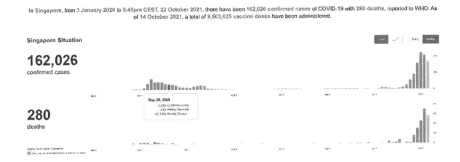

Figure 4.2: Singapore infection rates and death rates October 2021
Source: WHO[17]

Similarly, in Vermont, despite having the highest vaccination rate in the United States, the infection rate was higher than it has ever been in the entire pandemic. Their seven-day average case rate was 30 per 100,000 of the population. In September 2021, around 75% of the people in Vermont who died from COVID-19 were fully vaccinated.[18]

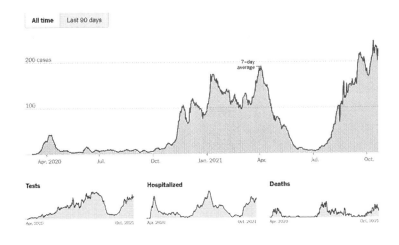

Figure 4.3: Vermont infection rates and death rates September 2021
Source: Vermont Department of Health[18]

Were these trends in Vermont and Singapore in the fall of 2021 isolated incidences of the COVID-19 vaccines not being effective at either preventing infections or deaths?

Facts versus Government Suppositions and Conjecture

C. S. Lewis stated that "One of the most cowardly things ordinary people do is to shut their eyes to facts." What are the facts? What are the factual, biomedical, and ethical arguments for and against mandating COVID-19 vaccines?

In any legal dispute, facts are essential! The Merriam-Webster Dictionary defines a fact as "something that truly exists or happens; something that has actual existence."[19] Black's Law Dictionary defines a fact as "a circumstance, event or occurrence as it actually takes or took place; a physical object or appearance, as it actually exists or existed. An actual and absolute reality, as distinguished from mere supposition or opinion; a truth, as distinguished from fiction or error."[20] Therefore, a fact is not opinion (based on who said it) but based on what transpired in reality.

It is important to distinguish fact from supposition and opinion before addressing the legal issues. In layman's language, a fact stands for "something which is real, tangible like an actual event," and in a lawsuit, "a fact is the information of the case concerning an event or a circumstance."[19,20] In most common law jurisdictions, the concept of fact and its analysis reflect bedrock principles of legal philosophy. It is also supported by various well-established standards. Under common law jurisdictions, the matters of fact have numerous practical applications, which include:

- Facts are required in legal proceedings to demonstrate a cause of action.
- Facts help in the determinations of judicial oversight bodies after evaluating admissible evidence.
- Facts establish whether a law has been transgressed or not.
- Facts determine culpability and liability.

The international legal system resolves disputes by applying the codified law to the facts of the case. As the *brocard* appropriately declares "*e facto oritor ius*" (law arises from fact). Facts are important to determine which law or international covenant should be applied to a case and to determine what specific international legal obligation has been breached by a State Party.

The COVID-19 vaccination debate has two distinct positions, one the official government "pro-mandate view," backed mainly by government decree and conjectures, and the "pro-choice view," backed by facts and objective scientific data[†].

Pro-Mandate
Government Decree and Conjecture

1. COVID-19 is a deadly disease that has killed millions of people across the globe.

Mandatory vaccination is justifiable in the face of such a killer disease that has a devastating impact on life expectancy.

People who elect not to vaccinate are selfish, irrational, and threaten the right to life and right to health of others with deadly disease.[21]

2. Mandatory vaccination is typically justified on arguments relating to the greater good and the do no harm principle.

According to John Stuart Mill, a justifiable "ground for the use of State coercion (and restriction of liberty) is when one individual risks harming others."[27] Erwin Chemerinsky, dean and professor of law at the UC Berkeley School of Law, summed up this argument as follows: "It is time to focus on the duty we all have to protect each other and to end this pandemic……..we should remind everyone that freedom does not include a right to endanger others."[28]

Those who decide not to take the COVID-19 vaccine ignore this concern and therefore act immorally and against the interest of the greater good.

3. Government officials and public health authorities such as the CDC and the FDA are best qualified to make vaccination decisions.

Government is responsible for public health and should ensure that a sufficiently high percentage of people vaccinate to preserve societal herd immunity.[21]

Never mind individual liberties, there is a deadly virus on the loose, and that is justification enough for the State to mandate that you get a COVID shot.

4. COVID-19 vaccines are 95% to 99% effective and protect people from getting infected with COVID-19 and transmitting SARS-CoV-2.

In April 2021, the CDC claimed that the COVID-19 vaccines are 99% effective

---

† Given the US CDC's disqualifying conflicts of interest as co-owners of numerous COVID-19 vaccine patents that directly profit from the sale of COVID-19 vaccines, any research conducted by and funded by the CDC or any of their corporate partners are not a credible source of independent, objective, academic research. For a list of CDC partners see: https://www. cdcfoundation.org/partner-list/corporations.

while Pfizer CEO Albert Bourla was "Excited to share that updated analysis from our Phase 3 study with BioNTech also showed that our COVID-19 vaccine was 100% effective in preventing #COVID19."[32] By March 2022, the position of the CDC was still that all COVID-19 vaccines currently available in the United States "are effective at preventing COVID-19 as seen in clinical trial settings."[32]

According to the CDC, "vaccine effectiveness studies provide a growing body of evidence that mRNA COVID-19 vaccines offer similar protection in real-world conditions as they have in clinical trial settings, reducing the risk of COVID-19, including severe illness, among people who are fully vaccinated by 90% or more."[32]

5. COVID-19 vaccines are overwhelmingly safe, and the benefits vastly outweigh the risks.

According to the CDC, COVID-19 vaccines are safe. "While COVID-19 vaccines were developed rapidly, all steps have been taken to ensure their safety and effectiveness. The WHO, EU, United States, and other health authorities approved the vaccine, and therefore it is safe."[40]

Over 403 million doses of the COVID-19 vaccine have been given in the United States from December 14, 2020, through October 12, 2021, since they were authorized for emergency use by the FDA.[38] By March 28, 2022, 11.2 billion vaccine doses have been administered globally, and more than 4.5 billion people have been fully vaccinated in 217 countries.[41-43]

"Serious side-effects that could cause long-term health problems are extremely unlikely following COVID-19 vaccination."[40]

6. VAERS data for COVID-19 vaccines show a disproportionate amount of adverse events due to the number of COVID-19 vaccines administered.

Billions of COVID-19 vaccines have been administered and as such the adverse events relating to these vaccines cannot be accurately compared to other vaccines that have been administered in much lower quantities.

7. COVID-19 vaccines are not experimental. They went through all the required stages of clinical trials.

Extensive testing and monitoring have shown that these vaccines are safe and effective. "COVID-19 vaccines were developed using science that has been around for decades."[22]

8. Healthy people in low-risk groups need to be vaccinated given the risk of symptomless spread to those in vulnerable groups.

Although most healthy people who contract COVID-19 will survive the infection, they should further improve their chances – and reduce their likelihood of infecting someone else – by getting vaccinated. Even a small percentage of deaths can still translate to many deaths, in absolute terms, if the infection rate escalates out of control.

9. COVID-19 vaccination reduce the spread of disease.

All healthy people that can be vaccinated should be mandated to curb the spread of COVID-19.[12]

10. Most COVID-19 hospital patients and deaths are unvaccinated.

More than 99% of recent deaths were among the unvaccinated, infectious disease expert Dr. Anthony Fauci said in July 2021, while Dr. Rochelle Walensky, the CDC's director, noted that unvaccinated people accounted for over 97% of hospitalizations.[69]

11. Natural immunity does not provide sufficient protection. At least 70% to 90% of the population needs to be vaccinated to achieve herd immunity.

Irrespective of whether people have already been infected with COVID-19 and already have antibodies in their system, they need to be vaccinated.[41,43]

CDC Director Rochelle Walensky, in her October 2020 published Lancet statement, argued that "there is no evidence for lasting protective immunity to SARS-CoV-2 following natural infection" and that "the consequence of waning immunity would present a risk to vulnerable populations for the indefinite future."[76]

12. The COVID-19 vaccines prevent serious illness and death.

As of September, 2022 the CDC maintains its position that "Vaccines reduce the risk of COVID-19, including the risk of severe illness and death among people who are fully vaccinated" and that "COVID-19 vaccines are working well to prevent severe illness, hospitalization, and death."[41,43]

13. Mass mandatory vaccinations are the only way for society to return to normal.

Getting an inoculation to protect yourself and others from COVID-19 is both a social responsibility and the only way to bring about the end of the global pandemic.

14. There is no right to free and informed consent.

Vaccine exemptions based on religious and other objections should be abolished. People should lose their freedoms if they choose not to vaccinate. They should not be allowed to travel, attend public events, or resume life as normal.[12]

Pro-Choice
Relevant Dispositive Facts and Scientific Data

1. COVID-19's Crude Mortality Rate ranges between 0.003% and 0.3%.

At least 99.85% of all people under the age of 70 who contract COVID-19 will survive! No mass nor mandatory vaccinations are reasonably required to combat a disease with a crude mortality rate of less than 0.3%.[5,12,17,22,23] According to the US CDC, the COVID-19 infection fatality rate is: 0-19 years old, 0.003%; 20-49 years old, 0.02%; 50-69 years old, 0.5 percent; 70 years old or older, 5.4%.[5,17,22,23] To put matters into global perspective, as of December 2020:

- World population: 7.8 billion
- Total COVID-19 cases: 182 million
- Total COVID-19 deaths: 3.94 million[23]

Percentage of world's population that got infected with COVID-19: **2.3%** (182 million divided by 7.8 billion = 0.023)

Percentage of people infected with COVID-19 that died from COVID-19: **2.1%** (3.94 million divided by 182 million = 0.0216)

Chances of getting COVID-19 and dying from it: **0.0497%** (0.023 times 0.0216 = 0.000497)

The median age of "COVID-19 death" is more than the normal life expectancy. The average age of a "COVID-19 death" in Italy is 86. In Australia, it is 82. Canada, 86. Germany, 83. Switzerland, 86. The United States, 78. The United Kingdom, 82.5. In virtually all instances, the average age of a "COVID-19 death" is greater than the national life expectancy. For most countries around the globe, the COVID-19 pandemic has had little-to-no impact on average life expectancy. Compare this with the Spanish flu, which saw a 28% reduction in life expectancy in the United States in just over a year.[24]

Statistical analyses from the United Kingdom and India have shown that the curvature for a COVID-19 death follows the curve for expected mortality:

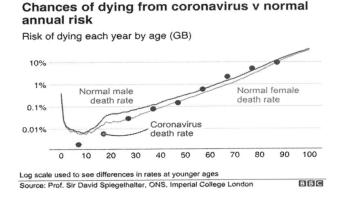

Chances of dying from coronavirus v normal annual risk

Risk of dying each year by age (GB)

Log scale used to see differences in rates at younger ages
Source: Prof. Sir David Spiegelhalter, ONS, Imperial College London

Figure 4.4: Chances of dying from coronavirus vs. normal annual risk
Source: BBC, Prof Sir David Spiegelhalter at the
University of Cambridge, Imperial College of London[25]

COVID-19 death counts were artificially inflated during 2020 and 2021. Countries around the world have been defining a COVID-19 death as a "death by any cause within 28/30/60 days of a positive PCR test". Healthcare bureaucrats from the United States, the United Kingdom, Italy, Germany, Ireland, and others have all confessed to this practice. Removing any distinction between "dying of COVID" and "dying of something else" such as a fatal gunshot or car accident after testing positive for COVID-19 will obviously lead to over-counting of COVID-19 deaths.[26]

2. Individuals must be left free from State control except where necessary and in the interest of the society.

COVID-19 poses a risk of death to approximately 0.15% of the infected population.[5,12,17,22] All vulnerable people have access to COVID-19 vaccines (that governments and vaccine manufacturers initially claimed to be 99% to 100% effective) and can take other necessary precautionary measures to reduce their risk of infection, such as self-isolation and protective clothing. Considering the aforementioned, the argument that healthy people pose a risk to vulnerable groups or are in some way a threat to them is patently absurd. It does not hold water by any rational standard.

To violate the vast majority of the population's human rights and civil liberties does not serve the greater good at all. In philosophy and political science, the greater good (common good) requires practical, rational reasoning and actions that are beneficial for all or most community members. A policy that adversely affects and violates the fundamental rights and freedoms of 99.85% of a community to protect 0.15% of a community does not serve the common interest.

3. Vaccination choice is a fundamental human right only an individual may decide how, when, and whether to exercise.

Because vaccination poses a risk to a person's life, liberty, and security, only an individual may decide how, when, and whether to vaccinate. The theory of herd immunity is not an adequate rationale for State compulsion to vaccinate.[12]

When dealing with a disease with a global infection fatality rate of approximately 0.15%, natural infection is preferable for all people not in vulnerable groups.[21] It is not the State's duty or function to intervene in personal health. It is each person's own responsibility to protect their health through individual choices. It is the government's duty to protect individual liberties and freedoms. When you trade liberty for security or health, you will end up losing both.[12]

Global and government agencies such as the WHO, CDC, FDA, and NIH are compromised organizations with extreme conflicts of interest that focus not on public health but on transnational pharmaceutical profit promotion.[29,30]

4. Data from across the globe indisputably prove that COVID-19 vaccines are not effective and do not prevent infection nor transmission.[6,31]

While initial results indicated that the Pfizer and Moderna vaccines were effective against COVID-19 infection (76%, 86% respectively) and hospitalization (85%, 91.6%), the effectiveness against infection by July 2021 dropped to 42% and 76% respectively.[33] In a nursing home study done in August 2021, CDC researchers found that "the efficacy of the two-dose vaccines from Pfizer-BioNTech and Moderna for preventing any coronavirus infection – mild or severe – dropped from 74.7% to 53.1%."[34]

In the United Kingdom, COVID-19 deaths among the vaccinated went from "rare" to two-thirds of all deaths by July 2021, while in Israel, by August 2021, over 60% of the severely ill were fully vaccinated.[31,35]

The trend of significantly increased infection and death rates following mass vaccination campaigns was evident in numerous countries across the globe. In September 28, 2021, data from Johns Hopkins University showed major spikes in COVID-19 deaths in 40 countries following mass vaccination campaigns.[5,17,22,36,37]

By October 2021, more than 44 independent peer-reviewed studies confirmed that the infection explosion that was experienced globally – post double vaccination in Israel, the United Kingdom, the United States, and other countries – was due to the vaccinated spreading COVID-19 as much or more than the unvaccinated.[6]

On October 11, 2022, Pfizer's Janine Small (President of International Developed Markets) confessed to the European Parliament that at the time of introduction, the COVID-19 vaccine had never been tested to determine whether it prevents the transmission of the virus.

Rob Roos, (Member of the European Parliament) from the Netherlands, questioned Small: "Was the Pfizer COVID vaccine tested on stopping the transmission of the virus before it entered the market? If not, please say it clearly. If yes, are you willing to share the data with this committee?"

Small replied: "Regarding the question around, did we know about stopping immunization before it entered the market? No."

This stunning admission eliminates the entire rationale for the COVID-19 vaccine mandates!

5. COVID-19 vaccines are unsafe, ineffective and the risks significantly outweigh the benefits for most people.

The COVID-19 vaccines have been invented, developed, and approved at a lightning-fast pace in less than one year. Testing of vaccine efficacy and safety were limited and insufficient. The average development time for almost all other safe vaccines have been between 10 and 15 years.

Adverse events are regularly occurring, and deaths, harms, and adverse events such as myocardial infarction (heart attacks), myocarditis, blood clots, perimyocarditis, Guillain-Barré syndrome anaphylaxis, autoimmune disorders, immunosuppression, DNA virus reactivation, acute venous thromboembolism, vaccine-induced thrombotic thrombocytopenia, and vaccine-induced immune deficiency syndrome to name a few are being reported in thousands of peer-reviewed research papers globally.[38]

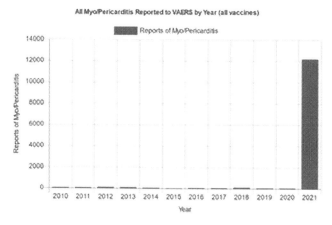

Figure 4.5: All Mayocarditis/Pericarditis reported to VAERS by Year.
Source: VAERS.

French virologist and Nobel Prize Winner Dr. Luc Montagnier in May 2021 warned that the COVID-19 vaccines cause antibody-dependent enhancement (ADE) that will lead to more (serious) infection and higher death rates in vaccinated persons.[39]

As can be seen from the CDC's Vaccine Adverse Events Reporting System (VAERS) table below, there were 16,766 COVID-19 vaccine-related deaths reported to VAERS between late December 2020 and October 9, 2021.[45] To put this into perspective, there were more COVID-19 vaccine-related deaths in fewer than 10 months than deaths from all other vaccines over 15 years.[44,45] A 2010 Harvard-executed study commissioned by the Department of Health and Human Services (HHS) found that "fewer than 1% of vaccine injuries" are reported to VAERS, suggesting the real numbers of fatalities and adverse events are significantly higher than reported.[46]

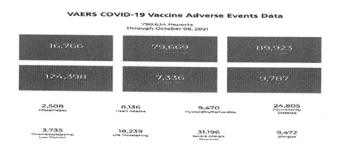

Figure 4.6: COVID-19 vaccine adverse events data October 2021
Source: VAERS

In Taiwan, the amount of people dying after their COVID-19 injection surpassed the number of deaths from the virus itself in September 2021. Taiwan's health authorities reported that deaths after vaccination reached 865, while deaths from the virus were 845.[47]

Data from the Centers for Medicare & Medicaid Services (CMS), released by whistleblowers in September 2021 which contains the records of some 59.4 million Medicare beneficiaries, showed that nearly 50,000 Medicare patients died within 14 days of getting "vaccinated", but these deaths were never logged or published in the government datasets.[48]

In the EU, data from the EnduraVigilance system, that is the EU-wide database for recording vaccine injury reports (jointly run by both the FDA and the CDC), showed that as of August 14, 2021, the system had collated 2,074,410 reports of injuries related to the COVID-19 vaccines, including 21,766 fatalities across the 27 Members States.[49]

By October 7, 2021, the WHO's publicly accessible database recording reported potential side-effects of medicinal products showed over two million possible COVID-19 vaccine injuries in 2021 alone, with 69% of the cases occurring in female patients.[50]

On December 20, 2021, the Office for National Statistics (ONS) distributed a dataset comprising specifics on "deaths by vaccination status in England" between January 1 and October 31, 2021.[51] The ONS data shows fully vaccinated teenagers aged 15 to 19 were statistically "three times more likely to die than unvaccinated teenagers, but children aged 10 to 14 were statistically 52 times more likely to die than unvaccinated children, recording a death rate of 238.37 per 100,000 person-years."[52]

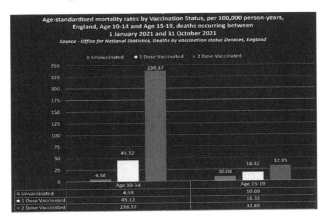

Figure 4.7: UK mortality rates by vaccination status January 2021 to October 2021
Source: United Kingdom ONS[48]

By January 19, 2022, there had been more than 1000 peer-reviewed papers evidencing a multitude of adverse events in COVID-19 vaccine recipients, including indisputable evidence of myocarditis and myocardial infarction following COVID-19 mRNA vaccination.[53] During February 2022 eminent American cardiologist and former vice chief of internal medicine at Baylor University Medical Center and professor at Texas A&M University, Dr. Peter McCullough noted that "I've seen a tenfold increase of myocarditis in association with the vaccine. Some of it incontrovertible."[54]

The correct method to evaluate vaccine effectiveness and safety is all-cause mortality. Deaths from all causes are compared between a control unvaccinated group and the vaccinated group. By the end of January 2022 data showed "a very significant above average number of deaths" across the United States that could not be attributed to COVID-19.[55] All-cause mortality in the 18 to 64 age group was 40% higher during the third and fourth quarters of 2021 than during pre-pandemic levels. For reference, a 10% increase would have been a one-in-200-year event.[55]

By March 20, 2022, official COVID-19 figures from the government of Canada showed the double vaccinated population was "on average 3.8 times more likely to be infected with COVID-19 and 3.3 times more likely to die of COVID-19 than the unvaccinated population," while the triple-vaccinated population was "on average 3.7 times more likely to be infected with COVID-19 but 5.1 times more likely to die of COVID-19 than the unvaccinated population."[56,57]

By May 13, 2022, data made available by the United States government and CDC strongly suggested that some fully vaccinated Americans were developing acquired immunodeficiency syndrome. AIDS-related diseases and cancers reported to VAERS increased between 1,145% and 33,715% in 2021.[55]

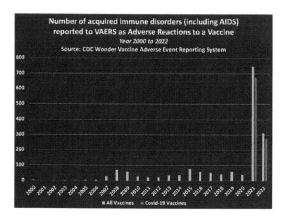

Figure 4.8: Number of acquired immune disorders reported to VAERS 2000 to 2022
Source: VAERS. The Expose

During August 2022, a peer-reviewed study published in "The Journal of Food and Chemical Toxicology" confirmed "evidence that [COVID-19] vaccination induces a profound impairment in type I interferon signaling, which has diverse adverse consequences to human health. We also identify potential profound disturbances in regulatory control of protein synthesis and cancer surveillance. These disturbances potentially have a causal link to neurodegenerative disease, myocarditis, immune thrombocytopenia, Bell's palsy, liver disease, impaired adaptive immunity, impaired DNA damage response and tumorigenesis."[58]

6. Comparing the data relating to adverse events per 100 000 doses ensures accurate proportionate analysis and comparison.

Over time, billions of other vaccines have also been administered without causing such volume adverse events.

CDC Data for instance confirms that between the 2008/2009 flu season and the 2019/2020 flu season, there were a total of 1.7204 billion doses of the flu vaccine administered in the United States.[59] According to "Our World in Data", as of August 9, 2022, 606 million doses of the COVID-19 vaccines have been administered in the United States. This means there have been nearly three times as many flu vaccines administered between 2008 and 2020 than COVID-19 injections since the end of 2020. The CDC data further confirms that between 2008 and 2020, there were just 64 events related to cancer reported as adverse reactions to the influenza vaccines compared to 2,579 cancer-related adverse reactions to the COVID-19 vaccines.[59] The number of adverse events related to cancer reported per 100,000 doses of COVID-19 vaccine administered equates to 0.43 per 100,000 doses compared to 0.0003 per 100,000 doses for the flu vaccine. The COVID-19 vaccination is therefore 1,433 times more likely to cause cancer than the flu vaccination.[59]

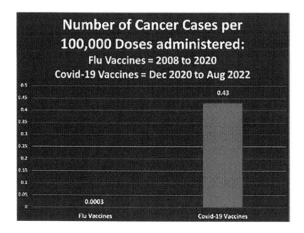

Figure 4.9: Number of cancer cases per 100, 000 doses
Source: VAERS, CDC, The Expose

7. COVID-19 vaccines are experimental by all scientific, medical and legal standards.

Dr. Robert Malone, one of the inventors of the mRNA technology, is on record stating, "The question that most troubles and perplexes me at this point is why the biological consequences …associated clinical adverse effects were not thoroughly investigated before widespread administration of random pseudouridine-incorporating 'mRNA'-like molecules to a global population. Biology, and particularly molecular biology, is highly complex and matrix-interrelated. Change one thing over here, and it is really hard to predict what might happen over there. That is why one must do rigorously controlled non-clinical and clinical research. Once again, it appears to me that the hubris of 'elite' high status scientists, physicians and governmental 'public health' bureaucrats has overcome common sense, well established regulatory norms have been disregarded, and patients have unnecessarily suffered as a consequence."[60]

The mRNA vaccines are new biotechnology with unknown long-term real-world consequences. mRNA has never been licensed for use in humans. According to the CDC "we will continue to provide updates as we learn more about the safety of the vaccines in real-world conditions," essentially admitting that the health authorities are busy with a "real-world" medical experiment.[43]

Until the end of August 2021, all COVID vaccines were merely EUA-authorized, not approved, or licensed. "EUA products are by definition experimental, which requires people be given the right to refuse them in terms of federal law, Title 21 U.S.C. § 360bbb-3(e)(1)(A)(ii)(I-III) of the Federal Food, Drug, and Cosmetic Act." Despite the fact that the FDA approved Comirnaty at the end of August 2021 and Spikevax at the end of January 2022, medium- and long-term safety and efficacy have not been proven in any COVID-19 vaccine.[12]

If the COVID-19 vaccines are not experimental and if they are extremely safe, why are pharmaceutical companies and healthcare providers protected from liability vis-à-vis the COVID-19 vaccines?[44]

8. You do not vaccinate people who aren't at risk from a disease. Only people in high-risk groups should be vaccinated.

According to Dr. Michael Yeadon (former vice president and chief scientist of Pfizer), "You do not vaccinate people who aren't at risk from a disease" and "Asymptomatic transmission is epidemiologically irrelevant. It's not necessary to argue it never happens; it is enough to show that if it occurs at all, it is so rare as not to be worth measuring."[12,61-65]

COVID-19's global survival rate is more than 99.8%. No mass vaccinations are reasonably required to combat a disease with a population-level crude mortality rate ranging between 0.0003% and 0.3%. It is further well noted that symptomless COVID-19 cases are not the drivers of the pandemic. A determinative study conclusively refuting the theory of "asymptomatic" spread in COVID-19, which was published in "Nature", showed that in a sample of 10 million, when all positive "asymptomatic" cases were followed and all close contacts were traced, there were zero (0) instances of asymptomatic spread.[66]

9. Data from countries across the globe show that high vaccination rates did not have any effect on the reduction in infections or deaths.

According to data from Johns Hopkins University, most countries across the globe saw a significant increase in the rate of infection following mass vaccination of the population. Countries with the highest vaccination rates globally, such as Israel, now have the highest infection rates.[5,67]

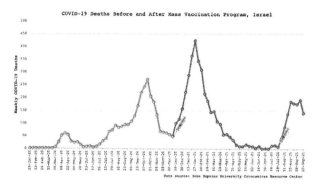

Figure 4.10: COVID-19 deaths before and after mass vaccination, Israel 2021
Source: Johns Hopkins University[5,67]

The phenomenon of countries experiencing sudden surges in new COVID-19 infections and deaths after a recent high degree of vaccine administration has become a universal trend.[5,36,67]

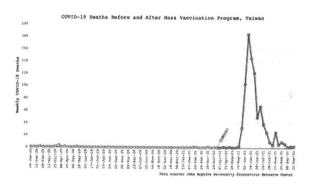

Figure 4.11: COVID-19 deaths before and after mass vaccination, Taiwan 2021
Source: Johns Hopkins University[5,36,67]

A peer-reviewed study published in the "European Journal of Epidemiology" that investigated data from 68 countries and 2,947 counties in the United States found no relation between vaccination level and fewer COVID cases.[68] The researchers concluded: "….that countries with higher percentage of population fully vaccinated have higher COVID-19 cases per 1 million people. The lack of a meaningful association between percentage population fully vaccinated and new COVID-19 cases is further exemplified, for instance, by comparison of Iceland and Portugal. Both countries have over 75% of their population fully vaccinated and have more COVID-19 cases per 1 million people than countries such as Vietnam and South Africa that have around 10% of their population fully vaccinated."[68]

Albert Einstein correctly asserted that the definition of insanity is "doing the same thing over and over again and expecting different results." To continue with a vaccination program that is not providing immunity nor reduce transmission is insane!

10. Based on the actual data most COVID-19 hospital patients and deaths are in fact fully vaccinated.

A CDC study released on September 17, 2021, found that most patients hospitalized with COVID-19 had been fully or partially vaccinated.[70] In the United Kingdom, from February 2021 through August 2021, 62% of all COVID-19 deaths were among the fully vaccinated.[70] Similarly, in Israel, 60% of all people hospitalized were fully vaccinated.[71] Another peer-reviewed study found that "Fully vaccinated patients had a higher rate of co-morbidities and immunosuppression compared with previously reported non-vaccinated hospitalized individuals with COVID-19."[72]

By March 2022, official UK data showed 90% of COVID-19 deaths were among the vaccinated and boosted.[73,74]

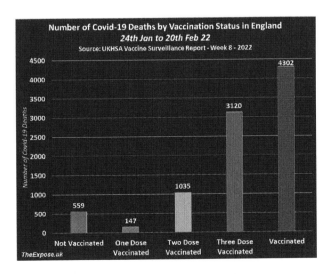

Figure 4.12: Number of COVID-19 deaths by vaccination Status January 24 to February 20, 2022
Source: UKHSA Surveillance Report -Week 8 2022, The Expose[73,74]

In total, there were 4,861 COVID-19 fatalities between January 24 and February 20, 2022, and the triple inoculated citizens accounted for 3,120 of them, while the unvaccinated citizens accounted for just 559. Overall, the vaccinated citizens accounted for 89% of all COVID-19 fatalities during these four weeks, with 4,302 verified deaths. This indicates the vaccinated population now accounted for nine in every 10 COVID-19 deaths, and the triple vaccinated population accounted for four in every five.[75]

11. Naturally acquired immunity is more robust and superior to existing vaccines. There is no need to vaccinate people that recovered from COVID-19 and already have natural immunity.

By April 2021, it was already well-known that significantly fewer people needed to be vaccinated to achieve herd immunity. 55% of Americans already had COVID-19 and already have antibodies in their system. There is no need to vaccinate people that already have antibodies. Theoretically, assuming the vaccines were effective, only 25% to 45% of Americans needed to be vaccinated to achieve herd immunity and not the CDC's 70% to 90%.[77-80]

In August 2021, an authoritative Israeli study found that natural immunity is significantly better than vaccine-induced immunity. The study found that the vaccinated were six to 13 times more likely to get infected than unvaccinated people who were previously infected with the coronavirus.[81] The risk of developing symptomatic COVID-19 was 27 times higher among the vaccinated, and the risk of hospitalization was eight times higher. Natural immunity affords longer-lasting and stronger protection against infection, symptomatic disease, and hospitalization due to COVID-19 compared to the two-dose vaccine-induced immunity, the authors wrote.[77,81]

By February 2022, more than 150 independent peer-reviewed studies confirmed that naturally acquired immunity is superior to vaccine-induced immunity.[77,82]

12. The COVID-19 vaccines significantly increase excess mortality and death.

The COVID-19 vaccines are not preventing deaths but in fact the cause of excess deaths.

By April 2022, data from "Our World in Data" (the flagship output of the University of Oxford's Oxford Martin Programme on Global Development which developed a unique and constantly evolving overview of all the major sources of data on the COVID-19 coronavirus) showed an irrefutable direct correlation between COVID-19 vaccines and excess deaths like the two samples below in all major Western democracies.[83]

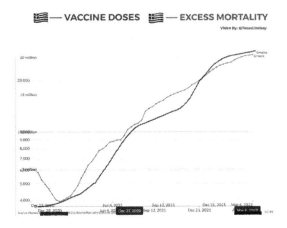

Figure 4.13: Correlation between COVID-19 vaccines and excess deaths – Greece 2021
Source: Our World in Data extracted by Texas Lindsay[83]

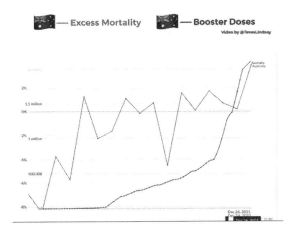

Figure 4.14: Correlation between COVID-19 vaccines and excess deaths – Australia 2021
Source: Our World in Data extracted by Texas Lindsay[83]

In a comprehensive study relating to excess mortality in Germany between 2020 and 2022 the researchers from the University of Regensburg and the University of Osnabruck which applied "sophisticated actuarial analysis to the publicly available all-cause mortality data provided by the German government" found that "In 2020, the observed number of deaths was close to the expected number with respect to the empirical standard deviation. By contrast, in 2021, the observed number of deaths was two empirical standard deviations above the expected number. The high excess mortality in 2021 was almost entirely due to an increase in deaths in the age groups between 15 and 79 and started to accumulate only from April 2021 onwards...the maybe most surprising fact is that the second year[2021] produces in all age groups a significant mortality increase, which is in sharp contrast to the expectation that the vaccination should decrease the number of COVID-19 deaths."[84] The researchers observe that "Something must have happened in April 2021 that led to a sudden and sustained increase in mortality in the age groups below 80 years."[84]

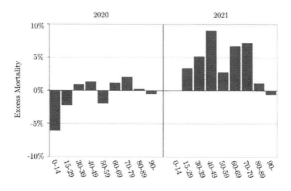

Fig. 1: Excess mortality in 2020 (left panel) and 2021 (right panel) in different age groups

Figure 4.15: German excess mortality in 2020
(pre-COVID-19 vaccines) and 2021 (post COVID-19 vaccines)
Source: Kuhbandner et al.[84]

Applying the Bradford Hill Criteria (a set of principles to establish the relationship between suspected causes and observed effects in the field of public health) conclusively points to the COVID-19 vaccines as the cause of the excess deaths.[85]

13. There are numerous other options for society to return to normal.
The contention that mandatory mass vaccination is the only way for society to return to normal is absurd, patently false, and denies scientific reality:

- The protect-the-vulnerable approach, as advocated by numerous eminent doctors, scientists and epidemiologists, is the most logical approach for society to immediately return to normality.[86]
- To achieve herd immunity, children and other people not in vulnerable groups can become naturally infected as they do with other pathogens that have a crude mortality rate of 0.3%.[44,77]

- Effective early outpatient treatment options and safe and effective drugs such as Ivermectin can be given as prophylaxis, as proven by numerous peer-reviewed studies and meta-analyses.[7,87-91]

None of the countries that achieved high vaccination rates returned to normal or ended emergency measures by February 2022.

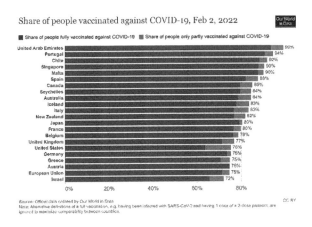

Figure 4.16: Share of people vaccinated against COVID-19
Source: Our World in Data[92]

The promise that a 70% to 80% vaccination rate would end the pandemic and return society to normal was a lie![92]

14. Individuals have the right to free and informed consent for all medical interventions.

Individuals have a non-derogable right to free and informed consent for all medical experiments and interventions, including COVID-19 vaccination, as guaranteed and required by the International Covenant on Civil and Political Rights and the Nuremberg Code.[12,93,94]

Misinformation and Disinformation

Maximilien de Robespierre (1758–1794), a French lawyer and statesman who was one of the most influential figures of the French Revolution, emphasized that "The secret of freedom lies in educating the people whereas the secret of tyranny is in keeping them ignorant," while English-born American philosopher, political theorist, and revolutionary author of the book "Common Sense" (1776), Thomas Paine (1736–1809) wisely pointed out that "Reason obeys itself; and ignorance submits to whatever is dictated to it."

According to mainstream media outlets and Western States, there is a great deal of "misinformation" about COVID-19 in circulation. The UNHRC, in their April 19, 2020, communication, also urged governments to craft measures "to regulate misinformation on COVID-19" and combat the spread of misinformation through independent fact-checking education and media literacy. "It is essential that governments and internet companies address this issue [of] misinformation in the first instance by themselves providing clear, reliable, fact-based information," the UNHRC noted.[95]

Stephan Lewandowsky, a professor of psychology at the University of Bristol in the United Kingdom notes that "The fundamental problem with misinformation is that once people have heard it, they tend to believe and act on it, even after it's been corrected,…Even in the best of all possible worlds, correcting misinformation is not an easy task."[96] Research further showed that people are more likely to view misinformation as truth, when they fail to carefully analyze and deliberate on the accuracy of the information provided to them.[97]

This raises three critical questions: What is the definition of this "misinformation"? Who decides what qualifies as "misinformation"? Who is spreading this "misinformation"?

What is the definition of this "misinformation"?

The Cambridge Dictionary of Linguistics defines "misinformation" as "wrong information" and as "information intended to deceive."

Who decides what qualifies as "misinformation"?

In the COVID-19 years, the groups that are using the term "misinformation" the most and constantly expressing concern regarding the spread of "misinformation" are governments, public health authorities, and their multinational corporate sponsors (big tech, big pharma, and the mainstream media). According to these highly conflicted groups that have also appointed themselves as the sole arbiters of "misinformation," any information that does not strictly support and confirm the official government narrative qualifies as "misinformation." No debate or differing points of view are permitted. A crepuscular international censorship network called the Trusted News Initiative (TNI), (whose members include the "AP, AFP, BBC, CBC/Radio-Canada, European Broadcasting Union (EBU), Facebook, Financial Times, First Draft, Google/ YouTube, The Hindu, Microsoft, Reuters, Reuters Institute for the Study of Journalism, Twitter, The Washington Post)", censors any "disinformation which threatens human life or disrupts democracy during elections."[98] The TNI articles strictly align with the "COVID-19 health policy from the world's major public health agencies."[98] To justify specific acts of suppression, "down-rank-ing" and "filtering," the search engine and social media behemoths refer to the CDC, ECDC, FDA, NIH, and WHO declarations, policies, and guidelines, determining how news flows to billions of people.[98] The crude corporate censorship underscores the vast power monopoly technology platforms have amassed and the blatant opacity with which they exercise it.[98]

Any information and articles on the following seven topics were the most severely suppressed to protect the prescribed narrative:

- the source and origins of SARS-CoV-2;
- cheap and effective early treatment options for COVID-19;
- the voices of imminent and respected dissenting health professionals, academics, scientists, clinicians and independent researchers;
- the record number of post-vaccine side-effects and death;
- the fact that natural immunity is stronger and more effective than vaccine-induced immunity;
- the central role of pre-existing co-morbidities in official COVID-19 death counts;
- the illegal and disproportionate nature of all COVID-19 emergency measures.[98]

The following prominent professors and researchers with formidable research publication credentials and conflict-of-interest-free records were among those extensively censored and ridiculed:

- Dr. Didier Raoult, microbiologist, and director, IHU Méditerranée Infection; Professor at Aix Marseille Université;
- Dr. Harvey A. Risch, Prof. Epid., Yale School of Public Health;
- Dr. Jay Bhattacharya, epidemiologist, Stanford University;
- Dr. Geert Vanden Bossche, former head of the Vaccine Development German Center for Infection Research;
- Dr. Knut M. Wittkowski, biometrician, 20-year head, biostatistics/

epid., Rockefeller University;

- Dr. Luke Montagnier, French virologist and Nobel-Winning Co-Discoverer of H.I.V.
- Dr. Martin Kulldorff, epidemiologist, Harvard;
- Dr. Michael Yeadon, former VP of respiratory research, Pfizer;
- Dr. Paul E Merik, Professor of Medicine (Deans' Endowed Chair), Chief of Pulmonary and Critical Care Medicine, East Virginia Medical School;
- Dr. Peter A. McCullough, former Vice-Chair Int. Med., Baylor Univ;
- Dr. Paul E Alexander, McMaster University, Ontario, Canada;
- Dr. Robert W. Malone, inventor of mRNA technology platform;
- Dr. Sucharit Bhakdi, former head of the Institute of Medical Microbiology, Univ. of Mainz;
- Dr. Sunetra Gupta, infectious disease epidemiologist, Oxford University.[98]

The TNI has also robustly suppressed frontline doctors who have saved thousands of lives with early COVID-19 therapies: Drs. George Fareed and Brian Tyson in California, Dr. Vladimir Zelenko in New York, Dr. Ryan N. Cole in Boise, Idaho, Dr. Richard Bartlett in West Texas, America's Frontline Doctors, founded by Dr. Simone Gold; and the Frontline COVID-19 Critical Care Alliance (FCCCA), led by Dr. Pierre Kory.[98] In addition, prominent international lawyers such as Dr. Robert F. Kennedy Jr. and Dr. Reiner Fuellmich were scorned, suppressed, and derided.

History demonstrates that the main protagonists of "misinformation" are immoral regimes and greedy large corporations that abuse their positions of authority and influence to either advance an ideology or to accumulate more power and wealth for themselves. Now they expect citizens to believe that whistleblowers, academics, scientists, and medical experts risking their careers are behind "misinformation." If you dig beneath the surface, however, you quickly realize that the organizations responsible for collecting, monitoring, and censoring COVID-19 "misinformation" are either funded by or part of the government apparatus or a foundation or multinational corporation that have a direct or indirect material financial benefit from mass global testing and vaccination programs and keeping the official mainstream COVID-19 narrative alive. Many of the so-called "fact-checkers" are, for instance, sponsored by big pharma, big tech, George Soros, the Bill and Melinda Gates Foundation, and other major beneficiaries and proponents of mandatory mass vaccination.[98-100] On December 20, 2021, a New York Post article reported that "The fact-check industry is funded by liberal moguls such as George Soros, government-funded nonprofits, and the tech giants themselves. The checkers are not the unbiased arbiters of truth; they are useful distractions."[100] The monopolized mainstream media and transnational tech companies have completely disgraced themselves throughout the COVID-19 pandemic and were nothing more than shameless propaganda peddlers.[86] Robert F. Kennedy Jr. noted that, "The term 'disinformation' is just a euphemism for anything that departs from official government proclamations or pharmaceutical industry profiteering and profit ambitions. It has nothing to do whether it's factually correct or not."

Who is spreading the "misinformation"?

The major disseminators of "misinformation" have been the State Parties and the mainstream media, big tech, and big pharma operating within their legal jurisdiction. Throughout the COVID-19 pandemic, governments have been propagating a biased, false narrative, denying the scientific realities, and suppressing all scientific studies that do not align with the mainstream narrative.

Regarding COVID-19 government and mainstream misinformation, Dr. Piers Robinson, co-director of the Organization for Propaganda Studies, stated that:

> It wouldn't be an underestimation to say that this is probably one of the biggest propaganda operations that we have seen in history.[98]

Two examples are worth highlighting:

A. Misinformation: COVID-19 is a pandemic of the unvaccinated

The narrative behind the contention that COVID-19 is "a pandemic of the unvaccinated" is a classic case of how fake statistics originate and proliferate and offers valuable insights around the perils of blind trust in public officials.[101]

In June 2021, the Associated Press (AP) printed an article titled, "Nearly All COVID Deaths in the US Are Now Among Unvaccinated." Authored by Carla K. Johnson and Mike Stobbe, it was reprinted or quoted by more than 100 media outlets and so-called fact-checkers such as Bloomberg, the Boston Globe, PBS, the Los Angeles Times, FactCheck.org, Snopes, Yahoo News, and WebMD. The article asserted that the AP performed an "analysis" that found only "1.1% of all C-19 hospitalizations and 0.8% of C-19 deaths in May" were due to "breakthrough infections in fully vaccinated people." Absurdly, the article included a qualification that "the AP calculated these rates based on figures provided by the Centers for Disease Control and Prevention, but that the CDC has not published such rates due to limitations in the data."[101] The AP's numbers were therefore pointless given that they were based on substantially inadequate data.[101]

Despite this glaring flaw in the "analysis," Dr. Fauci appeared on the July 4, 2021 edition of NBC's Meet the Press and echoed the AP's false statistics without mentioning its qualifications. "If you look at the number of deaths," proclaimed Fauci, "about 99.2% of them are unvaccinated. About 0.8% are vaccinated." Instead of correcting the AP article and Fauci for contriving and distorting CDC data, the director of the CDC, Dr. Rochelle Walensky, amplified it. During a July 16, 2021, White House press conference with Fauci by her side, she declared that "over 97% of people who are entering the hospital right now are unvaccinated" and that COVID-19 "is becoming a pandemic of the unvaccinated." In turn, media outlets acted as loudspeakers for Fauci and Walensky without any critical assessment. This involved reports from ABC News, CNN, NPR, The Guardian, The Hill, Politico, Microsoft News (MSN), Rolling Stone, USA Today, The Washington Post, and The New York Times.[101]

Contrary to assertions from Dr. Anthony Fauci that fully vaccinated people comprise only 1% of those being hospitalized or killed by COVID-19, a CDC study found that the vast majority of patients hospitalized with COVID-19 had been fully or partially vaccinated.[102] In the United Kingdom, one of the most vaccinated countries in the world against COVID-19 by mid-2021 (and therefore a good benchmark for other Western nations), a report released by Public Health England (PHE) in July 2021 highlighted the following facts:

- the mortality rate for fully vaccinated people was 0.636%, which was 6.6 times higher than the unvaccinated mortality rate of 0.0957%.
- fully vaccinated people were also found to be more susceptible to hospitalization than their unvaccinated counterparts (of the 4,087 fully vaccinated individuals, 2.05% [84 people] ended up in a hospital; among the 35,521 unvaccinated individuals, only 1.48% [527 people] were hospitalized).[101]

By March 2022, the pandemic among the unvaccinated was essentially over, whereas it was just getting started among the boosted. Data from the UK health authorities as well as data from other major Western health authorities showed that far from being protective, COVID-19 vaccines made all age groups significantly more vulnerable to infections and death![103,104]

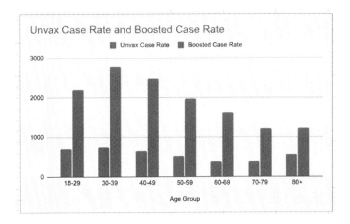

Figure: 4.17: Unvaccinated case rate vs. boosted case rate
Source: UKHSA Vaccine Surveillance Report Week 11 2022 extracts by Igor Chudov

Table 12. COVID-19 deaths (a) within 28 days and (b) within 60 days of positive specimen or with COVID-19 reported on death certificate, by vaccination status between week 7 2022 and week 10 2022
Please note that corresponding rates by vaccination status can be found in Table 13.
(a)

Death within 28 days of positive COVID-19 test by date of death between week 7 2022 (w/e 20 February 2022) and week 10 2022 (w/e 13 March 2022)	Total**	Unlinked*	Not vaccinated	Received one dose (1 to 20 days before specimen date)	Received one dose, ≥21 days before specimen date	Second dose ≥14 days before specimen date¹	Third dose ≥14 days before specimen date¹
	[This data should be interpreted with caution. See information below in footnote about the correct interpretation of these figures]						
Under 18	2	0	1	0	1	0	0
18 to 29	5	0	1	0	1	2	1
30 to 39	15	0	10	0	0	3	3
40 to 49	34	2	9	1	3	12	7
50 to 59	100	1	25	0	5	24	45
60 to 69	177	0	33	0	7	37	100
70 to 79	503	5	58	0	11	84	347
80 or over	1,584	3	102	0	29	220	1,230

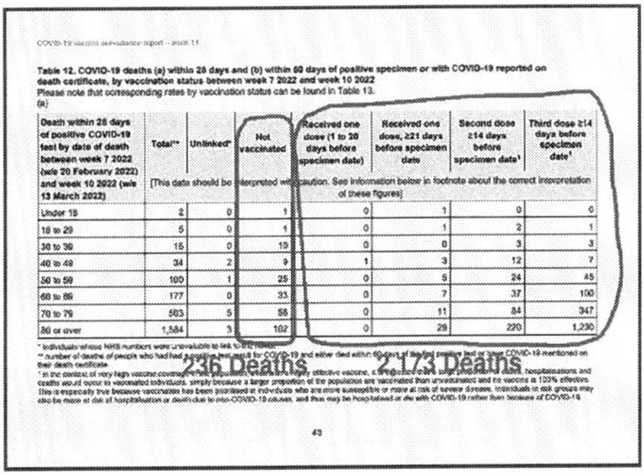

Figure: 4.18: Unvaccinated vs. vaccinated COVID-19 deaths week 7 – 10 2022
Source: UKHSA Vaccine Surveillance Report Week 11 2022 extracts by Igor Chudov

From a credibility and integrity perspective it is obvious that State officials with this level of duplicity and dishonesty cannot be trusted.

B. Misinformation: Ivermectin is a horse deworming medicine and dangerous to individuals

In 2015, in its only award for treatments of infectious diseases since six decades prior, the Nobel Committee for Physiology or Medicine honored the discovery of Ivermectin, a multifaceted drug deployed against some of the world's most devastating tropical diseases.[105] Ivermectin is a chemical anti-parasitic agent first discovered in 1975. It is on the WHO's list of "Essential Medicines" – medications the WHO deems safe and that should be commonly available in all countries – and is used to treat a wide variety of parasitic diseases in humans and animals. Merck's patent on Ivermectin expired in 1996 and as such Ivermectin is an "incredibly cheap" drug that is off-license, generic, and could easily be made widely available to give billions of people access to it.

By January 2021, it was well-known that more than 20 randomized clinical trials (RCTs) tracked the inpatient and outpatient treatments of COVID-19 since March 2020. Six of seven meta-analyses of Ivermectin treatment RCTs reported during 2021 found "notable reductions in COVID-19 fatalities, "by an average 83% (95% CI, 65% to 92%) compared with no Ivermectin treatment (5 RCTs, 1107 participants)."[106] During mass Ivermectin medication campaigns in Peru, excess deaths fell by a mean of 74% over 30 days in its 10 States with the most extensive medications. Decreases in deaths correlated with the extent of Ivermectin distributions in all 25 Peruvian States.[107]

The widely available, safe, and effective Ivermectin early treatment protocol presented a major problem to the global elite and the pharmaceutical industry. In terms of the FDA's rules and regulations, in order for any medical product to be to be granted an EUA, "there must be no adequate, approved, and available alternative to the candidate product for diagnosing, preventing, or treatment of the disease or condition." Acknowledging Ivermectin as a safe and effective treatment for COVID-19 meant that there could not be an EUA approval for the COVID-19 vaccines. In other words, Ivermectin stood in the way of actualizing the billions of dollars in profits, that led to Pfizer expecting "a record $100 billion in revenue, thanks to the COVID-19 vaccines and treatments." Ivermectin also threatened the global biopolitical developments relating to continued emergency measures and connected trillion-dollar taxpayer-funded spending implemented across the West as well as the WEF's "Great Reset."

Following early reports that Ivermectin could be used to reduce COVID-19 symptoms and be used as part of an effective early treatment protocol, the States, public health regulators, the global pharmaceutical industry, transnational corporations, and their mainstream media colluders (that during 2020 received $4.58 billion [75% of their budget] for television advertising from big pharma) "turned their collective fire on it."[108] The "Disinformation Playbook" as detailed in a 2021 peer-reviewed article published in the "Journal of Public Health Policy" was indeed expertly executed.[109] According to the researchers the five main disinformation tactics used by big pharma to attack and obscure true science are:

- **Faking science:** conducting—or paying others to conduct—flawed or biased scientific studies or hiding research with unfavorable conclusions. (The Fake)
- **Harassing scientists:** personally targeting, attempting to silence, or diminishing the credibility of scientists responsible for research findings inconvenient to industry. (The Blitz)
- **Manufacturing uncertainty:** questioning credibility, or emphasizing uncertainty, of independent science unfavorable to industry interests. (The Diversion)
- **Buying credibility:** using scientific credibility of academic institutions to push corporate agendas while leveraging funding to secure support from the scientific community. (The Screen)
- **Manipulating government officials:** inappropriately influencing policymakers to undermine the role of independent science in policy. (The Fix)[109,110]

Any doctor, academic, or scientist whose research and practical experience showed the efficacy of Ivermectin or anyone claiming to be healed by Ivermectin was said to be a charlatan and heretic "spreading dangerous misinformation." Numerous eminent medical doctors such as Dr. Paul E. Marik (regarded as the most published intensivist in the world with more than 513 peer-reviewed publications and 27,350 citations) who prescribed Ivermectin were investigated, suspended, fired, prosecuted, and some even had their medical licenses revoked. Medical experts such as Dr. Robert Malone, who dared to present the true facts on social media platforms, such as Twitter, had their accounts suspended.

High-impact medical journal editorial staff were getting orders to censor Ivermectin studies from big pharma and "philanthropists" such as Bill Gates.[111,112] Various medical journals such as The Lancet, The New England Journal of Medicine (NEJM), The Journal of the American Medical Association (JAMA), the British Medical Journal (BMJ) Nature, and The Cochrane Library did the following to suppress the evidence of the efficacy of early treatment:

1. Rejected all positive trials of Ivermectin, specifically the high-quality trials, with "statistically significant" results supporting the use of Ivermectin or Hydroxychloroquine, since May of 2020.[111,112]
2. Retracted positive Ivermectin research even after they passed rigorous peer-review and in certain instances after they were already published.[111,112]

3. Published fraudulent trials and fraudulent meta-analyses relating the use of Ivermectin or Hydroxychloroquine.[111,112]
4. Published copious anti-Ivermectin editorials that were not subject to any form of peer review but were widely misused by the mainstream media and government bureaucrats.[111,112]

Public health officials and the mainstream media proclaimed that "Ivermectin was used only on animals" and "anti-vaxxers" were openly mocked for "drinking horse de-wormer."[113,114] News anchors at ABC, CNN, CNBC, and other mainstream media outlets, falsely stated that not only is Ivermectin ineffective but "it can kill you". The most blatant example of this misinformation campaign was a story in Rolling Stone, which stated that emergency room departments in Oklahoma were so over-run with Ivermectin intoxication that they were turning gunshot patients away.[113] This tale was shared far and wide until Rolling Stone was compelled to retract it, when a letter from one of the hospitals involved was distributed, stating that "not only were they not 'overrun' with Ivermectin overdoses," but they had also never seen a single case.[114]

On August 21, 2021, the US FDA deceptively tweeted, "You are not a horse. You are not a cow. Seriously, y'all. Stop it."[115] The FDA included a link to their website where they have a section on "Why you should not use Ivermectin to prevent or cure COVID-19." They state that:

> The FDA has not authorized or approved Ivermectin for use in preventing or treating COVID-19 in humans or animals. Ivermectin is approved for human use to treat infections caused by some parasitic worms and head lice and skin conditions like rosacea. Currently available data do not show Ivermectin is effective against COVID-19.[116]

This was followed by a CDC national advisory on August 26, 2021, warning against the use of Ivermectin and recommending to the public to:

> Be aware that currently, ivermectin has not been proven as a way to prevent or treat COVID-19. Seek immediate medical attention or call the poison control center hotline (1-800-222-1222) for advice if you have taken ivermectin or a product that contains ivermectin and are having symptoms.

> Get vaccinated against COVID-19. COVID-19 vaccination is approved by FDA and is the safest and most effective way to prevent getting sick

and protect against severe disease and death from SARS-CoV-2, the virus that causes COVID-19.

Figure 4.19: Fauci warns Americans against dangerous horse drug Ivermectin
Source: CNN

On CNN, Dr. Antony Fauci declared that "There is no clinical evidence that indicates that this [Ivermectin] works." The truth, however, is that a peer-reviewed study conducted in June 2020 clearly showed that Ivermectin, "an FDA-approved anti-parasitic having broad-spectrum anti-viral activity in vitro, is an inhibitor of the causative virus (SARS-CoV-2), with a single addition to Vero-hSLAM cells 2 h post infection with SARS-CoV-2 able to effect ~5000-fold reduction in viral RNA at 48 h," and a peer-reviewed meta-analysis in August 2021, found: "that large reductions in COVID-19 deaths are possible using Ivermectin.[117-120] Using Ivermectin early in the clinical course may reduce numbers progressing to severe disease. The apparent safety and low cost suggest that Ivermectin is likely to have a significant impact on the SARS-CoV-2 pandemic globally."[118,119]

Based on the studies indicating "efficacy in prophylaxis, combined with the known safety profile of Ivermectin, a citywide prevention program using Ivermectin for COVID-19 was implemented in Itajaí in Brazil in the State of Santa Catarina" between July and December of 2020. "The objective of this study was to evaluate the impact of regular Ivermectin use on subsequent COVID-19 infection and mortality rates. Of the 223,128 citizens of Itajaí considered for the study, a total of 159,561 subjects were included in the analysis: 113,845 (71.3%) regular Ivermectin users and 45,716 (23.3%) non-users."[120] The researchers concluded that the regular use of Ivermectin led to an "up to a 92% reduction in COVID-19 Mortality Rate in a Dose-Response Manner" and that "non-use of ivermectin was associated with a 12.5-fold increase in mortality rate and a seven-fold increased risk of dying from

COVID-19 compared to the regular use of ivermectin. This dose-response efficacy reinforces the prophylactic effects of ivermectin against COVID-19."[120]

In August 2021, the Indian press touted that "Uttar Pradesh, India's most populous State with about 230 million people, was nearly COVID-19 free"– an amazing accomplishment demonstrating how early treatment contributed to overcoming the Delta variant-based surge in India from April to May 2021. Early treatment home kits containing Ivermectin and Doxycycline wiped out an outbreak of COVID-19, reducing cases by 99% in just three weeks.[121] Public health workers made regular visits to houses in towns and districts across Uttar Pradesh, proactively testing and treating the condition immediately. Even the WHO praised the effort yet failed to acknowledge the use of Ivermectin.[87,116] On August 25, 2021, the Indian media noticed the discrepancy between Uttar Pradesh's massive success and other States, like Kerala's, comparative failure. Although Uttar Pradesh was only 5% vaccinated to Kerala's 20%, Uttar Pradesh had (only) 22 new COVID cases, while Kerala was overwhelmed with 31,445 in one day. It became apparent that the early home treatment kits containing the Ivermectin must have been extremely effective.[87,121]

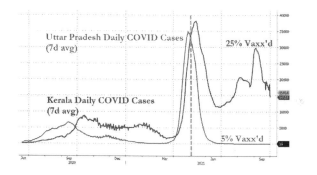

Figure 4.20: Uttar Pradesh vs. Kerala new cases
Source: TS News and News 18

In March 2021, a group of Japanese scientists from the Tanioka Clinic, Bunkyo-Ku and National Institute of Sensory Organs, Tokyo Medical Center, conducted a "retrospective statistical analysis study of the impact of Ivermectin against COVID-19 between the 31 onchocerciasis-endemic countries using the community-directed treatment with ivermectin and the non-endemic 22 countries in Africa." The scientists concluded that:

The morbidity and mortality in the onchocerciasis endemic countries are lesser than those in the non-endemic ones. The community-directed onchocerciasis treatment with ivermectin is the most reasonable explanation for the decrease in morbidity and fatality rate in Africa. In areas where ivermectin is distributed to and used by the entire population, it leads to a significant reduction in mortality.[122]

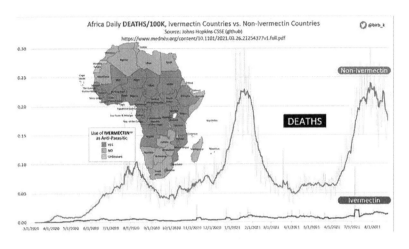

Figure 4.21: Africa daily deaths/100k, Ivermectin vs. non-Ivermectin countries
Source: Tanioka *et al.* Johns Hopkins University

Whenever there is clear evidence that a lifesaving drug works, public health officials have an ethical obligation to immediately inform the public and give them access. Shockingly, despite this clear evidence of the ability to save lives with the early treatment of Ivermectin, the WHO, Western democracies' public health agencies and big pharma did not disclose this lifesaving data to the public nor try to implement this strategy globally. Not only that, for the first time in history medical doctors were prohibited and prevented from prescribing lifesaving medication and forced to stand idly by, and see their patients die. Commenting on the success of Ivermectin in Itajaí in Brazil, Dr. Paul E. Marik noted that "We Could Have Saved 600-800k Lives (in the United States). The human cost is enormous and the reason this was denied is simply profiteering and making money for big pharma and their interests."

My family's personal experience with Ivermectin and the I-Mask Ivermectin protocol is that it saved the life of my frail elderly father.[123] My father is 79 years of age and chronically ill. He is both a prostate cancer and heart attack survivor living with a pacemaker. My father, permanently on morphine and other prescription pain medication, has numerous serious medical conditions following several unsuccessful back and abdomen operations. His digestive system only allows him to eat soup or soft food twice daily. When my father was diagnosed with COVID-19 on June 23, 2021, we all feared for his life. In terms of the mainstream narrative, my father had a near 0% chance of survival. We decided that we would not send my father to any hospital and that we would treat him at home. We immediately started my father on a course of Ivermectin (0.6mg per kg/day) combined with Zink (100mg/day), Vitamin D (3500 IU/day), and Vitamin C (2000mg/day). On June 27, 2021, his blood oxygen levels fell to 75. We placed him on a home oxygen machine and his oxygen levels recovered to 95 within a couple of hours. My father improved over the next eight days and recovered completely by July 5, 2021. If my father, with all his ailments and frail state, can survive COVID-19, there is no reason any person should die from this disease. In our circle of family, friends, business associates, and colleagues, we have lost eight dear people to COVID-19. All of them followed the official government advice to remain at home with no treatment and to then go to the hospital when breathing becomes difficult. Conversely, all in our circle of family and friends who started using Ivermectin, Zink, Vitamin D, and Vitamin C once diagnosed with COVID-19 survived irrespective of age and medical vulnerabilities. Governments and their ultra-wealthy handlers are expecting us not to "believe our lying eyes!"

The most abhorrent and criminal COVID-19 leadership failure of all is that the WHO, NIH, CDC, ECDC, and FDA have consistently denied the existence of lifesaving, effective, cheap, and safe readily available early treatments such as Ivermectin. "Their only recommended option until November 2020 – a month before the vaccines arrived – was to sicken at home until you couldn't breathe then go to the hospital."[111,112] Once the COVID-19 vaccines arrived, they were promoted as the only solution. Bruce Coville aptly asserted that "Withholding information is the essence of tyranny. Control of the flow of information is the tool of the dictatorship."

There is no other conclusion than that those public officials entrusted to protect and inform the public were untrustworthy and instead of acting with the required *uberimma fides* they were acting with *mala fides*. Government officials with prestigious credentials, big pharma, big tech, prestigious medical journals, and prominent media outlets repeatedly misreported the facts propagating the official false narrative with life-or-death consequences for millions of people around the globe. Dr. Pierre Kory surmised it well when he wrote that:

The NEJM, Lancet, BMJ, JAMA, Cochrane Library all have blood on their hands. As the world came under attack by a novel and highly transmissible respiratory virus, the medical journals had a critical, life-saving responsibility to publish any and all studies of treatments that were either potentially effective or substantively effective in either preventing or treating the disease. They abdicated their primary responsibility. Millions have died as a result.[111,112]

Historical Perspective on the Ramifications of "Misinformation"

History is the most outstanding teacher and predictor of the future. In 1500, the Roman Catholic Church was all-powerful in Western Europe and warily guarded its authoritarian position of dominance and control. Unexamined myths and misinformation insidiously determined prevailing norms that were deemed to be unassailable and sacrosanct by the religious/political establishment. Whoever dared to criticize or question the corrupt practices of the Catholic Church was labeled a heretic and burned at the stake. In the medieval period, moral, social, and (what we would today call) political thought all took place almost exclusively within religious institutions. Exploiting the illiteracy, ignorance, and superstition of the middle and lower class, the aristocracy and papacy used pseudo-Christian justifications that had no basis in the Bible to enrich themselves to coerce and dominate the public. A system of "indulgences" (in terms of which freedom from God's punishment for sin could be purchased with money) and numerous bureaucratic religious regulations were foisted upon the public to keep up the luxurious lifestyles of the pope, bishops, and clergy. Corruption was thriving, and enormous amounts of money were used to finance wars, build palaces, and commission art. To protect their powers, political and religious life was dominated by doom and gloom if one failed to obey the church's pseudo-religious mandates. Legal moralism (that is the theory of jurisprudence that the entire nation should be governed by one morality, with dissent from the official view being punishable as a crime) was the philosophy of law. Sacraments, rituals, and cults around saints kept the people mystified. The language of the Bible, Latin, was not accessible to most. Coercion masquerading as religious piety was the bedrock of religious politics. What enabled the corrupt elites to maintain power was their censorship and control of information through a monopoly of the communications channels of the time.

The Reformation began in 1517 when a German monk, Martin Luther, published his "95 Theses", exposing corrupt practices of the governing elite and the sale of indulgences. Luther's ideas eventually became synonymous with the notion of *sola scriptura* (the Bible is the source for Christian faith). The Church accused Luther of heresy in August 1518 and summoned him to Rome. Frederick III of Saxony interceded to keep him in German lands, where he continued to debate critics and translated the New Testament into German. The Edict of Worms of May 1521 "condemned Luther and officially banned citizens of the Holy Roman Empire from defending or propagating his ideas."[124] Many were burned at the stake for exposing the mainstream lies and deception. The barbaric executions were unable to quench the rebellion and became a catalyst for the spread of the truth. The Reformation movement was greatly supported by the invention of the Gutenberg printing press, which by now had spread all over Europe. The aristocracy no longer had a monopoly on the communication channels of the time as a growing number of ordinary people were able to acquire and read the Bible and other books in their mother tongue. Possessing forbidden books would lead to exile and, from 1527, the death penalty. The Reformation reached its pinnacle when the lower and middle classes recognized that they had been lied to and manipulated. They revolted against the feudal order and called for an end to many of the governing elite's extractive practices, including serfdom, the foundation of the rural economy that tied peasants to the aristocracy and offered them few rights. Frustration on the side of the elite rulers led to brute force with more regional "tribunals" and executions, which only fueled the resentment and gave people the courage to confront the tyranny and change the course of history. The Reformation led to the Dutch War of Independence, the Thirty Years War (one of the most destructive wars in European history with an estimated eight million casualties), the Holy Roman Empire losing supremacy, and eventually the Enlightenment. The Lutheran Reformation, which ended the Roman Catholic Church's control over Christian theology, had a wide-ranging effect, not only on religious practice, but also on the social, political, and intellectual life of the Western world.[125–128]

In 2022, the global political and corporate elite are all powerful and wearily guards its corrupt serfdom. Pseudo-Christianity has been replaced by a religion of health and pseudo-biomedical science. Religious apparatus has been replaced by emergency public health apparatus. Unexamined COVID-19 misinformation insidiously determines prevailing norms that are deemed unassailable and sacrosanct by the biomedical-political establishment. Whoever dares to criticize the mainstream public health narrative is yet again labeled a heretic and science denier. Exploiting the lack of knowledge, ignorance, and misconceptions of the middle and lower class regarding their fundamental human rights and health, the ultra-rich global elite uses pseudo-medical scientific justifications that have no basis in medical science to enrich themselves and coerce and dominate the public. To protect their powers, political and medical life is dominated by doom and gloom if one fails to obey the State's pseudo-biomedical mandates. Legal moralism is once again the philosophy of societal law. Non-stop mainstream media propaganda regarding COVID-19, new variants, and a proliferation of new public health mandates, keep the people mystified and occupied. Biomedical data is not comprehensible to most, and complex epistemological terminology further confuses most people. More than 600 years after the Reformation, we are again faced with a dire situation where corrupt global elites maintain power through the dissemination of misinformation and by censoring and controlling the flow of information through ownership and monopolistic control of modern communication channels such as Google, which has a 95% worldwide market share.[129] Google's algorithms effectively determine what people can and cannot see, with 80% of search traffic going to the top 10 listings on the first page.[130] In the modern day, those who control the media, the social media, and search engines controls the minds of the public!

Figure 4.22: Search engine market share 2021
Source: Statcounter

In the Middle Ages, behaviors were allowed and prohibited based on being "virtuous" or "wicked," subjectively determined by corrupt clergy. Today, behaviors are permitted or forbidden based on being "noninfectious" or "contagious," subjectively determined by corrupt public health officials.

Coercion masquerading as biomedical treatment is the bedrock of biomedical politics. A new "religion of health" where the religious apparatus is biomedical pseudo-science, and the juridical political apparatus to facilitate and legitimize the lawlessness is a perpetual "state of emergency". This period in history will be remembered as one of the most disgraceful moments in the Western world, and those who led and governed the major world powers during it as reckless, amoral, despicable individuals. As with the Reformation, the stronghold of the global elite will be broken once the lower and middle class recognize that they have been swindled.

Chapter Conclusion

The COVID-19 epidemic will notoriously be remembered as one of most manipulated international events in human history, typified by lies, deception, misinformation, and disinformation in a never-ending stream, coordinated by the global elite, State Parties, medical journals, medical associations, medical boards, global health agencies, big tech, big pharma, and big media.[108]

Danish theologian, philosopher, poet, social critic, and religious author Soren Kierkegaard (1813–1855) said that "There are two ways to be fooled. One is to believe what isn't true; the other is to refuse to believe what is true."

According to a peer-reviewed study published in the Lancet medical journal in April 2021, the 95% efficiency rate touted by the governments and pharmaceutical companies was highly misleading, to say the least.[131] The efficiency rate propagated refers to relative risk reduction rather than the standard absolute risk reduction. The table below shows Relative Risk Reduction compared to Absolute Risk Reduction.

THE SCALE OF THE COVID-19 INJECTION
EFFICACY LIE

	What they told you it did	What it actually does
	THE MARKETING LIE	THE LANCET STUDY
Jab Type	Relative Risk Reduction	Absolute Risk Reduction from Jab
Pfizer/BioNtech	95.03%	0.84%
Moderna (NIH)	94.08%	1.24%
Janssen	66.62%	1.19%
AstraZeneca/Oxford	66.84%	1.28%

Source: www.thelancet.com/journals/lanmic/article/PIIS2666-5247(21)00069-0/fulltext
For more information please visit: doctors4covidethics.org

Figure 4.23: The scale of the COVID-19 efficacy lie
Source: The Lancet[105]

This means that after receiving the COVID-19 vaccine, you were 99% just as likely to get COVID-19 as an unvaccinated person.

This raises three questions:

- By getting a vaccine, how would you be helping other people?
- If you have natural immunity against COVID-19 with a 99.85% probability of surviving, why do you still need the vaccine?
- If the vaccine does not stop the spread, why would any State continue to mandate it?

Any person who applies a moment of critical thinking can come to no other conclusion than anyone advocating for vaccine mandates are either uninformed, irrational, or has an ulterior motive.

It is evident that vaccine mandates are not based on data or medical science but on arbitrary political policies that do not have the best interests of ordinary citizens at heart.

C.S. Lewis adduced that "To be cured against one's will and cured of states which we may not regard as disease is to be put on a level of those who have not yet reached the age of reason or those who never will; to be classed with infants, imbeciles, and domestic animals."[132] Lewis further pointed out that if governments can use the concept of "disease" as a means for terming any actions that they dislike as "crimes", they can inflict a totalitarian rule in the name of biomedical therapy.

> For if crime and disease are to be regarded as the same thing, it follows that any state of mind which our masters choose to call "disease" can be treated as crime; and compulsorily cured. It will be vain to plead that states of mind which displease government need not always involve moral turpitude and do not therefore always deserve forfeiture of liberty. For our masters will not be using concepts of Desert and Punishment but those of disease and cure …. It will not be persecution. Even if the treatment is painful, even if it is life-long, even if it is fatal, that will be only a regrettable accident; the intention was purely therapeutic. Even in ordinary medicine there were painful operations and fatal operations; so, in this. But because they are "treatment," not punishment, they can be criticized only by fellow-experts and on technical grounds, never by men as men and on grounds of justice.[132]

After more than 24 months of the most extensive, coerced mass vaccination program in the history of humanity, the following facts are indisputable from a data and scientific perspective:

1. The COVID-19 vaccines do not prevent infection.
2. The COVID-19 vaccines do not prevent transmission.
3. The COVID-19 vaccines do not prevent death or hospitalization.
4. Natural immunity affords longer-lasting and more robust protection against COVID-19 infection than vaccine-induced immunity.
5. The COVID-19 vaccines have caused more death and adverse events in less than a year than all other vaccines combined over 80 years.

The main purpose of any vaccine is to provide immunity and to prevent the spread of the disease. Given that the COVID-19 vaccines do not confer immunity nor prevent transmission, vaccine mandates and mass vaccination programs defy common sense and rational government behavior based on all relevant facts.

Despite overwhelming data irrefutably disproving the validity of the COVID-19 mainstream narrative, some continue to argue that:

> People in the crisis-management field have made peace with blanket one-size-fits-all policies that some individuals don't like. When a ship is going down, passengers aren't given the luxury of quibbling with the color or design of the life vest, and they can't dither forever about whether to put one on or not. Emergencies invariably force people to make some choices that they might not consider ideal but asking everyone to get vaccinated against a potentially lethal virus is not a big imposition.[133]

Applying this same analogy to actual COVID-19 data and statistics since March 2020, the fact is that the ship is not sinking at all! There are only 0.15% of the passengers on board who are confronted with a life-threatening medical event, and the ship is fully equipped to isolate and treat these passengers effectively! There is no reasonable rationale to treat the other 99.85% of the passengers with an experimental drug with potentially deadly side-effects or to disrupt their journey or fundamental human rights.

"If you must be persuaded, reminded, pressured, lied to, incentivized, forced, bullied, socially shamed, guilt-tripped, threatened, punished, and criminalized to gain your compliance, you can be absolutely certain that what is being promoted is not in your best interest."[134]

5. LIMITS ON LIMITATIONS: THE ESSENCE OF FUNDAMENTAL HUMAN RIGHTS AND THE PROPORTIONALITY TEST

"To argue with a man who has renounced the use and authority of reason, and whose philosophy consists in holding humanity in contempt, is like administering medicine to the dead, or endeavoring to convert an atheist by scripture."

— Thomas Paine, *The Crisis*

The normative standards in international human rights obligate governments to respect, protect, and fulfill the human rights of all people in their territory. WHO declared COVID-19 a pandemic on March 11, 2020, which was followed by many States across the globe introducing harsh lockdown containment measures with severe wide-ranging interference with fundamental human rights. Democratic and totalitarian State Parties misused their emergency powers with a flagrant disregard for constitutional limits to policymaking. COVID-19-related regulations infringed the fundamental rights of billions of people worldwide.[1-3]

Generally, it is recognized that public order, safety, health, and democratic values justify the imposition of restrictions on the exercise of fundamental human rights and, as such, not all infringements are unlawful.[2,3] An infringement that takes place in line with a valid ratio that is recognized as a legitimate justification in terms of international human rights norms will not be regarded as illegal.[2,3] Articles 29 and 30 of the UDHR contain a series of limitations to human rights. Article 29(2) states:

In the exercise of his rights and freedoms, everyone shall be subject only to such limitations as are determined by law solely for the purpose of securing due recognition and respect for the rights and freedoms of others and of meeting the just requirements of morality, public order and the general welfare in a democratic society.

Two primary concerns drive the reasonable restriction of human rights. On the one hand, for the rights enshrined in IHRL to have real meaning, the courts must be willing to defend them vigorously and subject restrictions to close scrutiny. On the other hand, the State should be permitted sufficient room to craft legislation and undertake actions that serve pressing public interests.[2,3] It must, however, be emphasized that fundamental human rights cannot be limited for any reason. The rationale and *ratio decidendi* for limiting human rights, such as the right to human dignity, privacy, security of the person, opinion, and movement, needs to be exceptionally strong.[2,3] The limitation must serve a purpose regarded by society as extremely important.[2,3] There are also certain fundamental human rights that can never be violated at their essence under any circumstances, such as the right to be free from torture, cruel inhumane punishment, and from medical experimentation without prior informed consent.

Vaccine passports and other COVID-19 pseudo-medical regulations limit a wide array of inalienable fundamental human rights guaranteed by the ICCPR[4], that include:

- The right to equality. Vaccine passports create two classes of citizens: the vaccinated and the unvaccinated, with the latter being stripped of certain rights and freedoms.
- The inherent right to life. One of the side-effects of the COVID-19 vaccines can be death, which violates the inalienable right of all human beings not to be arbitrarily deprived of his or her life.
- The right not to be tortured or to be subjected to cruel and inhuman or degrading treatment nor to be subjected to medical and scientific experimentation without prior free consent. All COVID-19 vaccines are experimental with no long-term safety data, and COVID-19 vaccine mandates amount to medical experimentation without free consent.
- The right to liberty and security of person. Numerous people across the globe have been arbitrarily detained in "health hotels" and "quarantine facilities" as a result of not adhering to vaccine mandates.

- The right to freedom of movement. The right to liberty of movement is subject to adherence to arbitrary vaccine mandates and numerous countries required vaccine passports to enter and leave a country.
- The right not to be subjected to indiscriminate interference with privacy. Vaccine mandates interfere with the most intimate aspects of private life, bodily autonomy, and personal medical decisions.
- The right to freedom of thought, conscience, and religion. Any thoughts contrary to the official government narrative relating to vaccine mandates have been censored, silenced, and vilified. Many countries severely restricted religious activities based on vaccination status, essentially prohibiting religious gatherings.
- The right to peaceful assembly. Numerous State Parties enacted health regulations prohibiting peaceful assembly and demonstrations in opposition to lockdowns, mask mandates, and vaccine mandates.[5,6]

Most fundamental human rights are not absolute but subject to restriction by other rights and the legitimate needs of society, if the restrictions: are provided by law; are necessary to protect national security, public order (*ordre public*), public health, or the rights and freedoms of others; and are consistent with the other rights recognized in the ICCPR. Therefore, it is necessary to determine what IHRL asserts regarding the limitation of human rights.

IHRL obligates State Parties to prevent, detect, and respond to infectious disease, but also to have laws in place to balance individual rights and public health. Guidance and a legal framework to assess the legality of restrictive measures in response to national emergencies are provided by the Siracusa Principles on the Limitation and Derogation Provisions in the International Covenant on Civil and Political Rights; the Paris Minimum Standards; Article 4 of the ICCPR; ICCPR General Comment 29; and the Human Rights Committee Statement on Derogations from the Covenant in Connection with the COVID-19 pandemic on April 30, 2020.[6-9] The requirements for any measures derogating from covenant obligations is that they should, *inter alia*:

- respond to a pressing public or social need;
- be prescribed by law and not imposed arbitrarily;
- be proportionate to the threat;
- be strictly required by the exigencies of the situation;
- be no more restrictive than required to achieve the purpose;
- be non-discriminatory to any specific group.[6-9]

In order to determine whether a State may impose measures such as vaccine passports (that limit a broad array of fundamental human rights) it is essential to investigate whether such measures respect the essence of the fundamental right and subsequent to that consider the proportionality of such measures. The principle of proportionality prescribes that all statutes that affect human rights should be proportionate or reasonable. A proportionality analysis entails a balancing exercise, where the right affected is balanced against the public interest.[1,2]

Respect for the Essence of International Human Rights

IHRL determines that in no case may the restrictions on fundamental human rights be employed in a way "that would impair the essence of a covenant right."[10,11] Article 52(1) of the Charter of Fundamental Rights of the European Union, for instance, reads as follows:

> Any limitation on the exercise of the rights and freedoms recognized by this Charter must be provided for by law and respect the essence of those rights and freedoms. Subject to the principle of proportionality, limitations may be made only if they are necessary and genuinely meet objectives of general interest recognized by the Union or the need to protect the rights and freedoms of others.

Therefore, the starting point to determine the legality of a State mandate that violates basic human rights is to apply the "respect for the essence test", which requires for an examination of the essence of a fundamental human right in light of the international treaty obligations.[10,11]

The notion of the essence of a fundamental human right functions as a continuous reminder that certain core values set out in the ICCPR are absolute. That is to say, they are not up for balancing. According to Professor Koen Lenaerts (President of the Court of Justice of the European Union and Professor of European Union Law), in his article "Limits on Limitations: The Essence of Fundamental Rights in the EU" published in the "German Law Journal": "Where an infringing measure imposes a limitation on the exercise of a fundamental right that is so profound that it deprives the right *in casu* of its essence," that measure is incompatible with the ICCPR.[10] This is so without the necessity for a balancing exercise of competing interests, since a regulation that infracts "the very essence of a fundamental right is automatically disproportionate."[10]

i.) Respect for the Essence Test

Respect for the essence of basic human rights is one of the key conditions that must be satisfied for a limitation of a fundamental right to be justified. In order for the notion of "respect for the essence" to operate in a legally meaningful manner, international, regional, and domestic courts must apply the "respect-for-the-essence test" prior to undertaking a proportionality analysis.[10-14]

The essence of a fundamental human right entails that every basic human right has a "hard core" that guarantees to each and every human being a sphere of freedom that must always stay free from State intrusion. Once it is determined that the essence of a fundamental right has been impaired, the State mandate or regulation in question is incompatible with IHRL and must be annulled or declared invalid.[10,14] However, the fact that a State measure "respects the essence of a fundamental right" does not necessarily mean that it complies with the proportionality principle.[10] The respect-for-the-essence test and a proportionality analysis are two different types of inquiry.[10-12,15,16] Where a government measure complies with the proportionality principle, such a measure can also be seen as respecting the essence of the fundamental right at issue.[10] In fact, it is not possible for a State regulation to be a proportionate limitation on a fundamental human right, while depriving the right of its essence. Conversely, where a mandate or regulation violates the essence of a fundamental human right, it automatically constitutes a breach of the proportionality principle.[10] However, a mandate or regulation may respect the essence of a fundamental human right and yet still breach the proportionality principle.[10]

Therefore, from a methodological perspective, one needs to first examine whether the infringing State action respects the essence of the fundamental rights in question and only proceed with a proportionality analysis once it has been confirmed.[10,17,18] The purpose of this process of assessment is not mere empty formalism, but to emphasize the fact that the essence of a fundamental human right is absolute and not subject to balancing.[10,11]

ii.) The Essence of Civil and Political Rights

Although the ICCPR does not explicitly mention the term "essence" there are important rules laid down in Article 4 ICCPR and Article 5 ICCPR that speak implicitly to the concept of the essence of internationally protected fundamental human rights. According to Article 4(1) of the ICCPR, in times of public emergency that threatens the life of the nation the State Parties may take actions derogating from their commitments under the ICCPR "to the extent strictly required by the exigencies of the situation," provided that such actions are not incompatible with their other legal duties under international law. Article 4(2) ICCPR goes on to stipulate that "[n]o derogation from articles 6, 7, 8 (paragraphs 1 and 2), 11, 15, 16 and 18 may be made under this provision."[11] When attempting to identify the "essence of rights" within IHRL, these non-derogable rights that include the right to life, the embargo on torture and cruel, inhumane, or degrading treatment, the prohibition of medical experimentation without free consent, and the ban on slavery need to be considered with particular care.[10,11]

Articles 4(1) and 4(2) of the ICCPR are noteworthy as they offer one distinct interpretation of the concept of essence. Essence here implies that a right in its entirety is deemed essential for the fulfillment of civil and political rights.[10,11] These enumerated fundamental rights are absolute and uninfringeable as a whole, and no limitation can ever be permitted.[10,11] Some fundamental human rights are of such paramount significance for the promotion of fundamental human rights in general that they can never be derogated from, not even in extreme circumstances like the stated purpose of safeguarding "the health of the nation." These core group of human rights should be recognized as a restricted number of civil rights, absolved from the accord principle of IHRL. The extent and substance of these essential human rights are the same.[10,11]

Article 5(1) of the ICCPR determines that "no State may engage in any activity or perform any act aimed at the destruction of any of the rights and freedoms recognized" in the ICCPR or at their limitation "to a greater extent than is provided for in covenant."[11] Article 5(1) thus implies that there is an inviolable or sacred part within fundamental human rights and that this core may never be impaired, broken, or dishonored.[11] In other words, fundamental human rights hold a sacrosanct core. In his article "The Essence of International Human Rights", Professor Pierre Thielbörger (professor of public international law at Ruhr University Bochum, Germany) asserts that:

> These rights must be understood as a very limited number of core human rights, exempt from the consensus principle of international law. For these rights, their scope and their essence are identical. ...At the macro level, Article 4(1) and 4(2) ICCPR identify a small number of rights that are essential for the realization of civil and political rights altogether. They are in their entirety sacrosanct. At the micro level, Article 5(1) ICCPR forbids any act to be aimed at the destruction of civil political rights. It thereby establishes a core within each civil political right.[11]

The Siracusa Principles on the Limitation and Derogation of Provisions in the International Covenant on Civil and Political Rights, still considered as the leading methodology to understanding the derogation provisions of the ICCPR, specifically state that:

> [t]he scope of a limitation referred to in the Covenant shall not be interpreted so as to jeopardize the essence of the right concerned.[19]

Similarly in General Comment No. 31 on the "nature of the general legal obligations imposed on State Parties to the Covenant," the UNHRC stated that:

> State Parties must refrain from violation of the rights recognized by the Covenant, and any restrictions on any of those rights must be permissible under the relevant provisions of the Covenant. Where such restrictions are made, States must demonstrate their necessity and only take such measures as are proportionate to the pursuance of legitimate aims in order to ensure continuous and effective protection of Covenant rights. In no case may the restrictions be applied or invoked in a manner that would impair the essence of a Covenant right.[20]

In further interpreting lawful limitations under the ICCPR, the UNHRC, in its General Comment No. 27 on the freedom of movement in relation to Article 12 ICCPR, remarked that:

> …adopting laws providing for restrictions permitted by article 12, paragraph 3, States should always be guided by the principle that the restrictions must not impair the essence of the right t (cf. art. 5, para. 1); the relation between right and restriction, between norm and exception, must not be reversed. The laws authorizing the application of restrictions should use precise criteria and may not confer unfettered discretion on those charged with their execution.[21]

While the UNHRC explicitly only dealt with Article 12 of the ICCPR here, due to the focal point of the General Comment, the same logic should apply to other fundamental human rights.[11,21] By introducing the notion that a rule and exception may never be reversed, the UNHRC pointed out important case constellation in which the essence of a right would usually be infringed: "When the rule protecting the right becomes the exception and the rule limiting the right becomes the norm."[11,21]

iii.) Three crucial implications

The respect-for-the-essence principle has three important consequences:

- **First,** a mandate that violates "the essence of a fundamental right may not be justified on any ground," not even where the health of the nation is at stake.[10] State Parties may only implement public health policy that respects the essence of the fundamental rights in question. In practical terms, this means that State Parties' COVID-19 regulations should leave untouched the essence of the fundamental rights to equality, life, privacy, security, movement, religion, and also the right to be free from medical experimentation without free and informed consent.[10]

- **Second,** in respect of fundamental rights that are absolute, such as human dignity, the right to life, the prohibition of torture, the prohibition of inhuman or degrading treatment, and the prohibition of medical and scientific experimentation without free consent, one may reason that, since no limitation may be enacted upon those rights, in terms of Article 4 of the ICCPR, their content and their essence are, in legal effect, contiguous.[10,11]

- **Third,** regarding fundamental rights that may be subject to limitations, such as the right to respect for private life and the right to freedom of movement, "the essence of those rights is only compromised where the limitation in question empties those rights of their content or calls their very existence into question."[10] In other words, "respect for the essence of a fundamental right" indicates that the human right "is not called into question as such."[10,11]

It follows from international jurisprudence that "the essence of a fundamental right places an absolute limit" on the restrictions that may be imposed on a fundamental human right.[10,11] "Where a measure violates the essence of a fundamental right," such as vaccine mandates, it is *per se* irreconcilable with the ICCPR and IHRL, "without there being a need to carry out a balancing exercise between competing interests."[10]

The Proportionality Test[‡]

Similar to reasonableness review, a proportionality test is a contextual standard for the judicial safeguarding of fundamental human rights.[22,23] Over the past 60 years, the proportionality test – an analytical procedure similar to "strict scrutiny" in the United States – has become the standard legal test for adjudicating constitutional and human rights disputes in the world.[24]

Proportionality has become the central doctrine of contemporary human rights law and has been accepted by virtually all constitutional courts in Central and Eastern Europe and is increasingly employed in Central and South American jurisdictions.[22-28] The importance of proportionality is such a predominant principle that it has been said to be "the most important general principle of the communitarian law."[27]

In the common law systems, the principle is often called the "principle of reasonableness." The principle of proportionality prescribes that all statutes that affect human rights should be proportionate or reasonable.[27] The proportionality analysis involves a two-step inquiry.[25] Firstly, it needs to be established whether a particular government measure or mandate infringes a protected fundamental human right. If it does, the second step is concerned with whether the interference with the human right can be reasonably justified. The proportionality test provides a framework for analyzing the second question and consists of four sub-principles, exploring:

- whether the legislative measures pursue a legitimate goal (the legitimacy principle);
- whether there is a causal connection between the measure and the policy goal (the adequacy principle);
- whether the measure infringes human rights no more than absolutely necessary to accomplish this goal (the necessity principle); and
- whether the measure does not have a disproportionately adverse effect (the proportionality *stricto sensu* principle).

In principle, each element is assessed cumulatively, and failure of a legislative measure to comply with any one of the sub-principles will render the

---

‡ Portions of this chapter are republications of the content of two peer-reviewed articles by the author Dr. Willem van Aardt, "COVID-19 School Closures and The Principles of Proportionality and Balancing" published in the Journal of Infectious Diseases & Therapy in 2021 and "Limiting human rights during COVID-19 – is it only legitimate if it is proportional?" published in the De Rebus Attorneys Journal in 2021.

measure unjustified and illegitimate.[25-28]

i.) Legitimacy

The first element of legitimacy establishes that the measure that interferes with a right has to have a legitimate aim and an objective of sufficient public importance.[27] The limitation of rights that does not serve the purpose of or contribute to a society based on human dignity, equality, and freedom cannot be justifiable.[2,3] A limitation must serve a legitimate purpose that all reasonable citizens would agree to be of sufficient importance to infringe the fundamental human rights question.[2,3]

The Siracusa Principles, which were developed by eminent international law scholars convened by the International Commission of Jurists and other partners, specifically determine that:

> Public health may be invoked as a ground for limiting certain rights in order to allow a state to take measures dealing with a serious threat to the health of the population or individual members of the population. These measures must be specifically aimed at <u>preventing disease</u> or <u>injury</u> or <u>providing care for the sick</u> and <u>injured.</u>[7]

Unquestionably, State Parties have an obligation to prevent, detect, and respond to an infectious disease that poses a "serious threat to the health of the population or individual members of the population." It is, however, indisputable that a disease with a crude mortality rate of less than 0.3% does not represent a "serious threat to the health of the population" that would warrant the limitation of fundamental human rights and freedoms of 100% of the population in order to protect 0,3% of the population. By the end of October 2021, it was already an indisputable biomedical fact that the COVID-19 vaccines did not prevent disease nor hospitalization nor death and as such do not meet the basic criteria of "preventing disease" or "providing care for the sick."

The fiduciary criterion of legitimacy is a useful standard for assessing the normative legitimacy of government action. The criterion demands that State actions should have a representational character in that, for them to be legitimate, they must be intelligible as reasonable actions taken in the name of, or on behalf of, the persons subject to them. The government position that a disease with a global infection fatality rate of 0.15% is "a serious threat to the health of the population" and that a vaccine that does not prevent infection, transmission, hospitalization, or death should be mandated is not intelligible as a reasonable action taken in the name of, or on behalf of, the persons subject to them, but defies common sense.[29]

It is further important to note that in terms of Article 4 of the ICCPR, the right to life and the right to freedom from scientific and medical experimentation can never be violated, and public health regulation that seeks to violate these rights through a mandatory vaccine with side-effects that include blood clots and heart attacks that might lead to death, would be illegitimate and not pass the legitimacy test. As noted, but worth repeating, Article 5 of the ICCPR specifically determines that:

> Nothing in the present Covenant may be interpreted as implying for any State, group or person any right to engage in any activity or perform any act aimed at the destruction of any of the rights and freedoms recognized herein or at their limitation to a greater extent than is provided for in the present Covenant.[4]

The UNHRC have also made it clear that State Parties may in no circumstances act in violation of humanitarian law or peremptory norms of international law by imposing collective punishments through arbitrary deprivations of liberty. The COVID-19 era fines for not being vaccinated and detention in quarantine camps for the "crime" of being healthy and in the vicinity of someone who tested positive for a disease with a survival rate of 99.85% are prime examples of this type of illicit State action.[9]

Verdict: Vaccine mandates and related quasi-medical regulations are not legitimate and therefore unlawful.

ii.) Adequacy

The second element of adequacy establishes that the restrictive measure that limits the fundamental human right must be appropriate to achieve the aim, and there needs to be a crucial level of certainty that it will achieve the aim. That is to say, once the government has defined the end that it aimed for and the means that the government has designed to obtain such an end, then it must be verified whether the means are capable of achieving such an end. In other words, adequacy requires the existence of a reasonable connection between the measures taken by public authorities and the aim these measures seek to achieve. There must be a reasonable probability that the infringing government action will achieve its aim and produce the desired end result.[28] Irrespective of how important the purpose of the limitation is, restrictions on human rights will not be justifiable unless there is a compelling reason to conclude that the restrictive measure will achieve the purpose it is designed to achieve.[3,25-28] In the case of COVID-19, the measures enforcing mandatory vaccination were designed to achieve herd immunity, reduce infection rates, and, ultimately, crude mortality rates.

If a State Party's action, measure, or law does not serve the purpose it intends to serve; then it cannot be a reasonable limitation. Those who wish to limit fundamental human rights must present evidence of how the limitation serves the purpose.[2,3,27] If the State action, measure, or law only marginally contributes to achieving its purpose or fails to achieve its purpose, it will not be adequate to qualify as a legitimate limitation.[2,3,27]

With more than 10 billion COVID-19 vaccine doses having been administered in more than 184 countries globally[30] and various mass mandatory vaccination campaigns across globe, the relevant facts, as set out in Chapter 4, show:

- The COVID-19 vaccines do not confer immunity as fully vaccinated people can still be infected with SARS-CoV-2.
- The COVID-19 vaccines do not limit the spread of the virus as fully vaccinated people are still able to spread SARS-CoV-2.
- The COVID-19 vaccines do not prevent hospitalizations and death. Numerous peer-reviewed studies found that 60% to 90% of hospitalizations and deaths are fully vaccinated individuals.

The COVID-19 vaccines do not perform the absolute primary function of a vaccine as they do not confer sterilizing immunity and prevent the spread of a disease. For sterilizing immunity to be achieved, a vaccine needs to trigger a specific immunologic response, typically in the form of neutralizing antibodies. These are defensive proteins synthesized by the immune system that specifically target and neutralize a disease-causing organism such as a virus.[31] This is clearly not what transpired with the experimental COVID-19 vaccines.

The facts clearly show that mandatory mass vaccination campaigns did not achieve the desired end result of reducing infection, hospitalization, and deaths rates and returning society to normality.[32] It is therefore impossible to conclude that vaccine passports would be adequate, as there is certainty that the measures do not achieve the intended aim. The intrusive measures did not achieve the purpose they were designed to achieve, and therefore, the measures cannot be deemed proportional and therefore fail the adequacy requirement.

Verdict: Vaccine mandates and related quasi-medical regulations are not adequate and therefore unlawful.

iii.) Necessity

Whether the State Party chose, among the means capable of obtaining the desired end, the one that is the least restrictive, needs to be evaluated in the third prong of the proportionality test[15]. To determine whether the limitation does more damage than is reasonable for achieving its purpose requires a factual assessment of the extent of the limitation.[3,27] The restrictive measure should impair the fundamental human right as little as possible.[3,33] The infringement will not be considered necessary if there are less restrictive but equally effective or more effective means to achieve the same purpose.[34]

Article 4 of the ICCPR explicitly states that public policies limiting and violating fundamental human rights ought to be commenced only when such public policies are, "strictly necessary and required by the exigencies of the situation." The Siracusa Principles also emphasize that in applying a limitation, a State Party shall use no more restrictive means than are required for the achievement of the purpose of the limitation, and the burden of justifying a limitation upon a right guaranteed under the covenant lies with the State.[7,35] The tenaciously repeated Latin adage *necessitas legem non habet* (necessity has no law) in terms of contemporary IHRL is transmuted to justify a single specific case of derogation (a *bona fide* objectively verifiable "necessity") by means of an exception, rather than rendering the illicit, licit.

Several less restrictive choices than mass vaccine mandates and indiscriminate lockdowns could have been implemented, such as the focused protect-the-vulnerable approach, natural herd immunity, effective early treatment protocols, and the Swedish approach:

- **A focused protect-the-vulnerable approach:** The Great Barrington Declaration advocates that adopting targeted measures to protect the vulnerable should be the central aim of public health responses to COVID-19, while those in non-vulnerable groups continue life as normal.[36] The ethical methodology would be to only vaccinate those in vulnerable groups after they have given their informed consent and all other people who choose to be vaccinated. Those not in vulnerable groups are not at risk and do not need to be vaccinated to achieve the required public health goal.

- **Natural herd immunity:** To achieve herd immunity, children and other people not in vulnerable groups can become naturally infected as they do with other pathogens with a global infection fatality rate of 0.15%. Numerous peer-reviewed studies around the globe have proven that natural immunity is significantly superior to vaccine-induced immunity.[36,37] Given that the infection fatality rate (IFR) is close to zero for children and young adults, an obvious alternative to and less intrusive measure than mandatory mass vaccinations would be the acquisition of immunity if and when exposed to COVID-19 naturally. Children below 18 have a 99.997% probability of recovering from COVID-19 and will have only mild symptoms, while at the same time developing naturally acquired immunity that is superior to that which might be caused by a vaccine.[32,37] This approach would also accelerate the development of the much-needed herd immunity.

- **Effective early treatment protocols:** Safe and effective drugs such as Ivermectin and Hydroxychloroquine can be given as prophylaxis to significantly reduce infection rates, as indisputably proven by the success of such measures in India's Uttar Pradesh province and through numerous peer-reviewed studies and meta-analysis across the globe.[38-42]

- **The Swedish approach:** Sweden never imposed hard lockdowns, left their economy largely open, and made COVID-19 vaccines voluntary.[43] From the data, it is evident that, despite Sweden following a less restrictive approach of neither enacting a hard lockdown nor enacting vaccine mandates, the country's deaths per million of the population and infections per million of the population are not any worse than countries that enacted stringent lockdowns and enforced vaccine mandates.[44] In fact, according to WHO statistics, by November 2020 and February 2022 respectively, Sweden's death rate and the number of cases per million of the population were lower than those of the United States, United Kingdom, France, Belgium, and Spain, which all enacted repressive lockdowns and enforced mandatory vaccinations.[44-47]

November 20, 2020

Country	Deaths per 1 million population	Cases per 1 million population	Absolute 2020 excess mortality per 100,000
Sweden	627.77	19,907.88	13
USA	750.96	34,482.47	132
Spain	904.53	32,871.48	108
France	716.68	31,388.80	56
Belgium	1311.17	47,470.74	116
UK	792.14	21,407.36	100

March 20, 2022

Country	Deaths per 100 000 population	Cases per 100 000 population	Estimated 2020/2021 excess mortality per 100,000
Sweden	176.12	24,030.16	56
USA	293.31	23,947.51	140
Spain	215.96	24,313.70	11
France	213.41	37,712.47	63
Belgium	266.85	33,043.76	77
UK	243.02	30,913.85	109

Table 5.1: Sweden's death rate and the number of cases per million of the population compared to those of the United States, United Kingdom, France, Belgium, and Spain
Source: WHO

It is clear from the above that there were less restrictive choices available to tyrannical lockdowns and mass mandatory vaccination campaigns. Researchers at Johns Hopkins University have concluded that lockdowns have done little to reduce COVID-19 deaths but have had "devastating effects" on economies and caused numerous social ills. The study, titled "A Literature Review and Meta-Analysis of the Effects of Lockdowns on COVID-19 Mortality," found "no evidence that lockdowns, school closures, border closures, and limiting gatherings" in Europe and the United States have "had a noticeable effect on COVID-19 mortality." The study further noted that lockdowns "are ill-founded and should be rejected as a pandemic policy instrument" due to the fact that "[t]hey have contributed to reducing economic activity, raising unemployment, reducing schooling, causing political unrest, contributing to domestic violence, and undermining liberal democracy."[48]

The Siracusa Principles specifically determine that a measure is not strictly required by the exigencies of the situation where ordinary measures would be adequate, and the principle of strict necessity should be applied in an objective manner.[7] In other words, what is strictly necessary must be determined with reference to actual objective facts and data. Each measure should be directed to an actual, clear, present, or imminent danger and should not be imposed merely because of an apprehension of potential danger on the basis of predictive modeling or infections that do not cause significant mortality.[7] According to the relevant facts and data, the global IFR or survival rate of COVID-19 is 99.85%.

The Siracusa Principles specifically state that "In determining whether derogation measures are strictly required by the exigencies of the situation, the judgment of the national authorities cannot be accepted as conclusive."[7] The response to COVID-19 has once again shown the world how quickly governments can abuse their powers if not held to account by existing international legal rules and regulations.

Given that COVID-19 vaccines do not confer sterilized immunity nor prevent transmission and the fact that there are less restrictive, equally or more effective means to achieve the same purpose of reducing infection rates and returning society to normality, the vaccine mandates instituted by numerous States that adversely infringed individuals' fundamental human rights in the most pervasive, intrusive, damaging, and restrictive manner cannot be viewed as necessary.[32]

Verdict: Vaccine mandates and related quasi-medical regulations are not necessary and therefore unlawful.

iv.) Proportionality *stricto sensu*

Once it has been established that the infringing containment measure has complied with, the first, second, and third elements of the proportionality test, it needs to be determined whether the measure is reasonable *stricto sensu* or not. Professor Juan Cianciardo articulates it well:

> The doctrine and the jurisprudence have defined this sub-principle as an examination of the balance between the advantages and disadvantages brought about by the law. The subprinciple of proportionality stricto sensu means that the application of a given instrument or means to achieve a given end or objective should not be unreasonable in its reciprocal relationships. The interpreter must evaluate whether this balance is proportional, in other words, reasonable, or not.[27]

Proportionality *stricto sensu* requires that the harm done by State action, measure, or law should be weighed against the benefits that the State's action, measure, or law seeks to achieve.[1,3,27] Importantly, the measure has to represent a net gain, when the reduction in enjoyment of the right is weighed against the actual realization of the aim of the measure.[1,3,23-28] The limitation of fundamental human rights must achieve benefits that are proportional to the cost of the limitation.[1,3,23-28]

"Fundamental human rights differ in weight. A balance has to be achieved between the public interest and the interest of the individual. Where the limitation to a right is fundamental to a democratic society, a higher standard of justification is required; so too, where a law interferes with the intimate aspects of private life."[1] Moreover, greater scope is allowed in areas such as morals or social policy. Rights such as the right to life, the right to be free from medical experimentation, the right to freedom of opinion and expression, the right to security of the person, the right to privacy, the right to freedom of movement, and the right to freedom of religion, that are of particular importance to create an open and democratic society based on human dignity, freedom, and equality, carry a great deal of weight in the proportionality exercise. It will, therefore, be more difficult to justify the limitation of such rights.[1,3] The central issues, therefore, are weight and proportionality. To be of sufficient importance, and therefore reasonable in outweighing the human right concerned, the societal impact of the restricting measure should represent a net gain to a society based on human dignity and freedom.[1,3]

In order to determine proportionality *stricto sensu*, IHRL thus requires that the advantages and the disadvantages of the measure under analysis should be weighed. In French law, this is called the "balance between costs and benefits" (*La théorie du bilan coûts / avantages*).[1,3,27,49] A balance between costs and benefits means that any measure with a cost proportionate to its benefits is reasonable and legitimate, while a measure with a cost that is disproportionate to its benefits is unreasonable and illegitimate.[1,2,27]

This may be evaluated with the following formula: Using a scale of RC1 to RC10 to evaluate the degree of restriction and societal cost (**Restriction Cost**) of the infringing measure or regulation (RC10 being the most restrictive and costly measure), a scale of SB1 to SB10 to evaluate the **Societal Benefit** derived from the infringing measure (an SB10 deriving the most benefit), a scale of HR1 to HR10 to evaluate the societal importance of the affected **Human Right** (HR10 meaning a human right of extreme importance) and a scale of SI1 to SI10 to evaluate the **Societal Importance** of the public policy being pursued (SI10 meaning the most important state interest):

- If Measure A's degree of restriction and the societal cost is RC1 and the societal benefit SB5, and the relative importance of the affected human rights and state interest being pursued are HR10 and SI10, then the Measure would be considered proportional;
- If Measure B's degree of restriction and the societal cost is RC5 and the societal benefit SB6 and the relative importance of the affected human rights and state interest being pursued are HR10 and SI10, then the Measure would still be considered proportional given that there is a net gain;
- If Measure C's degree of restriction and the societal cost is RC5 and the societal benefit SB4 and the relative importance of the affected human rights and state interest being pursued are HR10 and SI10, then the Measure would not be considered proportional given that there is not a net gain and therefore the Measure is disproportional and illegal; and
- If Measure D's degree of restriction and the societal cost is RC10 and the societal benefit SB1 and the relative importance of the affected human rights and state interest being pursued are HR10 and SB10, then the Measure would be considered disproportional and illegal.[1,15]

In terms of the above formula, the harm done by the mass COVID-19 vaccine mandates would equate to RC10, SB1, HR10, and SI5 as depicted in Table 5.2 below.

Human Right Affected	Societal Importance of Human Right	Societal Benefit	Societal Cost	Societal Importance of COVID-19 Mandates
Right to Equality	HR10	SB 1	RC 10	SI 5
Right to Life	HR10	SB 1	RC 10	SI 5
Right to be Free from Medical Experimentation	HR10	SB 1	RC 10	SI 5
Right to Freedom and Security of the Person	HR8	SB 1	RC 8	SI 5
Right to Freedom of Movement	HR8	SB 1	RC 8	SI 5
Right to Freedom of Religion	HR8	SB 1	RC 8	SI 5
Right to Freedom of Opinion	HR9	SB 1	RC 8	SI 5

Table. 5.2: Table of Proportionality Formula Values as Applied to COVID-19 Mandates
Source: Dr. Willem van Aardt adapted from Prof. Cianciardo's formula[27]

It is impossible to contemplate the formulation of a credible argument justifying proportionality *stricto sensu,* which requires intrusive COVID-19 measures to result in a net gain and the existence of a balance between conflicting rights and interests. Moreso in light of the facts that the COVID-19 vaccines are ineffective and unsafe and mandatory mass vaccinations infringe a wide range of the human rights of 100% of the population to combat a disease with a crude mortality rate of less than 0.3%.[44-46]

The restriction of a human right is proportional *stricto sensu* if it is balanced because more benefits or advantages for the general interest are derived from it than damages against other goods or values in conflict.[1,3,23-28] Vaccine mandates effectively discriminate against and deny approximately 35% of the world's population their most basic human rights to life, liberty, and free consent to combat a disease with a global infection fatality rate of 0.15%.

By July 2021, it has become evident that the 95%+ efficiency rate publicized by the governments and the pharmaceutical companies was woefully inaccurate, erroneous, and vastly overstated the efficacy of the COVID-19 vaccines. According to a Lancet peer-reviewed study, Pfizer's number needed to vaccinate (NNV) is 117.[50] Meaning 117 people need to be vaccinated to prevent one COVID-19 case. That is, to prevent a COVID-19 *case*, not a COVID-19 death. Since the median survival rate of the virus itself is 99.85%, this means that 999 out of 1,000 cases survive. In order to prevent one death, you would therefore need to prevent 1,000 COVID cases. This means you would need to vaccinate 117,000 people to save one life (NNV = 117; Survival Rate = 999/1,000; 117 x 1,000 = 117,000). By the first half of 2021, 134 million people in America had been fully vaccinated, and over the same period, 10,355 people had died from the COVID-19 vaccinations (56 people each day).[51,52] Due to underreporting of vaccine-related deaths, whistleblowers estimated the number to be more than 50,000.[51,52] If we take the official numbers of 134 million (fully vaccinated) divided by 10,355 (vaccine deaths) = 12,940. This means that COVID-19 vaccines kill one out of every 12,940 people that are vaccinated.[51,52] So, if you vaccinated 117,000 people to save one life, 9.04 people would die from the vaccine. You are, therefore 904% more likely to die from the COVID-19 vaccine than to have it save your life. That is bad enough with the official deflated numbers. With the more likely estimate of 51,800 deaths, as confirmed by the Medicare data, you are 4,520% more likely to die from the COVID vaccine than to be saved by it and the likelihood of developing a lifelong debilitating disease is significantly greater than that.[51,52]

The COVID-19 mass mandatory vaccination measures seeking to protect public health with vaccines with an absolute risk reduction ranging between 0.84% and 1.28% provide close to no benefit while grossly infringing and violating individuals' inherent rights to life, human dignity, and freedom of thought; their right to education; and their right to be free from medical and scientific experimentation; to name a few.[4] From the relevant facts and data as set out in Chapter 4, it is indisputable that the COVID-19 vaccines are neither safe nor effective and do not confer immunity nor prevent the spread of the virus, which makes any mandatory vaccination regulations irrational and capricious.

From a cost-benefit perspective, individuals not in vulnerable groups have a close to zero risk of severe malady or death and thus no benefit from the COVID-19 vaccine but could be exposed to potentially significant adverse side-effects from the vaccines. A 2021 peer-reviewed study by a group of researchers from universities in Greece, Italy, Romania, and Russia, that analyzed the VAERS data, conducted a non-traditional best-case scenario cost-benefit analysis of the COVID-19 vaccines for the 65+ demographic in the United States. In their incarnation of the cost-benefit analysis, the costs are the number of deaths resulting from the COVID-19 vaccines, and the benefits are the lives saved by the COVID-19 vaccines. The time span used was from December 2019 to end-of-May 2021. The researchers concluded that an "extremely conservative estimate for risk-benefit ratio relating to the COVID-19 vaccine is about 5/1." In other words, people in the 65+

demographic are five times more probable to die from the COVID-19 vaccine than from COVID-19. The researchers further pointed out that the deaths from the COVID-19 vaccines shown in VAERS are short-term only, and for children, extremely short-term. Medium and long-term deaths from antibody-dependent enhancement autoimmune effects, blood clotting, strokes, vascular diseases, etc., which take time to develop are still to be determined. As such, "the long-term cost-benefit ratio under the best-case scenario could well be on the order of 10/1, 20/1, or more for all the demographics, increasing with decreasing age, and an order-of-magnitude higher under real-world scenarios!"[53]

Additionally, according to the WHO's VigiAccess Data, 2,199,476 adverse effects following vaccination against COVID-19 were reported by October 2021, with 866,558 (39%) of the injuries being reported in 18- to 44-year-olds, and 1,517,989 (69%) of all injuries occurring in women.[54] The nature of the injuries that have been reported includes blood and lymphatic system disorders; cardiac disorders; musculoskeletal disorders; connective tissue disorders; reproductive system and breast disorders; and respiratory, thoracic, and mediastinal disorders. The shocking number of injuries involved manifestations of "vaginal hemorrhaging, myocarditis, brain neoplasms (tumors), spontaneous abortion, fetal death, stillbirth, pulmonary embolism, renal failure, fetal growth restriction, deep vein thrombosis, as well as the onset of COVID-19, influenza, pneumonia, and over 100 other conditions."[54]

In the presence of such potential life-threatening risks, taking even a "moderate" risk of severe side-effects – from a vaccine with no medium and long-term safety data to combat a disease with a near-zero crude mortality rate for the vast majority of the population – cannot be viewed as proportionate *stricto sensu*. The cost-benefit argument against using such a vaccine is heavily in favor of risk and virtually no benefit.

Verdict: Vaccine mandates and related quasi-medical regulations are not proportionate *strictu* sensu and therefore unlawful.

Chapter Conclusion

The legal standards in IHRL obligate governments to respect, protect and fulfill the human rights of all people in their territory. The human rights standards that governments need to adhere to are unambiguous concerning how restrictions on fundamental human rights during pandemics should be treated.[4,7,8] The limitation of fundamental human rights is legitimate only if it respects the essence and is also proportional.[10,11,23,55]

The global health community has spent decades implementing evidence-based strategies to contain the spread of disease and protect the public's health without violating human rights. There was no reason to respond differently to COVID-19 than to other infectious diseases with similar mortality rates, such as flu, pneumonia, and other respiratory-related illnesses.[2]

Human rights norms and principles, such as the Siracusa Principles, specific to public health emergencies, contain effective, practical standards that State Parties need to adhere to in order to honor their covenant obligations with regard to protecting and ensuring fundamental human rights to all within their respective borders. What is of crucial importance is that these international norms are built into decision-making by public authorities when measures to prevent the spread of low-risk infectious disease are instituted in the future. All governments have a responsibility to focus on public policy that respects, protects, and ensures fundamental human rights, in line with their international covenant obligations. Numerous governments around the globe, almost all State Parties to the ICCPR, have taken disproportionate, extensively harsh, and repressive public health measures that infringe individuals' right to life, right to freedom of movement, and freedom from medical experimentation, without any credible explanations regarding the legitimacy, adequacy, necessity, or proportionality *stricto sensu* of such measures.[1,2]

A respect-for-the-essence test revealed that vaccine mandates and related quasi-medical regulations do not respect the essence of the fundamental human right to be free from medical experimentation without free consent. Additionally, the proportionality analysis indicates that mass mandatory vaccination regulations have breached and continue to breach IHRL, as set out in the ICCPR and the Siracusa Principles, to the detriment of hundreds of millions of people worldwide. COVID-19 vaccine mandates are not proportionate to the threat, not strictly necessary, not based upon an objective assessment of the actual situation, and not the least restrictive choice. Importantly, the harm done by the vaccine mandates significantly outweighs the benefits derived.

Governments and public health officials should be held accountable and liable for the egregious human rights violations perpetrated by both State and non-State actors during the course of 2020, 2021, and 2022 in order to ensure that in the future, State Parties honor their international covenant obligations and moreover, to ensure that public health responses by both State and non-State actors within their territories are legitimate, adequate, necessary, and proportionate, consistent with Siracusa and the ICCPR. International human rights and bioethical moral and legal obligations, properly construed, demand this approach.

6. LEGITIMIZING LAWLESSNESS: THE COVID-19 STATE OF EMERGENCY AS PARADIGM OF GOVERNMENT

"Every collectivist revolution rides in on a Trojan horse of "emergency". It was the tactic of Lenin, Hitler, and Mussolini. And "emergency" became the justification of the subsequent steps. This technique of creating emergency is the greatest achievement that demagoguery attains."

— Herbert Hoover

Recent events across the globe have again brought the world's attention to the complex interrelationship between the "state of emergency" (*iustititium, ausnahmezustand, notstand*, state of exception, or state of necessity) and the protection of fundamental human rights. The threat from COVID-19 has been conceived by many States as a direct "threat to the life of the nation."

To respond to this threat, many governments officially declared a "state of emergency" and bypassed an array of human rights legal obligations as set out in the ICCPR, leading to the most egregious violation of fundamental human rights since the Second World War.[1] It seems that States' previous understanding of their international human rights obligations is no longer applicable in the COVID-19 era as public health authorities across the globe continue to violate citizens fundamental human rights with a flagrant disregard for international treaty obligations and peremptory norms.

It has long been observed that one of the primary mechanisms employed by States to suppress and deny the basic human rights and freedoms of citizens has been the unjustified and nefarious declaration of a state of exception.

Time and time again, these measures are taken under the pretense of the existence of a national emergency that threatens the life of the nation. In his book "Constitutional Government and Democracy", Carl Friedrich warned that all modern "constitutional emergency powers, that fail to conform to any exacting standard of effective limitations upon a temporary concentration of powers… are liable to be transformed into totalitarian schemes if conditions become favorable to it."[2]

The widespread abuse of emergency provisions enabling governments to violate basic human rights contained in the ICCPR since 2020 has again resulted in the need for a closer analysis of the conditions and justifications for legitimate derogations in order to achieve effective implementation of the rule of law.

The State of Emergency as a Technique of Government

Giorgio Agamben is the philosopher who has most rigorously reflected upon the now near global state of emergency that has been defined as a "legal civil war".[3] Agamben singles out the state of emergency as the "dominant paradigmatic form of government" in contemporary politics subject to a vicious cycle in which the emergency measures the State seeks to rationalize in the name of preserving the constitution are the identical ones that lead to its ultimate ruin.[3,6] During a state of emergency "[l]aw is suspended and obliterated in fact."[3,6] However, the complex analysis presented in the Agamben thesis goes far beyond the assertion that the state of emergency has become the rule; it elaborates a theory to account for the existence of a nefarious government technique, rather than an exceptional temporary measure, that *de facto* produces a juridical void or anomie, threatening the very consistence of the post-Second World War juridico-political order.[3]

Agamben distinguishes two major schools of thought on the lawfulness of the state of emergency: those who include the state of exception within the juridical order and those who consider it something external, that is, an essentially political, or extra-juridical, phenomenon.[3] Among the first group, the state of exception is understood to be part of positive law through the theories of State sovereignty and the theory of necessity.

- The theory of State sovereignty (linked to the classification of the sovereign as "he who decides on the exception") encompasses three related doctrines:

» The first entails that "the sovereign who can decide on the state of exception," ensures its anchorage to the juridical order.[3,6] The distinction between two fundamental elements of law: "norm" and "decision" is what inscribes the state of emergency within the juridical order.[3,6] Despite the "norm" being annulled by the "decision," both elements remain within the framework of the juridical.[3,4] Agamben adduced that since the choice here relates to "the very annulment of the norm" that is, because the state of emergency represents the incorporation and seizure of the space that is neither inside nor outside (the space that denotes the rescinded and suspended norm), the sovereign "stands outside of the normal juridical order, and yet belongs to it, for it is he who is responsible for deciding whether the constitution can be suspended *in toto*."[3,6] It is paradoxical given that the state of emergency leads to the "suspension of the juridical order" that "subtract[s] the sovereign from any consideration of law."[3,6]

» The second theory that has become a common global practice in recent years, sees the state of emergency as the lawful exercise of the State's right to its own defense or the defense of the nation's health. Legitimacy is derived from the delegation contained in the "full powers" (*pleins pauvoirs)* whereby laws passed by parliament or congress provide exceptionally broad regulatory power to the executive, particularly the power to issue mandates that have the "force of law." One of the essential characteristics of this theory is the provisional *de facto* abolition of the distinction between executive, judicial, and legislative powers with a historical tendency to become a lasting practice of government.[3]

» The third sovereignty theory unites the legal and the non-legal by means of an extra-legal sovereign decision "having the force of law." In this sense, the judicial order is maintained even while the law (*legge, recht*) itself is placed on hold. This can take effect in two different forms. In a "commissarial dictatorship" the law is momentarily put on hold in order that it may eventually be implemented.[3,6] Although not applied, the law continues to exist: the constitution offers a supra-legislative framework that declares its suspension legitimate. In a another conformation, a "sovereign dictatorship" seeks to engrave the state of emergency implicitly within a judicial context by justifying it in the delineation between "constituent power" and "constituted power."[6] Because the state of emergency suspends "the constitution *in concreto* in order to protect its concrete existence, the state of emergency ultimately has the function of creating State affairs in which law can be realized."[3,6] The difference between constituent power and constituted power is what anchors the *iustititium* to the juridical order. Constituent power is not "a simple question of force", it is rather a power that, "though it is not constituted in virtue of a constitution, is nevertheless connected to every existing constitution in such a way that it appears as the founding power....and for this reason it cannot be negated even if the existing constitution might negate it."[3,6] In practical reality, it is a space in time where no law rules other than the sovereign subjective judgement itself.[3,6]

- The Theory of Necessity, with its roots in Roman Law posits that necessity is the foundation of the state of emergency.[3]

  » According to the Latin adage *necessitas legem non habet* (necessity has no law) the theory of the state of exception is reduced to the theory of the *status necessitatis*, so that "the judgement concerning the existence of the latter resolves the question of the legitimacy of the former."[3] "Necessity is not a source of law, nor does it suspend the law, it merely releases a particular case from the literal application of the law."[3]

  » In modern times, the state of necessity is included as a "state of law" through derogation provisions in various national constitutions. The principle, according to which necessity defines a unique situation and the law loses its *vim obligandi*, is that necessity is reversed and seen as the very source of law and the foundation of the validity of mandates having the force of law issued by the executive in a state of exception. Proponents argue that "the necessity with which we are concerned here ... cannot be regulated by previously estab-lished norms. But if it has no law, it makes law....; which means that it itself constitutes a true and proper source of law."[3] The *status necessitatis* is an "ambiguous and uncertain zone in which extra or anti-juridical executive action become law and juridical norms blur with factual reality" – a threshold where fact and law seem to become undecidable. "The state of necessity is thus interpreted as a lacuna in public law, which the executive power is obligated to remedy...a principle that concerns the judiciary power is extended to the executive power."[3]

Among the second group the state of exception is understood to be essentially "extra juridical" *de facto* elements. A constitutional commendation of the state of emergency is a pragmatic recognition of limited constitutional authority. Past and present proponents argue that it is neither feasible nor necessary to regulate government action in times of crisis using traditional juridical accountability processes.[6] A legal "void" must instead be opened for unrestrained government action, "albeit only for the time it takes to restore the constitutional order."[6] Attempts to impose legal controls will merely taint ordinary rights protections with extraordinary flexibility. In practice, however, the norm is completely annulled.[3]

Agamben rejects both main theoretical approaches and convincingly posits that:

> The state of necessity is not a "state of law," but a space without law ... that results from the suspension of law.[3,6]

> If the state of exception's characteristic is a (total or partial) suspension of the juridical order, how can such a suspension be contained within it? How can an anomie be inscribed within the juridical order? And if the state of exception is instead only a *de facto* situation, and is as such unrelated or contrary to law, how is it possible for the order to contain a lacuna precisely where the decisive situation is concerned? And what is the meaning of this lacuna?[3,6]

> In truth, the state of exception is neither internal nor external to the juridical order, and the problem of defining it concerns precisely a threshold, or a zone of indifference, where inside and outside do not exclude each other but rather blur with one another. The suspension of the norm does not mean it's abolition, and the zone of anomie that it establishes is not (or at least claims not to be) unrelated to the juridical order. Hence ... the very limit of the juridical order is at issue.[3,6]

To lift the veil covering this "zone of anomie" in support of his postulates, Agamben offers a pedantic juridical genealogy of the state of exception: the recurring and varied attempts throughout the Western legal tradition to extract sovereign power entirely from the habitus of law or, in an associated effort, to legislate for the law's own suspension.[6] Agamben notes the medieval conception of the state of exception, citing Dante, Thomas Aquinas, and Gratian, as justifying "a single, specific case of transgression by means of exception," instead of rendering the illicit licit.[3,6] The contemporary construction of the state of emergency appears with a 1789 declaration of the French National Constituent Assembly (*Assemblée nationale constituante*), discerning a "state of peace" from a "state of siege" in which all the tasks assigned to the civil government for preserving law and order is transferred to the military commander in chief, who exercises them in his sole discretion."[3,6] From there the state of emergency is increasingly unshackled from its state of war setting and is announced in peacetime to ensure the sudden expansion of broad executive power to deal with social disorder, political dissidents, emergencies, and economic crises.[3,6] These points are demonstrated repeatedly in Agamben's analysis of the history of the *iustititium* in Europe and America between 1789 and 2001; from the First World War period (that coincided with a permanent state of emergency in the majority of warring countries) to states of exception to manage fiscal emergencies in Germany in 1923 and France in 1925, 1935, and 1937; to trade union action and societal turmoil in the United Kingdom in 1920, earthquakes in Messina and Reggio, Italy in 1908, passage of the US New Deal in 1933, and, perhaps most relevant, by Adolf Hitler – to provide a basis for Nazi policies and practices during the Third Reich between 1933 and 1945.[3,6] It is well understood that the final years of the constitutional federal German Republic (*Deutsche Republik*) passed completely under a regimen of a state of emergency; it is less well known that Hitler could probably not have taken power had the German politicians not used and abused Article 48 of the Weimar Constitution more than 250 times between 1919 and 1933.[3,6] Shortly after assuming power, Hitler declared a "legal" state of emergency (*Ausnahmezustand)* in terms of Article 48 of the Weimar Constitution, which was never repealed, which effectively suspended fundamental human rights (*Grundrechte*).[3,6] The text of Article 48 (that corresponds closely with contemporary derogation provisions) reads:

> If security and public order are seriously disturbed or threatened in the German Reich, the president of the Reich may take measures necessary to reestablish security and public order, with the help of the armed forces if required. To this end he may wholly or partially suspend the fundamental rights established in Articles 114,115,117,118,123,124, and 153.

The article added that a law would be passed that would detail the conditions and limitations under which executive power would be exercised. Since this law was never passed, Hitler's emergency powers remained indeterminate *de facto* leading to a "presidential dictatorship" and a legalized *coup d'état* utilizing Article 48 of the Weimar Constitution.[3] The difficulty of defining and subjugating the forces that govern the evolution from a "constitutional dictatorship" during a declared state of emergency, which seeks to safeguard the constitutional order to an "unconstitutional dictatorship" that leads to its overthrow, as in Germany, is the fundamental aporia of all theories of constitutional dictatorship.[3,6]

Agamben finds that "modern totalitarianism can be defined as the establishment, by means of the state of exception, of a legal civil war that allows for the physical elimination not only of political adversaries but of entire categories of citizens" who hold opposing views.[3] "Faced with the unstoppable progression of what has been called a 'global civil war,' the state of emergency tends increasingly to appear as the dominant paradigm of government in contemporary politics."[3,6]

Agamben's elaborate analysis shows how the state of emergency is being utilized to transform democratic regimes into totalitarian States and accurately predicts the COVID-19 paragon that the "instruments" of government "depicted as temporary crisis arrangements have in some countries and may eventually in all countries become lasting peacetime institutions."

The state of exception as practically implemented in the West during the COVID-19 pandemic is not a special kind of law, rather it is the suspension of the juridical order itself:

> …a space devoid of law, a zone of anomie in which all legal determinations – and above all the very distinction between public and private – are deactivated. Thus all those theories that seek to annex the state of exception immediately to the law are false….The state of necessity is not a "state of law" but a space without law….[3]

> …there is nothing but a zone of anomie, in which violence without any juridical form acts.[3]

""[T]he state of exception is therefore" as noted by Dr. Stephen Humphreys, associate professor of international law, LSE Law School, UK, (in his 2006 article entitled "Legalizing Lawlessness: On Giorgio Agamben's State of Exception") "a *fictio iuris* par excellence which claims to maintain the law in its very suspension' but produces instead a violence that has 'shed every relation to law.'"[6]

While Agamben's excellent, erudite, and hyper-intellectual 2005 scrutiny of the state of exception "technique of government rather than an exceptional measure" becoming the rule and transforming democratic societies into totalitarian States is thoroughly supported by empirical reference, conceptual clarification, and ample practical historical examples that recurred globally during the COVID-19 pandemic, it does not include any reference to IHRL nor *jus cogens* norms.

From an IHRL perspective, both the declaration of a state of emergency and State action during a state of emergency are included in the international juridical order through Article 4 of the ICCPR and Article 53 of the Vienna Convention on the Law of Treaties. In terms of IHRL, certain *jus cogens* norms such as the prohibition of slavery, piracy, genocide, crimes against humanity, murder, torture, cruel, inhuman, or degrading treatment or punishment; and medical or scientific experimentation without free consent can never be legitimately annulled given the fundamental values they uphold! – not even during a declared state of emergency.

When *jus cogens* norms are practically annulled, as *de facto* occurred during the past two and a half years, it is not that there is a "juridical void" but rather that political tyrants "deactivated and deposed the law" through unlawful State action accompanied by the corruption of the judiciary that is too remiss or impotent to apply the law.[3,6] The current "space devoid of law" needs to be brought back and reinstituted into the international juridical order through the effectual implementation and adjudication of IHRL. A law that exists but is no longer practiced or effected no longer has meaning and serves as the gateway to injustice.[3]

Derogation and International Human Rights Law

When a State Party is involved in a life and death battle, no one can demand that it refrain from taking extraordinary emergency actions, but how exactly is a legitimate public emergency "threatening the life of the nation" determined in terms of IHRL?

State of emergency or derogation provisions in IHRL allow for State Parties to lawfully suspend human rights guarantees to respond to a situation "that threatens the life of the nation."[1] Stephen Humphreys explains that:

> The existence of derogation-like clauses is generally represented as a "concession" to the "inevitability" of exceptional state measures in times of emergency, and also as a means to somehow control these. As such, they have been viewed as "one of the greatest achievements of contemporary international law". In practice, the derogation model "creates a space between fundamental rights and the rule of law", wherein states can remain lawful while transgressing individual rights

– effectively creating,... a "double-layered constitutional system".[6,7]

IHRL derogation provisions have been labeled as a "necessary evil", given that emergency derogations are by definition intentional acts by States to disregard established international human rights obligations in response to extraordinary circumstances. Derogation provisions in the ICCPR limit the actions of States, as obligations may only be set aside to respond to a specific state of exception that is temporary in nature and that threatens the day-to-day functioning of the State.

Article 4(1) of the ICCPR determines that:

> In time of public emergency which threatens the life of the nation and the existence of which is officially proclaimed, the State Parties to the present Covenant may take measures derogating from their obligations under the present Covenant to the extent strictly required by the exigencies of the situation, provided that such measures are not inconsistent with their other obligations under international law and do not involve discrimination solely on the ground of race, colour, sex, language, religion or social origin.[1]

Article 15 of the European Convention contains a similar provision:

> In time of war or other public emergency threatening the life of the nation any High Contracting Party may take measures derogating from its obligations under [the] Convention to the extent strictly required by the exigencies of the situation, provided that such measures are not inconsistent with its other obligations under international law.

IHRL employs a mix of rules and open-textured standards to monitor derogation in the time of national emergencies. Some derogation standards are purely rule-based, including the legal obligations that States publish a formal notice of derogation, abstain from malevolent discrimination, and fulfill their IHRL commitments.[8] These rules limit the choices available to national authorities *ex-ante* by delivering the benefits of "predictability, stability, and constraint."[8]

The UNHRC issued a General Comment on Article 4 in 1981 that was very concise, comprising of only three articles mainly reiterating the terms of Article 4 of the ICCPR.[9] The Comment does not indicate how to ascertain the presence of an emergency, but makes clear that emergency measures taken must be of an "exceptional and temporary nature" and that, "in times of emergency, the protection of human rights becomes all the more important, particularly those rights from which no derogations can be made."[9] In 2001, an updated General Comment was released, which was considerably extended to 17 paragraphs with more detailed information.[10] This subsequent UNHRC Comment mainly deals with actions taken in reaction to an emergency and also does not consider specifically what establishes or how to ascertain the existence of such an emergency. Notably, the UNHRC Comment determine that, "Not every disturbance, or catastrophe qualifies as a public emergency which threatens the life of the nation."[10] It further states "If State Parties consider invoking article 4,…. they should carefully consider the justification and why such a measure is necessary and legitimate in the circumstances."[10] In April 2020, the OHCHR released a Statement entitled "Emergency Measures and Covid-19 Guidance" that also did not define the criteria of a "threat to the life of a nation" but did highlight that:

> Emergency powers should be used within the parameters provided by international human rights law, particularly the International Covenant on Civil and Political Rights (ICCPR), which acknowledges that States may need additional powers to address exceptional situations. Such powers should be time-bound and only exercised on a temporary basis with the aim to restore a state of normalcy as soon as possible.

> The suspension or derogation of certain civil and political rights is only allowed under specific situations of emergency that "threaten the life of the nation." Some safeguards must be put in place including the respect of some fundamental rights that cannot be suspended under any circumstance.[11]

Through the General Comments, the UNHRC recognizes the sovereign right of the State to determine the presence of a public emergency permitting for Article 4 to be invoked.[8] The UNHRC leaves the initial determination of the existence of a national emergency to the State Party by only demanding that the State Party "carefully consider" the justification, necessity, and legitimacy of such a measure.[8] Derogation provisions further recognize the principal obligations of the State as the protector of society and that in extraordinary situations, certain human rights guarantees need to be suspended within defined limits while still meeting core human rights obligations. This creates a challenge for IHRL as it permits State Parties to disregard express treaty obligations without clearly defined criteria of how a threat to the life of the nation is determined.

The critical question that needs to be addressed is whether the threat posed by COVID-19 represents a public health "emergency that threatens the life of the nation".

States have a Margin of Appreciation

In establishing whether a legitimate "public emergency" exists, the ICCPR allows derogation only when prevailing conditions pose a verifiable "threat to the life of the nation."[8] Because the ICCPR does not define key terms such as "life of the nation," national authorities and international tribunals are forced to exercise judgment in determining whether a particular emergency qualifies as a crisis "threatening the life of the nation."[8]

To decide on both the existence of such an emergency and on the nature and scope of derogations necessary to overcome it, governments have a wide margin of appreciation.[12] However, governments do not enjoy an unlimited power in this respect but are subject to IHRL as set out in various binding covenants ratified by States around the globe. The European Court of Human Rights (ECtHR) held that:

> It falls in the first place to each Contracting State, with its responsibility for the life of [its] nation', to determine whether that life is threatened by a "public emergency" and, if so, how far it is necessary to go in attempting to overcome the emergency. In this matter, authorities have a wide margin of appreciation. Nevertheless, the States do not enjoy an unlimited power in this respect.[13]

The "margin of appreciation" that is allowed "varies depending upon the nature of the right and the nature and ambit of the restriction."[14] A balance must be achieved between the general interest and the individual's interest. Where the restriction is to a right essential to an egalitarian society, a greater level of justification is required; so too, where a law impedes with the personal aspects of private life, on the other hand, "in areas such as morals or social policy greater scope is allowed to the national authorities."[14,15]

The margin of appreciation is the discretion left to a particular State to implement its preventative protection program the way it sees fit or, in short, "the amount of latitude left to national authorities."[14,15] Under the margin of appreciation standard, the "burden lies on governments to rationalize and justify emergency declarations during ex post facto judicial review."[8,16] The absence of such a reasoned justification would be a sufficient ground for making a determination that IHRL has been breached. For example, in the case of Brannigan & McBride v. United Kingdom, it was held that the United Kingdom had abused its emergency powers since there was no adequate justification for the actions that were taken.[17] Similarly, in the case of Aksoy v. Turkey, the ECtHR reasoned that certain emergency actions that were taken "exceeded the government's margin of appreciation due to the fact that it could not be said to be strictly required by the exigencies of the situation."[8,18] In each of these situations, the court recognized the legitimacy of the government's primary role in creating temporary emergency measures, but also underscored that governments must be prepared to offer satisfactory, rational, and reasonable justifications. These verdicts stress the principle that States ultimately carry the onus to prove a credible and reasonable factual predicate for any purported "threat to the life of the nation" and to explain why the measures they have taken to deal with the emergency are reasonable and necessary.[8]

By empowering countries to decide when and how to derogate from their international legal obligations, IHRL trusts States with primary responsibility to ascertain what measures are needed to safeguard and realize human rights for their citizens during public emergencies. Broad derogation legal standards and guidelines are the mechanisms IHRL utilizes to structure its legal philosophy, empowering States to create temporary human rights regimes that are customized to specific emergencies. The role of human rights tribunals, in contrast, is more restricted: to ensure that countries do not abuse their discretionary power by imposing self-serving, biased, or arbitrary limitations on fundamental human rights. The margin of appreciation doctrine respects this designation of authority, ensuring that international tribunals give a measure of deference to the context-sensitive judgments of national decision-makers during temporary emergencies. However, judicial deference to national authorities cannot be employed indiscriminately. If national authorities fail to support their human rights derogations with reasoned and rational deliberation supported by objective facts and data, if governments' behavior reflects a pattern of arbitrary and abusive conduct, or if conflicts of interest have compromised their fiduciary duty, international courts should withhold deference. Therefore, a country's authority to derogate from human rights legal obligations during public emergencies is conditioned upon the government serving as a faithful trustee for its citizens.[8,14]

For this delegation of power to function well, governments must adhere to international human rights norms and standards. Deference to State derogations is not justified if circumstances suggest that national authorities abuse emergency powers for political and financial exploitation of its population, as is widely occurring in the COVID-19 epoch.

When does a public health emergency threaten the life of the nation?

With regards to what constitutes an emergency "threatening the life of a nation," the ECtHR held that: the natural and customary meaning of the words "public emergency threatening the life of the nation" is sufficiently clear; they refer to "an exceptional situation of crisis or emergency which affects the whole population and constitutes a threat to the organized life of the community of which the State is composed."[8,19,20,22]

In the Denmark, Norway, Sweden, and the Netherlands v. Greece case, the ECtHR gave some guidance and held that a public "emergency threatening the life of a nation" must be imminent or actual, its effects must affect the entire population, and the continuance of the organized life of the community must be threatened.[2] The court underscored that the crisis or danger must be exceptional in that "the normal measures or restrictions permitted by the Convention for the maintenance of public safety, health, and order, are plainly inadequate."[21]

The ECtHR stressed the extraordinary nature of a public emergency as being a situation where "normality" is unquestionably impossible, and the normal day-to-day life of society cannot be followed.[16] Although set forth during a quasi-judicial proceeding and officially lacking legal precedential authority, the criteria set out in the Greek case were confirmed as influential precedents in later cases and widely perceived to give guidance to States.[22]

After six years of study by a special subcommittee and two additional years of revision by the full Committee on the Enforcement of Human Rights Law, the 61st Conference of the International Law Association (ILA), held in Paris from August 26 to September 1, 1984, approved by consensus a set of minimum standards governing the declaration and administration of states of emergency that "threaten the life of a nation," including 16 articles setting out the non-derogable rights and freedoms to which individuals remain entitled even during states of emergency. These standards, designated the Paris Minimum Standards of Human Rights Norms in a State of Emergency, are intended to help ensure that, even in situations where a *bona fide* declaration of a state of emergency has been made, the State Parties concerned will refrain from suspending those basic human rights that are regarded as non-derogable under Article 4 of the ICCPR.[23] The ILA's Paris Minimum Standards of Human Rights Norms in a state of emergency define a public emergency as:

...an exceptional situation of crisis or public danger, actual or imminent, which affects the whole population or the whole population of the area to which the declaration applies and constitutes a threat to the organized life of the community of which the State is composed.[23,24]

A commanding construal of the IHRL derogation provisions under the ICCPR has also been provided in the American Association for the International Commission of Jurists (AAICJ) Siracusa Principles.[25] The AAICJ initiated a colloquium composed of 31 distinguished experts in international law, held at Siracusa, Italy, in the Spring of 1984. This meeting, the first of its kind, was co-sponsored by the International Commission of Jurists, the Urban Morgan Institute for Human Rights, and the International Institute of Higher Studies in Criminal Sciences. The participants examined the limitation and derogation provisions in the ICCPR, seeking to identify: (i) their legitimate objectives; (ii) the general principles of interpretation which govern their imposition and application; and (iii) some of the main features of the grounds for limitation or derogation. The participants noted that there is a close connection between respect for human rights and the maintenance of international law and order.[25] With regards to what constitutes a "public emergency which threatens the life of a nation," the Siracusa Principle determines that:

A threat to the life of the nation is one that: (a) affects the whole of the population and either the whole or part of the territory of the State; and (b) threatens the physical integrity of the population, the political independence or the territorial integrity of the State or the existence or basic functioning of institutions indispensable to ensure and protect the rights recognized in the Covenant.[26]

The Siracusa Principles further comprise the following general principles with regards to implementing a public emergency that threatens the life of a nation:

- Derogation from rights recognized under international law in order to respond to a threat to the life of the nation is not exercised in a legal vacuum. It is authorized by law and as such it is subject to several legal principles of general application.[27]

- A proclamation of a public emergency shall be made in good faith based upon an objective assessment of the situation to determine to

what extent, if any, it poses a threat to the life of the nation. A proclamation of a public emergency, and consequent derogations from
Covenant obligations, that are not made in good faith are violations
of international law.[28]

- The provisions of the Covenant allowing for certain derogations in a
  public emergency are to be interpreted restrictively.[29]

- In a public emergency the rule of law shall still prevail. Derogation
  is an authorized and limited prerogative to respond adequately to a
  threat to the life of the nation. The derogating State shall have the
  burden of justifying its actions under law.[30]

The emphasis on "objective assessment" leaves open the possibility for a
treaty-monitoring forum to become involved in adjudication of the existence
of a national emergency, removing the exclusive ability of the government in
adjudging this important issue.[22]

Did the threat from COVID-19 meet the criteria of an emergency "threatening the life of a nation?"

International human rights standards are clear that a public health crisis that
"threatens the life of the nation" must jeopardize or threaten some vital component of statehood or survival of the populace and contain the following
key criteria:

- It must be actual or imminent.
- Its effects must involve the whole nation.
- The continuance of the organized life of the society must be endangered.
- The threat or crisis must be exceptional, in that the ordinary measures
  or controls for the preservation of public health, order, and safety are
  clearly insufficient.[19-21,22,24,26]

A public health emergency that does not meet the above criteria would
not constitute a legitimate threat to "the life of the nation" and any human
rights infringing public health measures instituted pursuant to such a public
health emergency would be illegitimate in terms of international human rights
normative standards.[22]

i.) Was the threat from COVID-19 actual or imminent?

The initial justification for COVID-19 emergency measures was the predictive modeling done by the Imperial College of London. After that, arbitrary increases in positive Reverse-Transcriptase Polymerase Chain Reaction (PCR) test results were either used to extend existing emergency measures or introduce new ones.

Major policy decisions need model input, but models are valuable only to the extent that outputs are transparent, valid, based on accurately documented sources, rigorously evaluated, and yield robust and reliable projections.[31] By August 2020, it had become evident that the predictive modeling and limited data initially used by many governments around the globe to justify their emergency regulations, which *inter alia* comprised models that predicted more than 2,000,000 COVID-19-related deaths in the United States, 500,000 in the United Kingdom, 375,000 in South Africa, and 100,000 in Sweden before the end of 2020, were highly speculative, woefully inaccurate, erroneous and vastly over stated the potential mortality rates and the threat to the life of the nation.[32-38]

According to the US CDC and the WHO, by December 31, 2020, 352,225 Americans out of a population of 331,515,730 (or less than 0.15%) had died as a result of COVID-19.[39] In the United Kingdom, the official death toll stood at 72,548 at the end of 2020 out of a population of approximately 66 million citizens.[40,41] By December 31, 2020, South Africa, with a population of 60 million, recorded 28,033 deaths, and Sweden, with a population of 10.4 million, recorded 9,654 deaths.[42,43]

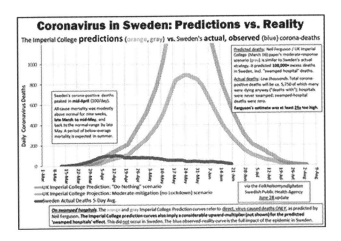

Figure 6.1: Coronavirus in Sweden: predictions vs. reality
Source: Swedish Public Health Agency (*Folkhalsomyndigheten*)

Numerous States used and continue to use arbitrary increases in the number of positive PCR tests, which amplifies fragments of live or dead virus found in nose and throat swabs, as justification to implement emergency measures. This is problematic since:

- **The PCR test was never intended to identify pathogens.** The PCR test is described in the media as the "gold standard" for SARS-CoV-2 diagnosis. However, the Nobel Prize-winning inventor of the process, Kerry Mullis, never intended it to be used as a diagnostic tool and stated, "I don't think you can misuse PCR. [It is] the results; the interpretation of it. If they can find this virus in you at all – and with PCR, if you do it well, you can find almost anything in anybody."[44]
- **PCR tests have a record of being incorrect and untrustworthy.**[45] The PCR tests for COVID-19 are known to produce false-positive results by reacting to DNA material that is not specific to SARS-CoV-2. A Chinese study, for instance, found that the same patient could get two different results from the same test on the same day.[46] In Germany, PCR tests are well-known to have reacted to ordinary flu viruses. A 2006 study found that PCR tests for one virus also responded to other viruses.[47] In 2007, reliance on PCR tests resulted in an "outbreak" of Whooping Cough that never actually existed. Some tests in the United States even reacted to the negative control sample.[48] The former President of the United Republic of Tanzania, John Magufuli, submitted particles of car lubricant, goat tissue, and pawpaw for PCR analysis and all came back positive for the COVID-19 virus.[49] As early as February 2020, specialists were acknowledging the PCR test was untrustworthy. President of the Chinese Academy of Medical Sciences, Dr. Wang Cheng, informed Chinese national television that "The accuracy of the tests is only 30-50%," while the Australian government's website claimed, "There is limited evidence available to assess the accuracy and clinical utility of available COVID-19 tests."[50] Moreover, a Portuguese court ruled that the PCR test "proves to be incapable of determining, beyond reasonable doubt, that such positivity does, in fact, correspond to the infection of a person with the SARS-CoV-2 virus" and should not be used for diagnosis.[44,51]
- **The CT values of the PCR are 100% faulty at 35 cycles.** It is widely documented and known that any test using a CT value over 35 is potentially meaningless.[52-54] Despite this and the CDC admitting that any tests over 28 cycles are not admissible for a reliable positive result,

almost all the labs in the United States were performing their PCR tests at least 37 cycles and at times as high as 45.[55] The NHS "standard operating procedure" for the PCR tests set the limit at 40 cycles.[56,57] This alone invalidates over 90% of the alleged positive COVID-19 cases.[44]

- **The WHO admitted PCR tests produced false positives.** In December 2020, the WHO released a memorandum on the PCR procedure directing laboratories to be cautious of high CT values producing false-positive outcomes.[44]

- **The Corman Drosten paper that is the root of every COVID PCR test in the world is dubious.** The genome of the SARS-CoV-2 virus was purportedly sequenced by Chinese researchers in December 2019, then made public on January 10, 2020. Less than 14 days later, Christian Drosten *et al.* had ostensibly used the genome to produce laboratory analysis for COVID-19 PCR tests. They penned a research article, "Detection of 2019 novel coronavirus (2019-nCoV) by real-time RT-PCR," which was submitted for peer review on January 21, 2020, and formally accepted on January 22, indicating the paper was superficially "peer-reviewed" in less than two days, a practice that normally takes weeks at minimum, but often months.[58] Since then, a consortium of over 20 scientists have pleaded for the revocation of the article, composing an extensive report specifying 10 major flaws in the article's scientific methodology.[59,60]

- **The CDC admitted that PCR tests "may not indicate the presence of an infectious virus,"** yet it is used to do precisely that in the case of COVID-19. A report by the research charity Collateral Global and Academics at Oxford University in February 2022 concluded that as many as one-third of all positive PCR cases may not have been infected with SARS-CoV-2 at all.[57,61]

- **Extreme corruption and conflicts of interest.** Those who profit from the tests are the same people continually promoting the incessant testing and continued emergency measures such as George Soros and Bill Gates, who own UK COVID-19 test company, Mologic.[60,62,63]

The significant percentage of asymptomatic COVID-19 infections, the well-known prevalence of severe comorbidities, and the potential for false-positive tests render the positive PCR results and death numbers extremely unreliable statistics and most definitely not credible to justify a legitimate state of emergency.

COVID-19 death numbers were artificially inflated globally by changing the definition relating to the cause of death by defining a "COVID-19 death" as a "death by any cause within 28/30/60 days of a positive test" and even counting "probable" or "presumed" COVID-19 deaths if test results were not available.[64] Healthcare officials from Italy, Germany, the United Kingdom, the United States, and others have all followed this practice.[65] Removing the distinction between "dying of COVID-19," and "dying of something else after testing positive for COVID-19" and in the USA "presumed to have died of COVID-19" leads to significantly over-counting "COVID deaths."[66] Lumping these statistics together inflated the impact of the virus and was often used, alongside positive PCR test numbers, to justify emergency measures. In the United Kingdom, for instance, during January 2022, the UK government released data showing that "deaths caused solely by COVID-19" between February 2020 and December 2021 in England and Wales amounted to only 6,183.[67] In the United States, a peer-reviewed study by Dr. Henry Ealy *et al.* published in the "Ethics in Science and Technology Journal" during October 2020 concluded that:

> The CDC has advocated for social isolation, social distancing, and personal protective equipment use as primary mitigation strategies in response to the COVID-19 crisis, while simultaneously refusing to acknowledge the promise of inexpensive pharmaceutical and natural treatments. These mitigation strategies were promoted largely in response to projection model fatality forecasts that have proven to be substantially inaccurate.

> The CDC published guidelines on March 24, 2020, that substantially altered how cause of death is recorded exclusively for COVID-19... As a result, a capricious alteration to data collection has compromised the accuracy, quality, objectivity, utility, and integrity of their published data.[68]

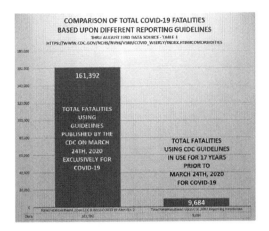

Figure 6.2 COVID-19 using the March 24, 2020, COVID-19 Guidelines
vs. using the 2003 Guidelines at the end of August 2020
Source: Ealy *et al*. Ethics in Science and Technology.

Finding: The threat from COVID-19 was neither actual nor imminent in relation to the scale and severity used as justification to enact a state of emergency.

ii.) Did the threat of COVID-19 involve the whole population?

After some initial uncertainty regarding the crude mortality rate and infection fatality rate of COVID-19 on different sections of the population, it soon became apparent that COVID-19 only poses a threat to a tiny segment of the population that falls in one of the vulnerable categories.

Infection fatality rates for COVID-19 depend heavily on age and underlying health conditions. By August 2020, it was evident that absolute risk of COVID-19 was extremely low for people younger than 65 years of age.[69] Dr. John Ioannidis, one of the world's most-published epidemiologists in a peer-reviewed study published in Science Direct during September 2020 noted that "People <65 years old have very small risks of COVID-19 death even in pandemic epicenters and deaths for people <65 years without underlying predisposing conditions are remarkably uncommon. Strategies focusing specifically on protecting high-risk elderly individuals should be considered in managing the pandemic."[69]

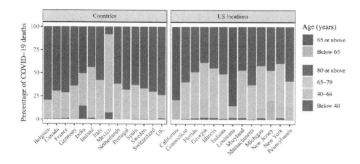

Figure 6.3 Proportion of COVID-19 deaths by specific age group category
Source: Ioannidis et al. Science Direct Journal September 2022

As of February 2021, the global infection fatality rate (IFR) was approximately 0.15% with 1.5 to 2.0 billion infections.[70]

Since the second half of 2020, it has been well known and documented that COVID-19's crude mortality rate ranged between 0.3% and 0.003% and that more than 99% of the population were never at risk of death from COVID-19.[71,72]

Country	Case Fatality	Crude Mortality
United States	1.6%	0.22%
United Kingdom	1.5%	0.21%
South Africa	3.1%	0.15%
Ethiopia	1.8%	0.005%
Sweden	1.3%	0.14%
France	1.6%	0.17%
India	1.3%	0.03%
Brazil	2.8%	0.28%

Table 6.1 COVID-19 case fatality and crude mortality rates
Sources: Johns Hopkins University, Mortality Analysis. (November 2020)

Finding: The threat from COVID-19 did not involve the whole population.

iii.) Was the continuance of the organized life of the community threatened by COVID-19?

The threat from COVID-19, as conceived by numerous governments around the globe, is related to a threat of overwhelming the capacity of hospitals and intensive care units to treat patients. The main argument used to defend emergency measures is that "flattening the curve" would prevent a rapid influx of cases and protect healthcare systems from collapse. However, most healthcare systems were never close to collapse at all. What is important to note is that we were dealing with the "concern about capacity, rather than the actual effect of COVID-19 on capacity."[73] Therefore, what was feared was a very limited and restricted "potential ICU capacity crisis" rather than "an emergency threatening the continuance of all elements of the organized life of the community."[73]

The "ICU capacity crisis" could have been easily overcome through the augmentation of ICU capacity by the allocation of resources to field hospitals as was done in New York City with the deployment of the Comfort hospital ship and the Army Corps of Engineers conversion of the 1,800,000-square-foot Jacob K. Javits Convention Center into an alternate care facility for more than 2,000 non-COVID-19 patients.[74,75] In both the United Kingdom and United States, millions were spent on temporary emergency hospitals that were never used.[76,77] The AP reported that:

> When virus infections slowed down or fell short of worst-case predictions, the globe was left dotted with dozens of barely used or unused field hospitals. Some public officials say that's a good problem to have — despite spending potentially billions of dollars to erect the care centers — because it's a sign the deadly disease was not nearly as cataclysmic as it might have been.[78]

To meet the threshold of "an emergency threatening the continuance of all elements of the organized life of the community," the threat should be so severe and impact the day-to-day life of the population in such a profound way that normalcy is no longer feasible.[22] This is a very high threshold as it means that the ordinary law and government institutions are no longer effective in controlling society as a whole.[22] This was never the case with COVID-19.

It was known early on in the pandemic that most deaths from COVID-19 would have occurred as part of the "normal" risks faced by people, particularly the elderly and those with chronic health problems. According to the CDC, 94% of Americans who died with COVID-19 had other "types of health conditions and contributing causes." Data on coronavirus-related deaths from the week ending February 1, 2020, through August 22, 2020 showed that only "for 6 percent of the deaths, COVID-19 was the only cause mentioned." In other words, 94% of Americans who died from COVID-19 had contributing conditions.[79] In most countries across the globe, COVID-19 did not have any meaningful impact on life expectancy and mortality curves, as can be seen from the statistical graph below.[44,80,81]

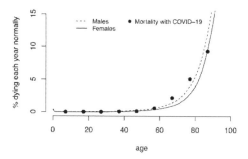

Figure 6.4: COVID-19 impact on life expectancy England and Wales
Source: David Spiegelhalter, ONS, Imperial College of London

The numbers of US deaths from or with COVID-19 (dark grey) and from all other causes (light gray), per age group, from February 2020 to February 2021, are depicted below:

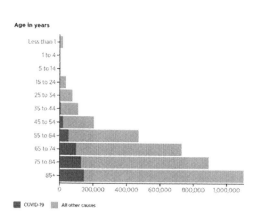

Figure 6.5: US deaths from or with COVID-19 compared with all other causes
Source: CDC, USA Facts

The following graph depicts the worldwide deaths proportional to other deaths in 2019.

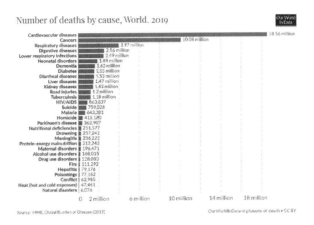

Figure 6.6: Number of deaths by cause 2019
Source: Our World in Data

According to Our World in Data, 58.8 million people died in 2019. The biggest killer by far was cardiovascular disease – responsible for more than 18.5 million deaths, or around a third of all deaths that year. Cancers killed more than 10 million people, or around one in six people, making it the second leading cause of death in the world. Respiratory disease killed 3.97 million people; lower respiratory infections killed 2.49 million people. John Hopkins University data shows that COVID-19 caused 1,88 million global deaths in 2020.[71,72]

It is evident that there are numerous other causes of death such as cancer, cardiovascular disease, and other respiratory diseases that had a significantly larger impact on society than COVID-19, yet these did not trigger any emergency measures. If emergency measures were not required due to people dying from heart disease, diabetes, cancer, the flu, or other respiratory illnesses, that caused significantly more deaths than COVID-19, then there was no reason to enact emergency measures for COVID-19.

Finding: COVID-19 did not threaten the continuance of the organized life of the community.

iv.) Was the COVID-19 crisis exceptional in that normal measures for public health and safety were plainly inadequate?

It is almost impossible to contemplate a rational *raison d'état* based on the notion that a disease with a crude mortality rate of less than 0.3% was such an extraordinary crisis that normal public health and safety measures were plainly inadequate.

Numerous normal measures could have and can still be taken to address the COVID-19 health threat and future coronavirus variants, such as:

- Cheap and effective prophylactics and early treatment protocols.[82-89]
- A protect the vulnerable approach.[90]
- Augmentation of the ICU capacity by allocating recourses to field hospitals.
- The Swedish approach.[91]
- The natural herd immunity approach.[92]

As described in detail in Chapter 4, Uttar Pradesh, India's most populous State with 230 million people, was nearly COVID-19 free following the proactive use of Ivermectin, included in home healthcare kits in 2021.[93]

Finding: The COVID-19 crisis was not exceptional in that normal measures for public health and safety were plainly adequate.

From the rudimentary analysis, set out in i. to iv. above, it is evident that the threat from COVID-19 never posed a "threat to the life of the nation" as it did not meet any of the international human rights criteria and thresholds.

Since the COVID-19 crisis does not meet the legal requirements of an emergency "threatening the life of a nation," derogation measures such as lockdown mandates, mask mandates, vaccine mandates, isolation mandates, and travel mandates are illegitimate contraventions of the ICCPR and IHRL. The COVID-19 era indeed saw a significant rise in emergency regimes where in the words of Agamben "the State continued to exist, but the law receded."[3]

The complex strategy of inscribing a state of exception into the law can only be valid if States adhere to international legal obligation and respect IHRL *jus cogens* norms. A state of emergency that does not meet the legal criteria as set out in IHRL is illicit and leads to anomie and a juridical void where law subsists only by encapsulating anomie.[3]

In his 1923 book "*Das Reichsstaatsrecht*", Julius Hatschek distinguishes between *objektive Notstandtheorie* according to which every act of State performed in conflict with the law during a state of emergency is illegitimate and, as such, is legally imputable, and a subjective *Notstandtheorie*, according to which emergency State powers are grounded in a "constitutional or pre-constitutional natural right" of the State, concerning which good faith is sufficient to guarantee immunity.[3,94] Post-Second World War IHRL codified the former and every illegal act committed during the COVID-19 pandemic by Western politicians and their corporate paymasters should be prosecuted to the full extent of the law.

Chapter Conclusion

The "paradoxical phenomenon" of the state of emergency has reached its maximum worldwide deployment during the COVID-19 pandemic, with nearly all United Nation Member States declaring a *justitium*. In the West specifically, the normative aspects of law were obliterated and contradicted with impunity by State violence that – while ignoring international law externally and producing a state of exception internally – still claims to be applying the law. Agamben deduced that these "attempts to reinsert a legal vacuum into the legal order's" only purpose is to protect illicit sovereign violence at all costs.[3] Agamben notes that:

> …alongside the movement that seeks to keep them in relation at all costs, there is a counter movement that, working in an inverse direction in law and life, always seeks to loosen what has been artificially and violently linked…. two opposite forces act, one that institutes and makes and one that deactivates and deposes. The state of exception is both the point of their maximum tension and-as it coincides with the rule- that which threaten today to render them indiscernible.[3]

IHRL objectively interpreted and applied does indeed "loosen what has been artificially and violently linked" by modern-day COVID-19 totalitarians such as Joe Biden, Justin Trudeau, Emmanuel Macron, Angela Merkel, Mario Draghi, Boris Johnson, Mark Rutte, Karl Nehammer, Jacinda Ardern, and Scot Morrison.

The bias intrinsic in individual countries deciding what constitutes an emergency that poses a "threat to the life of the nation" has proven disastrous during the COVID-19 crisis, as State officials abused emergency powers to the detriment of human rights protection around the globe. There is a fine line between governments' *bona fide* actions to secure the safety of the people and governments' *male fide* actions illegitimately abusing public health derogation provisions.

Determining whether a situation constitutes a public emergency "threatening the life of the nation" is seen predominantly as a political decision. However, the declaration of a state of emergency has substantial legal implications that too often have a disastrous adverse impact on fundamental human rights.[31] Leaving the determination of the presence of a national emergency exclusively to States weakens the universal protection of fundamental human rights, as recent events are clearly demonstrating.[22]

Human rights derogation can only be acceptable as a transient government technique for allowing States to safeguard fundamental human rights rather than as a mechanism for enabling national powers and their corporate handlers to advance their political and financial interests in a manner that impairs human rights protection.[8] Dr. Richard Burchill (former Director of the McCoubrey Centre for International Law at the University of Hull, UK) accurately contends that:

> Determinations of threats or public emergencies will give rise to new legal regimes that are likely to restrain human rights. Therefore, determination of the existence of a public emergency cannot be solely left to the political. It is incumbent upon international monitoring bodies to exert their supervisory role to determin[e] whether or not a State's belief in the existence of a public emergency is legitimate or not.[22]

From the crude mortality rate of COVID-19 that ranges between 0.3% and 0.003%, it is clear that the actual threat posed by COVID-19 does not constitute "a threat to the life of the nation." The position by most Western State Parties that COVID-19 represents an actual public emergency threatening the nation does not meet the standards previously established in IHRL. If a disease with a crude mortality rate similar to that of the common cold can be used to justify gross violations of fundamental human rights, then States *de facto* and *de jure* have latitude to completely disdain all international human rights responsibilities with impunity. Sadly, this is precisely what is going on. The COVID-19 crisis has been widely used to justify prevalent and pervasive human rights violations.[22] The state of exception continually assumes a "fictitious" or political nature, where a lexicon of war is maintained allegorically to rationalize recourse to broad executive powers.[6] The present "permanent state of emergency" should also be understood as a fiction sustained through the military metaphor of World War COVID-19.

To prevent future abuse, the role of ethical, uncompromised, independent, unbiased, and objective international monitoring bodies in determinations of public emergencies is crucial to avoid the subjectivity that appears to define the existence of threats from COVID-19. Professor Evan J. Criddle (Ernest W. Goodrich Professor of Law at William & Mary Law School, USA) was correct in 2014, when pointing out that:

> Robust scrutiny by international treaty bodies is necessary, to mitigate the conflicts of interest that arise between public institutions and political elites, whose survival is preserved, and their people, whose derogable human rights are sacrificed, during national crises. By asserting the ultimate prerogative to decide how general derogation standards apply to particular emergencies, international treaty bodies intercede as neutral arbiters between a State and its people to protect the integrity of HRL against erosion in State practice.[8]

The systematic violation of human rights undermines national security and public order and constitutes a threat to international peace and stability.[26] The inexplicable silence and inaction from the UNHRC and other regional human rights judicial forums in the face of the most pervasive abuse of emergency declarations and egregious violation of international human rights law by G20 nations is a cause for extreme concern; it is indicative that the current IHR juridical order and its various checks and balances have been severely compromised and are not functioning as they should. Above all, Agamben fears that efforts, both historically and present, to codify anomie – that is, to incorporate the non-legal within the law *(legge, recht)* – amount to a denial of the presence of an extra-legal reality. The hypothesis is expressed most distinctly in the final passage of the book:

> To show law in its nonrelation to life and life in its nonrelation to law means to open a space between them for human action, which once claimed for itself the name of "politics." Politics has suffered a lasting eclipse because it has been contaminated by law, seeing itself, at best, as constituent power (that is, violence that makes law), when it is not reduced to merely the power to negotiate with the law. The only truly political action, however, is that which serves the nexus between violence and law. And only beginning from the space thus opened will it be possible to question the use of law after the deactivation that, in the state of exception tied it to life.[3]

From a practical standpoint, the rampant abuse of emergency measures since the onset of the COVID-19 pandemic has confirmed the view that *de facto* there "are no ultimate institutional safeguards available for ensuring that emergency powers be used for the purpose of preserving the Constitution. Only the people's own determination to see them so used can make sure of that."[95]

7. COVID-19 VACCINE PASSPORTS: DEROGATING NON-DEROGABLE FUNDAMENTAL HUMAN RIGHTS

"Lex malla, lex nulla - A bad law is no law"

— Cassandra Clare

As billions of people were being inoculated against COVID-19, government officials in places as diverse as Austria, Canada, New York State, Israel, Greece, New Zealand, and China have introduced "vaccine passports" and there is talk of making them universal. The idea is simple: once citizens have received their COVID-19 vaccinations, their "vaccine passport" can then be used to gain entry to previously prohibited venues such as restaurants, theaters, sports arenas, offices, schools, and colleges. The digital vaccination certification, or "vaccine passport," is a "mobile app that instantaneously affirms the vaccinated status, COVID-19 test results, birth date, gender, and/or other identifiers of its holder. The information is usually mosaicked in a QR code, read by a proprietary scanner, and linked to a government registry." [1]

The European Parliamentary Assembly adopted Resolution 2361 on January 27, 2021 urging European Member States to "ensure that citizens are informed that the vaccination is not mandatory and that no one is under political, social, or other pressure to be vaccinated if they do not wish to do so" and "to ensure that no one is discriminated against for not having been vaccinated, due to possible health risks or not wanting to be vaccinated". However, in a call to action, on December 1, 2021, the European Commission President Ursula von

der Leyen said the EU's 27 Member States should consider mandatory vaccination in response to the spread of the "highly contagious" Omicron COVID
variant across Europe.[2,3] Shortly thereafter, the Greek Prime Minister Kyriakos
Mitsotakis announced that mandatory COVID-19 vaccination for all Greeks
above 60 years of age and those who refuse to get vaccinated would have to
pay a monthly fine of €100 ($114) for each month they did not get vaccinated,
starting January 16, 2022.[3] At the end of November 2021, it was reported that
those resisting vaccination in Austria might face harsh punishments, according
to a draft of the so-called COVID-19 Vaccination Protection Act. Under
the bill, anyone who refused to attend a scheduled vaccination appointment
would receive an official summons from local authorities. If an individual
failed to show up, they would be summoned one more time within the next
four weeks. Should the second official request be ignored, the person would
face a fine of €3,600 ($4,061) or four weeks in prison. The fine would increase
to €7,200 ($8,000) for those who had already been fined twice for violating
the vaccination requirement.[4] New Zealand Prime Minister Jacinda Ardern
heralded her country's "My Vaccine Pass" as the keycard to the kingdom. "If
you want to go to bars and restaurants, get vaccinated; if you want to get a
haircut – get vaccinated…. It's actually really straightforward. If you've got a
vaccine pass, you can do everything," she said, demonstrating what the Italian
philosopher Giorgio Agamben dubbed "techno-medical despotism" measures
"that are so focused on eliminating the risk of contagion to preserve mere
biological existence that they prohibit everything that makes human society
meaningful, from dating to democracy."[5-9]

Vaccine passports represent one of the most draconian aspects of the
irrational new normal that has metastasized amid an atmosphere of seemingly
endless pseudo-medical emergency measures. By including the vaccinated and
excluding the unvaccinated, the modern-day bio-political State distinguishes
the duteous subservient biocitizen from the excepted or *homo sacer* whose
"bare life" in the words of Agamben is a "life that is lived beyond recourse
to legal and political representation…and determining political element of
sovereign power."[8-10] *Homo sacer*, the rejected and therefore separate man
– set apart from others by pseudo-medical mandate – is, for Agamben, the
increasingly nascent figure of our era. An era in which we are witnessing the
effective re-emergence of largely unaccountable, illegitimate sovereign forms
of power.[9] An era defiled with malversation where the abrogation of individual
rights and freedoms is not the exception, but the emblematic norm.[11]

Despite vaccine passports being promulgated by purportedly estimable
leaders of Western democracies, they are nothing other than a form of political

delegitimization and illicit suspension (if not denial) of citizens' absolute human rights. From the perspective of IHRL, States that enforce exclusionary practices against those that insist on medical self-determination do so unlawfully. Lives lived on the margins of economic, social, political, and cultural borders – denied access to legal, economic and political redress in their Nation States during the COVID-19 era – are lives half lived. These lives exist in a limbo-like state that is largely preoccupied with acquiring and sustaining the bare essentials of life. The dispossessed, the silenced, the terminated, the coerced, and the victim of medical experimentation without free and informed consent all have been excluded, to different degrees, and appeal to the rule of law and recourse to IHRL norms for justice.[11]

Physical Integrity Rights are Core Peremptory Human Rights Norms *Jus Cogens*[§]

The norms of IHRL originate from a fiduciary relationship between the State and individuals subject to its powers. The State's primary duty is to provide a system of government that respects human rights norms. It fulfills this duty, in part, by governing through norms that conform to its international legal obligations.[12-15] As detailed in Chapter 3, several international treaties spell out the specific obligations of governments to respect the human rights of their citizens. The major assumptions behind the internationally recognized human rights in these treaties are that these rights are:

- Immutable – not being able to be taken away by any State Party.
- Universal – always applying to all persons.
- Interdependent and indissoluble – requiring respect for specific individual rights as mutual reinforcement for respect of all rights.[12-14,16-18]

As adduced in Chapters 5 and 6, while these assumptions would seem to dictate that respect for human rights must be unconditional, international law provides governments an exception, or loophole, whereby governments may deviate from the assumption of unconditional respect for some rights during declared states of emergency.[12] States of emergency are known to be correlates

§ Portions of this chapter are republications of the content of a peer-reviewed article by the author Dr. Willem van Aardt, entitled "Jus Cogens Norms, Public Policy and the Fiduciary Criterion of Morality" published in the De Rebus Attorneys Journal in July 2022.

of decreased respect for human rights and, for that reason, the international community specifically created laws and standards to govern State behavior during times of crisis, such as the COVID-19 pandemic.[12,19] In terms of IHRL, there are certain fundamental rights that can never be derogated from under any circumstances, not even in times of a public health emergency, given the fundamental values they uphold.[15-18] As noted in the previous chapter, these rights are known as non-derogable rights. The ICCPR specifies a list of seven fundamental human rights from which no derogation is allowed.[15-17] Included in all lists of non-derogable rights is a sub-category of globally recognized fundamental rights known as "physical integrity rights." The principle of bodily integrity entails the right of each human being to autonomy and self-determination over their own body. It considers an unconsented physical intrusion as a human rights violation. These rights are "the entitlements individuals have in international law to be free from arbitrary physical harm and coercion by their government" and include freedoms from torture and medical or scientific experimentation that includes the right not to be coerced to be injected with an experimental quasi-vaccine.[19]

Because of their normative specificity and status, non-derogable rights are core human rights *jus cogens* and obligations *erga omnes*.[12,16] As alluded to in Chapter 3, *jus cogens* is the legal term given to those norms that enjoy a higher rank and status in the international law hierarchy than treaty law and even ordinary customary law. It designates the peremptory norms from which no derogation is ever acceptable. It is a "super norm" that acts as a check on unbridled State power that renders any conflicting State action illegitimate.[14] Under case law and legal doctrine, *jus cogens* comprises a particular form of constitutional rule that every government is obligated to follow.[14-16] Being compelling law, it does not give a government the right to opt out, as is the case with other international norms deriving from custom or treaty. Peremptory norms limit the ability of the State to alter regulations or create ones, such as the rules relating to vaccine passports, which would be in contradiction with *jus cogens*. Any act, omission, or health policy of the State contrary to *jus cogens*, would represent a breach of international legal order.[12,15]

The rationale for treating non-derogable rights as privileged is functional and deductive: non-derogable rights should be seen as primary because all other rights are dependent on them. As the COVID-19 emergency measures again demonstrated, a governmental order in which the rights to life, physical security, freedom of movement, freedom of thought, and freedom from medical experimentation are frequently violated generates an intense and pervasive fear, which annuls the will to exercise other rights.[17]

Are the Novel COVID-19 Messenger RNA Vaccines Experimental or Not?

It is vital to differentiate between vaccines with long-term safety and efficacy data – such as the mumps, measles, and rubella vaccine; the polio vaccine; and others – and COVID-19 vaccines for which there is not yet medium- to long-term safety and efficacy data. To determine the legality of vaccine passports, a critical question to be answered is whether the COVID-19 vaccines are still experimental and in clinical trials or not.

The ascertainment and classification of a medical procedure as experimental or not is of paramount importance, given that IHRL states that experimental medical interventions always necessitate prior informed consent.

i.) Experiment Defined
The very definition of an experiment is a scientific procedure undertaken to discover or test a hypothesis.

The current hypothesis being tested with the recent real-world mass vaccination effort is that the Pfizer-BioNTech, Moderna, Oxford-AstraZeneca, and Johnson & Johnson's Janssen COVID-19 vaccines, most of which make use of advanced messenger RNA technology never used before, will not cause any serious medium- to long-term health problems.

ii.) COVID-19 mRNA Vaccine Development versus Standard Vaccine Development
Based on a typical vaccine development timeline, it takes 10 to 15 years to assess whether a vaccine is safe and effective in clinical trials, complete the regulatory authorization processes, and produce an adequate quantity of vaccine doses for common distribution.[21]

On January 10, 2020, the SARS-CoV-2 genetic sequence data were shared through the Global Initiative on Sharing Avian Influenza Data (GISAID), and by March 19, 2020, the global pharmaceutical industry had announced a major commitment to developing a vaccine to prevent COVID-19.[22] The clinical development, including safety and efficacy evaluations of COVID-19 vaccines, was completed in less than one year – about 10 to 15 times faster than a standard clinical vaccine development program.[21-23]

Years	Standard Vaccine Development Timeline	Years	COVID-19 Vaccine Development Timeline
2–5	Discovery Research	0–1	Discovery Research, Preclinical Trials, Phases 1–3 Clinical Trials, EUA**
2	Preclinical Trials	1–?	Post-EUA Vaccine Safety Monitoring and BLA Licensure
1–2	Phase 1 Clinical Trials: Are they safe?	1–?	Post-Licensure Vaccine Safety Monitoring
2–3	Phase 2 Clinical Trials: Do they activate an immune response?		
2–4	Phase 3 Clinical Trials: Do they protect against the disease?		
1–2	Regulatory Review and BLA Licensure		
1–?	Post-Licensure Vaccine Safety Monitoring		

* Biologics License Application (BLA) | ** Emergency Use Authorization (EUA)

Table 7.1: Comparative table of a standard vaccine development timeline and the COVID-19 development timeline
Source: World Economic Forum

From the above table, it is apparent there are no medium- or long-term safety and efficacy data available for the COVID-19 vaccines. These vaccines were created and authorized in less than one year, with the mass rollout of the COVID-19 vaccines only commencing in January 2021, thereby providing a further 12 months of real-world data as of January 2022.

The advancement and development of novel mRNA vaccines against infectious disease is unparalleled in numerous ways. A 2018 study by Young *et al.* funded by the Bill and Melinda Gates Foundation, postulated that vaccines are split into three classifications: Simple, Complex, and Unprecedented.

Simple and Complex vaccines denoted standard and modified applications of current vaccine technologies. Unprecedented denotes a category of vaccine against a disease for which there has never before been an appropriate vaccine. Vaccines against malaria, HIV, and COVID-19 fall into this category. As their study reveals, depicted in Figure 7.1 below, unprecedented vaccines are expected to take 12.5 years to develop. Even more portentously, they have a 5% estimated chance of making it through Phase II trials (evaluating efficacy) and, of that 5%, a 40% chance of making it through Phase III trials (evaluating population benefit). In other words, an unprecedented vaccine was expected to have a 2% probability of success at the stage of a phase III clinical trial. As the researchers candidly assert, there is a "low probability of success, especially for unprecedented vaccines."[24,25]

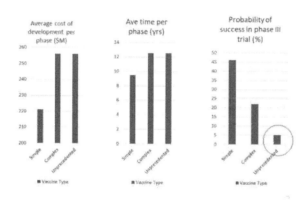

Figure 7.1: Probability of success of unprecedented vaccines
Source: International Journal of Vaccine Theory, Practice, and Research

Yet, within 18 months of the identification of the SARS-CoV-2 we had an unprecedented vaccine that claimed a 90 to 95% efficacy.[24,26] These claims of efficacy by public health authorities were the principal motivation behind public support for the COVID-19 vaccines. By January 2021, the British Medical Journal's Dr. Peter Doshi called attention to valid concerns over the efficacy of the COVID-19 vaccines.[24,27] A more objective, peer-reviewed analysis that was published in the Medicina journal, looked specifically at the issue of relative versus absolute risk reduction. While the high estimates of risk reduction are based upon relative risks, the absolute risk reduction is a more appropriate metric for a member of the public to ascertain whether a COVID-19 vaccination provides a meaningful risk reduction.[24,28] In that analysis, utilizing data supplied by the vaccine makers to the FDA, the Moderna vaccine at the time of interim analysis demonstrated an absolute risk reduction of 1.1% (p=0.004), while the Pfizer vaccine's absolute risk reduction was 0.7% (p<0.000).[24,28]

iii.) Emergency Use Authorization versus Biologics License Application

The traditional pathway to vaccine licensing in the United States is the FDA Biologics License Application (BLA) procedure. This is a thorough process that requires extensive data on a vaccine's safety and efficiency and various levels of evaluation by federal advisory committees. The BLA process has an excellent track record of promoting confidence and public trust in vaccines that are ultimately approved.[23]

The main COVID-19 vaccines utilized in the global mass vaccination campaigns received EUA only and not the time-tested BLA. An EUA does not require safety and efficiency data that are as thorough and comprehensive as the standard BLA procedure. For instance, EUA regulations for a COVID-19 vaccine required a median of two months of follow-up safety data, as opposed to two years under normal circumstances. The use of an EUA to make a vaccine available is almost unique, having been utilized only in 2005 to make the anthrax vaccine available.[29]

iv.) FDA-Issued EUA COVID-19 Vaccine Fact Sheets

For each COVID-19 vaccine authorized under an EUA, the FDA required that vaccine recipients or their caregivers be provided with an EUA Fact Sheet for Recipients and Caregivers. This fact sheet is similar in purpose and content to vaccine information statements (VISs) for licensed vaccines, but differs in that it is "specific to each authorized COVID-19 vaccine, is developed by the manufacturer of the vaccine, and is authorized by the FDA."[30-32] There is no VIS for COVID-19 vaccines authorized under an EUA. Instead, the FDA-approved EUA Fact Sheet for Recipients and Caregivers for each COVID-19 vaccine must be used.[30-32]

As of December 3, 2021, after 4.29 billion people, equal to about 55.9% of the world population, had received a dose of a COVID-19 vaccine, the EUA's fact sheets for Pfizer-BioNTech, Moderna, and Johnson & Johnson's Janssen still stated the following:

- "[T]he… COVID-19 vaccine is an unapproved vaccine that may prevent COVID-19. There is no FDA-approved vaccine to prevent COVID-19."
- "[T]he… COVID-19 vaccine is still being studied in clinical trials."
- "[T]he… COVID-19 vaccine is an unapproved vaccine in an ongoing clinical trial."

- "[T]he… COVID-19 vaccine has not undergone the same type of review as an FDA approved or cleared product."[30-32]

According to the official communications of CDC dated December 3, 2021, "the CDC continues to closely monitor the safety of COVID-19 vaccines"[33] and on June 2, 2021, the CDC confirmed it is "still in the process of learning: how well vaccines prevent you from spreading the virus that causes COVID-19 to others, how long COVID-19 vaccines protect people, how many people need to be vaccinated against COVID-19 before the population can be considered protected (population immunity), and how effective the vaccines are against new variants of the virus that causes COVID-19."[34-36]

As is abundantly clear from the above, the FDA, the CDC, and vaccine manufacturers are transparent and open that the COVID-19 vaccines are still in clinical trials and the experimental stage.

v.) "Comirnaty" (Pfizer) and "Spikevax" Moderna FDA "Approval" – Is it still experimental?

Some argue that the FDA approval of the Pfizer and Moderna vaccines at the end of August 2021 and January 2022 means that the Pfizer and Moderna vaccines are no longer experimental. This is not the case. All COVID-19 vaccines, including Pfizer and Moderna, have been used for less than 24 months and so are still experimental by definition and by any objective reasonable standard. Pfizer's vaccine, like Moderna's, is based on a "novel" experiment using messenger RNA to produce spike antibodies. There has never been anything like it used in humans before, and the COVID-19 vaccine with no medium- and long-term safety data is an experiment – whether conflicted government public health agencies acknowledge that or not.[35]

The fact is, Pfizer's clinical trials do not end until May 2023, and Moderna's only ends on October 27, 2022.[36,37] The phase III studies by Pfizer, Moderna, and Janssen are all of two years' duration. In its formal guidance during June 2020, the FDA confirmed that for licensure applications, it wanted participants followed for COVID-19 outcomes for "as long as feasible, ideally at least one to two years" after the first injection.[38]

Serious concerns have also been raised with regards to the following apparent flaws and deviation from long-established practices and procedures in the FDA approval process:

- The FDA did not adhere to its own guidance and standards relating to COVID-19 vaccine licensure to fast-track approval.

- There was no external review and a lack of data transparency.
- Approval was granted based on just six months of incomplete data.
- The trial is unblinded, and the placebo group no longer exists.
- At the time of BLA approval, it was well known, from real-world data, that the COVID-19 vaccines are ineffective and do not provide immunity, yet the FDA repeated Pfizer's claim that the vaccine is "95% effective" in their approval letter.
- Based on six months of data, approval represented one of the fastest for a novel vaccine in FDA history. Among the six "first in disease" vaccines approved by the FDA since 2006, pre-licensure pivotal trials were a median of 23 months in duration.
- The FDA granted approval prior to the conclusion of the two-year pivotal trials, with no reported data past March 13, 2021, unclear efficacy after six months due to unblinding, strong evidence of waning protection, and limited reporting of safety data.
- Regulatory approval of the RNA-based vaccines for SARS-CoV-2 was premature and the vaccine may cause much more harm than benefit.[24,27,39-44]

From an IHRL perspective, whether the COVID-19 vaccine is experimental or not is determined with reference to relevant objective facts irrespective of whether the vaccine has been "formally approved" by a potentially conflicted or corrupted governmental agency. By any objective legal and common-sense standards, the fact that the phase III studies by Pfizer, Moderna, and Janssen are all of two years' duration and still ongoing is a clear indication that the COVID-19 vaccines are still experimental.

vi.) Eminent Medical Experts and Researchers are on Record that the COVID-19 mRNA Vaccines are Experimental

Messenger RNA, or mRNA, is a molecule that tells the body how to make proteins. Vaccines based on mRNA are novel vaccines first made available to the public during the COVID-19 pandemic. These vaccines instruct your cells to make certain proteins from a virus or other microbe.

Dr. Robert Malone, one of the inventors of the mRNA technology used in the COVID-19 vaccine, on June 23, 2021, cautioned that:

> …the government is not being transparent with us about what those risks are. And so, I am of the opinion that people have the right to decide whether to accept vaccines or not, especially since these are experimental vaccines. This is a fundamental right having to do with

clinical research ethics,… And so, my concern is that I know that there are risks. But we don't have access to the data and the data haven't been captured rigorously enough so that we can accurately assess those risks. And therefore … we don't really have the information that we need to make a reasonable decision.[45]

On May 13, 2022, Dr. Malone read a joint statement, representing 17,000 physicians and medical scientists and declared that:

After two years of scientific research, millions of patients treated, hundreds of clinical trials performed and scientific data shared,… the data confirm that the COVID-19 experimental genetic therapy injections must end…these products do not prevent infection, replication and transmission…the vast majority of COVID infections are in those who have been vaccinated…the data now show that vaccination increases the risk of infection…..what has not been performed by the pharmaceutical industry is the required full battery of safety, toxicology , pharmacokinetic testing [showing] where does the RNA go and how long does it stay in your body…..the distribution of the m-RNA in the resulting spike-protein toxicology has not been well characterized and we do not understand even now what is happening in patients that receive these quasi vaccines…"[46]

Nobel Prize laureate for discovering AIDS, and arguably the top virologist in the world prior to his recent death, Professor Luc Montagnier, was invited to the Luxembourg Parliament to accompany petitioners speaking out against compulsory vaccination on January 12, 2022. Montagnier said in his speech:

These vaccines are poisons. They are not real vaccines. The mRNA allows its message to be transcribed throughout the body, uncontrollably. No one can say for each of us where these messages will go. This is therefore a terrible unknown. And in fact, we are now learning that …these mRNAs contain an area that we can call prion, which is an area capable of introducing protein modifications in an unpredictable way. There is therefore a known risk to human health.[47]

Dr. Michael Yeadon, a former Vice President and Chief Science Officer for Pfizer, warned "that the drive to inject the largest possible portion of the population with experimental COVID-19 vaccines" is "madness," and includes "crimes against humanity." Yeadon, who spent over 30 years leading novel "respiratory medicines research in some of the world's largest pharmaceutical companies, and who retired from Pfizer with the most senior research position in this field," wrote:

> There is absolutely no need for vaccines to extinguish the pandemic. I've never heard such nonsense talked about vaccines. You do not vaccinate people who aren't at risk from a disease. You also don't set about planning to vaccinate millions of fit and healthy people with a vaccine that hasn't been extensively tested on human subjects.[48]

> Gene-based agents are new in a public health application. Had I been in a regulatory role, I would have informed all the leading R&D companies that I would not approve these without extensive longitudinal studies, meaning they could not receive EUA before early 2022 at the earliest. I would have outright denied their use in children, in pregnancy, and in the infected recovered. Point blank. I'd need years of safe use before contemplating an alteration of this stance. The basic rules of this new activity, gene-based component vaccines, are:

> 1. to select part of the virus that has no inherent biological action—that rules out spike protein, which we inferred would be very toxic before they'd even started clinical trials;
> 2. select the genetically most stable parts of the virus....—again, this rules out spike protein;
> 3. choose parts of the virus which are most different from any human proteins. Once more, spike protein is immediately deselected, otherwise unnecessary risks of autoimmunity are carried forward.

> That all four leading actors chose spike protein, against any reasonable selection criteria, leads me to suspect both collusion and malign intent.[68]

World-renowned cardiologist, epidemiologist, former professor of medicine, and one of the top five most published medical researchers in America, Dr. Peter McCullough, on August 20, 2021, asserted that:

> This is something we've never seen in human medicine — a new product introduced and just going full-steam ahead with no check on why people are dying after the vaccine, I think this is malfeasance.[49]

Professor Joan-Ramón Laporte Roselló, an external expert for the European Medicines Agency on pharmacovigilance and honorary professor at the University of Barcelona, on February 7, 2022, stated that:

> Traditional vaccines are attenuated germs or portions of germs that stimulate the immune system, [whereas] messenger RNA vaccines introduce a nucleic acid that instructs cells in the vaccinated person to make this virus protein, the so-called spike protein, which in turn will stimulate the immune system.[50,51]

Laporte described the COVID-19 vaccines as "drugs based on a technology never used in therapeutics until now," and called mass vaccination against COVID "a global experiment unprecedented in human history." The pharmacovigilance expert also debunked the claim by governments, the mainstream media, and pharmaceutical companies that COVID-19 vaccines "save lives." He insisted that this is not what clinical trials have shown:

> No, ladies and gentlemen, clinical trials have not shown that the vaccines save lives.[50,51]

Dr. Tess Lawrie, whose firm the Evidence-Based Medicine Consultancy has worked with the World Health Organization, analyzed UK yellow card data and concluded that there is more than enough evidence to pull the injections from the market because they are not safe for human use. The report stated:

> It is now apparent that these products in the blood stream are toxic to humans. An immediate halt to the vaccination program is required whilst a full and independent safety analysis is undertaken to investigate the full extent of the harms, which the UK Yellow Card data suggest include thromboembolism, multisystem inflammatory disease, immune suppression, autoimmunity and anaphylaxis, as well as Antibody Dependent Enhancement (ADE).[52]

Stephanie Seneff Ph.D., a Senior Research Scientist at MIT's Computer Science and Artificial Intelligence Laboratory in Cambridge, Massachusetts, USA in her comprehensive peer-reviewed study entitled "Worse than the disease? Reviewing some possible unintended consequences of the mRNA vaccines against COVID-19" confirms that:

With the massive vaccination campaign well under way in response to the declared international emergency of COVID-19, we have rushed into vaccine experiments on a world-wide scale. At the very least, we should take advantage of the data that are available from these experiments to learn more about this new and previously untested technology. And, in the future, we urge governments to proceed with more caution in the face of new biotechnologies.[24]

It is clear that the world's most eminent medical researchers regard the COVID-19 vaccines as experimental.

Free Consent to Medical or Scientific Experimentation Is a Non-Derogable Human Right

As broached in Chapters 5 and 6, Article 4 of the legally binding ICCPR, which 173 governments worldwide, including the United States, committed to adhere to, is of paramount importance for the system of safeguarding human rights.[53] On the one hand, it allows for State Parties unilaterally to derogate temporarily from a part of their commitments under the Covenant. On the other hand, Article 4 subjects both this specific measure of derogation and its significant consequences to a definite regime of legal precautions.[53,54] As seen in the previous chapter, Article 4(1) of the ICCPR provides that in a time of public emergency that threatens the life of the nation, State Parties may take actions derogating from their duties under the Covenant to the degree strictly required by the pressures of the situation. Article 4(2), however, explicitly determines that "no derogation from Article 7 may be made under this provision."[18]

Article 7 of the ICCPR clearly dictates that "no one shall be subjected without his free consent to medical or scientific experimentation."[18] On April 30, 2020, the UNHRC again reiterated that:

State Parties cannot resort to emergency powers or implement derogating measures that violate obligations under international human rights treaties from which no derogation is allowed. State Parties cannot deviate from the non-derogable provisions of the Covenant such as article 7 or from other rights that are essential for upholding the non-derogable rights, even in times of public emergency.[55]

Therefore, a person's right to free consent to medical or scientific experimentation is a non-derogable fundamental human right that cannot be violated, not even in times of a public health emergency.

The Siracusa Principles on the Limitation and Derogation Provisions in the ICCPR specifically determine that:

> No State Party shall, even in a time of emergency threatening the life of the nation, derogate from the covenant's guarantees of the right to life and the right to freedom from torture; from cruel, inhumane, or degrading treatment or punishment, and from medical or scientific experimentation without free consent. These rights are not derogable under any circumstances, even for the stated purpose of safeguarding the life of the nation.[56]

The Siracusa Principles further establish that no State, including those that are not parties to the covenant, may suspend or infract, even in times of a public health emergency, the fundamental human right to freedom from medical or scientific experimentation without free consent.[46]

The Paris Minimum Standards of Human Rights Norms in a state of emergency, similarly instruct that, even in circumstances where a *bona fide* declaration of a state of emergency has been announced, the government concerned must refrain from suspending those basic human rights that are regarded as non-derogable under Article 4 of the ICCPR, Article 15 of the European Convention on Human Rights, and Article 27 of the American Convention on Human Rights.[57-59] The Paris Minimum Standards specifically determine that during the period of the existence of a public emergency, the government may not derogate from internationally prescribed rights that are by their own terms "non-suspendable" and not subject to derogation, and they confirm that the basic rights and freedoms guaranteed by international law, such as the right to free and informed consent for any medical experiment, shall remain non-derogable even during emergencies.[57]

Vaccine Passports and Proof of Vaccination Demanded by Non-State Actors

In terms of the "Doctrine of State Responsibility for Human Rights Abuses Committed by Non-State Actors", governments cannot sideline their international legal obligations not to derogate the non-derogable right to be free from medical experimentation without free consent.[60] Governments cannot coerce or allow private institutions such as colleges, schools, private employers, airlines, and others to mandate COVID-19 vaccination for citizens to be able to work and earn a living, to travel, to study at a college, to attend school, to attend sporting events, to attend concerts, or to get access to shopping malls. The choice between being vaccinated against COVID-19 or not being employed and losing one's livelihood, *or* the choice between being vaccinated or not attending school or college, is, in fact, no choice at all – but rather the same as mandating a vaccine – and thus a blatant and abrasive form of force, duress, overreach, and coercion, directly contravening all relevant *jus gentium* and *jus inter gentes* in relation to the derogation of non-derogable fundamental human rights.

Article 2 of ICCPR, Article 1 of the EU Convention, and Article 1 of the American Convention all determine that each State Party undertakes to respect and to ensure (secure) to all individuals within its territory and subject to its jurisdiction the rights recognized in the covenant, without distinction of any kind.[18,58,59]

In terms of this obligation, the State Party to the Covenant must prevent, investigate, and punish any violation of the fundamental human rights recognized and protected by the Convention, whether committed by State or non-State actors.[60] Significantly, the duty to ensure protected human rights and freedoms places a positive legal duty on State Parties to the Convention to protect individuals from the harmful acts and omissions of not only the State or its representatives but also private institutions.[60] The general obligation to ensure protected human rights consists of four principal State obligations:

- a duty to prevent;
- a duty to investigate;
- a duty to punish;
- a duty to remedy.[60]

Jus inter gentes governments have an international legal obligation "to take reasonable steps to prevent human rights violations" by public and private actors.[60] The duty to prevent includes all those means of an administrative, legal, and political nature that promote the protection of human rights and guarantee that any violations are considered and treated as illegal acts, which must lead to the punishment of those responsible and the legal duty to indemnify the victims for damages.[60,62,63]

On April 27, 2021, the OHCHR affirmed "that States should take measures to prevent human rights violations and abuses perpetrated" by State and non-State actors during the state of emergency. The OHCHR further reminded States that claims of such violations and abuses "should be investigated with a view to putting an end to the violation, bringing offenders to justice, and providing victims with protection and effective remedies."[20]

In terms of prevailing international law, it was and is illegal for any government to make COVID-19 vaccine passports mandatory or to allow non-State actors such as transnational corporations to make COVID-19 vaccine passports mandatory. Vaccine passports derogate the non-derogable fundamental human right to freedom from medical or scientific experimentation without free consent.[61]

Chapter Conclusion

In COVID-19 modernity, the Western public health establishment has illicitly refused citizens the basic human right to provide free and informed consent for the experimental mRNA COVID-19 vaccinations. Citizens were also deterred from gaining the information needed to recognize benefits and risks of the COVID-19 injections and their alternatives due to pervasive censorship and misinformation spread by authorities, public health bureaucrats and media.[46]

The pandemic has again shown governments' propensity to abuse fundamental human rights during a state of emergency. Some point out that state of emergency declarations is chiefly "deployed for the sake of preserving authoritarianism."[8,9] Considering the fact that major G20 nations are derogating non-derogable rights through vaccination passports, the safeguards from the unique legal status of non-derogable rights appear to be anemic, at best, during the COVID-19 pandemic. Obtaining an understanding of the correlation between non-derogability and emergency status is crucial to prevent further abuses and contraventions of IHRL.[12,19]

Vaccine mandates without any data or evidence on long-term safety, especially when the risks of either suffering acute illness or death from COVID-19 are close to zero for the vast majority of the population, would already be unlawful in terms of prevailing international human rights norms. Vaccine mandates in the face of overwhelming data and evidence that the COVID-19 vaccines being mandated neither confer sterilized nor near-sterilized immunity, nor prevent the spread of COVID-19, are patently absurd and devoid of any reason.

While it is common to encourage children to be vaccinated before attending public school, the calculus for mandating a COVID-19 vaccine is different. Vaccines such as the mumps, measles and rubella vaccine, the polio vaccine, and others all provide sterilizing or near-sterilizing immunity and have an important role in protecting human lives. These protections have resulted from a thorough tradition of testing combined with long-term assessment over periods of five, 10, and 15 years to establish both safety and efficacy. The COVID-19 vaccines do not have such a record of either safety or efficacy to warrant the large-scale vaccination in a bioethically responsible manner.[63-68]

From even the most conservative viewpoint of law and justice, the right not to be subjected to torture, cruel and inhumane treatment, and medical or scientific experimentation without free consent can "safely be considered as having attained the *jus cogens* status" to be respected by all States at all times, with no exceptions.[12,19] The denial of certain rights fundamental to human dignity, such as the right to free and informed consent to medical experimentation, must never be derogated in any conceivable emergency. Even apart from contravening international public law, making COVID-19 vaccines mandatory without medium- and long-term data was a mistake. Vaccine safety is fundamental to maintaining the public's trust in vaccines; mandating a vaccine with no medium- and long-term safety and efficacy data could have far-reaching ramifications.[64,65]

International human rights standards are explicit that all people should be afforded their non-derogable fundamental human right to free and informed consent and right of refusal in relation to any experimental medical procedure.[18] Respect for this fundamental right is essential to ensure the enjoyment of non-derogable rights and to provide an effective remedy against their violation.

Vaccine mandates are illegal and a gross violation of *jus cogens*, derogating norms from which no derogation is permitted. Normative legal and ethical perspectives dictate that State Parties should not make COVID-19 vaccination mandatory, nor allow citizens to be coerced into taking the COVID-19 vaccine by non-State actors in breach of international legal obligations.

8. PROOF OF COVID-19 VACCINATION TO ATTEND SCHOOL: A BIOMEDICAL ETHICAL PERSPECTIVE

"History shows that where ethics and economics come in conflict, victory is always with economics. Vested interests have never been known to have willingly divested themselves unless there was sufficient force to compel them."

— B. R. Ambedkar

Ethics seeks to find rational, reliable, and justifiable solutions to moral dilemmas. Judging medical interventions through the lens of medical ethics provides a simple, straightforward, and politically neutral approach to finding acceptable solutions and guiding prudent public health policy.[1] Although ethics, the study of morally acceptable standards of behavior and ethical judgment, should be seen as a branch of science, ethical laws are distinct from scientific laws. Ethical laws are dogmatic and prescriptive, and they dictate what ought to be. Ethical laws are normative, asserting standards and principles that need to be followed.[2]

Biomedical ethics is the interdisciplinary study of ethical issues emerging from medical advancements and their impact on society, public health policy, and medical practice.[2] Biomedical ethical normative standards should inform both public health policy and guidelines during times of crisis management and all experimental interventions.[2]

The origin of modern bioethics dates to the drafting of the Nuremberg code that followed the atrocities committed by German doctors in the name of public health in Nazi Germany. The principles of modern biomedical ethics emerged from two primary sources. The first was the Belmont Report of the National Commission for the Protection of Human Subjects of Biomedical and Behavioral Research, which was created by an Act of the US Congress in 1974 and charged with "identifying the basic ethical principles that should underlie the conduct of biomedical and behavioral research involving human subjects and developing guidelines."[2] The second was the book entitled "Principles of Biomedical Ethics" by James F. Childress and Tom L. Beauchamp.[3,4]

The four principles of Beauchamp and Childress – autonomy, beneficence, justice and non-maleficence– have been prominent in the area of biomedical ethics and are essential for understanding the contemporary approach to ethical assessment in healthcare."[2-4] Their approach is known as the principles or four-principles approach to biomedical ethics. The principles provide the most universal and complete norms intended to guide medical ethical actions. The difference between principles and rules is that "rules are more specific in content and more restricted in scope than principles."[3]

Across the United States, Europe, Australia, New Zealand, and Canada, many colleges and universities required proof of vaccination for all students attending in-person classes in 2021 and 2022, essentially making COVID-19 vaccines mandatory. This chapter provides perspective on whether the COVID-19 practice to mandate students to be vaccinated as a pre-condition to study is ethical in terms of the four principles.

To judge the four principles within the context of the COVID-19 vaccine mandates to attend school, it is necessary to first consider all the relevant facts that include the rationale for mandating COVID-19 vaccines to attend school and the relevant medical science and data applicable to children.

The Avowed Rationale for Mandating COVID-19 Vaccines to Attend School

As again demonstrated during the COVID-19 pandemic, almost all medical professionals in the United States blindly followed the recommendations of the CDC in treating their patients. During 2021 and 2022, the CDC maintained its recommendation that everyone five years and older "should get a COVID-19 vaccination to help protect against COVID-19". According to the CDC:

> Getting a COVID-19 vaccination can help protect your child from getting COVID-19. Early information shows that the vaccines may help keep people from spreading COVID-19 to others. They can also

help keep your child from getting seriously sick even if they do get COVID-19. Widespread vaccination is a critical tool to help stop the pandemic.[5]

For this recommendation to be rational, reasonable, and ethical public policy, the hypothesis is thus that:

i.   Children are at risk of becoming seriously ill from COVID-19 and therefore need to be protected through vaccination.

ii. Children are responsible for the transmission of SARS-CoV-2 and therefore other children, vulnerable children, teachers, parents, and grandparents need to be protected through the vaccination of children to keep children from spreading COVID-19 to others.

iii. Vaccinating children is critical to achieve herd immunity and can be achieved given that children are a substantial part of the population.

iv. COVID-19 vaccines are effective and preventing people from contracting and transmitting SARS-CoV-2.

v.   COVID-19 vaccines are safe and adverse events are extremely rare.

The Relevant Medical Science and Data applicable to Students[¶]

i). Are children at risk of becoming seriously ill from COVID-19?

Very early in the pandemic, doctors and policymakers became aware that COVID-19 is much less dangerous for children than for adults and the elderly.[1] In fact, a vital aspect of the pandemic was that children and young people were infected by SARS-CoV-2 far less frequently than adults and, when infected, typically had no symptoms at all or mild symptoms.[1,6-9]

A general pattern has been reported from multiple countries: that children who test positive for COVID-19 experience no symptoms or a mild form of the disease. It follows that children and younger adults have a much lower risk of severe forms of COVID-19 than other age groups.[10-12] Children have

---

¶ Given the CDC's disqualifying conflicts of interest as co-owners of numerous COVID-19 vaccine patents that directly profit from the sale of COVID-19 vaccines any research conducted by and funded by the CDC and/or their corporate partners is not a credible source of independent, objective, academic research.

a different reaction to the SARS-CoV-2 virus compared to adults. Children and adults' immune systems are different with respect to their makeup and functional receptiveness.[13]

COVID-19's case fatality and crude mortality rate for children ranges between 0.003% and 0.0003%, respectively, and in the case of healthy children with no co-morbidities, it is 0%.[10] A total of 99.997% of all school children under the age of 18 who contract COVID-19 will have mild to no symptoms and survive.[10]

It is an irrefutable medical fact that children are not at risk of acute ailment from COVID-19.[9] A detailed State-level data report by the American Academy of Pediatrics published during September 2020 showed that:

> Children were 0.00%-0.19% of all COVID-19 deaths, and 10 [US] State's reported zero child deaths. In State's reporting, 0.00%-0.003% of all child COVID-19 cases resulted in death.[10]

According to a March 2022 report published by the Murdoch Children's Research Institute, Finland has demonstrated that there have been zero COVID-19 deaths in young people throughout the entire pandemic.[14] A December 2021 German study assessed the absolute risk of COVID for children and presented the following statistics regarding healthy children and COVID-19 in Germany:

- For healthy children, the risk of going to the hospital is 51 per 100,000.
- For healthy children, the risk of going to the ICU is eight per 100,000.
- For healthy children, the risk of death is three per 1,000,000 with no deaths reported in children older than 5.
- Children 5 to 11 have a lower risk than children younger than five and adolescents 12 to 17.
- Children 5 to 11 have a risk of going to the ICU of two in 100,000.
- Zero children died.[15]

This data correlates with and corroborates data across the globe since early in 2020. Children are at the lowest risk from COVID, at least not any more at risk than from other common viruses similar to the flu, many of which are types of coronaviruses. A peer-reviewed study from July 2021 concluded that your risks of dying from COVID-19 if you are infected with it, in the following age groups is:

- 0-19 = 0.0027%
- 20-29 = 0.014%
- 30-39 = 0.031%
- 40-49 = 0.082%
- 50-59 = 0.27%
- 60-69 = 0.59%
- 70+ = 2.4%[16]

Children and young people are not at risk of becoming seriously ill from COVID-19.[12] There is, therefore, no medical basis or rationale for vaccinating school and college students against COVID-19 "to protect them" or "keep them safe."

ii.) Are children responsible for the transmission of SARS-CoV-2?

A further cardinal question to determine the credibility of the CDC recommendation to vaccinate all children above the age of five is the ability of infected children to spread SARS-CoV-2. Numerous independent peer-reviewed studies have shown that children and young people do not readily transmit the SARS-CoV-2 virus, and the theory of symptomless spread has been debunked, especially for children.[12-23]

In May 2020, it was already well known that children do not readily spread the SARS-CoV-2 virus. A medical meta-analysis research paper that reviewed more than 700 scientific research articles published in May 2020 found that: "Opening up schools and kindergartens is unlikely to impact COVID-19 mortality rates in older people."[12]

The medical and scientific data perspicuously show that school children, if infected, do not spread SARS-CoV-2 to other children or adults in any significant way.[17-22] Several international family cluster studies "found that children were not likely to be the index case in households, only being responsible for around 10% of infections."[17,18] Data from Guangzhou, China, have "supported this, finding an even lower rate of children as index cases in households at 5%."[19] A case study of a cluster in France included a child with COVID-19 "who failed to transmit it to any other person, despite exposure to more than a hundred children."[17,20] In a school study from New South Wales, Australia, a proportion of 863 close contacts of nine children and nine teachers were followed for seroconversion as a marker of recent exposure.[17] No evidence of children infecting teachers were found.[17,21] "In the Netherlands, separate data from primary care and household studies suggest SARS-CoV-2 is mainly spread between adults and from adult family members to children."[17] In the Republic of Ireland, results echo the experience of other countries, where children are not considerable drivers of the transmission of COVID-19. In a study among 1,001 child contacts, there were no confirmed cases of COVID-19. The study found "no evidence of secondary transmission of COVID-19 from children attending school in Ireland."[23] A comprehensive study in Sweden comparing the differences in infection rates of children, parents, and teachers in open and closed school settings also found statistically insignificant differences between open and closed school system infection, hospitalization, and mortality rates per 1,000 of the population.[24] In a study done in the federal State of Baden-Württemberg in southwest Germany, which has a population of 10.8 million, researchers assessed the viral transmission role of SARS-CoV-2-infected children who attended schools and childcare facilities after reopening. The researchers concluded that child-to-child transmission in schools and childcare facilities is uncommon and not the primary cause of SARS-CoV-2 infection in children.[25]

The fact that symptomless COVID-19 cases are not responsible for the spread of the SARS-CoV-2 virus has been well documented and researched.[26] A comprehensive study "involving SARS-CoV-2 nucleic acid screening in nearly 10 million residents of Wuhan, China," with regards to the symptomless contagion of COVID-19, showed zero instances of symptomless infection.[26] The researchers found that:

> Compared with symptomatic patients, asymptomatic infected persons generally have low quantity of viral loads and a short duration of viral shedding, which decrease the transmission risk of SARS-CoV-2.

> All close contacts of the asymptomatic positive cases tested negative, indicating that the asymptomatic positive cases detected in this study were unlikely to be infectious.[26]

In a further study investigating SARS-CoV-2 transmission in US childcare workers, researchers compared the spread of SARS-CoV-2 in childcare workers who continued with direct in-person childcare during the first three months of the COVID-19 pandemic in the United States of America with those who did not. Data were collected from 57,335 US childcare workers reporting whether they had ever tested positive for COVID-19 along with their level of exposure to childcare. The researchers found that:

No association was found between exposure to childcare and COVID-19... exposure to childcare during the early months of the US pandemic was not associated with an elevated risk for COVID-19 transmission to providers.[27]

The hypothesis that students are responsible for the substantial community spread of SARS-CoV-2 at school and other public venues is incorrect.

iii.) Is vaccinating children critical to achieve herd immunity?

Historically, vaccinations with effective vaccines ensured that a large portion of the population-maintained immunity to certain contagious diseases.

The disputation that States can only get to herd immunity by vaccinating children is preposterous. Children can become naturally infected as they do with other pathogens that cause innocuous infections.[23,28]

Children have a 99.997% probability of recovering from COVID-19 and will have no to only mild symptoms while at the same time developing naturally acquired immunity that is superior to that which might be caused by a vaccine.[28,29] An authoritative Israeli study published at the end of August 2021 showed that natural immunity was 13 times stronger than having two doses of the Pfizer-BioNTech inoculation. This study again clearly demonstrated that natural immunity confers longer lasting and significantly more robust protection against infection, symptomatic disease, hospitalization, and death.[30] Inexplicably, public health officials have consistently downplayed and ignored natural immunity among children. By October 2021, 81 peer-reviewed research studies confirmed that natural immunity to COVID-19 is equal or superior to any vaccine-induced immunity.[31]

Students becoming naturally infected with a disease that poses no risk to them would accelerate the development of herd immunity.[28,29] No mass vaccinations of children and young people are reasonably required to combat a disease with a population-level crude mortality rate ranging between 0.0003% and 0.3%.[28,32,33]

iv.) Are the COVID-19 vaccines effective at preventing children from contracting and transmitting COVID-19?

As set out in detail in Chapter 4, following the most extensive mass vaccination campaign in human history and numerous countries across the globe achieving vaccination rates in excess of 65% to 85% of the population, the indisputable medical and scientific facts are that the COVID-19 vaccines do not prevent people from contracting COVID-19 nor from them transmitting the disease to others.

As broached in Chapter 4, a "comprehensive study published at the end of September 2021 in the "European Journal of Epidemiology" that investigated the relationship between the percentage of the population fully vaccinated and new COVID-19 cases across 68 countries and 2,947 counties in the United States" concluded that:

> There appears to be no discernable relationship between percentage of population fully vaccinated and new COVID-19 cases... In fact, the trend line suggests ... that countries with higher percentage of population fully vaccinated have higher COVID-19 cases per 1 million people.[7]

COVID-19 vaccines are ineffective at preventing children from contracting or transmitting SARS-CoV-2, which renders any recommendation to vaccinate children absurd and devoid of reason.

The efficacy of COVID-19 vaccines is so dismal that, according to some researchers, these vaccines do not meet the legal definition of a vaccine. A vaccine is legally defined as any substance intended to be administered to an individual for the prevention of one or more diseases. A January 2000 patent application that defined vaccines as "compositions or mixtures that when introduced into the circulatory system of an animal will evoke a protective response to a pathogen" was rejected by the US Patent Office in light of the fact that "The immune response produced by a vaccine must be more than merely some immune response but must be protective. As noted in the previous Office Action, the article recognizes the term 'vaccine' to be a compound which prevents infection."[32]

By the end of 2021, many eminent medical researchers use the term "inoculated" rather than vaccinated when referring to COVID-19 vaccines, given that the COVID-19 inoculations prevent neither viral infection nor transmission of SARS-CoV-2, and their function in real-world circumstances appears at best to be a "medical treatment" that leads to symptom suppression and at worst an experimental inoculation with significant potentially lethal adverse events.[32]

v) Are the COVID-19 vaccines safe and adverse events extremely rare?

On May 16, 2022, the UK Office for National Statistics (ONS) distributed a dataset including specifics on "deaths by vaccination status in England" between January 1, 2021, and March 31, 2022. The dataset comprises several tables illustrating details such as, "Monthly age-standardized mortality rates by vaccination status for deaths involving COVID-19," and "Monthly age-standardized mortality rates by vaccination status for non-COVID-19 deaths."[34] The data shows that between those dates, double-vaccinated children aged 10 to 14 "were statistically up to 39 times more likely to die than unvaccinated children, and double vaccinated teenagers aged 15 to 19 were statistically up to four times more likely to die than unvaccinated teenagers."[34-36]

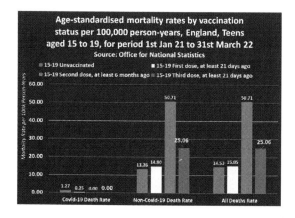

Figure 8.1: Aged standardized mortality rates by vaccination status per 100 000 person years, England, teens aged 15-19 January 1, 2022 – March 31, 2022. Source: Office National Statistics, The Expose

However, it is the triple injected statistics that are genuinely startling when it comes to children. The ONS data indicate that between January 1, 2021, and March 31, 2022, triple injected "children aged 10 to 14 were statistically 303 times more likely to die" than unvaccinated children of COVID-19, "69 times more likely to die of any cause other than COVID-19 than unvaccinated children, and 82 times more likely to die of all-causes than unvaccinated children."[34-36]

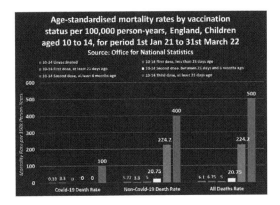

Figure 8.2: Aged standardized mortality rates by vaccination status per 100,000 person years, England, children aged 10-14 January 1, 2022 – March 31, 2022.
Source: Office of National Statistics, The Expose

This implies that three doses of a COVID-19 vaccination increase the risk of all-cause mortality for children "by an average of 8,100%, and the risk of dying of COVID-19 by an average of 30,200%" whilst two doses of the COVID-19 vaccine increase the risk of all-cause mortality "by an average of 3,600%."[34-36]

Official mortality statistics from 29 European countries further show that there has been a disturbing 691% surge in excess deaths among children since the European Medicines Agency (EMA) granted the EUA of the COVID-19 vaccine for children aged 12 to 15 in May 2021.[37]

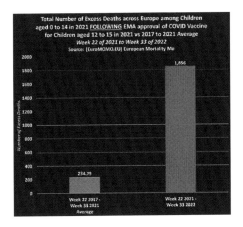

Figure 8.3: Total number of excess deaths among children aged 0-14 in 2021 following the EMA Approval
Source: EuroMomo.EU, The Expose.

According to Dr. Michael Yeadon, "COVID-19 gene-based 'vaccines' are toxic. The basic rules of selecting vaccine candidates are the agent has no inherent biological action (non-toxic); the agent should be the genetically most stable part of the virus; and the agent should be most different from human proteins. Spike protein used as the vaccine does not fit any of these criteria."[38]

Biomedical Ethical Considerations**

As alluded to at the beginning of the chapter, "ethics is the application of values and moral rules to human activities."[3-5] By distinction, biomedical ethics is a subsection of ethics that uses ethical principles and decision-making for solving actual or anticipated dilemmas in medicine and biology.[39-41]

In terms of the four-principles approach, biomedical ethics is based on four joint, moral commitments: respect for autonomy, beneficence, non-malefi-cence, and justice that offers a universal, essential moral analytical framework and principles that should compel policymakers, doctors, and other healthcare workers to make morally sound decisions.[40] If any one of the principles is violated by a medical intervention it would be deemed unethical and immoral.

a) Respect for Autonomy

Individual autonomy "refers to self-governance, to self-rule that is free from both controlling interference by others and from limitations, such as inade-quate understanding, that prevent meaningful choice."[39] Respect for autonomy is the moral duty to respect the autonomy and freedom of others.[39-42]

In his book "Four Principles' Approach to Healthcare Ethics", Tom Beauchamp asserts that:

> To respect an autonomous agent is to recognize with due appreciation that person's capacities and perspectives, including his or her right to hold certain views, to make certain choices and to take certain actions based on personal beliefs.[43]

** Portions of this chapter are republications of the content of a peer-reviewed article by the author Dr. Willem van Aardt, entitled "The Mandatory COVID-19 Vaccination of School Children: A Bioethical and Human Rights Assessment" published in the Journal of Vaccines and Vaccination in 2021.

Autonomy is the capability of a patient to act of their own free will. In the context of biomedical ethics, it is an ethical principle that patients should be given accurate information to make free and informed decisions regarding their own healthcare. Autonomy in biomedical ethics is built into the legal standard of "informed consent," which requires that all patients be informed of the risks of any medical mediation and be free to decline medical mediations.[3]

As postulated by Beauchamp and Childress, the principle of respect for autonomy entails various more specific moral rules that include:

- Telling the truth.
- Respecting the privacy of others.
- Protecting confidential information.
- Obtaining informed consent.
- Helping others to make important decisions when asked to do so.[3,40-43]

To require students to be vaccinated under the pretext that COVID-19 poses a grave mortal danger to students is simply not the truth – it is a blatant lie and unethical! Requiring students to disclose their vaccination status as a pre-condition to attend school violates the specific rules relating to privacy and confidentiality.

To require proof of vaccination to attend school, in effect coercing and forcing students to get vaccinated with an experimental vaccine (with no medium- or long-term safety and efficacy data), contravenes the moral obligation to respect the patient's right to free and informed consent. It also violates the Nuremberg Code, the WMA code of conduct, the WHO Guidance for Managing Ethical Issues in Infectious Disease Outbreaks, the UDBHR, and the European Union Convention on Human Rights and Biomedicine which all determine that the voluntary consent of the human subject is essential, and no one may be coerced to participate in a medical procedure without their free and informed consent.[28]

From a medical ethical perspective, the COVID-19 practice to vaccinate students under threat and duress, against a disease that poses no risk to them, with a vaccine proven to be neither safe nor effective, is highly unethical and morally reprehensible.

Beneficence and Non-Maleficence

The Hippocratic apothegm to physicians, "Bring benefit and do no harm," expresses the principles of beneficence ("bring benefit") and nonmaleficence ("do no harm").[3] This Hippocratic dictum has long been a vital principle of biomedical ethics. French physiologist Claude Bernard (1813-1878) extended it to the sphere of research, stating that one should not injure one person irrespective of the benefits that might come to others.

b) Beneficence

Beneficence in biomedical ethics describes the principle that medical interferences should be done to the patient's benefit. This limits permissible medical interferences so as not to include interferences that benefit only the medical providers, public health institutions, the pharmaceutical industry, or the public at large. The pervasive COVID-19 era practice where major public health policy is largely driven by the political and financial benefit of the global elite is highly unethical.

The principle of beneficence "asserts the [positive] duty to help others further their important and legitimate interests."[3] In terms of the principle of beneficence:

- A medical professional must prevent evil or harm.
- A medical professional must remove evil or harm.
- A medical professional must do or promote good.

As asserted by Beauchamp and Childress, the principle of beneficence also contains several more specific moral rules which include:

- Defending and protecting the rights of others.
- Preventing injury or harm from happening to others.
- Eliminating conditions that will cause injury or harm to others.
- Assisting individuals with disabilities.
- Rescuing individuals in danger.[3,40-43]

Research clearly demonstrates that there is no benefit to children getting a COVID-19 vaccine, and that in reality, the COVID-19 vaccines can cause probable harm, adverse effects, and even death. According to Pfizer's own research trial data, the probability of death in children from the COVID-19 vaccines is 107 times higher than death from COVID. [36] In December 2021, the UK ONS dataset containing details on "deaths by vaccination status in England" per 100,000 people between January 1, 2021, and October 31, 2021, showed that "vaccinated children aged 10 to 14 were statistically 10 times more likely to die than unvaccinated children, and vaccinated teenagers aged 15 to 19 were statistically twice as likely to die than unvaccinated teenagers."[36] The ONS data further revealed "teenagers aged 15 to 19 who had two COVID-19 vaccines were statistically three times more likely to die than unvaccinated teenagers, while children aged 10 to 14 who were double vaccinated were statistically 52 times more likely to die than unvaccinated children."[36]

The fact that medical practitioners continue to recommend the Pfizer vaccine in the face of trial data showing "that the COVID-19 vaccines kill more people than they save is irreconcilable with the principle of beneficence."[33,44-46] It is evident to any objective observer that in the COVID-19 era, where we are witnessing medical practitioners refusing to treat patients with cheap lifesaving effective drugs such as Ivermectin, while profiting financially by actively coercing children to be vaccinated with COVID-19 vaccines (that have side-effects that include blood clots, heart attacks, myocarditis, antibody-dependent enhancement, acquired immunodeficiency syndrome, and death), that the ethical principle relating to beneficence is pro-actively being violated on a grand scale by thousands of medical professionals around the globe.

c) Nonmaleficence

The principle of non-maleficence refers to the duty to refrain from causing harm. It underlies the medical maxim *primum non nocere*: "above all do no harm."[3]

The principle of non-maleficence exclaims, "One ought not to inflict evil or harm," to another. As advocated by Beauchamp and Childress, the principle of non-maleficence also contains several more specific moral rules which include:

- Do not kill.
- Do not cause pain or suffering.
- Do not incapacitate.
- Do not offend.
- Do not deprive others of the goods of life.[3]

Independent analysis of the US pharmacovigilance indicated that between December 14, 2020 and May 7, 2021, more than 190,000 adverse events and 4,057 deaths were reported to the US Vaccine Adverse Event Reporting System or VAERS.[46-48] There were more COVID-19 vaccine-related deaths in less than five months than deaths from all other vaccines over a period of 15 years.[46] The causal connection between the COVID-19 vaccines and adverse events are indisputable when applying the Bradford Hill Criteria.[49,50] Shortly after commencing the mass COVID-19 vaccination campaigns safety signals indicated that the vaccines cause harm and excess deaths.

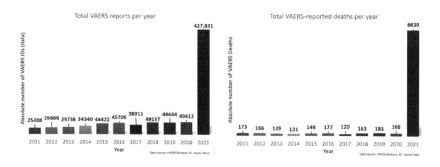

Figure 8.4: Bar plots showing the number of VAERS reports (left)
and reported deaths (right) per year for the past decade (2021 is partial data set)
Source: VAERS, Dr Jessica Rose[48]

Following a detailed analysis of the VAERS database during 2021, Dr. Jessica Rose, in her seminal article "Critical Appraisal of VAERS Pharmacovigilance: Is the U.S. Vaccine Adverse Events Reporting System (VAERS) a Functioning Pharmacovigilance System?" concluded that:

> It cannot be stressed enough when referring to VAERS data collected in the context of the COVID-19 injectable products that effective antiviral responses against the nCoV-2019 virus in the form of both cellular and humoral immune responses have been reported in peer-reviewed studies. Because of the low Infection Fatality Rate, indicating effective and robust immune responses, it remains unclear why multiple experimental mRNA vaccines have been fast-tracked through conventional testing protocols and are also being fast-tracked through production and administration into the public. With repurposed drugs like hydroxychloroquine and Ivermectin showing extremely positive results in patients, it is also unclear why these drugs are not being more extensively promoted as effective tools in the fight against this virus. What is clear is that the injectable products are proving unsafe for many individuals and inefficacious in others.[48]

Across the globe at the end of 2021, it has been widely reported that young men developed heart muscle inflammation, called myocarditis, following the COVID-19 vaccine, and the world had witnessed an unprecedented number of young and healthy athletes collapsing and dying while playing sports.[51,52]

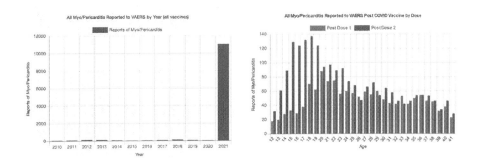

Figure 8.5: All Myo/Pericarditis reported to VAERS by year
Figure 8.6: All Myo/Pericarditis reported to VAERS post COVID-19 vaccine dose
Source: VAERS, European Journal of Preventive Cardiology

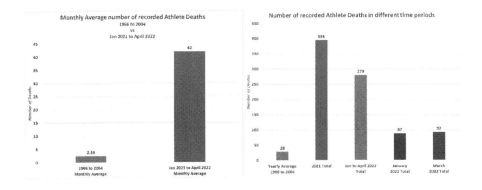

Figure 8.7: Monthly average number of recorded athlete deaths
Figure 8.8: Number of recorded athlete deaths in different Time Periods
Source: VAERS, European Journal of Preventive Cardiology, The Expose

Data published by the ONS show that between January 2021 and January 2022, double vaccinated 18- to 39-year-olds were on average 92% more likely to die than unvaccinated young adults.[53]

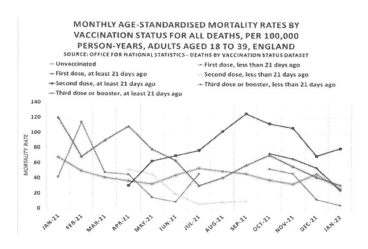

Figure 8.9: Monthly Age-Standardized Mortality Rates by Vaccination Status for all Deaths, Per 100,000 Person-Years, Adults
Source: Office for National Statistics, The Expose

By January 2021, the death rate per 100,000 person-years among the unvaccinated equated to 67.7. For individuals who had received one dose of the COVID-19 vaccine at least 21 days prior to their demise, the death rate per 100,000 person-years equated to 119.9 or 77% higher than the death rate amongst the unvaccinated. This decreased to 68.3 deaths per 100,000 in February 2021, before increasing to 90.1 in March 2021, then 108.8 in April 2021. At this point, the death rate amongst the partly vaccinated was 193.3% higher than the death rate amongst the unvaccinated.[53] The highest death rate amongst the double vaccinated occurred in September 2021, with 125.9 deaths per 100,000 person-years. In the same month, the death rate amongst the unvaccinated equated to 46.8. The double vaccinated mortality rate was therefore 169% higher than the unvaccinated death rate.[53] By the end of January 2022, there had been more than 1000 peer-reviewed papers evidencing a multitude of serious adverse events in COVID-19 vaccine recipients.[54] By March 18, 2022, the VAERS showed that there were unprecedented increases in recorded deaths and injuries following COVID-19 vaccines for the past 15 months since they were issued EUA's, as compared to recorded deaths and injuries reported following all FDA-approved vaccines for the previous 30 years:

- 68,000% increase in strokes.
- 44,000% increase in heart disease.
- 6,800% increase in deaths.
- 5,700% increase in permanent disabilities.
- 5,000% increase in life threatening injuries.
- 4,400% increase in hospitalizations.[55]

According to Emeritus Professor of Medical Ethics at Imperial College London, Professor Raanan Gillon, "the conventional moral imperative of medicine is to provide net medical benefit to patients with minimal injury."[42] The practical application of non-maleficence is for public health officials to weigh the benefits against burdens of all interventions and treatments, abandon those potentially inappropriately burdensome, and choose the best course of action for the patient.[41] To achieve this moral objective, public health policy-makers are obligated to ensure that their policies and recommendations can, in fact, provide the benefits they profess to be able to provide.[3,40-42] Whenever public health officials attempt to help others, they inevitably risk harming them. Public health officials committed to helping others must therefore consider the principles of beneficence and non-maleficence together.[39,40]

In order to provide each patient with a net benefit, it is essential to consider each patient's unique circumstances and medical condition. What represents a benefit for one patient may be harmful to another.[3,41] For example, an experimental COVID-19 vaccine may constitute a prospective net benefit for those above 85 or people with co-morbidities, while for children that are not at risk from COVID-19, it provides no benefit at all while introducing risk, given the fact that there are no medium or long-term safety and efficacy data available. The responsibility to provide a net benefit to patients also requires public health policymakers and medical practitioners to be clear about risk and probability in assessing harm and benefit.[42]

From a net benefit perspective, children have close to zero risks of severe ailment or death and thus no benefit from the vaccine but are exposed to potentially significant adverse side-effects from the COVID- 19 vaccines.[28,58]

In a comprehensive peer-reviewed study examining COVID-19 inoculations for children, the researchers performed a cost-benefit analysis and found as follows:

> Thus, our extremely conservative estimate for risk-benefit ratio is about 5/1. In plain English, people in the 65+ demographic are five times as

likely to die from the inoculation as from COVID-19 under the most favorable assumptions! This demographic is the most vulnerable to adverse effects from COVID-19. As the age demographics go below about 35 years old, the chances of death from COVID-19 become very small, and when they go below 18, become negligible.

It should be remembered that the deaths from the inoculations shown in VAERS are short-term only (˜six months for those inoculated initially), and for children, extremely short-term (˜one month). Intermediate and long-term deaths remain to be identified, and are possible from ADE, autoimmune effects, further clotting and vascular diseases, etc., that take time to develop. Thus, the long-term cost-benefit ratio under the best-case scenario could well be on the order of 10/1, 20/1, or more for all the demographics, increasing with decreasing age, and an order-of-magnitude higher under real-world scenarios! In summary, the value of these COVID-19 inoculations is not obvious from a cost-benefit perspective for the most vulnerable age demographic and is not obvious from any perspective for the least vulnerable age demographic."[32]

A study conducted by scientists from the California University, Harvard University, Johns Hopkins University, Oxford University, and the University of Toronto published in September 2022, confirmed that the COVID-19 vaccines were up to 98 times worse than the virus itself. The researchers criticized the booster mandates for American university students in the fall of 2022, stating that the COVID-19 booster mandates may cause a net expected harm:

> …per[1]hospitalization prevented in previously uninfected young adults, we anticipate 18 to 98 serious adverse events, including 1.7 to 3.0 booster-associated myocarditis cases in males, and 1,373 to 3,234 cases of grade ≥3 reactogenicity which interferes with daily activities.[56]

Contrasting the fact that children are not at risk even when contracting COVID-19 with the significant risks and known adverse events associated with COVID-19 vaccines (that include blood clots, heart attacks, myocarditis, antibody-dependent enhancement, and death), it would be impossible to credibly argue that COVID-19 vaccines present children and young people with a net benefit. COVID-19 vaccine passports violate the principles relating to both beneficence and non-maleficence.

d) Justice

The principle of formal justice is universal to all theories of justice and is usually ascribed to Aristotle. Justice in healthcare is commonly interpreted as requiring fair, equitable, and appropriate treatment of persons or, as Aristotle said, "Giving to each that which is his due." Who should be given the benefits of medical research and bear its burdens? This is a matter of justice, in the sense of what is deserved or "fairness in distribution." An injustice ensues when some benefit to which a person is entitled is refused without good reason or when some burden is imposed unjustifiably.[3,40-43] There are several widely accepted interpretations of just ways to distribute burdens and benefits. These include:

- To each individual an equal share.
- To each individual according to individual need.
- To each individual according to individual effort.
- To each individual according to societal contribution.
- To each individual according to merit.

Another way of conceiving the principle of justice is that equals ought to be treated equally. However, Aristotle argued that justice is more than mere equality. People can be treated unjustly even if they are treated equally. It is crucial to treat equals equally and to treat unequal's unequally in proportion to the morally relevant inequalities.[3,41-43]

In the context of the COVID-19 response, it is essential to point out that equality is at the heart of justice. To treat children and young adults who are not at risk of serious illness from SARS-CoV-2 the same as 75- to 95-year-old at-risk sections of the population is unnecessary, irrational, unreasonable, and unethical.[28]

Chapter Conclusion

More than a thousand years prior to the lifetime and teachings of Hippocrates (called the father of Western medicine), medicine in pre-1000 BCE Mesopotamia was a well-established profession that included diagnosis, pharmaceutical applications, and the proper treatment of wounds.[57] The practices of *asu* physicians were so widespread and commonplace that their services and fees were regulated by law. The Babylonian Code of Hammurabi (*circa* 1950 BC) that *inter alia* had legal rules relating to the punishment for malpractice as well as proper payment for physicians, governed that:

If the doctor has treated a man for a severe wound with lances of bronze and has caused the man to die or has opened an abscess of the eye for a man and has caused the loss of the man's eye, one shall cut off his hands.

If he has opened his abscess with a bronze lance and has made him lose his eye, he shall pay money, half his price.[58,59]

Such regulations point on the one hand to established medical treatment, but on the other, in the inclusion of biomedical treatment among "injuries," was an attempt to apply the *lex talionis* – the legal *quid pro quo* principle – to medical practice. If this ancient code that included corporal punishment for "errors of omission or commission" would have been applied today, we would have millions of bankrupt medical practitioners without hands!

Despite it being settled science from very early on in the COVID-19 pandemic that children are not at risk from COVID-19 and that children are not responsible for spreading the disease in any meaningful way, universities, colleges, and schools across the globe have implemented COVID-19 vaccination policies targeting students. These policies continued to be implemented when emerging scientific evidence on the real-world effectiveness of COVID-19 vaccines proved that the COVID-19 vaccines prevented neither infection nor transmission and that the potential harms significantly outweighed any potential benefits.

The implementation of these policies by medical practitioners is unethical and immoral, measured against the four biomedical ethical principles of autonomy, non-maleficence, beneficence, and justice.

In addition, these unethical policies are a direct violation of various international bioethical and human rights norms cited in Chapter 3, including:

- The Nuremberg Code, which states that "The voluntary consent of the human subject is essential. This means that the person involved should have legal capacity to give consent; should be so situated as to be able to exercise free power of choice, without the intervention of any element of force, fraud, deceit, duress, overreaching, or other ulterior form of constraint or coercion; and should have sufficient knowledge and comprehension of the elements of the subject matter involved as to enable him to make an understanding and enlightened decision."[1,28]
- The WMA's Declaration of Helsinki, the WHO's Guidance for

Managing Ethical Issues in Infectious Disease Outbreaks, the UDBHR, and the European Union Convention on Human Rights and Biomedicine, which specifically determine that any preventive, diagnostic, or therapeutic medical intervention is "to be carried out only with the prior, free, and informed consent of the person concerned," judged on adequate information.[1,28,59]

- The ICCPR, which clearly dictates that "no one shall be subjected without his free consent to medical or scientific experimentation."

International bioethical norms and human rights standards with regard to informed consent for all medical interventions logically apply to the vaccination of students with COVID-19 vaccines, an invasive medical procedure that carries significant known and unknown risks. COVID-19 vaccines are experimental, and parents and students have the right to refuse such a vaccine.[28]

Our children, who are humanity's future, deserve the implementation of evidence-based, ethically sound public health policies in the best interest of children and young people. Each one of the four principles of ethics is to be taken as a *prima facie* obligation that must be fulfilled.[40-43] Whatever the personal philosophy, politics, financial interest, religion, moral theory, or life stance of public health policymakers, they need to commit to uphold and adhere to the four biomedical ethical principles: respect for autonomy, beneficence, non-maleficence, and justice, constantly reflecting on their scope and application.[60]

The public health response to the COVID-19 pandemic again highlights the need for State Parties to abide by universal ethical guidelines and normative standards in the field of bioethics and the need to promote shared values in relation to the formulation and implementation of public health policies. Normative medical ethical perspectives dictate that public health policymakers should not allow children and students to be coerced into taking the COVID-19 vaccines in breach of international biomedical ethical standards.

9. MASK MANDATES: FOLLOWING THE SCIENCE OR IMPOLITIC AND ILLICIT?††

*"There can be no keener revelation of
a society's soul than the way in which it treats its children."*

— Nelson Mandela

Governments worldwide have implemented many nonpharmaceutical interventions (NPIs) to mitigate the spread of severe acute respiratory syndrome coronavirus 2 (SARS-CoV-2). Many countries introduced the mandatory requirement to wear masks to contain SARS-CoV-2.[1] Shocking video evidence from across the Western world surfaced throughout the pandemic, showing police officers violently assaulting, arresting, and jailing citizens for the "crime" of not wearing a mask or not wearing a mask properly.[2,3] In Australia, an elderly man suffered a heart attack while being forcibly arrested for not wearing a mask outdoors while in the United Kingdom a screaming man was violently pinned to the floor by five police officers as he was arrested for refusing to wear a mask in a train station.[4,5]

In most Western nations all students, staff, and teachers were required to wear masks in schools. In the United States, a five-year-old autistic child in

---

†† Portions of this chapter are republications of the content of a peer-reviewed article by the author Dr. Willem van Aardt, entitled "COVID-19 Mask Mandates for School Children - Following the Science or Impolitic?", published in the International Journal of Epidemiology and Public Health Research in January 2022.

Arizona "was prevented from boarding the school bus for not wearing a face mask" while in California a four-year-old child "was removed from school by police after he refused to wear a facemask."[6,7] Never before have billions of children been forced to wear face masks for extended periods of time. Some argue that mask mandates that violate an array of children's fundamental human rights are especially cruel and inhumane to young children and that two years of near permanent mask-wearing scarred them psychologically and physically, with children suffering from hypoxia, Mask-Induced Exhaustion Syndrome (MIES), anxiety, panic attacks, and severe depression while the prolonged pressure from the elastic straps left other young children with permanently protruding ears.[8] By concealing teachers' mouths and dampening their speech, mask-wearing makes it harder for young children to develop crucial linguistic skills and prevents special needs children with hearing impairments from lip-reading.[9] Unable to see important facial expressions, children and teachers misread and misunderstand one other, a particularly dire problem for children with special needs. Children cannot develop social skills when they cannot see one another's faces and facial expressions while interacting.[10]

The CRC and the ICCPR ensure certain basic human rights to all children. Mask mandates infringe on a child's fundamental human right to education directed towards the development of the child's personality, talents, and mental and physical abilities to their fullest potential.[5] Other fundamental human rights infringed by mask mandates include *inter alia*:

- the right of the child to be free from torture or any other cruel, inhumane, and degrading treatment;[11-13]
- the right of the child not to be subjected without his or her free consent to medical or scientific experimentation;[11-13]
- the right of the child to form his or her own views to express those views freely in all matters affecting the child;[11-13]
- the right of the child to freedom of expression;[11-13]
- the right of the child to engage in play and recreational activities appropriate to the age of the child;[11-13]
- the right of the child to be protected from all forms of physical or mental violence, injury or abuse, neglect or negligent treatment, maltreatment, or exploitation;[11-13]
- the right of the child not to be subjected to arbitrary or unlawful interference with his or her privacy.[11,13]

At the start of the pandemic, the CDC, the WHO, British health authorities, and the ECDC all refrained from recommending widespread mask usage, often discouraging it. Dr. Anthony Fauci emailed in February 2020 that the typical mask "is not really effective in keeping out virus, which is small enough to pass through the material." In a March 8 interview on "60 Minutes" he said that "there's no reason to be walking around with a mask."[14] In March 2020, the US Surgeon General stated that face masks, worn by the public at large, were "not effective" in stopping people from getting SARS-CoV-2.[13] The position of the US public health officials (who constantly profess they are merely following the science and the data) changed over time and, as the pandemic developed, the public experienced first-hand the consequences of the politicization of science and the prevalence of government public-health misinformation.[13] The official line across the Western world became that masks must be mandatory for the vaccinated and the unvaccinated, given that the SARS-CoV-2 infection is transmitted predominately by inhaling respiratory droplets generated when people cough, sneeze, sing, talk, or breathe.[13,15]

CDC Director Robert Redfield, MD, touted "Cloth face coverings are one of the most powerful weapons we have to slow and stop the spread of the virus – particularly when used universally within a community setting."[14] Numerous other world leaders and public health officials continually reiterated that they were merely following "the science." Joe Biden even proclaimed that "Wearing masks is not a political statement, it is a scientific imperative."[14]

Across the globe, government officials, mainstream media, and big tech have convinced people that mask mandates are legitimate and that masks effectively prevent the spread of the SARS-CoV-2 virus.[13] But has the "science" regarding mask effectiveness and the legality regarding mask mandates been settled as decisively as we have been directed to believe?[16] In May 2022, a joint statement representing more than 17,000 scientists and medical physicians, for instance, categorically stated that "masks are not and have never been effective protection against an airborne respiratory virus in the community setting."[13,17]

Before investigating the science and IHRL implications of mask mandates it is worth investigating the contemporary COVID-19 epistemological philosophy of "the science" subscribed to by Western health officials.

Following "the Science"

Albert Einstein, widely acknowledged to be one of the greatest physicists of all time and best known for developing the theory of relativity and for his important contributions to the development of the theory of quantum mechanics, said that "Blind belief in authority is the greatest enemy of truth".

In an October 18, 2021 interview, Dr. Anthony Fauci, President Joe Biden's chief medical adviser and the longtime head of the National Institute of Allergies and Infectious Diseases (NIAID), righteously proclaimed that his critics are "really criticizing science because I represent science. ... I have stood for making science, data, and evidence be what we guide ourselves by. ... [B]ecause what I do, I try very hard, is to be guided by the truth...."[18] Yet eminent scientists found no science behind the CDC's mask mandates that Fauci endorsed.

- Dr. Vinay Prasad, MD, MPH, and Associate Professor of Medicine at the University of California San Francisco on June 29, 2021, stated that "The CDC cannot 'follow the science' because there is no relevant science. The proposition is at best science-y; a best guess based on political pressure, pundit anxiety, and mechanistic understanding."[19]
- Dr. Martin Kulldorff, Professor of Medicine at Harvard Medical School on July 13, 2021, affirmed that "Mandating children to wear masks is detrimental to their health, and claimed benefits to public health lack scientific evidence. ... Triple stumble by Fauci: 1. No scientific evidence that masking children is effective; 2. Even if effective, children have low disease risk, minuscule mortality risk and do not transmit much...."[20]
- Dr. Scott Balsitis, Ph.D., Viral Immunologist, and former CDC fellow, on August 26 and 27 2021, also pointed out that "We now have three studies on masking kids, and none show a significant benefit ... in spite of having no data showing it works. Therein lies the problem. It doesn't matter how many people want something to be true, it matters if it is true. That's why most medical experts in many other countries are recommending against masking kids."[21]
- Dr. Marty Makary, Professor at Johns Hopkins School of Medicine, and Dr. H. Cody Meissner, Chief of Pediatric Infectious Disease at Tufts Children's Hospital and a Professor of Pediatrics at Tufts University School of Medicine, on August 8, 2021 asserted that "We have been encouraging Americans to wear masks since the beginning of the pandemic. But special attention should be paid to the many children who struggle with masks. Public-health officials claim to base their decisions and guidance on science, but there's no science behind mask mandates for children."[22]

Despite public health authorities consistently and insistently proclaiming that they are merely following "the science," numerous arbitrary, irrational public health policies have been implemented during 2020, 2021, and 2022. Though scientific evidence can be a sound justification for State action, the correlation between politics, society, and science is considerably more intricate than the States would have us believe. As a starting point, there is no such thing as "the science." Scientists frequently differ concerning various issues, from study design and theoretical approaches to methodologies and conclusions.[23] Instead of citing scientific studies to justify mandates for masks, lockdowns, and vaccines, government officials cite unrelated or subjective research and recommendations of discredited and conflicted organizations such as the WHO, CDC, FDA, and NIH. Multiple federal and international investigations have documented the obfuscation, coverups, and financial entanglements with pharmaceutical companies that have made these organizations "cesspools of corruption".[24] According to Open Books the NIH and hundreds of individual scientists received an estimated $350 million in undisclosed royalties from third parties (primarily drug companies) between 2010 and 2020. The NIH grants over $32 billion in funding to research institutions around the world and employs thousands of scientists to conduct research inhouse.[25] These research grants combined with research grants from other US agencies, global "philanthropic foundations" and the pharmaceutical industry ensure that academic institutions toe the official line.[25] For any independent and objective researcher, it is patently obvious that actual science is not being followed.

A contemporary Massachusetts Institute of Technology (MIT) study that investigated "coronavirus sceptics" deployed data to advocate for radical policy changes, which best encapsulates how the Western governments viewed "the science" and "epistemology."[26] Their critique of the academic researchers, data analysts and scientists who do not come to the same conclusion dictated by public health officials ("coronavirus sceptics," "anti-mask groups," or "unorthodox scientists") included the following (emphasis added):

- Most fundamentally, **the groups we studied believe that science is a process, and not an institution**. As we have outlined in the case study, these groups mistrust the scientific establishment ("the Science") because they believe that the institution has been corrupted by profit motives and politics. The knowledge that the CDC and academics have created cannot be trusted because they need to be subject to increased doubt, and not accepted as consensus.

- While previous literature in visualization and science communication has emphasized the need for data and media literacy to combat misinformation, this study finds that [these groups] **practice a form of data literacy in spades. Within this constituency, unorthodox viewpoints do not result from a deficiency of data literacy; sophisticated practices of data literacy are a means of consolidating and promulgating views that fly in the face of scientific orthodoxy.** Not only are these groups prolific in their creation of counter-visualizations, but **they leverage data…to advocate for and enact policy changes.**
- **These groups argue for open access to government data** (claiming that CDC and local health departments are not releasing enough data for citizens to make informed decisions), and they use the language of **data-driven decision-making to show that …mandates are both ill-advised and unnecessary.**
- [These groups] **use "data-driven" narratives to justify their heterodox beliefs.** [They] are acutely aware that mainstream narratives use data to underscore the pandemic's urgency; they believe that these data sources and visualizations are fundamentally flawed and seek to counteract these biases [with accurate data interpretation and virilization].
- [These groups] express mistrust for academic and journalistic accounts of the pandemic, proposing to rectify alleged bias by **"following the data"** and creating their own data visualizations … [and insist that] that discussions can be **"guided solely by the data."** In other words, [they] **value unmediated access to information and privilege personal research and direct reading over "expert" [mainstream] interpretations.**
- These groups **highly value scientific expertise** they also see **collective analysis of data** as a way to bring communities together within a time of crisis and **being able to transparently and dispassionately analyze the data is crucial for democratic governance.** In fact, the explicit motivation for many of these followers is to find information so that they can make the best decisions for their families—and by extension, for the communities around them.
- **Data literacy is a quintessential criterion for membership within the community** they have created [and they display] **skill in accessing, interpreting, critiquing, and visualizing data, as well as the pro-social willingness to share those skills with other interested parties.** This is a community of practice focused on acquiring and transmitting expertise….
- While academic science is traditionally a system for producing knowledge within a laboratory, validating it through peer review, and sharing

results within subsidiary communities, [these groups] reject this hier-
archical social model. **They espouse a vision of science that is radically
egalitarian [unbiased classless, democratic] and individualist.** This
study forces us to see that coronavirus skeptics **champion science as
a personal practice that prizes rationality and autonomy; for them,
it is not a body of knowledge certified by an institution of experts.**
- These groups were predisposed to digging through the scientific literature and highlighting the uncertainty in academic publications that
media organizations elide[ignore].[26]

What the authors describe above as unacceptable, "unorthodox science," and
heresy is, in essence, authentic science. The very definition of scientific research
is the "diligent and systematic inquiry or investigation into a subject in order
to discover or revise facts, theories, applications, etc." The Merriam-Webster
Dictionary defines the "Essential Meaning of Science" as "knowledge about
or study of the natural world based on facts learned through experiments and
observation." To not allow any critical thinking or opposite views or discourse
or investigation is not "science."

According to the MIT researchers, absurdly, the solution to combating
"misinformation" is not total transparency of all data sets but less transparency, given the skill and proficiency of the "anti-maskers" in analyzing and
interpreting data. Giving such people more data would presumably only
further incentivize them to strengthen their counter-consensus arguments.
In other words, more transparency would allow "anti-maskers" to expose
the false narratives propagated by the public health authorities, mainstream
media, and academic establishment. According to the MIT researchers, the
solution to combatting "misinformation" is not total transparency but rather
to improve the mainstream "visualization" projected to the public.[26] In other
words, mainstream government propaganda should be improved.

The authors of the MIT study conclude that these groups are in essence
the same as the January 6, 2021, rioters, and that:

There is a fundamental epistemological conflict between maskers
[orthodox scientist/ academic establishment] and anti-maskers
[unorthodox scientist], who use the same data but come to such different conclusions...data is not a neutral substrate that can be used
for good or for ill. Indeed, anti-maskers [unorthodox scientist] often
reveal themselves to be more sophisticated in their understanding of
how scientific knowledge is socially constructed than their ideological

adversaries, [and] espouse naive realism about the "objective" truth of public health data…Put differently, there is no such thing as dispassionate or objective data analysis…. Objective numbers and data visualizations—is part of a broader battleground about scientific epistemology and democracy in modern American life."[26]

Orthodox science, according to the Western democratic States in the COVID-19 era, is science narrowly tailored and packaged to achieve a predestined ideological outcome. This epistemological view of science is the same world view held by tyrants such as Hitler, Stalin, Mussolini, Pol Pot, Pinochet, Ceausescu, Mao Zedong, Kim Jong Il, and others.

Despite it being extremely obvious to any independent objective observer, the authors refused to follow their analysis to its logical conclusion: the world was misled and lied to by public health authorities, the mainstream media, conflicted multinational corporations and foundations, and the academic establishment. The empirical data relating to COVID-19 simply do not support the mainstream narrative. The "unorthodox scientists" have skillfully proven this fact and showed millions of people across the globe that the "emperor has no clothes!" As aptly asserted by Dr. Mike Yeadon, "I tried to follow the science, but it was not there. I then followed the money, that's where I found 'the science.'" Albert Einstein was correct when he said that "Three great forces rule the world: stupidity, fear, and greed."

The table below summarizes the difference between the COVID-19 "science" practiced and preached throughout the pandemic, and real science:

THE COVID-19 "SCIENCE"	REAL SCIENCE
An institution	A process of investigation, conjecture and criticism
Body of knowledge certified by the establishment	Body of knowledge obtained through sophisticated scientific analysis and investigation
Science is settled and predetermined	Sciences evolves and improves as more data and knowledge are obtained
Science depends on ideology and corporate paymasters	Science depends on data analysis
No transparency: only selective data analyzed and published	Total transparency; all data analyzed and results of all experiments published

By dictate, no debate allowed	Debate and dissent the only means of progress
Outcomes predetermined by the official narrative and corporate interest	Outcomes depend on results of data analysis and evidence
Extreme conflict of interest	No conflict of interest
Irrational and arbitrary	Rational
Conflicting conclusions of the same data set viewed as heresy that should be silenced, censored and punished	Conflicting conclusions of the same data set welcomed to eventually come to the best conclusion
Biased	Unbiased
Subjective	Objective
Unethical and unprincipled	Ethical and principled
Dishonest, mixture of truth and lies	Honest, based solely on truth

Table 9.1 The differences between the COVID-19 "science"
practiced and preached throughout the pandemic, and real science
Source: Dr. Willem van Aardt, based on the MIT article[26]

Alec Zeck correctly contended that "Coercion is not science! Withholding data is not science! Manipulating data is not science! Cherry-picking studies is not science! Fearmongering is not science! Pharma propaganda is not science!" Dr. Marcia Angell, a former editor in chief of the NEJM, resigned in 2000 after two decades in the position, because of what she described as the "indefensible influence being exerted by Pharma" on the NEJM. In her book "The Truth About Drug Companies: How They Deceive Us and What to Do About It" published in 2005, she explained:

Now primarily a marketing machine to sell drugs of dubious benefit, big pharma uses its wealth and power to co-opt every institution that might stand in its way, including the US Congress, the FDA, academic medical centres and the medical profession itself…It is simply no longer possible to believe much of the clinical research that is published or to rely on the judgment of trusted physicians or authoritative medical guidelines.[28]

A 2018 research paper published in the BMJ that "examined how much money editors of the world's most influential medical journals received from industry sources" revealed that more than 50% of the editors of the journals that could be assessed, "were receiving money from the pharmaceutical industry – in some cases, hundreds of thousands of dollars."[29] While most citizens across the globe, in good faith, believed that they were being provided with "the science" with regards to COVID-19, they were actually provided with paid promotional ads by trillion-dollar industries and corrupt government institutions that make up their own science. And the majority of that "science" benefits them, not the citizens. It is profit before people! Pharmaceutical corporations violate more criminal laws than any industry in history, as measured by their criminal settlements with US federal prosecutors.[30] The sentiment that "our universities, our academics, and the medical journals are now prostitutes of corporate money... fake studies and fake news reports have been pharma's standard operating procedure for decades" is indeed accurate.[30] According to Richard Smith, a former editor of the BMJ, a cofounder of the UK Committee on Medical Ethics and a member of the board of the UK Research Integrity Office, some medical studies are entirely fiction, with the participants and the results being made up.[31] Smith asserts that:

The business model of journals and publishers depends on publishing, preferably lots of studies as cheaply as possible. They have little incentive to check for fraud and a positive disincentive to experience reputational damage—and possibly legal risk—from retracting studies. Funders, universities, and other research institutions similarly have incentives to fund and publish studies and disincentives to make a fuss about fraudulent research they may have funded or had undertaken in their institution—perhaps by one of their star researchers.

The time may have come to stop assuming that research actually happened and is honestly reported and assume that the research is fraudulent until there is some evidence to support it having happened and been honestly reported.[31]

The Government Rationale for COVID-19 Mask Mandates

According to the US CDC, "masks were mainly intended to lessen the emission of virus-laden droplets (source control)," which is especially relevant for asymptomatic wearers, such as children.[11,15] The contention was that masks also help reduce inhalation of these droplets by the wearer ("filtration for wearer protection").[15] Therefore, the grounds for enforcing mask mandates as part of a comprehensive prevention strategy were as follows:

- to protect all individuals from contracting the SARS-CoV-2 virus and becoming extremely sick or dying of COVID-19 and
- to stop the viral transmission and amplification of SARS-CoV-2 by individuals in public venues.[15]

For mask mandates to be judicious and rational public-health policies, that meet the required legitimacy, adequacy, necessity, and proportionality criteria the contention is that:

- masks are efficient at preventing both contraction and transmission of SARS-CoV-2;
- mask wearing has no significant adverse health effects for wearers; and
- mask mandates are associated with lower COVID-19 case growth rates.

It is therefore important to investigate whether the above presuppositions are correct and supported by actual science and data. If these principal points of departure are incorrect, it follows that mask mandates would be irrational, unnecessary, unreasonable, and therefore anti-juridical and unlawful in terms of IHRL.

Government Contention a): Masks are efficient at preventing both contraction and transmission of SARS-CoV-2

A systemic review of interventions to combat the spread of respiratory viral diseases by the highly regarded Cochrane Library found that medical/surgical mask-wearing makes little or no difference to the outcome of influenza or influenza-like illnesses compared to not wearing a mask:

The pooled results of randomized trials did not show a clear reduction in respiratory viral infection with the use of medical/surgical masks during seasonal influenza. There were no clear differences between the use of medical/surgical masks compared with N95/P2 respirators in healthcare workers when used in routine care to reduce respiratory viral infection.[32]

Clinical trials have consistently found that masks do not protect people from respiratory viruses.[13] In a 2012 systematic review of the scientific evidence by the UK Department of Health into whether the use of masks prevents transmission of influenza, the researchers concluded that:

> Six of eight randomized controlled trials found no significant differences between control and intervention groups (masks with or without hand hygiene; N95/P2 respirators) .... None of the studies we reviewed established a conclusive relationship between mask/respirator use and protection against influenza infection.[32]

A randomized RCT relating to the efficacy of cloth masks published in 2015 that investigated cloth and surgical masks used by healthcare workers in Vietnam was the initial randomized trial to investigate the use of cloth masks.[13,33] The investigators found healthcare workers who wore cloth masks were more likely to contract viruses than those who wore surgical masks, as well as a third control group who were not obliged to wear masks at all.[13,33] They discovered that cloth masks blocked only 3% of droplets while medical masks blocked just over half, and the N95 masks blocked 99.9% to 99.99%.[13,33] The investigators established that healthcare workers should not use cloth masks as protection against respiratory infection since the physical properties of a cloth mask, reuse, frequency, and effectiveness of cleaning, and increased moisture retention may increase the infection risk.[33]

In February 2020, Hong Kong–based scientists reviewed 10 experimental trials between 1946 and 2020 that investigated whether masks outside hospital settings protected their wearers against the flu.[13,34] The scientists pooled the results of the ten trials into a meta-analysis and concluded the following:

> We did not find evidence that surgical-type face masks are effective in reducing laboratory-confirmed influenza transmission, either when worn by infected persons (source control) or by persons in the general community to reduce their susceptibility.[34]

On April 1, 2020, the University of Minnesota's Center for Infectious Disease and Research Policy (CIDRAP) published an article describing the differences between cloth face coverings, surgical masks, and respirators. CIDRAP's Dr. Lisa Brosseau, who is a national expert on respiratory protection and infectious diseases, analyzed "the science" presented by the CDC in her article entitled "Masks-for-all for COVID-19 not based on sound data" and pointed out that:

Data from laboratory studies that indicate cloth masks or face coverings offer very low filter collection efficiency for the smaller inhalable particles we believe are largely responsible for transmission, particularly from pre- or asymptomatic individuals who are not coughing or sneezing. At the time we wrote this article, we were unable to locate any well-performed studies of cloth mask leakage when worn on the face—either inward or outward leakage. As far as we know, these data are still lacking.

The guidelines from the Centers for Disease Control and Prevention (CDC) for face coverings initially did not have any citations for studies of cloth material efficiency or fit, but some references have been added since the guidelines were first posted. We reviewed these and found that many employ very crude, non-standardized methods... or are not relevant to cloth face coverings because they evaluate respirators or surgical masks. (Leung 2020, Johnson 2009, Green 2012).

The CDC failed to reference the National Academies of Sciences Rapid Expert Consultation on the Effectiveness of Fabric Masks for the COVID-19 Pandemic (NAS 2020), which concludes, "The evidence from...laboratory filtration studies suggests that such fabric masks may reduce the transmission of larger respiratory droplets. There is little evidence regarding the transmission of small, aerosolized particulates of the size potentially exhaled by asymptomatic or pre-symptomatic individuals with COVID-19." As well, the CDC neglected to mention a well-done study of cloth material filter performance by Rengasamy et al. (2014), which we reviewed in our article.[16]

In other words, not only did the CDC not have any data or evidence to support their recommendations, but they fallaciously referenced irrelevant studies, while neglecting to reference studies that disproved their theory.

In November 2020, a group of Danish researchers (widely quoted out of context by those supporting mask mandates as proof of the efficacy of masks) published an investigator-initiated, unblinded RCT that covered almost 6,000 people in Denmark.[13,35] A total of 3,030 participants were randomly assigned to the recommendation to wear high-quality surgical face masks, and 2,994 were assigned not to wear face masks; 4,862 participants (80.7%) completed the study.[13,35] Trial participants were followed for a month to see if they had been infected with SARS-CoV-2. 42 participants (1.8%) in the mask group and 53 (2.1%) in the control group contracted SARS-CoV-2.[13,35] The between-group difference was −0.3% in favor of the mask group.[13,35] In analyzing the data, the researchers clearly make the following point:

> In this community-based, randomized controlled trial conducted in a setting where mask wearing was uncommon and was not among other recommended public health measures related to SARS-CoV-2, a recommendation to wear a surgical mask when outside the home among others did not reduce, at conventional levels of statistical significance, incident SARS-CoV-2 infection compared with no mask recommendation.[35]

It is further noteworthy that the participants in this RCT were given high-quality surgical face masks to wear and not the cloth masks used by most of the general population.[13,35]

By October 2021, after more than 18 months' worth of data and numerous peer-reviewed studies, the University of Minnesota's CIDRAP, which continuedly monitored the effectiveness of masks concluded that:

> Cloth and surgical masks offer a very limited degree of source control, because, while they limit the number of larger respiratory particles in a space, they do not prevent the emission of most small particles (aerosols) exhaled during breathing, talking, singing, coughing, or other respiratory actions.

> The data are clear that most cloth face coverings and surgical masks offer very limited source control (protection of others from pathogens by limiting emissions from an infected person) and personal protection against small inhalable infectious particles.[36]

Finding: The contention that masks are efficient at preventing both contagion and transmission of influenza-type viruses is not supported by the scientific data.

Government contention b):
Mask wearing has no adverse health effects for wearers

In 2020, a peer-reviewed study by a group of Italian professors warned that face masks are causing prominent ear deformities in young children.[8,13] Small children mostly wear masks with elastic ear loops or strips of fabric with lateral slits (side cuts at the ears). The researchers found that these masks cause constant compression on the ear skin and, consequently, on the auricle's cartilage, leading to erythematous and painful lesions of the retro auricular skin when the masks are worn for many hours.[8,13] Pre-adolescent children have undeveloped ear cartilage with less resistance to deformation; lengthy pressure from the elastic loops of the mask can influence the outer ear's growth and angulation.[8,13] This prolonged pressure can increase the outer auricle's angle. The researchers further found that the "single band" masks (that wrap around the neck) slide downwards and do not keep the nose covered; furthermore, if these masks are used in summer, they tend to produce a humid microenvironment favoring the development of dermatitis and eczema.[13,37]

A comprehensive 2021 study by a group of German researchers published in the "International Journal of Environmental Research and Public Health," titled "Is a Mask That Covers the Mouth and Nose Free from Undesirable Side Effects in Everyday Use and Free of Potential Hazards?" reveals that there are clear, biomedical scientifically demonstrable adverse effects for mask wearers, on psychological, social, and physical levels.[13,37] The comprehensive meta-analysis on the scientifically proven related side-effects of wearing masks that referenced 44 mostly experimental studies for quantitative evaluation and 65 publications for substantive evaluation revealed significant adverse effects of masks in numerous disciplines. In the paper, researchers refer to the psychological and physical deterioration, as well as multiple symptoms described because of their consistent, recurrent, uniform presentation from different disciplines as MIES.[37] The researchers' objectified evaluation "evidenced changes in respiratory physiology of mask wearers with significant correlation of O_2 drop and fatigue ($p < 0.05$), as well as clustered co-occurrences of respiratory impairment and O_2 drop (67%), N95 mask usage and CO_2 rise (82%), N95 mask and O_2 drop (72%), N95 mask and headache (60%), respiratory impairment and temperature rise (88%), but also temperature rise and moisture (100%) under the masks."[13,37] The researchers found *inter alia* that:

Extended mask-wearing by the general population can have an adverse effect on the wearer's blood gases sub-clinically and in some cases also clinically manifest and, therefore, have a negative effect on the basis of all aerobic life, external and internal respiration, with an influence on a wide variety of organ systems and metabolic processes with physical, psychological and social consequences for the individual human being. With the advent of the so-called SARS-COV-2 pandemic, we have seen a number of medical practices that have little or no scientific support as regards reducing the spread of this infection. One of these measures is the wearing of facial masks, either a surgical-type mask, bandana or N95 respirator mask. Several studies have indeed found significant problems with wearing such a mask. This can vary from headaches, to increased airway resistance, carbon dioxide accumulation, to hypoxia, all the way to serious life-threatening complications.[37]

In an additional study of the effect of surgical masks, researchers found that the masks reduced the blood's oxygen levels significantly. The lengthier the time spent wearing the mask, the greater the fall in blood oxygen levels.[38] The significance of these findings is that a drop in oxygen levels (hypoxia) is associated with immunity impairment.[39,40] Additionally, studies have also demonstrated that hypoxia can impede the main type of immune cell used to fight viral infections, called the CD4+ T-lymphocyte.[39] This occurs as the hypoxia increases the level of a compound called the hypoxia inducible factor-1 (HIF-1), which inhibits T-lymphocytes and stimulates immune inhibitor cells (Tregs). This increases the risk of infections for mask wearers.[40]

Apart from these serious adverse health effects, comparison between areas where mask mandates were implemented and areas where they were not implemented revealed that mask mandates increased death rates. An authoritative observational study by Dr. Zacharias Foegen into the effect of mask wearing on the Case Fatality Ratio (CFR) compared data between counties in the State of Kansas (with its 2.8 million residents) that had mask mandates (MMC) and those that did not have mask mandates (noMMC) during which the State of Kansas issued mask mandates but allowed 105 counties to either opt out or issue their own mask mandates.[41] The study found that contrary to the mainstream narrative that mask mandates reduce infection rate and therefore also death rates "mask mandates actually caused 1.5 times the number of deaths or 50% more deaths compared to no mask mandates," as can been seen in Figure 9.1 below:

No-MMC[†]	MMC[‡]	
9880	13665	Infected
95	241	Deaths
0	111	Thereof additional deaths by mask mandate[§]
73	101	85% deaths with COVID-19[¶] as underlying cause of death without mask mandate[**]
73	212	deaths with COVID-19 as underlying cause of death[‡‡]
0,74%	1,55%	CFR[§§] (for deaths with COVID-19 as underlying cause of death)
	2,10	RR[¶¶] (for deaths with COVID-19 as underlying cause of death)

[†] counties without mask mandate
[‡] mask mandated counties.
[§] As calculated in step 4b
[¶] coronavirus disease 2019.
[**] ([total deaths] * 85% − [additional deaths by mask mandate]) * [infected in group]/ [infected total].
[‡‡] Total of the two rows above
[§§] case fatality rate
[¶¶] risk ratio (MMC/noMMC).

Figure 9.1 Effects of Mask Mandates on Death Rates in the State of Kansas
Source: Dr Zacharias Foegen, Medicine Journal February 2022

Dr. Foegen explains that:

The mask mandates themselves have increased the CFR by 1.85 or by 85% in counties with mask mandates. It was also found that almost all of these additional deaths are attributed solely to COVID-19. [The reason] for the increased [deaths] by mandating masks is that virions that enter or those coughed out in droplets are retained in the facemask tissue, and after quick evaporation of the droplets, hypercondenced droplets or pure virions (virions not inside a droplet) are re-inhaled from a very short distance…the "Foegen effect." In the "Foegen effect" the virions spread (because of their smaller size) deeper into the respiratory tract. "They bypass the bronchi and are inhaled deep into the alveoli, where they can cause pneumonia instead of bronchitis, which would be typical of a virus infection…."[41]

Moreover, the researchers noted that "the 'Foegen effect' could increase the overall viral load because virions that should have been removed from the respiratory tract are returned. Viral reproduction *in vivo* including the reproduction of the re-inhaled virions, is exponential compared with the mask-induced linear droplet reduction."[41]

The parallelization analysis based on county level data showed that in Kansas, counties with mask mandates "had significantly higher case fatality rates than counties without mask mandate, with a risk ratio of 1.85 (95% confidence interval [95% CI]: 1.51-2.10) for COVID-19 related deaths."[41]

A peer-reviewed study by Beny Spira, an Associate Professor at the

University of São Paulo entitled "Correlation Between Mask Compliance and COVID-19 Outcomes in Europe" confirmed Dr. Foegen's findings. Published in the "Cureus Journal of Medical Science" on April 19th, 2022, the paper analyzed "the correlation between mask usage against morbidity and mortality rates in the 2020-2021 winter in Europe."[42,43]

Data from 35 European countries (with a total of 602 million people) on mask usage, ill health, and mortality, during a six-month period were studied.[42,43] Professor Spira's research revealed that:

> ...countries with high levels of mask compliance did not perform better than those with low mask usage in the six-month period that encompassed the second European wave of COVID-19.

> ...the lack of negative correlations between mask usage and COVID-19 cases and deaths suggest that the widespread use of masks at a time when an effective intervention was most needed, i.e., during the strong 2020-2021 autumn-winter peak, was not able to reduce COVID-19 transmission.[42]

In addition to finding "no benefit to mask mandate compliance in curtailing the spread of COVID-19," the paper found a "moderate positive correlation between the use of masks and COVID-19 deaths":

> Moreover, the moderate positive correlation between mask usage and deaths in Western Europe also suggests that the universal use of masks may have had harmful unintended consequences...

> The positive correlation between mask usage and cases was not statistically significant (rho = 0.136, p = 0.436), while the correlation between mask usage and deaths was positive and significant (rho = 0.351, p = 0.039). The Spearman's correlation between masks and deaths was considerably higher in the West than in East European countries: 0.627 (p = 0.007) and 0.164 (p = 0.514), respectively.[42]

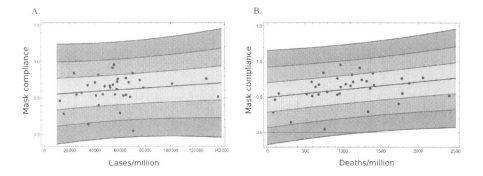

Figure 9.2: Correlation between average mask compliance and cases/million (A) or deaths/million (B) in 35 European countries. [Each dot represents a country. The blue line represents the fitted regression line and the areas above and below indicate 1 σ (yellow), 2 σ (green), or 3 σ (red)]
Source: Professor Beny Spira, Cureus Journal of Medical Science

Professor Spira also made clear that confounding factors such as disparate vaccination rates and COVID-19 infection rates between countries, were irrelevant:

It could be argued that some confounding factors could have influenced these results. One of these factors could have been different vaccination rates among the studied countries. However, this is unlikely given the fact that at the end of the period analysed in this study (March 31, 2021), vaccination rollout was still at its beginning, with only three countries displaying vaccination rates higher than 20%: the UK (48%), Serbia (35%), and Hungary (30%), with all doses counted individually.

It could also be claimed that the rise in infection levels prompted mask usage resulting in higher levels of masking in countries with already higher transmission rates. While this assertion is certainly true for some countries, several others with high infection rates, such as France, Germany, Italy, Portugal, and Spain had strict mask mandates in place since the first semester of 2020. In addition, during the six-month period covered by this study, all countries underwent a peak in COVID-19 infections (Figures 1, 2), thus all of them endured similar pressures that might have potentially influenced the level of mask usage.[42]

In other words, not only do mask mandates have adverse effects for wearers, but they actually increased the death rate of people that contract COVID-19, which means that the use of face masks as an epidemiologic intervention is contraindicated.

> **Finding:** The contention that mask wearing has no significant adverse health effects is untrue. Objective scientific data show that there are significant adverse ramifications to masking and that mask mandates may lead to higher death rates.

Government contention c):
Mask mandates are associated with lower
COVID-19 case growth rates

A 2021 University of Louisville study hypothesized that "statewide mask mandates and mask use are associated with lower COVID-19 case growth rates." To test this hypothesis, "they compared COVID-19 case growth in the 33 States that imposed statewide mask mandates on or before August 2, 2020, with those that imposed mask mandates after this date and those that didn't have mask mandates at all, using data from the CDC and the Institute for Health Metrics and Evaluation at the University of Washington."[44]

The researchers found that:

> Contrary to our hypothesis, early mandates were not associated with lower minimum case growth. Maximum case growth was the same among states with early, late, and no mandates. This indicates that mask mandates were not predictive of slower COVID-19 spread when community transmission rates were low or high. We wondered if mask mandates were associated with smaller or slower surges in case growth. Differences between minimum and maximum case growth were similar among early, late, and no mandate states, and surges from minimum to maximum growth occurred at similar rates. These findings suggest that mask mandates are not predictive of smaller or slower shifts from low to high case growth.[44]

The study confirmed that mandating mask use made no difference, as "case growth was not significantly different between mandate and non-mandate states at low or high transmission rates." The researchers concluded that their findings "do not support the hypothesis that SARS-CoV-2 transmission rates decrease with greater public mask use."[44]

Interestingly, a May 2021 study by the CDC found that incidence of COVID-19 for students in schools mandating masks "Was not statistically significant compared with schools where mask use was optional."[45] The study "covered more than 90,000 elementary-school students in 169 Georgia schools from November 16 to December 11 and was, according to the CDC, the first of its kind to compare COVID-19 incidence in schools with certain mitigation measures in place to other schools without those measures."[45,46] Instead of transparently reporting the finding, the CDC buried the study's finding of "null effects of a student masking requirement by omitting it from the studies' summary."[46]

A May 2021 study by Brown University researchers who investigated "the correlation of mitigation practices with staff and student COVID-19 case rates in Florida, New York, and Massachusetts during the 2020-2021 school year," did not find any correlations between mask mandates and COVID-19 case rates among students:

> This paper reports on the correlation of mitigation practices with staff and student COVID-19 case rates in Florida, New York, and Massachusetts during the 2020-2021 school year. We analyze data collected by the COVID-19 School Response Dashboard and focus on student density, ventilation upgrades, and masking. We find higher student COVID-19 rates in schools and districts with lower in-person density but no correlations in staff rates. Ventilation upgrades are correlated with lower rates in Florida but not in New York. We do not find any correlations with mask mandates. All rates are lower in the spring, after teacher vaccination is underway.[47]

By December 2021, Dr. Paul Elias Alexander analyzed and chronically compiled more than 167 peer-reviewed articles relating to COVID-19 face mask requirements and concluded that:

> It is not unreasonable to conclude that surgical and cloth masks, used as they currently are being used (without other forms of PPE protection), have no impact on controlling the transmission of COVID-19 virus. Current evidence implies that face masks can be harmful. The body of evidence indicates that face masks are largely ineffective.

My focus is on COVID face masks and the prevailing science that we have had for nearly 20 months. I present the masking "body of evidence" below (n=167 studies and pieces of evidence), comprised of comparative effectiveness research as well as related evidence and high-level reporting. To date, the evidence has been stable and clear that masks do not work to control the virus and they can be harmful and especially to children.[48]

Finding: The contention that mask mandates are associated with lower COVID-19 case growth rates is untrue and not supported by objective independent science and data.

Mask Mandates for School Children:
An Illicit Violation of Constitutional Law and IHRL

The WHO's 2017 report entitled "Advancing the Right to Health: The Vital Role of Law" determines that international health regulations require countries to exercise their health powers in a transparent and non-discriminatory manner, with full respect for the dignity, human rights, and fundamental freedoms of persons.[49,50]

The mandatory masking of school children represents a violation of and limitation on children's fundamental human rights guaranteed by the CRC and the ICCPR.[11-13] As detailed in Chapters 5 to 7 of this book, the Siracusa Principles, which contain criteria for limiting fundamental human rights to advance various public purposes, offer State Parties standards for acceptable limitation on rights to reduce the spread of infectious disease.[51] They *inter alia* require that restrictions should respond to a pressing public or social need, pursue a legitimate aim, be necessary, be the least restrictive and be proportionate.[51] Importantly, the ICCPR and Siracusa specifically determine that "No state, including those that are not parties to the Covenant, may suspend or violate, even in times of public emergency freedom from torture or cruel, inhuman or degrading treatment or punishment and from medical or scientific experimentation."[49,51] Both the WHO and US CDC acknowledged that there is no scientific evidence supporting the use of masks and that mandatory mask-wearing was experimental.[52] Never before have millions of children been forced to wear face masks for extended periods of time. The potential adverse biomedical ramifications of near permanent mask-wearing by children while at school while exercising outside and while playing sports were unknown. In contravention of international bioethical norms and IHRL, public health authorities were conducting a large-scale biomedical experiment without the required prior informed consent and with detrimental effects on children.[13]

If a rudimentary proportionality analysis, which is the typical legal test for resolving human rights disputes, had been applied, the illegality of mask mandates would have been evident. As postulated in Chapter 5, the proportionality analysis examines the four sequential questions once a *prima facie* infringement of a fundamental human right has been found. First, does the infringing public policy pursue a legitimate aim? (legitimacy); second, is the public policy suitable and rationally connected to the fulfilment of policy goals? (adequacy or efficacy); third, is the infringing policy necessary and the least restrictive option? (necessity); and fourth, do the benefits of the policy measures outweigh the cost? (proportionality *"strictu sensu"*). If the answer to any one of the four questions is no, then the measure is illegitimate.

- **Do mask mandates for children pursue a legitimate goal? (legitimacy)** It is a legitimate goal of State Parties to take action to safeguard the public against an infectious disease that represents a serious threat to the health of the population.[11,13,49] However, a disease with a crude mortality rate of less than 0.3% does not represent a "serious threat to the health of the population" and, as such fails the legitimacy requirement.
- **Would mask mandates for children be adequate to achieve the purpose? (adequacy)** The objective science set out earlier in the chapter clearly shows that mask mandates neither prevent contraction nor transmission of COVID-19 and therefore are inadequate to achieve the stated objective of "preventing both contraction and transmission of SARS-CoV-2." Mask mandates therefore fail the adequacy requirement.
- **Are mask mandates for children the least intrusive and least restrictive measure available that will accomplish the public health goal?** Given that the IFR is close to zero for children and young adults, an obvious alternative and less intrusive measure to mass mandatory masking would simply have been to make masking optional. Several studies also showed that by simply opening windows and improving ventilation in classrooms, case numbers were reduced.[46,47,48] Given that there were numerous less intrusive measures available, mask mandates are unnecessary and therefore illicit.
- **Are mask mandates for children a proportionate response?** The restriction of a human right is proportional *stricto sensu* if it is

"pondered" or balanced because more benefits or advantages for the general interest are derived from it than damages against other goods or values in conflict. From a cost-benefit perspective, a schoolchild has a close to zero risk of severe malady or death and thus no benefit from the mask but are exposed to significant adverse side-effects from masking (that includes hypoxia, MIES, anxiety, panic attacks, severe depression, facial deformity and psychological damage) as reported in numerous peer-reviewed studies. Dr. Elissa Schechter-Perkins, MD, MPH, the director of Emergency Medicine and Infectious Disease Management at Boston Medical Center, in an August 2021 interview confirmed that:

[T]here are real downsides to masking children for this long, with no known end date, and without any clear upside…. I'm not aware of any studies that show conclusively that kids wearing masks in schools has any effect on their own morbidity or mortality or on the hospitalization or death rate in the community around them.[46]

In the presence of such potential risks (to combat a disease with a near zero case fatality rate in school children), mask mandates cannot be viewed as proportionate *stricto sensu*. The cost-benefit argument against using an essentially untested mask reveals heavy risk and virtually no benefit to masking.

Given the glaring irregularity of mask mandates, the question that comes to mind is: Why were these irrational and illegal policies ever implemented?

When a US Federal Court in April 2022 ruled that "the national public health agency had exceeded its legal powers in issuing the mandate…" and declared mask mandates unlawful, Dr. Anthony Fauci's response was telling. Fauci warned that the court ruling goes "against public health principles" and sets a "bad precedent." "We are concerned about that – about courts getting involved in things that are unequivocally public health decisions."[53] In other words, "public health" and "public health officials" are above the law. It is this ignorance and misguided arrogant attitude by public officials in positions of power and influence that is at the core of the lawlessness that caused immeasurable suffering during the COVID-19 pandemic.

All the pain, emotional trauma, physical deformity, and anxiety inflicted on children around the globe by public health bureaucrats could have been averted by applying well-established IHRL norms and principles. It is not that there were no laws. The laws were in place, but those in position of power and authority chose to ignore the law and to act lawlessly and above the law!

Chapter Conclusion

Masking was the single most common non-pharmaceutical intervention in the course of the COVID-19 pandemic.[42] Most countries implemented recommendations or mandates regarding the use of masks in public spaces "at an unprecedented global scale as an important tool to curb viral transmission among potential susceptible persons."[42] When numerous governments around the globe "followed the science" by implementing mandatory mask wearing, most available independent authoritative studies on the subject conducted pre-COVID-19 (between 1946 and 2020) concluded that wearing a mask does not prevent the transmission of influenza-type viruses. Florida's Governor Ron DeSantis (one of the few State leaders that followed the real science) was indeed correct when he noted that "the medical science didn't change, the political science did."

> You now hear a lot of chatter in other states about lifting mask mandates on these little children as if somehow, they had an epiphany or even some suggest that the science changed. And let me just tell you: the science has not changed one iota, we knew from the beginning and that's why Florida never imposed a forced masking policy on school children, and that's why we fought to liberate the masked kids.[54]

Mask mandates were never about science but maintaining political control.[13] Alas, many States politicized and commercialized the COVID-19 response.[13] Only narrowly tailored subjective "scientific opinions" that support and justify the irrational COVID-19 public health policies that were embarked on were acceptable, while the actual objective science was ignored and much-needed robust scientific debate was repressed.[55] Suppression of science and lack of open debate has impinged enormously on the finding of balanced, ethical solutions during the COVID-19 pandemic.[55] Government public health policymakers, aided by the mainstream media and censorship by tech giants, controlled the scientific narrative, even when the "science" that was followed and relied upon was at complete odds with the views of many eminent world-class scientists.[56,57]

From the actual objective and independent biomedical science and data, it was and remains evident that masks are inefficient at preventing both contagion and transmission and masks have significant adverse health effects for wearers. To the disgrace of many so-called Western democracies, instead of "following the science," politicians and public health bureaucrats perverted science and followed the politics of profit. In certain instances, impressionable "scientists" were led by politics to somehow conjure up "data" to support official policy despite contradicting scientific data from the preceding six decades. Despite insistently and relentlessly proclaiming to "follow the science," self-serving government officials, big pharma, media barons, and tech monopolies betrayed the public trust. They made themselves guilty of the most pervasive anti-science and misinformation campaign in more than a century. The only acceptable biomedical scientific views were those that supported and justified the official government response to the COVID-19 pandemic. Any dissenting scientific views or contradictory scientific data (irrespective of the credibility of the data) were censored by governments, public health authorities, the mainstream media, and big tech to the detriment of the public.[13,55]

True science that was practiced by Leonardo Da Vinci, Galileo Galilei, Albert Einstein, Izaak Newton, Louis Pasteur, Marie Curie, Friedrich Nietzsche, and many others is conducted in an unbiased, objective, and neutral manner, rather than merely to provide subjective supportive justification for political decisions and conclusions reached in advance.[58-64] As highlighted by the 1965 Physics Nobel Prize winner Richard Feynman:

> Scientist's statements are approximate, never certain. We must leave room for progress and doubt, or there is no progress and no learning. There is no learning without having to pose a question, and a question requires doubt. Before you begin an experiment, you must not know the answer. If you already know the answer there is no need to gather any evidence, and to judge the evidence, you must take all of it, not just the parts you like.[66]

That major funders of health research also profited financially from the pandemic, raise legitimate questions about transparency, and criminal conflicts of interest.[67-70] There is a need for increased transparency about who the major funders of health research are globally and what influence the exert on research findings. With just three organizations, the Bill and Melinda Gates Foundation ($51,9 billion assets), the Wellcome Trust ($46,2 billion assets) and the NIH ($43 billion annual budget), all strong and vocal supporters and financial beneficiaries of the COVID-19 policies, sponsoring two-thirds of the worlds non-commercial biological research, numerous academics were intimidated and feared the loss of research grants if they dared to speak out against the official narrative.[67-70] In August 2020, it was reported that representatives "of the NIH's COVID-19 Treatment Guidelines Panel (comprised of physicians, statisticians, and other experts who are developing treatment guidelines on COVID-19 intended for healthcare providers) have financial ties to a company behind clinical trials of a drug to treat COVID-19, as well as to another large pharmaceutical company involved with developing a COVID-19 vaccine".[71] In a 2021 peer-reviewed study titled "Big pharma and healthcare: unsolvable conflict of interests between private enterprise and public health" published in the "Israel Journal of Psychiatry and Related Sciences," the researchers note that:

> The industry, funding over 80% of trials, sets up a research agenda guided more by marketing than by clinical considerations. Smart statistical and epidemiological tactics help obtain the desired results. Budget for marketing is by far greater than for research. Massive advertising to physicians and to the public gets increasingly sophisticated: ghost writing, professional guidelines, targeting of consumer groups and manipulating media for disease mongering. Pervasive lobbying and political ties limit the independence of regulatory bodies.[69]

In a shocking but accurate call for the "COVID-19 state of medical emergency to be lifted, scientific integrity restored, and crimes against humanity addressed," a group of by 17,000 physicians and medical scientists who represent a much larger, enlightened global medical community who refused to be compromised on May 11, 2022, stated that:

> [T]he disastrous COVID-19 public health policies imposed on doctors and our patients are the culmination of a corrupt medical alliance of pharmaceutical, insurance, and healthcare institutions, along with the financial trusts which control them. They have infiltrated our medical system at every level and are protected and supported by a parallel alliance of big tech, media, academics and government agencies who profited from this orchestrated catastrophe.

> This corrupt alliance has compromised the integrity of our most prestigious medical societies to which we belong, generating an illusion of scientific consensus by substituting truth with propaganda. This alliance continues to advance unscientific claims by censoring data and intimidating and firing doctors and scientists for simply publishing actual clinical results or treating their patients with proven, life-saving medicine. These catastrophic decisions came at the expense of the

innocent, who are forced to suffer health damage and death caused by intentionally withholding critical and time-sensitive treatments, or as a result of coerced genetic therapy injections, which are neither safe nor effective.[17]

The notion that a hypothesis ought to be examined, assessed, simulated, scrutinized and the results then published in a peer-reviewed journal – has always been a beacon of objectivity, and supposed to be free of bias by its very nature. Unfortunately, in the COVID-19 era the scientific community faces frightening realities: the public's ability to distinguish science from corporate-sponsored pseudoscience has been eroded *in toto*, corporate efforts to influence evidence-based policymaking are ubiquitous and effectively determine global health policy, and foundational processes to protect science – such as the integrity and independence of peer review systems and advisory committees – have been subverted and corrupted.[65]

In a scathing but factual indictment of the US public health agencies, Dr. Harvey Risch, Professor Emeritus of Epidemiology in the Department of Epidemiology and Public Health at the Yale School of Public Health, during an October 2022 interview, commentated:

I have zero trust in the CDC, and I have zero trust in the FDA. They have shown their complete corruption with regards to industry sponsors, and it's despicable. I believe that the people in charge of those agencies should be prosecuted in court for that degree of corruption that has shown that their allegiance has been to their companies and not to the American people.

The CDC, which was supposed to be an elite intellectual medical public health institution, has put out garbage study after garbage study after garbage study. It publishes these studies in Morbidity and Mortality Weekly Report. When I was in medical school, the MMWR was the public health standard — what one looked to see what was happening in public health every week. Now it's the publication of nonsense. It puts out studies that are fatally flawed. Week in after week out, fatally flawed studies: studies with 8% response rates, studies using the wrong study design, studies using the wrong controls. It's bizarre that these institutions would put out material like this, think that this passes for scientific evidence and that it would just breeze through without criticism.[72]

To find public health solutions, open, transparent, and robust scientific debate is needed. Credible biomedical science is all about questioning various hypotheses.[13] Narrow "scientific views" tailored to official policy and not allowed to be subjected to vigorous peer and public scrutiny are not credible science! More than 200 years ago, Immanuel Kant asserted that:

> Ours is an age of criticism, to which everything must be subjected. … [T]he authority of legislation, [is] by many regarded as grounds for exemption from the examination of this tribunal. But, if they are exempted, they become the subjects of just suspicion, and cannot lay claim to sincere respect, which reason accords only to that which has stood the test of a free and public examination.[73]

It is disconcerting that many Western democracies, including the United States and the United Kingdom, have regressed and, throughout the pandemic, chosen to exempt official public health policy from juridical scrutiny.

10. COVID-19 LEGAL PATERNALISM AND FUNDAMENTAL HUMAN RIGHTS

"That government is best which governs least."

— Henry David Thoreau

In his manuscript, "Principles of Morals and Legislation", the eighteenth-century theorist, lawmaker, and social reformer Jeremy Bentham (regarded as the founder of modern utilitarianism) divided all regulations into three categories: (i) regulations intended to shield you from injury caused by others; (ii) regulations intended to shield you from harm caused by yourself; and (iii) regulations forcing you to assist and help others. Bentham held that only the first category of decrees was lawful.[2] Bentham argued convincingly against the third category of regulations, but he also condemned regulations of the second category.[2] Regulations intended to save citizens from themselves is called "paternal legislation," while the opinion that such mandates are lawful is called "legal paternalism" and the practice of judges to enforce such regulations "paternalistic jurisprudence."[1,2]

In response to the COVID-19 pandemic, the world saw an unprecedented wave of paternalistic government public health policies being implemented around the globe.[3] As noted in Chapter 1, while private medicine focuses on individual wellbeing, public health is concerned with the wellbeing of the whole nation. Thus, in contrast to the main fiduciary duty to the individual observed in clinical medicine, public health is established on a collective responsibility to promote and protect the health of the population. On the basis of this difference, many pundits have indicated that one major issue that distinguishes public health morals from clinical morals is identifying when paternalistic interferences that override individual autonomy are ethically and legally justified.[4]

Paternalistic government policies are often criticized on the grounds that they infringe on civil liberties. Some of these policies violate derogation provisions, and others even violate non-derogable rights that are regarded as core human rights, *jus cogens*, and obligations *erga omnes*.[3]

Legal paternalism implies that since the State knows the interests of individual citizens better than the citizens themselves, it stands as a permanent guardian of those interests *in loco parentis*.[4] But what kind of paternalism is compatible with an open and democratic society based on freedom and equality and a legal system that recognizes fundamental human rights as espoused in the ICCPR? Do authorities have the right to control citizens' conduct through isolation mandates, mask mandates, travel mandates, social distancing mandates, vaccine mandates, and stay-at-home mandates? Or does this create an authoritarian State, leading to infantilization, demotivation, and severe breaches of individual autonomy and freedom?[3]

This chapter examines critical issues related to the appropriateness of paternalistic public health measures during the COVID-19 pandemic and investigates under what circumstances paternalistic policies may be justified.[3]

Legal Paternalism Defined‡‡

"Paternalism" comes from the Latin word "*pater*" and means to act like a father or to treat another person as a child.[3] In modern philosophy and jurisprudence, it is to act for another person's good without that person's consent, as parents do for children.[3] It is contentious because its end is altruistic, and its means are coercive. Paternalists advance people's interests relating to their health, safety, and life at the expense of their fundamental freedoms. Paternalists reason that they can make wiser and better decisions than the people for whom they act.[3,5,6] David Buchanan in his article "Autonomy, paternalism, and justice: ethical priorities in public health" contends that:

---

‡‡ Portions of this chapter are republications of the content of a peer-reviewed article by the author Dr. Willem van Aardt, entitled "The new era of COVID-19 legal paternalism and the limitation of fundamental human rights" published in the De Rebus SA Attorneys Journal in February 2022.

Paternalism is the usurpation of decision-making power, by preventing people from doing what they have decided, interfering in how they arrive at their decisions, or attempting to substitute one's judgment for theirs, expressly for the purpose of promoting their welfare. The moral concern is that the presumption that one is right, and therefore justified in seeking to override other people's judgment, constitutes treating them as less than moral equals. It denies people the right to choose their own ends of action, because it would not be necessary to supplant their decision if they shared the public health professionals' goals.[4]

Paternalistic policies have three essential elements:

- They involve interference in a person's ability to choose.
- They are enacted to further the person's perceived good or welfare.
- They are enacted without the consent of the person concerned.[7]

Put in a different way, State Party A acts paternalistically towards Citizen B by imposing Mandate M:

- M interferes with the self-rule or autonomy of B.
- A does so without the permission of B.
- A does so since A thinks M will improve the health and wellbeing of B (or in some other way serve the safety, interests, values, welfare or good of B).[7,8]

According to Thomas Matthew and Luke Buckmaster in their research paper "Paternalism in social policy: when is it justifiable?," hard paternalism denotes that in certain instances, it is acceptable for the government to interfere in a person's actions, even when that person is acting knowledgeably and voluntarily, while soft paternalism denominates to the concept that the only circumstances under which the government is permitted to interfere in individual decision-making are those in which a person is making choices that are either ill-informed or in-voluntary.[7]

Pure paternalism alludes to government interferences where "the class being protected is identical with the class being interfered with," while in the case of impure paternalism, the group of individuals being interfered with is greater than the group being safeguarded.[8]

Narrow paternalism refers solely to government paternalism and the use of legal compulsion, while broad paternalism implies any paternalist action, irrespective of whether it is performed by a State on non-State actor.

Weak paternalism refers to paternalists who deem it legal to restrict the means through which an individual "is seeking to achieve a particular objective if it is believed by authorities that these means will not achieve their desired ends" (for instance, a ban on early treatment medication such as Ivermectin for COVID-19).[7] By contrast, strong paternalism believes that people may have mistaken or irrational ends and it is justifiable to intervene to block them from realizing those ends.[7]

With regards to the COVID-19 practice of enforcing medical therapy, Tom Beauchamp and James Childress, in their book "Principles of Biomedical Ethics," write that:

> Medical paternalism consists in the judgement that the principle of beneficence trumps the principle of autonomy. Weak medical paternalism involves interference on the grounds of beneficence only to prevent substantially non-autonomous conduct.... that includes cases of consent and refusal that is not adequately informed, severe depression that precludes rational deliberation and addiction that presents free choice. Strong paternalism, by contrast involves interventions to benefit a person, despite the fact that the persons risky choices ...are informed voluntary and autonomous.[9]

According to them, strong paternalism can be justified in public healthcare if the following conditions are fulfilled:

- A patient is at risk of serious preventable harm.
- The paternalistic action will probably prevent the harm.
- The projected benefits to the patient of the paternalistic action outweigh its risks to the patient.
- It is the least autonomy-restrictive alternative that will secure the benefits and reduce the risk is adopted.[9]

In the COVID-19 era, most paternalistic policies are an example of strong impure paternalism, given their mandatory nature and that less than 0.3% of the population are at risk of death from SARS-CoV-2.[3]

The Conundrum with COVID-19 Biomedical Legal Paternalism

i) Conditions not satisfied to justify strong medical paternalistic intervention

None of the conditions listed by Beauchamp and Childress were satisfied. Most of the population were never at risk from COVID-19! It has also been proven beyond any doubt that COVID-19 vaccine mandates did not prevent any harm. From a cost-benefit perspective, the risks associated with the COVID-19 vaccines significantly outweigh any potential benefits. The adoption of vaccine mandates and other exclusionary practices such as lockdowns and mandatory quarantine represented the riskiest and most autonomy restrictive regulations that could possibly be introduced by State Parties.

ii) The individual is better placed to know what is best

Paternalist policies are controversial principally because they are premised on the notion that the State is better able to make decisions in a person's interests than the person themselves. Such policies offend a fundamental tenet of liberal societies: namely, that the individual is best placed to know what is in his or her interests.[3,10] Government bureaucrats make mistakes and sometimes err in their judgement! The COVID-19 vaccine mandates are an excellent example of this. The official public narrative in relation to effectiveness went from 99% effective to real live conditions showing not effective at all, with no positive impact of vaccination on transmission. Similarly, in relation to safety, the narrative went from public officials claiming overwhelming safety to the most vaccine adverse events in the history of humanity within six months. To expose large numbers of people to the potentially deadly consequences (due to the ineptitude of public officials) through strong medical paternalism can never be justified.

iii) Biomedical legal paternalism is incompatible with the respect for human dignity and fundamental human rights

Respect for human dignity implies free will at its core. From the recognition of human dignity descends the right and the freedom to make one's own decisions. By imposing choices based on what someone else thinks is good for a person, legal paternalism violates the equal dignity of all human beings and given the interdependence and indivisibility of human rights, adversely affects all human rights. Therefore, as Immanuel Kant argues, "a government that was established on the principle of regarding the people in the same way that a father regards his children's welfare, … a paternal government, is the worst despotism we can think of …a constitution that subverts all the freedom of the subjects, who would have no freedom whatsoever… [The sovereign who] wants to make people happy in accord with his own concept of happiness… becomes a despot."[3,11]

The notion of "happiness" (or the "greater good") is far too vague and variable to provide a balanced standard for political decision-making. State Parties who attempt to ground regulation on "happiness" (or the "greater good") and what it deems to be in the best interest of individuals rather than on fundamental human rights will inexorably judge "happiness" and what it deems to be in society's best interest by their own self-serving subjective standards, which in turn will lead to unjustified legal paternalism.

iv) Biomedical legal paternalism violates intimate aspects of private life

Respect for a person's autonomy and free will is respect for his unrestricted voluntary choice as the only rightful determinant of his actions, except where the interests of others need protection from him.[3,12] The reason why the government should not interfere in principally self-regarding affairs is not that such meddling is self-defeating and probable to cause more harm than it prevents, but rather that it would itself be an injustice and a violation of the private sanctuary that is every person's self. [3,12] This is true irrespective of what the calculus of harm and benefits might show.[3,12]

John Stuart Mill in his celebrated essay "On Liberty" penned:

> Neither one person, nor any number of persons is warranted in saying to another human creature of ripe years, that he shall not do with his life for his own benefit what he chooses to do with it. … He cannot rightfully be compelled to do or forbear because it will be better for him to do so, because it will make him happier, because, in the opinion of others, to do so would be wise, or even right.[13]

Mill further asserts that:

> There is a part of the life of every person who has come to years of discretion, within which the individuality of that person ought to reign uncontrolled either by any other person or by the public collectively.

A man's mode of laying out his existence is the best, not because it is best in itself, but because it is his own mode. . ... It is the privilege and proper condition of a human being, arrived at the maturity of his faculties, to use and interpret experience in his own way.

Society can and does execute its own mandates: and if it issues wrong mandates instead of right, or any mandates at all in things with which it ought not to meddle, it practices a social tyranny more formidable than many kinds of political oppression, since, though not usually upheld by such extreme penalties, it leaves fewer means of escape, penetrating much more deeply into the details of life, and enslaving the soul itself.[13]

Mill here is confirming something about what it means to be human, an independent free agent. Coercing a human being for his own good denies this status as an autonomous individual; so much so that Mill objects to it so firmly and in such absolute terms. "To be able to choose is a good that is independent of the wisdom of what is chosen."[2,14]

When there is a limitation of a right fundamental to a democratic society, a higher standard of justification is required; more so, where a pseudo-medical paternalistic State mandate interferes with the "intimate aspects of private life."[3,15-18]

v) Biomedical legal paternalism has unintended consequences

A further related argument against legal paternalism is that there is no guarantee that it will improve people's health and welfare; indeed, it may make it worse. Mill argues that: "[T]he strongest of all arguments against the interference of the public with purely personal conduct, is that when it does interfere, the odds are that it interferes wrongly, and in the wrong place."[2,14]

In the case of the COVID-19 lockdowns, for instance, the unintended consequences included economic devastation, hunger, disruption in education, significant spikes in suicides and mental health issues, and increased domestic violence, while in the case of vaccine mandates, the unintended consequences included significantly increased cases of anaphylaxis, blood clots, cancer, coronary artery disease, heart attacks, heart failure, myocarditis, pericarditis, thrombosis with thrombocytopenia syndrome, stroke, sudden adult death syndrome, vaccine induced auto immune deficiency syndrome, and excess deaths.[3,19-22]

vi) Biomedical legal paternalism is vulnerable to corrupt practices

While sincere, *bona fide* legal paternalism may sometimes be justified, *male fide* paternalistic State actions that are fraught with conflicts of interest, institutionalized corruption, exploitation, and profiteering can never be legitimate. In light of the well-documented corruption of major global and national health regulators and the corruption and undue influence of the transnational pharmaceutical industry on global health it would be immoral and indefensible to subdue the unsuspecting public to biomedical paternalistic mandates that could have fatal long-term health consequences.[23]

vii) Biomedical legal paternalism transgresses the voluntary consent criterion

The COVID-19 legal paternalism significantly infringed on the individual's right to medical self-determination in direct violation of the Nuremberg Code principal tenet that the voluntary consent of the human subject is absolutely essential. This means that the person involved:

- should have legal capacity to give consent;
- should be so situated as to be able to exercise free power of choice, without the intervention of any element of force, fraud, deceit, duress, overreaching, or other ulterior form of constraint or coercion; and
- should have sufficient knowledge and comprehension of the elements of the subject matter involved as to enable him to make an understanding and enlightened decision.

In his article "Libertarianism and Legal Paternalism", the late Professor John Hospers (former Professor Emeritus in Philosophy at the University of Southern California) contends that "the greater the degree to which a person's action (or a proposed action, or a thought-of action) is voluntary, the less are other persons (or institutions, especially the law) justified in behaving paternalistically toward that person."[2] In other words, if a person has the ability to make a voluntary decision, he should be left free from State interference to do so. But the key word here is "voluntary." The contemporary conception of voluntariness, which is shared by most COVID-19 medical paternalists only skims the surface of this important criterion. The popular conception, embedded also in most State policy, is that vaccine mandates are acceptable if i.) the disease presents a grave threat to public health, ii.) there is an expectation of positive comparative usefulness, and iii.) voluntary consent is obtained through "proportionate coercion."[24,25] We know for a fact that i.) and ii.) are not true for COVID-19 and the COVID-19 vaccines, but the unethical practice of "proportionate coercion" warrants some further elucidation. Hospers identifies three essential indicators to determine the voluntariness of a decision: I.) Freedom from Coercion and Pressure. II.) Informed and Educated Consent. III.) Healthy Psychological State.[2]

i. Freedom from coercion and pressure. When any form or degree of coercion takes place, the decision is not voluntary.[2] The ultimate case of coercion is one in which, for example, the Biomedical State physically arrests you and medical officers forcibly inject you with a deadly pathogen. You resisted, but without success. In that instance it is not your conduct at all, but the conduct of the individual who impelled you.[2] Still, you were pressured. More characteristically coercion comprises not of blatant corporal action but of the threat of it or some other adverse ramifications: "If you don't get into the vehicle to be transported to the quarantine facility, you will be forcibly arrested and criminally prosecuted," or "If you do not take the COVID-19 vaccine you will not be able to partake in social activities." In contrast with the first instance, in threat instances there is a choice. But it is not much of a choice. Getting into a vehicle to be transported to a quarantine facility or getting the COVID-19 vaccine to be able to socialize is not a choice we would have made except for the coercion. We were compelled to do something we would not willingly have done. Threats, too, are a matter of gradation.[2] Threat of death is a more serious than threat of loss of freedom; and a threat of injury is more serious than threat of loss of employment.[2] Many COVID-19 paternalists are inclined to label it coercion only if there is bodily injury or threat of bodily injury, but this is far too narrow.[2] A threat of loss of employment may not be much of a threat if you can easily obtain another job; but if no others are obtainable due to recession, the threat of loss of employment could be exceptionally serious. In any event, it's not a position you would willingly have left – but for the coercion. To be clear, any kind of pressure put on you interferes, impedes, and therefore nullifies the voluntariness of your decision irrespective of the degree.[2] Hospers correctly notes that:

> Any influence, whether pressure or outright coercion, which keeps the process of decision-making from "filtering through your mind" and thus triggers the decision with partial or no

cooperation from your untrammeled decision-making faculties, inhibits the full voluntariness of the decision.

ii. Informed and educated consent. The decision must be well-informed, based on all the relevant facts, purged of false and misleading information.[2] If a conman sells you what he proffered to be a blue diamond when it is actually blue glass, and you pay the price of a rare blue diamond, your decision to pay is not voluntary. You would not have paid that much voluntarily. At least not for a piece of blue glass. It is not that you were coerced, you were defrauded, that is, you were provided with false and misleading information in making your decision. Similarly, if a public health quack sells you what he proffers to be a 99.9% "effective" and "safe" vaccine that prevents infection and transmission when it prevents neither infection nor transmission and has deadly side-effects, your decision to receive the vaccine is not voluntary. It is indeed a textbook case of "fraud in the inducement" or *dolus dans locum in contractui* that occurs when a company tricks a counterparty into signing an agreement to their detriment by making use of fraudulent statements and misrepresentations.[2] Since fraud invalidates the "meeting of the minds" needed for a contract (without the fraudulent inducement the agreement would not have been executed at all), the injured party can seek damages or terminate the contract.[2] If a vaccine manufacturer materially misrepresents (*dictim et promissa*) the efficacy and safety of their product, consent has also not been obtained given the "fault in the conclusion of the contract." (*culpa in contrahendo*)

In addition to fraud and material misrepresentation, there are many other instances where informed consent will not be present. You are of the opinion that you are drinking craft beer; it was craft beer you ordered and the host at the gathering handed you a Belgian glass of pale-golden liquid that appeared to be craft beer, only it contained cyanide.[2] Even though no undue force was set upon you, it is not sensible to conclude that you are voluntarily drinking cyanide.[2] Drinking the cyanide in this instance is not a voluntary act; drinking craft beer would have been.[2] When a valetudinarian agrees to take part in a medical experiment such as the COVID-19 vaccinations – he is not threatened; not pressured – but if some of the potential serious adverse side-effects have been hidden from him, one would not be able to contend that he consented voluntarily to take the COVID-19 vaccine. There must not only be uncoerced consent, but there also needs to be fully informed consent with sufficient knowledge and comprehension of all relevant facts to enable him to make an enlightened decision.[2] If consent is not informed; it is not voluntary. How informed must it be to be "fully informed"? According to Hospers:

> The general formula is: he must be told all the relevant facts prior to making his decision. But this too turns out to be a matter of degree: one could go on forever citing medical facts which might turn out to be relevant; can one ever be quite sure one has reached an end of citing such facts? Even if the physician or researcher has cited all the facts he knows, there may still be others he doesn't know which are highly relevant to the patient's decision, even to his life or death. It would seem, then, that a patient can have "informed consent" but not "fully informed consent." If full (complete) information is required for voluntariness, the patient's consent must always be something less than fully voluntary.[2]

Whether public health officials or vaccine manufacturers provided all the relevant facts and known side-effects will be a factual determination. When biomedical medical paternalists pressured citizens to take the experimental COVID-19 vaccines through threats of punishment if you do not and promises of reward if you do, it failed voluntariness on both counts.[2]

Given the contemporary practice to allow minors as young as 11 in certain US States to receive a COVID-19 vaccine without parental consent, the principle of voluntary consent relating to children needs some explication.[26] It would barely be an exaggeration to maintain that the consent of children to participate in a medical experiment relating to never-before-used highly complicated mRNA gene therapy can never be voluntary, and that "voluntary consent," though it may have been acquired in such a case, could never be given. Even if the child recites all the possible "Side Effects After Getting a COVID-19 Vaccine" provided by a loquacious amoral doctor, the child is not in a position to understand and comprehend the short- and long-term consequences. Children simply do not have the emotional, intellectual, and experiential fortitude to understand the full force of a simple statement like "Severe allergic reactions after COVID-19 vaccination are rare" or to recognize the glaring factual inaccuracy of the CDC's claim: "The known risks of COVID-19 (for children) far outweigh the potential risks of having a rare adverse reaction to vaccination, including the possible risk of myocarditis or pericarditis."[27] Children can make all kinds of confident declarations, bets, and accept challenges, not realizing what they actually mean. When the 11-year-old is offered some cocaine instead of sherbet candy with the promise that "It is harmless and will give you a marvelous high" he may accept it enthusiastically, just as a toddler might play with a loaded handgun.[28] For this reason, contrary to what some modern-day biomedical paternalists enacted, all such pseudo-medical allowances to children should be prohibited by rule of law, for the child's safety. A young person cannot provide informed consent, much less "educated consent" – and those who exploit and profit from the child's vulnerability should be prosecuted in terms of the criminal law instead of leading States and parading the world stage.[2] To profess that an 11-year-old child can give "informed consent" (without the permission of his or her parents), to medical procedures that can have fatal long-term side-effects is preposterous and makes a mockery of medical ethics and the law.[26]

iii. Healthy psychological state. An individual might not be under coercion, and he might be fully informed of the pertinent facts, and yet he may make his decision in what can only be described as an irrational, psychological state. An individual suffering from schizophrenia may be mentally disturbed; but lacking this extreme, a person may be in demented, confused, intoxicated, senile, or in a severe state of manic depression. Generally, when a person is in such a state, he cannot be labeled as "fully informed."[2] His "consent" would lack volition by the second standard.[2] There may even be instances when the individual is not coerced and all of the relevant facts are openly before him or her, and yet he or she is in no position to make a sound judgment given his or her psychological state.[2] An individual in a state of manic depression might be quite articulate as to the facts, yet a recitation of typically shocking statistics, such as his own impending demise or the extermination of the entire planet, may well not distress him.[2] When a human being is in such a psychological state, his decisions cannot be described as fully voluntary.[2] A deranged person in an extremely hysterical phase may jump from a tenth-story balcony without compulsion and in complete possession of the relevant facts as to the probable effects of his action.[2] It is mostly because of the psychological state of such an individual, not because of intimidation or paucity of facts and information, that we simply cannot rationally portray his actions as fully voluntary.[2] It is similarly the case where individuals are suffering from mass delusion or Mass Formation Psychosis (MFP) in a nation subjected to large-scale government propaganda and "menticide" designed to influence emotions, motives, objective reasoning, and behavior such as occurred in Nazi Germany, the Soviet Union, North Korea, and Cambodia and cannot be seen as making voluntary decisions.[29-31] Dr. Joos Meerloo (1903-1976), renowned Dutch psychoanalyst, author, and former Professor of Psychiatry at the New York School of Psychiatry, researched the techniques by which organized mental pressure brings citizens to subservient submission, and by which totalitarians imprint their idiosyncratic "truth" on their victims' psyches. According to Meerloo "the totalitarian systems of the 20th century represent a kind of collective psychosis."[31] In his best-known book "The Rape of the Mind: The Psychology of Thought Control, Menticide and Brainwashing", he asserts that:

> It is interesting to note that the phenomenon of institutionalized mass delusion has so far received little scientific treatment, although the term is bandied about wherever the problems of political propaganda are discussed. But science has shied away from scrutinizing the collective mental aberration we call mass delusion when it is connected with present-day affairs; it is the historical examples, such as witchcraft and certain forms of mass hysteria, that have been examined in great detail.

> In our era of warring ideologies, in a time of battle for man's mind, this question demands attention. What is mass delusion? How does it arise? What can we do to combat it? The fact that I have made an analogy between the totalitarian frame of mind and the disease of mental withdrawal known as schizophrenia indicates that I consider the totalitarian ideology delusional and the totalitarian frame of mind a pathological distortion that may occur in anyone. When we tentatively define delusion as the loss of an independent, verifiable reality, with a consequent relapse into a more primitive state of awareness, we can see how the phenomenon of totalitarianism itself can be considered delusional.

For it is delusional (un-adapted to reality) to think of man as an obedient machine. It is delusional to deny his dynamic nature and to try to arrest all his thinking and acting at the infantile stage of submission to authority. It is delusional to believe that there is any one simple answer to the many problems with which life confronts us, and it is delusional to believe that man is so rigid, so unyielding in his structure that he has no ambivalences, no doubts, no conflicts, no warring drives within him.[31]

Instead of opinions and beliefs that correspond to the factual reality the victim of mass delusion becomes overrun by misconceptions that are false beliefs considered to be true despite the presence of data that proves the opposite. Mass delusion brought about by the crime that Meerloo coined "menticide" has been induced many times throughout history.[31] According to Meerloo, "menticide is an old crime against the human mind and spirit but systematized anew. It is an organized system of psychological intervention and judicial perversion through which a [ruling class] can imprint [their] own opportunistic thoughts upon the minds of those [they] plan to use and destroy. It is simply a question of reorganizing and manipulating collective feelings in the proper way." He explains that:

> …he who dictates and formulates the words and phrases we use, he who is master of the press and radio, is master of the mind. Repeat mechanically your assumptions and suggestions, diminish the opportunity for communicating dissent and opposition. This is the formula for political conditioning of the masses.[31]

Never in history have such effective means existed to manipulate a society into mass delusion. Television, the internet, smart phones, social media, and apps, all in conjunction with non-stop propaganda and sophisticated algorithms that censor the flow of truth and contradictory information, allow those in authority to easily assault the minds of the masses. The addictive nature of these technologies further ensures that most people willingly subject themselves to the governing elite's misinformation propaganda with an astonishing frequency.[32]

Preparing the populace for the crime of menticide commences with the propagating of fear. Mortal dangers - true, imagined, or manufactured - are utilized to spread fear, but an especially effective method is to make use of "waves of terror". Under this method, the propagation of fear is staggered with intervals of calm, but each of these intervals of calm is followed by the fabrication of an even more extreme spell of fear. The introduction of harsh COVID-19 lockdown, isolation, and social distancing mandates that were intermittently relaxed and then reintroduced with the arrival of more "dangerous variants" is a good example of this technique. As Meerloo writes,

> Each wave of terrorizing creates its effects more easily, after a breathing spell, than the one that preceded it because people are still disturbed by their previous experience. Morality becomes lower and lower, and the psychological effects of each new propaganda campaign become stronger; it reaches a public already softened up…there is in fact much that is comparable between the strange reactions of the citizens of [totalitarianism] and their culture as a whole on the one hand and the reactions of the…sick schizophrenic on the other.[31]

The fear and anxiety drive the individual members of society into a state of panic that is too emotionally exhausting to endure for a protracted period. To evade the anxiety, terror, and fear of the panic state, a negative reaction in the form of a psychotic break sometimes takes place.[32] A psychotic event is not a downward spiral into a state of chaos, but rather a re-arrangement of one's existential frame of reference "which blends fact and fiction, or delusions and reality" to remove the fear, anxiety, and panic.[32] A phase of panic followed by a phase of psychotic insight.[33] Silvano Arieti (1914-1981), former Professor of Psychiatry at New York Medical College, explains:

> [the] phase of panic – when the patient starts to perceive things in a different way, is frightened on account of it, appears confused, and does not know how to explain "the strange things" that are happening.

> [the] phase of psychotic insight – when the patient succeeds in "putting things together" [b]y devising a pathological way of seeing reality, [which allows him] to explain his abnormal experiences. The phenomenon is called "insight" because the patient finally sees meaning and relations in his experiences.[33]

The insight, however, is psychotic as it is founded on delusions and not on factual reality. The delusions permit the individual to get away from the flood of negative feelings associated with the extreme state of fear and anxiety, but at the cost of losing touch with reality.[33]

Eminent Swiss psychiatrist and psychoanalyst, Carl Jung (1865-1971), who coined the term "analytical psychology", also studied the historical phenomenon when mental illness becomes the norm, rather than the exception in a society, a situation that Jung termed a "psychic epidemic."

> Indeed, it is becoming ever more obvious that it is not famine, not earthquakes, not microbes, not cancer but man himself who is man's greatest danger to man, for the simple reason that there is no adequate protection against psychic epidemics, which are infinitely more devastating than the worst of natural catastrophes.[34]

Jung noted that the individuals in a state of collective psychosis "become morally and spiritually inferior," they "sink unconsciously to an inferior...intellectual level," they become "more unreasonable, irresponsible, emotional, erratic, and unreliable, ...Crimes the individual alone could never stand are freely committed by the group."[32,34] Jung further explained that "Heightened suggestibility mean individual bondage, because the individual is at the mercy of environmental influences. The discriminative capacity is weakened, and so is the sense of personal responsibility."[35] In his 1946 essay titled "After the Catastrophe", in which he assessed the madness that had prevailed during years of war with Germany, he writes:

> The phenomenon we have witnessed in Germany was nothing less than [an] outbreak of epidemic insanity. . . No one knew what was happening to him, least of all of the Germans, who allowed themselves to be driven to the slaughterhouse by their leading psychopaths like hypnotized sheep.[34]

In a 1955 letter to Dr. Hans Illing addressing the same topic, Jung wrote that:

> Since the sole carrier of life and the quintessence of any kind of community is the individual, it follows that he and his quality are of paramount importance. The individual must be complete

and must have substance, otherwise nothing has substance, for any number of zeros still do not amount to more than zero.

A group of inferior people is never better than anyone of them; it is just as inferior as they, and a State composed of nothing, but sheep is never anything else but a herd of sheep, even though it is led by a shepherd with a vicious dog.[35]

According to Belgian clinical psychologist and professor in clinical psychology at Ghent University, Professor Dr. Mattias Desmet , in "The Psychology of Totalitarianism," MFP is the phenomenon where about 30% of the population becomes entranced with the dominant State narrative, rendering a large fraction of the population completely unable to process objective scientific data and facts.[29,30] Individuals hypnotized by this process are unable to recognize the lies and misrepresentations they are being bombarded with daily, and actively attack anyone who has the temerity to share information with them that contradicts the government propaganda they have come to embrace. Studies suggest that mass formation follows a general distribution:

- 30% are brainwashed, hypnotized, indoctrinated by the group narrative.
- 40% in the middle are persuadable and may follow if no worthy alternative is perceived.
- 30% fight against the narrative.[29,30]

In a December 2021 article that explicated Professor Dr. Desmet's MFP theory, Dr. Robert Malone highlighted that:

Left unabated, a society under the spell of mass formation will support a totalitarian governance structure capable of otherwise unthinkable atrocities in order to maintain compliance. A note: mass formation is different from group think. There are easy ways to fix group think by just bringing in dissenting voices and making sure you give them platforms. It isn't so easy with mass formation. Even when the narrative falls apart, cracks in the strategy clearly aren't solving the issue, the hypnotized crowd can't break free of the narrative. This is what appears to be happening now with COVID-19. The solution for those in control of the narrative is to produce bigger and bigger lies to prop up the solution. Those being controlled by mass formation no longer are able to use reason to break free of the group narrative.[36]

Voluntariness, like so many other notions, is not an over-simplified yes-or-no concept, but a matter of degree and cognizance of all the relevant facts. Coercion itself encompasses a broad range of permutations, from the application of physical force at one end, to the application of subtle emotional pressure on the other. Edward Bernays (1891-1995) pioneered the scientific technique of shaping and manipulating public opinion. He famously dubbed this "the engineering of consent" which provides leaders that "understand the mechanisms and motives of the group mind" the means to "control and regiment the masses according to our will without their knowing about it." This not free and informed consent but manipulated, coerced and illegitimate consent.[37] Bernays noted that:

> The conscious and intelligent manipulation of the organized habits and opinions of the masses is an important element in democratic society. Those who manipulate this unseen mechanism of society constitute an invisible government which is the true ruling power of our country.[37]

Justification for paternalistic policies

Is there any good reason at all for legal paternalism? When and to what extent can the State restrict fundamental freedoms? What kinds of conduct may the legislature make criminal without infringing on the moral autonomy of individual citizens? Is there a limit to biomedical legal paternalism that the State must not exceed?

Mill presents that what is probably the best answer to this question: the "harm principle." This principle protects self-regarding acts, carving out a space for the freedom that should be shielded from outside intervention. Other-regarding acts, though, might be subject to interference by others.[3] Mill writes: "The only part of the conduct of anyone, for which he is amenable to society, is that which concerns others. In the part which merely concerns himself, his independence is, of right, absolute. Over himself, over his body and mind, the individual is sovereign."[3,12-14]

According to Mill, legal paternalism is only justified to maintain and sustain fundamental rights and autonomy of a specific person. He, for instance, held that an agreement by which a person agrees to sell himself into permanent slavery should be null and void – as indeed it would be declared by effectively any court in a constitutional democracy. But why, if a person enters such an agreement, should anyone impede his actions?

> The reason for not interfering, unless for the sake of others, with a person's voluntary acts is consideration for his liberty. . .. By selling himself for a slave, he abdicates his liberty; he foregoes any future use of it beyond that single act. He therefore defeats, in his own case, the very purpose which is the justification of allowing him to dispose of himself. ...The principle of freedom cannot require that he should be free not to be free. It is not freedom to be allowed to alienate his freedom.[13]

The reason for not respecting such an agreement is the need to preserve the autonomy and freedom of the person to make future choices. According to Hospers, Legal Paternalism is warranted at time t, in order to preserve a wider range of individual human rights and freedoms for that person at times $t_2, t_3, t_4, t_5, t_6, t_7$, etc.[2] In other words, fundamental human rights cannot be violated for a reason other than their increased protection.

Professor Julian Savulescu, of Oxford University's Uehiro Centre for Practical Ethics, noted that the primary reason for employing coercive measures during an epidemic was preventing harm to others. "You're not entitled to shoot a gun into the air risking harm to other people and likewise, you can't shoot Covid that might kill other people into a crowd," he said. Savulescu qualified his statement by confirming that four ethical conditions must be met to justify coercive policies like vaccine or mask mandates. "First of all, the problem has to be significant, so you have to have a grave emergency or real risk of harming people. Secondly, you have to have a safe and effective intervention," he told CNBC. "Thirdly, [the outcome] has to be better than fewer liberties and more restrictive measures. And lastly, the level of coercion has to be proportionate to the level of risk and the safety and effectiveness of the intervention."[38] The fact is, COVID-19 cannot be compared to a gun being shot into a crowd. A bullet through the head or heart will kill 100% of its victims whereas COVID-19 poses a risk of death to fever than 0.3% of the population. Secondly, COVID-19 vaccines, mask mandates, and lockdowns all proved to be either unsafe and/or ineffective. Thirdly, the outcomes of the COVID-19 measures did significantly more harm than good. And lastly, the demonstrably ineffective measures were egregiously disproportional to combat a disease that posed no risk of mortality or morbidity to 99% of the population. At the time Savulescu made his comments in November 2021, this was a well-known fact.[39,40]

Gostin *et al.*, in their 2002 article entitled "The Model State Emergency Health Powers Act: planning for and response to bioterrorism and naturally occurring infectious diseases", specified four principled justifications for paternalistic policies. Such public health interventions must be: (i) required to prevent material risk, first, in the opinion of health bureaucrats but, ultimately, to the contentment of an independent judge; (ii) well-tailored to deal with the threat and "not going further than what is necessary;" (iii) authorized in a manner allowing public oversight; and (iv) amendable in the case of a miscalculation. Contrariwise, they observed that such violations would not be justified if: (i) the problem was not as serious as initially believed, (ii) the measure taken was unresponsive to the problem, or (iii) the regulatory action was more constrictive than needed to diminish the risk.[41,42]

All vulnerable people have access to COVID-19 vaccines or can take other proven effective precautionary measures to reduce their risk of infection, such as self-isolation, prophylactic medication, and protective apparel.[3] Considering the aforementioned and the fact that the theory of symptomless spread as major driver of the pandemic has been debunked *in toto,* the argument that healthy people pose a risk to vulnerable groups and therefore need to be subjected to paternalistic policies that infringe a wide array of fundamental human rights and freedoms such as freedom of movement, freedom of religion, and freedom to bodily autonomy is irrational and unreasonable.[3,39-42]

IHRL and the Thesis of Implied Limitations

It is important to distinguish between (i) ethical justification and (ii) justification in terms of IHRL. Although there is some overlap and shared principles between the two, a violation of the first may still be legal while a violation of the second would be illegal. In terms of the thesis of "implied limitations" of a fundamental human right, the only permitted legal limitations to human rights are those necessary for their existence as a whole. The theory of "implied limitations" is a consequence of the inviolability and interdependence of fundamental human rights. If a fundamental right could be restricted for reasons other than their overall protection – for instance, for a general social benefit – they would no longer be inviolable.[3,12]

Fundamental rights are constitutively inalienable; they exist necessarily, inhere in every person, and cannot be taken away from him or her.[3] Therefore, they cannot be limited for a reason other than their overall protection. This does not imply, of course, that their exercise does not meet some limits, but such limits cannot find their justification outside the system of fundamental rights themselves.[9] Paternalistic policies can consequently only be lawful if the policy strictly complies with the derogation and limitation provisions set out in Article 4 of the ICCPR.[3] It must, therefore, be shown that the paternalistic policy or law in question serves a "constitutionally-acceptable" purpose, that it respects the essence of the fundamental human right, and that there is sufficient proportionality between the harm done by the law or State action and the benefits it is designed to achieve.

The limitation of human rights for a purpose that is reasonable and necessary in a democratic society involves the weighing up of competing values and, ultimately, an assessment based on proportionality.[3,16-18] The principle of proportionality prescribes that all statutes that affect human rights should be proportionate or reasonable. As set out in Chapter 5, the proportionality analysis applied to paternalistic policy examines the following set of sequential questions once a *prima facie* infringement of a fundamental human right has been found. First, does the infringing paternalistic policy pursue a legitimate aim (legitimacy)? Second, is the paternalistic policy suitable and rationally connected to the fulfillment of policy goals (efficacy)? Third, is the infringing paternalistic policy necessary and the least restrictive option (necessity)? And fourth, do the benefits of the paternalistic policy measures outweigh the cost (proportionality, "*strictu sensu*", or "balancing")?[3,17] In their article "Public health ethics: mapping the terrain", Childress *et al.* list five criteria aligning with the IHRL and that public health mediations that infringe on individual autonomy need to adhere to in order to be ethically justified: (i) effectiveness, (ii) proportionality, (iii) necessity, (iv) least infringement, and (v) public justification.[43] In Chapters 4, 5, 6, and 7, I have demonstrated that vaccine mandates and other COVID-19 mandates do not meet any of these legal and ethical standards.

Chapter Conclusion

Under the paternalistic guise of protecting the vulnerable members of society – children, the elderly, the frail – States oppressed and injured not only them but healthy, productive members of society. Instead of offering "protection" to the vulnerable and respecting their human rights and freedoms, States "waged civil war" against all people who refused biomedical paternalistic treatments and who insisted on medical self-determination.[44,45] This war has allowed the State to discriminate against those people in the name of "greater good" medical therapy. Just as grievously, millions of people were deprived of the lifesaving medications they needed because effective early treatment options have been made illegal or available only through a prescription that most medical doctors were afraid to provide lest they come under the scrutinization of State medical boards and lose their licenses.

The biomedical paternalistic State has grown in reach and power since 2020, with its pseudo-scientific biological theories and gene therapy mandatory vaccinations having led to the exploitation, suppression, coercion, and antagonization of the global population. Obeisance to the therapeutic State now renders us a "nation of victims."[46] Far from succeeding in its avowed program of producing and maintaining "zero infections," public health officials instead have created nations of irrational, self-pitying, imprudent, pseudo-medical victims increasingly inept at living free, self-determining, and healthy lives – the very kind of lives that, paradoxically, public health claims as its goal for a nation.[46]

Justice, or the protection and enforcement of individual human rights (especially the "inherent" right to freedom of choice), is the very purpose of an ideal State and the standard by which a State Party should determine appropriate regulation. The present-day arguments for restricting individual autonomy to promote public health are principally misguided, from an ethical, empirical and legal perspective:

- On **empirical grounds**, there can be no debate that people who exercise the highest degree of individual autonomy are also the healthiest.[4] Contrariwise, people with the least individual autonomy – with a meager measure of control over their employment circumstances or other major life conditions – have the poorest health. The obvious inference is that, to promote public health, public officials should focus on finding ways to expand individual autonomy, not constrain it.
- On **ethical grounds**, many different philosophical theories identify autonomy as a defining element in human well-being and the essential precondition for moral agency.[4] Crucially for our objectives here, in the works of both John Stuart Mill and Immanuel Kant, the state of autonomy offers the crucial link between standards of the rule of law and the notion of free and equal individuals. Autonomy or self-rule is the *sine qua non* that allows moral agents to give free and informed

consent to any proposed public health interventions.[3] Autonomy here is equated with positive freedom, independence, and self-mastery. The key point is "being in the position of deciding, not being decided for."[4]

- On **juridical grounds** it is apparent from the relevant facts that the COVID-19 public health "medical model," of pseudoscientific justifications for managing and controlling every aspect of human behavior violates IHRL. Moreover, paternalistic mandatory vaccination policies do not meet the legal standards set out in Article 4 of the ICCPR, the proportionality analysis, and infringe the essence of the right to free and informed consent prior to medical experimentation.

Paternalism, as such, is not incompatible with the legal order of a constitutional State, but in such a legal order, a paternalistic purpose for the greater good cannot be considered a sufficient reason to restrict personal freedom.[3] History teaches that "for the common good is the most common excuse for uncommon evil," and that "the more corrupt the State, the more numerous the laws."[47,48] Fundamental human rights may only be restricted in line with international emergency derogation and limitation provisions and the principle of proportionality.[49,50]

Where governments interfere in individuals' autonomy, it is important that paternalistic policies should be subjected to rigorous scrutiny to determine their legitimacy, efficacy, necessity, and proportionality. If the limitation of rights does not serve the purpose of and contributing to a society based on human dignity, equality, and freedom, it cannot be justifiable.[3,49-51] More significantly, to achieve public health objectives, greater attention must be directed toward advocating a common perception of a just and lawful society, in relation to which there are deep divisions in contemporary Western society.

The eminent Professor Joel Feinberg (former Regents Professor of Philosophy and Law, University of Arizona) viewed as "one of the most influential figures in American jurisprudence" highlighted that:

The principle of legal paternalism justifies State coercion to protect individuals from self-inflicted harm, or in its extreme version, to guide them, whether they like it or not, toward their own good. Parents can be expected to justify their interference in the lives of their children… on the ground that *"daddy knows best."* …Put in this blunt way, paternalism seems a preposterous doctrine. If adults are treated as children, they will come in time to be like children. Deprived of the right to choose for themselves, they will soon lose the power of rational judgment and decision. Even children, after a certain point, had better not be "treated as children," else they will never acquire the outlook and capability of responsible adults.[5,53]

As espoused in the UN Vienna Declaration, "Human rights and fundamental freedoms are the birthright of all human beings; their protection and promotion is the first responsibility of governments." Paternalistic States do not have the right to decide if and when people are entitled to enjoy their fundamental human rights. Governments' only duty is to protect fundamental rights and freedoms.[2,3,52]

11. AN UNJUST LAW IS NO LAW AT ALL

"Human law is law only by virtue of its accordance with right reason; and thus, it is manifest that it flows from the eternal law. And in so far as it deviates from right reason it is called an unjust law; in such case it is no law at all, but rather a species of violence."

— Thomas Aquinas

Governing through law and governing in accordance with the rule of law are two very different things. All government is unavoidably by law, as power that fails to be authorized by law is not government power. It follows that all law promulgated by the executive cannot automatically be characterized as morally meritorious or governance in accordance with the "rule of law".[1,2] The Nazi era laws enacted in Germany in the 1930s all met the formal conception of law but lacked the substance and the virtue of law that aligns with the "rule of law".[1,2]

Channeling State power through statutory law means adhering to certain formal features of legal rules. The formal component of law is satisfied when laws conform to certain formal and procedural requirements. Laws should *inter alia* be duly promulgated, general in application, prospective, clear, unambiguous, stable, transparent, and be presided over by an independent judiciary. The rule of law, however, is not satisfied by procedural and formal requirements only. While insisting on these requirements, an exercise of State power that pays "credible tribute" to the rule of law additionally demands that law be substantively just.[1,2] Typically, this means that the law must align with the natural law, be rational, and inherently respect fundamental human rights and freedoms.[1,2]

Vaccine passport laws turn every society into a dystopian nightmare, forcing unvaccinated people to live like fugitives, unable to work and earn a living, study, dine at restaurants, attend a ball game, or in certain instances buy groceries, fuel, medicine, or even clothing, due to being banned from almost every retail establishment. Vaccine passport laws are illogical, non-scientific, and futile in preventing either contagion or transmission of COVID-19. On the contrary, vaccine passports give people carrying them a false sense of security that they cannot be infected with COVID-19 nor infect others, while more and more scientific data and everyday lived experience confirms that these vaccines are useless.[3] It is apparent to any objective observer that vaccine passports are not about our health. There is no rational, objective, sensical, scientific, or epidemiological basis for continuing a vaccination campaign with ineffective vaccines that neither confer immunity nor prevent contagion. The vaccine passports are all about politics, control, illegitimately stripping citizens' fundamental human rights, and enriching a corrupt global elite. All around the globe, unjust public health policies have been enacted that have severely encroached on fundamental human rights and freedoms and deprived ordinary people of going about their everyday lives. Governments are blackmailing, shaming, and coercing their citizens and openly admitting that people who refuse to be vaccinated with an experimental vaccine with death as a potential side-effect will be discriminated against. During 2021 and 2022, numerous State Parties around the globe are unashamedly making it abundantly clear that people who choose not to be vaccinated and experimented on will have little to no fundamental human rights.[4-6] To these States, they are a subclass of human beings not worthy of and not entitled to a normal life. In their perverse view, citizens are only entitled to enjoy fundamental rights and freedoms and enjoy everyday life if they take all vaccines prescribed by COVID-19 government autocrats. Human rights and fundamental freedoms are subject to having an up-to-date vaccine passport!

The idea that healthy people are endangering others simply by breathing and going about their everyday lives, that they therefore need to be injected with a vaccine proven to be ineffective against a disease with a survival rate of 99.7% or risk being stripped of inalienable fundamental human rights, is the greatest swindle and chicanery in the history of the world. Citizens worldwide have been deceived and tricked into believing that the various COVID-19 mandates were in their best interest and that these pseudo-scientific public health measures to combat a disease that poses no threat to more than 99.85% of the world's population were lawful. However, vaccines mandates, mask mandates, and lockdowns are illegitimate and not authorized by natural law, the social contract, or IHRL. They are a collection of unjust laws, and an unjust law is no law at all.

Clearly, in the COVID-19 era, conceptions of the law and mandates – which emphasize law's formal conceptions rather than the substantive merits of law – are favored among contemporary Western States. These formal conceptions are attuned to the positivist outlook that insist that law and morality, rationality and reason do not need to coincide.[2]

Jurisprudential compositions on the "rule of law" is vast and this chapter does not attempt to provide a comprehensive overview. Rather, this chapter will explicate how the rule of law has been conceived both historically and in modern legal theory in order to help illuminate certain features of current debates about the rule of law. In particular, I will focus attention on the historic association between the rule of law and concepts of natural law and modern concepts of substantive justice.

The Rule of Law and Tyranny

Almost 2,400 years ago, the Greek philosophers Plato and Aristotle studied political philosophy and wrestled with many of the same political problems that we are faced with in the COVID-19 era.[7,8]

Two of the various political topics that these men wrote about were "the rule of law" and "tyranny:"

- The rule of law is the notion that no one is above the law, even those who are in a position of authority and power.[7]
- Tyranny ensues when absolute power is allowed to go unchecked. In a tyrannical State, the rulers become immoral and corrupt and utilize their power to further their interests instead of the interest of the citizens subject to their rule.[7]

The rule of law serves as a safeguard against tyranny because just laws such as IHRL *jus cogens* and obligations *erga omnes* that are respected and adhered to ensure that States and public officials do not become corrupt, and if they do, they can be held to account.

Both Plato's and Aristotle's arguments in support of the rule of law are the arguments of a natural law theorist. Both philosophers' rule of law theories encapsulated an understanding that the rule of law aligns with the natural law.[2]

Plato (c. 428–347 BC)

Plato's most significant work on politics, his book "The Republic," was published about 380 BC. "The Republic" explores the meaning of justice and looks at different types of government.[7] The Ancient Greeks recognized the existence of a higher law (*nomos*). This higher law was derived through reason from nature (*phusis*), and they regarded this law as being universal, divine, and immutable. According to Plato, human law is at best only an imperfect image of the ideal law of nature.[2,8] According to Plato, "the state in which the rulers are most reluctant to govern is always the best and most quietly governed, and the state in which they are most eager, the worst." Plato deemed tyranny the "worst disorder of a state" as tyrants lack "the very faculty that is the instrument of judgment" – reason.[7]

In determining whether a government has become tyrannical, a good test is "sound reason" or put differently "rationality." Can the government edicts and mandates be rationally explained and defended when confronted with independent, objective data and facts? To mandate citizens to be injected with an experimental vaccine that has been proven to be ineffective and unsafe to combat a disease with a greater than 99.5% survival rate is not only irrational and unreasonable, but patently absurd and devoid of any reason. Plato noted that the tyrannical ruler is enslaved because the best part of him (reason) is enslaved, and likewise, the authoritarian State is enslaved because "it too lacks reason and order." As we have again witnessed over the past two and a half years, when the government "lacks reason" and issues irrational, unreasonable mandates, such as vaccine mandates, mask mandates, and lockdowns, society will fall into disorder.[7]

No outside governing power limits the tyrant's egotistical conduct in a tyrannical government. To Plato, the only solution is respect for and adherence to the rule of law, as the rule of law shields citizens against oppression and tyranny. In "The Republic", he described the law as an "external authority" that serves as the ally of all the citizens in a country.[7]

In his work "The Statesman" – a discourse wherein the analysis of the rule of law, in particular, has been argued to be of significance to modern-day political theory – Plato surmised that the goodness of the State is entirely a function of whether the sovereigns "govern on the basis of expert knowledge and what is just" irrespective of "whether they rule according to laws or without laws."[2,9] Plato's claim that laws must always be followed by government officials seems to refer to the principal meaning of law – that is to say, "good law." Platonic dialogues make use of the word "law" in this sense, asserting that it is only "those who don't know" who identify as "law" that which is not "correct."[2,9,10]

From this viewpoint, a society can only claim to have the "rule of law" when its mandates, rules and decrees have come about in a way that ensures that they will be substantively good: "by trial and error, on the good advice of experts, and after securing popular approval through persuasion."[2,9] Plato referred to laws that come into existence with "advisers ... having given advice on each subject in an attractive way." For the reason that the advice must be "attractive," (sound, rational, reasonable, moral, objective) the test for a just law in conformity with the *"rule of law"* remains in the final analysis substantive.[2]

In his final book "Laws," Plato links the "rule of law" tenet with the "natural law."[11,12] Law must have "virtue" or "complete justice" as its goal in order to conform with the "rule of law." In discussing laws that are "sound" or "good", Plato acknowledges that laws may also be "unsound" and "bad." But the latter are in reality not laws, but "spurious laws" and it is futile to argue that they have any legal authority. The "Laws" test for differentiating spurious laws from real laws is entirely substantive. Having thus clarified how properly to recognize law, Plato further asserts that:

> Where the law is subject to some other authority and has none of its own, the collapse of the state, in my view, is not far off; but if law is the master of the government and the government is its slave, then the situation is full of promise and men enjoy all the blessings that the gods shower on a state.[7]

The text also proceeds to note that a good State requires not only the rule of law but government officials adroit to administer the laws.

During the COVID-19 era, the world saw an unprecedented wave of governing politicians acting lawlessly by placing the financial interest of their corporate backers above the law and right reason, openly contravening IHRL, by instituting various unreasonable government mandates that have no basis in reason.

Aristotle (384–322 BC)

Aristotle is "generally regarded as the founder of the Rule-of-Law tradition".[2] Academic scholars of the rule of law often cite him and he is said to have provided the first "coherent description" or unambiguous clarification of the rule of law as a normative ideal.[2]

The State was a Greek citizen's whole scheme of association, a city wherein all his needs, material, physical, and spiritual, were fulfilled. When Aristotle used the term "State" he comprehended within it all that we connote by the terms State, government, society, economic activity, and religion. To him, government needed to be substantively just. The State existed, according to Aristotle, not merely to make life possible but to make life good. The State was the individual's means of realizing his own dreams and aspirations. For Aristotle, *"eudaimonia"* or "happiness" was a core concept in defining both human perfection and the goal of a community or a State. The main goal of the best constitution (politeia) was happiness, defined by Aristotle as "the perfect...activity and employment of virtue."[8]

In his famous work "Politics," a collection of essays on government intended to provide direction for leaders, statesmen, governments, and politicians, Aristotle analyzed the divergent governments in Greece's numerous city-States and identified six different systems of government.[7,8] Aristotle classified the different systems of government as either "true" or "defective and perverted." He, among other things, stated that:

> Governments which have a regard to the common interest are constituted in accordance with strict principles of justice and are therefore true forms; but those which regard only the interest of the rulers are all defective and perverted forms, for they are despotic.

"True" governments served the common interests of all citizens, while "Despotic" governments served only the selfish interests of a particular person or group of persons. Figure 11.1 below shows the "despotic" and "true" constitutions.[7,8]

Aristotle's 'True' vs. 'Despotic' Forms of Government		
Number of Rulers	**'True' (Common Interest)**	**'Despotic' (Selfish Interest)**
one	Monarchy	Tyranny
few	Aristocracy	Oligarchy
many	Polity	Democracy

Figure 11.1: Aristotle's true vs. despotic forms of government
Source: Aristotle, Constitutional Rights Foundation

To Aristotle, tyranny is the illogical, capricious, and arbitrary power of a government that is "…responsible to no one, [and that] governs with a view to its own advantage, not to that of its subjects, and therefore against their will." Aristotle believed that tyranny is the "very reverse of a constitution." He noted that where the laws have no authority, there is no constitution or legitimate legal construct.[7] The law should be supreme and apply to both the government and the governed. Laws should reign supreme "when good" but when "laws miss the mark" they are not binding.[2,13] Aristotle emphasized that these laws must uphold just principles and standards, such that "true forms of government will of necessity have just laws, and perverted forms of government will have unjust laws."[7,13] The proliferation of irrational, arbitrary, and unjust laws such as vaccine, mask, and self-isolation mandates, is clear evidence that State and public institutions have become perverted and corrupted.

According to Aristotle, any form of government will be perverted when the "rule of law" is not respected and adhered to. Aristotle warned that in democracies without law, as we are again witnessing in the COVID-19 era, where numerous world governments are flouting IHRL, demagogues (leaders appealing to emotions) will take over.

> For in democracies where the laws are not supreme, demagogues spring up…. [T]his sort of democracy…exercise a despotic rule over the better citizens. The decrees of the [demagogues] correspond to the edicts of the tyrant. Such a democracy is fairly open to the objection that it is not a constitution at all; for where the laws have no authority, there is no constitution. The law ought to be supreme over all![7]

Aristotle made the same argument about oligarchies and noted that "When the rulers have great wealth and numerous friends, … individuals rule and not the law."[7,13] In an October 2021, Newsweek article, Carol Roth accurately reported that:

> When historians look back on the decisions made beginning in March 2020 and still going strong, this period will be remembered as the "Great Consolidation"—the acceleration of a historic wealth transfer and power concentration out of the hands of the middle class and into those with political power and connections. The "connected" form a powerful bloc comprised of big government, big business and big special interests. And though their monikers label them "big," they are comprised of relatively small elites. And they are seeking to use their power to benefit themselves at your expense.[14]

Big companies have more lobbying dollars and more connections, and thus more ability to play the political game.... As a result, big firms were deemed "essential" and allowed to stay open during the pandemic, while small businesses were subjected to punishing lockdown orders and forced to close, in part or completely. Many of the examples were infuriating given the absurd hypocrisies they presented. For example, big box pet retailers like PetSmart that groomed pet hair and nails were deemed essential—while salons owned by small business owners that served humans were not.... Spending that couldn't be done at closed businesses was shifted to the ones that were open, which were by and large big businesses, many of which saw a substantial increase in their revenue.[14]

During the COVID-19 pandemic, we have witnessed firsthand the perversion of democracy and democratic institutions on a national and international level, as the political elite and their corporate cronies and paymasters enriched themselves at the expense of the middle class and to the detriment and suffering of the poor and the vulnerable.[8] About 97 million more people are living on less than $1.90 a day because of the pandemic, increasing the global poverty rate from 7.8% to 9.1%.[15] In contrast, in the United States of America, billionaires have grown $2.1 trillion richer during the COVID-19 pandemic, their collective fortune increasing by 70% — from just short of $3 trillion at the start of the COVID-19 emergency on March 18, 2020, to over $5 trillion on October 15, 2021, according to Forbes data analyzed by Americans for Tax Fairness (ATF) and the Institute for Policy Studies Program on Inequality (IPS). The $5 trillion in wealth now held by 745 billionaires is two-thirds more than the $3 trillion in wealth held by the bottom 50% of households estimated by the Federal Reserve Board.[15]

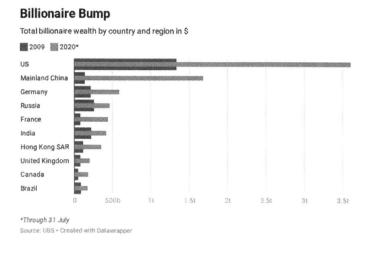

Figure 11.2: Total billionaire wealth by country and region 2009 and 2020
Source: UBS, Forbes

Interestingly, in addition to law, Aristotle believed a sizeable middle class would protect against the excesses and profligacy of oligarchy and democracy. He explains that:

> [T]he best political community is formed by citizens of the middle class, and that those states are likely to be well-administered in which the middle class is large, and stronger if possible than both the other classes . . .; for the addition of the middle class turns the scale and prevents either of the extremes from being dominant.[7]

Aristotle correctly posited that "the rule of law" is preferable to the rule of any individual or group of individuals, for the reason that individuals possess shortcomings and could unjustly tailor the State to their interests, whereas the "rule of law" is objective and impartial. Government leaders ought to be "the servants of the laws," because "law is order, and good law is good order."[7,8]

Thomas Aquinas (1225-1274)

As witnessed throughout the ages, political rulers are sometimes just and sometimes unjust. In the thirteenth century, Thomas Aquinas (1225-1274) commented that if rational laws govern a community for the common good, such government will be classified as just. On the other hand, if the community is directed not for the common good but in the financial and political interest of a small corporate and political kleptocratic elite, it is a perversion of government and no longer just.[16]

According to Aquinas, when the government is unjustly exercised by a small minority who seeks personal profit from their position instead of the real good of the community, such a government is called a tyrannical government. The tyrants oppress their citizens through numerous arbitrary, irrational, unjust laws instead of ruling justly.[16]

The COVID-19 pandemic government overreach is a first-rate example of such tyrannical powers in progress, establishing absolute control over the population by deceit and subversion, in contravention of all peremptory norms and covenants protecting those rights unbeknown to the majority of the citizens of the world.

The doctrine of natural law has been pivotal in the just regulation of civil society for more than 800 years. In terms of the doctrine of natural law, it is the principal duty of the State to protect and improve the fundamental human rights of its citizens. The government acts contrary to its natural purpose, the function for which it exists, if it hurts rather than helps a single one of its citizens for the sake of benefiting all the others.[16] The government or State is always subject to the rule of law in relation to what type of mandates it may issue (*quantum ad vim directivam*), and the *vim directivam* is directly related to the rule of law.[16] Any human laws or mandates are nothing more than the expression of the natural order of justice, which limits the State's authority. The concept of the rule of law is inseparable from the concept of natural law.[16] The State must always obey the natural law and cannot exercise power over anyone unless the law permits it. There must be a rational law that aligns with the natural law sanctioning everything the State does. The State cannot create or abolish inviolable human rights by law, mandate, or convention (as many governments across the globe professed during the COVID-19 pandemic); they can only confirm the existence of fundamental human rights and protect these rights. The role of the State is no more than declaratory.[16] Fundamental human rights have always existed within humans and exist independently of the State or any of its mandates. Foreign and even stateless persons cannot, lawfully, be deprived of these sacrosanct rights. The existence or continuation of basic human rights does not depend on the extrajudicial will or whims of public officials.[16]

The State, therefore, cannot lawfully act erratically, irrationally, or arbitrarily. To do so would be incompatible and contradictory with the basic concept of the rule of law, which is a central value of any constitutional democracy. The rule of law requires that the government exercise its powers rationally and respect the individual's human rights.[16] "Every law is ordained for the common-wellbeing of men, and only for this does it have the reason of law (*vim et rationem legis*); if it fails in this regard, it has no capacity to bind (*virtutem obligandi non habet*)."[16]

As we again witnessed during the COVID-19 pandemic, the misuse of the law may occur in two ways:

- First, when that which is mandated by law is opposed to the object for which that law was constituted. A law that violates fundamental human rights such as the rights to bodily autonomy and to be free from medical experimentation and forced vaccination is opposed to the object of the law and therefore unjust. According to Aquinas, in such a situation, not only is there no obligation or responsibility to obey the law, but one is obligated to defy it, as did the holy martyrs who suffered death rather than obey the immoral commands of tyrants.[16]

- Secondly, when those in authority enact laws that exceed the competence of their authority. When a government demands adherence to a law that it did not have the legal and constitutional authority to make in the first place (as the legal pre-requisite criteria as set out on Article 4 of the ICCPR for an "emergency" was not met), such as stay at home mandates, mask mandates, and social distancing mandates, the citizens are free to obey or disobey.[16]

A line has been crossed in the global response to the COVID-19 pandemic. We have seen a shift towards a different and incorrect understanding of human rights and fundamental freedoms and a false understanding of the relationship between the individual and the State. Many so-called Western democracies have now crossed the line into an absurd lawless realm where the assumption is that human rights are something that is granted to the individual by the State as a prize for good behavior and total subservience to all government mandates irrespective of how irrational or arbitrary those mandates may be. The contention is that our ability to go about our everyday life is not something that we can take for granted, something that is ours, but is something that is given to us by the State in return for full compliance. According to the COVID-19 tyrants, our body is also something that is owned by the State and by the majority, and what we do with our bodies is determined by the State's vague and subjective notion of the "common good," which is very malleable and changes in line with the government's illegitimate agenda from day-to-day.

The shift, as mentioned above, is illegitimate and not in line with the basic rule of law, as that which is ordered by COVID-19 law is opposed to the object for which the law is constituted, that is the protection of fundamental human rights. It is not within the State's legitimate power to grant or take away human rights depending on good behavior or adherence to extra-juridical pseudo-medical mandates. The objective of the rule of law is always to protect individual rights by requiring the government to act in accordance with the law. This is a fundamental principle of the rule of law, which is a basic principle of constitutional law. Tyranny is the exercise of totalitarian power over citizens, which is not warranted by law.[9] Central to the conception of the constitutional order is that the executive and every sphere of government are constrained and restricted by the principle that they may exercise no power and perform no function outside that conferred upon them by the rule of law. The State cannot exert control over its citizens unless the law permits it to do so. If the State acts without legal authority, it acts lawlessly, something that a constitutional democracy cannot tolerate.[16]

Fuller's Theory of the Rule of Law – An Irrational Law is Void *Ab Initio*

In January 2022, prior to his death, the world's top virologist, Professor Luc Montagnier, who received a Nobel Prize in 2008 for discovering the HIV virus, commented that "It would be irrational, legally indefensible and contrary to the public interest for the government to mandate [COVID-19] vaccines absent any evidence that the vaccines are effective in stopping the spread of the pathogen they target."[17]

The principle of rationality and non-arbitrariness is an important ordering principle in IHRL. In his 1964 book "The Morality of Law," Lon Fuller, (former professor of Law at Harvard University) regarded as "one of the four most important American legal theorists of the last hundred years," envisaged law as a form of social ordering that uses respected and authoritative mandates to "create the conditions essential for a rational human existence."[18,19]

Fuller contends that for mandates to be moral (to satisfy the demands of "external morality"), they must promote the objectives of humanity. In expanding his theory of the rule of law, Fuller accentuated the requirement for policymakers to respect rationality and human autonomy. Respecting rationality and human autonomy was not merely a normative principle, but also a pragmatic necessity for those who sought to create a legitimate legal system. For the law to succeed as a form of social ordering, States must appeal to the rational dimensions of individuals by empowering those individuals to understand why the law has been enacted and what the law demands so they can conform their actions to its demands. Only when the State treats the law's subjects as rational, self-regulating representatives will its directives lead to compliance, thereby nurturing a culture of legality.[19,20]

According to Fuller's social theory of law, there is an "internal morality" that "makes law possible." If citizens do not feel a moral obligation to obey the law, then the law could not survive.[21] Government mandates must contain specific moral standards to be regarded as moral and legitimate. The mandates must therefore:

1. express general, not *ad hoc*, commands;
2. be publicized and communicated;
3. not be applied retroactively;
4. be intelligible and rational;
5. not be contradictory to other laws;
6. not require conduct impossible to comply with or "conduct beyond the power [rights] of the affected party;"
7. be relatively stable and not be frequently changed;
8. be administered in a just, congruent manner.[19,20-22]

A mandate that fails to satisfy any one of these eight *sine qua non* (essential elements) or desiderata would be "futile" from the standpoint of contributing to a genuine "legal system," for the reason that it would offer no rational basis for people to orientate their behavior in retort.[19,20] The eight essential elements are also morally consequential since an individual's moral duty to obey directives from governments would depend upon whether the mandates could rationally attract compliance. As Fuller expounds,

> [T]here can be no rational ground for asserting that a man can have a moral obligation to obey a legal rule that came into existence only after he had acted, or was unintelligible, or was contradicted by another rule of the same system, or commanded the impossible, or changed every minute.[19,20]

Fuller noted that these elements of a legitimate "legal system establish a kind of reciprocity between government and the citizen with respect to the observance of rules."[19,20] Should governments fail to govern with directives that satisfy the eight *sine qua non*, their relationship with their citizens would lack the reciprocity required to create legal authority. No legislator, even a despot, can disregard these standards entirely and succeed. It follows that some compliance with moral principles is necessary to make law, even bad law.[20] According to Fuller's theory, when this "bond of reciprocity" is entirely broken by the State, nothing is left on which to ground the citizen's sense of duty to observe laws.[19,20]

To merit recognition as legitimate law, mandates from States must offer rational grounds for compliance. Directives that violate citizens' fundamental human rights *jus cogens* cannot satisfy this requirement. For example, there is no rational basis for concluding that people have moral obligations to comply with mandates that authorize their own torture, enslavement, arbitrary detention, or being injected with an experimental vaccine with death or acute ailment as a potential side-effect. These kinds of mandates do not offer rational grounds for compliance and cannot credibly be interpreted as actions taken in the best interest of the individuals subject to them. Accordingly, arbitrary detention, torture, slavery, medical experimentation without free and informed consent, and other violations of international *jus cogens* norms undo the reciprocity that is essential to sustain legal order.

International human rights norms do not exist for the benefit of States but for the benefit of human beings subject to their control. With regards to the legitimacy of vaccine mandates, for instance, the appropriate inquiry is whether the purported incongruence between the positive norm against being subjected to medical or scientific experimentation without free consent and the COVID-19 mandatory inoculation State practices gives people who are subject to government power a rational reason to submit to cruel, inhumane, or degrading treatment and medical experimentation at the direction of their own government. The answer is, of course, self-evident. States cannot rationally assume that their citizens have a moral obligation to submit to their authority when the outcome involves being injected with an experimental COVID-19 vaccine that may lead to death, acute ailment, or disability. Accordingly, when States mandate COVID-19 vaccines without free consent or other violations of peremptory norms of international law, these mandates are illicit and unlawful. They are void *ab initio*, as embodied in the doctrine of *jus cogens*.[20,23,24] As previously mentioned, the unique function of these peremptory norms is to render void any State action that conflicts with such a peremptory norm. The peremptory norm designates the ascendancy of the law, which even the sovereign can neither abrogate nor modify and renders any contradictory

State edict illegitimate. Consequently, the *jus cogens* norm acts as a check on unauthorized State power. It is further crucial to note that *jus cogens* principles apply not only to treaties but also to "any other act or action of States."[25-27]

The various COVID-19 vaccine mandates that have been issued across the globe violate peremptory norms of international law and are therefore illicit and void *ab initio* in terms of the doctrine of *jus cogens*.

"The Prohibition on Unilateralism and the Fiduciary Criterion of Legitimacy"[§§]

In order to determine whether State action is legitimate and lawful or not, eminent legal scholars and authors of the book "Fiduciaries of Humanity", Professor E. J. Criddle and Professor E. Fox-Decent argue that the "prohibition on unilateralism principle" and "fiduciary criterion of legitimacy" test should be analyzed.[8,20]

According to their legal theory, the prohibition on unilateralism and the fiduciary criterion is embedded in the juridical structure of IHRL. Criddle and Fox-Decent explain:

> The prohibition on unilateralism is a legal principle that denies one party any authority or entitlement to dictate terms to another party of equal standing. The fiduciary criterion of legitimacy is a standard of adequacy for assessing the normative legitimacy and lawfulness of the actions of international public actors. The criterion demands that public actions have a representational character in that, for them to be legitimate and lawful, they must be intelligible as actions taken in the name of, or on behalf of, the persons subject to them.[20]

Adherence to these principles is integral to legitimate State authority under international law, such that contraventions of these standards compromise a State's claim to exercise lawful authority.

---

§§ Portions of this chapter are republications of the content of a peer-reviewed article by the author Dr. Willem van Aardt, entitled "Jus Cogens Norms, Public Policy and the Fiduciary Criterion of Morality" published in De Rebus SA Attorneys Journal in July 2022.

i) The Prohibition of Unilateralism

When a country acts unilaterally, it refuses to involve other State Parties in its foreign affairs. If a government implements a policy without the advice of any outside groups, objective facts, or independent experts, it is adopting a policy of unilateralism. Any action described this way is entirely one-sided, and the roots of the word unilateralism reflect this — "*uni*" means "one" in Latin, and "*lateralism*" comes from "*latus*" or "side."[28,29]

The prohibition on unilateralism principle operates as a structuring concept of international law at various levels and throughout a number of disciplines. At the international or interstate level, the principle explains the foundational dogma of sovereign equality according to which governments have legal equality and independence from one another since independent equals cannot dictate terms to one another. Governments are thus barred by international law from violating the territorial integrity of other States and meddling unilaterally in the internal affairs of other nations.[8] When disputes arise, States are required to engage in good-faith negotiations, with recourse to impartial third-party arbitration or adjudication if necessary.[8,20]

At the national or intrastate level, the prohibition on unilateralism principal bars parties from dictating terms to one another.[20] If one party were legally entitled to impose terms of interaction on another, the principle of legal equality would be violated. The dominant party to the interaction would possess a legal privilege not enjoyed by the other party.[20] On a Kantian understanding, the prohibition on unilateralism principle follows Kant's inherent right to equal freedom; the mere subjection of one party to the will of another (even if the other is acting in good faith and reasonably) is an unjust compromise of equal liberty.[20] From a Hobbesian point of view, unilateralism's infringement of the principle of legal equality is enough to establish its wrongfulness.[20]

According to Professors Criddle and Fox-Decent:

> The prohibition on unilateralism may be understood to have two aspects. One is captured by the Kantian principle that **no person may be treated as a mere means, but only as an end,** which is the principle of non-instrumentalization. The other aspect is the republican principle of non-domination, according to which **one person may not be subject to the arbitrary will of another.** The Kantian principle condemns actual abuse. The republican principle condemns the possession of arbitrary power that would make abuse possible, whether or not the power is ever in fact used abusively.[20] (my emphasis)

International law mitigates the risk of governmental tyranny by subjecting State Parties to several legal frameworks protective of fundamental human rights, such as IHRL and international law's regime for regulating states of emergency. As demonstrated in Chapter 3 and 6 within this legal framework, some norms, such as the prohibitions on torture, slavery, arbitrary detention, and medical experimentation without free and informed consent, are regarded as *jus cogens* and are of a type from which no derogation is permitted.[8]

Two questions immediately come to mind. First, on what basis can we differentiate peremptory (*jus cogens*) from non-peremptory norms? Second, how can we differentiate lawful State action from unlawful imitations that constitute government abuse? Professors Fox-Decent and Criddle argue that their "fiduciary criterion of legitimacy" provides a useful, practical measure to answer these questions.[20]

ii) The Fiduciary Criterion of Legitimacy

In layman's terms, "when someone has a fiduciary duty to someone else, the person with the duty must act in a way that will benefit that other person. The person who has a fiduciary duty is called the fiduciary, and the person to whom the duty is owed is called the beneficiary." If the fiduciary breaches the fiduciary duties, the beneficiaries are typically entitled to restitution and damages.[29]

According to Professor Vincent Johnson, (Distinguished Professor of Law, St. Mary's University, San Antonio, Texas),"regardless of whether specific rules of government ethics have been adopted, public officials have a broad fiduciary duty to carry out their responsibilities in a manner that is faithful to the public trust."[30] The duties of public officials extend beyond minimum compliance with codified ethics rules. Even if no ethics code has been implemented or adopted, public officials must act in a manner that comports with their common-law fiduciary-duty responsibilities. Government ethics laws, criminal provisions, and other legislation should be construed and applied in light of the requiring loyalty duties that are imposed on public officials as fiduciaries.[30]

By their very nature, peremptory norms make illegal public policies that violate core human rights that could never be understood to be implemented in the name of, or on behalf of, the individuals subject to them.[8,20,23-27] Genocide, torture, slavery, arbitrary detention, and medical experimentation without free and informed consent, for example, are not rationally comprehensible as policies that could be adopted in the name of, or in the best interest, of their victims. In the case of COVID-19 vaccine mandates, for instance, it would be morally reprehensible to mandate citizens to be subjected to a medical experiment that may potentially cause death, disability, or acute ailment.[8] By distinction, policies that modestly limit fundamental human rights for rational reasons (for example health warnings on cigarette packages, rules relating to seatbelts, the prohibition against acquiring or selling drugs deemed harmful) are intelligible as public policies that could be adopted in the name of, and in the best interest of, the persons subject to them.[8] Publicly justifiable limitations on certain human rights can therefore be consistent with fiduciary norms of stewardship and representation that govern public agencies on condition, as Professors Criddle and Fox-Decent explain:

> These limitations embody the principles of integrity and formal moral equality and demonstrates due regard for the legitimate interests of the people on whose behalf and in whose name authorities govern.[20]

In the case of peremptory norms, no such justification is possible because any violation of these norms represents a wrongful violation of fundamental human rights *jus cogens*, and as such cannot be an action taken in the name of, or for the benefit of the persons made to suffer it.[8] The fiduciary criterion of legitimacy consequently emerges as a measure that takes its cues from the norms that constitute and regulate fiduciary representation, which are also norms that are incompatible with public policies that infringe fundamental human rights. The nature of public power is fundamentally representational, and therefore the "fiduciary principle" within international law can be seen as analogous to the power-conferring rule *pacta sunt servanda* that transmutes international accords into binding treaties.[8] The fiduciary principle permits States to retain and utilize public powers, but on the condition that those powers (when objectively assessed) are judged to be used in the name of or in the best interest of their citizens.[20]

In this context, the fiduciary criterion of legitimacy is a valuable normative standard to determine the legitimacy of government policy and practice.[8] In synopsis, the fiduciary criterion of legitimacy articulates a representative ideal that serves as a normative standard of legitimacy. While it is always concerned with fiduciary norms arising from representation, the criterion is also suitable for the critical assessment of complex interactions of law and social facts, as seen in the case of vaccine mandates during the COVID-19 era. The criterion presupposes that if it is not satisfied, the relevant government policy will be illicit.

It is self-evident that no reasonable and rational fiduciary would mandate an ineffective, unsafe vaccine that has death, acute ailment, and disability as a potential side-effect.

The Efficacy of Law versus The Force of Law

It is important to distinguish between laws (mandates) that possess the "efficacy of the law" – which entails valid rational legislative acts by the executive – and laws (mandates) that lack efficacy yet possess the "force of the law" – which entails illicit irrational legislative acts by the executive.[31]

From a legal technical perspective, laws (mandates) that lack "the efficacy of the law" do not qualify as "law" that aligns with the "rule of law" even though they contain the "force the law" given that they meet the formal requirements of law and are enforced by the executive. Put differently: for a law to align with the "rule of law," it substantively requires inherent moral value in addition to meeting the formal criteria of law. Agamben encapsulates the principle well:

> That is to say, the concept of "force of law" as a technical legal term defines a separation of the norm's *vis obligandi*, or applicability, from its formal essence, whereby decrees, provisions, and measures which are not formally laws nevertheless acquire their "force."[31]

A good example of this phenomenon was the Fascist Third Reich in which Adolf Eichmann never tired of repeating that "the words of the Fuhrer have the force of law."[31] During the first six years of Hitler's dictatorship, government at every level – Reich, State, and municipal – adopted hundreds of laws, decrees, directives, guidelines, and regulations that increasingly restricted the civil and human rights of the Jews in Germany. The first major law to curtail the rights of Jewish citizens was the "Law for the Restoration of the Professional Civil Service of April 7, 1933," which excluded Jews and the "politically unreliable" (those with opposing views) from the civil service.[32] The numerous inhumane antisemitic Nazi-era laws that were duly passed by the German *Reichstag* between 1933 and 1939, such as the *Reich* Citizenship Law and the Law for the Protection of German Blood and Honour, by which German Jews: lost their German citizenship, were classified *Staatsangehörige* ("State subjects"), were forbidden to marry or have sexual relations with German non-Jews, were forbidden to employ non-Jewish women under age 45 in their homes, and were forbidden to fly the German flag, as it represented an offense against German honor, had the "force of law" even though they lacked the "efficacy of the law." COVID-19 public health measures that violate peremptory IHRL norms are contemporary examples of laws that contain the "force of law" but lack the "efficacy of law."

As penned by Professor of Law and Social Theory, Aleardo Zanghellini, in the "Yale Journal of Law & the Humanities":

> Placed in the context of the substantive natural law tradition, "rule of law" conveys the moral imperative that states should govern not only through law that credibly complies with certain formal and institutional requirements, but substantively good—justice-orientated–law.[2]

Recent events again demonstrated that ruling through laws (mandates) that lack the "efficacy of the law" creates an anomic society in which there is a disintegration or disappearance of the juridical norms and values, where the "force of law" is applied without the "rule of law."

Chapter Conclusion

"True" governments serve the common interests of all citizens, while "despotic" governments serve only the selfish interests of a particular person or group of persons.[7,8] The law, as applied during the COVID-19 pandemic, to a large extent corresponds with the radical leftist Critical Legal Studies (CLS) theory, in the sense that COVID-19 laws are being exposed: not as a rational system but an ideology that supports and makes possible an unjust political system. The law, according to CLS, is merely a tool used by the establishment to achieve its political and financial objectives and maintain its power and domination over an unequal status quo: "[a]n instrument for oppression used by the wealthy and the powerful to maintain their place in the hierarchy."[33] The COVID-19 mandates perpetuated the established power relations of society and covered the injustices perpetrated with a mask of legitimacy.[33-38] But this type of "law" is in fact not "law" at all but pseudo-law devoid of the essence of law.

According to Thomas Aquinas, all State power should be a ministry or service because it is derived from God for the happy ordering of the life of its citizens.[16] The purpose of the State is therefore moral because of its origin and its originator.[16] It is the duty of the government to enact rational laws that individuals may live a happy and fulfilling life, which is the true end of civil society.[16] The State must lay the foundations of the happiness of its citizens by maintaining law and order, through just, rational governance that aligns with natural law.[16]

Martin Luther King Jr. asserted that:

A just law is a man-made code that squares with the moral law, or the law of God. An unjust law is a code that is out of harmony with the moral law. ... An unjust law is a human law that is not rooted in eternal and natural law. Any law that uplifts human personality is just. Any law that degrades human personality is unjust.

Promoting the rule of law at the international level means instituting lawful relationships between governments, on the one hand, and the individuals who are subject to them, on the other.[20] As Fuller acknowledged, these relationships can only be understood to be governed by the rule of law if governments treat people as rational, self-determining agents by establishing rules that satisfy specific formal criteria.

The rule of law also requires that public powers respect the prohibition against unilateralism and the fiduciary criterion.[20] Put differently, governments respect the rule of international law when they treat people subject to their jurisdiction as equal beneficiaries of the international legal order. The fiduciary criterion also supplies a valuable standard for assessing the exercise of lawful sovereign authority, as manifested in peremptory norms of IHRL that govern fundamental human rights.[20]

Professor Jeremy Waldron (professor of law and philosophy at the New York University School of Law) suggested that "the lead idea of the rule of law is that respect for law can take the edge off human political power, making it less objectionable, less dangerous, more benign and more respectful."[39] In normative terms, the rule of law is a requirement that States rule through just laws rather than otherwise.[2] Respect for and adherence to the rule of law by all governments across the globe is imperative, as the rule of law shields citizens against oppression and tyranny. During the COVID-19 pandemic, we have witnessed the deterioration of the rule of law and the perversion of democracy and democratic institutions on a national and international level.

During the COVID-19 epoch, Western political leaders contended that the "rule of law" was purely a procedural concept.[40] They claimed that the State may strip its citizens of their fundamental human rights or violate their freedoms as long as this was done by way of duly implemented legal procedures. At the Nuremberg trials, to justify their biomedical atrocities against German dissidents and Jews, some of the former Nazi officers argued that they had broken none of the duly implemented German laws. It was only by evoking the rule according to a higher law that the Allied trial lawyers were able to defeat such legal defenses.[40-42] Thus, "the rule according to a higher law" may well provide a pragmatic legal measure to identify the instances of political reasoning when a State, even though acting in conformity with clearly defined and properly enacted legal mandate, produces results that are substantially unjust.

A State's disregard for fundamental human rights is a conclusive marker of the absence of the rule of law in that State. This absence of legality is also a failure of justice as respect for fundamental human rights is paradigmatic of the requirements of justice. Conversely, honoring fundamental human rights means that both law and justice effectively rule. Through a proliferation of irrational, unjust laws that lack the efficacy of law, the political elite and their ultra-wealthy corporate overlords enriched themselves at the expense of the middle class and to the detriment and suffering of the poor and the most vulnerable. There needs to be a return to the rule of law and those in positions of power who contravened the rule of law need to be tried and held to account.

12. GLOBAL BIOMEDICAL FASCISM AND THE TYRANNY OF THE THERAPEUTIC STATE

"Fascism should more appropriately be called
Corporatism because it is a merger of State and corporate power"

— Benito Mussolini

In an uncanny 1980's prediction of future threats of authoritarianism, Bertram Gross (1912-1997), American social scientist and professor of political science, in his book "Friendly Fascism," which analyzed political and economic power trends, identifies global capitalist growth and inappropriate responses to global crises as the new source of despotism.[1] His prognostication could not have been more accurate:

> I see [as] a more probable future a new despotism creeping slowly across America. Faceless oligarchs sit at command posts of a corporate-government complex that has been slowly evolving over many decades. In efforts to enlarge their own powers and privileges, they are willing to have others suffer the intended or unintended consequences of their institutional or personal greed. For Americans, these consequences include chronic inflation, recurring recession, open and hidden unemployment, the poisoning of air, water, soil and bodies, and, more important, the subversion of our constitution. More broadly, consequences include widespread intervention in international politics through economic manipulation, covert action, or military invasion.[1]

Gross knew that an unbridled transnational corporate superpower would inexorably lead to corporate fascism. The political theorist Sheldon Wolin (1922-2015), refining Gross's theory in 2003, described this commercial fascism as a "managed democracy."[1,2] It is, as Gross and Wolin indicated, typified by duplicity, chicanery, and fraud; it claims to pay homage to the international legal order, democratic government, the constitution, human rights protection, and the rule of law, but internally had captured all the levers of power to render the citizen powerless.[1] Gross cautioned that the means by which we have been immobilized and fettered would be incremental and often unnoticed until it was done:

> [A] friendly fascist power structure in the United States, Canada, Western Europe, or today's Japan would be far more sophisticated than the "*caesarism*" of fascist Germany, Italy, and Japan. It would need no charismatic dictator nor even a titular head ... it would require no one-party rule, no mass fascist party, no glorification of the State, no dissolution of legislatures, no denial of reason. Rather, it would come slowly as an outgrowth of present trends in the establishment.[1]

Gross also predicted the peril of our corporate-produced electronic delusions. He anticipated that the technological innovations in the hands of colossal corporations would be used to deceive the public to the point of "collective insanity" so that "almost every individual would get a personalized sequence of information injections at any time of the day-or night."[1] This is, of course, what Apple, Google, Microsoft, Facebook, Twitter, CNN, CNBC, Fox, and others are doing. He warned that it would be too late when we woke up. It has been more than 40 years since Gross's book was published. It was a warning that was disregarded, but remains critical as a description of what has transpired since 2020, how we arrived at this point, and how the predominant forces of corporate fascism function to subjugate humanity. It is impossible to combat structures of illegitimate control until we analyze and comprehend how those structures operate.[1]

One of the major forces in global politics is the WEF, a lobbying organization whose members and alumni are the global political elite and global monopoly capital that includes transnational corporations such as Apple, Amazon, Amex, AstraZeneca, Blackrock, Cisco, Citigroup, Facebook, IBM, Intel, Johnson & Johnson, Google, Goldman Sachs, Microsoft, Moderna, Pfizer, Vanguard, State Street, Walmart, and many others. The WEF believes that a globalized world is best managed by a self-selected coalition of multinational corporations,

States, and charitable foundations that manage the globe through PPPs. It promotes the interests of its partners globally, which it expresses through initiatives like the "Great Reset" and the "Global Redesign." It sees periods of global instability and human suffering – such as the COVID-19 pandemic – as "windows of opportunity" to intensify its efforts in the self-interest of the global plutocrats and political elite.[3-5] Professor Klaus Schwab, Founder and Executive Chairman, WEF, declared that: "The pandemic represents a rare but narrow window of opportunity to reflect, reimagine, and reset our world."[5]

Gross predicted the duplicity and deception that would ensue:

> [T]he operating rules of modern capitalist empire require ascending rhetoric about economic and social development, human rights, and the self-effacing role of transnational corporations in the promotion of progress and prosperity. The more lies are told, the more important it becomes for the liars to justify themselves by deep moral commitments to high-sounding objectives that mask the pursuit of money and power. The more a country like the United States imports its prosperity from the rest of the world, the more its leaders must dedicate themselves to the sacred ideal of exporting abundance, technology, and civilization to everyone else. The further this myth may be from reality, the more significant it becomes—and the greater the need for academic notables to document its validity by bold assertion and self-styled statistical demonstration.[1]

Since the beginning of the COVID-19 pandemic, the West saw a rapid replacement of democratic forms of government with biomedical fascist forms of rule enacting medical-political solutions in the form of numerous public health mandates, monitored and censored by major transnational technology corporations that progressively and unavoidably erode fundamental human rights and freedoms. Although the biomedical therapeutic State as a mechanism to obtain and sustain autocratic totalitarian rule-following collusion between the political elite and the ultra-wealthy is not new, what is unique in the COVID-19 era is the worldwide implementation of pharmacratic principles in nearly all UN Member States and newfound advanced technology to enforce and monitor mandatory biomedical procedures, paving the way for a technologically advanced fascist world order.

The combination of neoliberal ideology, corporate lobbying, political corruption, big business-appeasing fiscal and regulatory policies, tax avoidance and evasion by the ultra-rich through "charitable" foundations in recent decades has led to a substantial weakening of the public sector and its capacity to provide essential services and to fulfill its international human rights obligations. This combination also facilitated an extraordinary accumulation of individual and corporate wealth that increased market concentration and monopoly capital. The proponents of PPPs, such as the WEF, represent the private sector as the most effective way to deliver the required means for implementing global sustainable development goals and the future of global governance. However, history has shown that PPPs between the ultra-wealthy corporate elite and the political elite extirpate respect for fundamental human rights and freedoms with calamitous ramifications.[6]

George Santayana's aphorism that "Those who cannot remember the past are condemned to repeat it" is remarkably relevant in 2022 given the frightening similarities between Nazi Germany's public health (*Volksgesundheit*) biomedical policies and practices in the 1930s and *modus operandi* followed by a host of States since the beginning of the COVID-19 pandemic.[7] History is complicated but certainly not incomprehensible. Facing the past with courage obliges us to raise questions of the past based on the agony of the present and questions of the present based on the agony of the past.[8]

Figure 12.1: Photos of Adolf Hitler and IBM founder Thomas Watson and Immanuel Macron and Microsoft founder Bill Gates
Source: Isurvived.org and Paris Match

The Dawn of Nazi Germany's Private-Public Partnerships (PPPs)

One early admirer of the Italian Fascists was Adolf Hitler, who, less than a month after the March on Rome, through which Mussolini became Prime Minister of Italy, began to model himself and the National Socialist German Labor Party (Nazi Party) upon Mussolini and the Fascists.[9,10] The Nazis, led by Hitler and the German war hero Erich Ludendorff, attempted a "March on Berlin" modeled upon the March on Rome, which resulted in the failed Beer Hall Putsch in Munich in November 1923.[11]

Despite the increased following and appeal of the Nazi Party by 1933, regime change and power could come only through an alliance with the ultra-wealthy industrialists and the bankers. Knowing this, Herman Goering sent telegrams to Germany's 25 ultra-rich industrialists, inviting them to a secret meeting at his official residence in Berlin on February 20, 1933 (*Geheimtreffen vom 20. Februar 1933*). Hitler addressed the group, vowing to protect and expand their monopoly capital position, asserting that in his vision for Germany, "private enterprise [not owned by the ultra-wealthy] cannot be maintained in a democracy," and promised he would also eliminate trade unions. According to Robert Jackson, the former Supreme Court Justice and chief US prosecutor at Nuremberg, "The industrialists became so enthusiastic that they raised three million Reichsmarks [more than $30 million today] to strengthen and confirm the Nazi Party in power."[12] It was well understood that the ultra-rich would retain control behind the scenes if Hitler were left free to manage the political show.[11,12]

This meeting was the beginning of an evolving national Fascist State in which the ultra-rich German corporate elite colluded with soon-to-be centralized State power to take advantage of and swindle the populace in the name of "public health" and the "greater good." Within months, the newly established Fascist State subverted and annihilated constitutional democracy and the "rule of law" in Germany.

Stoking the Fears and Declaring a State of Emergency

On the evening of February 27, 1933, "fire broke out" in the Reichstag chambers. Capturing the burning of the Reichstag building, the Nazi regime deployed the mainstream radio, press, and newsreels to fuel widespread fear among the general German population of a pending "communist uprising," then exploited the fears and anxieties of the general public for political gain by declaring a state of emergency (*Ausnahmezustand*).[13]

The decree, officially the "Order of the Reich President for the Protection of People and State" (*Verordnung des Reichspräsidenten zum Schutz von Volk und Staat*), invoked the authority of Article 48 of the Weimar Constitution, which allowed the *Reichspräsident* to take any appropriate measure to remedy dangers to public health and safety.[14] The decree's Section 1 and 4 determined that:

> On the basis of Article 48 paragraph 2 of the Constitution of the German Reich, the following is ordered in defense against Communist State-endangering acts of violence:
>
> § 1. Articles 114, 115, 117, 118, 123, 124 and 153 of the Constitution of the German Reich are suspended until further notice. It is therefore permissible to restrict the rights of personal freedom [*habeas corpus*], freedom of opinion, including the freedom of the press, the freedom to organize and assemble, the privacy of postal, telegraphic and telephonic communications, and warrants for house searches, orders for confiscations as well as restrictions on property, are also permissible beyond the legal limits otherwise prescribed.
>
> § 4 Whoever provokes, appeals for, or incites the disobedience of the orders given out by the supreme state authorities or the authorities subject to them for the execution of this decree, or the orders given by the Reich government according to § 2, can be punished – insofar as the deed is not covered by other decrees with more severe punishments – with imprisonment of not less than one month, or with a fine from 150 to 15,000 Reichsmarks.
>
> Whoever endangers human life by violating § 1 is to be punished by sentence to a penitentiary, under mitigating circumstances with imprisonment of not less than six months and, when the violation causes the death of a person, with death, under mitigating circumstances with a penitentiary sentence of not less than two years. In addition, the sentence may include the confiscation of property.
>
> Whoever provokes or incites an act contrary to the public welfare is to be punished with a penitentiary sentence, under mitigating circumstances, with imprisonment of not less than three months.[14]

A month later, the Reichstag passed the "Enabling Act," (*Gesetz zur Behebung der Not von Volk und Reich*, the Law to Remedy the Distress of People and Reich) allowing Hitler's cabinet to rule without the Reichstag's consent. Although intended as a temporary measure, the state of emergency was extended twice and remained a paradigm of Nazi government until 1945.[15]

The state of emergency nullified most German citizens' fundamental human rights *(Grundrechte)* and was soon followed by a proliferation of mandates in the name of "public health" and the "greater good."

Dramatic Similarities Between Pharmacratic Controls in Nazi Germany and COVID-19 Public Health Measures

The Nazis were absolutely obsessed with health. Even the Nazi symbol the Svastica or *Hakenkreuz*, comes from the sanskrit: स्वस्तिक, romanized: svastika, meaning conducive to "well-being" ("the state of being comfortable, healthy and happy").

The classic work on public health policies in Nazi Germany is "Health, Race, and German Politics between National Unification and Nazism" (1870–1945) by Paul Weindling.[15,16] Weindling convincingly argues that German eugenics neither had its roots in German nationalist racial movements nor its natural consequence in an alliance with Nazism. Rather, its history is "better understood from the perspectives of public health, social policy, and of the bio-medical sciences".[16] The espoused vision of technocratic social engineering with the object of creating a healthy social organism of "biologically based collectivism" is what enabled the transformation in German society.[15,16]

War and persistent socio-economic and political instability decisively shifted the balance, first, in favor of "welfare oriented" biomedical solutions that aligned with the German social welfare system, and then, once the depression hit, in favor of even more repressive forms of biomedical interventions and "medicine as 'integral to the final solution.'"[15,16] Both doctors and scientists were affected by the inflation and the depression, and they found it advantageous to bolster their status by embracing Nazi biomedical racial hygiene policies. Thus, as Weindling argues, eugenics and other medical atrocities could thrive "in this crisis atmosphere as a medically regulated solution to problems" threatening the nation's future.[15] Many of Weindling's observations and remarks about Nazi Germany seem as if they refer to conditions during the COVID-19 pandemic. He writes:

Scientifically educated experts acquired a directing role as prescribers of social policies and personal lifestyle…science and medicine provided an alternative to party politics, by forming a basis for collective social policies to remedy social ills.

Medicine was transformed from a free profession…to the doctor carrying out duties of State officials in the interests not of the individual patient but of society and of future generations…Doctors became a part of a growing State apparatus.[15,16]

In Nazi Germany, as in the COVID-19 era, public health took complete precedence over individual human rights. *Reichgesundheitsführer,* Leonardo Conti (1900–1945) declared that "no one had the right to regard health as a personal private matter, which could be disposed of according to individualistic preference. Therapy had to be administered in the interests of the race and society rather than of the sick individual".[15,16] Nazism was "applied biology," stated Hitler deputy Rudolf Hess. All professional associations concerned with the administration of law and order were amalgamated into the "National Socialist League of German Jurists" (*Nationalsozialistischer Rechtswahrerbund*), while the "Academy of German Law" and eminent Nazi legal academics, such as Carl Schmitt, promoted the Nazification of German law.[15-17] Judges were enjoined to let the "health of the nation sentiment" (*gesundes Volksempfinden*) guide them in their decisions. On July 14, 1933, the "Law for the Prevention of Genetically Diseased Offspring" was enacted.[17] Individuals who "suffered" from conditions assumed to be hereditary, such as feeblemindedness, schizophrenia, manic-depressive disorder, genetic epilepsy, fatal dementia, genetic blindness, genetic deafness, physical deformity, and alcoholism, were deemed a threat to the nation's health and targeted for sterilization. The medical profession benefited considerably from the push for sterilization, both financially and politically.[15,16] Special hereditary health courts lent a veneer of due process to the cruel and inhumane public health mandates. Tribunals of two doctors and a lawyer mandated sterilization irrespective of the patient's wishes as the emergency declaration removed the legal basis for the inviolability of a citizen's bodily autonomy. The highly elastic and subjective diagnosis of "feeblemindedness" provided "legal grounds" in most cases. Vasectomy was the usual sterilization method for men, and for women, tubal ligation, an invasive procedure that resulted in the deaths of thousands of women.[18-20]

To build public support for this inhumane public health policy, nationwide posters, documentary films, and high-school biology textbooks argued the case for mandatory sterilization: "an easy surgical procedure, a humane means by which the nation can be protected from boundless misery."[18] The mainstream media propaganda portrayed its victims as less than fully human.[18] Analogous to the COVID-19 global media practice to publish no information that contradicts the official government narrative, the German media giant Bertelsmann and other mainstream media outlets of the time's film, radio, theater, and press offices operated in strict compliance with government public health mandates and published material only following directives issued by the "*Reich Ministry for Public Enlightenment and Propaganda*" (*Reichsministerium für Volksaufklärung und Propaganda*). In terms of the "Editors Law" *(Schriftleitergesetz)* of October 4, 1933, Nazi officials expected editors and journalists to register with the Reich Press Chamber to work in the field and follow the mandates and instructions handed down by the ministry.[19,21,22] In Clause 14 of the law, the government called for editors to exclude anything "calculated to weaken the strength of the *Reich* abroad or at home."[21] Even the AP opted to placate the Nazi authorities, firing all of its German-based Jewish staff and altering its news reporting to align with Nazi propaganda. Among those alterations was softening the reporting of the daily bigotry endured by Jews, and by the end of 1933, the AP was refusing to make public images portraying such bigotry.[18,19,21,22]

As in the COVID-19 era, when "public health experts" such as Dr. Antony Fauci repeatedly propagated false COVID-19 narratives such as vaccines being safe and effective, prominent medical and public health "experts" of the time such as Dr. Eugen Fischer, Dr. Ernst Rudin, and Dr. Arthur Gut decried Germany's "biologic degeneration" and proposed laws and mandates to improve the quality and quantity of the population. Thousands of physicians, medically trained academics, and nurses legitimized and helped implement Nazi policies aiming to "cleanse" German society of individuals perceived as biological threats to the "nation's health." Many in the medical community embraced the new prominence of biology, bio-surveillance, bio-medical solutions, eugenics, increased government and corporate research funding, and new career opportunities – including openings created by the elimination of those with opposing views and Jews from the medical and public health fields.[18,22,23]

On August 12, 2021, the "United States National Education Association" with its more than three million members who "include public school educators, support members, faculty and staff members at the university level, retired educators, administrators, and college students becoming teachers," endorsed COVID-19 vaccine requirements for school workers, aligning itself with the Biden administration's push to get more Americans vaccinated.[24,25] Comparable to the groundswell of support for human-rights-violating COVID-19 public health policies from teachers unions, Ivy League schools, major medical research institutions, and public universities such as Harvard, Brown, Columbia, Dartmouth, Duke, Emory, Johns Hopkins, Princeton, Stanford, Tufts, the University of Michigan, and Yale, which all enforced CDC guidelines and required students to get COVID-19 vaccines before returning to campus in 2021; on November 11, 1933 "The Vow of Allegiance of the Professors of the German Universities and High-Schools to Adolf Hitler and the National Socialistic State" was presented at the Albert Hall in Leipzig, confirming the unequivocal support of major academic institutions and academics for Nazi policies.[26,27] Dr. Martin Heidegger, regarded as one of the most influential and most original German philosophers of the 20th century, told his students and colleagues that Germany's soul needed fresh air to breathe and National Socialism would provide it.[25] As in the COVID-19 era, when intellectuals admonished that the unvaccinated and those insisting on human rights protections were selfish, Heidegger reasoned that freedom of thought and freedom of expression were harmful and egocentric ideas. Instead, he urged his students to live up to their national responsibilities to the community in both "thought and deed."[27] According to historian Richard Evans, 15% of university teachers had lost their jobs by fall of 1933. Most were fired because of their political beliefs.[27]

Akin to the strong support for mandatory COVID-19 government policies from the ultra-wealthy global elite and their multinational corporations such as Amazon, Amex, Blackrock,[28] ¶¶ Cisco, Citigroup, Microsoft,[29] *** Moderna,

---

¶¶ BlackRock, the world's largest funds manager with $US10 trillion in assets under management, is the second largest shareholder in Pfizer. It is also one of the top two stakeholders in four of the six major American media companies including News Corp, Disney, Comcast, and Time Warner. It also owns a stake in the New York Times.

*** Microsoft founder Bill Gates's foundation is the second-largest contributor to the WHO. As of September 2021, it had invested nearly $780 million in its programs in that year. Germany, the biggest contributor, had contributed more than $1.2 billion, while the US donated $730 million.

Apple, Google, Goldman Sachs, Facebook, Pfizer, Vanguard,[30][†††] State Street,[31][‡‡‡] Walmart, and many others, that all insisted on strict adherence to all COVID-19 mandates as widely covered in the mainstream media, the German corporate elite played a crucial role in Hitler's Germany. In a sense, Nazism was a manifestation of "monopoly capitalism" that used the Nazis as a tool to enrich themselves.[22,32,34,35] The following well-known companies were Nazi contributors and collaborators and profited significantly under Nazi rule: Krupp, IG Farben, BASF, Bayer, Hoechst, Agfa, IBM, Siemens, Bertelsmann, BMW, Audi, Daimler-Benz, Deutsche Bank, Ford, Kodak, Hugo Boss, Porsche, Volkswagen, and the Associated Press.[22,36-40]

Figure 12.2: Henry Ford receiving the
Grand Cross of the German Eagle from Nazi officials, 1938
Source: Centre for Online Jewish Studies (COJS)

German businesses were granted extraordinary privileges to control their workers, collective bargaining was abolished, and wages were capped.[32] Business profits soared rapidly, as did corporate investment.[32] Real wages dropped by 25% between 1933 and 1938.[32] State and corporate advertising money ensured that in the eyes of the general public the Nazi policies were

††† The Vanguard Group, the world's second-largest asset manager with total global assets under management (AUM) of $8.2 trillion as of December 1, 2021, is the biggest stakeholder in Pfizer pharmaceuticals with $ 20 billion worth of shares at December 2021. It also has ownership in four major media companies in the United States including News Corp, Disney, Comcast, Time Warner, and The New York Times. The Vanguard Group is also the largest shareholder of BlackRock shares. The wealthiest families in the world are associated with Vanguard Group funds.

‡‡‡ State Street is the third-largest asset manager in the world with $2.7 trillion in assets under management. It is the third largest shareholder in Pfizer in December 2021.

not only the only solution, but they were fashionable, sophisticated and the "current thing".

Figure 12.3: Hugo Boss designed Nazi uniforms 1934
Source: warhistoryonline.com

Kindred to the Biden administration's 2021 COVID-19 vaccination mandate for federal contractors in the United States and COVID-19 "no jab, no job" policies in other Western democracies that led to millions of government employees across the globe losing their jobs, on April 7, 1933, the *Reichstag* passed the "Law for the Restoration of the Professional Civil Service" *(Berufs-beamtengesetz).*[18,23] The Civil Service law abolished the employment rights of "biologically inferior" non-Aryan German and Jewish public servants. In effect, it prevented all people who held an opposing view from working as judges, doctors in State-run hospitals, lawyers in government departments, and teachers in State schools.[18,23]

Western COVID-19 public health regulations allowed for the apprehension and forced detention in a "quarantine facility" of "anyone who may be a danger to public health" without any due process, prior notice, judicial warrant, judicial review or the ability to independently and objectively verify the public health authority's decision to arrest.[41-45] Gross human rights violations such as the forced detentions in terms of Canada's "Quarantine Act" and when the Australian police arrested three teenagers who escaped from a Australian quarantine facility (the "Centre for National Resilience" in Howard Springs, Northern Territory) during November 2021, after being deemed close contacts, occurred throughout the West.[41,42,43,44,45] In Nazi Germany, "protective custody" (*Schutzhaft*) laws facilitated the extra-juridical arbitrary arrest and imprisonment of dissidents, political opponents, Jews, and those deemed a threat to the "nation's health." Officially defended as being necessary to "protect" detainees from the "righteous" wrath of the German population, *Schutzhaft* did not require a judicial warrant, nor prior notice nor any judicial review. Those "relocated" under *Schutzhaft* were sent to concentration camps. "Protective custody" prisoners were not quarantined within the regular prison system but in "concentration camps" under the specific authority of the SS (*Schutzstaffel*; the influential guard of the Nazi *Reich*).[17] The conditions in the camps were *conditio inhumana* and the detainees defined outside the boundaries of the German rule of law.[46]

As during the COVID-19 pandemic, the Nazi public health effort was integrated into a comprehensive media campaign continually trumpeting "medical experts'" dire warnings of impending "national death" if the biological threats to the nation's health were not removed.[18] In a further development, the "Reich Citizenship Law and the Law for the Protection of German Blood and German Honor" announced in Nuremberg on September 15, 1935, criminalized marriage or sexual relations between Jews and non-Jewish Germans, while the "Marital Health Law" of October 1935 banned unions between the "hereditarily healthy" and persons deemed "genetically unfit."[18] Mainstream media propaganda heralding the new crime of "racial defilement" portrayed Jews as black and the "biological inferior" as subhuman (*untermenschen*). The film *Der ewige Jude* (The Eternal Jew) (1940), directed by Fritz Hippler, portrayed Jews as cultural parasites who carry contagion and devour precious resources.[17] To enforce its racial hygiene measures, hundreds of "hereditary and racial care clinics" (comparable to the modern day COVID-19 "testing centers") were established to conduct bio-surveillance to identify those posing a "biological threat". Staffed by thousands of physicians and assistant physicians, the clinics operated under the guidance of local public health authorities and established extensive hereditary data banks for the government's future use.[18] What had been private or moral spheres were subjugated to a biological social pathology under State control.[15,16]

By 1939, Nazi public health measures took a profound turn, from controlling reproduction and marriage to the mass murder of persons regarded as "biological threats."[15,18] "Reliable helpers were recruited from the ranks of psychiatrists," who defined lying for the State, similar to Dr. Antony Fauci's lies relating to the efficacy of masks and the risks of outdoor spread of the virus, as a higher form of morality.[15,16,47] "Each euthanasia institution had a registry office to issue the false [death] certificates."[15,16] In addition to the millions of innocent Jews murdered between 1939 and 1945, an estimated

200,000 people – who included babies born with Down syndrome, individuals with other genetic disabilities and elderly psychiatric patients considered to be "incurably ill" – were massacred in "euthanasia" programs. Fatal doses of drugs, malnourishment, and gassing were the main techniques of killing administered by medical doctors, public health officials and nurses.[18,33] By 1945 over 200 German "Health Courts" had also mandated the forced sterilization of over 400,000 individuals, most found to be "simple-minded."[8,12,18] The more power medical doctors, scientists, and public health officials exercised, the more inebriated with power they became. Weindling notes: "The doctor was to be a Führer of the Volk to better personal and racial health… Terms like 'euthanasia' and 'the incurable' were a euphemistic medicalized camouflage with connotations of relief of the individual suffering of the terminally ill."[15] Amid all the death and destruction, the Nazis remained preoccupied with public health and they even established "[a] plantation for herbal medicines" at the Dachau concentration camp.[15,16]

One of the enduring puzzles of the Nazi era is how an evil ideology with public health policies incorporating biosurveillance, mandatory sterilizations, euthanasia, and murder was practiced in a nation with the history of Germany's cultural and scientific achievement. Linked to this question is what led to the support and participation of so many German medical doctors in carrying out some of the most evil barbarities of the Nazi regime. Karl Kessler in his article "Physicians and the Nazi Euthanasia Program" published in the "International Journal of Mental Health" in 2007, concludes that: "Physicians became Nazified more thoroughly and much sooner than any other profession, and as Nazis they did more in the service of the nefarious regime than any of their professional peers."[48] Physician membership in the Nazi Party was higher than for any other profession. The 45% membership in the party for physicians compares with 25% for lawyers, 24% for teachers, 22% for musicians, and the average of 9% for the general population.[48]

The cruel and inhumane Nazi public health policies were not advanced by a narrow set of actors or promoted and practiced by a handful of bigoted Nazi public health officials whose actions were left unchecked, but instead were popular policies that were fully supported by the ultra-wealthy German elite, the major German corporations, the medical establishment, academic luminaries, and society at large. Nazi public health policy was based on the premise that the "biogenetically inferior" were a cancer and a threat to the "greater good" and the future wellbeing of the nation who had to be removed at any cost. COVID-19 public health policy was based on the premise that the individual who refused to adhere to arbitrary mandates, epitomized by the unvaccinated, is a threat to the well-being of the nation, who must be "cured" or "removed" from society at any cost.[16]

Nazi Germany's history proves that when the 1% of the 1% big business corporate elite and big government political elite collude and become bedfellows through PPPs, gross human rights violation, lawlessness, unjust laws, social turmoil, inflation, recession, unemployment, poisoning of the environment, food shortages, medical experiments, eugenics, death, and destruction is the denouement.

This raises some disturbing issues for the modern day COVID-19 public health practices. The most obvious of these, and the most troubling for its contemporary resonance, is the social prejudice that marks activities pursued in the name of public health and the extent to which inhumane health and medical policies are absorbed and replicated as prevalent logic and acceptable practice and not viewed as *contra bonos mores*.

Your Body Belongs to the State

Hitler recognized that the seizure of private property elicits powerful emotional and civil resistance. One of the secrets of his rise to power was that he managed to portray the National Socialist movement as opposed to such a measure. Hitler understood well that there was no need to nationalize property when you can "nationalize the people" through indoctrination and constant propaganda.

Hitler famously proffered: "Through clever and constant application of propaganda, people can be made to see paradise as hell and also the other way around, to consider the most wretched sort of life as paradise." With respect to the relationship between health and the State, Hitler's basic goal was the same as the modern-day COVID-19 public-health zealots – namely, abolishing the boundary between private and public health. Popular Nazi slogans included:

- "Your body belongs to the nation!"
- "Your body belongs to the Führer!"
- "You have the duty to be healthy!"
- "Food is not a private matter!"
- "We have the duty, if necessary, to die for the Fatherland; why should we not also have the duty to be healthy? Has the Führer not explicitly demanded this?"
- "Nicotine damages not just the individual but the population as a whole!"[16,49]

The COVID-19 health ideology and practices closely mirror the Nazi public health ideology and practices. Each rest on the same premise – that the individual is unqualified to make personal health decisions and therefore needs the intervention of the paternalistic State, thus perverting what should be private health decisions to be subject to public health policy.[16] Robert Paxton affirms that:

> [F]ascism redrew the frontiers between private and public, sharply diminishing what had once been untouchably private. It changed the practice of citizenship from the enjoyment of constitutional rights and duties to participation in mass ceremonies of affirmation and conformity. It reconfigured relations between the individual and the collectivity, so that an individual had no rights outside community interest. It expanded the powers of the executive—party and State—in a bid for total control.[50]

The Nazi public-health ethic demanded respect for health and sacrifices for the "greater good" of the nation and illustrates the connection between politicized and corporatized biomedical health solutions and the disdain of fundamental human rights. The civil, political, social, and economic implications of the biomedical therapeutic character of Nazism and the use of similar public health policies in Western democracies during the past two years should not be ignored or underestimated.

The dramatic similarities between pharmacratic controls in Germany under National Socialism and those in the West over the past two and a half years are self-evident and striking.[16] It was biomedical pietism that enabled the Nazis to wage biomedical wars against the Jews, the genetically inferior, the physically disabled, and those who held opposing views. This is a vital point. Once a society begins to revere public health as a universal good – a superior moral value that trumps all others, especially freedom – it becomes sanctified as a kind of worldly holiness.[16] This, Thomas Szazs points out, allows the therapeutic State "to devour everything human on the ostensibly rational ground that nothing falls outside the province of the nation's health, just as the theological State had devoured everything human on the entirely rational ground that nothing falls outside the province of God and religion."[16]

A Familiar Fascistic Pattern Emerges

The pattern and sequence of events that lead a nation that respects fundamental human rights and freedoms to a fascist nation that rules through medical tyranny and commits atrocities in the name of "public health" or "the greater good" follow the same basic pattern:

1. Collusion between the corporate and political elite to exploit the population through big business-big government PPPs.
2. Creating mass fear and hysteria through propagating a false narrative in the mainstream media.
3. Declaring a state of emergency that gives government officials the power to disregard and suspend fundamental human rights and the rule of law.
4. Implementation of tyrannical "rule by mandate" through a proliferation of new legislation and the arbitrary exercises of unchecked authority in the name of the "greater good" and the "nation's health."
5. Maintenance of the bio-medical tyranny State through corrupt PPPs with the ultra-wealthy elite, continued mass media propaganda, and the support of the corporate and State-controlled, major academic, medical, and educational establishments.
6. The biomedical tyranny getting progressively more absurd, irrational, unethical, barbaric and deadly as corporate greed increases and public officials with unbridled power and authority do as they please.
7. The despots and their corporate backers are eventually exposed as lawless criminals and enemies of humanity masquerading as political leaders, business magnates, philanthropists, and public health officials and brought to justice.

The Global Palingenesis of Biomedical Fascism

The Fascist State took distinct forms depending on the regions in which it was implemented.[51] However, in all cases, it maintained specific common attributes, such as close collaboration with the corporate elite, taking advantage of a "crisis" to impose its movement, cultivating unfounded fear, providing a "solution" to address the fear, discriminating against a pseudo-subclass, and nurturing elitism and corporatism through the abuse of corrupted State power.[51]

Governments in fascist nations use religious (theocratic), political (ideological), economic (socialistic), and biomedical (pharmacratic) justifications as a tool to manipulate public opinion and legitimize cohesive domination. Rhetoric such as "It is God's will! It is the will of the people! It is social justice! It is for the health of the nation! It is for the greater good!" are common from government leaders, even when the major tenets and ethical principles of the religion, ideology, or philosophy (or medical profession in the case of COVID-19) are diametrically opposed to the regime's policies or actions.[16]

Political scientist Dr. Lawrence Britt, in 2003, studied the authoritarian regimes of Hitler (Germany), Mussolini (Italy), Franco (Spain), Suharto (Indonesia), and Pinochet (Chile), which followed the fascist or protofascist model in obtaining, expanding, and maintaining power and found they all had specific identifying characteristics in common:

1. Disregard for the Respect of Fundamental Human Rights
2. Identification of Enemies and Scapegoats as a Unifying Cause
3. Supremacy of the Public Health Authority, Military and Police
4. Controlled and/or Colluding Mainstream Media
5. Obsession with National Health, Safety and Security
6. Manipulation of Public Opinion
7. Collusion between Corporate Elite and Government Elite
8. Freedom of Association and Assembly Suppressed
9. Ousting of Intellectuals with Opposing Views
10. Obsession with Mandates, Laws and Punishment
11. Rampant Cronyism and Pervasive Corruption
12. Fraudulent Elections
13. Profits and Power of Large Corporations Protected and Expanded
14. Non-stop Monopolized Propaganda
15. Promotion and Establishment of Totalitarian Governance Structures[51]

All the main characteristics of traditional fascism were extensively practiced during the COVID-19 pandemic:

1. Disregard for the Respect of Fundamental Human Rights

Fundamental human rights were disregarded and violated on a grand scale. The rights to freedom of movement, freedom from medical experimentation without prior free consent, freedom of thought, conscience, religion, freedom of assembly, freedom from arbitrary or unlawful interference with privacy, freedom to hold opinions without interference, freedom from arbitrary detention, and freedom from cruel, inhumane or degrading treatment were grossly violated on a global scale never seen in the history of humanity. Through the clever use of propaganda, exaggerating the actual threat from the "enemy" (COVID-19) and "greater good" arguments, the population was made to accept these human rights abuses by ostracizing, even demonizing, those being targeted, such as the unvaccinated and those who held opposing views. To obscure the extent of human rights abuse, concealment, denial, and mass State and corporate disinformation campaigns were used.[51]

2. Identification of Enemies and Scapegoats as a Unifying Cause

Citizens were rallied into a unifying nationalistic hysteria over the need to win the COVID-19 "war" and combat the perceived common "enemy" that was damaging the nation. United States President Joe Biden continually admonished the unvaccinated and the opposition for "actively working to undermine the fight against COVID-19."[52] "If the unvaccinated are not to blame, who is?" asked CNN news anchor John Berman.[53a] In a tacit compact, the State and its supporters united to create enemies by alienating large parts of their own populations. "They" are causing disease. "They" are "diseases," caused by their vaccination status, opposing views, genes, or their biological state. "They" are wicked. We are virtuous.[16] "This is now a pandemic of the unvaccinated. It is now a pandemic of choice – the choice not to get vaccinated. And it's a choice that's having a profound impact, a bad one on the rest of us," British Prime Minister Boris Johnson echoed the sentiment and called for a "national conversation" about how Britain's NHS can cope with new COVID variants in the face of "stubborn anti-vaxxers." Reflective of the animosity created in the West, Canadian journalist Mark Slapinski said that unvaccinated people are "dirty [and] disgusting" and proposed "the final solution" to the antivaxxer question:

> Take little stickers and put them on all [their] houses just so people know who they are and where they live. Put them on cattle cars and ship them off to work camps. Segregate them. Remove them from society. [Strip] them of all their rights. Loot them and use their assets.[53b]

"Forbes" magazine's Enrique Dans in his June 2021 article "What are we going to do with the anti-vaxxers" called the unvaccinated "irresponsible idiots" and "denialist" and proposed that "denialism must be tackled, isolated and neutralized, as the uncivil and unacceptable behaviour that it is."[53c] Expressing the same sentiment, the director of the Institute of Global Health Innovation at Imperial College, London, Ara Darzi in October, 2022 penned an article in "The Times" entitled "Antivaxers are a global menace who must be defeated."[53d] Across the major Western democracies scapegoating was effectively used to divert people's attention away from previous lies, ineptitude, shift blame for failures, and channel frustration in controlled directions. States pandered to social frustration by providing solutions to eradicate the "threat" in the form of social assistance, health mandates, and COVID-19 vaccines.[51]

3. Supremacy of the Public Health Authority, Military, and Police

Directives and guidance from public health authorities such as the CDC were effectually turned into law and were the final word on any matter. No constructive scientific debate or any form of disagreement with the government narrative was allowed – irrespective of the irrationality or absurdity of the public health mandates, they were implemented without question. According to an article published in April 2022 in the peer-reviewed, international medical journal Surgical Neurology International, "Hospitals were ordered by the CDC to follow a treatment protocol that resulted in the deaths of hundreds of thousands of patients, most of whom would have recovered had proper treatments been allowed."[54] Extensive biosurveillance measures were implemented through invasive mandatory PCR tests to detect "biological threats" and provide "surveillance data streams from varied sources in, helping to determine baseline prevalence rates".[55] Surveillance architectures that included integrated information sharing systems and advanced mobile geo-tracking technologies were also developed to enforce medical dictates.[55] Even when other domestic social challenges were prevalent, public health authorities, the military, and/or police were given disproportionate amounts of government funding to combat and detect the "enemy," while the domestic real-need social agenda was neglected. The freedom of healthy citizens with no symptoms of disease was arbitrarily deprived through arrest and forced detention at "quarantine facilities" or "health hotels."[41-45]

Medical doctors and nurses were glamorized as the war "heroes of the nation" on the forefront of the "war" by the mainstream media and all hospitals in the United States displayed massive banners proclaiming that "Heroes Work Here."

Shockingly, when the "heroes" served their purpose and refused to be injected with the experimental COVID-19 vaccine, they were summarily dismissed! In September 2021, France suspended 3,000 unvaccinated health workers without pay while in the United States, New York Mayor Bill de Blasio said that "roughly 10 percent" of the city's public-hospital workforce, or about 5,000 people, remained unvaccinated and were not allowed to work and suspended without pay. During January 2022, one of the top-ranked hospitals in United States, Mayo Clinic, also terminated the employment of 700 of its employees for refusing to get COVID-19 vaccinations.[56,57]

4. Controlled and/or Colluding Mainstream Media

Sometimes the mainstream media is directly controlled by the State; in other cases, the media is indirectly controlled by government regulation, and in other instances, such as occurred during the COVID-19 pandemic, the corporate owners of the mainstream media outlets are bedfellows with the fascist governance system. The Western world's monopolized trillion-dollar mainstream media propaganda machine's non-stop lies and misinformation around COVID-19 worked in lockstep to inform the people exactly what to think and when to think it. Taxpayer-funded add campaigns ensured that the mainstream media ceaselessly disseminated the approved morale-sapping daily salvo of gloom-laden COVID-19 propaganda through well-known "news" anchors, actors, and executives. In fiscal year 2021, the US Congress appropriated $1 billion for the secretary of health to spend on activities to "strengthen vaccine confidence in the United States." As part of a "comprehensive media campaign," the Biden administration purchased ads on TV, radio, in print, digital, and on social media from hundreds of news organizations "to build vaccine confidence". Following a Freedom of Information Act (FOIA) lawsuit filed by Judicial Watch against the US Department of Health and Human Services (HHS) the Biden Administration's extensive 2021 "Propaganda Plan to Push [the] COVID Vaccine" through a "Public Education Campaign" was uncovered on October 4, 2022. The *modus operandi* to allocate vast amounts of corporate and government spending towards COVID-19 propaganda, essentially buying the mainstream media, was followed throughout the West.[54,58-61] Censorship, especially in "war" time, is pervasive as we have again witnessed during "World War COVID-19," where the leading Silicon Valley monopolies Google, Facebook (Meta), Twitter, and many other large corporations "censored" any views opposing the public health authorities' approved narrative.[62-64] Enormous amounts of taxpayer-funded government spending was directed to mainstream media outlets and "fact checkers" to propagate the official COVID-19 public health narrative and combat the truth (relabeled as "disinformation") that contradicted the official narrative.[58-61]

5. Obsession with National Health, Safety, and Security

Fascist governance structures need to prepare the nation for "war" or constantly remind the nation that they are at "war," causing a sense of insecurity and paranoia in the population. As noted by Julian Assange, the goal is not to have a "successful war" but "an endless war!" The Nazi State declared civil servants to be "administrative soldiers," schoolteachers "soldiers of education," and doctors "soldiers of medicine."[16] During World War COVID-19, fear was also used as a motivational tool to unite the masses to struggle for the same cause with thoughtless action.[51] The COVID-19 experience has shown that once a "threat" to health is in place, people are willing to accept limitations to their freedom that they would never previously have endured – not even during the two world wars and totalitarian dictatorships.[46] Education was designed to glorify the fascist movement's policies and practices, and students were indoctrinated to be obedient and submissive to the State irrespective of the irrationality or absurdity of the dictates. In the United States education departments such as the New York City Department of Education actively promoted and enforced CDC guidelines and as at the end of August 2022 still "Encourage[d] up to date COVID-19 vaccination for everyone six months or older" and still required vaccination "for all visitors entering school buildings."[65] Any criticism of the regime or the "greater good' policies were considered treason and unpatriotic while contravention of the COVID-19 mandates were criminalized.

6. Manipulation of Public Opinion

The faceless oligarchy enjoyed unprecedented power over the minds, beliefs, personalities, and behavior of men, women, and children across the globe. Advanced and sophisticated technological and psychological control techniques were used during COVID-19 to spread fear, mislead, and manipulate the public opinion.[66] Lockdowns, isolation mandates, mask mandates and incessant unending mainstream media fear-mongering, lies, and deception gave rise to decoupling of societal connections (isolation), lack of sense-making (meaninglessness), constant free-floating anxiety, and constant free-floating psychological discontent resulting in mass delusion and mass formation psychosis (MFP).[66] As noted in Chapter 10, according to Professor Dr. Mattias Desmet, MFP occurs from the dynamic of citizens acting as a crowd in projecting their personal free-floating anxieties, frustration and aggression onto the social construct of a COVID-19 "pandemic" and providing a sense of renewed "social belonging" to mitigate the anxiety.[66] In his article "COVID, Politics and Psychology" Phil Shannon explains:

In MFP, sacrifice (lockdown, for example) and heroism (such as self-quarantine) are called upon whilst opportunities for virtuous behavior proliferate ("I'm masking up, getting jabbed, self-isolating for your benefit"). All participants in the COVID-driven MFP reinforce the mass psychosis by passing on their latest traumatic fears to each other in a closed-system, positive-feedback loop ("Oh my God, now it's Omicron! It's highly contagious! Run for the hills!") whilst thrashing around for scapegoats to make them feel subjectively safer because all their pet interventions have delivered nothing of any benefit.[67]

While fear primed a populace for menticide, the use of State sponsored propaganda to spread misinformation and create confusion with regard to the source of the dangers, and the nature of the pandemic, aided to break down the minds of the people.[68] Government officials and the mainstream media used blatant lies, contradictory reports, and non-sensical information to create confusion that led to the heightened susceptibility of a descent into the delusions of totalitarianism.[68] As psychoanalyst Dr. Joost Meerloo, who spent more than two years under the pressure of Nazi-occupied Holland, witnessing firsthand the Nazi methods of mental manipulation, elucidates:

Delusions, carefully implanted, are difficult to correct…There is another important weapon the totalitarians use in their campaign to frighten the world into submission. This is the weapon of psychological shock. Hitler kept his enemies in a state of constant confusion and diplomatic upheaval. They never knew what this unpredictable madman was going to do next. Hitler was never logical, because he knew that was what he was expected to be. Logic can be met with logic, while illogic cannot—it confuses those who think straight. The Big Lie and monotonously repeated nonsense have more emotional appeal … than logic and reason. While the [people are] still searching for a reasonable counterargument to the first lie, the totalitarians can assault [them] with another.[69]

The intellectuals and medical doctors willingly (maybe unwittingly) were invaluable change agents in subverting fundamental human rights and freedoms during the pandemic. Similar to the Nazi strategy of offering a biomedical solution to solve the Third Reich's problems, offering a "medicalized solution" to address the COVID-19 anxiety was extremely popular and received widespread support from the intelligentsia and the public at large.[27] Medicalization was mindlessly equated, especially by the cognoscenti, with scientific, moral, and social progress that contributed further to its popularity.[15,16]

In his 1949 dystopian novel "Nineteen Eighty-Four," George Orwell envisioned a totalitarian super State in which the oligarchs in coming times would use linguistic debasement as a conscious method of control. The party leaders imposed "doublethink" on the population and made extensive use of "newspeak" in all propaganda. Doublethink is a process of indoctrination whereby the individual is manipulated to simultaneously accept two opposite and mutually contradictory beliefs as correct, believing in both simultaneously and absolutely, in denial of reality, while "newspeak" is a controlled language of restricted vocabulary designed to limit the individual's ability to think and to mask all ideological content from the speaker by introducing new meanings to words to serve a despot's agenda.[70,71] This semantic strategy of control, used extensively in Nazi Germany, was also used with remarkable success during the COVID-19 pandemic to distort inconvenient realities.

"Doublethink" included:

- "COVID-19 vaccines being 99.9% to 100% safe and effective" while at the same time believing the "unvaccinated posed a mortal danger to the vaccinated."
- "Masks are protecting wearers from infection" while at the same time believing "the anti-maskers posed a mortal danger to those that wear masks."
- "Social distancing of six feet apart is absolutely needed to save lives and prohibit transmission in outdoor settings," while at the same time believing "it is safe to fly on an airplane that follows the CDC guidance (despite social distancing being a practical impossibility)."
- "Attending a church service is irresponsible behavior that may lead to contagion and death" while at the same time believing "attending a BLM rally with thousands of other people is no issue at all."
- "Going to the gym is dangerous and selfish" that leads to the spread of COVID-19 while at the same time believing that "shopping at COSTCO is perfectly safe."
- "Small business owners being open during lockdowns present a real threat to the nation's health" while at the same time believing that "large multinational retailers such as Walmart being open is an essential service to the public."
- "COVID-19 vaccines provide sterilized immunity against SARS-CoV-2" while at the same time believing "you need a COVID-19 vaccine or booster shot every six months to protect yourself and your family against SARS-CoV-2."

"Newspeak" included:

- "Treatable common corona virus" becoming the "deadly COVID-19 virus,"
- "Nobel Prize winning cheap and effective early treatment medication" becoming "Dangerous horse deworming medicine,"
- "Life-threatening experimental mRNA gene therapy" becoming "lifesaving vaccine,"
- "Experimental risky and ineffective" becoming "proven, safe, and effective,"
- "Healthy individual" becoming "asymptomatic carrier,"
- "Authoritative academic expert with indisputable contrary objective

facts" becoming "disseminator of misinformation,"
- "Detention center" becoming "health hotel,"
- "Propaganda" becoming "public health education" etc., etc., etc.

7. Collusion between Corporate Elite and Government Elite

The ultra-wealthy business aristocracy of a fascist movement are often the ones who put the government leaders into power, creating a mutually beneficial private-public partnership and power elite. One constant thread that runs through all of the authoritarian COVID-19 policies, the PPPs, the totalitarian logic and messaging, has been the role of the WEF and its acolytes. Many of its partners actively used COVID-19 as an excuse to implement the "Great Reset" as detailed in Schwab's writings. The WEF, whose ultra-wealthy partners (such as Amazon, Amex, Blackrock, Cisco, Citigroup, Microsoft, Moderna, Apple, Google, Goldman Sachs, Facebook, Pfizer, Vanguard, State Street, Walmart, and many others), which were extraordinarily enriched through World War COVID-19, use graduates of its youth programs to "penetrate" governments worldwide to further their globalist corporate agenda.[72] Head of the WEF Klaus Schwab at Harvard's John F. Kennedy School of government in 2017 stated: "What we are very proud of, is that we penetrate the global cabinets of countries with our WEF Young Global Leaders… like Trudeau."[72]

The WEF's Global Leaders program has produced notable world leaders like Canadian PM Justin Trudeau, Governor of California Gavin Newsom, US Transportation Secretary Pete Buttigieg, New Zealand Prime Minister Jacinda Ardern, former German Chancellor Angela Merkel, President of France Emmanuel Macron, Prime Minister of Australia Scott Morrison, Prime Minister of the Netherlands Mark Rutte and Human Rights Watch director Kenneth Roth to name a few.[72] The WEF's acolytes include business leaders such as Blackrock CEO Larry Fink, Microsoft founder Bill Gates, former Microsoft CEO Steven Ballmer, Amazon founder Jeff Bezos, Google co-founders Sergey Brin and Larry Page, Tesla and SpaceX founder Elon Musk, former Google CEO Eric Schmidt, Wikipedia co-founder Jimmy Wales, PayPal co-founder Peter Thiel, eBay co-founder Pierre Omidyar, Facebook founder and CEO Mark Zuckerberg, Facebook COO Sheryl Sandberg, Moderna CEO Stéphane Bancel, Pfizer CEO Albert Bourla, and Pfizer VP Vasudha Vats.[72]

The correlation between the most repressive COVID-19 measures in the West and the country location of WEF corporate and political partners is noteworthy.

8. Freedom of Association and Assembly Suppressed

Because the organizing power of civil society is the only real threat to a fascist government, labor unions (with opposing views) and the ability to assemble and demonstrate are either eliminated, declared illegal, or severely repressed.[51] During COVID-19, arbitrary public health regulations included hundreds of people congregating at transnational retailers being "legal" and "safe" but tens or hundreds of people attending church or attending a social gathering at a private residence being "dangerous," "unsafe," irresponsible, and illegal. On January 2, 2021, it was reported that

> Disturbing video out of Canada shows police violently raiding a family's home for supposedly violating local COVID capacity rules. The now-viral footage from Gatineau, Quebec on New Year's Eve shows several masked police forcibly removing a man from the home after a COVID snitch reported the gathering of six people. The police are then seen subduing the man outside, pinning his face against the asphalt and snow.[73]

Numerous pastors were arrested for holding Sunday service in violation of COVID-19 mandates. In the United States for instance, Pastor Rodney Howard-Browne was arrested and charged with "unlawful assembly and violation of a public health emergency orders" during March 2020 while in Canada, Pastor Artur Pawlowski "was arrested in the middle of a busy highway on his way home from his Calgary church and dragged into a police van after he refused to allow health bureaucrats to interrupt his service" during June 2021.[74,75] Another Canadian, Pastor James Coats, who refused to comply with public health orders during the pandemic, was jailed and fined for not complying with the Alberta province's restrictions around capacity, masks, and social distancing. Coates defended his stance before the judge saying, "I'm simply here in obedience to Jesus Christ, and it's my obedience to Christ that has put me at odds with the law. The court is aware that I'm contesting the legitimacy of that law."[76]

Traditional spiritual and community ties were usurped by artificial ties to the State and its COVD-19 ideology. As diversity and independence fade away, most people supported the State's sacred biological ideology and religion of health. Human beings are more easily conditioned into new patterns of behavior and thought when isolated. Meerloo noted that "Where thinking is isolated without free exchange with other minds and can no longer expand, delusion may follow." He further writes that:

> Pavlov made another significant discovery: the conditioned reflex could be developed most easily in a quiet laboratory with a minimum of disturbing stimuli. Every trainer of animals knows this from his own experience; isolation and the patient repetition of stimuli are required to tame wild animals. . . . The totalitarians have followed this rule. They know that they can condition their political victims most quickly if they are kept in isolation.

> The mind that is open for questions is open for dissent. In the totalitarian regime the doubting, inquisitive, and imaginative mind has to be suppressed. The totalitarian slave is only allowed to memorize, to salivate when the bell rings.[69]

9. Ousting of Intellectuals with Opposing Views

The fascist ideology promotes open hostility to any intellectuals in higher education and academia who hold an opposing view. The hostility against Dr. Martin Kulldorff, professor of medicine at Harvard University, Dr. Sunetra Gupta, professor at Oxford University, and Dr. Jay Bhattacharya, professor at Stanford University Medical School, when they opposed the mainstream COVID-19 narrative with their "Great Barrington Declaration" is one of many examples.[77] Any opposing views were branded as "dangerous" or "disinformation" that aim to jeopardize the noble "war" effort and destroy the nation. Dr. Antony Fauci for instance opined that these eminent scholars' views were "nonsense and very dangerous" while the Guardian's wholly unqualified "Chief Leader Writer" Sonia Sodha opined that their views were "unsupported by existing scientific evidence" and that "The kindest interpretation is these are three politically naive but self-important scientists with little idea about how to engage with the real world. But they have done science a profound disservice."[78,79] Corporate monopoly capital research grants and government funding ensured that most academic institutions, academic journals, and cognoscenti eagerly promoted the fascist COVID-19 agenda. Research articles, written by leading scientific experts, who dared to question the accepted dogma by the controllers of scientific publications – especially concerning the safety, alternative treatments, or efficacy of vaccines – were retracted from major medical and scientific journals weeks, months and even years after publication.[54] As noted by Dr. Russel Blaylock in his April 2022 peer-reviewed article "COVID UPDATE: What is the truth":

> Another unprecedented tactic is to remove dissenting doctors from their positions as journal editors, reviewers and retracting of their scientific papers from journals, even after these papers have been in print….the vast majority promoting alternatives to official dogma, especially if the papers question vaccine safety….. Websites have been removed, highly credentialed and experienced clinical doctors and scientific experts in the field of infectious diseases have been demonized, careers have been destroyed and all dissenting information has been labeled "misinformation" and "dangerous lies", even when sourced from top experts in the fields of virology, infectious diseases, pulmonary critical care, and epidemiology. These blackouts of truth occur even when this information is backed by extensive scientific citations from some of the most qualified medical specialists in the world.[54]

Given that the COVID-19 pandemic was initiated and sustained through lies, manipulation and deception, intellectuals that put forward the actual data and facts and attempted to expose the illegitimacy were mostly attacked *ad hominem* and seldom *ad rem*.

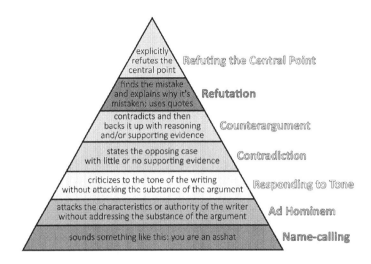

Figure 12.4: Hierarchy of argumentation
Source: P. Graham, how to disagree, http://www.paulgraham.com/disagree.html, 2008

10. Obsession with Mandates, Laws, and Punishment

In the "war" against the SARS-CoV-2 virus, the public health author-ities, police, and military were given limitless power to enforce newly enacted arbitrary laws and health mandates to control the popula-tion and punish or eradicate the opposition.[51] Participation in the States' "greater good" initiatives such as the COVID-19 public health guidelines were at first strongly encouraged and then mandated, and non-compliance penalized. In October 2020, New York City Mayor Bill de Blasio announced that "the fines for mass gatherings in vio-lation of State rules would be up to $15,000 a day, and the fines for not wearing face coverings and maintaining social distancing would be $1,000 a day."[80] In January 2022, the Council of Ministers of Italy enacted a law that "Citizens aged over 50 in Italy who have not been vaccinated will be fined €100, and those who try to go to work without having received the jab face penalties of between €600 and €1,500. According to the new measures adopted by the Government, those who access stores without at least presenting a negative Covid test could be fined up to €1,000."[81] In February 2022, Austria promul-gated a law making it compulsory for adults to get vaccinated against the coronavirus, imposing criminal fines of up to $15,862 a year on citizens who refuse the COVID vaccination.[82] A consequence of the tendency to sugar-coat any arbitrary law in a "public health," "greater good," or "disease prevention" disguise is a society in which virtually any conduct can be legally classified and punished as a crime so that everyone (except the plutocratic power elite and public officials) becomes a potential criminal through illogical mandates.[16] During the course of the COVID-19 pandemic, the following basic human activities were criminal offences subject to fines and punishment in various major Western democracies:

- Walking outside.
- Not wearing a face mask.
- Surfing in the sea.
- Refusing to be inoculated with an experimental mRNA vaccine.
- Holding a church service.
- Servicing customers in a small business.
- Allowing customers to frequent a gym.
- Meeting with more than five friends at home.
- Jogging in the park or on the beach.
- Children playing outside their house.
- Standing less than six feet from a friend.
- Posting an invitation to an anti-lockdown event on Facebook.
- Going to work without having received a COVID-19 vaccine.
- Entering a retail store without having received a COVID-19 vaccine.
- Utilizing public transport without having received a COVID-19 vaccine.
- Attempting to enter a nightclub without having received a COVID-19 vaccine.
- Allowing an unvaccinated child to attend a daycare facility.
- Refusing to be detained at a quarantine facility after testing negative for COVID-19 etc. etc. etc.

Ian Smith, co-owner of New Jersey-based Atilis Gym, was fined $1.2 million in January 2022 after refusing to close his gym during the Garden State's lockdown. The defiant gym owner that never backed down, going so far as to remove the gym's doors so police couldn't lock them said:

> No government official will ever tell me that I am not able to provide for my family. I do not answer to public servants – no matter what

threats or punishments they impose. I am a free man. I do not ask for permission. I do not ask for forgiveness. You work for us. The only way you'll ever close these doors is when you close my casket.[83]

On September 2, 2020, a pregnant woman in Australia was hand-cuffed and arrested in her own home (while still in her pajamas) in front of her two children for the "crime" of promoting an anti-lock-down human rights event on Facebook. The gathering was promoted as a "peaceful protest," with the goal of "ending lockdowns and standing up for human rights." Police informed Zoe Buhler, 28, that she was under arrest for "incitement" and that they would be confiscating all laptops and cellular phone devices on the property. Local media reported that Zoe faced a $20,000 fine and that "Victoria police chief commissioner Shane Patton was unapologetic as he explained that police had in some instances even been smashing car windows due to people inside the cars not cooperating with police or following the newly imposed health guidelines."[84]

11. Rampant Cronyism and Pervasive Corruption

The rampant corruption at various levels of government across the globe to financially exploit citizens by mandating an experimental COVID-19 vaccine that neither prevents infection nor transmission is well documented.[85,86] By August 2020, US Federal spending on COVID-19 vaccine candidates exceeded $9 billion, spread among seven companies, and total global spending on COVID-19 vaccines is projected to reach $157 billion by 2025, driven by mass manda-tory vaccination programs and "booster shots" expected every two years.[85,86] Lobbying ensures that government implements the policies and PPPs dictated by big business, leading to corporations increasingly assuming governmental functions and services, increasing profits while reducing State responsibility for the welfare of the citizens.[6] The veiled corruption works both ways; the political elite receives benefits from the corporate elite, who benefit from government favoritism.[51] The fact that former senior CDC and FDA employees have lucra-tive careers in the pharmaceutical industry following their departure from State regulators is no coincidence. For instance, current Board Member of Pfizer Scott Gottlieb used to be the FDA commissioner regulating Pfizer.

12. Fraudulent Elections

Elections in nations engrossed in biomedical fascism are a complete charade. During COVID-19, emergency legislation was used to control and manipulate mail-in ballots and in-person voting numbers to allegedly facilitate pervasive election fraud in the world's largest economy.[87,88] The mainstream media and social media platforms were also extensively used to "promote" the candidate supported by the fascist overlords and their corporate allies. According to political commentators, one of the most successful disinformation campaigns in modern American electoral history "led by democratic officials, ex-CIA 'reporters' (which usually means current CIA 'contractors') acting in collusion with big tech and the legacy media" occurred in the weeks prior to the 2020 presidential election to obscure the corrupt and criminal business practices of Joe Biden and his son, Hunter, in the Ukraine.[88-90] In September 2022, an article in the Washington Examiner reported on "growing body of evidence that Democrats, the FBI, Big Tech, and legacy media worked together – right out in the open – to put President Joe Biden in the White House."[88] As asserted by Bertram Gross:

> In the West, it is all a vast show. Choreographed political vaudeville, which cost billions of dollars, is called free elections. Cliché-ridden slogans, which assure us that the freedoms we cherish remain sacrosanct, dominate our national discourse as these freedoms are taken from us by judicial and legislative fiat. It is a vast con game.[1]

13. Profits and Power of Large Corporations Protected and Expanded

Fascism endorses corporatism or *corporativismo*, which is the theory and practice of organizing society into "corporations" in PPPs with the State.[91,92] Although the personal life of ordinary citizens was upended, criminalized, and under strict control, the ability of large corporations to operate in freedom was not compromised during the COVID-19 pandemic. In fact, due to corrupt dealings with the political-elite and mandates that ensured increased sales and product take-up, transnational corporations made super-profits, and the ultra-rich global elite's wealth grew exponentially between 2020 and 2022. Given the collusion between the corporate and political elite, the elite are under-regulated or corruptly regulated while the citizens are over-regulated. The boundless diversity among citizens is obscured and replaced by mass compliance (or at minimum, acquiescence) to the convictions and conduct permitted by the global elite.[91,92]

14. Non-Stop Monopolized Propaganda

Hitler's regime was the first regime in the age of technology, that employed to perfection the instruments of technology to dominate its people.[1] In his analysis of previous totalitarian regimes, Dr. Joost Meerloo pointed out:

> …he who dictates and formulates the words and phrases we use, he who is master of the press and radio, is master of the mind…. radio and television tend to take away active affectionate relationships between men and to destroy the capacity for personal thought, evaluation, and reflection. They catch the mind directly, giving people no time for calm, dialectical conversation with their own minds, with their friends, or with their books.[69]

One of the striking features of the COVID-19 pandemic was the extent to which the corporate and political elite controlled all major channels of information technology and communication globally, due to the concentration of media ownership such as Google that has a 95% worldwide market share.[93] Googles algorithms effectively determine what people can and cannot see with 80% of search traffic going to the top 10 listings on the first page.[94] Those who control the media, the social media, and search engines control the minds of the public! Non-stop monopolized propaganda was extensively used on a never-before-seen global scale to manipulate the nations of the earth to acquiescence and thoughtless action.[51] Mainstream media replaced news with ceaseless indoctrination, diversion, and entertainment. Biomedical fascist propaganda used all available mass media: internet, television, movies, radio, social media, theater, newspapers, magazines, brochures, billboards, posters, podcasts, mobile, transit channel, digital channel, drama, paintings, and even songs. The extent to which the propaganda machinery of a State or States has been brought under the control of one group of allied organizations is a useful measure of the degree to which totalitarianism dominates it, and of the extent to which constitutional democracy and the rule of law has been eradicated.[51]

15. Promotion and Establishment of a Totalitarian Governance Structure

During the COVID-19 pandemic, totalitarian State practices that permit no real individual freedom and exercise an extremely high degree of control and regulation over public and private life for the "greater good" were implemented across the globe through arbitrary business closures, lockdowns, isolation mandates, travel mandates, mask mandates, and vaccine mandates.[91,92] Historian Robert Conquest describes a totalitarian State as "a State that recognizes no limit on its authority in any sphere of public or private life and extends that authority to whatever length it considers feasible."[92] Totalitarianism is juxtaposed with other forms of authoritarianism that are "only concerned with political power, and as long as it is not contested it gives society a certain degree of liberty.... does not attempt to change the world and human nature."[95,96] In contrast, totalitarianism aims to penetrate and envelop "the deepest reaches of societal structure", and "to completely control the thoughts and actions of its citizens."[97] During the COVID-19 pandemic, everyday activities such as traveling, family gatherings, social gatherings, religious gatherings, working, attending school or college, and shopping were all considered "regulated" behaviors that could lead to "increased infections" and jeopardize the "greater good." Non-stop mainstream media "coverage" made abundantly clear to citizens what they were allowed to think, say, and do! Any dissent or honest criticism was ridiculed and branded immoral and seditious. A "USA Today" article published on July 2, 2021, for instance, noted that "George Washington and Benjamin Franklin would disapprove of COVID vaccine resistance" while Christopher Beem, the managing director of the McCourtney Institute, in August 2021 penned an article in The Conversation arguing that "Refusing [the] COVID-19 vaccine isn't just immoral, it's un-American."[98,99]

Totalitarian governance perverts and subjugates all political, social, and legal institutions to pursue some popular sacrosanct unassailable goal, such as the "biological war" to eradicate SARS-CoV-2, to the exclusion of all others. Vast amounts of the State capital were directed toward its realization, regardless of the monetary or human cost.[100-102] In the US alone, an estimated $5 trillion of pandemic stimulus money was spent, with the global humanitarian fallout of the COVID-19 measures leading to an additional six to seven million children suffering from acute malnourishment and wasting and an estimated 810 million poverty-stricken people being undernourished in 2020.[103-105] Whatever could advance the goal is endorsed; whatever could thwart the goal is spurned with contempt. This fixation on the sacred goal leads to a philosophy that justifies everything in terms of the goal. The ensuing popular support allows the State the broadest latitude of action. Any opposition is outlawed and labeled "wicked." Because the pursuit of the unassailable goal is the only ideological foundation for the totalitarian State, achieving the goal can never be acknowledged. As we have already been told with COVID-19, even if case numbers are down, there may be some new variants on the way or even worse, an even more deadly pathogen than COVID-19 that would require a rejuvenated "war" effort and continued state of emergency!

Some critics of fascism hold the view that much of the ideology is simply the result of unprincipled opportunism disguised in "the public's best interest" and that fascism is ideological dishonesty and highly irrational.[106-109] Although true, the COVID-19 crisis has, however, again shown that it is a calculated, shrewd ideology directed to maintain and expand the interests and the perpetuity of the political and corporate elite, in the face of baseless fear.

COVID-19 Inverted Totalitarianism versus Nazi Totalitarianism

Nazi "right-wing" authoritarian ultranationalist fascism and modern "left-wing" COVID-19 public health fascism are fundamentally indistinguishable political practices that are not antagonistic but two similar types of fascist totalitarianism – one nationwide, traditional totalitarianism and the other worldwide, inverted totalitarianism. Both kinds of totalitarianism are extraordinarily effective in bypassing the constitutional limits of their power and undermining individual freedom, fundamental human rights, and the rule of law.[46,110-114]

Sheldon Wolin coined the term "inverted totalitarianism" to describe the corporate subversion and corruption of constitutional democratic principles through the phenomena of "managed democracy"[2] - a political form in which the rulers bypass the constitutional limits of their powers and governments are staged, managed, and controlled within corporate capitalism, and citizens are oblivious of those who exercise real power.[115-117]

Although principally and effectually identical, Nazi totalitarianism and COVID-19 inverted totalitarianism differ in the following aspects:

Nazi Totalitarianism	COVID-19 Inverted Totalitarianism
National, occurring in one country with regional implications.	Global, occurring in most Member States of the United Nations simultaneously through a combination of US global hegemony and transnational monopoly capital coercion and seduction resulting in the subservience of many States.[2]
The focus is on strengthening and enriching the German economy and German ultra-wealthy industrialists and their national corporations.	The focus is on consolidating the power of the global political elite and their ultra-rich colluders and on maximizing the profitability of their transnational corporations.
Replaced the weak Weimar democratic government and supplanted democracy with socialism.	Preserve existing democratic governments to maintain the illusion of a free and democratic society.[2]
Open subversion: ousted the established democratic governance system and structures through revolution.	Subtle subversion: corrupts, undermines, and then manipulates, manages and controls established democratic governance structures to defeat the original purpose.[2]
Government was a structured and coordinated whole.[2]	Global system of managed (manipulated) and controlled democracies.[2]
Propaganda formally managed and regulated through propaganda laws. Mainstream corporate colluders adhere to all laws.	State propaganda only part of the phenomenon. Concentration of media ownership allows propaganda to be largely managed and distributed by the ultra-wealthy's transnational corporations, creating the delusion of a "free press." More advanced capabilities of governing and deceiving the public.[2,115]
Although also strongly supported and funded by the ultra-wealthy German national corporations, Hitler dominated or at minimum had the ability to dominate the plutocrats.	Transnational corporations through lobbying, political contributions, and the revolving door dominate States including the United States, with governments being subservient to large international corporations.[2]
A tight Government-Big Business oligarchy that required a charismatic strong leader such as Hitler ("Fuhrer") to implement the ideology.	An integrated Big Business-Big Government (PPP) power structure that does not depend on a specific leader but produces leaders who are close to and colluding with the corporate leaders.[2]
Social policy for the working class incorporated an aim to full German employment.	Exploits the poor through pseudo-health and social programs and weakening working conditions.

Political or ideological opponents and scapegoats were crudely punished through murder and imprisonment.	Political or ideological opponents and scapegoats are punished through termination of employment, character assassinations, cancel culture, stigmatization, sanctions, humiliation, discreditation, condemnation, ostracizing, financial war, financial destabilization, and ruin.[116]
Ideology included the biological superiority of German people as part of the "Master Race" (*Herrenrasse*) entitled to special treatment.	Ideology does not include a "Master Race." All organic and biological resources that include human beings are commodified and plundered by the ultra-wealthy and their transnational corporations.
The ultra-wealthy German puppeteers and their German corporations had an allegiance to Germany.	The ultra-wealthy global aristocratic exploiters and their transnational corporations have no allegiance to any country.[117]
Committed its abhorrent human rights abuses and biomedical mass experimentation pre-IHRL, UDHR, and ICCPR.	Commits its human rights abuses and mandatory biomedical mass experimentation, post-IHRL, UDHR and ICCPR, openly breaching IHRL obligations *erga omnes* and violating *jus cogens* norms.
Never dominated the League of Nations nor professed to be adhering to all the Leagues Treaties. Resigned from the League of Nations in 1935.	Financially penetrated, subverted, corrupted and now dominates the United Nations, and its various specialized agencies such as the IMF, WHO UNICEF, UNESCO, and the UNHRC. Subservient States maintain membership of the United Nations and superficially claim that all covenant obligations are adhered to while actively breaching IHRL.
Funded by the German State and the German corporate elite.	Infinitely better funded through PPPs that include the world's only superpower, all Western States and the largest transnational corporations on earth.

Table 12.1: Comparison between
Nazi totalitarianism and COVID-19 inverted totalitarianism
Source: Dr. Willem van Aardt, adapted from
the work of Sheldon Wolin and Bertram Gross[2,3]

In modern-day inverted totalitarianism, transnational corporate control, surveillance, coercion, seduction, and mass manipulation, which far surpass those employed in Nazi Germany, are effectively masked by concentrated global mainstream media propaganda, political play-acting, scientific fraud, technocratic censorship, technology addiction, sensationalism, perversion of biology, sham wokeness, and superfluous consumerism that pacify and manipulate the public to relinquish their individual human rights and freedoms.[117]

The United States, as the world's only superpower, played a vital role in the globalization of inverted totalitarianism, culminating in the lockstep worldwide comportment and subservience of numerous States to implement COVID-19 policies. The superpower claims both democracy and global hegemony.[2] Democracy and hegemony are coupled by means of the nefarious corporate manipulation of the US democracy resulting in the United States no longer being a liberal constitutional democracy but a fundamentally undemocratic illiberal democracy ("managed democracy") that ignores and bypasses the constitutional limits of its power.[2] Under a managed democracy, despite "elections" being held, the electorate has no real power to impact any State policies and practices due to behind-the-scenes amoral corporate control and manipulation of the elections and the State.[1,2] One of the critical global totalizing dynamics of the COVID-19 pandemic is the US worldview (established during the global war on terror) that it has the right to launch preventative conventional wars and biomedical "wars" and any attempt by any State to resist its dominance and control is "illicit." Once the transnational corporations corrupted and perverted the US democracy, global domination by the power elite followed naturally.

The potential sociopolitical and socioeconomic ramifications of not adhering to the demands and expected behaviors of the United States and its Western allies (that provide the vast majority of the funding to the United Nations and its various specialized agencies such as the WHO, OHCHR, UNHRC, IMF, and World Bank) contributed to widespread global mimicking of Western COVID-19 measures and adherence to CDC and WHO advisories.

Managed Democracies Managing the United Nations

When reviewing the UN's major funders, the fact that the profit before people agenda of the corporate elite and its "managed" State allies are robustly endorsed by the United Nations comes as no surprise.

72% of UN funding comes from governments. The United States on its own is responsible for paying 22% of the UN's general budget, and together with its Western allies controls more than 60% of the UN budget. There are, however, non-State organizations under the control of the ultra-wealthy elite that also contribute, including the Gates Foundation, which donated $276 million in 2019.[118]

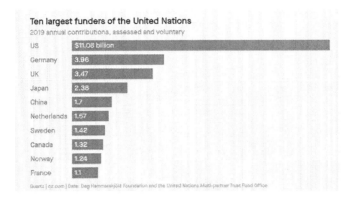

Figure 12.5 The largest funders of the United Nations
Source: The United Nations

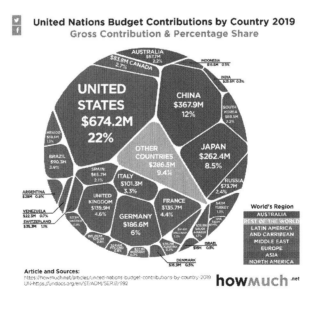

Figure 12.6: UN budget contributions by country, 2019
Source: The United Nations

The OHCHR (which is supposed to act as guardian of the human rights norms and covenant obligations) is partially funded through assessed contributions from Member States to the United Nations regular budget and partially through voluntary contributions (extrabudgetary funding) from donors, the majority of which are Member States. In 2020, UN Human Rights' total income was US$340.9 million. Of this total, 65.8% came from voluntary contributions (that included contributions from Bill Gates's Microsoft and George Soros's Open Society Foundation) and 34.2% came from the UN regular budget. The United States and its Western allies that include Sweden, the European Commission, Norway, the Netherlands, Denmark, Germany, Canada, the United Kingdom, Switzerland, Finland, and Belgium are responsible for more than 90% of all voluntary contributions. This explains the deafening silence by the OHCHR in the face of the most egregious human rights violations by major Western democracies.[119] While the OHCHR is supposed to promote fundamental rights around the world and intensely scrutinize the fundamental rights situations in countries such as Somalia and Zimbabwe, there is scant action so far in case of serious fundamental rights violations by the United States, its Western allies, China, and other large contributors. The glaring deficiencies and corruption of the existing structure have been elucidated by the brazen violation of human rights during the COVID-19 pandemic without any material condemnation or action from the OHCHR.

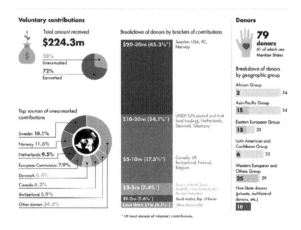

Figure 12.7: Voluntary contributions to the Office of the
United Nations High Commissioner for Human Rights 2020
Source: The United Nations Human Rights Commission

The rampant corruption of the pharmaceutical industry has been well documented for many years.[120] In 1988, Halfdan Mahler (WHO director general for the period of 1973 to 1988) in the Danish paper "*Politiken*" cautioned humanity against the power the multinational pharmaceutical companies had over the WHO: "the industry is taking over WHO," he stated.[121] Very few believed him, since the general public did not comprehend the convoluted and duplicitous subversion strategies being deployed by the global elite.

The WHO is guiding the public health services of 194 Member States and a number of other countries, regarding their usage of pharmacologic medicines, vaccines, and non-drug treatment (psychotherapy, physiotherapy, alternate medicine etc.). In 2005, the WHO altered its monetary policy and allowed private contribution funding, instead of only allowing financial support from the Member States.[121] This effectively brought the WHO under the control of the ultra-wealthy global elite and their multinational pharmaceutical companies.[120] More than half of its annual budget now comes from voluntary contributions such as the contributions from the Gates Foundation and the GAVI vaccine alliance that has the "noble goal" of introducing and increasing "access to vaccines so that they are able to protect every child with a full package of WHO-recommended life-saving vaccines" and "introducing new vaccines into the routine schedules of national immunization programmes" that their members profit from.[122,123]

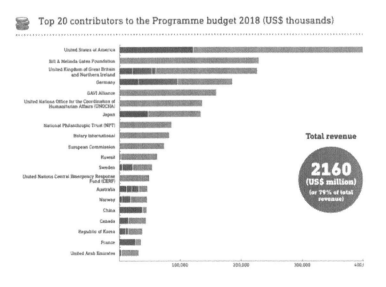

Figure 12.8: Top 20 contributions to the WHO 2018
Source: The United Nations[123]

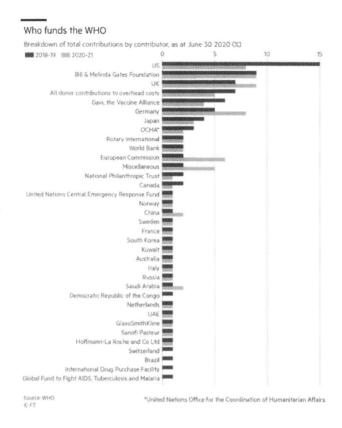

Figure 12.9: Who funds the WHO 2018 -2021
Source: WHO

For Bill Gates, vaccines are a strategic philanthropy that feed his many vaccine-related businesses (including Microsoft's ambition to control a global vaccination ID enterprise).[124] In 2010, at the time of pledging $10 billion to the WHO, Gates stated that "We must make this the decade of vaccines." Shortly thereafter Gates opined that "new vaccines could reduce [the global] population."[124] In 2014, Kenya's Catholic Doctors Association blamed the WHO for chemically sterilizing millions of unwilling Kenyan women with a "tetanus" vaccine campaign. Independent test centers found a sterility formula in every vaccine tested. After initially denying the allegations, the WHO ultimately conceded it had been developing the sterility inoculations for more than 10 years.[124] Similar accusations came from Mexico, Nicaragua, and Tanzania. "The Gates Foundation's focus on underdeveloped, poor countries is not viewed by the local population as an example of beneficence, but rather as abominable human exploitation."[124] Professor Patrick Bond, a political economist at the

University of Witwatersrand, Johannesburg, South Africa, (who was part of Nelson Mandela's government), described Gates's business-philanthropic practices and agenda of the Gates Foundation as "ruthless and immoral".[125] Professor Bond noted that:

> [Gates's] influence is so pervasive that many actors in international development, which would otherwise critique the policy and practice of the foundation, are unable to speak out independently as a result of its funding and patronage.[125]

In his 2013 book, "Deadly Medicines and Organised Crime: How Big Pharma Has Corrupted Healthcare", the former Danish director of the Nordic Cochrane Center openly addressed what he called "the criminal practices of the pharmaceutical industry" and documented that "'big pharma' already has taken patient's lives and caused harm to patients from the use of poisonous, poorly documented, and ineffective medicine."[126]

A January 2015 peer-reviewed study by Dr. Seren Ventegodt pointed out that the "WHO's Model List of Essential Medicines" was biased towards recommending drugs and vaccines from pharmaceutical companies - as opposed to other cheap and effective generic drugs - despite the fact that these "recommendations" did not align with independent meta-analysis relating to the positive and negative effects of these drugs and vaccines.[121,126] Ventegodt pointed out:

> The results from the Cochrane reviews, which most researchers regard as a much more reliable source of information on medicine than the data coming from the pharmaceutical industry itself, clash harshly with the recommendations of WHO in its drug directories. The Cochrane meta-analyses have systematically found less effect and more harm from the pharmaceutical drugs than the pharmaceutical industry does, when it documents its own products, also when the industry's own data is used.

> Many drugs listed in the WHO drug directories, like "WHOs model list of essential medicines," have no value as medicine according to Cochrane reviews, since the drugs are dangerous, often harmful, and without significant beneficial effects for the patient. You can even say that the lack of effect and the danger of the drugs are well documented! Today after the Swine Flu Scandal the pharmaceutical industry has gained control over the WHO system, leading to an

extreme bias towards the use of not only ineffective and unnecessary influenza vaccines and medicines, … which according to independent meta-analyses and … reviews are found to be without significant beneficial effect – and often harmful.[121,126]

Despite it being a well-known fact that the international Swine Flu Scandal in 2009 was directly caused by the WHO, resulting in hundreds of States paying billions of dollars for needless vaccinations, and in spite of thousands of victims suffering severe harmful consequences of these treatments, the WHO concluded "that all went well and happened according to the plans from 2005 and that no errors had been made in the WHO system."[127,128] There is no doubt that when reflecting on the "practices" during the COVID-19 pandemic a similar incredulous conclusion would be-reached by the WHO and their corporate masters.

The WHO that is widely regarded as the world's most powerful international organization, surpassing the UN Security Council (in relation to the ability to get a desired worldwide outcome), has been suborned by the global elite to issue advisories and make declarations and pronouncements that put profit before people.[129] Having honed their debased practices over many years, including the 2009 Swine Flu "pandemic" scandal, the global elite manufactured and managed the COVID-19 pandemic flawlessly in their self-interest. Based on the WHO's advice and recommendations, more than 64% of the world population has received at least one dose of the experimental and ineffective COVID-19 mRNA vaccine with more than 11 billion doses administered globally by March 2022 and resulting in super profits for the ultra-wealthy global elite!

We are living in a time of unbridled global inverted totalitarianism, in which the tools used to advance the agenda of the rich and the powerful are much more subtle and technologically advanced to hide the real agenda, which is to commodify and exploit every natural resource and human by immoral and lawless transnational corporations and their unruly ultra-wealthy owners.[117,130]

COVID-19 Global Biomedical Fascism

COVID-19 biomedical fascism, with its morally unopposable sacrosanct "greater good" crusade is a political project rather than an unintended effect of sincere public health policies, "an elite strategy reflecting a belief in the responsibility of the State and the corporate elite to regulate and restrain personal behavior."[109]

"Global biomedical fascism" can be defined as the oppression of personal liberty, choice, and behavior, particularly private medical and moral choices, for the financial and political gain of the global corporate and political elite. This modern form of fascism is established and sustained through government and corporate coercion and rationalized by an elitist ideology and rhetoric of the "greater good" and the supremacy of public health. Public health fascism, as manifestly observed during the COVID-19 era, appears as an equivalent to the Nazi era public health fascism, but co-occurring in almost all UN Member States. It is global in scope and involves biomedical "weapons" (gene-editing biotechnology) that Hitler could imagine but never attain. It is based on a global coalition of multinational technology, pharmaceutical and financial corporations, dominant States, the global corporate elite, ultra-wealthy foundations, science, academia, public health regulators, and the Western medical and military-industrial complex that the old-fashioned fascists could barely approximate.[1]

A "greater good" moral dictate executed by the government and justified on public health grounds is the essence of neo-global public health fascism. Global biomedical fascism, *via* its moral absolutism, abrogates the ethical principle that the "freedom of action that is the condition of moral merit includes the freedom to act wrongly [or] moral esteem would be meaningless without freedom."[109] Kant correctly argued that the capacity to make moral choices lay within the presence of freedom, affirming that if we are not able to make our own choices, those choices could not be moral as we were never free to make that choice in the first instance.[109]

> If we are to have free will, we must have the ability to make a decision that is unhindered; if God did not give us free will then our decisions cannot be considered immoral or moral as we would have had to act in the way we did. Thus, we cannot be held responsible; a good moral action cannot be praised as you had no other option, whilst an immoral action cannot be punished as …there was no free choice.[109]

Global biomedical fascism is a despotic order backed up by naked coercion and sophisticated manipulation that intentionally created and utilized the COVID-19 crisis to accelerate the tendencies toward a repressive global corporate society. The mixture of public health, global politics, and huge transnational corporations, specifically, coercion for financial and political benefit in the public health sphere, provides a basis for this neo-medical fascism. To a certain extent, it permits freedom of opinion and individual choices in the free-market economy, but not in the public health sphere. As noted by Noam Chomsky:

> The smart way to keep people passive and obedient is to strictly limit the spectrum of acceptable opinion but allow very lively debate within that spectrum - even encourage the more critical and dissident views. That gives people the sense that there's free thinking going on, while all the time the presuppositions of the system are being reinforced by the limits put on the range of the debate.[131]

The practical effects on the individual are conformism and passivity in the areas that matter and non-conformism in the areas that do not. History shows that the combination of public health and corporatized politics leads to professional authoritarianism and fascism that destroys individual freedoms. *Prima facie*, the combination is perilous to freedom and democracy because it supplies a design, instrument, or rationalization for the violation of fundamental human rights and freedoms. Technocratic and pharmacratic social engineering with the purpose of creating a healthy social organism of "biologically based collectivism" once again enables the modern-day transformation to a fascist State.[16]

The dualism between an under-regulated ultra-wealthy corporate class and an over-regulated moral or private sphere of the masses indicate the fascist's preoccupation and systemic obsession with people's private lives and medical and moral choices. This is exemplified in their persistent technocratic monitoring of compliance and criminalization and penalization of the contravention of COVID-19 public health mandates.

In a modern biomedical fascist State, the rule of medical discretion and "therapy" replaces "the rule of law."[16] The classification of behavior as the cause of disease or disease itself provides an ideological rationalization for State-subsidized social control. As was evident during the COVID-19 era, what States labeled "dangerous disease posing a risk to the vast majority of citizens" was not a fact, but a strategy; not a condition, but a fascist public policy in which disapproved thoughts and actions are repressed through pseudo-public-health interventions.[132,133]

Overall, modern public health fascism is characterized by an "unholy alliance" between the world's ultra-rich global elite and the political elite to improve global public health through a combination of technocratic and pharmacratic forms of government that diminishes citizens to a powerless mass with limited fundamental human rights and freedoms. On account of this alliance, the COVID-19 new world order resembles less of the values of post-Second World War Western liberal democracies and more of the values of Nazi Germany. Such is the perversity of the modern medical fascists that while preaching the "greater good" message, they destroy the fabric of society and exploit the population for the benefit of the rich and powerful.

Capitalist Politics Wearing a "Public Health" Disguise

As in Nazi Germany, the globe has seen capitalist politics wearing a "public health" disguise to cover up a creeping despotism in which the ultra-rich global corporate elite merged with centralized State power to manipulate and exploit hard-working ordinary people and trample on their fundamental human rights. This corporate authoritarianism is in the process of subverting constitutional democracy on a global scale. However, unlike the violent and sudden usurpations that led to totalitarianism in the days of Lenin, Hitler, Stalin, Mussolini, Pinochet, Ceausescu, and others, this new "corporate" breed of fascism gains ground through gradual infringements on the fundamental rights and freedoms of the people in the name of the "greater good" and a "public health emergency."

The COVID-19 public health practices perpetuated society's class structure and patterns of domination through corporate control over health institutions and the pharmaceutical industry. Monopoly capital influence is apparent in the financial penetration, subversion, and exploitation of the WHO and national health regulators such as the CDC by large corporations and the "medical-industrial complex."[134] The modern public health fascist State's intervention in healthcare perversely protects and advances the capitalist domination at the expense of the health and safety of the nation.[127]

The aphorism that "Fascism is the marriage of corporation and State" is indeed true. In this marriage, law and science are distorted to condone the illegitimate usurpation of power. Facts and opinions become interchangeable. Truth is no longer based on provable facts or actual data; it is based on dogma and sentiment. Lies become the truth. "Collective insanity" becomes the new normal.[1] The world is turned upside down and allows the elite to cannibalize the State as it profits from futile and useless "wars" against the next "virus strain."[1,50,135]

In the 1930s, many supposedly sophisticated Europeans rushed to embrace fascist States. Since the beginning of 2020, many people again rushed to embrace the therapeutic State, but this time on a global scale. As Thomas Szasz warned, "By the time they discover that the therapeutic State is about tyranny, not therapy, it will be too late."[16] Mandating COVID-19 vaccines, masks or lockdowns has got nothing to do with public health. It is all about tyrannical control and financial gain by the so-called global political and corporate elite. An Oxfam report revealed that 32 of the world's largest companies saw their profits increase by $109 billion more in 2020 as the COVID-19 pandemic laid bare an economic model that delivers profits for the wealthiest on the backs of the poorest.[105] These people are neither upper class nor elite. They are narcissistic international criminals, despots, and enemies of humanity who should be prosecuted and held to account. As noted by Thomas Paine in his 1776 "Common Sense" pamphlet that examined some of the atrocities committed by the plutocratic elites:

> In England, a king hath little more to do than to make war and give away places, which in plain terms, is to impoverish the nation and set it together by the ears……Of more worth is one honest man to society and in the sight of God, than all the crowned ruffians that ever lived.

Chapter Conclusion

During the COVID-19 pandemic, sizable imbalances were created between government power and civil society due to the fact that ordinary people were lied to and deceived through plutocratically funded propaganda to obey illegitimate, unjust laws.

Many citizens across the globe were utterly taken aback by the global response to COVID-19 and how Western democracies went from protecting and respecting fundamental human rights to imposing arbitrary, irrational mandates that grossly violated these very rights in a matter of months. To understand why events are unfolding contrary to reasonable expectations, it is always important to follow the money (*sequere pecuniam*) and to investigate who benefits (*qui bono*) and who advances (*qui prodest*). The truth is that the difficulties faced by billions of people worldwide are the result of years of unlawful predatory actions by the ruling elites in the West: their greed, myopia, lawlessness, and malevolent ambitions. These global elites are not considering how to better the lives of their people; they are obsessed and preoccupied with their self-serving agenda and realizing super-profits.

History teaches us that we ought to be circumspect about embracing an ideology that appoints bio-medical experts as our protectors: they often degrade, coerce, and hurt their beneficiaries and do their best to render them despairingly dependent on their oppressors.[16] Transforming numerous United Nations Members States from constitutional democracies into fascist therapeutic States during the COVID-19 pandemic has shifted the internal balance of power in favor of the government and against the individual and fundamental human rights and freedoms. Ironically, as in Nazi Germany, this shift has been accompanied by widespread support from the literati and the general public. They mistake "greater good" public health policies for what is, in reality, greediness by ruthless modern fascists and international industrialists engendered by the growth of pharmacratic regulations and the therapeutic State.[16]

The similarities between Nazi Germany's "greater good" biomedical practices and the COVID-19 "greater good" public health policies are striking. They cannot be dismissed as irrelevant given the incremental death and destruction that such, in principle, totalitarian policies would cause if tolerated and sustained. The glaringly obvious truth is that the Nazi health ideology and practices closely resemble the COVID-19 health ideology and practices.[16] It is not difficult to understand the perils represented by transnational powers that have at their disposal the unlimited biometric and genetic information of most citizens in the Western world. With such information at hand, the annihilation of the Jews, which was undertaken on the basis of incomparably less efficient bioinformation technology, would have been total and extremely swift.

The Nuremberg war crime trials that prosecuted some of the Nazi officers, public health officials, and their ultra-rich corporate backers spurred the creation of a collection of international human rights instruments, treaties, and peremptory norms that remain central to human rights protection to this day. The Vienna Convention on the Law of Treaties and ICCPR, that encompasses binding IHRL and non-derogable peremptory norms, were explicitly put in place to prevent a recurrence of the medical atrocities and cruel human rights violations in the name of public health that occurred following close collaboration between the corporate and political elite in Nazi Germany. Yet despite all these international covenants and *jus cogens* norms that were created, this is indeed what has recurred since the beginning of 2020, only this time on a global scale.

The various national and international organizations that have a fiduciary duty to act as the guardians of civil liberties and fundamental human rights and to be a check on unbridled State power have been wholly corrupted by the political elite and their corporate paymasters through various well-funded foundations and government lobbyists, coercing governmental processes with undisclosed interest, resulting in the transformation of good cause initiatives like the United Nations, the WHO, the OHCHR, and UNICEF away from their foundational principles to serving the interest of the global elite. It is not that there were no rules or that the rules were vague. It is that the powerful elite ignored the unambiguous rules and acted as if they were above the law.

It is necessary to counter current global trends, re-claim public policy, and take courageous measures to bolster national and international human rights protection and weaken the grip of unbridled corporate power on people's lives.[6]

13. EPILOGUE

"Civil disobedience becomes a sacred duty when the state has become lawless or corrupt. And a citizen who barters with such a state shares in its corruption and lawlessness."

— Mahatma Gandhi

The concept of the State and government officials in power as the guardians protecting civil society from internal and external enemies is a basic notion of Western political philosophy. However, history also shows that *"Power tends to corrupt, and absolute power corrupts absolutely."* What prevents the guardians of society from succumbing to the temptation to exploit and harm the people they are supposed to protect? What prevents the guardians from becoming anti-juridical and abusing emergency provisions? Roman poet Decimus Junius Juvenalis posed the classic question: *"Quis custodiet ipsos custodes?"* - "Who shall guard the guardians?"

The rule of law and specifically IHRL is there to keep the guardians in check and to hold them accountable to specific peremptory norms. Regrettably, recent global events demonstrated that there are no uncompromised, effective, ethical international defenses that guard against the guardians, specifically when the State guardians are the dominant political and monopoly capital of the West that fund and control the very international institutions that are supposed to guard against them. Once a political juridical system has been corrupted by those in power, the only and ultimate guardians to ensure adherence to IHRL principles are "we the people." It is up to the citizenry to guard and defend the constitutional order *in extremis* to ensure a restoration to law and order. Thomas Paine said that "The duty of a patriot is to protect his country from his government," while Thomas Jefferson affirmed that "When once a Republic is corrupted, there is no possibility of remedying any of the growing evils but by removing the corruption and restoring its lost principles; every other correction is either useless or a new evil."

The Anglo-American legal tradition has endorsed the idea that sometimes the people, rather than the government, may best represent the constitution.[1] Locke's doctrine of resistance grows out of the idea that when the government seeks to subvert the terms of the social contract, then it becomes an aggressor against the people, who accordingly have a right to resist. When elected officials break their oath to uphold the constitution it is not the patriotic citizen that is in rebellion but the governing official.[2]

The purpose of a citizenry acting as guardians is to protect the rule of law against abrogation and sabotage by corrupt government officials, not to necessarily create a new politico-legal order but to facilitate a return to law and order. According to Professor Christine Korsgaard, the former Arthur Kingsley Porter Professor of Philosophy at Harvard:

> The duties of justice require us to obey the powers that be, because only in the political state can human rights and freedom be realized. But the virtue of justice requires us to make human rights our end. When a political society itself violates human rights, the virtue of justice is turned against itself, and the person who makes human rights his end may be driven to take the law into his own hands.[3]

The rule of law should have multiple protectors – the government in ordinary times, the citizenry in extraordinary ones.[3] It is only "we the people's" own determination that will see a return from a state of lawlessness to a state of law. When public powers violate the rights and fundamental liberties guaranteed by IHRL, resistance to oppression is the right and duty of the citizen. If one does not speak out when injustice occurs, on the grounds that "it's not happening to me (yet)," pretty soon events will prove that view short-sighted. Consider the poem by the Nazi dissident and pacifist Lutheran pastor Martin Niemoller:

**First, they came for the socialists, and I did not speak out—
Because I was not a socialist.
Then they came for the trade unionists, and I did not speak out—
Because I was not a trade unionist.**

> **Then they came for the Jews, and I did not speak out—**
> **Because I was not a Jew.**
> **Then they came for me—and there was no one left to speak for me.**

Conformity is the proclivity to embrace the opinions, actions, and mindsets of those around you. Commonly, conformity entails a revision of your own opinions in submission to social pressures. According to the late Professor Solomon Eliot Asch (1907-1996) (founder of the Institute for Cognitive Studies at Rutgers University, New Jersey) "people conform for two main reasons: they want to fit in with the group (normative influence) and[or] because they [mistakenly] believe the group is more informed than they are (informational influence)."[39-41]

The pathological conformity, witnessed in the West throughout the COVID-19 pandemic, is years in the making and the consequence of a conflux of various factors. It is fueled by a modern society in which social acceptance and affirmation occupies a prominent position.[4,5] It is furthered by the widespread use of social media platforms whose success is dependent on promoting "virtue signaling" and conforming to the "current thing".[4,5] Social media users move from news story to news story, issue to issue, and strongly "support" whatever "current thing" dominates the mainstream news. It is the product of a society that promotes the rights of the majority over the rights of the individual.[4,5] These factors, combined with a disregard for the rule of law by the ruling elite, have created a society of extreme conformists.[4,5] In his article "Enforcing Social Conformity: A Theory of Authoritarianism", Professor Stanley Feldman (professor of political science, Stony Brook University, New York) asserts that:

> …people who value social conformity… support the government when it wants to increase its control over social behavior and punish noncon-formity…valuing social conformity increases the motivation for placing restrictions on behavior…the desire for social freedom is now subservient to the enforcement of social norms and rules. Thus, groups will be targeted for repression to the extent that they challenge social conformity…[5]

Many people hold the view that to be a decent person equals being a compliant person and to do exactly what one is told to do by government bureaucrats. This view however fails to distinguish between just moral laws and unjust immoral laws, driven by greed, politics, and corruption.[4]

When most of society advocates for the enforcement of conformity (legal moralism), a society places itself in a "continuum of destruction".[5,6] As the State utilizes intimidation and force to penalize the non-compliant minority, the majority (incited by mainstream propaganda) justifies their support of such repressive measures by demonizing the non-compliant, leading to more severe measures.[5] In Nazi Germany, government measures such as outlawing minority groups from theaters, sports arenas, restaurants, and other public places, imposing restrictions, ousting them from their careers, making them to pay fines, and impeding their freedom of assembly and freedom of movement, served as the initial measures on a "continuum of destruction that resulted in mass-condemnation, mass-incarceration and mass-murder.[6]

Our present-day predicament is again an overwhelming predisposition toward conformity and subservient submission to lawless rulers.[5]

Civil disobedience becomes a sacred duty when the State has become lawless

Historically, the most horrendous crimes against humanity, such as the Holocaust, genocide, slavery, enforced sterilization, enforced disappearances, torture, and other inhumane acts of a similar character intentionally causing great suffering, have resulted not from disobedience to government but from obedience. Mark Passio explains:

> [T]he order-follower always bears more moral culpability than the order-giver, because the order-follower is the one who actually performed the action, and in taking such action, actually brought the resultant harm into physical manifestation. Order-following is the pathway to every form of evil and chaos in our world. It should never be seen as a "virtue" by anyone who considers themself a moral human being. Order-followers have ultimately been personally responsible and morally culpable for every form of slavery and every single totalitarian regime that has ever existed upon the face of the earth.[7]

Our problem today is once again not one of civil disobedience but of inappropriate subservient civil obedience to unjust, arbitrary mandates. Rollo May declared that "The hallmark of courage in our age of conformity is the capacity to stand on one's own convictions" while Carl Jung professed: "The true leaders of mankind are always those who are capable of self-reflection,"[8,9] To rectify the lawlessness created by the global elite, civil disobedience is required against any biomedical dictates that do not comply with IHRL. As Oscar Wilde pointed out, "Disobedience, in the eyes of anyone who has studied history, is man's original virtue. It is through disobedience that progress has been made."[10]

On the topic of civil disobedience to bring about a return to the rule of law, it is worth heeding the advice of eminent civil dissidents such as Henry David Thoreau, Mahatma Gandhi, Martin Luther King Jr., Nelson Mandela, and Howard Zin.

In his famous essay, "On the Duty of Civil Disobedience", published in 1849, American transcendentalist Henry David Thoreau noted that:

- Disobedience is the true foundation of liberty. The obedient must be slaves.
- Unjust laws exist: shall we be content to obey them, or shall we endeavor to amend them, and obey them until we have succeeded, or shall we transgress them at once?
- There will never be a really free and enlightened state until the state comes to recognize the individual as a higher and independent power, from which all its own power and authority are derived.[2]

Mahatma Gandhi, leader of India's movement against British colonialism in the 1930s and 1940s contended that civil disobedience becomes a sacred duty when the State has become lawless or corrupt and is the inherent right of a citizen:

- Civil disobedience is the inherent right of a citizen.[11]
- An unjust law is itself a species of violence. Arrest for its breach is more so.[12]
- Civil disobedience is the assertion of a right which law should give but which it denies.[13]

Martin Luther King Jr., leader of the American civil rights movement from 1955 until his assassination in 1968, said that:

- One may well ask: 'How can you advocate breaking some laws and obeying others?' The answer lies in the fact that there are two types of laws: just and unjust. I would be the first to advocate obeying just laws. One has not only a legal, but a moral responsibility to obey just laws. Conversely, one has a moral responsibility to disobey unjust laws. I would agree with St. Augustine that 'an unjust law is no law at all.' A just law is a manmade code that squares with the moral law or the law of God. An unjust law is a code that is out of harmony with the moral law.[14]

- Of course, there is nothing new about this kind of civil disobedience. It was seen sublimely in the refusal of Shadrach, Meshach and Abednego to obey the laws of Nebuchadnezzar because a higher moral law was involved. It was practiced superbly by the early Christians who were willing to face hungry lions and the excruciating pain of chopping blocks, before submitting to certain unjust laws of the Roman empire.[15]
- In no sense do I advocate evading or defying the law, as would the rabid segregationist. That would lead to anarchy. One who breaks an unjust law must do so openly, lovingly, and with a willingness to accept the penalty. I submit that an individual who breaks a law that conscience tells him is unjust, and who willingly accepts the penalty of imprisonment to arouse the conscience of the community over its injustice, is in reality expressing the highest respect for law.[15]

South African anti-apartheid activist and 1993 Nobel Peace Prize winner Nelson Mandela, who served as the first black president of South Africa from 1994 to 1999, propounded that "When a man is denied the right to live the life he believes in, he has no choice but to become an outlaw" and judiciously noted that:

- Freedom can never be taken for granted. Each generation must safe-guard it and extend it…Use this precious right to ensure that the darkness of the past never returns…It is in your hands to create a better world for all who live in it.[16]
- I learned that courage was not the absence of fear, but the triumph over it. The brave man is not he who does not feel afraid, but he who conquers that fear.[17]
- For to be free is not merely to cast off one's chains, but to live in a way that respects and enhances the freedom of others.[17]

The words spoken by the Second World War veteran, the late Professor Howard Zin in 1970, are more relevant today than ever:

Protest beyond the law is not a departure from democracy; it is abso-lutely essential to it…. Our problem is civil obedience. Our problem is the numbers of people all over the world who have obeyed the dictates of the leaders of their government … and millions have been killed because of this obedience…. Our problem is that people are obedient all over the world, in the face of poverty and starvation and stupidity, and war and cruelty. Our problem is that people are obedient while the jails are full of petty thieves, and all the while the grand thieves are running the country. That's our problem. We recognize this for Nazi Germany. We know that the problem there was obedience, that the people obeyed Hitler. People obeyed—that was wrong. They should have challenged, and they should have resisted; if we were only there, we would have showed them.[18]

In 2022 we are faced with the dilemma of "grand thieves," running not only the country but indeed also world affairs. In a certain sense corrupt totalitarian governments are not the problem! People obeying tyrants is the only problem! The people have the power and always will have the power. They just need to be made aware of this fact, realize it, and act upon it!

The Natural Right and Constitutional Right to Revolution

Political theorists, from Aristotle to Sheldon Wolin and Bertram Gross, have warned against the rule of the ultra-wealthy elite and their political minions. Once the corrupt plutocrats take over, Aristotle writes, the only options are tyranny and "revolution". The Merriam Webster dictionary defines revolution several different ways:

a. "a sudden, radical, or complete change;"
b. "a fundamental change in political organization (the overthrow or renunciation of one government or ruler and the substitution of another by the governed);"
c. "activity or movement designed to effect fundamental changes in the socioeconomic situation;"
d. "a fundamental change in the way of thinking about or visualizing something: a change of paradigm."

A pertinent question is whether the citizens have a right to revolution (to fundamental change) within a constitutional democracy.[19] Revolution is certainly a state of fact that "cannot be regulated in its course by those it tends to subvert and destroy" and in a sense by definition anti-juridical even when it is just.[20] Although it may seem paradoxical at first sight, revolution (movement designed to effect fundamental change) that seeks to reinstate the rule of law is justified in terms of the natural law and in conformity with both the written and the unwritten positive law.[19]

It is commonly argued that the moral right to revolution cannot be a constitutional right since the notions of constitution and revolution are, at their roots, *contradictio in terminis*. An established juridical order or constitution, inevitably, strives to entrench that order firmly to prevent change, while a revolution, axiomatically, seeks to alter the fundamental politico-legal order. Put differently, the objectives of a constitution and a revolution are profoundly irreconcilable: a constitution seeks to maintain a specific order, a revolution to undo that order.[20] According to this point of view, constitution and revolution are intrinsically in tension, and a constitutional right to revolution is a contradiction.[19] Professor of Law at the Indiana University School of Law, David C. Williams, in his article "The Constitutional Right to 'Conservative' Revolution" calls this view "the inconsistency claim":

> …the inconsistency claim is overbroad, because it fails to distinguish between two critically different types of revolution. With regard to the goals of revolution, while all revolutions aim to overthrow government, the inconsistency claim is wrong in maintaining that all revolutions aim to destroy the existing constitutional order. On the contrary, some revolutions are made to preserve the traditional order against the efforts of innovative government officials to change it; indeed, the American revolutionaries began their war as professed defenders of the British Constitution. Armed revolt against such a government is therefore not an attack on the constitution but an attempt to protect it.[19]

The principal error made by those who support "the inconsistency claim" is to assume that the State and constitution are the same thing, so that action against one is necessarily an action against the other.[19,20] In fact, the two are quite different from one another.[19,20] In certain instances, the government may be actively violating the constitution and the rule of law.[19,20] Therefore, the law recognizes the right to revolution as a right to protect the preexisting constitutional order against State officials who would subvert it.[20] When a State has set itself against the constitution by violating it, such a revolutionary movement is more law-abiding than the corrupt government itself. Therefore, according to Professor Williams, there is nothing conceptually incoherent in the idea of a constitutional right to revolution.[19,20]

In terms of both the natural law and constitutional law, citizens have the right to revolution when the office holders are corrupt and sabotaging the existing legal order or waging war against the citizenry.[19,20] Whether citizens have a natural right to revolution is separate from having a constitutional right to revolution.[19,20] Citizens may have a moral right to oust a tyrannical regime and institute a new one, but the constitution may in no way create, limit, regulate, or safeguard such a right.[19] Natural law is those rights that belong to all individuals at all times and places by virtue of being human, while constitutional law comprises written legal norms that are deemed to be fundamentally superior and of higher rank than all other legal norms within a particular society.[19] Therefore, natural rights differ from constitutional rights in three crucial ways:

i. The contents of natural rights and constitutional rights may overlap, or they may differ. Constitutional rights may (ought to) include some or all natural rights but may not. Additionally, a constitution may codify the scope of natural rights and define the content of an equivocal natural right with greater exactness. Lastly, a constitution may include constitutional rights in addition to natural rights.[19]

ii. The sources of natural rights and constitutional rights are different despite both ultimately deriving from natural rights. Natural law is that law (*lege*) applicable to human beings by virtue of their moral status as human beings; and is therefore operative in all locations, situations, and circumstances. Constitutional law, by distinction, is the constitution of a specific legal community; it is binding on its citizens by virtue of its inclusion in an ongoing, historically situated, civil society. A constitution, even when it does incorporate natural law, adds an additional element of responsibility and obligation by making it part of the positive law for a particular society rather than just a universal law.[19]

iii. The sources for verifying and construing natural rights may differ from those for constitutional rights. To discern the scope and content of natural rights, natural law is analyzed. By contrast, to determine the scope and content of constitutional rights, the text of the constitution itself, related documents, and relevant judicial rulings are analyzed. For the UN Member States that signed and ratified the ICCPR in particular, one might consult the text of the particular State constitution, and its amendments, Supreme Court cases, the documentary history of the parliaments, and the various international treaties the State signed and ratified.[19]

Professor Williams asserts that these differences have the following impli-
cation in relation to citizens having both a constitutional and natural right
to revolution when those in power subvert the natural law and constitutional order:

i. The type of right affects its enforceability. A natural right to revolution
    is the inherent right of all citizens at all times and in all countries
    when the State has been corrupted and is actively violating the social
    contract. By distinction citizens regard a constitutional right as a
    matter settled and legally binding among themselves, by themselves,
    and for themselves at a given time and within a specific country. Such
    a right is legitimized by the very act of protecting the norms and values
    espoused in their constitution as a single legal community.[19]

ii. Given the different sources used in the analysis of a natural right
    and constitutional right to revolution respectively, the nature of the
    inquiries would be distinct. Inquiry into a natural right to revolution
    would involve the examination of natural rights and the social contract,
    rationality, fundamental human rights, and freedom. Inevitably, such
    a direct inquiry into natural rights is more abstract and unstructured.
    By distinction, the determination of a constitutional right to revolution
    would be documentary in nature, designed to determine the meaning
    of a preexisting feature of our constitutional order. Importantly, irre-
    spective of whether any State constitution specifically provides for a
    "right to revolution", all citizens have both a constitutional and natural
    right to revolution due to the fact that "natural law transcends and
    controls all such culturally and historically specific acts as the consti-
    tution. If the materials of constitutional law fail to safeguard a natural
    right, then the constitution is simply inadequate."[19]

iii. Third, the relationship between citizens during a natural revolution
     and constitutional revolution differs. Natural law revolutionaries must
     petition to others as human beings who have rights merely by virtue
     of being human. Their course is potentially global. In theory, every
     human being in the world would have the same right or duty to take
     part in every battle of liberty. A natural law revolution would be reg-
     ulated not by shared, historical legal tradition, but by direct appeal to
     natural law. By contrast, constitutional revolutionaries must appeal to
     other citizens within their own country, citizens sharing a particular
     historical legal tradition and owing one another particular, historically
     contingent obligations.[19]

Both the natural law and constitutional law appropriately interpreted reject the antonymous view that revolution and constitution are inherently, conceptually incompatible. All citizens always hope and trust that their government will be faithful to its constitutional and IHRL mandate, but if it is not, it is up to the people as the ultimate guardians of the "rule of law" to force a restoration.

There are, however, crucial intrinsic limits for a revolution to be legitimate. First, the goal of any such revolution must always and only be to preserve the constitutional order and the rule of law.[19] Second, the form and method of a legitimate revolution should be governed by peremptory norms. Revolution is a civil activity, and there are various ways to order such activity: revolutionary movements can be democratic, peaceful, non-violent, respectful of human rights, and decentralized. For a revolution to be lawful, the revolution must conform to the *jus cogens* norms.[19] Thus, the citizens do not create a lawful revolution in the aggressive, unrestrained exercise of self-rule; rather, they act within the dictates of a constitutional democracy nationally and IHRL internationally, that adhere to the natural law, and respect fundamental human rights and freedoms.[19]

Making Your Voice Heard

For many across the West, the IHRL guarantees relating to inalienable fundamental human rights are worthless paper guarantees given the widespread violation of these rights during the COVID-19 pandemic. This, however, does not mean that the ideal to turn this right into a practical reality should not be pursued vigorously, or that society should have a lax attitude towards the authoritarians who undermine these fundamental human rights.

In order to bring an end to lawlessness it is also crucial for ordinary citizens to be willing to engage with the corrupt bureaucracy and call out governments and their multinational corporate allies for the human rights violations that occurred during the COVID-19 pandemic. Standing up for what is right starts by speaking out against injustice and the violation of fundamental rights such as the right to be free from medical experimentation without free and informed consent. A means to place lawless bureaucrats on notice that people across the world understand what their inalienable human rights are and that they will not tolerate their further violation is to submit vast numbers of individual complaints to national and international human rights organizations. International complaints should be submitted to the UN Human Rights Council and the UN Human Rights Committee.

The UN Human Rights Committee considers **individual complaints** relating to a violation of an individual's rights under the ICCPR.[21] A complaint can be brought against a State Party that satisfies two conditions:

- The State must be a Party (through ratification or accession) to the ICCPR providing for the rights which have been violated.[22]
- The State Party must have recognized the competence of the Human Rights Committee to receive and consider complaints from individuals.[22]

As of September 2022, 116 States are party to the Optional Protocol to the International Covenant on Civil and Political Rights. Western States subject to the Optional Protocol either through ratification or accession include Australia, Belgium, Canada, Finland, France, Germany, Iceland, Italy, Ireland, Greece, Netherlands, New Zealand, and others.[22]

To submit an individual complaint, the complaint form in Annexure i may be used, and should include:

- Information on the complainant.
- The State Party against which the complaint is directed.
- The fundamental human rights set out in the ICCPR that have been violated (See Chapters 3,5,6, and 7 of this book).
- Steps taken to exhaust national remedies or evidence that domestic remedies have not been exhausted on grounds that their application would be ineffective or unreasonably prolonged.
- A list of facts on which the complaint is based.
- A checklist of supporting documents.

Any individual can also submit a complaint in terms of the complaint procedure of the United Nations Human Rights Council. The overall source for this complaint procedure of the Human Rights Council is the UDBHR and "consistent patterns of gross and reliably attested violations of all human rights and fundamental freedoms occurring in any part of the world and under any circumstances."[23]

This complaint procedure is a universal complaint procedure encompassing all human rights and all fundamental freedoms in all Member States of the United Nations. According to the UNHRC, "A complaint can be submitted against any country irrespective of whether the country has ratified any particular treaty or made reservations under a particular instrument."[23]

The complaint form set out in Annexure ii can be utilized to submit a complaint and must include:

- Information on the complainant.
- Details of a consistent pattern of gross violations of fundamental human rights and freedoms.
- A description of the facts, covering: the identification of the victims and perpetrators of the violation, accompanied by a detailed description of the events when the violation took place.
- Evidence, such as written declarations by the victims, their families, or witnesses of the IHRL violation, or medical reports detailing the consequences of the violation.
- The UDHR rights that have been violated (See Chapters 3,5,6 and 7 of this book).
- Steps taken to exhaust national remedies or evidence that domestic remedies have not been exhausted on grounds that their application would be ineffective or unreasonably prolonged.

Joost Meerloo, who escaped from prison in Nazi-occupied Holland during the Second World War pointed out that "Freedom can never be completely safeguarded by rules and laws. It is as much dependent on the courage, integrity, and responsibility of each of us as it is on these qualities in those who govern. Every trait in us and our leaders which points to passive submission to mere power betrays democratic freedom."[24]

Addressing the COVID-19 Human Rights Abuses and Restoring Law and Order

Over the past two years, millions of people across the West lost their jobs, were injured, and died as a direct or indirect result of illicit public policies that were implemented. Once the miscreant COVID-19 era bureaucrats have been ousted from their positions of power through lawful civil and political action, it is imperative to deal judiciously with the widespread human rights violations that occurred during the COVID-19 era.

The exhortation by Emily Oster in her October 21, 2022 article in "The Atlantic" to "Declare a Pandemic Amnesty" and forgive and forget what happened over the past two and a half years is not an appropriate nor reasonable course of action.[38] Oster's contention that any "misstep wasn't nefarious. It was the result of uncertainty", is simply not true.[38] A group of corrupt supercilious political and corporate global elite willfully and lawlessly contravened IHRL and trampled on the dignity and human rights of millions of people in the pursuit of power and profit. In the interest of truth, justice, reparation, and non-recurrence these international criminals and their accomplices, that are the enemies of humanity, need to be investigated, prosecuted, and held to account in terms of the rule of law.

Although there is no standard model for dealing with the past (DWTP), the 2004 report of the UN Secretary-General on "The Rule of Law and Transitional Justice in Conflict and Post-Conflict Societies" provides some guidance.[25] The report determines that effective transitional justice strategies must be both inclusive in scope and all-encompassing in nature, involving all pertinent State actors and non-State actors in developing a "single nationally owned and led strategic plan."[26] The report further emphasizes that the practical definition of transitional justice should be expanded to include "judicial and non-judicial mechanisms, with differing levels of international involvement (or none at all) and individual prosecutions, reparations, truth-seeking, institutional reform, vetting and dismissals, or a combination thereof."[25]

On December 16, 2005, the UN General Assembly adopted Resolution 60/147 entitled the "Basic Principles and Guidelines on the Right to a Remedy and Reparation for Victims of Gross Violations of International Human Rights Law and Serious Violations of International Humanitarian Law."[27] Significantly, this document outlines the State's obligations concerning gross violations of international human rights and humanitarian law. Principle 8 defines the term victim as:

> …persons who individually or collectively suffered harm, including physical or mental injury, emotional suffering, economic loss or substantial impairment of their fundamental rights [and] also includes the immediate family or dependents of the direct victim and persons who have suffered harm in intervening to assist victims in distress or to prevent victimization.

The "Basic Principles and Guidelines" expand the rights offered to victims by combining entitlements allowed under both IHRL and international humanitarian law (IHL).[25,26,27] In the 2006 case of DRC v Rwanda, the International Court of Justice (ICJ) affirmed the complimentary application of IHRL and IHL.[29,30]

In 2006, 2007, and 2009 the UN Human Rights Council also addressed the issue of the "right to truth" in a series of studies, reports, and resolutions aimed at strengthening "the right to truth" as a principle of international law and a standalone fundamental right of the individual that should not be subject to limitations.[31-33]

In his 2010 article entitled "A Conceptual Framework for Dealing with the Past", Jonathan Sissol proposes that the "Joinet/Orentlicher principles against impunity", formulated by Louis Joinet (1997) and further refined by Diane Orentlichter (2005) at the behest of the Commission on Human Rights, and the right to truth principles, could be utilized as a framework for dealing with the past.[25,34,35] Importantly, these principles are based on the IHRL concept of primary State responsibility to protect and respect fundamental human rights and the inherent right of remedy for individual victims of serious human rights infringements. As such, the principles do not involve new international or national judicial obligations but identify procedures and processes for the implementation of existing judicial obligations under IHRL.[25]

The "Joinet/Orentlicher" principles provide a helpful framework, from both a juridical and normative point of view, to deal with the insidious human rights violations that occurred during the COVID-19 pandemic. The principles identify four critical rights for juridically dealing with the past: i.) the right to know, ii.) the right to justice, iii.) the right to reparation, and iv.) the guarantee of non-recurrence.[25]

i. The Right to Know – The right of victims, their families and of the public at large to know the truth and the duty of the State to conserve remembrance.[25]

The Right to Know includes the right on the part of specific victims of human rights violations and their families to learn the truth about what happened to them or their loved ones, in particular with respect to severe injuries and death due to mandatory COVID-19 vaccination policies.[25] It is based on the right on the part of the public at large to know the truth about the circumstances, decisions, and actions that led to the commission of widespread and systematic human rights violations in order to avoid their recurrence. In addition, the right to know obligates the State to undertake measures to conserve the collective memory from extinction, such as securing archives and other evidence, to shield against the advancement of similar inhumane public policies in the future. To ensure this right, quasi-judicial com-missions of inquiry (in practice, often called "truth" commissions) should be established. Given the prevalent human rights abuses relating to COVID-19, both national and international "COVID-19

Truth Commissions" should be established. The commissions would serve a twofold purpose: 1) to disassemble the State and non-State machinery and institutions that facilitated and orchestrated the human rights violations to ensure that they do not recur; and 2) to gather, archive, and preserve evidence of serious human rights infringements for the judiciary to utilize in subsequent civil and criminal prosecutions.[25]

ii. The Right to Justice – The right of victims to a fair legal remedy and the duty of the State to investigate, indict, and duly punish the criminals.[25]

The Right to Justice means that any victim can claim their fundamental human rights and get a reasonable and effective remedy, including the expectation that those responsible will be held legally liable in line with the doctrine of *versari in re illicita* and that damages will be paid.[25] The right to justice also involves legal obligations on the part of the State to investigate human rights violations, arrest and prosecute the offenders and, if their guilt is proven, punish them. The politicians, public officials, corporations, and public figures who contravened *jus cogens* norms and defrauded the public with false claims of safety and efficacy should be prosecuted to the full extent of the law. The super-profits made directly and indirectly by various corporations that propagated false narratives and contravened bedrock human rights norms should be forfeited and recuperated through heavy penalties and utilized to compensate victims and restore law and order. National courts have primary responsibility, but international criminal tribunals may exercise concurrent jurisdiction if needed. The right to justice further imposes restrictions on amnesty, asylum, extradition, *non bis in idem*, due obedience, official immunity, prescription, and other measures, insofar as they may be exploited to obstruct justice and shield the perpetrators from prosecution.[25]

iii. The Right to Reparation – The right of specific victims or their children and relatives to reparation and the duty of the State to provide satisfaction.[25]

The Right to Reparation necessitates remedial measures for individual victims or their dependents or relatives. This includes the duty to restore the victim to their previous situation,[25] - for instance, reappointing citizens who lost their jobs due to the vaccine mandates and compensating those families whose breadwinners died or were disabled. It further entails monetary compensation for mental or physical injury, medical care, including physiotherapy and psychological treatment, moral damage due to defamation, lost career opportunities, education, social benefits, legal expenses, and other expert assistance to enforce fundamental human rights. The duty to provide satisfaction relates to communal measures of reparation. These entail symbolic actions, such as an annual tribute to the COVID-19 victims of mass mandatory vaccination policies and building remembrance memorials and museums. It further consists of the acknowledgment by the State of its accountability in the form of a public apology (to help to restore victims' dignity) and the inclusion of a truthful account of the biomedical human rights violations that occurred during the COVID-19 era in all public educational materials at all levels.

iv. The Guarantee of Non-Recurrence – The right of victims and the public at large to be safeguarded from further abuses and the duty of the State to ensure the rule of law.[25]

The Guarantee of Non-Recurrence centers on the need to remove senior government officials from office who are implicated in serious human rights violations, to fundamentally reform or disband the various corrupt government and non-government institutions that facilitated the human rights violations, and to repeal state of emergency laws and regulations. It further requires reforming laws and State institutions in accordance with the norms of IHRL and the rule of law. In particular, the reform of global and national public health agencies, judicial bodies responsible for the protection of fundamental human rights, and the eradication of conflicts of interest should be a priority. The screening of senior public officials must comply with the requirements of the rule of law and the principles of meritocracy, non-discrimination, and complete transparency. All public officials with conflicts of interest and those who breached IHRL and their fiduciary duties to the public during the COVID-19 pandemic should be removed from their positions and prosecuted. The funding structures of global and national public health organizations, major academic institutions, and high-impact academic journals should be reformed to eliminate undue political and corporate influence. Of particular importance is the enactment of more robust competition and anti-monopoly regulations and the dismantling of the global pharma, global technology, global social media, global mainstream media, and global financial monopolies that played a key role in the human rights defilements during the pandemic. The judiciary's independence should be strengthened and reintroduced to hold politicians, public officials, powerful corporations, and their elite owners accountable.[25]

Figure 13.1, adapted from a design by Swiss Peace, a division of Human Security of the Swiss Federal Department of Foreign Affairs, illustrates some of the main mechanisms and procedures associated with the four principles above.[25]

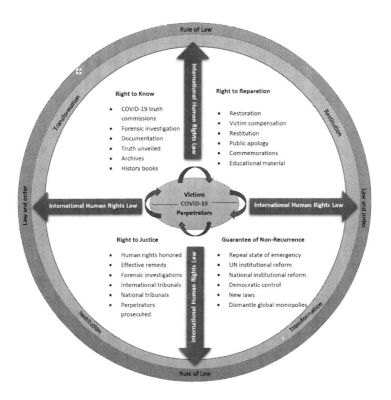

Figure 13.1 Conceptual framework for dealing with COVID-19 IHRL violations
Source: Dr. Willem van Aardt, Adapted from Swiss Peace
diagram dealing with impunity.[25]

Dealing with a culture of human rights abuses is one of the most complex tasks facing citizens in transitioning from inherently fascist forms of government to true democratic forms of administration that protect and respect fundamental human rights.[25] The "principles of international law recognized in the Charter of the Nuremberg Tribunal and in the judgment of the Tribunal" adopted by the International Law Commission in 1950 specifically determine:

i.   Crimes against international law are committed by men, not abstract entities, and only by punishing individuals who commit such crimes can the provisions of international law be enforced.
ii. Criminal liability exists under international law even if domestic law does not punish an act that is an international crime.
iii. The principle of international law, which under certain circumstances, protects the representatives of a state, cannot be applied to acts that are condemned as criminal by international law. The authors of these acts cannot shelter themselves behind their official position in order to be freed from punishment in appropriate proceedings.
iv. The fact that a person acted pursuant to order of his Government or of a superior does not relieve him from responsibility under international law, provided a moral choice was in fact possible to him.[36,37]

To restore confidence and accountability in the world, it is necessary to admit publicly the gross abuses that have taken place during the COVID-19 pandemic and to hold those responsible and liable who have committed, planned, ordered, executed, and profited from such abuses, and to compensate victims. This process of dealing with the past is an essential prerequisite for re-establishing the rule of law.[25]

POSTSCRIPT

"There are two potential violators of man's rights: the criminals and the government. The great achievement of the United States was to draw a distinction between these two — by forbidding to the second the legalized version of the activities of the first."

— Ayn Rand

The question of course is: What kind of policies, strategies and structural changes are necessary to ensure the primacy of human rights and to counter the current global state of lawlessness?

The globalization of the world economy, increased market concentration, monopoly capital, corporate deregulation, global elite tax avoidance, and PPPs have facilitated the disproportionate global power of a small group of elites and the transnational corporations (TNCs) they control at the expense of the Nation State, the rule of law and the protection of fundamental human rights.

One of the key enablers of the pervasive human rights abuses that were committed during the COVID-19 era was the monopolistic control of the global media, technology, pharmaceutical, medical, and financial industries and their corrupt influence on national and global public institutions. Through societies, foundations, NGOs, and think tanks such as the WEF, monopoly capital dominates the UN's specialized agencies, obdurate effective human rights protection, and coerces governmental processes with undisclosed interest, resulting in transformation of good cause initiatives like the UN, away from its foundational principles to private financial gain. Having mastered the art of manipulation through subversion and deceit, eroding the governments the people entrusted to protect their fundamental human rights, with gross violations of natural law, the social contract, and IHRL; they impose their anti-juridical world view and exploitative *modus operandi* upon the citizens of the world.

In a 2020 peer-reviewed study published in the journal of "Sustainable

Development Goals and Human Rights," Jens Martens highlighted that trillion-dollar institutional investors are drivers of a new generation of PPPs in public health and infrastructure, forcing States to fulfill the needs of these investors rather than fulfilling their primary duty to respect and ensure the fundamental human rights of their citizenry.[1] An analysis of the relationships between 43,000 TNCs by the Swiss Federal Institute of Technology back in 2011 revealed that "transnational corporations form a giant bow-tie structure and a large portion of control flows to a small tightly-knit core of financial institutions." At the center of the bow tie, a core group of 147 corporations controls 40% of the network's wealth, while just 737 companies control 80%.[2] Over the past decade monopolistic control increased exponentially with control and ownership of the largest global corporations now vesting in a small number of index funds.[3] According to various statistics of the largest national economies, there are more private corporations than countries among the 50 largest global economic entities. The assets under management by the world's three largest asset management companies, BlackRock, Vanguard, and State Street, amounted to US$ 21 trillion at the end of 2021. This is more than the GDPs of Australia, France, Germany, the Netherlands, Italy, the United Kingdom, and New Zealand.[3-5]

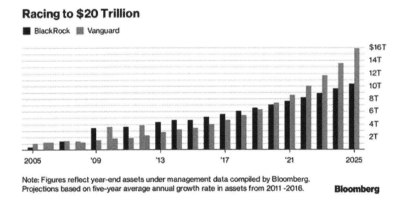

Figure 14.1: Blackrock and Vanguard projected assets under management
Source: Bloomberg

Current underlying global social and economic structures, power relations, and governance arrangements significantly impede the protection of human rights[6]. In the context of the United Nations Agenda 2030, the difference between those who value the rule of law and those who advocate for increased corporate influence, monopolistic control, and PPPs as the ultimate solution is not just semantic but reflects two fundamentally different cognitive orientations or world views of the role of the State. Those who value the rule of law view the State as the primary duty-bearer to ensure fundamental human rights and act as the central provider of public goods and services. The States fiduciary duty is to its citizens who democratically elected it.[6] On the other hand, the proponents of the PPP model view the State and its ability to regulate society as a tool to be misused to increase profitability. The TNC's fiduciary duty is towards its global elite shareholders with only one aim: maximization of profits. A further significant difference between the two world views and value systems is that the former views human beings as unique and invaluable with inalienable natural rights and immense potential to do good, while the latter views human beings as a disposable natural resource to be exploited for profits.

The WEF's vision for the world lies in a "public-private" United Nations, in which certain specialized agencies of the United Nations would function under joint State and non-State governance systems and where certain "issues would be taken off the agenda of the United Nations" to be addressed by "plurilateral, often multi-stakeholder, coalitions of the willing and able."[1,5] In other words, "issues" such as global and food security, global health, and global security should be entrusted to a small group of unelected officials and monopoly-capital-funded groups with the ultimate purpose of increasing profits at the expense of the global population.

A textbook case of how such a "multi-stakeholder coalition of the willing and able" would operate in practice is the response to the COVID-19 pandemic. A POLITICO special report published in September 2022 revealed that four non-governmental organizations (NGOs) "chartered the step by step journey through which much of the international response to the COVID-19 pandemic passed from governments to a privately overseen global constituency of non-governmental" with dire ramifications for the protection of fundamental human rights and freedoms.[6,7] The report also described the considerable monetary and political networks that empowered them to attain such influence at the highest levels of the WHO, the European Commission and the United States government.[7]

The four NGOs were the Bill & Melinda Gates Foundation, GAVI (the global vaccine alliance that Gates helped to establish), the Wellcome Trust (that had worked with the Gates Foundation in previous years), and the Coalition for Epidemic Preparedness Innovations, or CEPI, that Gates and Wellcome both helped to set up in 2017.[7]

According to the probe, based on more than 48 interviews with US and European bureaucrats and global health authorities, NGOs' "extensive politicking and financial might in the US and Europe helped to enable them to direct the international response to the most important health event of the past century."[7]

> Armed with expertise, bolstered by contacts at the highest levels of Western nations and empowered by well-grooved relationships with drug makers, the four organizations took on roles often played by governments — but without the accountability of governments.

> [T]he groups identified potential vaccine makers and targeted investments in the development of tests, treatments and shots. And they used their clout with the World Health Organization to help create an ambitious worldwide distribution plan.[7]

The WHO was critical to the power grab by these unelected NGOs. All had established connections to the specialized agency. The board of directors of both GAVI and CEPI have a specifically assigned WHO delegate. There is also a revolving door between employment in the organizations. Former WHO personnel currently work at CEPI and the Gates Foundation.[6] The investigation further found that much of the four NGOs' undue influence over the WHO emanates from monetary contributions. Since the onset of the COVID-19 pandemic, the Gates Foundation, GAVI, and the Wellcome Trust have jointly donated more than $1.4 billion to the WHO – a substantially larger sum of money than most official Member States, including the United States and the European Commission.[7]

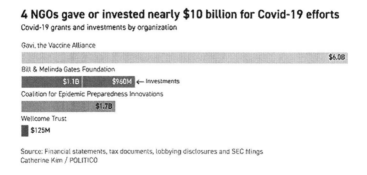

4 NGOs gave or invested nearly $10 billion for Covid-19 efforts
Covid-19 grants and investments by organization

Gavi, the Vaccine Alliance
$6.0B

Bill & Melinda Gates Foundation
$1.1B $960M ← Investments

Coalition for Epidemic Preparedness Innovations
$1.7B

Wellcome Trust
$125M

Source: Financial statements, tax documents, lobbying disclosures and SEC filings
Catherine Kim / POLITICO

Figure 14.2: The Four NGO's that gave or invested $ 10 billion for COVID-19 efforts
Source: Politico

When civil society organizations working in poorer States, such as Doctors Without Borders voiced uneasiness with the notion that Western-dominated elite groups, would be making life-and-death decisions impacting citizens in poorer nations and insisted on reduced cost for poorer nations, Bill Gates and the Gates Foundation protected the interests of big pharma and opposed efforts for a total waiver of intellectual property rights.[7-9] Working directly with the WHO, and public health agencies in major Western democracies, the four groups played a key role in dictating, controlling, and profiting from the global response to COVID-19 while also continuously protecting the interest of monopoly capital at the expense of the poor and vulnerable.[7-11]

Lawrence Gostin, a Georgetown University professor who specializes in public-health law, stated correctly that "we should be deeply concerned... putting it in a very crass way, money buys influence, and this is the worst kind of influence." Such power is "anti-democratic, because it's extraordinarily non-transparent, and opaque" and "leaves behind ordinary people, communities and civil society."[7]

Instead of further accepting the disingenuous and inherently anti-juridical and anti-democratic solution of "multi-stakeholderism" and PPPs between partners with fundamentally different fiduciary duties and legal obligations, a radical change of direction is necessary to restore the rule of law globally. This includes, *inter alia,* the following steps:

i. Effective enforcement of existing IHRL, jus cogens norms and covenant obligations

States should honor their primary duty to protect and ensure the fundamental human rights of all those within their jurisdiction. Governments should take their international legal obligations seriously and comply with the legally binding ICCPR that specifically regulates the protection of fundamental human rights during a public health emergency.

It is not that there was no international law relating to the bioethical norms that were breached during the pandemic. Instead, the global and political elite transgressed the unambiguous and clear rules and regulations with disdain and impunity. The aftermath of the catastrophic COVID-19 human rights abuses offers a historic opportunity for Western governments to demonstrate that they put fundamental human rights over the interests of big business by prosecuting and holding to account all those public officials and corporations who violated the ICCPR and the *jus cogens* norms in IHRL.

ii. Dismantling disproportionate global corporate power and global elite monopolies

Existing anti-trust and competition laws have evidently been too weak to prevent mega-mergers and to curtail the growth of financial, technological, pharmaceutical, and media monopolies with disproportionate undue influence on global affairs, public sentiment, and policy.[1] Some of the leading architects of the ubiquitous human rights abuses during the COVID-19 era were the monopolistic control of:

- the pharmaceutical industry and its influence on global and national public health agencies,
- the mainstream media industry that deceived and misled the public through non-stop propaganda,
- social media and technology companies that impeded free speech and restricted the flow of truth and lifesaving information, and
- philanthropic foundations funded by the global elite to buy political influence, corrupt and distort science and engineer social change.

To reinforce the role of the State as the primary duty-bearer to ensure the fundamental human rights of its citizens, States must take efficient measures to dismantle corporate power and prevent the further existence of corporate "too big to fail" entities.[1] Public funds should be invested to establish national and international companies to increase competition and eradicate the major monopolies. National and international legislation should also be enacted to outlaw any conglomerate, fund, company or associates directly or indirectly holding more than a 10% national market share and no more than a 5% global market share. National, regional, and global anti-trust laws, anti-monopoly laws and legal frameworks, and competition regulators should be strengthened.[1] At the international level, this should include the development of a "UN Convention on Competition and the Prevention of Global Monopolies" with an inherent anti-humanity agenda. In curbing global and national monopolies, specific attention should be directed towards the limitation of conglomerates in industries that can destabilize the global economy, the global health system, the global food supply, the global security system, the global media system, and the global communication and information systems.

iii. Strengthening national public finance

To prevent the further weakening of the State, governments must be enabled to expand their fiscal policy. States should approach the matter from a revenue (tax policy) and expenditure (budget policy) perspective. Proactive tax policies to fulfill their primary human rights obligations should be implemented.[1] This includes forms of fair taxation that are sensitive to the welfare of low and middle-income citizens and the increased taxation of TNCs and the ultra-wealthy global elite, many of whom pay virtually no income tax at all.[6] It should also entail the taxation of the extraction and depletion of natural and non-renewable resources. Fiscal policy should be further strengthened by eliminating corporate tax incentives to TNCs, monopolies, and other dominant corporates and phasing out harmful subsidies. Prudent budgetary policies can become a powerful instrument to strengthen the Nation State. The strengthening of public finance is necessary at all levels of government. The improvement of the national fiscal systems should coincide with global tax cooperation to counter various schemes of tax avoidance and evasion by the global elite, including the use of so-called philanthropic foundations that actively fund national and international public institutions for their ultimate owners to profit directly or indirectly.

iv. Eradicating and criminalizing corruption at the United Nations and public health and human rights institutions

Member States should provide the United Nations and its specialized agencies with stable and predictable funding to enable them to fulfill their mandates. In particular, States should reverse the tendency toward voluntary contributions and the reliance on philanthropic and corporate funding that led to widespread corruption and subversion of the UN system.[1]

Member States and the United Nations should develop a regulatory framework for interactions between the United Nations and TNCs and the lobby groups and think tanks that represent their interests that should set minimum standards for the collaboration between TNCs and philanthropic foundations with the UN specialized agencies such as the WHO and the UNHRC. These standards should prevent undue corporate influence on UN policies and prevent companies that violate IHRL from participating in UN initiatives and eligibility for UN procurement. An essential element of such a legal framework should be the criminalization of corrupt practices, the prohibition of conflicts of interest with a direct or indirect monetary interest, and a mandatory public disclosure policy for all interactions with TNCs and other non-State actors.

v. Public policy that advances fundamental human rights instead of investors rights

Corporate lobby groups such as the WEF have been advocating vigorously against overregulation of TNCs and for the continuance of precisely those investment, trade, financial, and other regulations that have destabilized the global economy, worsened inequalities, facilitated public health corruption, and led to the most pervasive human rights abuses since the Second World War.[1,6] In addition to the lax regulation of TNCs and PPPs during the COVID-19 era, lawless practices led to the over-regulation of citizens through various illicit mandates to increase product take-up and the profitability of TNCs. The fascist trend to overregulate citizens while underregulating TNCs and their ultimate owners should be reversed.

Governments should reconsider and amend their approach toward trade, investment, and capital allocation to TNCs and monopolies in order to place human rights and the principles of sustainable national growth at the center of all trade and investment decisions. This should include implementing manufacturing policies to encourage the development of a solid domestic corporate sector. There must be a clear-cut distinction between those who should regulate and the party to be regulated. Any proposition that obscures the fact that TNCs have fundamentally different primary interests and fiduciary duties from Nation States, public health administrations, the United Nations, and its specialized agencies, should be rejected.

vi. Finding alternatives to PPPs

The WEF, international financial institutions (IFIs), corporate think tanks, TNCs and lobbyists (all with inherent conflict of interest) have been steadily promoting PPPs as the primary model for sustainable development. Unfortunately, many States have followed their advice with deleterious ramifications for the protection of fundamental human rights.[1-4] Some argue that the PPP model in essence amounts to legalized criminal conspiracy to exploit the citizenry and funnel the tax they paid to TNCs and other monopolies. In the aftermath of the

COVID-19 pandemic and the detrimental corporate influence and public health PPPs that led to pervasive human rights violations and the death, disability, injury, suffering, and poverty of millions of people globally, it is essential to subject the PPP model to IHRL norms and standards.[1]

States should rethink their approach toward private sector participation in public health and infrastructure investment and explore alternative means of public financing in compliance with human rights standards.[1] This may include service charges, user fees, and the issuance of public bonds to subsidize different public services.[1]

vii. Creating additional binding international legal obligations relating to biomedical technology, bioethics, and transnational corporations

Experience shows voluntary normative guidelines, such as the UNESCO UDBHR have failed to hold corporations, public health officials, and medical practitioners accountable. In light of the recent biomedical technological advances and the death, destruction, suffering, and destabilization that some of these advances hold for humanity if abused by modern-day biomedical collectivists, there is a need for a legally binding convention that expands existing ICCPR provisions and *jus cogens* norms to specifically regulate biotechnology, bioethics, and biomedical science. The various relevant bioethical norms and standards set out in the UDBHR, the OVIEDO Convention, the Nuremberg Code, and the ICCPR should be expanded using 2022 knowledge and combined in an updated legally binding "Bioethical and Biomedical Science Convention" to bring about additional human rights protection and severe criminal penalties for perpetrators. Given the severe adverse ramifications caused as a result of scientific fraud during the course of the COVID-19 pandemic, specific rules should also be enacted to criminalize the censorship of objective biomedical research and the collusion between big pharma and academic institutions and journals.

The measures listed above are not an exhaustive list but certainly crucial to thwarting the increasing, non-monitored, non-democratic undue influence of a small corporate elite on the execution of the global agenda that since 2020 has led to an egregious violation of the post-Second World War juridical order and IHRL. It is important to re-establish the rule of law and equal justice at national and international levels and to restore the integrity of the various national and global public institutions.

SUMMARY

The principal arguments in this book and their implications may be summarized as follows:

1. The irrational pseudo-medical emergency measures enacted to combat COVID-19 violate the social contract and infringe absolute natural rights in contravention of constitutional legal norms developed over the past 1,000 years.
2. In the aftermath of the Second World War, there have been numerous international human rights instruments setting out adequate legal peremptory norms, bioethical standards, and practices, many of which have tragically been totally disregarded during the COVID-19 pandemic.
3. The issue is not that there were no bioethical and legal rules to follow or that the rules were ambiguous but rather that numerous governments, public health agencies, conflicted multinational pharmaceutical companies, vaccine manufacturers, NGOs, and "philanthropic foundations" maliciously contravened clear bioethical rules, guidelines, and norms for political and financial gain.
4. International commitment to human rights protection is in the process of undergoing a paradigm shift towards lawlessness and non-adherence to IHRL that will have significant adverse ramifications for the international legal and political arena if allowed to proceed unchallenged.
5. The legal standards in IHRL obligate governments to respect, protect, and fulfill the human rights of all people in their territory. In terms of IHRL, certain fundamental rights can never be derogated from under any circumstances, even in times of a public health emergency. Because of their normative specificity and status, non-derogable rights are core human rights *jus cogens* and obligations *erga omnes*.
6. The limitation of fundamental human rights is legitimate only if it respects the essence and is also proportional. A respect-for-the-essence

test revealed that vaccine mandates and related quasi-medical regulations do not respect the essence of the fundamental human right to be free from medical experimentation without free consent. Additionally, the proportionality analysis indicates that mass mandatory vaccination regulations have breached IHRL to the detriment of hundreds of millions of people worldwide. COVID-19 vaccine mandates are not proportionate to the threat, not strictly necessary, not based upon an objective assessment of the actual situation, and not the least restrictive choice. Importantly, the harm done by the vaccine mandates significantly outweigh the benefits derived.

7. Article 4(1) and (2) of the ICCPR, which 173 governments worldwide have committed to adhere to, is of paramount importance for the system of safeguarding human rights. The subjectivity inherent in individual States determining what constitutes an emergency that poses a "threat to the life of the nation" has proven disastrous during the COVID-19 crisis, as State officials contravened Article 4 and abused emergency powers to the detriment of human rights protection around the globe. Utilizing an illicit state of emergency as nefarious government technique, rather than an exceptional temporary measure, *de facto* produces a juridical anomie, threatening the existence of the post-Second World War juridico-political order.

8. The principle of bodily integrity entails the right of each human being to autonomy and self-determination over their own body. It considers an unconsented physical intrusion as a human rights violation. These rights are "the entitlements individuals have in international law to be free from arbitrary physical harm and coercion by their government" and include freedoms from torture and medical or scientific experimentation that includes the right not to be coerced to be injected with an experimental vaccine. The human right to freedom from torture, cruel, inhumane treatment, and medical experimentation without free and informed consent can never be legitimately violated in terms of IHRL.

9. Vaccine mandates without any data or evidence on long-term safety, especially when the risks of either suffering acute illness or death from COVID-19 are close to zero for the vast majority of the population, would already be unlawful in terms of prevailing IHR norms. Vaccine mandates in the face of overwhelming data and evidence that the COVID-19 vaccines neither confer sterilized nor near-sterilized immunity nor prevent the spread of COVID-19 are patently absurd and devoid of any reason.

10. The four principles of biomedical ethics – autonomy, beneficence, non-maleficence, and justice – that are supposed to be the cornerstones of biomedical ethics in healthcare practice, were widely contravened during the COVID-19 pandemic. The public health response to the COVID-19 pandemic again highlights the need for State Parties to abide by universal ethical guidelines and normative standards in the field of bioethics and the need to promote shared values in relation to the formulation and implementation of public health policies.

11. The COVID-19 legal paternalism significantly infringed on the individual's right to medical self-determination in direct violation of the Nuremberg Code and *jus cogens* norms. Coerced consent is not consent. Promoting COVID-19 vaccines as effective and safe while knowing they do not confer sterilized immunity and have deadly side-effects is a textbook case of "fraud in the inducement" or *dolus dans locum in contractui* that occurs when a company tricks a counterparty into an agreement to their disadvantage by using fraudulent statements and representations.

12. Where governments interfere in individuals' autonomy, it is important that paternalistic policies should be subjected to rigorous scrutiny to determine their legitimacy, efficacy, necessity, and proportionality. If the limitation of rights does not serve the purpose of and contribute to a society based on human dignity, equality, and freedom, it cannot be justifiable.

13. Fundamental rights are constitutively inalienable; they exist necessarily, inhere in every person, and cannot be taken away from him or her. Therefore, they cannot be limited for a reason other than their overall protection. This does not imply that their exercise does not meet some limits, but such limits cannot find their justification outside the system of fundamental rights themselves. If a fundamental right could be restricted for reasons other than its overall protection – for instance, for a general social benefit –it would no longer be inviolable.

14. Orthodox science, according to the Western democratic States in the COVID-19 era, is science narrowly tailored and packaged to achieve a predestined ideological outcome. This epistemological view of science is the same world view held by tyrants such as Hitler, Stalin, Mussolini, and others. To find public health solutions, open, transparent, and robust scientific debate is needed. Credible biomedical science is all about questioning various hypotheses. Narrow "scientific views" tailored to official policy and not allowed to be subjected to vigorous

peer and public scrutiny are not credible science!

15. Governing through law and governing in accordance with the rule of law are two very different things. The formal component of law is satisfied when laws conform to certain formal and procedural requirements. Laws should *inter alia* be duly promulgated, general in application, prospective, clear, unambiguous, stable, transparent, and be presided over by an independent judiciary. The rule of law, however, is not satisfied by procedural and formal requirements only. While insisting on these requirements, an exercise of State power that pays "credible tribute" to the rule of law additionally demands that law be substantively just. Typically, this means that the law must align with the natural law, be rational, and inherently respect fundamental human rights and freedoms.

16. A line has been crossed in the global response to the COVID-19 pandemic. We have seen a shift towards a different and incorrect understanding of human rights and fundamental freedoms and a false understanding of the relationship between the individual and the State. Many so-called Western democracies have now crossed the line into an absurd lawless realm where the assumption is that human rights are something that is granted to the individual by the State as a prize for good behavior and total subservience to all government mandates irrespective of how irrational or arbitrary those mandates may be.

17. The State must always obey the natural law and cannot exercise power over anyone unless the law permits it. There must be a rational law that aligns with the natural law sanctioning everything the State does. The State cannot create or abolish inviolable human rights by law, mandate, or convention (as many governments across the globe professed during the COVID-19 pandemic); they can only confirm the existence of fundamental human rights and protect these rights. The role of the State is no more than declaratory. Fundamental human rights have always existed within humans and exist independently of the State or any of its mandates. Foreign and even stateless persons cannot, lawfully, be deprived of these sacrosanct rights. The existence or continuation of basic human rights does not depend on the extra-judicial will or whims of public officials.

18. A State's disregard for fundamental human rights is a conclusive marker of the absence of the rule of law in that State. This absence of legality is also a failure of justice as respect for fundamental human rights is paradigmatic of the requirements of justice. Conversely, honoring

fundamental human rights means that both law and justice effectively rule. Through a proliferation of irrational, unjust COVID-19 laws that lack the efficacy of law, the political elite and their ultra-wealthy corporate colluders enriched themselves at the expense of the middle class, the poor, and the most vulnerable.

19. Nazi "right-wing" authoritarian ultranationalist fascism and modern "left-wing" COVID-19 biomedical fascism are fundamentally indistinguishable political practices that are not antagonistic but two similar types of fascist totalitarianism – one nationwide, traditional totalitarianism and the other occurring in multiple countries at the same time – inverted totalitarianism. Both kinds of totalitarianism are extraordinarily effective in bypassing the constitutional limits of their power and undermining individual freedom, fundamental human rights, and the rule of law. These similarities cannot be dismissed as irrelevant given the incremental death and destruction that such, in principle, totalitarian policies would continue to cause if tolerated and sustained.

20. "Global biomedical fascism" can be defined as the oppression of personal liberty, choice, and behavior, particularly private medical and moral choices, for the financial and political gain of the global corporate and political elite. This modern form of fascism is established and sustained through government and corporate coercion and rationalized by an elitist ideology and rhetoric of the "greater good" and the supremacy of public health.

21. *Jus inter gentes* governments have an international legal obligation "to take reasonable steps to prevent human rights violations" by public and private actors. In terms of the doctrine of State responsibility for human rights abuses committed by non-State actors, governments are legally liable for the death, injury, and damages suffered as a result of the human rights abuses committed by non-State actors during the course of the COVID-19 pandemic.

22. All citizens always hope and trust that their government will be faithful to its constitutional and IHRL mandate, but if it is not, it is up to the people as the ultimate guardians of the "rule of law" to force a restoration.

23. The rule of law should have multiple protectors-the government in ordinary times, the citizenry in extraordinary ones. It is only the people's own determination that will see a return from a state of lawlessness to a state of law. When public powers violate the rights and

fundamental liberties guaranteed by IHRL, resistance to oppression is the right and duty of the citizen.

24. In terms of both the natural law and constitutional law, citizens have the right to revolution (to fundamental change) when the office holders are corrupt and sabotaging the existing legal order or waging war against the citizenry. When a State has set itself against the constitution by violating it, such social movement for change is more law-abiding than the corrupt government itself.

25. Crimes against international law are committed by people, not abstract entities, and only by punishing individuals who commit such crimes can the provisions of international law be enforced. Once the unprincipled COVID-19 era officeholders have been ousted from their positions of control through legitimate civil and political action, it is important to deal judiciously with the pervasive human rights abuses that occurred during the COVID-19 era.

26. Governments, public health officials, and other offenders who have committed, planned, ordered, executed, and profited from the egregious human rights violations during the course of 2020, 2021, and 2022 should be prosecuted and victims should be compensated in order to restore the rule of law and ensure that in the future, State Parties honor their international covenant obligations. International human rights and bioethical moral and legal obligations, properly construed, demand this approach.

27. Instead of further accepting the inherently deceptive, anti-juridical, and anti-democratic WEF solution of elitest control of major sustainable global development policy and initiatives, a radical change of direction is necessary to root out corruption, restore the credibility of global public institutions, and reinstate the rule of law globally.

ANNEXURE I. HUMAN RIGHTS COMMITTEE
COMPLAINTS FORM

For communications under:

- Optional Protocol to the International Covenant on Civil and Political Rights
  - Convention against Torture, or
- International Convention on the Elimination of Racial Discrimination

Please indicate which of the above procedures you are invoking: ....

Date: ....

i. Information on the complainant:

Name: ....   First name(s): ....
Nationality: ....   Date and place of birth: ....
Address for correspondence on this complaint: ....

Submitting the communication: ....
on his/her own behalf: ....
on behalf of another person: ....

If the complaint is being submitted on behalf of another person:

Please provide the following personal details of that other person

Name: ....   First name(s): ....
Nationality: ....   Date and place of birth: ....
Address or current whereabouts: ....

If you are acting with the knowledge and consent of that person, please provide that person's authorization for you to bring this complaint ....

Or

If you are not so authorized, please explain the nature of your relationship with that person: .... and detail why you consider it appropriate to bring this complaint on his or her behalf: ....

ii. State concerned/Articles violated

Name of the State against which the complaint is directed: ....
Articles of the Covenant or Convention alleged to have been violated: ....

iii. Exhaustion of domestic remedies/Application to other international procedures

Steps taken by or on behalf of the alleged victims to obtain redress within the State concerned for the alleged violation – detail which procedures have been pursued, including recourse to the courts and other public authorities, which claims you have made, at which times, and with which outcomes: ....

> If you have not exhausted these remedies on the basis that their application would be unduly prolonged, that they would not be effective, that they are not available to you, or for any other reason, please explain your reasons in detail: ....

Have you submitted the same matter for examination under another procedure of international investigation or settlement (e.g. the Inter-American Commission on Human Rights, the European Court of Human Rights, or the African Commission on Human and Peoples' Rights)? ....

> If so, detail which procedure(s) have been, or are being, pursued, which claims you have made, at which times, and with which outcomes: ....

iv. Facts of the complaint

Detail, in chronological order, the facts and circumstances of the alleged violations. Include all matters which may be relevant to the assessment and consideration of the particular case. Please explain how you consider that the facts and circumstances described violate your rights.

....

Author's signature: ....

[The blanks under the various sections of this model communication simply indicate where your responses are required. You should take as much space as you need to set out your responses.]

v. Checklist of supporting documentation (copies, not originals, to be enclosed with your complaint):

- Written authorization to act (if you are bringing the complaint on behalf of another person and are not otherwise justifying the absence of specific authorization): ....
- Decisions of domestic courts and authorities on your claim (a copy of the relevant national legislation is also helpful): ....
- Complaints to and decisions by any other procedure of international investigation or settlement: ....
- Any documentation or other corroborating evidence you possess that substantiates your description in Part IV of the facts of your claim and/or your argument that the facts described amount to a violation of your rights: ....
- Please include, if necessary, an indication in a UN language (Arabic, Chinese, English, Spanish, French and Russian) of the contents of the accompanying documentation. Your communication should not exceed 50 pages (excluding annexes). In case your application exceeds twenty pages, you must also file a short summary. All individual complaints should be submitted to the Petitions Team mailing address: ....

Petitions and Inquiries Section
Office of the High Commissioner for Human Rights
United Nations Office at Geneva
1211 Geneva 10, Switzerland
e-mail: petitions@ohchr.org, TB-petitions@ohchr.org, ccpr@ohchr.org, and registry@ohchr.org .

ANNEXURE II. HUMAN RIGHTS COUNCIL COMPLAINT PROCEDURE FORM

You are kindly requested to submit your complaint in writing in one of the six official UN languages (Arabic, Chinese, English, French, Russian and Spanish) and to use these languages in any future correspondence;

- Anonymous complaints are not admissible.
- It is recommended that your complaint does not exceed eight pages, excluding enclosures.
- You are kindly requested not to use abusive or insulting language.

I. Information concerning the author (s) of the communication or the alleged victim (s) if other than the author

Individual ▢   Group of individuals ▢   NGO ▢   Other ▢
Last name: ....
First name(s): ....
Nationality: ....
Address for correspondence on this complaint: ....
Tel and fax: (please indicate country and area code) ....
E-mail: ....
Website: ....

Submitting the complaint:

On the author's own behalf: ▢
On behalf of other persons: ▢   (Please specify: ....)

II. Information on the State concerned
Name of the State concerned and, as applicable, name of public authorities responsible for the alleged violation(s): ....

III. Facts of the complaint and nature of the alleged violation(s)

The complaint procedure addresses consistent patterns of gross and reliably attested violations of all human rights and all fundamental freedoms occurring in any part of the world and under any circumstances.

Please detail, in chronological order, the facts and circumstances of the alleged violations including dates, places and alleged perpetrators and how you consider that the facts and circumstances described violate your rights or that of the concerned person(s).

....

....

....

....

....

....

IV. Exhaustion of domestic remedies

Steps taken by or on behalf of the alleged victim(s) to exhaust domestic remedies–please provide details on the procedures which have been pursued, including recourse to the courts and other public authorities as well as national human rights institutions, the claims made, at which times, and what the outcome was:................

If domestic remedies have not been exhausted on grounds that their application would be ineffective or unreasonably prolonged, please explain the reasons in detail: ....

V. Submission of communication to other human rights bodies

Have you already submitted the same matter to a special procedure, a treaty body or other United Nations or similar regional complaint procedures in the field of human rights? ....

If so, detail which procedure has been, or is being pursued, which claims have been made, at which times, and the current status of the complaint before this body: ....

VI. Request for confidentiality

In case the communication complies with the admissibility criteria set forth in Council resolution 5/1, kindly note that it will be transmitted to the State concerned so as to obtain the views of the latter on the allegations of violations.

Please state whether you would like your identity or any specific information contained in the complaint to be kept confidential.

Request for confidentiality *(Please tick as appropriate)*:   Yes ☐   No ☐

Please indicate which information you would like to be kept confidential

Date: ....   Signature: ....

N.B. The blanks under the various sections of this form indicate where your responses are required. You should take as much space as you need to set out your responses. Your complaint should not exceed eights pages.

VII. Checklist of supporting documents

Please provide copies (not original) of supporting documents (kindly note that these documents will not be returned) in one of the six UN official languages.

- Decisions of domestic courts and authorities on the claim made (a copy of the relevant national legislation is also helpful): ☐
- Complaints sent to any other procedure mentioned in section V (and any decisions taken under that procedure): ☐
- Any other evidence or supporting documents deemed necessary: ☐

VIII. Where to send your communications?

Office of the United Nations High Commissioner for Human Rights
Human Rights Council Branch-Complaint Procedure Unit
OHCHR- Palais Wilson
United Nations Office at Geneva
CH-1211 Geneva 10, Switzerland
Fax: (+41 22) 917 90 11
E-mail: CP@ohchr.org
Website: http://www.ohchr.org/EN/HRBodies/HRC/Pages/HRCIndex.aspx

GLOSSARY

absolute rights
: inalienable fundamental human rights that belong to individuals in a state of nature.

actio iniuriarum
: an action aimed at the protection the personality interest (bodily integrity, dignity or reputation) of the plaintiff.

ad idem
: of one mind.

adverse event
: any untoward or unfavorable medical occurrence in a human study participant, including any abnormal physical exam or laboratory finding, symptom, or disease temporally associated with the participant's involvement in the research, whether or not considered related to participation in the research.

anomie
: a social condition defined by an uprooting or breakdown of any moral values, standards. Greek: nomia (*ἀνομία*, "lawlessness").

anti-juridical
: contempt for judicial proceedings and the application of the rule of law.

aristocracy
: form of government that places strength in the hands of a small, privileged, corrupt, ruling class, the aristocrats. The term derives from the Greek *aristokratíā*.

aristocrat
: "ruling" social class.

bio citizen
: bio citizenship; health citizenship; therapeutic citizenship – describes forms of belonging, rights claims, and demands for access to resources and care that are made on a biological basis such as an injury, shared genetic status, or disease state.

bioethics
: the ethics of medical and biological research.

biomedical
: relating to both biology and medicine.

biomedical fascism
: the oppression of personal liberty, choice, and behavior, particularly private medical and moral choices, for the financial and political gain of the corporate and political elite

biomedical collectivism	utilizing unjust laws to oppress personal medical choices and deny bodily autonomy based on society's collective judgment of what medical procedures should be mandated.
biotechnology	the integration of natural sciences and engineering sciences in order to achieve the application of organisms, cells, parts thereof, and molecular analogues for products and services.
bona fides	good faith.
boni mores	good morals.[3]
causa	underlying reason or cause.
civil obligation	a legal obligation enforceable by a right of action in a court of law.
collectivism	the practice of giving group priority over each individual within the group.
commission per omissionem	conduct in a form of an omission or failure to act.
constitution	a set of written or unwritten legal norms that are considered to be more fundamental than and superior to all other legal norms within a given polity.
contra bones mores	contrary to good morals.
COVID-19	coronavirus disease of 2019, the disease caused by the novel coronavirus SARS-CoV-2.
COVID-19 vaccine	an inoculation that prevents neither viral infection nor transmission of COVID-19. Its main function in practice appears to be symptom suppression, it is operationally a "treatment".
culpa in contrahendo	"fault in the conclusion of the contract". Legal doctrine imposing a duty of good faith on parties when negotiating a contract. The objective is to prevent a party from concluding a contract to his or her detriment. In other words, a person must not induce or provide misleading information to another in the pre-contractual phase leading the other party to enter into an agreement to his or her detriment.
culpa lata	gross negligence.
culpa	negligence or fault.
dictum et promisum (*pl dictim et promissa*)	materially false statement made by seller to buyer during negotiations.[2]

dirrito	the juridical order (broader than "the law") a thoroughly heterogeneous ensemble of the various institutions, regulatory decisions, mandates, administrative measures, scientific statements, philosophical, techniques, media, academia, moral and philanthropic propositions which enhance and maintain the exercise of power within the social body. (Michel Foucault)
dispositive fact	a fact that is decisive when answering a question of law. Sometimes used to refer to facts that resolve a legal dispute altogether (once they are proven with necessary certainty).
dolus dans locum in contractui	fraud (misrepresentation) that induces a contract in the sense that without the fraudulent inducement the contract would not have been concluded at all.
dolus	fraud or bad faith.
elite	small group of powerful people who hold a disproportionate amount of wealth, privilege, political power. (Latin: eligere, to select or to sort out). Decision-makers whose power is not subject to control by any other body in the society.
erga omnes	towards all. Specific commitments that States have towards the international community as a whole.
error facti	error of fact.
ex lege	as a matter of law.
ex post facto	after the event.
extra-juridical	something which is done, given, or effected outside the course of regular judicial proceedings.
fascism	a form of authoritarianism, characterized by collusion between the ultra-wealthy, the political elite, and dictatorial power, forcible suppression of opposition, and strong regimentation of society.
fictio iurus	a legal fiction, a presumption of law.
fraud in the inducement	occurs when a person tricks another person into signing an agreement to one's disadvantage by using fraudulent statements and representations. Because fraud negates the "meeting of the minds" required of a contract, the injured party can seek damages or terminate the contract.
global elite	relatively small, loosely connected group of corrupt, lawless individuals, corporations, and foundations who dominate North American, European, and global policymaking.

globalist	a globalist believes in the centralization of finance, money, social access production, and government. They deride the Nation State concept and argue that global centralization would create a "fairer" system for everyone, but in reality, they desire a system in which they have total control over every aspect of life. Globalists, more than anything, want to dominate and micro-manage every detail of civilization and socially engineer humanity in the image they prefer.
good faith	a standard of judging the behavior of parties to an agreement according to which they should behave honestly, openly, and fairly in their dealings with one another.
government	the governing body of a Nation State.
herd immunity	the general protection of a population from a disease due to enough individuals possessing antibodies (whether by previous infection and recovery or by immunization).
homo sacer	the accursed man. A figure of Roman law: a person who is banned and may be killed by anybody but may not be sacrificed in a religious ritual.
illiberal democracy	a governing system in which, although elections take place, citizens are cut off from knowledge about the activities of those who exercise real power because of the lack of basic human rights. The rulers of an illiberal democracy may ignore or bypass constitutional limits on their power. They also tend to ignore the will of the minority, which is what makes the democracy illiberal. Elections in an illiberal democracy are often manipulated or rigged, being used to legitimize and consolidate the incumbent rather than to choose the country's leaders and policies.
inter alia	among other things.
international human rights law	body of international law created to promote and protect human rights at the international, regional, and domestic levels. They are mainly obligations that States are bound to obey. It is primarily made up of treaties, agreements between States, and customary international law. Declarations, guidelines, and principles adopted at the international level contribute to the understanding, implementation, and development of international law. Enforcement of international human rights law can occur on domestic, regional,

or international level.

international law   a body of rules established by custom or treaty and recognized by nations as binding in their relations with one another.

inverted totalitarianism   a system in which democracy is corrupted and subverted by the ultra-wealthy and corporations and politics is trumped by economics.

jus cogens   "compelling law." It designates norms from which no derogation is permitted by way of particular agreements. Designates certain legal rules that cannot be contracted out, given the fundamental values they uphold. The 1969 and 1986 Vienna Conventions on the Law of Treaties stipulate that a treaty is void if it conflicts with *jus cogens* (Arts 53 and 64). The same is true for unilateral declarations, following the guiding principles adopted by the International Law Commission in 2006 (Principle 8). According to the Articles on Responsibility finalized by the same commission in 2001 and 2011, States as well as international organizations shall cooperate to bring to an end any serious breach of *jus cogens* and shall not recognize as lawful a situation created by such a breach, nor render aid or assistance in maintaining such situation (Arts 41/2001 and 42/2011). Moreover, if States or international organizations are to violate *jus cogens*, they cannot invoke any circumstance precluding the wrongfulness of their conduct, such as necessity or *force majeure* (Art. 26).

jus gentium   law of nations.

jus inter gentes   law between the peoples.

justitium   derived from the Latin term *juris statio* is a concept of Roman law, equivalent to the declaration of the state of emergency. Some scholars also refer to it as a state of exception, stemming from a state of necessity.

lawless   not regulated by or based on law, not restrained, or controlled by law: unruly, illegal.

lawlessness   a state of disorder due to a disregard of the rule of law.

legal liberalism   which holds that laws may only be used to the extent that they protect fundamental human rights.

legal moralism   the philosophy of law that holds that laws may be used to prohibit or require behavior based on society's collective

	judgment of whether it is moral.
legge	the law. (German: *Recht*, Gezets; French: *droit, loi.*).
mala fides	bad faith.
managed democracy	the application of corporate managerial skill to the basic democratic political institution of popular elections. A political form in which governments are legitimated by elections that they have learned to control. Under managed democracy, the electorate is prevented from having a significant impact on policies adopted by the State because of the opinion construction and manipulation carried out by means of technology, social science, contracts, and corporate subsidies. Managerial methods are also the means by which State and global corporations unite so that corporations increasingly assume governmental functions and services and corporations become still more dependent on the State. A main object of managed democracy is privatization and the expansion of the private, together with reduction of governmental responsibility for the welfare of the citizens (Sheldon Wolin).
non-derogable rights	human rights can be characterized as derogable or non-derogable. Article 4 of the International Covenant on Civil and Political Rights (ICCPR) provides for a derogation power, which allows governments to temporarily suspend the application of some rights in the exceptional circumstance of a "state of emergency" and subject to certain conditions. Certain rights, however, are non-derogable, that is, they cannot be suspended even in a state of emergency. Article 4(2) of the ICCPR provides that no derogation is permitted for *inter alia*: the right to life (Art. 6); freedom from torture or cruel, inhuman and degrading treatment or punishment; and freedom from medical or scientific experimentation without consent (Art. 7).
obligation *erga omnes*	those obligations for which all States have a legal interest in fulfilment by reason of the importance of their subject-matter to the international community. Peremptory norms that States have a duty to respect irrespective of any treaty, because the obligatory duty of compliance is understood as being owed to the international community as a whole. In view of the importance of the rights

involved, all States can be held to have a legal interest in their protection. Such obligations derive, for example, in contemporary international law, from the outlawing of acts of aggression, and of genocide, as also from the principles and rules concerning the basic rights of the human person, including protection from slavery, cruel and inhumane treatment, medical experimentation without free consent and racial discrimination.

pacta sund servanda agreements freely and seriously entered must be honored and enforced (sanctity of contract).

paradoxical phenomena self-contradictory occurrence (Such as claiming to be maintaining and enforcing the law while acting lawless).

parri passu at the same time.

pathology mental, social, or linguistic abnormality or malfunction.

peremptory norm also called *jus cogens*. Latin for "compelling law". A fundamental principle of international law that is accepted by the international community of States as a norm from which no derogation is permitted.

pharmacovigilance the process of collecting, monitoring, and evaluating adverse effects for safety signals to reduce harm to the public in the context of pharmaceutical and biological agents.

pharmacracy rule by medicine or physicians. In a theocracy, people perceive all manner of human problems as religious in nature, susceptible to religious remedies; similarly, in a pharmacracy people perceive all manner of human problems as medical in nature, susceptible to medical remedies. (Thomas S. Szasz)

physical integrity rights integrity rights, sometimes referred to as personal integrity rights, are entitlements codified in international law according to which individuals are to be protected from arbitrary physical harm and coercion by their own government.

plutocrat a person whose power derives from their wealth.

polity an organized society; a state as a political entity.

populus the people.

pseudo-medical any system of treatment of physical ailments, or substances prescribed for such treatment, purported to be medical or supported by critical medical science but which cannot be shown to be effective.

pseudo-science a claim, belief, or practice that is presented as scientific, but does not adhere to a valid scientific method, lacks supporting evidence or plausibility, cannot be reliably tested, or otherwise lacks scientific status. Pseudoscience is often characterized by the use of vague, exaggerated or unprovable claims, an over-reliance on confirmation rather than rigorous attempts at refutation, a lack of openness to evaluation by other experts, and a general absence of systematic processes to rationally develop theories.

rechtsstaat   "Constitutional State" in which the exercise of governmental power is constrained by the law. Closely related to "constitutionalism" while it is often tied to the Anglo-American concept of the rule of law, but differs from it in also emphasizing what is just (a concept of moral rightness based on ethics, rationality, law, and natural law). In a *Rechtsstaat*, the power of the State is limited in order to protect citizens from the arbitrary exercise of authority.

relative rights   rights that are incidental to persons as members of society and standing in various relations to each other.

rule of law   the restriction of the arbitrary exercise of power by subordinating it to well-defined and established laws (the mechanism, process, institution, practice, or norm that supports the equality of all citizens and government before the law, secures a nonarbitrary form of government, and more generally prevents the arbitrary use of power).

scilicet   by way of explanation.

sanctity of contract   the principle that agreements legitimately entered into should be upheld and enforced.

state of emergency   a situation of national danger or disaster in which a government suspends normal constitutional procedures in order to regain control.

state of exception   state of emergency also referred to as a state of necessity.

State Party   a country that has ratified a treaty or convention and is therefore legally bound by its provisions.

statism   a political system in which the State has substantial centralized control over social and economic affairs.

statist   an advocate of statism.

statum di diritto   state of law, rule of law, state ruled by law.

substantive law   body of rules and established principles governing society that create and define rights and obligations of persons.

thanatopolitics	the use of death for mobilizing political life.
therapeutic State	the transformation of the dominant political ideology from a democratic welfare State legitimized by the rule of law to an autocratic therapeutic State legitimized by bio-medicine and biomedical mandates (Thomas S. Szasz).
totalitarian	a system of government that is centralized and dictatorial and requires complete subservience to the State.
uberrima fides	utmost good faith
ultra-wealthy global elite	the global elite, the 0,1% of the 1% corporate aristocracy.
vaccination	the act of introducing a vaccine into the body to produce immunity to a specific disease.
vaccine	any substance designed to be administered to a human being for the prevention of one or more diseases.
versari in re illicita	the common law doctrine that holds that a person is criminally liable for all the adverse consequences caused by an initial illegal activity irrespective of whether those consequences were intended or foreseen.[1]
videliset	in other words.
vis compulsiva	force exerted to compel another to do something against their will; menacing force exerted by terror.
void	of no legal force and effect. Null.
weltanschauung	a particular philosophy or view of life; the worldview of an individual or group.

FIGURES AND TABLES

REFERENCES

Preface

1. Van Aardt, W. (2004). *State responsibility for human rights abuses committed by non-State actors under the Constitution.* PhD diss., North-West University. Also see van Aardt, W. (2022) Public policy, jus cogens norms and the fiduciary criterion of legitimacy. De Rebus Attorneys Journal. July 1, 2022.

2. Ioannidis, J. P. A. (2021). "Reconciling estimates of global spread and infection fatality rates of COVID-19: an overview of systematic evaluations." *European journal of clinical investigation* 51, no. 5: p 13554.

3. Hoffer, E. (1976).*The temper of our time.*Buccaneer Books.

4. Wiśniewski J B (2020).Quote. Available at: https://www.goodreads.com/author/quotes/14121943.Jakub_Bo_ydar_Wi_niewski. (Accessed: September 1 2022).

5. Action Against Hunger. (2021).World Hunger: Key facts and Statistics Available at: https://www.actionagainsthunger.org/world-hunger-facts-statistics (Accessed: June 15, 2022).

6. Gross, B. M. (1980). *Friendly fascism: The new face of power in America.* South End Press.

7. Wolin, S. S. (2008). *Democracy Incorporated: Managed Democracy and the Specter of Inverted Totalitarianism.* Princeton: Princeton University Press.

8. Szasz, T. (1984). *The therapeutic State.* Buffalo: Prometheus Books.

9. Weindling, P. (1993). *Health, race and German politics between national unification and Nazism, 1870-1945.* Cambridge University Press.

10. Agamben, G. (2021). *Where Are We Now? The Epidemic as Politics.* Rowman & Littlefield.

11. Agamben, G. *State of exception.* In State of Exception. University of Chicago Press.

12. Wolin, S. S. (2004). *Politics and Vision: Continuity and Innovation in Western Political Thought* (expanded ed.). Princeton: Princeton University Press.

13. Chomsky, N. (2013). *How the World Works,* Soft Skull Press. p 78

14. Chomsky, N. (2016). *Who Rules the World?,*Metropolitan Books. p54.

15. Frost,T. (2019). "The Dispositif between Foucault and Agamben. Law, Culture and the Humanities." 15(1): p151-171.

16. Foucault, M. (1980). The Confession of the Flesh. Power/Knowledge. Selected interviews and other writings, 1972–1977. Ed. Colin Gordon. Trans. Colin Gordon, Leo Marshall, John Mepham, Kate Soper. New York: Harvester Wheatsheaf, pp.194-228. Also see Agamben, G. (2009). "On the Limits of Violence," Diacritics 39 (2009), p 103–111.

17. Foucault, M. (2003)."Society Must Be Defended," Lectures at the Collège de France, 1975–76, David Macey (tr.).(London: Penguin Books, 2003), p. 259. Also see Agamben,G. (1998). *Homo Sacer: Sovereign Power and Bare Life,* Daniel Heller-Roazen (tr.).Stanford, CA: Stanford University Press.

18. Benjamin, N. (2005). *The Culture of Death.* New York: Berg Press, p. 54.

19. Campbell, T. (2011). *Improper Life: Technology and Biopolitics from Heidegger to*

   Agamben. Minneapolis, MN: University of Minnesota Press, p. 29.
20. United Nations, Office of the High Commissioner of Human Rights. (2022).Status of Ratification Interactive Dashboard: International Covenant on Civil and Political Rights. Available at: https://indicators.ohchr.org/ (Accessed: January 27, 2022).
21. Diakonia International Humanitarian Law Centre. (2021). "Easy Guide to International Humanitarian Law". (4th revised edition). Available at: 2021https:// apidiakoniase.cdn.triggerfish.cloud/uploads/sites/2/2021/06/Easy-Guide-to-IHL. pdf (Accessed: January 28, 2022).
22. Martens, J. (2020). "The Role of Public and Private Actors and Means in Implementing the SDGs: Reclaiming the Public Policy Space for Sustainable Development and Human Rights." In: Sustainable Development Goals and Human Rights, pp. 207-220. Springer, Cham, 2020. Also see World Economic Forum (2010) Everybody's business: strengthening international cooperation in a more interdependent world - report of the global redesign initiative. Geneva. http:// www3.weforum.org/docs/WEF (Accessed: September 16, 2022).
23. Mills, C. W. and Wolfe, A. (2000). *The power elite*. Vol. 20. Oxford University Press.
24. Johns Hopkins Bloomberg School of Public Health, Event 201. The Center for Health Security Available at: https://www.centerforhealthsecurity.org/event201/ (Accessed: January 28, 2022).
25. Hedges, C. (2018).*The Rule of the Uber-Rich Means Either Tyranny or Revolution*. Truthdig. Available at: https://www.commondreams.org/views/2018/10/22/rule-uber-rich-means-either-tyranny-or-revolution. (Accessed: January 29, 2022).
26. World Economic Forum. (2022).*Our Partners. 2022.* Available at: https://www. weforum.org/partners#search (Accessed: January 31, 2022).
27. Buxton, N. (2016). *Davos and its danger to Democracy.* January, 18 2016 Available at: https://www.tni.org/en/article/davos-and-its-danger-to-democracy (Accessed: January 17, 2022).
28. The World Economic Forum. (2020).The Great Reset. Available at: https://www. weforum.org/focus/the-great-reset (Accessed: January 17, 2022).
29. McArthur, J., Snower, D. (2010). "Everybody's business: Strengthening international cooperation in a more interdependent world, creating employment, eradicating poverty and improving social welfare." In World Economic Forum.
30. Sisson, J. (2010). "A conceptual framework for dealing with the past." Politorbis 50, no. 3: p. 11-15.

Chapter 1

1. Aristotle. Politics. pp. 3, 6–7, 12.
2. Aquinas, T. (2005). *Summa Theologiae*. pp. 1, 2. 90. 2 and 4 also see Chapmen, B. (2014).St. Thomas and the Common Good Dominicana. Available at: https://www. dominicanajournal.org/st-thomas-and-the-common-good/ (Accessed: November 14, 2021).
3. Waldemar, Hanasz (2010). "The common good in Machiavelli". History of Political Thought. 31 (1): p 57–85.
4. Publius. Federalist. pp. 10, 51.
5. The Vatican. (2004). Compendium of the Social Doctrine of the Church. Chapter 4. Available at: www.vatican.va/roman_curia/pontifical_councils/justpeace/ documents/rc_pc_justpeace_doc_20060526_compendio-dott-soc_en.html (Accessed: November 15, 2021)
6. Alighieri, D. (1965). "Monarchia, 1312-1313." PG Ricci (a cura di), Milano, Mondadori.

7. Landler, M. (2021). Vaccine Mandates Rekindle Fierce Debate Over Civil Liberties. *New York Times.* December 10, 2021. Available at: https://www.nytimes.com/2021/12/10/world/europe/vaccine-mandates-civil-liberties.html (Accessed: January 4, 2022).

8. World Health Organization. (2021). WHO Coronavirus (COVID-19). Dashboard. Available at: https://covid19.who.int/ (Accessed: January 27, 2022).

9. UN General Assembly. (1948). Universal Declaration of Human Rights, 10 December 1948, 217 A (III).

10. UN General Assembly. (1966). International Covenant on Civil and Political Rights, 16 December 1966, United Nations, Treaty Series, vol. 999, p. 171.

11. Kennedy, J F. (1961). Inaugural address: Friday, January 20, 1961. Western Standard Publishing Company, 1999.

12. Jose, R. (2021). Sydney's unvaccinated warned of social isolation when COVID-19 lockdown ends. Reuters. Available at: https://www.reuters.com/world/asia-pacific/sydneys-unvaccinated-warned-social-isolation-when-lockdown-ends-2021-09-28/ (Accessed: October 15, 2021).

13. Bloomberg. (2022). More Than 10 Billion Shots Given: Covid-19 Tracker. January 28, 2022. Available at: https://www.bloomberg.com/graphics/covid-vaccine-tracker-global-distribution/ Accessed: January 28, 2022.

14. USA Facts US Coronavirus vaccine tracker. Accessed: January 27, 2022. https://usafacts.org/visualizations/covid-vaccine-tracker-States/

15. Bleier, B, S. et al. (2021). "COVID-19 vaccines may not prevent nasal SARS-CoV-2 infection and asymptomatic transmission." Otolaryngology–Head and Neck Surgery 164, no. 2: 305-307.

16. Alexander, P, E. (2021). "146 Research Studies Affirm Naturally Acquired Immunity to Covid-19: Documented, Linked, and Quoted." Brownstone Institute.

17. Blazquez-Navarro, A. *et al.* (2021). "Superior cellular and humoral immunity toward SARS-CoV-2 reference and alpha and beta VOC strains in COVID-19 convalescent as compared to the prime boost BNT162b2-vaccinated dialysis patients." Kidney International 100, no. 3: p 698-700.

18. VAERS. (2021).Data Sets. Available at: https://vaers.hhs.gov/data/datasets.html. Accessed: January 18, 2022. Also see http://vigiaccess.org/, https://www.ema.europa.eu/en. https://dailyangle.com/articles/30-000-covid-vaccine-deaths-recorded-by-europe-database

19. The Expose. (2022). MHRA confirms the UK has recorded 5 times more Deaths in 12 months due to Covid-19 Vaccination than it has Deaths due to every other Vaccine combined in 21 years. *The Expose.* January 18, 2022. Available at: https://dailyexpose.uk/2022/01/18/uk-5-times-more-deaths-due-to-covid-vaccines (Accessed: January 20, 2022).

20. Times Of Israel Staff. (2022). Israel world #1 in daily COVID cases per capita; exposed schoolkids won't quarantine. January 20, 2022. Times of Israel. Available at: https://www.timesofisrael.com/israel-world-1-in-daily-covid-cases-per-capita-exposed-schoolkids-wont-quarantine/. (Accessed: January 21, 2022)

21. The RIO Times. (2022). South Africa: Only 26% of the population is vaccinated, but the Government has overcome wave of Omicron cases. RIO Times. January 3, 2022. Available at: https://www.riotimesonline.com/brazil-news/modern-day-censorship/south-africa-with-only-26-of-the-population-vaccinated-the-Government-has-overcome-the-wave-of-omicron-cases-the-Government-announced/ (Accessed: January 22, 2022).

22. John Hopkins University. Covid 19 Deaths Before and After Mass Vaccination John Hopkins Data March 2020 – Sept 2021.

23. Kennedy, R, F. Jr. (2021).*The Real Anthony Fauci: Bill Gates, Big Pharma, and the*

Global War on Democracy and Public Health (Children's Health Defense). Sky Horse Publishing.

24. Mercola, J, and Cummins, R. (2021)."The Truth About COVID-19: Exposing the Great Reset, lockdowns, vaccine passports, and the new normal." Chelsea Green Publishing.

25. C19Protocols. Reducing Risk of COVID-19 Infection and Severity: Early Treatment Protocols. 2021. Available at: https://c19protocols.com/treatment-protocols/. (Accessed: January 21 , 2022)

26. Alexander, P, E. (2022). "Early Outpatient Treatment for COVID-19: The Evidence." January, 20, 2022. Brownstone Institute. Available at: https://brownstone.org/articles/early-outpatient-treatment-for-covid-19-the-evidence/ (Accessed: January 23, 2022).

27. Bryant, A., Lawrie, T.A., Dowswell, T., Fordham, E.J., Mitchell, S., Hill, S.R. and Tham, T.C., (2021). Ivermectin for prevention and treatment of COVID-19 infection: a systematic review, meta-analysis, and trial sequential analysis to inform clinical guidelines. American journal of therapeutics, 28(4), p.e434.

28. Lagier, J.C., Million, M., Gautret, P., Colson, P., Cortaredona, S., Giraud-Gatineau, A., Honoré, S., Gaubert, J.Y., Fournier, P.E., Tissot-Dupont, H. and Chabrière, E., (2020). Outcomes of 3,737 COVID-19 patients treated with hydroxychloroquine/azithromycin and other regimens in Marseille, France: A retrospective analysis. Travel medicine and infectious disease, 36, p.101791.

29. Derwand, R., Scholz, M. and Zelenko, V., (2020). COVID-19 outpatients: early risk-stratified treatment with zinc plus low-dose hydroxychloroquine and azithromycin: a retrospective case series study. International Journal of Antimicrobial Agents, 56(6), p.106214.

30. Fonseca, S.N.S., de Queiroz Sousa, A., Wolkoff, A.G., Moreira, M.S., Pinto, B.C., Takeda, C.F.V., Rebouças, E., Abdon, A.P.V., Nascimento, A.L. and Risch, H.A.,(2020). Risk of hospitalization for Covid-19 outpatients treated with various drug regimens in Brazil: comparative analysis. Travel medicine and infectious disease, 38, p.101906.

31. HQ Meta. (2022). HCQ for COVID-19: real-time meta-analysis of 340 studies, Version 207. Available at: hcqmeta.com. Accessed: May 3, 2022.

32. Blaylock RL. (2022). "COVID UPDATE: What is the truth?" Surg Neurol Int. Apr 22;13: p. 167.

33. Alexander, P, E. (2021). 40 Studies on Vaccine Efficacy that Raise Doubts on Vaccine Mandates. Brownstone Institute. Available at: https://brownstone.org/articles/16-studies-on-vaccine-efficacy/. (Accessed: October 28, 2021).

34. Vergara, R. J. D., Sarmiento, P.J.D and Lagman, J.D.N. (2021)."Building Public Trust: A Response to COVID-19 Vaccine Hesitancy Predicament." Journal of Public Health. Oxford, England.

35. Hall, M. A., and D. M. Studdert. (2021). "'Vaccine Passport' Certification—Policy and Ethical Considerations." New England Journal of Medicine.

36. King, J. *et al*, (2021). "Mandatory COVID-19 vaccination and human rights." The Lancet.

37. Hindupost. (2021).Europe: Mass Protests Against Covid-19 Vaccine 'Passports'. Available at: https://hindupost.in/world/europe-mass-protests-against-covid-19-vaccine-passports/ (Accessed: October 10, 2021).

38. Dror, A. A., N. Eisenbach, S. Taiber, N. G. Morozov, M. Mizrachi, A. Zigron, S. Srouji, and E. Sela. (2020). "Vaccine Hesitancy: The Next challenge in the Fight against COVID-19." European Journal of Epidemiology 35, no. 8: p. 775–779.

39. Office of the United Nations High Commissioner for Human Rights.(2020). Emergency Measures and Covid-19 Guidance.

40. UNESCO International Bioethics Committee (IBC) and the UNESCO World Commission on the Ethics of Scientific Knowledge and Technology (COMEST). (2021). "Statement on COVID-19: Ethical Considerations from a Global Perspective."

41. Rand, A. *et al.* (1986).*Capitalism: The unknown ideal.* Penguin.

42. Members of the EU Parlement. (2021). Members of the European Parliament supporting the rights of workers against mandatory Digital Certificates. Press Conference. October 29, 2021. Available at: https://www.youtube.com/watch?v=GtnGntLmPRE. Accessed: January 15, 2022)

43. Rose, G., (1981). Strategy of prevention: lessons from cardiovascular disease. British medical journal (Clinical research ed.), 282(6279), p.1847

44. Rose, G. (2001). "Sick individuals and sick populations." International journal of epidemiology 30, no. 3 : p. 427-432.

45. BioNTech Form F-1 United States Securities and Exchange Commission. September 9, 2019. SE https://www.sec.gov/Archives/edgar/data/1776985/000119312519241112/d635330df1.htm

46. Paget, J., Spreeuwenberg, P., Charu, V., Taylor, R.J., Iuliano, A.D., Bresee, J., Simonsen, L. and Viboud, C., (2019). Global mortality associated with seasonal influenza epidemics: New burden estimates and predictors from the GLaMOR Project. Journal of global health, 9(2).

47. Lefebvre, A., Fiet, C., Belpois-Duchamp, C., Tiv, M., Astruc, K. and Glélé, L.A., (2014). Case fatality rates of Ebola virus diseases: a meta-analysis of World Health Organization data. Médecine et maladies infectieuses, 44(9), pp.412-416.

48. Ross, J; Schell H. (2020). How Many People Die Each Day? Visual Capatilist. Available at: https://www.visualcapitalist.com/how-many-people-die-each-day/ (Accessed: January 18 , 2022).

49. Szasz, T. (1984). *The therapeutic State.* Buffalo: Prometheus Books.

50. Macron, E M. (2020). "We are at war" with COVID-19, says President in national broadcast. Paris. March, 16 2020. Available at: https://uk.ambafrance.org/We-are-at-war-with-COVID-19-says-President-in-national-broadcast (Accessed: January 17 , 2022).

51. Ataman, L; Mawad, D and Picheta, R. (2022). Macron says he wants to 'piss off' the unvaccinated, as tensions rise over new French vaccine pass. CNN. January 5, 2022. Available at: https://www.cnn.com/2022/01/05/europe/macron-unvaccinated-comments-vaccine-pass-intl/index.html (Accessed: January 10, 2022).

52. Chapel, B. (2020). 'We Are At War,' WHO Head Says, Warning Millions Could Die From COVID-19. NPR. March 26, 2020. Available at: www.npr.org/sections/corona virus-live-updates/2020/03/26/822123471/we-are-at-war-who-head-says-warning-millions-could-die-from-covid-19 (Accessed: January 17, 2022).

53. NDTV Staff. (2021). "We Are at War" Against COVID-19, Says UN Chief. May 24, 2021. NDTV. Available at: https://www.ndtv.com/world-news/we-are-at-war-against-covid-19-un-chief-antonio-guterres-2448351 (Accessed: January 17, 2022).

54. Szasz, T. (2007). *The medicalization of everyday life: Selected essays.* Syracuse University Press.

55. Szasz, T. (2007). *Pharmacracy in America.* Society, 41(5), 54-58.

56. Szasz, T. (2003). *Pharmacracy: Medicine and politics in America.* Syracuse University Press.

57. Agamben, G. (2008). *State of exception.* In State of Exception. University of Chicago Press.

58. Korab, A. (2021). Dr. Fauci Just Said This About Your "Individual Freedom". October 7, 2021. YahooLife. Available at: https://www.yahoo.com/lifestyle/

dr-fauci-just-said-individual-121519548.html (Accessed: January 20, 2022).

59. World Tribune Staff. Fauci declares that 'individual freedom is superseded by the State'. November 16, 2021. Available at: https://www.worldtribune.com/fauci-declares-that-individual-freedom-is-superseded-by-the-State/ (Accessed: January 20, 2022).

60. Hitler's antisemitism. Why did he hate the Jews? Anne Frank house. Available at: https://www.annefrank.org/en/anne-frank/go-in-depth/why-did-hitler-hate-jews/#source-392916 (Accessed: January 20, 2022).

61. Martin, K. (2022).The Strange History of Roman Medical Treatments. Available at: https://www.healthyway.com/content/the-strange-history-of-roman-medical-treatments/ (Accessed: January 20, 2022).

62. Time Magazine. (1946). "The Clyster Craze" Time. July 1, 1946.

63. Malone, R, W. (2022). We the people, demand to see the data! Substack. Available at: https://rwmalonemd.substack.com/p/we-the-people-demand-to-see-the-data. Accessed: February 22, 2022.

64. Ohe, M. (2022). 'Multi-drug Treatment for COVID-19-induced Acute Respiratory Distress Syndrome.' Turk J Pharm Sci. Feb 28;19(1): p. 101-103.

65. Oster ME, Shay DK, Su JR, et al. (2022). 'Myocarditis Cases Reported After mRNA-Based COVID-19 Vaccination in the US From December 2020 to August 2021.' JAMA. 2022;327(4):p.331–340.

66. World Economic Forum. Our Partners. 2022. Available at: https://www.weforum.org/partners#search (Accessed: February 22, 2022).

67. Buxton, N. (2016). Davos and its danger to Democracy. January, 18 2016 Available at: https://www.tni.org/en/article/davos-and-its-danger-to-democracy (Accessed: February 22, 2022).

68. The World Economic Forum. The Great Reset. 2020. Available at: https://www.weforum.org/focus/the-great-reset (Accessed: February 22, 2022).

69. Martens, J. (2020). "The Role of Public and Private Actors and Means in Implementing the SDGs: Reclaiming the Public Policy Space for Sustainable Development and Human Rights." In Sustainable Development Goals and Human Rights, Springer, Cham, pp. 207-220.

70. Ioannidis, J, PA. (2021). "Reconciling estimates of global spread and infection fatality rates of COVID-19: an overview of systematic evaluations." European journal of clinical investigation 51, no. 5: p. 13554.

71. Assembly, UN General Assembly. (1948). "Universal declaration of human rights." UN General Assembly 302, no. 2: p. 14-25.

72. Assembly, UN General. "International covenant on civil and political rights." (1966): 171.

73. Van Aardt, W. (2004). State responsibility for human rights abuses committed by non-State actors under the constitution. Doctoral dissertation, North-West University. p 86 -115 .

74. Wolin, S.S., (2008). Managed democracy and the specter of inverted totalitarianism.

75. Kennedy, D, W. (2005).'Speaking Law to Power: International Law and Foreign Policy,' 23 Wis. Int'l L.J. p. 173.

76. Fitzpatrick, J. (2003). 'Speaking Law to Power: The War Against Terrorism and Human Rights,' European Journal of International Law, Volume 14, Issue 2, April 2003, P. 241–264

Chapter 2

1. New York Trust Co. v. Eisner, 256 U.S. 345 (1921).
2. Van Aardt, W. (2004)." State responsibility for human rights abuses committed by non-State actors under the constitution." PhD diss., North-West University, 2004 at: 17.
3. Mcaffee, L G, Mcaffee, M. (2019). The Bible's Impact on Human Rights, *Christianity Today.*
4. The Holy Bible—New International Version. (also include 1998, New American Library, New York, NY.
5. Catholic Culture. (1997). Catechism of the Catholic Church, Catholic Culture at 475 Available at: https://www.catholicculture.org/culture/library/catechism/index.cfm?recnum=5497 (Accessed: September 17, 2021).
6. Cicero, Rep. III, 22, 33.
7. Swartz, N P. (2010). "Thomas Aquinas: on law, tyranny and resistance." Acta Theologica 30, no. 1.
8. Biblia Sacra. Vulgate Editionis. Epistoli Beati Pauli ad Romanos, Caput XIII, 1. "...all things that are, are set in order by God".
9. Biblia Sacra. Vulgate Editionis. Epistoli Beati Pauli Apostoli ad Romanis, Caput XIII, 1. "For all power is from the Lord God".
10. Krishef, D, J.B. (2017). Ethics and Religion Talk: Do human rights come from God or from the government? The Rapidian. Available at: https://www.therapidian.org/november-20-2017-ethics-and-religion-talk-do-human-rights-come-god-or-government. (Accessed: September 20, 2021).
11. Thomas Aquinas, Summa theologiae, Ia-IIae, q. xciii, art. 3, ad 2m.
12. Thomas Aquinas. Commentum in Quatuor Libros Sententiarum. Liber Secun dus. Dist. XLIV, Q. II, A. 2. (Translated by J.G. Dawson).
13. Henkin, L. (2019).*The rights of man today.* Routledge. p 10.
14. Coke, E. (1809).Institutes
15. Heyman, S.J., (1991). First Duty of Government: Protection, Liberty and the Fourteenth Amendment, The. Duke LJ, 41, p.507. footnote 1 quoting the CONG. GLOBE, 39th Cong., 2nd Sess., 101 (1867), remarks of Rep. Farnsworth (debating the reconstruction Act of 1867)';
16. Bigelow, A.M. (1993). In the Ghetto: The State's Duty to Protect Inner-City Children from Violence. Notre Dame JL Ethics & Pub. Pol'y, 7, p.533.
17. Wood, G.S., (2011). *The creation of the American republic, 1776-1787.* UNC Press Books.
18. Reid, J.P., (1986). Constitutional history of the American revolution: the authority to legislate (Vol. 3). Univ of Wisconsin Press. p 55-60.
19. Hobbes, T. (1651). *Leviathan.* At xiv
20. Locke, J 1690(b).*Two Treatises of Government.* At ch. II s 4
21. Strong, C F. (1960). *Modern political constitutions: an introduction to the comparative study of their history and existing form.* Sidgwick & Jackson. p 35 -38
22. Rousseau, J, J. (1762). *Social Contract* At Chapter 6 (emphasis added).
23. Hutcheson, F. (1772). *A Short Introduction to Moral Philosophy.* Vol. 1. Robert&Andrew Foulis, 1772 at 302
24. Burlamaqui, J.J., (1780). The principles of natural law. J. Nourse.: Part I Chap. V
25. Wilson, J. (1774). "Considerations on the Nature and Extent of the Legislative Authority of the British Parliament." Collected Works of James Wilson 1 (2007): 3-30.
26. Tandon, R. (2021). COVID-19 and suicide: just the facts. Key learnings and guidance for action. Asian journal of psychiatry, 60, p.102695.

27. McIntyre, R.S. and Lee, Y. (2020). Projected increases in suicide in Canada as a consequence of COVID-19. Psychiatry research, 290, p.113104.
28. Kuehn BM. (2020). Surge in Child Abuse, Harm During COVID-19 Pandemic Reported. JAMA. 2020;324(7): p 621.
29. Mittal, S, and Tushar S. (2020). "Gender-based violence during COVID-19 pandemic: a mini-review." Frontiers in Global Women's Health 1: p. 4.
30. Telles, L.E., Valenca, A.M., Barros, A.J. and da Silva, A.G., (2020). Domestic violence in the COVID-19 pandemic: a forensic psychiatric perspective. Brazilian Journal of Psychiatry, 43, pp.233-234.
31. Dubey, M J, et al. (2020). "COVID-19 and addiction." Diabetes & Metabolic Syndrome: Clinical Research & Reviews 14, no. 5 (2020): 817-823.
32. Blackstone, W., (1830). Commentaries on the Laws of England (Vol. 2). Collins & Hannay.
33. Stanford Encyclopedia of Philosophy. (2016).Kant's Moral Philosophy, Stanford Encyclopedia of Philosophy. Available at: https://plato.stanford.edu/entries/kant-moral/index.html. (Accessed: August 30, 2021).
34. Kant, I., (1983). On the proverb: That may be true in theory, but is of no practical use. Perpetual peace and other essays, pp.61-92.
35. Van Aardt, W. (2022). "The new era of COVID-19 legal paternalism and the limitation of fundamental human rights." De Rebus Attorneys Journal. The Law Society of South Africa, Feb 1, 2022.
36. Smith, G H. (2016). Immanuel Kant on Our Duty to Obey Government. Libertarianism.org. Available at: https://www.libertarianism.org/columns/immanuel-kant-our-duty-obey-government (Accessed: August 31, 2021).
37. Bailyn, B. (2017).The ideological origins of the American Revolution. Harvard University Press at 34-54.
38. Scott, P.B. (1987). "The Right of Revolution: The Development of the People's Right to Reform Government." W. Va. L. Rev., 90, p.283.
39. Hill, H. (1938), GEORGE MASON CONSTATUTIONALIST. P. 141 quoting the first draft of the Virginia Declaration of Rights)
40. Mason, George. (1776). Virginia Declaration of Rights. Section 3. Virginia Foundation for the Humanities and Public Policy, 1990.
41. Wills, G. (2018).Inventing America: Jefferson's declaration of independence. Vintage. p. 52 -55.
42. Jefferson, Thomas. (1776). The declaration of independence. at para. 25.
43. Becker, Carl Lotus. (1922). The Declaration of Independence: A study in the history of political ideas. Harcourt, Brace.
44. Williams, D C. (1997). "The Constitutional Right to "Conservative" Revolution" (1997). Articles by Maurer. Faculty. P. 674.
45. Hatschek, J., (1923). Das Reichsstaatsrecht (Vol. 1). Berlin Stilke.
46. Agamben, G. (2005). "State of exception." Chicago. University of Chicago Press.
47. Schellhammer, M. (2005).JOHN ADAMS'S RULE OF THIRDS. Journal of the American Revolution. February 11, 2013.
48. William M. (2005). Only 1/3rd of Americans Supported the American Revolution? History news Network. August 8, 2005. Available at: https://historynewsnetwork.org/article/5641 (Accessed: September 12, 2021).
49. Paine, T. (1776). Common Sense. Philidelphia: W. and T. Bradford.
50. Hamilton, A., (1775). The farmer refuted. The Works of Alexander Hamilton, 1, pp.51-128.

Chapter 3

1. Nowak, M. (2003). *Introduction to the international human rights regime*, Leiden, Boston: Martinus Nijhoff Publishers, 2003, p. 36.
2. van Aardt, W. (2004). "State responsibility for human rights abuses committed by non-State actors under the constitution." PhD diss., North-West University. p. 76 - 110.
3. Tasioulas, J. (2015)."Custom, jus cogens, and human rights." Custom's Future: International Law in a Changing World, Curtis A. Bradley (ed.), Cambridge University Press, Forthcoming.
4. van Aardt, W. (2021). The Mandatory COVID-19 Vaccination of School Children: A Bioethical and Human Rights Assessment. J Vaccines Vaccin. 12: p. 457
5. United Nations, General Assembly. (1948). Universal Declaration of Human Rights.
6. van Aardt, W. (2021). "Limiting human rights during Covid-19- is it only legitimate if it is proportional". De Rebus SA Attorneys Journal. The Law Society of South Africa. May 2021. Pp 14 -16.
7. van Aardt, W., (2021). COVID-19 School Closures and the Principles of Proportionality and Balancing. J Infect Dis Ther 9: S3:002.
8. Vienna Declaration and Programme of Action Adopted by the World Conference on Human Rights in Vienna on 25 June 1993
9. Martens, J. (2020). "The Role of Public and Private Actors and Means in Implementing the SDGs: Reclaiming the Public Policy Space for Sustainable Development and Human Rights." In: Sustainable Development Goals and Human Rights, pp. 207-220. Springer, Cham, 2020.
10. United Nations. (1998). Analytical Report of the Secretary-General submitted pursuant to Commission on Human Rights Resolution 1997/21 Commission on Human Rights, U.N. Doc. E/CN.4/1998187 p. 16-17.
11. Meron, T, (1984). "Towards a humanitarian declaration on internal strife." American Journal of international law, 78(4), pp.859-868.
12. UN Human Rights Committee. (2004). General comment no. 31, The nature of the general legal obligation imposed on States Parties to the Covenant, 26 May 2004, CCPR/C/21/Rev.1/Add.13
13. Vienna Convention at article 26: "*Pacta Sunt Servanda*". Every treaty in force is binding upon the parties and must be performed by them in good faith'.
14. Lagerwall, A. and Carty, A., 2015. Jus cogens. Oxford Bibliographies-International Law, 1.
15. Zenović, P, (2012). "Human rights enforcement via peremptory norms–a challenge to State sovereignty." Riga Graduate School of Law Research Papers, (6).
16. Criddle, E, J. Fox-Decent, E. (2009)." A fiduciary theory of jus cogens" 34 Yale J. Int'l L. p. 331, 332, 339.
17. Mwenedata, A, Sehorana, J. (2016)." The Determination and Enforcement of Jus Cogens Norms For Effective Human Rights Protection." IOSR Journal Of Humanities And Social Science.
18. United Nations, Vienna Convention on the Law of Treaties, 23 May 1969, United Nations, Treaty Series, vol. 1155, p. 331.
19. Yearwood, L. (2009). "State Accountability for Breaching Jus Cogens Norms," University of Exeter.
20. Meron, T. (1986). "On a Hierarchy of International Human Rights," 80 AM. J. INT'L L., p. 19-2.
21. Stephens, P.J., (2004). "A Categorical Approach to Human Rights Claims: Jus Cogens as a Limitation on Enforcement." Wis. Int"l LJ, 22, p.245.

22. Yearbook of the International Law Commission, (1966).ii, at 248 (UN Doc A/CN.4/ SER.A/1966/Add. 1).
23. Bianchi, A., (2008). "Human rights and the magic of jus cogens." European journal of international law, 19(3), pp.491-508.
24. Orakhelashvili, A., 2006. *Peremptory norms in international law* (pp. 50-51). Oxford: Oxford University Press. p 50-51.
25. International Covenant on Civil and Political Rights (ICCPR). G.A. Res. 2200A (XXI).(1966).
26. United Nations Office of the High Commissioner of Human Rights. (2022). International Human Rights Law. Available at: https://www.ohchr.org/en/ instruments-and-mechanisms/international-human-rights-law (Accessed: September 22, 2022)
27. UN Committee on Economic, Social and Cultural Rights (CESCR), General Comment No. 3: The Nature of States Parties' Obligations (Art. 2, Para. 1, of the Covenant), 14 December 1990, E/1991/23
28. Jecker, N.S., Jecker, N.S., Jonsen, A.R. and Pearlman, R.A., (2011). Bioethics. Jones & Bartlett Publishers. p 3.
29. The Medical Dictionary. (2021).Available at: https://medical-dictionary. thefreedictionary.com/bioethics. (Accessed: October 20, 2021)
30. The Nuremberg Code (1947).In: Mitscherlich A, Mielke F. Doctors of infamy: the story of the Nazi medical crimes. New York: Schuman, 1949: xxiii-xxv.
31. Universal Declaration on Bioethics and Human Rights (UDBHR). Adopted by acclamation on 19 October 2005 by the 33rd session of the General Conference of UNESCO.
32. Andorno, R. (2005). "The Oviedo Convention: A European Legal Framework at the Intersection of Human Rights and Health Law" Journal of International Biotechnology Law 2: 135.
33. Council of Europe. (1997).The Convention for the Protection of Human Rights and Dignity of the Human Being with regard to the Application of Biology and Medicine: Convention on Human Rights and Biomedicine (OVIEDO).
34. World Medical Association. (2022). About Us. 2022. Available at: https://www. wma.net/who-we-are/about-us/ (Accessed: October 20, 2021).
35. World Medical Association. (1948). *WMA Declaration of Geneva*. Available at: https://www.wma.net/what-we-do/medical-ethics/declaration-of-geneva/ (Accessed: October 20, 2021).
36. World Medical association. (1964).WMA Declaration of Helsinki - Ethical Principles for Medical Research Involving Human Subjects. Available at: https:// www.wma.net/what-we-do/medical-ethics/declaration-of-helsinki/ (Accessed: October 20, 2020).
37. WMA Declaration of Helsinki at: Article 16 – 18
38. World Health Organization. (2021). Vigiaccess. Available at: http://vigiaccess.org/ (Accessed: October 20, 2021).
39. NewsRescue. (2021). WHO Database Reports Over 2 million Potential COVID Jab Injuries in 2021, Vast Majority in Women. Available at: https://newsrescue.com/ who-database-reports-over-2-million-potential-covid-jab-injuries-in-2021-vast-majority-in-women/ (Accessed : January 10, 2022).
40. World Health Organization. (2016). Guidance for Managing Ethical Issues in Infectious Disease Outbreaks 2016. WHO: p. 35 -38
41. Richards, D.L. and Clay, K.C., (2012). "An umbrella with holes: Respect for non-derogable human rights during declared states of emergency, 1996–2004." Human Rights Review, 13(4), pp.443-471.
42. Koji, T. (2001). "Emerging Hierarchy in International Human Rights and Beyond:

From the Perspective of Non-derogable Rights." European Journal of International Law 12, no. 5:p 917-941.

43. Schwab, K. (2016).*Fourth Industrial Revolution*. World Economic Forum.
44. United Nations. Office of the High Commissioner of Human Rights. (1993). Address by the Secretary-General of the United Nations at the opening of the World Conference on Human Rights. Available at: www.ohchr.org/en/statements/2009/10/ address-secretary-general-united-nations-opening-world-conference-human-rights. (Accessed: January 20, 2021).

Chapter 4

1. Senat. (2021). Commission Des Affaires Sociales. 4 Octobre 2021. Available: https://www.senat.fr/amendements/commissions/2020-2021/811/Amdt_COM-1. html (Accessed: October 12, 2021).
2. Pettypiece, S, Przybyla, H, and Egan, L. (2021). President Joe Biden on ThursdNBC News. Biden announces sweeping vaccine mandates affecting millions of workers. NBC News. September 9, 2021. Available at: https://www.nbcnews.com/politics/ white-house/biden-announce-additional-vaccine-mandates-he-unveils-new-covid-strategy-n1278735 (Accessed: October 12, 2021).
3. New York State. (2021). Frequently Asked Questions: Proof of Full Vaccination or Mask Requirement for Businesses and Venues. Available at: https://coronavirus. health.ny.gov/frequently-asked-questions-proof-full-vaccination-or-mask-requirement-businesses-and-venues (Accessed: October 12 2021).
4. Stableford, D. (2021). NYC to require proof of COVID vaccination for indoor activities. Yahoo News - Aug 3, 2021.Available at: https://www.msn.com/en-us/ money/other/nyc-to-require-proof-of-covid-vaccination-for-indoor-activities/ ar-AAMTkIR (Accessed: October 17, 2021).
5. John Hopkins university and Medicine. (2021).Corona Viris Resource Centre. Mortality Analysis. Available https://coronavirus.jhu.edu/data. (Accessed monthly 2020, 2021, 2022)
6. Alexander, P, E. (2021)."42 Studies on Vaccine Efficacy that Raise Doubts on Vaccine Mandates". Brownstone Institute. October 28, 2021, Available at: https:// brownstone.org/articles/16-studies-on-vaccine-efficacy/
7. Alexander P, E. (2022). "Early Outpatient Treatment for COVID-19: The Evidence." Brownstone Institute. January 22, 2022. Available at; https:// brownstone.org/articles/early-outpatient-treatment-for-COVID-19-the-evidence/ (Accessed: February 19, 2022).
8. Alexander P, E. (2021). "75 Studies and Articles Against COVID-19 School Closures." Brownstone Institute. Available at: https://brownstone.org/articles/75-studies-and-articles-against-COVID-19-school-closures/ (Accessed: February 19, 2022).
9. Alexander P, E. (2021). "More than 150 Comparative Studies and Articles on Mask Ineffectiveness and Harms". December 20, 2021. Brownstone Institute. Available at https://brownstone.org/articles/more-than-150-comparative-studies-and-articles-on-mask-ineffectiveness-and-harms/ (Accessed: February 19, 2022).
10. Alexander P, E. (2021). "More Than 400 Studies on the Failure of Compulsory Covid Interventions" (Lockdowns, Restrictions, Closures).Brownstone Institute. Available at; https://brownstone.org/articles/more-than-400-studies-on-the-failure-of-compulsory-covid-interventions/ (Accessed: February 19, 2022).
11. Alexander P, E. (2021). Sweden and Germany: No Deaths In Children Due to Covid. Brownstone Institute. December 8, 2021. Available at: https://brownstone.

org/articles/sweden-and-germany-no-deaths-in-children-due-to-covid/ (Accessed: February 19, 2022).

12. van Aardt, W. (2021). "Can Government mandate the COVID-19 vaccine against your will? A discussion on international human rights law" De Rebus SA Attorneys Journal. The Law Society of South Africa. July 2021. Pp 14 -17.

13. King, W.C., Rubinstein, M., Reinhart, A. and Mejia, R., (2021). COVID-19 vaccine hesitancy January-May 2021 among 18–64-year-old US adults by employment and occupation. Preventive medicine reports, 24, p.101569. Also see Unheard. (2021).The most vaccine-hesitant group of all? PhDs. Available at: https://unherd.com/thepost/the-most-vaccine-hesitant-education-group-of-all-phds/. (Accessed: January 10, 2022).

14. Quinnipiac University Poll. (2021). Nearly 7 In 10 Say Recent Rise In COVID-19 Deaths Was Preventable, Quinnipiac University National Poll Finds; Job Approval For Supreme Court Drops To All-Time Low. Quinnipiac University. September 15, 2021. Available at: https://poll.qu.edu/poll-release?releaseid=3820 (Accessed: December 15, 2021).

15. Aljazeera. (2021).Singapore vaccinates 80 percent of population against COVID-19. August 29, 2021. Available at: https://www.aljazeera.com/news/2021/8/29/singapore-vaccinates-80-percent-of-population-against-COVID-19 (Accessed: December, 15, 2021).

16. Walia, A. (2021). Vermont – The Most Vaccinated State – Sets Single Day COVID Case Record. The Pulse. October 19, 2021. Available at: https://thepulse.one/2021/10/19/vermont-the-most-vaccinated-State-sets-single-day-covid-case-record/ (Accessed: December 5, 2021).data confirmed at: https://www.mayoclinic.org/coronavirus-COVID-19/vaccine-tracker

17. World Health Organisation. (2021).WHO Coronavirus (COVID-19).Dashboard. (2021). Available at: https://covid19.who.int/ (Accessed monthly 2020, 2021, 2022);

18. Vermont Department of Health, (2021). COVID-19 Data. Available at: https://www.healthvermont.gov/COVID-19 .(Accessed: January 14, 2022).

19. Dictionary, Merriam-Webster. (2002). "Merriam-webster." Available at: https://www.merriam-webster.com/dictionary/fact (Accessed: December 5, 2021).

20. Black, H C. (1910). Law dictionary. Vol. 1188. St. Paul, Minn.: West Publishing Company.

21. Habakus, L. K., Holland, M., & Rosenberg, K. M. (Eds.). (2011).Vaccine Epidemic, How Corporate Greed, Biased Science, and Coercive Government Threaten Our Human Rights, Our Health, and Our Children. Simon and Shuster.

22. US Department of Health and Human Sciences, Centers for Disease Control and Prevention. (2021). Demographic Trends of COVID-19 Cases and Deaths in the US Reported to CDC. Available at: https://covid.cdc.gov/covid-data-tracker/#datatracker-home (Data as at: June 20, 2021).

23. Loannidis JPA. (2020). Global perspective of COVID-19 epidemiology for a full-cycle pandemic. Eur J Clin Invest.Dec;50(12): p13423.

24. Swiss Policy Research. (2021).Studies on COVID-19 Lethality. Available at: https://swprs.org/studies-on-COVID-19-lethality/#age. (Accessed: January 18, 2022).

25. Triggle, N. (2020). Coronavirus: How to understand the death toll. BBC News. April 16, 2020. Available at: https://www.bbc.com/news/health-51979654 (Accessed: February 5, 2022).

26. Lee, J. (2020). "How to understand – and report – figures for 'Covid deaths'" The Spectator. March 29, 2020.

27. Savulescu J (2021). "Good reasons to vaccinate: mandatory or payment for risk?" Journal of Medical Ethics; 47: p 78-85.

28. English, C. (2021). Mandatory COVID Vaccines: Why Forcing People to Get A Shot May Backfire. *American Council on Science and Health*. April 23, 2021.

29. Kennedy, R F. (2021). "The Real Anthony Fauci: Bill Gates, Big Pharma, and the global war on democracy and public health." Skyhorse Publishing.

30. Gøtzsche, P C. (2012)."Corporate crime in the pharmaceutical industry is common, serious and repetitive." BMJ 345

31. Hollander, B. (2021). "The real-world effectiveness of the Moderna and Pfizer (mRNA).vaccines appears to be sinking like a stone, *Real Clear Science*." August 23, 2021. Available at: https://www.realclearscience.com/articles/2021/08/23/lets_stop_pretending_about_the_COVID-19_vaccines_791050.html (Accessed: January 24, 2022).

32. US Department of Health and Human Sciences, Centers for Disease Control and Prevention (2021). Vaccine Effectiveness. Available at: https://www.cdc.gov/coronavirus/2019-ncov/vaccines/effectiveness.html? (Accessed monthly 2021 and 2021). Also see https://twitter.com/AlbertBourla/status/1377618480527257606.

33. Puranik, A., Lenehan, P.J., Silvert, E., Niesen, M.J., Corchado-Garcia, J., O'Horo, J.C., Virk, A., Swift, M.D., Halamka, J., Badley, A.D. and Venkatakrishnan, A.J., (2021). Comparison of two highly-effective mRNA vaccines for COVID-19 during periods of Alpha and Delta variant prevalence. MedRxiv.

34. Nanduri, S., Pilishvili, T., Derado, G., Soe, M.M., Dollard, P., Wu, H., Li, Q., Bagchi, S., Dubendris, H., Link-Gelles, R. and Jernigan, J.A., (2021). Effectiveness of Pfizer-BioNTech and Moderna vaccines in preventing SARS-CoV-2 infection among nursing home residents before and during widespread circulation of the SARS-CoV-2 B. 1.617. 2 (Delta).variant—National Healthcare Safety Network, March 1–August 1, 2021. Morbidity and Mortality Weekly Report, 70(34), p.1163.

35. Delaney P. (2021). Brief video illustrates dramatic spikes in COVID-19 deaths after jabs in 40 nations , Lifesite , October 23, 2021. Available at: https://www.lifesitenews.com/news/brief-video-illustrates-dramatic-spikes-in-COVID-19-deaths-following-jabs-in-40-nations/ (Accessed: November 25, 2021)

36. Smalley, J. (2021).COVID Deaths Before and After Vaccination Programs. September 26, 2021. Available at: https://www.youtube.com/watch?v=WR-pqrMWu3E (Accessed: November 25, 2021)

37. Smalley, J. (2021).COVID Deaths Before and After Vaccination Programs. September 26, 2021. Available at: https://twitter.com/RealJoelSmalley (Accessed: November 25, 2021)

38. Alexander, P, E.(2021). Here are hundreds of studies proving thatCOVID-19 jabs do harm. February 18, 2022. *Lifesite News*

39. Montagnier, L and Rubenfeld, J.(2022).Omicron Makes Biden's Vaccine Mandates Obsolete. Wall Street Lournal January,9. 2022. Available at: https://www.wsj.com/articles/omicron-makes-bidens-vaccine-mandates-obsolete-covid-healthcare-osha-evidence-supreme-court-11641760009. (Accessed: March, 5 2022)

40. US Department of Health and Human Sciences, Centers for Disease Control and Prevention (2021, 2022). Vaccine Benefits. Available at: https://www.cdc.gov/coronavirus/2019-ncov/vaccines/vaccine-benefits.html (Accessed: Monthly 2021 and 2022).

41. US Department of Health and Human Sciences, Centers for Disease Control and Prevention (2021, 2022). Vaccine Safety. https://www.cdc.gov/coronavirus/2019-ncov/vaccines/safety/safety-of-vaccines.html (Accessed: Monthly 2021 and 2022).

42. Pharmaceutical technology. COVID-19 Vaccination Latest news, daily rates, information and update. March 28, 2022. https://www.pharmaceutical-technology.com/COVID-19-vaccination-tracker/

43. US Department of Health and Human Sciences, Centers for Disease Control

and Prevention (2021).Possible Side Effects After Getting a COVID-19 Vaccine. Available at: https://www.cdc.gov/coronavirus/2019-ncov/vaccines/expect/after. html (Accessed monthly 2021, 2022).

44. Van Aardt, W. (2021). *"The Mandatory COVID-19 Vaccination of School Children: A Bioethical and Human Rights Assessment."* Journal of Vaccines & Vaccination 12, no. 3.

45. Vaccine Adverse Event Reporting System. (2021).Centers for Disease Control and Prevention (CDC).and the U.S. Food and Drug Administration (FDA). Available at: https://vaers.hhs.gov/ (Accessed monthly 2021, 2022).

46. Lazarus, R. (2010).Electronic Support for Public Health–Vaccine Adverse Event Reporting System. Harvard Pilgrim Health Care, Inc. Submitted to: The Agency for Healthcare Research and Quality (AHRQ).U.S. Department of Health and Human Service. Available at: (Accessed: October 20, 2021). https://digital.ahrq. gov/sites/default/files/docs/publication/r18hs017045-lazarus-final-report-2011.pdf

47. Meier, T. (2021). More Die After Vaccination Than From COVID-19 in Taiwan. NTD. October 13, 2021. Available at: https://www.ntd.com/more-die-after-vaccination-than-from-covid-19-in-taiwan_688004.html (Accessed: October, 20, 2021).

48. Delaney P, (2021). Nearly 50k Medicare patients died soon after getting COVID shot: whistleblower, Lifesite News. September 28, 2021. Available at: https://www. lifesitenews.com/news/nearly-50k-medicare-patients-died-soon-after-getting-covid-shot-whistleblower/ (Accessed: October 20, 2021).

49. Macloone David. COVID shots linked to 2 million injuries, 21,766 deaths in Europe, EU reports *Lifesite News.* August 26, 2021. Available at: https://www. lifesitenews.com/news/covid-shots-linked-to-2-million-injuries-21766-deaths-in-europe-eu-reports/ (Accessed: October, 23, 2021).

50. Bingham,J. (2021). WHO database reports over 2 million potential COVID jab injuries in 2021, vast majority in women. Lifesite News. October 7, 2021. Available at: https://www.lifesitenews.com/news/who-database-reports-over-2-million-potential-covid-jab-injuries-in-2021-vast-majority-in-women/ (Accessed: October 23, 2021).

51. UK Office for National Statistics. (2022).Deaths by vaccination status, England, 20 December 2021. Available at: https://www.ons.gov.uk/ peoplepopulationandcommunity/birthsdeathsandmarriages/deaths/datasets/ deathsbyvaccinationstatusengland (Accessed: March 5, 2022).

52. The Expose. (2022). Official Data shows Children are up to 52 times more likely to die following COVID-19 Vaccination than Unvaccinated Children & the ONS is trying to hide it. *The Expose.* January 29, 2022.

53. Informed Choice Australia. (2022). 1000 Peer Reviewed Studies Questioning COVID-19 Vaccine Safety. January 19, 2022. Available at: https://www. informedchoiceaustralia.com/post/1000-peer-reviewed-studies-questioning-COVID-19-vaccine-safety (Accessed: June 15, 2022).

54. McCullough, P. (2022). https://twitter.com/P_McCulloughMD. Also see Gab TV. Dr. Peter McCullough | "I'm telling you, the vaccines are causing large numbers of deaths" | Bradford Hill Tenets of Causality | 2/3/2022 https://sage.gab.com/channel/constitution1a/view/ dr-peter-mccullough-im-telling-624c83ef7fc2doefc8a3eb2d

55. The Expose.(2021). AIDS-related Diseases & Cancers reported to VAERS increased between 1,145% and 33,715% in 2021. Available at: https://expose-news.com/2022/05/13/33715percent-increase-aids-related-disease-usa/ (Accessed: May, 14, 2022).

56. Government of Canada.(2022).COVID-19 daily epidemiology update. March

28. 2022. Available at: https://health-infobase.canada.ca/src/data/covidLive/ Epidemiological-summary-of-COVID-19-cases-in-Canada-Canada.ca.pdf (Accessed: May 14, 2022).

57. The Expose. (2022).Official Government of Canada data is truly terrifying; it suggests the Triple Vaccinated have developed AIDS & are now 5.1x more likely to die of COVID-19 than the Unvaccinated. March 20, 2022.Available at: https:// dailyexpose.uk/2022/03/20/gov-canada-data-triple-vaccinated-have-a-i-d-s/ (Accessed: May 15, 2022).

58. Seneff S, Nigh G, Kyriakopoulos AM, McCullough PA. (2022).Innate immune suppression by SARS-CoV-2 mRNA vaccinations: The role of G-quadruplexes, exosomes, and MicroRNAs. Food Chem Toxicol Jun;164: p 113008.

59. The Expose. (2022).U.S. Government data confirms a 143,233% increase in Cancer cases due to COVID Vaccination. Available at: https://expose-news. com/2022/08/16/us-gov-covid-vaccination-risk-cancer-143233-percent/ (Accessed: August 17, 2022).

60. Mallone, R, W. (2022). When is mRNA not really mRNA? Substack March 28, 2022.

61. Yeadon, M. (2022).The Covid Lies.

62. Lawrence, R.(2021). "Single most qualified mRNA expert speaks about vaccine risks after he says YouTube banned his video", Washington Examiner, June , 24 2021.

63. National Herald. (2020).No need for vaccines, COVID pandemic is over, says Former Vice President of Pfizer. November 27, 2020. Available at: www. nationalheraldindia.com/health/no-need-for-vaccines-the-covid-pandemic-is-over-says-former-vice-president-of-pfizer (Accessed: June 15, 2022).

64. Stecklow, S. (2021).The ex-Pfizer scientist who became an anti-vax hero. Reuters. March 18, 2021.

65. American Institute of Economic Research. Staff. (2020). Open Letter from Medical Doctors and Health Professionals to All Belgian Authorities and All Belgian Media. September 20, 2020. AIER. Available at: www.aier.org/article/ open-letter-from-medical-doctors-and-health-professionals-to-all-belgian-authorities-and-all-belgian-media/. (Accessed: May 16, 2022).

66. Cao, S., Gan, Y., Wang, C. et al. (2020). "Post-lockdown SARS-CoV-2 nucleic acid screening in nearly ten million residents of Wuhan, China". Nat Commun 11, p. 5917.

67. Toledo, A. (2021).Johns Hopkins data PROVES distribution of COVID-19 vaccines led to spikes in infections and deaths. Vaccine Deaths October 14, 2021. Available at: https://www.vaccinedeaths.com/2021-10-14-data-proves-vaccine-distribution-led-to-deaths.html (Accessed: April 10, 2022). also see reference 35.

68. Subramanian, S. V., and Akhil Kumar. (2021)."Increases in COVID-19 are unrelated to levels of vaccination across 68 countries and 2947 counties in the United States." European Journal of Epidemiology 36, no. 12: p. 1237-1240.

69. Agresti, J, D. (2021). "COVID-19 Is Not a "Pandemic of the Unvaccinated"." Just Facts. September 27, 2021. Available at: https://www.justfactsdaily.com/COVID-19-is-not-a-pandemic-of-the-unvaccinated. (Accessed: September 30, 2021).

70. Kindle MD, R., Kozikowski, L.A., DeSouza, L., Ouellette, S. and Thornton-Thompson, S., (2021). Comparative Effectiveness of Moderna, Pfizer-BioNTech, and Janssen (Johnson & Johnson).Vaccines in Preventing COVID-19 Hospitalizations Among Adults Without Immunocompromising Conditions-United States, March-August 2021.

71. Erica Carbajal.(2021). Nearly 60% of hospitalized COVID-19 patients in Israel fully vaccinated, data shows. Hospital Review. August 19, 2021. Available at: https://www.beckershospitalreview.com/public-health/nearly-60-of-hospitalized-COVID-19-patients-in-israel-fully-vaccinated-study-finds.html (Accessed: September 20, 2021).

72. Brosh-Nissimov, T., Orenbuch-Harroch, E., Chowers, M., Elbaz, M., Nesher, L., Stein, M., Maor, Y., Cohen, R., Hussein, K., Weinberger, M. and Zimhony, O., (2021). BNT162b2 vaccine breakthrough: clinical characteristics of 152 fully vaccinated hospitalized COVID-19 patients in Israel. Clinical Microbiology and Infection, 27(11), pp.1652-1657.

73. UK Health Security Agency. (2022). COVID-19 vaccine surveillance report Week 11. March 17. 2022. Available at: https://assets.publishing.service.gov.uk/Government/uploads/system/uploads/attachment_data/file/1061532/Vaccine_surveillance_report_-_week_11.pdf (Accessed: March 15, 2022).

74. The Expose.(2022).Whilst you've been distracted by Russia's Invasion, the UK Gov. released a Report confirming the Fully Vaccinated now account for 9 in every 10 COVID-19 Deaths in England. March 1, 2020. The Expose. Available at: https://dailyexpose.uk/2022/03/01/russia-distraction-uk-gov-revealed-triple-vaccinated-account-9-in-10-covid-deaths/ (Accessed: March 10, 2022).

75. UK Health Security Agency. (2022). COVID-19 vaccine surveillance report Week 8. February 24 2022 Available at: https://assets.publishing.service.gov.uk/Government/uploads/system/uploads/attachment_data/file/1057599/Vaccine_surveillance_report_-_week-8.pdf. (Accessed: August 10, 2022).

76. US Department of Health and Human Sciences, Centers for Disease Control and Prevention (2021).Frequently Asked Questions about COVID-19 Vaccination. Available at: https://www.cdc.gov/coronavirus/2019-ncov/vaccines/faq.html (Accessed monthly 2021, 2022).

77. Alexander, P, E. (2021). 150 Research Studies Affirm Naturally Acquired Immunity to COVID-19: Documented, Linked, and Quoted. Brownstone Institute. October 17, 2021. Available at: https://brownstone.org/articles/79-research-studies-affirm-naturally-acquired-immunity-to-COVID-19-documented-linked-and-quoted/ (Accessed: November 20, 2021).

78. Bendix, A. (2021). A Johns Hopkins professor predicts the US will reach herd immunity by April, but many experts aren't so optimistic. Business Insider. February 20, 2021. Available at: https://www.businessinsider.com/johns-hopkins-professor-herd-immunity-us-april-2021-2 (February 28, 2021).

79. Doshi, P. (2020). "COVID-19: Do many people have pre-existing immunity?" Bmj 370.

80. Asiz, S. 92021). "Significant underestimation": Canada's COVID-19 case count likely much higher than reported. Global News. February 12, 2021. Available at: https://globalnews.ca/news/7635145/real-coronavirus-cases-columbia-university-modelling/ (Accessed: March, 31 2021).

81. Gazit, S., Shlezinger, R., Perez, G., Lotan, R., Peretz, A., Ben-Tov, A., Cohen, D., Muhsen, K., Chodick, G. and Patalon, T., (2021). Comparing SARS-CoV-2 natural immunity to vaccine-induced immunity: reinfections versus breakthrough infections. MedRxiv.

82. Alejo, J.L., Mitchell, J., Chang, A., Chiang, T.P., Massie, A.B., Segev, D.L. and Makary, M.A., (2022). Prevalence and durability of SARS-CoV-2 antibodies among unvaccinated US adults by history of COVID-19. JAMA, 327(11), pp.1085-1087.

83. Texas Lindsey. (2022). "Around the World In Data…All My Covid Videos in One Place…". May 9, 2022. Substack. Available at: https://texaslindsay.substack.com/p/around-the-world-in-data (Accessed: May 10, 2022). Also see: Gilbert G B, (2022). All Cause Mortality in the United States During 2021. American Institute for Economic Research. January 30, 2022.

84. Kuhbandner, C. and Reitzner, M., Excess mortality in Germany 2020-2022.

85. Hill, A, B. (1965). "The Environment and Disease: Association or Causation?".

Proceedings of the Royal Society of Medicine. 58 (5): 295–300.

86. Kulldorff, M *et al.* (2020)."Great Barrington Declaration." Available at: https://gbdeclaration.org/ (Accessed: January 15, 2021).

87. Trialsite Staff. (2021). MSN Showcases the Amazing Uttar Pradesh Turnaround—The Ivermectin-based Home Medicine Kits. *Trialsite News.* September 19, 2021.

88. Alam, M.T., Murshed, R., Gomes, P.F., Masud, Z.M., Saber, S., Chaklader, M.A., Khanam, F., Hossain, M., Momen, A.B.I.M., Yasmin, N. and Alam, R.F., (2020). Ivermectin as pre-exposure prophylaxis for COVID-19 among healthcare providers in a selected tertiary hospital in Dhaka–an observational study. European Journal of Medical and Health Sciences, 2(6).

89. Morgenstern, J., Redondo, J.N., Olavarria, A., Rondon, I., Roca, S., De Leon, A., Canela, J., Tavares, J., Minaya, M., Lopez, O. and Castillo, A., (2021). Ivermectin as a SARS-CoV-2 Pre-Exposure Prophylaxis Method in Healthcare Workers: A Propensity Score-Matched Retrospective Cohort Study. Cureus, 13(8).

90. Morgenstern, J., Redondo, J.N., Olavarria, A., Rondon, I., Roca, S., De Leon, A., Canela, J., Tavares, J., Minaya, M., Lopez, O. and Castillo, A., (2021). Ivermectin as a SARS-CoV-2 Pre-Exposure Prophylaxis Method in Healthcare Workers: A Propensity Score-Matched Retrospective Cohort Study. Cureus, 13(8).

91. McCullough, P.A., Alexander, P.E., Armstrong, R., Arvinte, C., Bain, A.F., Bartlett, R.P., Berkowitz, R.L., Berry, A.C., Borody, T.J., Brewer, J.H. and Brufsky, A.M., 2020. Multifaceted highly targeted sequential multidrug treatment of early ambulatory high-risk SARS-CoV-2 infection (COVID-19). Reviews in cardiovascular medicine, 21(4), p.517.

92. Our World in Data.(2022) Available at: https://ourworldindata.org/vaccination. (Accessed: February 2, 2022).

93. International Covenant on Civil and Political Rights (ICCPR). G.A. Res. 2200A (XXI). (1966). Article 4 and 7.

94. Nuremberg Code (1947).

95. United Nations Office of the High Commissioner of Human Rights. (2020). EMERGENCY MEASURES AND COVID-19: GUIDANCE. April 27, 2020.

96. Abrams, Z. (2021). "Controlling the spread of misinformation." Monit Psychol 52:p. 44.

97. Bago, B., Rand, D. G., & Pennycook, G. (2020). Fake news, fast and slow: Deliberation reduces belief in false (but not true).news headlines. Journal of Experimental Psychology: General, 149(8), p. 1608–1613.

98. Woodworth, E. (2021). "COVID-19 and the Shadowy "Trusted News Initiative." Global Research. Centre for Research on Globalization.

99. BBC. (2020).Trusted News Initiative (TNI).to combat spread of harmful vaccine disinformation and announces major research project. December 10, 2020. Available at: https://www.bbc.com/mediacentre/2020/trusted-news-initiative-vaccine-disinformation (Accessed: March 1, 2022).

100. New York Post. (2021).Facebook admits the truth: 'Fact checks' are really just (lefty).opinion. New York Post. December 14, 2021. also see Gielen,T (2021). Monopoly, Who Owns the World. Available at: https://www.youtube.com/watch?v=ruigMHQE21Q (Accessed: March 15, 2022).

101. Agresti, J,D. (2021). COVID-19 Is Not a "Pandemic of the Unvaccinated". *Just Facts Daily.* September 27, 2021.

102. Bajema, K.L., Dahl, R.M., Evener, S.L., Prill, M.M., Rodriguez-Barradas, M.C., Marconi, V.C., Beenhouwer, D.O., Holodniy, M., Lucero-Obusan, C., Brown, S.T. and Tremarelli, M., (2021). Comparative effectiveness and antibody responses to moderna and Pfizer-BioNTech COVID-19 vaccines among hospitalized veterans—five Veterans Affairs Medical Centers, United States, February 1–September 30,

2021. Morbidity and Mortality Weekly Report, 70(49), p.1700.

103. Chudov, I. (2022). UK will HIDE Vaccinated Cases and Deaths. Substack. March 17, 2022. Available at: https://igorchudov.substack.com/p/uk-will-hide-vaccinated-cases-and?s=r (Accessed: March 18, 2022)

104. Chudov, I. (2022). UK: Pandemic is Over for the Unvaccinated. March3, 2020. Available at: https://igorchudov.substack.com/p/uk-pandemic-is-over-for-the-unvaccinated?s=r (Accessed: March 18, 2022).

105. Tambo, E., Khater, E.I., Chen, J.H., Bergquist, R. and Zhou, X.N., 2015. Nobel prize for the artemisinin and ivermectin discoveries: a great boost towards elimination of the global infectious diseases of poverty. Infectious diseases of poverty, 4(1), pp.1-8.

106. Lawrie, T. (2021). "Ivermectin reduces the risk of death from COVID-19-a rapid review and meta-analysis in support of the recommendation of the Front Line COVID-19 Critical Care Alliance." Published 5 January.

107. Santin, A.D., Scheim, D.E., McCullough, P.A., Yagisawa, M. and Borody, T.J., 2021. Ivermectin: a multifaceted drug of Nobel prize-honoured distinction with indicated efficacy against a new global scourge, COVID-19. New microbes and new infections, 43, p.100924.

108. Blaylock RL. (2021). 'COVID UPDATE: What is the truth?' Surg Neurol Int. 2022 Apr 22; 13: p.167.

109. Reed, G., Hendlin, Y., Desikan, A., MacKinney, T., Berman, E. and Goldman, G.T., (2021). The disinformation playbook: how industry manipulates the science-policy process—and how to restore scientific integrity. Journal of Public Health Policy, pp.1-13.

110. Union of Concerned Scientists. (2017). The Disinformation Playbook. How Business Interests Deceive, Misinform, and Buy Influence at the Expense of Public Health and Safety. Published Oct 10, 2017, Updated May 18, 2018. Available at: https://www.ucsusa.org/resources/disinformation-playbook (Accessed: September 18, 2022)

111. Kori, P. (2022) The Criminal Censorship of Ivermectin's Efficacy by The High-Impact Medical Journals - Part 1. Pierre Kory's Medical Musings. Substack. Available at: https://pierrekory.substack.com/p/the-criminal-censorship-of-ivermectins. (Accessed: September 23, 2022).

112. Wilson. R. (2022). Dr. Pierre Kory: The Editors of High-Impact Journals Had Standing Orders Not to Publish Positive Data on Repurposed Drugs. The Expose. September 17, 2022. Available at: https://expose-news.com/2022/09/17/editors-of-journals-had-standing-orders/. (Accessed: September 18, 2022).

113. Peter, W. 92021). One Hospital Denies Oklahoma Doctor's Story of Ivermectin Overdoses Causing ER Delays for Gunshot Victims. RollingStone. September 5, 2021.

114. Golden, C, D. (2021).Rolling Stone Offers Pathetic 'Update' to Ivermectin Overdose Story They Got Totally Wrong, Bury the 1 Fact That Killed It. Western Journal. September 6, 2021.

115. U.S. FDA on Twitter (2021). "You are not a horse. You are not a cow. Seriously, y'all. Stop it." Available at: https://twitter.com/US_FDA/status/1429050070243192839 (Accessed: January 8 2022).

116. US Food and Drug Administration. (2021). Why You Should Not Use Ivermectin to Treat or Prevent COVID-19. US FDA. Available at: www.fda.gov/consumers/consumer-updates/why-you-should-not-use-ivermectin-treat-or-prevent-COVID-19 (Accessed: December 2, 2021).

117. Caly L, Druce JD, Catton MG, Jans DA, Wagstaff KM. (2020). The FDA-approved drug ivermectin inhibits the replication of SARS-CoV-2 in vitro. Antiviral Res.

Jun;178: p. 104787.
118. Bryant, A., Lawrie, T.A., Dowswell, T., Fordham, E.J., Mitchell, S., Hill, S.R. and Tham, T.C., (2021). Ivermectin for prevention and treatment of COVID-19 infection: a systematic review, meta-analysis, and trial sequential analysis to inform clinical guidelines. American journal of therapeutics, 28(4), p.e434
119. Alam, M.T., Murshed, R., Gomes, P.F., Masud, Z.M., Saber, S., Chaklader, M.A., Khanam, F., Hossain, M., Momen, A.B.I.M., Yasmin, N. and Alam, R.F., (2020). Ivermectin as pre-exposure prophylaxis for COVID-19 among healthcare providers in a selected tertiary hospital in Dhaka–an observational study. European Journal of Medical and Health Sciences, 2(6).
120. Flávio, C., Baldi, F., Lôbo, R.B. and Chamie, J., Ivermectin prophylaxis used for COVID-19 reduces COVID-19 infection and mortality rates: A 220,517-subject, populational-level retrospective citywide.
121. Durden, T. (2021). India's Ivermectin Blackout: The Secret Revealed | *ZeroHedge*. May 7 , 2021. ; also see Sharma, A. (2021).Tale of Two States: Kerala, Uttar Pradesh Paint A Contrasting Picture of Covid-19.August 25, 2021.*News18.com*.
122. Tanioka, H., Tanioka, S. and Kaga, K., 2021. Why COVID-19 is not so spread in Africa: How does Ivermectin affect it?. medRxiv.
123. I-MASK+ Prophylaxis & Early Outpatient Treatment Protocol for COVID-19 [v18 – updated October 12, 2021] Available at: covid19criticalcare.com. (Accessed: January, 20, 2022).
124. Fahlbusch, E, and Bromiley, G W. (2003). *The Encyclopedia of Christianity*, Volume 3. Grand Rapids, Michigan: Eerdmans. p. 362.
125. Maanen, H van (2002). *Encyclopedie van misvattingen*, Boom, p. 68.
126. Parker, G. (1984). The Thirty Years' War (1997 Ed.). Routledge.
127. LærdómsöEggertsdóttir, M. (2006). "From Reformation to Enlightenment." A history of Icelandic literature 5: p174-250.
128. Flannelly, K.J., (2017). The Reformation and The Enlightenment. In Religious Beliefs, Evolutionary Psychiatry, and Mental Health in America (pp. 19-27). Springer, Cham.
129. Statcounter. (2022). Search Engine Market Share Worldwide. Available at: https://gs.statcounter.com/search-engine-market-share (Accessed: September 1, 2022).
130. Jessica L. (2013). No. 1 Position in Google Gets 33% of Search Traffic [Study]. Search Engine Watch.
131. Olliaro, P., Torreele, E. and Vaillant, M., (2021). COVID-19 vaccine efficacy and effectiveness—the elephant (not).in the room. The Lancet Microbe, 2(7), p.279-e280.
132. Lewis, C.S., (1953). The humanitarian theory of punishment. Res Judicatae, 6, p.224.
133. Kayyem, J. (2021).Vaccine Refusers Don't Get to Dictate Terms Anymore. *The Atlantic*.
134. Watson, I., (2004). A Guide to the Methodologies of Homeopathy. *Cutting Edge Publications*.

Chapter 5

1.   van Aardt W. (2021). "Limiting human rights during Covid-19- is it only legitimate if it is proportional" *De Rebus SA Attorneys Journal*. The Law Society of South Africa. May 2021. Pp 14 -16.
2.   van Aardt W. (2021). "COVID-19 School Closures and the Principles of Proportionality and Balancing. *J Infect Dis Ther* 9: S3 :002

3. Willem van Aardt. (2004). *State Responsibility for Human Rights Abuses Committed by Non-state Actors under the Constitution*, PhD diss., North-West University 360-395.

4. International Covenant on Civil Political Rights (ICCPR), (1966).G.A. Res. 2200A (XXI).Art.4.

5. Newsrescue. (2021). Nigeria's Edo State Announces No More Church, Mosque, Parties Without Vaccine Passport. Available at: https://newsrescue.com/breaking-nigerias-edo-state-announces-no-more-church-mosque-parties-without-vaccine-passport-video/ (Accessed; September 10, 2021). Also see: Evans, Z. (2021).Supreme Court Lifts California Restrictions on Private Religious Gatherings. Yahoo News. Available at: https://news.yahoo.com/supreme-court-lifts-california-restrictions-125544852.html (Accessed: April 15, 2021).

6. International Commission of Jurists. (1984). Siracusa Principles on the Limitation and Derogation Provisions in the International Covenant on Civil and Political Rights. Available at https://www.icj.org/wp-content/uploads/1984/07/Siracusa-principles-ICCPR-legal-submission-1985-eng.pdf. (Accessed: April 17, 2021).

7. Lalich, R. (1985). The Paris Minimum Standards of Human Rights Norms in a State of Emergency. American Journal of International Law, 79(4), 1072-1081.

8. CCPR General Comment No. 29: Article 4: Derogations during a State of Emergency* Adopted at the Seventy-second Session of the Human Rights Committee, on 31 August 2001 CCPR/C/21/Rev.1/Add.11, General Comment No. 29.

9. UN. Human Rights Committee. (2020) Statement on derogations from the Covenant in connection with the COVID-19 pandemic. United Nations. CCPR/C/128/2. Distr.: General 30 April 2020 Original: English.

10. Lenaerts, K. (2019). "Limits on Limitations: The Essence of Fundamental Rights in the EU". German Law Journal, 20(6), p. 779-793.

11. Thielbörger, P. (2019). "The Essence" of International Human Rights." German Law Journal 20, no. 6 (2019): p. 924-939.

12. Charter of Fundamental Rights of the European Union, Oct. 26, 2012, 2012 O.J. (C 326).44.

13. von BogdandyS et al., (2012). "Reverse Solange—Protecting the Essence of Fundamental Rights Against EU Member States", 49 common mkt. l. rev. 489, p. 510 (noting that Article 2 of the Treaty on European Union ("TEU"). aims at: safeguarding the essence of fundamental rights).

14. ECJ, Case C-362/14, Schrems v. Data Protection Commissioner, ECLI:EU:C:2015:650, Judgment of 8 October 2015.

15. ECJ, Joined Cases 293 & 594/12, Digital Rights Ireland Ltd. V. Minister for Commc'ns, ECLI:EU:C:2014:238, Judgment of 8 Apr. 2014; ECJ, Joined Cases 2013 & 698/15,

16. Tele2 Sverige AB v. Post-och telestyrelsen and Others, ECLI:EU:C:2016:970, Judgment of 21 Dec. 2016.

17. Sky Österreich, Case C-283/11 at: paras. 48–50; Digital Rights Ireland, Joined Cases 293 & 594/12 at: paras. 39–45; ECJ, Case C-129/14 PPU, Spasic, ECLI:EU:C:2014:586, Judgment of 27 May 2014, paras. 56–60; Léger, Case C-528/13 at: paras. 51–55; Delvigne, Case C-650/13 at: paras. 46–49; ECJ, Case C-157/14, Société Neptune Dist. V. Ministre de l'Économie et des Finances, ECLI:EU:C:2015:823, Judgment of 17 Dec. 2015, paras. 68–76; N., Case C-601/15 PPU at: paras. 50–54; ECJ, Case C-477/14, Pillbox 38 v. Sec'y of State for Health, ECLI:EU:C:2016:324, Judgment of 4 May 2016, paras. 160–62; ECJ, Case C-547/14, Philip Morris Brands and Others v. Sec'y of State for Health, ECLI:EU:C:2016:325, Judgment of 4 May 2016, paras. 149–53; ECJ, Joined Cases

439 & 488/14, SC Star Storage SA and Others v. Institutul Naţional de Cercetare-Dezvoltare în Informatică (ICI).and Others, ECLI:EU:C:2016:688, paras. 49–51; ECJ, Case C-201/15, AGET Iraklis v. Y pourgos Ergasias, Koinonikis Asfalisis kai Koinonikis Allilengyis, ECLI:EU:C:2016:972, Judgment of 21 Dec. 2016, paras. 82– 89; Tele2 Sverige AB, Joined Cases 203 & 698/15 at: paras. 101–07; ECJ, Case C-258/14, Florescu and Others v. Casa Judeţeană de Pensii Sibiu and Others, ECLI:EU:2017:448, Judgment of 13 June 2017, paras. 53– 57; Fries, Case C-190/16 at: paras. 36–39; K., Case C-18/16 at: paras. 34–37; ECJ, Case C-73/16, Puškár v Finančné riaditeľstvo Slovenskej republiky and Kriminálny úrad finančnej správy, ECLI:EU:C:2017:725, Judgment of 27 Sept. 2017, paras. 62–65; ECJ, Case C-380/16, Comm'n v. Germany, ECLI:EU:C:2018:76, Judgment of 8 Feb. 2018, paras. 65–71; Menci, Case C-524/15 at: paras 43–46; Garlsson Real Estate, Case C-537/16 at: paras. 45–48.

18. UN Human Rights Committee (HRC), (2007)Yeo-Bum Yoon and Myung-Jin Choi v. Republic of Korea, UN Doc. CCPR/C/88/D/1321-1322/2004 (Jan. 23, 2007)

19. UN Commission on Human Rights. (1984).The Siracusa Principles on the Limitation and Derogation Provisions in the International Covenant on Civil and Political Rights, para. 58, U.N. Doc. E/CN.4/1985/4 (Sept. 28, 1984).

20. UN Human Rights Committee (HRC), General comment no. 31, The nature of the general legal obligation imposed on States Parties to the Covenant, 26 May 2004, CCPR/C/21/Rev.1/Add.13, Also see United Nations. Office of the High Commissioner for Human Rights, and International Bar Association. Human Rights in The Administration Of Justice: A Manual On Human Rights For Judges, Presecutors And Lawyers. No. 9. New York and Geneva: United Nations, 2003.

21. UN Human Rights Committee (HRC), CCPR General Comment No. 27, Freedom of Movement, para. 13, U.N. Doc. CCPR/C/21/Rev.1/Add.9 (Nov. 2, 1999).

22. Jackson, V C., Tushnet, M. (2017).Proportionality: New frontiers, new challenges. Cambridge University Press. p 256.

23. Barak A. (2010). "Proportionality and principled balancing". 4(1).Law and Ethics of Human Rights 1;

24. Sweet, A,S; Mathews, J. (2008)."Proportionality Balancing and Global Constitutionalism," Colum. J. Transnat'l L.: 47 72.

25. Urbina, F J. (2012). "A Critique of Proportionality," Am. J. Juris. 57: 4-5.

26. de Jaegere. (2019). "Proportionality Analysis, In Judicial Review and Strategic Behaviour: An Empirical Case Law Analysis of the Belgian Constitutional Court": p. 283-326.

27. Cianciardo, J. (2010). "The Principle of Proportionality: The Challenges of Human Rights," J. Civ. L. Stud. 3: p. 177 -190.

28. Luka Anđelković. (2017). "The Elements of Proportionality as a Principle of Human Rights Limitations," FACTA UNIVERSITATIS-Law and Politics 15, 3: p. 235-244.

29. Criddle, E J., Fox-Decent, E. (2016).Fiduciaries of humanity: how international law constitutes authority. Oxford University Press.

30. Bloomberg. (2021). More Than 8.23 billion Shots Given: Covid-19 Tracker Updated: December 7, 2021, 5:35 AM CST. Available at: https://www.bloomberg.com/graphics/covid-vaccine-tracker-global-distribution/ (Accessed: December 8, 2021).

31. Myhre, J, Sifris, D MD. (2020).Sterilizing Immunity and COVID-19 Vaccines. Verywellhealth. December 24, 2020. Available at: https://www.verywellhealth.com/covid-19-vaccines-and-sterilizing-immunity-5092148 (Accessed: January 7, 2022).

32. Van Aardt, W. (2021). "The Mandatory COVID-19 Vaccination of School Children: A Bioethical and Human Rights Assessment." Journal of Vaccines &

Vaccination 12, no. 3.

33. Barak, A. (2012).*Proportionality Stricto Sensu (Balancing), In Proportionality: Constitutional Rights and Their Limitations.* p. 340-370.

34. van Aardt, W. (2020). "Are the stringent COVID-19 lockdown regulations unconstitutional and unjustifiable?" *De Rebus SA Attorneys Journal.* The Law Society of South Africa. September 2020. Pp 26 – 28.

35. Yu, W, Keralis, J. (2020).Controlling COVID-19: The Folly of International Travel Restrictions, Viewpoint, *Health and Human Rights Journal.*

36. Martin Kulldorff et al. (2020).The Great Barrington Declaration

37. Alexander, P. E. (2021).150 Research Studies Affirm Naturally Acquired Immunity to Covid-19: Documented, Linked, and Quoted. Brownstone Institute. October 17, 2021. Available at: https://brownstone.org/articles/79-research-studies-affirm-naturally-acquired-immunity-to-covid-19-documented-linked-and-quoted/ (Accessed: November 8, 2021).

38. Wang, L., Zhou, T., Zhang, Y., Yang, E.S., Schramm, C.A., Shi, W., Pegu, A., Oloniniyi, O.K., Henry, A.R., Darko, S. and Narpala, S.R., (2021). Ultrapotent antibodies against diverse and highly transmissible SARS-CoV-2 variants. *Science*, 373(6556), p.eabh1766.

39. Trialsite Staff. (2021). MSN Showcases the Amazing Uttar Pradesh Turnaround— The Ivermectin-based Home Medicine Kits. *Trialsite News.* September 9, 2021. Available at: www.trialsitenews.com/msn-showcases-the-amazing-uttar-pradesh-turnaround-the-ivermectin-based-home-medicine-kits (Accessed: November 8, 2021).

40. Alam, M.T., Murshed, R., Gomes, P.F., Masud, Z.M., Saber, S., Chaklader, M.A., Khanam, F., Hossain, M., Momen, A.B.I.M., Yasmin, N. and Alam, R.F., (2020). Ivermectin as pre-exposure prophylaxis for COVID-19 among healthcare providers in a selected tertiary hospital in Dhaka–an observational study. *European Journal of Medical and Health Sciences*, 2(6).

41. Morgenstern, J., Redondo, J.N., Olavarria, A., Rondon, I., Roca, S., De Leon, A., Canela, J., Tavares, J., Minaya, M., Lopez, O. and Castillo, A., (2021). Ivermectin as a SARS-CoV-2 Pre-Exposure Prophylaxis Method in Healthcare Workers: A Propensity Score-Matched Retrospective Cohort Study. *Cureus*, 13(8).

42. Santin, A.D., Scheim, D.E., McCullough, P.A., Yagisawa, M. and Borody, T.J., 2021. Ivermectin: a multifaceted drug of Nobel prize-honoured distinction with indicated efficacy against a new global scourge, COVID-19. *New microbes and new infections*, 43, p.100924.

43. Government Offices of Sweden. (2020). Folkhalsomyndigheten Public Health Agency of Sweden. FAQ about COVID-19. Available at: https://www.folkhalsomyndigheten.se/the-public-health-agency-of-sweden/communicable-disease-control/covid-19/covid-19-faq/ (Accessed: November, 7 2020).

44. World Health Organization (WHO). (2020). WHO Coronavirus Disease (COVID-19).Dashboard. Available at: https://covid19.who.int/ (Accessed: Monthly 2020, 2021, 2022).

45. Johns Hopkins University, Mortality Analysis. (2021). Available at: https://coronavirus.jhu.edu/data/mortality (Accessed: Monthly 2020, 2021, 2022)

46. US Department of Health and Human Sciences, Centers for Disease Control and Prevention. (2020). Demographic Trends of COVID-19 Cases and Deaths in the US Reported to CDC. https://www.cdc.gov/coronavirus/2019-ncov/covid-data/ (Accessed: Monthly 2020, 2021, 2022)

47. Parildar, U, Perara, R, Oke, J. (2021). Excess Mortality across Countries in 2020. *The Centre for Evidence-Based Medicine.* March 3, 2021. Available at: https://www.cebm.net/covid-19/excess-mortality-across-countries-in-2020/ (Accessed: June, 5

2021).

48. Kandasamy, A., Herby, J., Jonung, L. and Hanke, S.H., 2021. "A Literature Review and Meta-Analysis of the Effects of Lockdowns on COVID-19 Mortality." Studies in Applied Economics.

49. Lemasurier, J Cf. (1979). Expropriation:"Bilan-cout-avantages" et necessite publique, LA REVUE ADMINISTRATIVE, septembre-octobre 1979, at: 502 (Fr.).

50. Olliaro, P., Torreele, E. and Vaillant, M. (2021). COVID-19 vaccine efficacy and effectiveness—the elephant (not).in the room. *The Lancet Microbe*, 2(7), pp.e279-e280.

51. Horowitz, D. (2021). Dr. McCullough testifies in court that CMS data potentially signal much higher vaccine death toll. October 13 2021. BlazeMedia. Available at: https://www.theblaze.com/op-ed/horowitz-dr-mccullough-testifies-in-court-that-cms-data-potentially-signal-much-higher-vaccine-death-toll (Accessed: October 13, 2021).

52. Renz, T. (2021). Whistleblower Testimony: 45,000 Deaths Caused by the COVID-19 Vaccines. July. 17, 2021. Available at: https://pandemictimeline. com/2021/07/whistleblower-testimony-45000-deaths-caused-by-the-covid-19-vaccines/ (Accessed: October 13, 2021).

53. Kostoff, R. N., Calina, D., Kanduc, D., Briggs, M. B., Vlachoyiannopoulos, P., Svistunov, A. A., & Tsatsakis, A. (2021). Why are we vaccinating children against COVID-19?. *Toxicology reports*, 8, 1665–1684.

54. Bingham,J. (2021). WHO database reports over 2 million potential COVID jab injuries in 2021, vast majority in women. *Lifesitenews*. October 7, 2021. Available at: https://www.lifesitenews.com/news/who-database-reports-over-2-million-potential-covid-jab-injuries-in-2021-vast-majority-in-women/ (Accessed: October 13, 2021).

55. UN News (2021). "Human rights must be maintained in beating back the COVID-19 pandemic, 'without exception' ". UN experts. Available at: https://news.un.org. (Accessed: April 4, 2021)

Chapter 6

1. International Covenant on Civil Political Rights (ICCPR), (1966).G.A. Res. 2200A (XXI).

2. Friedrich, C J. (1941). *Constitutional Government and democracy; theory and practice in Europe and America.*

3. Agamben, G. (2008). State of exception." In State of Exception. University of Chicago Press, 2008.

4. Schmitt, C. (1922). *Politische theologie: vier kapitel zur lehre von der souveränität.* Vol. 1. Duncker & Humblot.

5. Schmitt, C.(1978*). Die Diktatur. Duncker et Humblot.*

6. Humphreys S. (2006). "Legalizing Lawlessness: On Giorgio Agamben's State of Exception." *European Journal of International Law*, Volume 17, Issue 3, 1 June 2006, p. 677–687.

7. Hickman, T.R., (2005). Between human rights and the rule of law: Indefinite detention and the derogation model of constitutionalism. *The Modern Law Review*, 68(4), pp.655-668

8. Criddle, E J. (2014). "Protecting human rights during emergencies: delegation, derogation, and deference." *Netherland's yearbook of international law* 45 (2014): p. 197-220.

9. UN Human Rights Committee (HRC). (1981). CCPR General Comment No. 5: Article 4 (Derogations), 31 July 1981.

10. UN Human Rights Committee (HRC). (2001). CCPR General Comment No. 29: Article 4: Derogations during a State of Emergency, 31 August 2001, CCPR/C/21/Rev.1/Add.11.
11. United Nations Office of the High Commissioner of Human Rights. (2020). Emergency Measures and Covid-19 Guidance. Office of the High Commissioner of Human Rights. April 27, 2020, Available at: https://www.ohchr.org/Documents/Events/EmergencyMeasures_COVID19.pdf (Accessed: May 12, 2021).
12. Brannigan and McBride v. United Kingdom, ECtHR, Nos. 14553/89, 14554/89, 25 May 1993, para 59 (citing Ireland v. United Kingdom and Klass and Others v. Germany). Also see Handyside v. United Kingdom, ECtHR, No. 5493/72, 7 December 1976, at: 22.
13. The Registry of European Court of Human Rights, Guide on Article 15 of the European Convention on Human Rights Derogation in time of emergency. 7. The European Court of Human Rights. April 30 2021. Available at: https://www.echr.coe.int/Documents/Guide_Art_15_ENG.pdf. (Accessed: June, 15, 2021). Specifically see references to Ireland v UK, Series A No. 25 (1970); Brannigan and McBride v. the United Kingdom, 1993, § 43; Mehmet Hasan Altan v. Turkey, 2018, § 91 and Şahin Alpay v. Turkey, 2018.
14. Van Aardt, W. (2004). *State responsibility for human rights abuses committed by non-State actors under the constitution.* Doctoral dissertation, North-West University. p 368 Also see *S v Makwanyane and Another* [1995] ZACC 3 at 151, 1995 (3) S.A. 391
15. Maclean, A. R. (2000). "The Human Rights Act 1998 and the individual's right to treatment." Medical law international 4, no. 3-4: p. 245-276.
16. Murray v. United Kingdom, ECtHR, 14310/88, 28 October 1994, para 38.
17. Brannigan and McBride v. United Kingdom, ECtHR , Nos. 14553/89, 14554/89, 25 May 1993,
18. Aksoy v. Turkey, ECtHR, No. 21987/93, 18 December 1996.
19. Lawless v. Ireland (no. 3), 1 July 1961, Series A no. 3.
20. Ireland v. the United Kingdom, 18 January 1978, Series A no. 25.
21. Denmark, Norway, Sweden and the Netherlands v. Greece (the "Greek case"), nos. 3321/67 and 3 others, Commission report of 5 November 1969, Yearbook 12.
22. Burchill, R. (2005). "When does an emergency threaten the life of the nation?: Derogations from human rights obligations and the war on international terrorism." *Yearbook of New Zealand Jurisprudence* 8, no. 1: 99-118.
23. Lillich, R B. (1985). "The Paris minimum standards of human rights norms in a State of emergency." *American Journal of International Law* 79, no. 4 (1985): 1072-1081
24. Paris Minimum Standards of Human Rights Norms in a State of Emergency paragraph 1 (a).and (b).
25. International Commission of Jurists. (1984). Siracusa Principles on the Limitation and Derogation Provisions in the International Covenant on Civil and Political Rights.
26. Siracusa Principles, para. 39.
27. Siracusa Principles, para. 61.
28. Siracusa Principles, para. 62.
29. Siracusa Principles, para. 63.
30. Siracusa Principles, para. 64.
31. Bustin, S., Coward, A., Sadler, G., Teare, L. and Nolan, T., (2020). CoV2-ID, a MIQE-compliant sub-20-min 5-plex RT-PCR assay targeting SARS-CoV-2 for the diagnosis of COVID-19. *Scientific reports,* 10(1), pp.1-13.
32. Ferguson, N., Laydon, D., Nedjati Gilani, G., Imai, N., Ainslie, K., Baguelin, M.,

Bhatia, S., Boonyasiri, A., Cucunuba Perez, Z.U.L.M.A., Cuomo-Dannenburg, G. and Dighe, A., (2020). Report 9: Impact of non-pharmaceutical interventions (NPIs) to reduce COVID19 mortality and healthcare demand.

33. Magness, P W. (2020). Imperial College Model Applied to Sweden Yields Preposterous Results. *American Institute of Economic Research*. April 30, 2020.

34. Ioannidis, J PA, Cripps, S and Martin A. Tanner. (2020). "Forecasting for COVID-19 has failed." *International journal of forecasting.*

35. Staff Writer. (2020).COVID-19 in South Africa – Predictions versus reality. MyBroadBand. July, 9, 2020. Available at: https://mybroadband.co.za/news/trending/359207-covid-19-in-south-africa-predictions-versus-reality.html (Accessed: July 12, 2020)

36. Miltimore, J.(2020).Modelers Were 'Astronomically Wrong' in COVID-19 Predictions, Says Leading Epidemiologist—and the World Is Paying the Price. *FEE Stories*. July 2 2020. Available at: https://fee.org/articles/modelers-were-astronomically-wrong-in-covid-19-predictions-says-leading-epidemiologist-and-the-world-is-paying-the-price/ (Accessed: July 12, 2020).

37. Curl, J. (2020). "Experts Finally Declare Imperial College Coronavirus Model That Predicted 2.2M Dead In U.S. 'Totally Unreliable'". May, 17, 2020. *The Daily Wire*. Available at: https://www.dailywire.com/news/experts-finally-declare-imperial-college-coronavirus-model-that-predicted-2-2m-dead-in-u-s-totally-unreliable (Accessed: July 12, 2022).

38. Jewell, N.P., Lewnard, J.A. and Jewell, B.L., 2020. Caution warranted: using the Institute for Health Metrics and Evaluation model for predicting the course of the COVID-19 pandemic. *Annals of internal medicine*, 173(3), pp.226-227.

39. US Department of Health and Human Sciences, Centers for Disease Control and Prevention. (2020). Demographic Trends of COVID-19 Cases and Deaths in the US Reported to CDC. https://www.cdc.gov/coronavirus/2019-ncov/covid-data/ (Accessed: Monthly 2020, 2021, 2022)

40. World Health Organization (WHO). (2022).*WHO Coronavirus Disease (COVID-19).Dashboard.* Available at: https://covid19.who.int/region/amro/country/us (Accessed monthly 2020, 2021, 2022).

41. United Kingdom Office For National Statistics. Population estimates. (2022). https://www.ons.gov.uk/peoplepopulationandcommunity/populationandmigration/populationestimates/

42. World Health Organization (WHO). (2022).*WHO Coronavirus Disease (COVID-19).Dashboard*. South-Africa. Available at: https://covid19.who.int/region/afro/country/za

43. World Health Organization (WHO). (2022).*WHO Coronavirus Disease (COVID-19).Dashboard.Sweden*. Available at: https://covid19.who.int/region/euro/country/se

44. Knightly, K. (2021).*30 facts you NEED to know: Your Covid Cribsheet*. September 22, 2021. Available at: https://off-guardian.org/2021/09/22/30-facts-you-need-to-know-your-covid-cribsheet/ (Accessed: October 18, 2021).

45. Shyu, D. et al. (2020).Laboratory tests for COVID-19: A review of peer-reviewed publications and implications for clinical use. *Missouri Med*. p. 117, 184–195.

46. Li Y, Yao L, Li J, Chen L, Song Y, Cai Z, Yang C. Stability issues of RT-PCR testing of SARS-CoV-2 for hospitalized patients clinically diagnosed with COVID-19. *J Med Virol*. (2020).Jul;92(7):p. 903-908.

47. Patrick, D.M., Petric, M., Skowronski, D.M., Guasparini, R., Booth, T.F., Krajden, M., McGeer, P., Bastien, N., Gustafson, L., Dubord, J. and MacDonald, D. (2006). An outbreak of human coronavirus OC43 infection and serological cross-reactivity with SARS coronavirus. *Canadian Journal of Infectious Diseases and*

Medical Microbiology, 17(6), pp.330-336.

48. Kolata, G. (2007).Faith in Quick Test Leads to Epidemic That Wasn't. January, *New York Times*. January, 22, 2007. Available at: https://www.nytimes.com/2007/01/22/health/22whoop.html (Accessed: October 17, 2021).

49. Reuters Staff. President queries Tanzania coronavirus kits after goat test. Reuters. May 3, 2020. Available at: https://www.reuters.com/article/us-health-coronavirus-tanzania-idUSKBN22F0KF (Accessed: October 17, 2021).

50. Australian Government Department of Health. (2020). COVID-19 Testing in Australia- Information for Health Professionals. Australian Government Department of Health. August 3, 2020. p 44.

51. TRL JUDGMENTS JUDGMENT OF THE LISBON COURT OF APPEAL Process: 1783/20.7T8PDL.L1-3 Reporter: MARGARIDA RAMOS DE ALMEIDA Descriptors: HABEAS CORPUS INTEREST IN ACT: SARS-COV-2, RT-PCR TESTS DEPRIVATION OF FREEDOM ILLEGAL DETENTION Agreement Date: 11/11/2020. Available at: https://indianbarassociation.in/wp-content/uploads/2021/10/MARGARIDA-RAMOS-DE-ALMEIDA-11-NOV-2020-RT-PCR-TEST-1-04.pdf (Accessed: February 17, 2022).

52. Knightly, K. (2020). WHO (finally).admits PCR tests create false positives. *Off Guardian*. December 18, 2020. Available at: https://off-guardian.org/2020/12/18/who-finally-admits-pcr-tests-create-false-positives/ (Accessed: February 17, 2022).

53. Rita Jaafar et al, (2021). "Correlation Between 3790 Quantitative Polymerase Chain Reaction–Positives Samples and Positive Cell Cultures, Including 1941 Severe Acute Respiratory Syndrome Coronavirus 2 Isolates," *Clinical Infectious Diseases*, Vol. 72, Issue 11, 1 June 2021, p92.

54. Swiss Policy Research. (2021). "The Trouble with PCR Tests," updated June 2021 Available at: https://swprs.org/the-trouble-with-pcr-tests (Accessed: February 17, 2022).

55. Trabert, D. CDC: maximum 28 CT for post-vaccine COVID PCR tests. The Sentinel. May 3, 2021. https://sentinelksmo.org/cdc-maximum-28-ct-for-post-vaccine-covid-pcr-tests/

56. NIH. (2021). "Therapeutic Management of Nonhospitalized Adults with COVID-19, last updated July 8, 2021" Available at: https://www.covid19treatmentguidelines.nih.gov/management/clinical-management/nonhospitalized-adults–therapeutic-management/ (Accessed: February 18, 2022)

57. Macfarlane, J. (2022).Did flawed PCR tests convince us Covid was worse than it really was? Britain's entire response was based on results - but one scientist says they should have been axed a year ago. *DailyMail*. March,12 2022. Available at: https://www.dailymail.co.uk/health/article-10606107/Did-flawed-tests-convince-Covid-worse-really-was.html (Accessed: April 10, 2022)

58. Corman VM, Landt O, Kaiser M, Molenkamp R, Meijer A, Chu DK, Bleicker T, Brünink S, Schneider J, Schmidt ML, Mulders DG, Haagmans BL, van der Veer B, van den Brink S, Wijsman L, Goderski G, Romette JL, Ellis J, Zambon M, Peiris M, Goossens H, Reusken C, Koopmans MP, Drosten C. (2020).Detection of 2019 novel coronavirus (2019-nCoV).by real-time RT-PCR. Euro Surveill. 2020 Jan;25(3): p. 2000045.

59. Borger et al. (2020). Cormen-Drosten review report, curated by an international consortium of scientist in life sciences (ICSLS). "Retraction request letter to Eurosurveillance editorial board." Available at: https://cormandrostenreview.com/retraction-request-letter-to-eurosurveillance-editorial-board/. (Accessed: 24 September 2022).

60. Woodworth, E. (2021). "COVID-19 and the Shadowy "Trusted News Initiative"." *Global Research*.

61. Mcnulty, I. (2021).PCR Tests and the Rise of Disease Panic. *Brownstone Institute.* December 2, 2021. Available at: https://brownstone.org/articles/pcr-tests-and-the-rise-of-disease-panic (Accessed: September 24, 2022).

62. Alex R, (2021). "Bill Gates and George Soros buy out UK Covid test company Mologic," *The Times,* 20 July 2021. Available at: https://www.thetimes.co.uk/article/bill-gates-andgeorge-soros-buy-out-uk-covid-test-company-mologic-70c3r736b (Accessed: September 24, 2022).

63. Breggin, P R, Breggin G R McCullough, P , Vliet, E L. (2021). *COVID-19 and the Global Predators.* Lake Edge Press.

64. Heneghan, C, Oke, J. (2020). "Public Health England Has Changed Its Definition of Deaths: Here's What It Means." *Centre for Evidence-Based Medicine:* 12.

65. Knightly, K. (2020).Covid19 Death Figures "A Substantial Over-Estimate" *Off Guardian.* April 5, 2020. Available at: https://off-guardian.org/2020/04/05/covid19-death-figures-a-substantial-over-estimate/ (Accessed: September 7, 2022).

66. US Department of Health and Human Sciences, Centers for Disease Control and Prevention. (2020).Guidance for Certifying Deaths Due to Coronavirus Disease 2019 (COVID–19).Available at: https://www.cdc.gov/nchs/data/nvss/vsrg/vsrg03-508.pdf. (Accessed: Monthly 2020, 2021, 2022). Also see Anderson, R.N., Warner, M., Anne, L. and Ahmad, F., 2020. Guidance for certifying deaths due to coronavirus disease 2019 (COVID-19).

67. UK Office for National Statistics. (2022).COVID-19 deaths and autopsies Feb 2020 to Dec 2021. United Kingdom Office for National Statistics. January 17, 2022. Available at: https://www.ons.gov.uk/aboutus/transparencyandgovernance/freedomofinformationfoi/covid19deathsandautopsiesfeb2020todec2021 (Accessed: February 18, 2022).

68. Ealy, H., McEvoy, M., Chong, D., Nowicki, J., Sava, M., Gupta, S., White, D., Jordan, J., Simon, D. and Anderson, P., (2020). COVID-19 Data Collection, Comorbidity & Federal Law: A Historical Retrospective. ETHICS, 2, pp.4-22.

69. Ioannidis, J.P., Axfors, C. and Contopoulos-Ioannidis, D.G., 2020. Population-level COVID-19 mortality risk for non-elderly individuals overall and for non-elderly individuals without underlying diseases in pandemic epicenters. Environmental research, 188, p.109890.

70. Ioannidis, J.P., 2021. Reconciling estimates of global spread and infection fatality rates of COVID-19: an overview of systematic evaluations. European journal of clinical investigation, 51(5), p.e13554.

71. Johns Hopkins University, Mortality Analysis. (2021). Available at: https://coronavirus.jhu.edu/data/mortality (Accessed: November 8, 2020 and February 8, 2022).

72. US Department of Health and Human Sciences, Centers for Disease Control and Prevention. (2020).COVID-19 Mortality Overview, Provisional Death Counts for Coronavirus Disease 2019 (COVID-19). Available at: https://www.cdc.gov/nchs/covid19/mortality-overview.htm (Accessed: Monthly 2020, 2021, 2022).

73. Stavrianakis, A. and Tessier, L.A., (2020). Go Suppress Yourself: A Chronicle. *Somatosphère: Science, Medicine, and Anthropology.*

74. Mulraney, F. (2020).Trump salutes the US Navy Comfort as the hospital ship begins its journey to New York where Gov. Cuomo says he will welcome it with 'open arms' despite a rift with the president over a State-wide quarantine. *Daily Mail.* March 28,2020. Available at: https://www.dailymail.co.uk/news/article-8163625/Trump-salutes-Navy-Comfort-hospital-ship-begins-journey-New-York.html (Accessed: September 14, 2021).

75. Lopez, C T. US department of Defence. Corps of Engineers Converts NYC's Javits

Center Into Hospital, April, 1, 2020. Available at: https://www.defense.gov/News/News-Stories/Article/Article/2133514/corps-of-engineers-converts-nycs-javits-center-into-hospital/ (Accessed: September 2, 2021).

76. BBC News. Covid-19: Nightingale hospitals to close from April. *BBC*. March 8, 2021. Available at: https://www.bbc.com/news/health-56327214; (Accessed: September 2, 2021).

77. Associated Press. Majority of field hospitals will be shut down after going unused. *New York Post*. April 30, 2020. Available at: https://nypost.com/2020/04/30/many-field-hospitals-went-largely-unused-will-be-shut-down/ (Accessed: September 2, 2021).

78. Sisak, M R. (2020). Many field hospitals went largely unused, will be shut down. *AP News*. April, 29, 2020. Available at: https://apnews.com/article/virus-outbreak-ap-top-news-international-news-weekend-reads-manhattan-e593ba57f37206b495521503d7e5e4c5 (Accessed: September 2, 2021).

79. Woods, A. (2020). 94% of Americans who died from COVID-19 had contributing conditions: CDC. *New York Post*. August 31, 2020. Available at: https://nypost.com/2020/08/31/94-of-americans-who-died-from-covid-19-had-contributing-conditions/ (Accessed: September 2, 2021).

80. Spiegelhalter, D. (2020).How much 'normal' risk does Covid represent? Winton Centre. May 21, 2020. Available at: https://medium.com/wintoncentre/how-much-normal-risk-does-covid-represent-4539118e1196 (Accessed: September 28, 2021).

81. Vasishtha, G., Mohanty, S.K., Mishra, U.S., Dubey, M. and Sahoo, U., 2021. Impact of COVID-19 infection on life expectancy, premature mortality, and DALY in Maharashtra, India. *BMC infectious diseases*, 21(1), pp.1-11.

82. C19Protocols (2021). Reducing Risk of COVID-19 Infection and Severity, Prevention Protocols 2021 Available at: https://c19protocols.com/prevention-protocols/

83. Alam, M.T., Murshed, R., Gomes, P.F., Masud, Z.M., Saber, S., Chaklader, M.A., Khanam, F., Hossain, M., Momen, A.B.I.M., Yasmin, N. and Alam, R.F., 2020. Ivermectin as pre-exposure prophylaxis for COVID-19 among healthcare providers in a selected tertiary hospital in Dhaka–an observational study. *European Journal of Medical and Health Sciences*, 2(6).

84. Kory, P., Meduri, G.U., Varon, J., Iglesias, J. and Marik, P.E., 2021. Review of the emerging evidence demonstrating the efficacy of ivermectin in the prophylaxis and treatment of COVID-19. *American journal of therapeutics*, 28(3), p.e299.

85. Million, M., Lagier, J.C., Gautret, P., Colson, P., Fournier, P.E., Amrane, S., Hocquart, M., Mailhe, M., Esteves-Vieira, V., Doudier, B. and Aubry, C., 2020. Early treatment of COVID-19 patients with hydroxychloroquine and azithromycin: a retrospective analysis of 1061 cases in Marseille, France. *Travel medicine and infectious disease*, 35, p.101738.

86. McCullough, P.A., Alexander, P.E., Armstrong, R., Arvinte, C., Bain, A.F., Bartlett, R.P., Berkowitz, R.L., Berry, A.C., Borody, T.J., Brewer, J.H. and Brufsky, A.M., 2020. Multifaceted highly targeted sequential multidrug treatment of early ambulatory high-risk SARS-CoV-2 infection (COVID-19). *Reviews in cardiovascular medicine*, 21(4), p.517.

87. Morgenstern, J., Redondo, J.N., Olavarria, A., Rondon, I., Roca, S., De Leon, A., Canela, J., Tavares, J., Minaya, M., Lopez, O. and Castillo, A., 2021. Ivermectin as a SARS-CoV-2 Pre-Exposure Prophylaxis Method in Healthcare Workers: A Propensity Score-Matched Retrospective Cohort Study. *Cureus*, 13(8).

88. C19 Protocols. (2021). Reducing Risk of COVID-19 Infection and Severity. (2021). Treatment Protocols 2021. Available at: https://c19protocols.com/treatment-protocols/

89. Lima-Morales, R., Méndez-Hernández, P., Flores, Y.N., Osorno-Romero, P., Sancho-Hernández, C.R., Cuecuecha-Rugerio, E., Nava-Zamora, A., Hernández-Galdamez, D.R., Romo-Dueñas, D.K. and Salmeron, J., (2021). Effectiveness of a multidrug therapy consisting of Ivermectin, Azithromycin, Montelukast, and Acetylsalicylic acid to prevent hospitalization and death among ambulatory COVID-19 cases in Tlaxcala, Mexico. *International journal of infectious diseases,* 105, pp.598-605.
90. Martin Kulldorff *et al.* (2020).The Great Barrington Declaration.
91. Government Offices of Sweden. (2020). Folkhalsomyndigheten Public Health Agency of Sweden. FAQ about COVID-19.
92. Alexander,P, E. (2021).*150 Research Studies Affirm Naturally Acquired Immunity to Covid-19: Documented*, Linked, and Quoted. *Brownstone Institute.* October 17, 2021.
93. Trialsite Staff. (2021). MSN Showcases the Amazing Uttar Pradesh Turnaround—The Ivermectin-based Home Medicine Kits. *Trialsite News.* September 9, 2021. Available at: www.trialsitenews.com/msn-showcases-the-amazing-uttar-pradesh-turnaround-the-ivermectin-based-home-medicine-kits (Accessed: September 24, 2022).
94. Hatchek J. (1923). *Das Reichsstaatsrecht.* Vol. 1. Stilke, P 158. SOC p 23
95. Friedrich, C J. (1941). *Constitutional Government and democracy; theory and practice in Europe and America.*

Chapter 7

1. Kulldorff M, Bhattacharya, J. (2021).Vaccine Passports Prolong Lockdowns. *Wallstreet Journal.* April 6, 2021.
2. European Parlentary Assembly. (2021).Resolution 2361 (2021).COVID-19 vaccines: ethical, legal and practical considerations. Assembly debate on 27 January 2021 (5th Sitting). (see Doc. 15212, report of the Committee on Social Affairs, Health and Sustainable Development, rapporteur: Ms Jennifer De Temmerman). Text adopted by the Assembly on 27 January 2021 (5th Sitting).
3. Barnes J, and N Allen. (2020).EU must consider mandatory vaccination, says Ursula van der Leyen *The Telegraph.* Available at:https://www.telegraph.co.uk/world-news/2021/12/01/eu-must-consider-mandatory-vaccination-says-ursula-von-der-leyen/ (Accessed: December 20, 2021).
4. Adl-Tabatabai, S. (2021).Unjabbed Austrians Now Face PRISON If They Do Not Comply. News Punch. December 1, 2021. Available at: https://newspunch.com/unjabbed-austrians-now-face-prison-if-they-do-not-comply/ (Accessed: December 20, 2021).
5. Levine, J. (2022).Vaccine Passports Are Here to Stay. Why Worry?. January 1, 2022. Available at: https://theintercept.com/2022/01/01/covid-vaccine-passports-surveillance/ (Accessed: January 7, 2021).
6. Agamben, G. (2020).Meet the Philosopher Who Is Trying to Explain the Pandemic. New York Times. August 21, 2020. Available at: https://www.nytimes.com/2020/08/21/opinion/sunday/giorgio-agamben-philosophy-coronavirus.html. (Accessed: December 20, 2021).
7. Hamilton,K. (2021)New Zealand Prime Minister Admits She Wants to Create Two Classes of Citizens Based on Vaccination Status. Breitbart. Available at: https://www.breitbart.com/politics/2021/10/24/new-zealand-prime-minister-admits-she-wants-create-two-classes-citizens-based-vaccination-status/ (Accessed: December 20, 2021)

8. Agamben, G. (2008). *State of exception.* University of Chicago Press.
9. Agamben, G. (2017). *The Omnibus Homo Sacer.* Stanford University Press.
10. Humphreys, S. (2006). "Legalizing lawlessness: On Giorgio Agamben's State of exception." European Journal of International Law 17, no. 3: p. 677-687.
11. Frost, T. ed., (2013). *Giorgio Agamben: Legal, political and philosophical perspectives.* Routledge.
12. van Aardt, W. (2022) Public policy, *jus cogens* norms and the fiduciary criterion of legitimacy. De Rebus Attorneys Journal. July 1, 2022. Also see Lagerwall, A, Carty, A. (2015). Jus cogens. Oxford Bibliographies-International Law, 1.
13. Orakhelashvili, A. (2006).*Peremptory Norms in International Law.* Oxford: Oxford University Press, 2006.
14. Bianchi, A. (2008). Human Rights and the Magic of Jus cogens, *European Journal of International Law,* Volume 19, Issue 3, June 2008, P 491–508,
15. Zenović, P. (2012). "Human rights enforcement via peremptory norms–a challenge to State sovereignty." Riga Graduate School of Law Research Papers 6.
16. Koji, T. (2001)."Emerging Hierarchy in International Human Rights and Beyond: From the Perspective of Non-derogable Rights." *European Journal of International Law* 12, no. 5: p. 917-941.
17. Farer,T. (1992). "The Hierarchy of Human Rights." American University International Law Review 8, no. 1: p. 115-119.
18. International Covenant on Civil and Political Rights (ICCPR). G.A. Res. 2200A (XXI), 1966.
19. Richards, D. L., Clay, K. C., (2012). "An umbrella with holes: Respect for non-derogable human rights during declared States of emergency, 1996–2004." *Human Rights Review* 13, no. 4 2012:p. 443-471.
20. Office of the United Nations High Commissioner for Human Rights. Emergency Measures and COVID-19 Guidance. 2020. Available at: https://www.ohchr.org/Documents/Events/EmergencyMeasures_COVID19.pdf (Accessed: December 15, 2021).
21. World Economic Forum. (2021). 5 charts that tell the story of vaccines today 2020. Available at: https://www.weforum.org/agenda/2020/06/vaccine-development-barriers-coronavirus/ (Accessed: December 15, 2021).
22. Le, T.T., Cramer, J.P., Chen, R. and Mayhew, S., 2020. Evolution of the COVID-19 vaccine development landscape. *Nat Rev Drug Discov, 19*(10), pp.667-668.
23. Walter, Emmanuel B., and M. Anthony Moody. "Vaccine development: steps to approval of an investigational vaccine." *North Carolina medical journal* 82, no. 2 (2021): 141-144.
24. Seneff, S. and Nigh, G., 2021. Worse than the disease? Reviewing some possible unintended consequences of the mRNA vaccines against COVID-19. *International Journal of Vaccine Theory, Practice, and Research, 2*(1), pp.38-79.
25. Young, R., Bekele, T., Gunn, A., Chapman, N., Chowdhary, V., Corrigan, K., Dahora, L., Martinez, S., Permar, S., Persson, J. and Rodriguez, B., 2018. Developing new health technologies for neglected diseases: a pipeline portfolio review and cost model. *Gates Open Research, 2.*
26. Baden, L.R., El Sahly, H.M., Essink, B., Kotloff, K., Frey, S., Novak, R., Diemert, D., Spector, S.A., Rouphael, N., Creech, C.B. and McGettigan, J., 2020. Efficacy and safety of the mRNA-1273 SARS-CoV-2 vaccine. *New England journal of medicine.*
27. Doshi, P., 2021. Peter Doshi: Pfizer and Moderna's "95% effective" vaccines—we need more details and the raw data. *The BMJ Opinion.*
28. Brown, R.B., 2021. Outcome reporting bias in COVID-19 mRNA vaccine clinical trials. *Medicina, 57*(3), p.199. Also see: Olliaro P, Torreele E, Vaillant M. COVID-19 vaccine efficacy and effectiveness—the elephant (not).in the room.

Lancet Microbe 2021; published online April 20.

29. Opel, D.J., Salmon, D.A. and Marcuse, E.K., 2020. Building trust to achieve confidence in COVID-19 vaccines. *JAMA network open*, 3(10), pp.e2025672-e2025672.

30. Food and Drug Administration (FDA), US Department of Health and Human Services. (2021).Fact Sheet for Recipients and Caregivers: Emergency Use Authorization (EUA).of Pfizer-BioNtech COVID-19 Vaccine to Prevent Corona Virus Disease 2019 (COVID-19).in Individuals 18 Years of Age and Older. Available at: https://www.fda.gov/emergency-preparedness-and-response/ coronavirus-disease-2019-COVID-19/COVID-19-vaccines (Accessed: December 20, 2021).

31. Food and Drug Administration (FDA), US Department of Health and Human Services. (2021).Fact Sheet for Recipients and Caregivers: Emergency Use Authorization (EUA).of Moderna COVID-19 Vaccine to Prevent Corona Virus Disease 2019 (COVID-19).in Individuals 18 Years of Age and Older. Accessed: December 20, 2021. Available at: https://www.fda.gov/emergency-preparedness-and-response/coronavirus-disease-2019-COVID-19/COVID-19-vaccines (Accessed: December 20, 2021).

32. Food and Drug Administration (FDA), US Department of Health and Human Services. (2021). Fact Sheet for Recipients and Caregivers: Emergency Use Authorization (EUA).of the Janssen COVID-19 Vaccine to Prevent Corona Virus Disease 2019 (COVID-19).in Individuals 18 Years of Age and Older. Accessed: December 20, 2021. Available at: https://www.fda.gov/emergency-preparedness-and-response/coronavirus-disease-2019-COVID-19/COVID-19-vaccines (Accessed: December 20, 2021)

33. Centers for Disease Control and Prevention (CDC), US Department of Health and Human Services. Safety of COVID-19 Vaccines. Accessed: July 13, 2021. Available at: https://www.cdc.gov/coronavirus/2019-ncov/vaccines/safety/safety-of-vaccines. html (Accessed: December 20, 2021).

34. CDC, US Department of Health and Human Services. Key Things to Know about COVID-19 Vaccines. Accessed: June 25, 2021. Available at: https://www.cdc.gov/ coronavirus/2019-ncov/vaccines/keythingstoknow.html (Accessed: December 20, 2021).

35. Peckford, B. (2021).10 reasons why the FDA approval for Pfizer jab isn't about health, but about forcing people to take the shot. *Peckford42*. August 25, 2021.

36. BioNTech, S. E. (2020). "Study to describe the safety, tolerability, immunogenicity, and efficacy of RNA vaccine candidates against COVID-19 in healthy individuals." ClinicalTrials. gov: NCT04368728.

37. ModernaTX, A. (2020). "A study to evaluate efficacy, safety, and immunogenicity of mRNA-1273 vaccine in adults aged 18 years and older to prevent COVID-19." ClinicalTrials. gov, jul./2020.

38. US Food and Drug Administration. (2020).Development and licensure of vaccines to prevent COVID-19: guidance for industry. 2020. Available at: https://www.fda. gov/media/139638/download (Accessed: December 20, 2021).

39. Iacobucci, G. (2021)."COVID-19: FDA set to grant full approval to Pfizer vaccine without public discussion of data." BMJ: *British Medical Journal (Online)*.374.

40. Doshi, P. (2021). "COVID-19 vaccines: In the rush for regulatory approval, do we need more data?" bmj 373.

41. Doshi, P. (2021). "Does the FDA think these data justify the first full approval of a COVID-19 vaccine?" *The BMJ Opinion*.

42. Food and Drug Administration (FDA), US Department of Health and Human Services. (2022).FDA Letter to Pfizer. Available at: https://www.fda.gov/

media/150386/download
43. Kesselheim, A.S., Darrow, J.J., Kulldorff, M., Brown, B.L., Mitra-Majumdar, M., Lee, C.C., Moneer, O. and Avorn, J., (2021). An Overview Of Vaccine Development, Approval, And Regulation, With Implications For COVID-19: Analysis reviews the Food and Drug Administration's critical vaccine approval role with implications for COVID-19 vaccines. *Health Affairs, 40*(1), pp.25-32
44. Classen, J.B., (2021). COVID-19 RNA based vaccines and the risk of prion disease. *Microbiol Infect Dis, 5*(1), pp.1-3.
45. Wood, E. (2021). mRNA vaccine inventor concerned over adolescents receiving vaccine; YouTube removes video. *The Christian Post.* June, 24 2021. Available at: https://www.christianpost.com/news/mrna-vaccine-inventor-concerned-over-adolescent-vaccination.html (Accessed: December 20, 2021).
46. Malone et al. (2021).GLOBAL COVID-19 Summit. Available at: https://globalcovidsummit.org/ (Accessed: 24 September 2022).
47. Montagnier L. (2022). "They Are Not Vaccines, They Are Poisons" – Speech To The Luxembourg Parliament. January 13, 2022.
48. Sones, M. (2021). "It's 'entirely possible' vaccine campaigns 'will be used for massive-scale depopulation": Former Pfizer VP. *Lifesite News.* March, 29 2021. Available at: https://www.lifesitenews.com/opinion/former-pfizer-vp-to-aflds-entirely-possible-this-will-be-used-for-massive-scale-depopulation/ (Accessed: December 21, 2021).
49. McCullough, P. (2021). The State of COVID Treatment. September 19, 2021. Available at: https://thetruthiswhere.wordpress.com/2021/09/19/dr-peter-mccullough-the-State-of-covid-treatment (Accessed: December 20, 2021).
50. Laporte is a pioneer of pharmacovigilance in Spain. He was the director of the Coordinating Center for the Spanish Pharmacovigilance System and member of the National Pharmacovigilance Commission until the creation of the Spanish Medicines Agency in 1999. Outside of Spain, Laporte was also chairman of the World Health Organization's essential medicines committee in 2004.
51. Boralevi, P. (2022). Spanish drug safety expert says mass COVID vaccination is unprecedented 'global experiment'. *Lifesite News.* February, 9, 2022. Available at: https://www.lifesitenews.com/news/spanish-drug-safety-expert-says-mass-covid-vaccination-is-unprecedented-global-experiment/ (Accessed: February 10, 2022).
52. Beck, S. (2022). Revealed, the vaccine safety alert that drugs watchdog is ignoring. *TCW.* September 1, 2022. Available at: https://www.conservativewoman.co.uk/revealed-the-vaccine-safety-alert-that-drugs-watchdog-is-ignoring/ (Accessed: September 20, 2022).
53. Burchill, R. (2005). When Does an Emergency Threaten the Life of the Nation? Derogations from Human Rights Obligations and the War on International Terrorism. *New Zealand Yearbook of Jurisprudence* 9 (2005): 96–114.
54. Human Rights Committee. (2001). General Comment 29, States of Emergency (article 4). U.N. Doc. CCPR/C/21/Rev.1/Add.11, 2001.
55. Human Rights Committee. (2020). Statement on Derogations from the Covenant in Connection with the COVID-19 Pandemic. International Covenant on Civil and Political Rights CCPR/c128/2, 2020.
56. International Commission of Jurists. (1984). Siracusa Principles on the Limitation and Derogation of Provisions in the International Covenant on Civil and Political Rights. UN Doc E/CN.4/1984/4, Annex at: 58, 1985.
57. Lillich, R B. (1985). The Paris Minimum Standards of Human Rights Norms in a State of Emergency. *American Journal of International Law* 79, no. 4 (1985): 1072–1081.
58. Council of Europe. (1953). Convention for the Protection of Human Rights and

Fundamental Freedoms, Rome." 4.XI.Nov. 4, 1950, 213 UNTS 222 (entered into force Sept. 3, 1953).

59. American Convention on Human Rights, opened for signature Nov. 22, (1969). (Entered into force: July 18, 1978).

60. Van Aardt, W. (2004). *State Responsibility for Human Rights Abuses Committed by Non-State Actors under the Constitution.* Doctoral dissertation, North-West University, 2004.

61. Nuremberg Code (1947).

62. Velasquez Rodriguez Case Judgement of 29 July 1988, Inter-Am. Ct. Hr. (Ser. C).No. 4 (1988).at para. 166.

63. Gur-Arie, R., Jamrozik, E. and Kingori, P. (2021). No jab, no job? Ethical issues in mandatory COVID-19 vaccination of healthcare personnel. *BMJ global health, 6*(2), p.e004877.

64. Opel, D.J., Diekema, D.S. and Ross, L.F., (2021). Should we mandate a COVID-19 vaccine for children?. *JAMA pediatrics, 175*(2), pp.125-126.

65. Van Aardt, W. (2021). The Mandatory COVID-19 Vaccination of School Children: A Bioethical and Human Rights Assessment. *Journal of Vaccines & Vaccination* 12, no. 3.

66. van Aardt, W. (2021). Proof of COVID- Vaccination to Study-A Biomedical Ethical Analysis. *Journal of Biology and Today's World* 10, no. 5: p 1-4.

67. van Aardt W. (2021). "Can Government mandate the COVID-19 vaccine against your will? A discussion on international human rights law" *De Rebus SA Attorneys Journal.* The Law Society of South Africa. July 2021. Pp 14 -17.

68. Wilson, R. (2022). Covid Lies: "Vaccines" Are Safe and Effective. May 24, 2022. *The Expose.*

Chapter 8

1. van Aardt, W. (2021). "Proof of COVID-19 Vaccination to Study-A Biomedical Ethical Analysis." *Journal of Biology and Today's World* 10, no. 5 (2021): 1-4.

2. United States National Commission for the Protection of Human Subjects of Biomedical, and Behavioral Research. (1978). The Belmont report: ethical principles and guidelines for the protection of human subjects of research. Vol. 2. Department of Health, Education, and Welfare, National Commission for the Protection of Human Subjects of Biomedical and Behavioral Research, 1978.

3. Beauchamp, T. L., and Childress, J, F. (2001). *Principles of biomedical ethics.* Oxford University Press, USA.

4. Jošt, M., Cox, T.S. (2000)."Food Production and Bioethics." Sociologija Sela 3, no. 4: p. 149.

5. US Department of Health and Human Sciences, Centers for Disease Control and Prevention. (2021).COVID-19 Vaccines for children and teens.

6. Morand, A., et al. (2020). "COVID-19 virus and children: What do we know?" *Archives de Pédiatrie* 27.3: p. 117.

7. Subramanian, S. V., Kumar , A. (2021). "Increases in COVID-19 are unrelated to levels of vaccination across 68 countries and 2947 counties in the United State s." *European Journal of Epidemiology* : 1-4

8. US Department of Health and Human Sciences, Centers for Disease Control and Prevention. (2021).COVID-19 Pandemic Planning Scenarios.

9. Esposito S, Principi N. (2020). To mask or not to mask children to overcome COVID-19. *Eur J Pediatr.* ;179(8):1267-1270.

10. American Academy of Pediatrics. (2021) "Children and COVID-19: State -level

data report." Available at: COVID-19 and Age (uvm.edu). (Accessed: October 1, 2022).

11. Brodin, P. (2020). *"Why is COVID-19 so mild in children?"* 109.6: p.1082-1083.

12. Ludvigsson, J. F. (2021). Children are unlikely to be the main drivers of the COVID-19 pandemic – A systematic review. Acta Paediatr: 109(8): p. 1525-1530.

13. Bunyavanich S, Do A, Vicencio A. (2020). Nasal Gene Expression of Angiotensin-Converting Enzyme 2 in Children and Adults. JAMA. 2020;323(23):p. 2427–2429. Also see: Loske, J., Röhmel, J., Lukassen, S. et al. (2022). Pre-activated antiviral innate immunity in the upper airways controls early SARS-CoV-2 infection in children. *Nat Biotechnol* 40,p. 319–324.

14. Murdoch Children's Research Institute. (2022). COVID-19 and Children's Surveillance Report. March 21, 2022. Available at: www.mcri.edu.au/sites/default/files/media/documents/covid-19_and_childrens_surveillance_report_13_210322-v2.pdf (Accessed: April, 20, 2022).

15. Sorg AL, Hufnagel M, Doenhardt M, Diffloth N, Schroten H, von Kries R, Berner R, Armann J. (2022). Risk for severe outcomes of COVID-19 and PIMS-TS in children with SARS-CoV-2 infection in Germany. *Eur J Pediatr.* 2022 Aug 13:p. 1–9. Also see Sorg, Anna-Lisa, Markus Hufnagel, Maren Doenhardt, Natalie Diffloth, Horst Schroten, Ruediger von Kries, Reinhard Berner, and Jakob Peter Armann. (2021). "Risk of Hospitalization, severe disease, and mortality due to COVID-19 and PIMS-TS in children with SARS-CoV-2 infection in Germany." medRxiv.

16. Axfors, C. and Ioannidis, J.P., (2021). Infection fatality rate of COVID-19 in community-dwelling populations with emphasis on the elderly: An overview PREPRINT. *medRxiv Epidemiology*, pp.1-34.

17. Munro, A.P., & Faust, S.N. (2021)."Children are not COVID-19 super spreaders: Time to go back to school." Archives Disease Childhood 105.7: p 618-619.

18. Zhu, Y., et al. (2020). "Children are unlikely to have been the primary source of household SARS-CoV-2 infections." SSRN Electronic J.

19. Jing, Q.L., et al. (2020). "Household secondary attack rate of COVID-19 and associated determinants in Guangzhou, China: A retrospective cohort study." The Lancet Infectious Diseases 20.10: p.1141-1150.

20. Danis, K., et al. (2020). "Cluster of coronavirus disease 2019 (COVID-19).in the French Alps, February 2020." Clin Infectious Diseases 71.15:p. 825-832.

21. National Centre for immunization research and surveillance. (2020). "COVID-19 in schools-the experience in NSW."

22. The National Institute for Public Health and the Environment (RVIM). (2020). "Children and COVID-19, 2020."

23. Heavey, L., et al. (2020). "No evidence of secondary transmission of COVID-19 from children attending school in Ireland, 2020." Eurosurveillance 25.20: p 2000903.

24. Vlachos, J., Hertegård, E. and Svaleryd, H.B., (2021). The effects of school closures on SARS-CoV-2 among parents and teachers. Proceedings of the National Academy of Sciences, 118(9).

25. Ehrhardt, J., Ekinci, A., Krehl, H., Meincke, M., Finci, I., Klein, J., Geisel, B., Wagner-Wiening, C., Eichner, M. and Brockmann, S.O., (2020). Transmission of SARS-CoV-2 in children aged 0 to 19 years in childcare facilities and schools after their reopening in May 2020, Baden-Württemberg, Germany. *Eurosurveillance,* 25(36), p.2001587.

26. Cao, S., et al. (2020). "Post-lockdown SARS-CoV-2 nucleic acid screening in nearly ten million residents of Wuhan, China." *Nat* 11.1: 1-7.

27. Gilliam, W.S., Malik, A.A., Shafiq, M., Klotz, M., Reyes, C., Humphries, J.E.,

Murray, T., Elharake, J.A., Wilkinson, D. and Omer, S.B., (2021). COVID-19 transmission in US childcare programs. *Pediatrics*, 147(1).

28. van Aardt, W. (2021). "The mandatory COVID-19 vaccination of school children: A bioethical human rights assessment." *J vaccines vaccin* 12(2021): p. 457

29. Jarjour, N. N., et al. (2021). "T cell memory: Understanding COVID-19." *Immunity* 54.1:p.14-18.

30. Gazit, S., Shlezinger, R., Perez, G., Lotan, R., Peretz, A., Ben-Tov, A., Cohen, D., Muhsen, K., Chodick, G. and Patalon, T., 2021. Comparing SARS-CoV-2 natural immunity to vaccine-induced immunity: reinfections versus breakthrough infections. *MedRxiv*.

31. Alexander, P.E. (2021). 150 Plus Research Studies Affirm Naturally Acquired Immunity to Covid-19: Documented, Linked, and Quoted. *Brownstone Institute*. October 17, 2021. Available at: https://brownstone.org/articles/79-research-studies-affirm-naturally-acquired-immunity-to-covid-19-documented-linked-and-quoted/ (Accessed: February 20, 2022).

32. Kostoff, R.N., Calina, D., Kanduc, D., Briggs, M.B., Vlachoyiannopoulos, P., Svistunov, A.A. and Tsatsakis, A., 2021. Why are we vaccinating children against COVID-19?. *Toxicology Reports*, 8, pp.1665-1684

33. John Hopkins University and Medicine. (2021). "Coronavirus Resource Centre, Mortality Analysis."

34. UK Office for National Statistics. (2022).Deaths by vaccination status, Deaths occurring between 1 January 2021 and 31 March 2022 edition of this dataset England Available at: www.ons.gov.uk/peoplepopulationandcommunity/birthsdeathsandmarriages/deaths/datasets/deathsbyvaccinationstatusengland.

35. UK Office for National Statistics. (2022).Mortality Analysis, Deaths occurring between 1 January 2021 and 31 March 2022 edition of this dataset England https://www.ons.gov.uk/peoplepopulationandcommunity/birthsdeathsandmarriages/deaths/bulletins/monthlymortalityanalysisenglandandwales/latest

36. The Expose. (2022). Children's risk of Death increases between 8100% and 30,200% following Covid-19 Vaccination compared to Unvaccinated Children according to official ONS data. *The Expose*. May 20, 2022.

37. The Expose. (2022). Europe officially records a shocking 691% increase in Excess Deaths among Children since EMA first approved COVID Vaccine for Children. *The Expose* September 8, 2022.

38. Rhoda Wilson. Covid Lies: "Vaccines" Are Safe and Effective. *The Expose*. May 24, 2022.

39. Iserson, K.V. (1999). "Principles of biomedical ethics." Emergency Med Clini 17.2. p. 283-306.

40. Beauchamp T, Childress J. (2019).Principles of Biomedical Ethics: Marking Its Fortieth Anniversary. *Am J Bioeth*. Nov; 19 (11): p. 9-12.

41. Varkey, B. (2021). "Principles of clinical ethics and their application to practice." *Medical Principles Practice* 30.1: p. 17-28.

42. Gillon, R. (1994). "Medical ethics: Four principles plus attention to scope." *BMJ* 309.6948:184.

43. Beauchamp, L. (2007). "The 'four principles' approach to health care ethics." Principles of health care ethics 29: 3-10.

44. Liberty Counsel. (2022). FDA Authorizes Pfizer Booster COVID Shot for Children. May 17, 2022. https://lc.org/newsroom/details/051722-fda-approves-pfizer-booster-covid-shot-for-children-1

45. Thomas, S J., et al. (2021). "Safety and efficacy of the BNT162b2 mRNA Covid-19 vaccine through 6 months." New England Journal of Medicine 385, no. 19p.: 1761-1773.

46. Steve K, Rose, J, Crawford, M. (2021). Estimating the number of COVID vaccine deaths in America. Available at: https://www.skirsch.com/covid/Deaths.pdf (Accessed: March 27, 2022).

47. Steve Kirch, (2022). 20 questions they don't want to answer. March 26, 2022. Substack. Available at: https://stevekirsch.substack.com/p/20-questions-they-dont-want-to-answer? (Accessed: March 27, 2022).

48. Rose, J. (2021). "Critical Appraisal of VAERS Pharmacovigilance: Is the US Vaccine Adverse Events Reporting System (VAERS) a Functioning Pharmacovigilance System?".

49. Rothman, K J., Greenland, S. (2005). "Hill's Criteria for Causality." *Encyclopedia of biostatistics* 4.

50. Fedak, K.M., Bernal, A., Capshaw, Z.A. and Gross, S., 2015. Applying the Bradford Hill criteria in the 21st century: how data integration has changed causal inference in molecular epidemiology. *Emerging themes in epidemiology*, 12(1), pp.1-9.

51. Vogel, G., & Couzin-Frankle, J. (2021). "Israel reports link between rare cases of heart inflammation and COVID-19 vaccination in young men." Sci.

52. Bille, K., Figueiras, D., Schamasch, P., Kappenberger, L., Brenner, J.I., Meijboom, F.J. and Meijboom, E.J., 2006. Sudden cardiac death in athletes: the Lausanne Recommendations. *European Journal of Preventive Cardiology*, 13(6), pp.859-875.

53. The Expose. (2022). Fully Vaccinated Young Adults suffer 73% increase in Heart Attacks & Strokes and 92% higher Mortality Rate compared to Unvaccinated. May 17 2022. *The Expose*. Available at: https://expose-news.com/2022/05/17/covid-jabs-increase-risk-heart-attack-death-young-adults / (Accessed: May 17, 2022).

54. Informed Choice Australia. (2022). 1000 Peer Reviewed Studies Questioning COVID-19 Vaccine Safety. January 19, 2022. Available at: https://www.informedchoiceaustralia.com/post/1000-peer-reviewed-studies-questioning-covid-19-vaccine-safety (Accessed: January 20, 2022).

55. Brian S. (2022). COVID-19 Vaccine Massacre: 68,000% Increase in Strokes, 44,000% Increase in Heart Disease, 6,800% Increase in Deaths Over Non-COVID Vaccines. *Global Research*, March 29, 2022

56. Bardosh, K., Krug, A., Jamrozik, E., Lemmens, T., Keshavjee, S., Prasad, V., Makary, M.A., Baral, S. and Høeg, T.B., (2022). COVID-19 Vaccine Boosters for Young Adults: A Risk-Benefit Assessment and Five Ethical Arguments against Mandates at Universities.

57. World Medical Association. (1964). "WMA declaration of Helsinki-ethical principles for medical research involving human subjects."

58. Teall, E. K. (2014). "Medicine and doctoring in ancient Mesopotamia." Grand Valley Journal of History 3, no. 1: p. 2.

59. Jastrow, M. (1914). "The medicine of the Babylonians and Assyrians." Proceedings of the Royal Society of Medicine 7, no. Sect_Hist_Med : p. 109-176.

60. Gillon, R. (2015). "Defending the four principles approach as a good basis for good medical practice and therefore for good medical ethics." J Medical Ethics 41.1: p. 111-116.

Chapter 9

1. Principi, N. and Esposito, S., (2021). Restrictive Measures for Children During the COVID-19 Pandemic: Are They Scientifically Supported? *Frontiers in Pediatrics*, 9.

2. Hurst, M. (2020). Mask protest melee at North Star Mall yields one arrest. *Kens5*. December 28, 2020. Available at: https://www.kens5.com/article/news/local/public-safety/

mask-protest-melee-at-north-star-mall-yields-one-arrest/273-fcc7c908-f617-482f-babc-970c44836025 (Accessed: September 2, 2022).

3. Mcarthur, T. (2020).Man who 'refused to wear face mask' on train pepper-sprayed after scuffle with police. Mirror September 4, 2020. Available at: https://www.mirror.co.uk/news/uk-news/man-who-refused-wear-face-22627930 (Accessed: September 2, 2022).

4. Steinbuch, Y. (2021). Man reportedly suffers heart attack while cuffed for not wearing mask outside. New York Post. August 4, 2021. Available at: https://nypost.com/2021/08/04/man-has-heart-attack-while-cuffed-for-not-wearing-mask-report/(Accessed: September 2, 2022). also see Brittany Chain. (2021). Elderly man collapses to the ground after being arrested for 'failing to wear a face mask' while walking in a park – as his desperate partner screams for help. Daily Mail Australia. Available at: https://www.dailymail.co.uk/news/article-9854585/Coronavirus-Australia-Elderly-QLD-man-collapses-hes-arrested-not-wearing-face-mask.html(Accessed: September 2, 2022).

5. Martin, H. (2021).He's trying to break my arm': Screaming man is pinned to the floor by police officers as he is arrested after refusing to wear a mask in chaotic scenes at train station Daily Mail. March 16 , 2021. https://www.dailymail.co.uk/news/article-9367403/Moment-group-police-officers-arrest-man-allegedly-not-wearing-mask.html

6. Snow D. (2020). 5-Year-Old Autistic Boy Kicked Off School Bus For Not Wearing Mask, Parents Say. August 28, 2020. Available at: https://www.ibtimes.com/5-year-old-autistic-boy-kicked-school-bus-not-wearing-mask-parents-say-3036228 (Accessed: September 2, 2022).

7. Laila, C. (2022). California: 4-Year-Old Boy Removed From School by Police For Refusing to Wear Mask (VIDEO). Gatewaypundit. August 20, 2022. Available at: https://www.thegatewaypundit.com/2022/08/california-4-year-old-boy-removed-school-police-refusing-wear-mask-video/ (Accessed: September 2, 2022).

8. Zanotti, B., Parodi, P.C., Riccio, M., De Francesco, F. and Zingaretti, N., (2020). Can the Elastic of Surgical Face Masks Stimulate Ear Protrusion in Children? Aesthetic plastic surgery, 44(5), pp.1947-1950;

9. Vlachos, J., Hertegård, E. and Svaleryd, H.B., (2021). The effects of school closures on SARS-CoV-2 among parents and teachers. Proceedings of the National Academy of Sciences, 118(9).

10. Mheidly, N., Fares, M.Y., Zalzale, H. and Fares, J., (2020). Effect of Face Masks on Interpersonal Communication During the COVID-19 Pandemic. Frontiers in Public Health, 8, p.898.

11. International Covenant on Civil and Political Rights (ICCPR). G.A. Res. 2200A (XXI). (1966).

12. UN General Assembly, Convention on the Rights of the Child, 20 November 1989, United Nations, Treaty Series, vol. 1577.

13. Van Aardt, W. (2022). "COVID-19 Mask Mandates for School Children-Following the Science or Impolitic?." International J of Epidemiology and Public Health Research 4, no. 1 (2022). Also see van Aardt W, "Proof of Covid-19 Vaccination to Study-A Biomedical Ethical Analysis" Journal of Biology and Today's World. (2021) Volume 10, Issue 5.

14. Zindberg, J. (2022). Point: There's No Evidence That Masks Work. Recordnet.com May 6, 2022. Available at: https://www.recordnet.com/story/opinion/2022/05/06/point-theres-no-evidence-masks-work/9677658002/ (Accessed: May 7, 2022).

15. US Department of Health and Human Sciences, Centers for Disease Control and Prevention (2021).Science Brief: Community Use of Cloth Masks to Control the Spread of SARS-CoV-2; Available at: www.cdc.gov/coronavirus/2019-ncov/

science/science-briefs/masking-science-sars-cov2.html (Accessed: Monthly 2020, 2021, 2022). ; US Department of Health and Human Sciences, Centers for Disease Control and Prevention (2021).Filtration for Wearer Protection Available at: www.cdc.gov/coronavirus/2019-ncov/science/science-briefs/masking-science-sars-cov2.html (Accessed: Monthly 2020, 2021, 2022). US Department of Health and Human Sciences, Centers for Disease Control and Prevention (2021).Source Control to Block Exhaled Virus Available at: www.cdc.gov/coronavirus/2019-ncov/science/science-briefs/masking-science-sars-cov2.html (Accessed: Monthly 2020, 2021, 2022).

16. Lisa M Brosseau, ScD; Angela Ulrich, PhD, MPH; Kevin Escandón, MD; Cory Anderson, MPH; and Michael T. Osterholm, PhD, MPH. COMMENTARY: What can masks do? Part 1: The science behind COVID-19 protection. October 14, 2021. CIDRAP. University of Minnesota. Available at: Available at: https://www.cidrap.umn.edu/news-perspective/2021/10/commentary-what-can-masks-do-part-1-science-behind-covid-19-protection (Accessed: December 20, 2021).

17. Global COVID Summit, Declaration IV. May 11, 2022. BY PHYSICIANS AND MEDICAL SCIENTISTS. Available at: https://globalcovidsummit.org/ (Accessed: May, 12, 2022).

18. Mack, E. (2021). Fauci Warns Unvaccinated Might Bring a Fifth COVID Wave. October 17, 2021. Available at: https://www.newsmax.com/newsfront/COVID-19-pandemic-anthonyfauci/2021/10/17/id/1040831/ (Accessed: October 19, 2021).

19. Prasad,P. (2021). "What's the Evidence Guiding CDC's Latest Mask Policy?" Medpage Today, 7/29/21

20. Kulldorff,M. (2021). Twitter, 4/11/21 and 7/13/21.

21. Scott J. Balsitis. (2021). Twitter, 8/26/21 and 8/27/21.

22. Makary, M and Meissner, H, D. (2021)."The Case Against Masks for Children," *The Wall Street Journal*, August, 8, 2021.

23. Bacevic, J. (2020). There's no such thing as just 'following the science' – coronavirus advice is political. *The Guardian*. April, 28, 2020.

24. Kennedy, R F. (2021). "The Real Anthony Fauci: Bill Gates, Big Pharma, and the global war on democracy and public health." Skyhorse Publishing.

25. The Expose. (2022). Corrruption: Goverment Scoentist have been paid $ 350 million to hide data. May 22, 2022. *The Expose* also see: Open the Books, May 9, 2022; Open the Books NIH Royalty Disclosures Fact Sheet.

26. Lee, C., Yang, T., Inchoco, G.D., Jones, G.M. and Satyanarayan, A., (2021), May. Viral visualizations: How coronavirus skeptics use orthodox data practices to promote unorthodox science online. In *Proceedings of the 2021 CHI conference on human factors in computing systems* (pp. 1-18).

27. Epistemological relating to the theory of knowledge, especially with regard to its methods, validity, and scope, and the distinction between justified belief and opinion. Epistemologists study the nature, origin, and scope of knowledge, epistemic justification, the rationality of belief, and various related issues. Epistemology is considered a major subfield of philosophy, along with other major subfields such as ethics, logic, and metaphysics.

28. Angell, M., (2005). *The truth about the drug companies: How they deceive us and what to do about it*. Random House Trade Paperbacks.

29. Liu, J.J., Bell, C.M., Matelski, J.J., Detsky, A.S. and Cram, P., (2017). Payments by US pharmaceutical and medical device manufacturers to US medical journal editors: retrospective observational study. bmj, 359.

30. Robert Yoho. (2020). Butchered By Healthcare. KDP.

31. Smith, R. (2021). "Time to assume that health research is fraudulent until proven otherwise." The *BMJ Opinion* 5.

32. Jefferson T. et al. (2020). Do physical measures such as hand-washing or wearing masks stop or slow down the spread of respiratory viruses? Cochrane Acute Respiratory Infections Group. *Cochrane Library*. Also see: Bin-Reza, F., Lopez Chavarrias, V., Nicoll, A. and Chamberland, M.E., (2012). The use of masks and respirators to prevent transmission of influenza: a systematic review of the scientific evidence. Influenza and other respiratory viruses, 6(4), pp.257-267

33. MacIntyre, C.R., Seale, H., Dung, T.C., Hien, N.T., Nga, P.T., Chughtai, A.A., Rahman, B., Dwyer, D.E. and Wang, Q., (2015). A cluster randomized trial of cloth masks compared with medical masks in healthcare workers. BMJ open, 5(4), p.e006577.

34. Xiao, J., Shiu, E.Y., Gao, H., Wong, J.Y., Fong, M.W., Ryu, S. and Cowling, B.J., (2020). Nonpharmaceutical measures for pandemic influenza in nonhealthcare settings—personal protective and environmental measures. Emerging infectious diseases, 26(5), p.967.

35. Bundgaard, H., Bundgaard, J.S., Raaschou-Pedersen, D.E.T., von Buchwald, C., Todsen, T., Norsk, J.B., Pries-Heje, M.M., Vissing, C.R., Nielsen, P.B., Winsløw, U.C. and Fogh, K., (2020). Effectiveness of adding a mask recommendation to other public health measures to prevent SARS-CoV-2 infection in Danish mask wearers: a randomized controlled trial. Annals of Internal Medicine.

36. Brosseau L, et al. (2021).What can masks do? Part 1: The science behind COVID-19 protection. CIDRAP. Available at: https://www.cidrap.umn.edu/ news-perspective/2021/10/commentary-what-can-masks-do-part-1-science-behind-covid-19-protection (Accessed: October 1, 2022).

37. Kisielinski, K., Giboni, P., Prescher, A., Klosterhalfen, B., Graessel, D., Funken, S., Kempski, O. and Hirsch, O., (2021). Is a Mask That Covers the Mouth and Nose Free from Undesirable Side Effects in Everyday Use and Free of Potential Hazards?. International journal of environmental research and public health, 18(8), p.4344.

38. Beder, A., Büyükkoçak, Ü., Sabuncuoğlu, H., Keskil, Z.A. and Keskil, S., (2008). Preliminary report on surgical mask induced deoxygenation during major surgery. Neurocirugia, 19(2), pp.121-126.

39. Westendorf, A.M., Skibbe, K., Adamczyk, A., Buer, J., Geffers, R., Hansen, W., Pastille, E. and Jendrossek, V., (2017). Hypoxia enhances immunosuppression by inhibiting CD4+ effector T cell function and promoting Treg activity. Cellular Physiology and Biochemistry, 41(4), pp.1271-1284;

40. Sceneay, J., Parker, B.S., Smyth, M.J. and Möller, A., (2013). Hypoxia-driven immunosuppression contributes to the pre-metastatic niche. Oncoimmunology, 2(1), p.e22355; Shehade, H., Acolty, V., Moser, M. and Oldenhove, G., (2015). Cutting edge: hypoxia-inducible factor 1 negatively regulates Th1 function. The Journal of Immunology, 195(4), pp.1372-1376.

41. Fögen, Z. (2022). "The Foegen effect: A mechanism by which facemasks contribute to the COVID-19 case fatality rate." Medicine 101, no. 7 (2022): e28924-e28924.

42. Spira, B. (2022). "Correlation Between Mask Compliance and COVID-19 Outcomes in Europe." Cureus 14, no. 4.

43. Winters,N. (2022).Study Finds Positive Correlation' Between Higher Mask Usage And COVID-19 Deaths. May 16, 2022. *The National Pulse*. https://thenationalpulse.com/2022/05/16/ study-finds-correlation-between-mask-compliance-and-covid-deaths/

44. Guerra, D, Guerra, D, J. (2021). "Mask mandate and use efficacy in state-level COVID-19 containment." medRxiv.

45. Gettings, J., Czarnik, M., Morris, E., Haller, E., Thompson-Paul, A.M., Rasberry, C., Lanzieri, T.M., Smith-Grant, J., Aholou, T.M., Thomas, E. and Drenzek, C., 2021. Mask use and ventilation improvements to reduce COVID-19 incidence in

elementary schools—Georgia, November 16–December 11, 2020. *Morbidity and Mortality Weekly Report, 70*(21), p.779.

46. David Z. (2021). "The Science of Masking Kids at School Remains Uncertain," *New York Magazine's Intelligencer,* 8/20/21)

47. Oster E, Jack R, Halloran C, Schoof J, McLeod D. COVID-19 mitigation practices and COVID-19 rates in schools: Report on data from Florida, New York and Massachusetts. medRxiv. 2021 Jan 1.

48. Alexander, PE. (2021). More than 150 Comparative Studies and Articles on Mask Ineffectiveness and Harms. December 20, 2021. *Brownstone Institute.* Available at: https://centerforneurologyandspine.com/do-masks-work-see-the-review-of-over-150-studies-below/ (Accessed: December 2, 2021).

49. Van Aardt, W. (2021). "The Mandatory COVID-19 Vaccination of School Children: A Bioethical and Human Rights Assessment." Journal of Vaccines & Vaccination 12, no. 3 (2021).

50. World Health Organization, (2017).Advancing the Right to Health: The Vital Role of Law", Switzerland

51. International Commission of Jurists. (1984). Siracusa Principles on the Limitation and Derogation of Provisions in the International Covenant on Civil and Political Rights, UN Doc E/CN.4/1984/4, Annex

52. World Health Organization. (2020). On June 5, 2020, the WHO released a statement entitled "Advice on the use of masks in the context of SARS-CoV-2" *inter alia* stating that "*At the present time, the widespread use of masks by healthy people in the community setting is not yet supported by high quality or direct scientific evidence, and there are potential benefits and harms to consider.* Available at: https://www.who.int/publications/i/item/advice-on-the-use-of-masks-in-the-community-during-home-care-and-in-healthcare-settings-in-the-context-of-the-novel-coronavirus-(2019-ncov)-outbreak (Accessed: January 7, 2022). According to the US CDC's "Science Brief: Community Use of Cloth Masks to Control the Spread of SARS-CoV-2, "*Experimental data support community masking to reduce the spread of SARS-CoV-2.*" See: US Department of Health and Human Sciences, Centers for Disease Control and Prevention (2021). Science Brief: Community Use of Cloth Masks to Control the Spread of SARS-CoV-2.] Both the WHO and US CDC admit that there is no scientific evidence supporting the use of masks and that mandatory mask-wearing is experimental.

53. Vlachou, M, (2022). Anthony Fauci Criticizes Court Ruling Voiding Federal Mask Mandate For Travel. *Huffpost.* April, 22, 2022. Available at: https://www.huffpost.com/entry/anthony-fauci-cricizes-ruling-on-masks_n_6262a43ee4b0ea625c063f77

54. Caden D, (2022).DeSantis on other states lifting school mask mandates: "The medical science didn't change, the political science did", *The Capitolist.* February 8, 2022. Available at: https://thecapitolist.com/desantis-on-other-states-lifting-school-mask-mandates-the-medical-science-didnt-change-the-political-science-did/

55. Abbasi K. (2020). Covid-19: politicisation, "corruption," and suppression of science. BMJ. 2020 Nov 13;371:m4425.

56. van Aardt, W. (2021). "Proof of COVID-19 Vaccination to Study-A Biomedical Ethical Analysis." Journal of Biology and Today's World 10, no. 5 (2021):p 1-4.

57. Alexander P, E. (2021).The Attack on Scientific Dissent Becomes Ever More Brutal. Brownstone Institute. October 22, 2021. Available at: https://brownstone.org/articles/the-attack-on-scientific-dissent-becomes-ever-more-brutal/ (Accessed: December 10, 2021).

58. Da Vinci, L., (2013). *Leonardo's notebooks: writing and art of the great master.*

Hachette UK."Iron rusts from disuse, stagnant water loses its purity, and in cold weather becomes frozen; even so does inaction sap the vigors of the mind." "All sciences are vain and full of errors that are not born of Experience, the mother of all Knowledge." — Leonardo da Vinci, Leonardo's Notebooks

59. Galileo Galilei ."It is surely harmful to souls to make it a heresy to believe what is proved.";"Who would dare assert that we know all there is to be known?"

60. Albert Einstein. "The important thing is to never stop questioning"; "Creativity is seeing what others see and thinking what no one else has ever thought."

61. Isaac Newton. "To arrive at the simplest truth requires years of contemplation."

62. Louis Pasteur."Little science takes you away from God but more of it takes you to Him."

63. Marie Curie."Nothing in life is to be feared, it is only to be understood. Now is the time to understand more, so that we may fear less."; "Be less curious about people and more curious about ideas. Marie Curie You can only analyze the data you have." ; "It was like a new world opened to me, the world of science, which I was at last permitted to know in all liberty."

64. Friedrich Nietzsche. "A thinker sees his own actions as experiments and questions--as attempts to find out something. Success and failure are for him answers above all." — Friedrich Nietzsche

65. Alexander Graham Bell. "Observe, Remember, Compare." ; "Great discoveries and improvements invariably involve the cooperation of many minds."

66. Feynman, R.P., (2005). The pleasure of finding things out: The best short works of Richard P. Feynman. Basic Books.

67. Willis. M (2022). The Truth About Ivermectin: A new short documentary. August 29, 2022. [interview with Dr Mike Yeadon] Available at: https://rumble.com/v1hu7xr-the-truth-about-ivermectin-a-new-short-documentary-by-plandemic-filmmaker-m.html (Accessed: September 1, 2022)

68. Schwab, T. (2021)."Covid-19, trust, and Wellcome: how charity's pharma investments overlap with its research efforts." bmj 372.

69. Brezis M. (2008). Big pharma and health care: unsolvable conflict of interests between private enterprise and public health. Isr J Psychiatry Relat Sci. 2008;45(2):83-9; discussion 90-4. PMID: 18982834.

70. Chumley, C. K. (2020). Bill Gates and his coronavirus conflicts of interest. April 2, 2020. The Washington Times.

71. Ballasy, M. (2020). Ten experts on a NIH COVID-19 panel have ties to companies involved in coronavirus treatment. Just the News. August 11, 2020.

72. Rish. H. (2022). Traditional Vaccines Now in Question: Dr. Harvey Risch Loses All Trust in the CDC and the FDA [VIDEO]. October 8, 2022. Vigilant Fox. Available at: https://www.redvoicemedia.com/2022/10/traditional-vaccines-now-in-question-dr-harvey-risch-loses-all-trust-in-the-cdc-and-the-fda-videos/. (Accessed: October 9, 2022)

73. Smith, N. K. (2011). Immanuel Kant's critique of pure reason. Read Books Ltd.

Chapter 10

1. Bentham, J., 1996. The collected works of Jeremy Bentham: An introduction to the principles of morals and legislation. Clarendon Press.

2. Hospers, J. (1980)."Libertarianism and legal paternalism." Journal of Libertarian Studies 4, no. 3 (1980): p. 255-265.

3. van Aardt, W. (2002). "The new era of COVID-19 legal paternalism and the limitation of fundamental human rights" De Rebus SA Attorneys Journal. The Law

Society of South Africa. February 2022. p. 43-44.

4. Buchanan, D, R. (2008). "Autonomy, paternalism, and justice: ethical priorities in public health." *American journal of public health* 98, no. 1 (2008): p. 15-21.

5. Feinberg,J. (1971). "Legal paternalism". 1 *Canadian Journal of Philosophy*. p. 105.

6. Suber, P. (1999). "Paternalism." *Philosophy of law: An encyclopedia*.

7. Matthew, T, Buckmaster, L. (2010). "Paternalism in social policy: when is it justifiable?" Commonwealth of Australia.

8. Dworkin, G. (1972). "Paternalism." the Monist :p. 64-84.

9. Beauchamp, T. L. and Childress, J. F. (2001). *Principles of biomedical ethics*. Oxford University Press, USA.

10. New B. (1999). "Paternalism and public policy." Economics & Philosophy 15, no. 1: p. 63-83

11. Kant, I., (1983). *Perpetual peace and other essays*. Hackett Publishing.

12. Bertrand Cattinari, E., 2015. The Doctrine of 'Implied Limitations' of Fundamental Rights: An Argument Against Legal Paternalism. *University of Leicester School of Law Research Paper*, (15-18).

13. Mill, J.S., 2021. *On Liberty: And Utilitarianism*. SSEL.

14. Dworkin, Gerald. (1998). *The theory and practice of autonomy*. Cambridge University Press.

15. S v Makwanyane and Another 1995 (6). BCLR 665 (CC).at [109]

16. van Aardt, W. (2004). "State responsibility for human rights abuses committed by non-State actors under the constitution". PhD diss., North-West University.

17. van Aardt, W. (2021). "Limiting human rights during Covid-19- is it only legitimate if it is proportional" *De Rebus SA Attorneys Journal*. The Law Society of South Africa. May 2021. Pp 14 -16.

18. van Aardt, W. (2020). "Are the stringent COVID-19 lockdown regulations unconstitutional and unjustifiable?" *De Rebus SA Attorneys Journal*. The Law Society of South Africa. September 2020. Pp 26 – 28.

19. Polombu B, (2020).4 Life-Threatening Unintended Consequences of the Lockdowns. FEE Stories. August 25, 2020. Available at: https://fee.org/articles/4-life-threatening-unintended-consequences-of-the-lockdowns/ (Accessed: August 29, 2020).

20. Talotta R. (2021). Do COVID-19 RNA-based vaccines put at risk of immune-mediated diseases? In reply to "potential antigenic cross-reactivity between SARS-CoV-2 and human tissue with a possible link to an increase in autoimmune diseases". *Clin Immunol*. 2021 Mar;224: p. 108665.

21. Edwards, E. (2021). Evidence grows stronger for Covid vaccine link to heart issue, CDC says. *NBC News*. June 10, 2021.

22. US Department of Health & Human Services. Centers for Disease Control and Prevention. (2022). Safety of COVID-19 Vaccines. Available at: https://www.cdc.gov/coronavirus/2019-ncov/vaccines/expect/after.html (Accessed: February 24, 2022).

23. Ventegodt, S. (2015). "Why the corruption of the World Health Organization (WHO).is the biggest threat to the world's public health of our time." J Integrative Med Ther 2, no. 1: p. 5.

24. Savulescu J, Giubilini A, Danchin M. (2021). Global Ethical Considerations Regarding Mandatory Vaccination in Children. *J Pediatr*. Apr;231: p. 10-16.

25. Pennings, S., & Symons, X. (2021). Persuasion, not coercion or incentivisation, is the best means of promoting COVID-19 vaccination. *Journal of medical ethics*, 47(10), p. 709–711.

26. Dutton, K. (2022). Bill Would Let Children Over 12 Get Vaccines Without Parents' Consent. *Newsweek*. January 21, 2022.

27. U.S. Department of Health & Human Services. Centers for Disease Control and Prevention. (2022). Safety of COVID-19 Vaccines. Available at: https://www. cdc.gov/coronavirus/2019-ncov/vaccines/safety/myocarditis.html (Accessed: April 4, 2022 and September 8, 2022). "*Should I Still Get Myself or My Child Vaccinated? Yes. CDC continues to recommend that everyone ages 5 years and older get vaccinated for COVID-19. The known risks of COVID-19 illness and its related, possibly severe complications, such as long-term health problems, hospitalization, and even death, far outweigh the potential risks of having a rare adverse reaction to vaccination, including the possible risk of myocarditis or pericarditis. If you have already gotten the first dose of Pfizer-BioNTech or Moderna vaccine, or if your child has already gotten the first dose of the Pfizer-BioNTech vaccine, it's important to get the second dose unless a vaccination provider or your doctor tells you not to get it.*"

28. Hartley-Parkinson, C. (2011). Schoolgirl, 10, takes dealer father's cocaine stash to show-and-tell session at school after he hid it in a bag of Haribo" *DailyMail.* Une 1, 2011. Available at: https://www.dailymail.co.uk/news/article-1392982/Schoolgirl-10-takes-drug-dealer-fathers-cocaine-hidden-Haribo-bag-tell.html (Accessed: April 8, 2022).

29. Desmet, M. (2021). Stopping Totalitarianism and Mass Formation Psychosis. December 9 , 2021. Available at: https://rumble.com/vqhgle-dr.-robert-malone-billions-of-people-have-been-brainwashed-and-dont-realize.html (Accessed: December 10, 2021).

30. Desmet, M. (2022). *The Psychology of Totalitarianism.* Chelsea Green Publishing.

31. Meerloo, J. (1956). *The rape of the mind: The psychology of thought control, menticide, and brainwashing.* Vol. 118. World Publishing Company.

32. Academy of Ideas. (2021). Is a Mass Psychosis the Greatest Threat to Humanity? February 26, 2021. *Academy of Ideas.*

33. Arieti, Silvano. (1955). *Interpretation of schizophrenia.*

34. Jung, C.G. (2014). *The symbolic life: Miscellaneous writings.* Routledge

35. Young, C. (1946). Letters Vol II P 217 -221.

36. Malone, R. (2021). MASS FORMATION PSYCHOSIS or... mass hypnosis-the madness of crowds. December 9, 2021. Substack. Available at: https:// rwmalonemd.substack.com/p/mass-formation-psychosis. (Accessed: September 5, 2022).

37. Bernays, E. L. (2018) *Propaganda.* Chile: Desert.

38. Taylor, C. (2021). Are Covid vaccine mandates ethical? Here's what medical experts think. CNBC. November 4, 2021. Available at: https://www.cnbc. com/2021/11/24/are-covid-vaccine-mandates-ethical-heres-what-medical-experts-think.html (Accessed: September 5, 2021).

39. Ioannidis, J. P. A. (2021)."Reconciling estimates of global spread and infection fatality rates of COVID-19: an overview of systematic evaluations." *European journal of clinical investigation* 51, no. 5: p 13554.

40. Cao, S., Gan, Y., Wang, C. *et al.* (2020). Post-lockdown SARS-CoV-2 nucleic acid screening in nearly ten million residents of Wuhan, China. Nat Commun 11, p. 5917.

41. Gostin LO, Sapsin JW, Teret SP, Burris S, Mair JS, Hodge JG Jr, Vernick JS. (2002). The Model State Emergency Health Powers Act: planning for and response to bioterrorism and naturally occurring infectious diseases. JAMA. 2002 Aug 7;288(5):p. 622-8.

42. Bayer R. (2003). Ethics of health promotion and disease prevention. In: Jennings B, Kahn J, Mastroianni A, Parker LS, eds. Ethics and Public Health: Model Curriculum. Washington, DC: Association of Schools of Public Health; 2003.

43. Childress, J.F., Faden, R.R., Gaare, R.D., Gostin, L.O., Kahn, J., Bonnie, R.J., Kass,

N.E., Mastroianni, A.C., Moreno, J.D. and Nieburg, P., (2002). Public health ethics: mapping the terrain. Journal of Law, Medicine & Ethics, 30(2), pp.170-178.

44. Agamben, G. (2021). Where are we now? The epidemic as politics. Rowman & Littlefield.

45. Agamben, G. (2008). "State of exception." In State of Exception. University of Chicago Press.

46. Baker, R A. (2003). "Psychiatry's gentleman abolitionist." The Independent Review 7, no. 3:p. 455-460.

47. Quote by Jakub Bożydar Wiśniewski also said: "For the greater good": the phrase that always precedes the greatest evil." Available at: https://www.goodreads.com/author/quotes/14121943.Jakub_Bo_ydar_Wi_niewski (Accessed: February 11, 2022).

48. Quote by Tacitus. Available at: https://www.brainyquote.com/authors/tacitus-quotes (Accessed: February 11, 2022).

49. van Aardt, W. (2020). "Separation of church and State: Making sense of freedom of religion under lockdown regulations" De Rebus SA Attorneys Journal. The Law Society of South Africa. November 2020. Pp 23 – 25

50. van Aardt, W. (2021). "Can Government mandate the COVID-19 vaccine against your will? A discussion on international human rights law" De Rebus SA Attorneys Journal. The Law Society of South Africa. July 2021. Pp 14 -17.

51. van Aardt, W. (2021). "COVID-19 School Closures and the Principles of Proportionality and Balancing" (2021). J Infect Dis Ther 9: S3:002.

52. Vienna Declaration and Programme of Action Adopted by the World Conference on Human Rights in Vienna on 25 June 1993. Available at: https://www.ohchr.org/EN/ProfessionalInterest/Pages/Vienna.aspx. (Accessed: October 1, 2022).

53. Harrison, J (2004) 'In Memoriam: Joel Feinberg, University of Arizona News, March 31, 2004

Chapter 11

1. Young, A.L., (2012). The Rule of Law in the United Kingdom: Formal or Substantive?. ICL Journal, 6(2), pp.259-280.

2. Zanghellini, A., (2016). The foundations of the rule of law. Yale JL & Human., 28, p.213.

3. Subramanian, S.V. and Kumar, A., 2021. Increases in COVID-19 are unrelated to levels of vaccination across 68 countries and 2947 counties in the United States. European journal of epidemiology, 36(12), pp.1237-1240.

4. The Telegraph Staff. (2021). Jacinda Ardern admits Covid plan will lead to two-tier society in New Zealand Our. The Telegraph. 24/10/2021. Available at: https://www.msn.com/en-gb/travel/news/jacinda-ardern-admits-covid-plan-creating-two-tier-system-in-new-zealand/ar-AAPTMGF (Accessed: September 2, 2022).

5. Isaac, L and Kennedy N. (2021). Austria to impose Covid lockdown for the unvaccinated age 12 and older, CNN. Available at: https://www.cnn.com/2021/11/14/europe/austria-lockdown-unvaccinated-intl/index.html (Accessed: September 1, 2022).

6. Walt, V and Warner, B. (2021). No jab, no job: Europe's workers face tough measures as politicians lay down the law. Forbes. October 14, 2021. Available at: https://fortune.com/2021/10/14/covid-vaccine-fired-europe-workers-france-italy-draghi-macron-green-pass/amp/ (Accessed: September 2, 2022).

7. The Constitutional Rights Foundation. (2010). Plato and Aristotle on Tyranny and the Rule of Law. The Constitutional Rights Foundation. Bill of Rights in Action.

(Volume 26, No. 1).

8. van Aardt, W. (2022) Public policy, jus cogens norms and the fiduciary criterion of legitimacy. De Rebus Attorneys Journal. July 1, 2022. Also see Van Aardt, W. (2004). "State responsibility for human rights abuses committed by non-state actors under the Constitution." PhD diss., North-West University.

9. Márquez, X., (2012). A Stranger's Knowledge: Statesmanship, Philosophy, and Law in Plato's Statesman: Statesmanship, Philosophy, and Law in Plato's Statesman. 34, 341-364.

10. Plato, Statesman, in Plato: Complete Works. 294, 337 (John M. Cooper ed., 1997).

11. Stalley, R, F. (1983). An Introduction to Plato's Laws. 27, 33-34 (pointing out Plato's contributions to the natural law tradition and arguing that, in supporting the rule of law in the Laws, he assumes that laws are capable of mirroring the requirements of reason). Also see: Fred D. Miller. (2012). Rule of Reason in Plato's Laws in Reason, Religeon and Natutal Law: From Plato to Spinosa (Jonathan A. Jacobs ed., 2012).(arguing that the Laws defends the rule of law insofar as the governing laws are in accordance with nature, that is, insofar as they are the work of an intelligent legislator aiming at the virtuous life).

12. Plato, Laws, in Plato: Complete Works 1318, 1325, 1393 (John M. Cooper ed., 1997).

13. Aristotle, Politics, in The Complete Works of Aristotle ARISTOTLE, VOL. 2, 1986, 2030 (Jonathan Barnes ed., 1995).

14. Roth, C. (2021). We're Living Through the Greatest Transfer of Wealth from the Middle Class to the Elites in History | Opinion. Newsweek. October, 24, 2021. Available at: https://www.newsweek.com/were-living-through-greatest-transfer-wealth-middle-class-elites-history-opinion-1641614 (Accessed: February 7, 2022).

15. Collins, C. (2021). Updates: Billionaire Wealth, U.S. Job Losses and Pandemic Profiteers. Inequality.org October 18, 2021. Available at: https://inequality.org/great-divide/updates-billionaire-pandemic/ (Accessed: February 8 , 2022). Also see: Sánchez-Páramo, C. *et al.* (2021). COVID-19 leaves a legacy of rising poverty and widening inequality. WorldBankBlog. October 7, 2021. https://blogs.worldbank.org/developmenttalk/covid-19-leaves-legacy-rising-poverty-and-widening-inequality

16. Swartz, N P. (2010). "Thomas Aquinas: on law, tyranny and resistance." Acta Theologica 30, no. 1. Also see: Aquinas, Thomas (1256). Commentum in Quatuor Libros Sententiarum. 1267. De Regimine Principum liber primus, 1265-1274. Summa Theologica.

17. Montagnier, L., Rubenfeld, J. (2022) Omicron Makes Biden's Vaccine Mandates Obsolete. Wallstreet Journal. January 9, 2022.

18. Summers, R. S. (1984). London: Edward Arnold, 1984, p. 1. (The other three, according to Summers, are Oliver Wendell Holmes, Jr., Roscoe Pound, and Karl Llewellyn.)

19. Fuller, Lon L. (1964)."The morality of law."

20. Fox-Decent, E, Criddle E. (2018)."The Internal Morality of International Law." *McGill Law Journal/Revue* de droit de McGill 63, no. 3-4: p765-781.

21. Dworkin, R. (1965). "The elusive morality of law." Vill. L. Rev. 10: 631.

22. Tucker, E.W. (1965). The morality of law, by Lon L. Fuller. Indiana Law Journal, 40(2), p.5.

23. Sinclair, I.M. and Sinclair, I.R. (1984). *The Vienna Convention on the law of treaties.* Manchester University Press.

24. Vienna Convention on the Law of Treaties, 23 May 1969, 1155, UNTS 331, art 53 (entered into force 27 January 1980). ("A treaty is void if, at the time of its conclusion, it conflicts with a peremptory norm of general international law.").

25. Yearwood, L. (2009). "State Accountability for Breaching *Jus Cogens* Norms", University of Exeter, 2009.

26. Meron, T. (1986). "On a Hierarchy of International Human Rights", 80 *AM. J. INT'L L.*,p. 19-21.

27. Stephens, P, J. (2004). "A Categorical Approach to Human Rights Claims: Jus Cogens as a Limitation on Enforcement." *Wis. Int'l LJ* 22: p. 245.

28. Vocabulary.com.(2022) Available at: https://www.vocabulary.com/dictionary/unilateralism (Accessed: September 16, 2022).

29. Cornel Law School, (2022). "fiduciary duty." Available at: https://www.law.cornell.edu/wex/fiduciary_duty (Accessed: September 16, 2022).

30. Johnson, V.R., (2018). The Fiduciary Obligations of Public Officials. *Mary's J. on Legal Malpractice & Ethics*, 9, p.298.

31. Agamben, G. (2008). *State of exception*. In State of Exception. University of Chicago Press.

32. United States Holocaust Memorial Museum, Antisemetic Legislation 1933–1939. United States Holocaust Memorial Museum, Washington, DC. Available at: https://encyclopedia.ushmm.org/content/en/article/antisemitic-legislation-1933-1939 (Accessed: August 26, 2022).

33. West's Encyclopedia of American Law, edition 2. S.v. "Critical legal theory." Available at: https://legal-dictionary.thefreedictionary.com/Critical+legal+theory. (Accessed: August 26, 2022).

34. Hobson, T, (2018). "Lawlessness: What Happens When Law Itself Becomes Lawless?" *Patheos*. February 26.

35. Unger, R M. (1986). *The Critical Legal Studies Movement*. Cambridge, Mass.: Harvard Univ. Press.

36. Oetken, J.P. (1990). Form and substance in critical legal studies. *Yale LJ, 100*, p.2209.

37. Tushnet, M. (1990). Critical legal studies: A political history. *Yale Lj, 100*, p.1515.

38. Hutchinson, A C., (1989). *Critical Legal Studies*. Totowa, N.J.: Rowman & Littlefield.

39. Waldron, J. (2002). Is the Rule of Law an Essentially Contested Concept (in Florida)?, 21 *LAW & PHIL*. P. 137.

40. Sellers, M., 2003. *Republican Legal Theory: The History, Constitution and Purposes of Law in a Free State*. Springer.

41. Bassiouni, M. C. (2001). 38 Affirmation of the Principles of International Law Recognized by the Charter of the Nuremberg Tribunal and the Judgement of the Trial, U.N. Doc. A/64/Add.1, A/Res/95(1)(11 Dec. 1946). In International Terrorism: Multilateral Conventions (1937–2001), Leiden, The Netherlands: Brill | Nijhoff.

42. Shklar, J.N. and Shklar, J.N., (1986). *Legalism: Law, morals, and political trials*. Harvard University Press.

Chapter 12

1. Gross, B. M. (1980).*Friendly fascism: The new face of power in America*. South End Press.

2. Wolin, S. S. (2008). *Democracy Incorporated: Managed Democracy and the Specter of Inverted Totalitarianism*. Princeton: Princeton University Press

3. World Economic Forum. (2022).Our Partners. Available at: https://www.weforum.org/partners#search. (Accessed: September 9, 2022).

4. Buxton, N. (2016).Davos and its danger to Democracy. January 18, 2016, Available

at: https://www.tni.org/en/article/davos-and-its-danger-to-democracy (Accessed: September 9, 2022).

5. The World Economic Forum. (2020).The Great Reset. Available at: https://www. weforum.org/focus/the-great reset Accessed: September 8, 2022).

6. Martens, J. (2020)."The Role of Public and Private Actors and Means in Implementing the SDGs: Reclaiming the Public Policy Space for Sustainable Development and Human Rights." In *Sustainable Development Goals and Human Rights*, pp. 207-220. *Springer*, Cham.

7. Santayana, G. (1905). *The Life of Reason*, rr, The Phases of Human Progress: Reason in society. Vol. 2. C. Scribner's sons.

8. Birn, A.E.; Molina, N., (2005). In the name of public health. *American Journal of Public Health*, 95(7), pp.1095-1097.

9. Kershaw, Ian (2000). *Hitler, 1889–1936*: Hubris. New York; London: W.W. Norton & Company.

10. Lyttelton, A. (2008). *The Seizure of Power: Fascism in Italy, 1919–1919*. New York: Routledge. pp. 75–77

11. Evans, R, J. (2003). *The Coming of the Third Reich*. New York: Penguin Books

12. Nuremberg Trials. (1946). The Trials of the War Criminals Before Nuremberg Military Tribunal (PDF). Vol. VII. Washington: United States Government Printing Office. pp. 16–17.

13. Order of the Reich President for the Protection of People and State (German: *Dehorning des Reichspräsidenten zum Schutz von Volk und Staat*).

14. The Decree of the Reich President for the Protection of People and State" (German: *Verordnung des Reichspräsidenten zum Schutz von Volk und Staat*).

15. Weindling, P. (1993). *Health, race and German politics between national unification and Nazism, 1870-1945*. Cambridge University Press.

16. Szasz, T. (1984).*The therapeutic State*. Buffalo: Prometheus Books.

17. United States Holocaust Memorial Museum, Washington, DC. (2022).THE BIOLOGICAL STATE: NAZI RACIAL HYGIENE, 1933–1939. Washington, D.C. Available at: https://encyclopedia.ushmm.org/content/en/article/the-biological-State-nazi-racial-hygiene-1933-1939 (Accessed: February 11, 2022).

18. Bachrach S. (2004).In the name of public health--Nazi racial hygiene. *N Engl J Med*. 2004 Jul 29;351(5): p. 417-20.

19. United States Holocaust Memorial Museum, Washington, DC SERIES: NAZI PROPAGANDA Available at: https://encyclopedia.ushmm.org/content/en/series/nazi-propaganda?parent (Accessed: February 11, 2022).

20. Bock G. (2004).Nazi sterilization and reproductive policies. In: Kuntz D, Bachrach S, eds. Deadly medicine: creating the master race. Chapel Hill: University of North Carolina Press: p. 61-87

21. United States Holocaust Memorial Museum, Washington, DC. (2022).THE PRESS IN THE THIRD REICH. Available at: https://encyclopedia.ushmm.org/content/en/article/the-press-in-the-third-reich (Accessed: February 11, 2022).

22. Elhassan, K. (2018).10 Famous Companies That Collaborated with Nazi Germany. History Collection. July 16, 2018. Available at: https://historycollection.com/10-famous-companies-collaborated-nazi-germany/9/(Accessed: February 11, 2022).

23. Proctor, R. (1988). Racial hygiene: medicine under the Nazis. Cambridge, Mass.: Harvard University Press.

24. Busser, C. (2021).NEA announces support for educator vaccine and testing requirement. NEA Press Release. August 12, 2021.

25. Meador, D. (2019). What Does the National Education Association Do? An Overview of the NEA. *Thoughtco*. June 11, 2019.

26. Burt, C. (2021). Harvard joins other elite institutions in vaccine mandate. May

6, 2021. Available at: https://universitybusiness.com/harvard-joins-other-elite-institutions-in-vaccine-mandate/ (Accessed: February 14, 2022). also see Burt C Heeding CDC guidance, top universities require masks as Delta variant surges. July 29, 2021 Available at: https://universitybusiness.com/heeding-cdc-guidance-top-universities-require-masks-as-delta-variant-surges/ (Accessed: February 14, 2022).

27. Richard, J. E. (2003). *The Coming of the Third Reich* (New York: Penguin, 2003), 421.

28. Yahoo Finance (2022). Available at: https://finance.yahoo.com/quote/PFE/holders (Accessed: February 11, 2022).

29. Mereli, A. (2021). The WHO is to Dependant on the Gates Foundation. Quarts. Available at: https://qz.com/2102889/the-who-is-too-dependent-on-gates-foundation-donations/ (Accessed: February 11, 2022).

30. Hanson, D. (2021). The Shocking Amount of Money Vanguard and BlackRock Control. MoneyInc. Available at: https://moneyinc.com/shocking-amount-of-money-vanguard-and-blackrock-control/ (Accessed: February 11, 2022).

31. Yahoo Finance. (2022). https://finance.yahoo.com/quote/PFE/holders (Accessed: February 11, 2022).

32. Tooze, A (2006). The Wages of Destruction: The Making and Breaking of the Nazi Economy. New York: Viking. Also DeLong, J. Bradford "Slouching Towards Utopia?: The Economic History of the Twentieth Century. XV. Nazis and Soviets". econ161.berkeley.edu. University of California at Berkeley.

33. Burleigh M. (1994). *Death and deliverance: euthanasia in Germany c.1900-1945.* Cambridge, England: Cambridge University Press.

34. Mathews, J. (2021). All the major companies requiring vaccines for workers. August 23, 2021. Fortune. Available at: https://fortune.com/2021/08/23/companies-requiring-vaccines-workers-vaccination-mandatory/ (Accessed: February 11, 2022).

35. Messenger, H. (2022).From Amex to Walmart, here are the companies mandating the Covid vaccines for employees. NBC News. January 25 2022. Available at: https://www.nbcnews.com/business/business-news/amex-walmart-are-companies-mandating-covid-vaccine-employees-rcna11049 (Accessed: February 11, 2022).

36. Records of the United States Nuremberg War Crime Trials. (1948). United States v Carl Krauch et al. (Case V1).August 14, 1947 – July 30, 1948. Available at: https://www.archives.gov/files/research/captured-german-records/microfilm/m892.pdf (Accessed: February 11, 2022).

37. LAW REPORTS OF TRIALS OF WAR CRIMINALS VOLUME X THE I.G. FARBEN AND KRUPP TRIALS PUBLISHED FOR THE UNITED NATIONS WAR CRIMES COMMISSION BY HIS MAJESTY'S STATIONERY OFFICE 1949 Available at: https://www.archives.gov/files/research/captured-german-records/microfilm/m892.pdf (Accessed: February 11, 2022).

38. Black, E. (2012). IBM and the Holocaust: The Strategic Alliance Between Nazi Germany and America's Most Powerful Corporation-Expanded Edition. Dialog press.

39. BBC News World Edition. (2002).Bertelsmann admits Nazi past. BBC News. October 8, 2002. Available at: http://news.bbc.co.uk/2/hi/business/2308415.stm (Accessed: February 15, 2022).

40. John, A. 10 Popular Companies that Profited in Nazi Concentration Camps. Wonderslist. Available at: https://www.wonderslist.com/10-popular-companies-profited-nazis/. (Accessed: February 15, 2022).

41. ABC News. (2021).Teenagers from remote NT community arrested after escape from Howard Springs COVID quarantine facility. November 30, 2021. Available

at: https://www.abc.net.au/news/2021-12-01/multiple-people-escape-howard-springs-quarantine-facility-darwin/100663994 (Accessed: September 10, 2022).

42. Bell, D. (2020). American charged under Quarantine Act amid accusations he ignored pandemic safety rules in Banff. CBC. Available at: https://www.cbc.ca/news/canada/calgary/u-s-man-charged-with-breaching-pandemic-rules-1.5692421 (Accessed: September 7, 2022).

43. Wolfe. R. (2021). Germans, Australians dragged to government 'quarantine centers' for COVID-19. Lidfesite. Available at: https://standby.lifesitenews.com/news/dozens-dragged-to-covid-quarantine-camps-in-germany-australia/ (Accessed: September 7, 2022).

44. Mek, A. (2021). Australia: Army Forcibly Throws Covid-Exposed Citizens in Quarantine Camps (Video). RAIR. Available at: https://rairfoundation.com/Australia-army-forcibly-throws-covid-exposed-citizens-in-quarantine-camps-video/. (Accessed: September 7, 2022).

45. Jarret. G (2021). New Zealand Announces 'Quarantine Camps' Where Positive Patients Will Be Forcibly Placed. Gregg Jarred Podcast. Available at: https://thegreggjarrett.com/new-zealand-announces-quarantine-camps-where-positive-patients-will-be-forcibly-placed/ (Accessed: September 7, 2022).

46. Agamben, G., (2021). *Where are we now?: The epidemic as politics*. Rowman & Littlefield

47. Lyman, B. (2021). "Fauci Lied": NYT Op-Ed Rebukes Fauci For COVID Misinformation. July 29, 2021. MSN News. Available at: https://www.msn.com/en-us/news/politics/fauci-lied-nyt-op-ed-rebukes-fauci-for-covid-misinformation/ (Accessed: September 1, 2022). also see Porter, J. (2022). Dr. Fauci Attempts to Defend His Legacy Of Lies, Gets Debunked With His Own Words. Lifezette. August 24, 2022. Available at:https://www.lifezette.com/2022/08/dr-fauci-attempts-to-defend-his-legacy-of-lies-gets-debunked-with-his-own-words-videos/ (Accessed: September 1, 2022).

48. Kessler, K. (2007). "Physicians and the Nazi euthanasia program." International Journal of Mental Health 36, no. 1: p. 4-16.

49. Proctor, R. N. (1999). *The Nazi War on Cancer*. Princeton: Princeton University Press.

50. Paxton, R O. (2004). *The Anatomy of Fascism* (First ed.). New York: Alfred A. Knopf.

51. Britt, L.(2003). "The 14 Characteristics of Fascism." *Free Inquiry*.

52. Chalfat, M. (2021). Biden blames unvaccinated for US's COVID-19. The Hill. sloghttps://thehill.com/policy/healthcare/571593-biden-blames-unvaccinated-for-covid-19s-slog/

53. MSN. (2021).CNN's Berman Asks: If Unvaccinated Not to Blame for Delta Surge Who Is. (MSN, July 29, 2021). Available at: https://www.msn.com/en-us/news/politics/cnn-s-berman-asks-if-unvaccinated-not-to-blame-for-delta-surge-who-is/ar-AAMHSIO (Accessed: August 10, 2021). Hill,J. (2022). Mark Slapinski says the unvaccinated should be looted and sent to work camps. Substack. Available at: https://hillmd.substack.com/p/mark-slapinski-says-the-unvaccinated. (Accessed: October 10, 2022).c. Dand, E. (2021) What Are We Going To Do With The Anti-Vaxxers?. Forbes. June 27, 2021. d. Darsi, A. (2022) Antivaxers are a global menace who must be defeated. The Times. October 3, 2022.

54. Blaylock, R.L. (2022). "COVID UPDATE: What is the truth?" Surg Neurol Int. 2022 Apr 22;13:167.

55. US department of Homeland Security. (2022).CBD Focus Areas – Biosurveillance. Available at: https://www.dhs.gov/science-and-technology/biosurveillance. (Accessed:October 2, 2022).

56. Parpia, R. (2022). Mayo Clinic Fires 700 Employees for Refusing to Get

COVID-19 Vaccinations. The Vaccine reaction. January 10, 2022. *The Vaccine Reaction*. Available at: https://thevaccinereaction.org/2022/01/mayo-clinic-fires-700-employees-for-refusing-to-get-covid-19-vaccinations/ (Accessed: January 12, 2022).

57. France 24. (2021). France suspends 3,000 unvaccinated health workers without pay. Available at: https://www.france24.com/en/france/20210916-france-suspends-3-000-unvaccinated-health-workers-without-pay. (Accessed: October 1, 2022). Also see Walsh, J D. (2021) I'm Not Changing My Mind': New York Fires Unvaccinated Health-Care Workers. INTELLIGENCER. Available at: https://nymag.com/intelligencer/2021/09/new-york-fires-unvaccinated-health-care-workers.html (Accessed: October 1, 2022).

58. U.S. Department of Health and Human Services (HHS). (2020). COVID-19 Public Education Campaign. Available at https://wecandothis.hhs.gov/resource/we-can-do-campaign-background (Accessed: January 12, 2022).

59. Karp, P. (2020). Morrison government spent $128m on advertising in 2019-20, figures reveal. The Guardian. Available at: https://www.theguardian.com/australia-news/2020/dec/25/morrison-Government-spent-128m-on-advertising-in-2019-20-figures-reveal (Accessed: December 9, 2021).

60. Thompson, E. (2020).Trudeau government to spend more than $88M on COVID-19 ads. CBC. Available at https://www.cbc.ca/news/politics/covid-pandemic-advertising-communications-1.5597690 (Accessed: January 7, 2022).

61. McKibben, A. (2021). The millions spent on 'disturbing' covid advertising. https://www.politics.co.uk/comment/2021/03/29/the-millions-spent-on-disturbing-covid-advertising/ Politics.co.uk. In 2020, the UK Government tripled its already bloated advertising budget, displacing corporate behemoths such as Unilever, Sky and Proctor & Gamble, by splurging a whopping £164 million. If you then add Public Health England's substantial 2020 ad spend of £80m, you get a good picture of how Government messaging has come to comprehensively dominate our lives.

62. Pesce, L.N (2020). Twitter, Facebook and YouTube are taking down that hydroxychloroquine video, and now Donald Trump Jr. can't tweet for 12 hours. Market Watch. Available at: https://www.marketwatch.com/story/why-twitter-facebook-and-youtube-are-taking-down-that-hydroxychloroquine-video-and-suspending-accounts-including-donald-trump-jr-that-shared-it-2020-07-28 (Accessed: October 2, 2022).

63. Kari, P. (2021). Facebook bans misinformation about all vaccines after years of controversy. The Guardian. Available at: https://www.theguardian.com/technology/2021/feb/08/facebook-bans-vaccine-misinformation (Accessed: October 2, 2022).

64. US Centers for Disease Control and Prevention (2020, 2021, 2022). Guidance Documents. Available at: https://www.cdc.gov/phlp/news/2020/2020-03-19.html; https://www.cdc.gov/coronavirus/2019-ncov/communication/guidance-list.html?Sort=Date%3A%3Adesc (Accessed monthly 2020, 2021, 2022).

65. NYC Department of Education. (2022).*DOE Fall 2022 COVID-19 Guidance*. Available at: https://www.schools.nyc.gov/school-life/health-and-wellness/covid-information/health-and-safety-in-our-schools (Accessed: August 31, 2022).

66. Desmet, M. (2022). *The Psychology of Totalitarianism*. Chelsea Green Publishing, 2022. Also see Desmet, M. (2022). Stopping Totalitarianism And Mass Formation Psychosis. Available at: https://rumble.com/vu2530-mattias-desmet-stopping-totalitarianism-and-mass-formation-psychosis.html (Accessed: February 4, 2022).

67. Planet, D., Windschuttle, K., Franklin, R., O'Sullivan, J., Daniels, A., Blair, T., Connor, M., Dolce, J., Colebatch, H., McCann, D. and Smith, P. (2022). Part Two: COVID, Politics and Psychology. February 5, 2022. *Quadrant Public Health*.

68. Academy of Ideas. (2021). "The Manufacturing of a Mass Psychosis – Can Sanity Return to an Insane World?" April 24, 2021. Available at: https://academyofideas. com/tag/mass-psychosis/. (Accessed: September 15, 2022)

69. Meerloo, JA M, Meerloo, J. (1956). *The rape of the mind: The psychology of thought control, menticide, and brainwashing.* Vol. 118. World Publishing Company.

70. Orwell, G. (1949). *Nineteen Eighty-Four.* London: Martin Secker & Warburg Ltd.

71. McArthur, Tom, ed. (1992). The Oxford Companion to the English Language. Oxford University Press. p. 321.

72. Conradson, J. (2022).Klaus Schwab's 'World Economic Forum' Cuts Off "All Relations" With Russia, Scrubs Putin from WEF Website.' March 10, 2022. *The Gateway Pundit.* Available at: https://www.thegatewaypundit.com/2022/03/ klaus-schwabs-world-economic-forum-cuts-off-relations-russia-scrubs-putin-wef-website/ (Accessed: September 17, 2022). also see Informed Choice Australia. (2021). WEF and their 'Young Global Leaders' program, who's on the list?. Available at: https://www.informedchoiceaustralia.com/post/wef-and-their-young-global-leaders-program. Accessed: September 15, 2022).

73. Newswars. (2022). O Canada: Police Raid House "Gestapo-Style" After COVID Snitch Reports Over 5 People In Home. *NewsWars.* Available at: https://www. newswars.com/o-canada-police-raid-house-gestapo-style-after-covid-snitch-reports-over-5-people-in-home/ (Accessed: October 2, 2022)

74. Lush, T O'Meara, C. (2020).Pastor arrested for holding Sunday service in violation of COVID-19 social distancing orders. *Associated Press.* March 30, 2020. Available at: https://www.police1.com/coronavirus-covid-19/articles/pastor-arrested-for-holding-sunday-service-in-violation-of-covid-19-social-distancing-orders (Accessed: September 17 , 2022)

75. Klett, L,M. (2021). 'It's insanity': Canadian pastor jailed for holding church service compares gov't actions to communist China. The ChristianPost. May 13, 2021. Available at: https://metrovoicenews.com/new-documentary-says-canadian-church-crackdown-similar-to-china/ (Accessed: September 17 , 2022)

76. Shellnut, K. (2022). Canadian Pastor Jailed Over COVID-19 Violations Released. Available at: https://www.christianitytoday.com/news/2021/february/canada-pastor-jail-arrest-gracelife-church-covid-order.html (Accessed: September 17 , 2022)

77. Kulldorff, M. *et al.* (2020). "Great Barrington Declaration." https://gbdeclaration.org

78. Rivas, K. (2020).Fauci calls coronavirus herd immunity approach 'nonsense, very dangerous. Fox News. October 15, 2020.Available at: www.foxnews.com/ health/fauci-coronavirus-herd-immunity-great-barrington-declaration-nonsense (Accessed: September 8, 2022).

79. Sodha, S. (2020). The anti-lockdown scientists' cause would be more persuasive if it weren't so half-baked. October 11, 2020. *The Guardian.* Available at: https://www. theguardian.com/commentisfree/2020/oct/11/the-rebel-scientists-cause-would-be-more-persuasive-if-it-werent-so-half-baked (Accessed: August 29, 2022).

80. Crane, E. (2020). NYC Mayor Bill de Blasio threatens fines of $15k if people living in locked down COVID-19 hotspot neighborhoods violate mass gatherings ban and $1,000 fines for no masks from tomorrow. DailyMail. Available at: https:// www.dailymail.co.uk/news/article-8815669/Bill-Blasio-threatens-fines-15k-violation-mass-gathering-bans.html (Accessed: August 29, 2022).

81. King, C. (2020). Italy to impose fines of up to €1,500 on unvaccinated citizens. EuroWeekly. Available at: https://euroweeklynews.com/2022/01/08/italy-to-impose-fines-of-up-to-e1500-on-unvaccinated-citizens/ (Accessed: August 29, 2022).

82. Reuters. (2022). Austrian COVID vaccine mandate to come into force on Saturday,

Reuters. Available at: https://news.yahoo.com/austrian-covid-vaccine-mandate-come-162007674.html (Accessed: August 29, 2022).

83. Barkoukis, L. (2022).NJ Gym Owner Who Refused to Close During Lockdown Has Finally Been Sentenced. TownHall. Available at: https://townhall.com/tipsheet/leahbarkoukis/2022/01/28/nj-gym-owner-who-refused-to-close-during-lockdown-has-finally-been-sentenced-n2602469 (Accessed: August 29, 2022).

84. Smeaton, P. (2020). Pregnant Australian woman arrested at: home for promoting anti-lockdown protest on Facebook. LifesiteNews. Available at: https://www.lifesitenews.com/news/pregnant-australian-woman-arrested-at-home-for-promoting-anti-lockdown-protest-on-facebook (Accessed: August 29, 2022).

85. Africa News. (2020). Africa's Covid-19 Corruption That Outweighs Pandemic. Africa News. Available at: https://www.africanews.com/2021/05/25/africa-s-COVID-19-corruption-that-outweighs-pandemic/ (Accessed: August 29, 2022).

86. UN Office of the High Commissioner of Human Rights. (2020). COVID-19 highlights deadly cost of corruption and the urgent need for companies to respect human rights: UN experts. Available at: https://www.ohchr.org/en/press-releases/2020/07/COVID-19-highlights-deadly-cost-corruption-and-urgent-need-companies-respect?LangID=E&NewsID=26064 (Accessed: August 29, 2022).

87. D Sousa. (2022). 2,000 Mules: They Thought We'd Never Find Out. They Were Wrong. Regnery Publishing. 2022.

88. Stauffer E. (2022). The FBI Whistleblowers and Biden's Tainted Election Washington Examiner September 1, 2022. Available at: https://www.realclearpolitics.com/2022/09/01/the_fbi_whistleblowers_and_bidens_tainted_election_578410.html (Accessed: August 29, 2022).

89. Greenwald, G (2022).The NYT Now Admits the Biden Laptop -- Falsely Called "Russian Disinformation" -- is Authentic. Substack. Available at: https://greenwald.substack.com/p/the-nyt-now-admits-the-biden-laptop?s=r (Accessed: August 29, 2022).

90. Smith, K. (2022). How Dem officials, the media and Big Tech worked in concert to bury the Hunter Biden story. New York Post. Available at: https://nypost.com/2022/03/18/how-big-tech-media-and-dems-killed-the-hunter-biden-story/

91. Pollard, J. (2005). *The Fascist Experience in Italy*. (n.p.): Taylor & Francis.

92. Conquest, R. (1999). Reflections on a Ravaged Century: Reign of Rogue Ideologies. p. 74.

93. Statcounter. (2022). Search Engine Market Share Worldwide. Available at: https://gs.statcounter.com/search-engine-market-share (Accessed: August 29, 2022).

94. Lee, J. (2013). No. 1 Position in Google Gets 33% of Search Traffic [Study]. Search Engine Watch.

95. The Editors of Encyclopaedia Britannica. (2022).Totalitarianism Government, Available at: https://www.britannica.com/topic/totalitarianism (Accessed: August 29, 2022)

96. Mussolini, B. (1935). *The Doctrine of Fascism*, Firenze: Vallecchi Editore. P 14.

97. Cinpoes, R. (2010). *Nationalism and Identity in Romania: A History of Extreme Politics from the Birth of the State to EU Accession*. London, Oxford, New York, New Delhi and Sydney: Bloomsbury.

98. Beem, C. (2021). Why refusing the COVID-19 vaccine isn't just immoral – it's 'un-American'. *The Conversation*. August 9, 2021. Available at: www.theconversation.com/why-refusing-the-covid-19-vaccine-isnt-just-immoral-its-un-american-165564 (Accessed: August 29, 2022).

99. Servitje, L, Lincoln, M and Yamey, G. (2021). 'Medical freedom' isn't an American value. The Founders promoted vaccines and public health. USA Today. Available at: https://www.usatoday.com/story/

opinion/2021/07/02/rejecting-covid-vaccine-unpatriotic-washington-madison-franklin/7793607002/?gnt-cfr=1 (Accessed: August 29, 2022).

100. Parlapiano et al. (2022). Where $5 Trillion in Pandemic Stimulus Money Went. *New York Times*. March 11 2022. Available at: https://www.nytimes.com/interactive/2022/03/11/us/how-covid-stimulus-money-was-spent.html (Accessed: August 29, 2022)

101. Weintraub, K, Weise E. (2020).Federal spending on COVID-19 vaccine candidates tops $9 billion, spread among 7 companies. USA Today. Available at: https://www.usatoday.com/story/news/health/2020/08/08/feds-spending-more-than-9-billion-COVID-19-vaccine-candidates/5575206002/ (Accessed: August 30, 2022)

102. Reuters. (2021). World to Spend 157 Billion on COCID-19 Vaccines.*Reuters*. Available at: https://www.reuters.com/business/healthcare-pharmaceuticals/world-spend-157-billion-COVID-19-vaccines-through-2025-report-2021-04-29/ (Accessed: August 30, 2022)

103. AIER Staff. (2020). Cost of Lockdowns: A Preliminary Report. AIER. November 18, 2020. Available at: https://www.aier.org/article/cost-of-us-lockdowns-a-preliminary-report/. (Accessed: August 31, 2022).

104. World Health Organization. (2021). UN report: Pandemic year marked by spike in world hunger. WHO. Available at: https://www.who.int/news/item/12-07-2021-un-report-pandemic-year-marked-by-spike-in-world-hunger (Accessed: August 30, 2022)

105. Oxfam International.(2020). Pandemic profits for companies soar by billions more as poorest pay price. 9th September 2020 Available at: www.oxfam.org/en/press-releases/pandemic-profits-companies-soar-billions-more-poorest-pay-price (Accessed: August 31, 2022).

106. Pipes, R. (1995). *Russia Under the Bolshevik Regime*. New York: Vintage Books, Random House.

107. Gerhard, S., Bernd, S., Detlef, V., Scott, M.D., Ewald, O., Louise, W. and PS, F. (1990). The Mediterranean, South-east Europe, and North Africa, 1939-1941. (From Italy's Declaration of Non-Belligerence to the Entry of the United States into the War). Oxford University Press.

108. Gillette, A (2001). *Racial Theories in Fascist Italy*. London; New York: Routledge.

109. Rushlau, I, D. (2017). 'Friendly Fascism': The Core of American Conservatism. DailyKos. September 3, 2017 Available at: https://www.dailykos.com/stories/2017/9/3/1695654/--Friendly-Fascism-The-Core-of-American-Conservatism. (Accessed: August 30, 2022)

110. Sarti, R. (1968). Fascism and the Industrial Leadership in Italy, 1919-40: A Study in the Expansion of Private Power Under Fascism.

111. Kershaw, I (2000). *Hitler, 1889–1936*: Hubris. New York; London: W.W. Norton & Company.

112. Griffin, R. (2013). Fascism, *Totalitarianism and Political Religion*. Routledge.

113. Pauley, B F. (2003). *Hitler, Stalin, and Mussolini: Totalitarianism in the Twentieth Century Italy*. Wheeling: Harlan Davidson, Inc.

114. Martinot, S. (2008). *The Question of Fascism in the US*. Available at: https://www.ocf.berkeley.edu/~marto/fascism.htm (Accessed: August 29, 2022).

115. Nyyssönen, H. and Metsälä, J., 2021. Liberal democracy and its current illiberal critique: The emperor's new clothes? *Europe-Asia Studies*, 73(2), pp.273-290.

116. Carey, A. (1997). *Taking the Risk Out of Democracy: Corporate Propaganda versus Freedom and Liberty*.

117. Hedges, C. and Sacco, J. (2012). *Days of Destruction, Days of Revolt*. Nation Books.

118. Dag Hammarskjöld Foundation. (2021). Chapter One: How is the United Nations funded? Available at: https://docs.daghammarskjold.se/time-to-meet-the-moment/

part-one-1.html (Accessed: August 31, 2022).

119. United Nations Office of the High Commissioner of Human Rights. (2021). United Nations OHCHR Report 2020. Annual Report 1 May 2021. Available at: https://www.ohchr.org/sites/default/files/Documents/Publications/OHCHRreport2020.pdf (Accessed: August31, 2022).

120. Gøtzsche, P C. (2012). "Corporate crime in the pharmaceutical industry is common, serious and repetitive." BMJ 345 : e8462

121. Ventegodt, S., 2015. Why the corruption of the World Health Organization (WHO).is the biggest threat to the World's public health of our time. J Integrative Med Ther, 2(1), p.5.

122. World Health Organization. (2022). How WHO is Funded. Available at: https://www.who.int/about/funding/ (Accessed: July, 17, 2022).

123. Singh, H. (2020).Who gives funding to World Health Organisation-WHO? Jagran Josh. May 1 2020. Available at: (Accessed: July 7, 2022). https://www.jagranjosh.com/general-knowledge/who-gives-funding-to-world-health-organisation-who-1587119413-1

124. Kennedy, R, F. (2020).Gates' Globalist Vaccine Agenda: A Win-Win for Pharma and Mandatory Vaccination. April 9, 2020. *Children's Health Defense.* Available at: https://childrenshealthdefense.org/news/government-corruption/gates-globalist-vaccine-agenda-a-win-win-for-pharma-and-mandatory-vaccination/ (Accessed: July 7, 2022)

125. Sharaf, V. (2020). The Vaccine Program: Betrayal of Public Trust & Institutional Corruption—Part 3 of 7. *Childrens Health Defense.* January 25, 2018. Available at: https://childrenshealthdefense.org/news/vaccine-program-betrayal-public-trust-institutional-corruption-part-3-7/ (Accessed: July 7, 2022)

126. Gøtzsche, P.C., Smith, R. and Rennie, D. (2019). *Deadly medicines and organised crime: how big pharma has corrupted healthcare.* CRC press.

127. World Health Organization (2005).*Strengthening global health security by implementing the International Health Regulations.* Available at: https://www.who.int/publications/i/item/9789241580410 (Accessed: September 1 2022)

128. World Health Organization (2011).*Report of the strengthening response to pandemics and other public-health emergencies.* Available at: https://www.who.int/publications/i/item/strengthening-response-to-pandemics-and-other-public-health-emergencies (Accessed: September 1, 2022).

129. Chan, Lai-Ha. (2010)."WHO: the world's most powerful international organisation?." Journal of Epidemiology & Community Health 64, no. 2 (2010): 97-98.

130. Flowers,M , Zeese, K (2013), "Lifting the Veil of Mirage Democracy in the United States", Truthout (article). Truthout. February 13, 2013.

131. Chomsky, N. (1998). "The common good."

132. Jacob S. (2000).Curing the Therapeutic State: Thomas Szasz interviewed by Jacob Sullum. Reason. July 2000. Available at: https://reason.com/2000/07/01/curing-the-therapeutic-State-t/ (Accessed: February 17, 2022)

133. Szasz, T. (2007). *The medicalization of everyday life: Selected essays.* Syracuse University Press.

134. Waitzkin, H. (1978). "A Marxist view of medical care." Annals of internal medicine 89, no. 2: p. 264-278.

135. Payne, S. G. (1995). A History of Fascism, 1914–45. *University of Wisconsin Press.*

Chapter 13

1. Williams, D C. (1997). "The Constitutional Right to "Conservative" Revolution" (1997). Articles by Maurer. Faculty. P. 674.

2. Thoreau, H. D.(1849). On the Duty of Civil Disobedience.
3. Korsgaard, C. (2008). "Taking the Law into our own Hands: Kant on the Right to Revolution."
4. Academy of Ideas. (2022). Obedience and the Rise of Authoritarianism. Academy of Ideas. January, 26 2022. Available at: https://academyofideas.com/2022/01/why-are-most-people-cowards-obedience-and-the-rise-of-authoritarianism/ (Accessed: September 20, 2022)
5. Feldman, S. (2003)."Enforcing social conformity: A theory of authoritarianism." Political psychology 24, no. 1p: 41-74. Also see Academy of Ideas. (2022). Why are Most People Cowards? | Obedience and the Rise of Authoritarianism. Available at: https://academyofideas.com/2022/01/why-are-most-people-cowards-obedience-and-the-rise-of-authoritarianism/ (Accessed: September 20, 2022).Staub, E. (2003).*The psychology of good and evil: Why children, adults, and groups help and harm others.* Cambridge University Press, 2003.
6. Staub, E. (2003). *The psychology of good and evil: Why children, adults, and groups help and harm others.* Cambridge University Press, 2003.
7. Pasio, M. (2014).The Painfill Truth. May 21. Available at: https://www.youtube.com/watch?v=vxTfvoaxjUY (Accessed: September 20, 2022).
8. Rollo, M. (2009). *Man's search for himself.* WW Norton & Company.
9. Jung, C.G., (2014). *Collected Works of CG Jung, Volume 10: Civilization in Transition* (Vol. 49). Princeton University Press.
10. Gide, A. (2012). *Oscar Wilde: Reminiscences.* Open Road Media.
11. Mahatma Gandhi (2012). "The Essential Gandhi: An Anthology of His Writings on His Life, Work, and Ideas", p.144, Vintage
12. Mahatma Gandhi (2007). "Gandhi on Non-Violence", p.88, New Directions Publishing
13. Gandhi, M. and Mukherjee, R. (1993). "The Penguin Gandhi Reader", p.148, Penguin Books India.
14. Martin Luther King, Jr. (1963). *Letter from a Birmingham Jail.*
15. Martin Luther King, Jr. (2011). Why We Can't Wait (ed. Beacon Press, 2011)
16. Nelson Mandela (2011). "Nelson Mandela By Himself: The Authorised Book of Quotations", p.160, Pan Macmillan
17. Nelson Mandela (2012). "Notes to the Future: Words of Wisdom", Simon and Schuster. P118.
18. Zinn, H. (1970). "The problem is civil obedience." Address at: John Hopkins University. Baltimore, Maryland.
19. Williams, D C. (1997) "The Constitutional Right to "Conservative" Revolution" (1997). Articles by Maurer Faculty. P. 674.
20. Scott, P.B., (1987). The Right of Revolution: The Development of the People's Right to Reform Government. W. Va. L. Rev., 90, p.283.
21. UN General Assembly (1966). Optional Protocol to the International Covenant on Civil and Political Rights, 19 December 1966, United Nations, Treaty Series, vol. 999, p. 171
22. United Nations. Individual Communications Human Rights Treaty Bodies Available at: https://www.ohchr.org/en/treaty-bodies/individual-communications (Accessed: September 20, 2022).
23. United Nations Office of the High Commissioner of Human Rights. (2022). Complaints about human rights violations. Available at https://www.ohchr.org/en/treaty-bodies/complaints-about-human-rights-violations (Accessed: September 20, 2022).
24. Meerloo, J.A.M. and Meerloo, J. (1956). The rape of the mind: The psychology of thought control, menticide, and brainwashing (Vol. 118). World Publishing Company.

25. Sisson, J. (2010). "A conceptual framework for dealing with the past." Politorbis 50, no. 3 (2010): 11-15.
26. United Nations. (2004). Report of the UN Secretary General on the Rule of Law and Transitional Justice in Conflict and Post-Conflict Societies (S/2004/616), p. 9.
27. UN General Assembly. (2005). Resolution 60/147, 16 December 2005
28. Bassiouni, M. C. (2006). "International Recognition of Victims' Rights". *Human Rights Law Review.* 6 (2): p. 204–5.
29. CJ Judgments. (2006). "(DRC v Rwanda).[2006] ICJ Rep 6"
30. van Boven, T (2006). Freshman; et al. (eds.). 'Victims' Rights to a Remedy and Reparation (PDF). Netherlands: Koninklijke Brill NV. p. 19–40.
31. Commission on Human Rights. (2006). Sixty-second session Item 17. Study on the right to the truth Report of the Office of the United Nations High Commissioner for Human Rights E/CN.4/2006/91 8 February 2006.
32. Human Rights Council. (2007). IMPLEMENTATION OF GENERAL ASSEMBLY RESOLUTION 60/251 OF 15 MARCH 2006 ENTITLED "HUMAN RIGHTS COUNCIL". Right to the truth Report of the Office of the High Commissioner for Human Rights A/HRC/5/7. 7 June 2007.
33. Human Rights Council. (2009).ANNUAL REPORT OF THE UNITED NATIONS HIGH COMMISSIONER FOR HUMAN RIGHTS AND REPORTS OF THE OFFICE OF THE HIGH COMMISSIONER AND THE SECRETARY-GENERAL Right to the truth Report of the Office of the High Commissioner for Human Rights* A/HRC/12/19. 21 August 2009.
34. Commission on Human Rights. (1997). THE ADMINISTRATION OF JUSTICE AND THE HUMAN RIGHTS OF DETAINEES. Question of the impunity of perpetrators of human rights violations (civil and political).Revised final report prepared by Mr. Joinet pursuant to Sub-Commission decision 1996/119. E/CN.4/Sub.2/1997/20/Rev.1. 2 October 1997.
35. Commission on Human Rights. (2005). PROMOTION AND PROTECTION OF HUMAN RIGHTS Impunity `Report of the independent expert to update the Set of principles to combat impunity, Diane Orentlicher* Addendum Updated Set of principles for the protection and promotion of human rights through action to combat impunity E/CN.4/2005/102/Add.1. 8 February 2005.
36. UN General Assembly. (1950). Affirmation of the Principles of International Law recognized by the Charter of the Nürnberg Tribunal, 11 December 1946. Available at: https://legal.un.org/ilc/texts/instruments/english/draft_articles/7_1_1950.pdf (Accessed: October 9, 2022).
37. Trial of the Major War Criminals before the International Military Tribunal, vol. I, Nürnberg 1947, page 222-224.
38. Oster, E. (2022) Let's declare a pandemic amnesty. The Atlantic. Available at: www.theatlantic.com/ideas/archive/2022/10/covid-response-forgiveness/671879/ (Accessed: November 4, 2022).
39. Asch, S. E. (1951). Effects of group pressure upon the modification and distortion of judgment. In H. Guetzkow (ed.) *Groups, leadership and men.* Pittsburgh, PA: Carnegie Press.
40. Asch, S. E. (1956). Studies of independence and conformity: I. A minority of one against a unanimous majority. *Psychological monographs: General and applied, 70(9),* 1-70.
41. Modern Therapy. (2019) Asch Conformity Experiment Explained. July 17, 2019. Experiments Explained. Available at: https://moderntherapy.online/blog-2/asch-conformity-experiment-explained. Accessed on October 31, 2022.

Postscript

1. Martens, J. (2020)."The role of public and private actors and means in implementing the SDGs: reclaiming the public policy space for sustainable development and human rights." In Sustainable Development Goals and Human Rights, pp. 207-220. Springer, Cham, 2020.
2. Vitali S, Glattfelder JB, Battiston S (2011).The network of global corporate control. PLoS ONE 6: p.10.
3. Boys D (2017).The new generation of PPPs in infrastructure – meeting the needs of institutional investors. In: Civil Society Reflection Group on the 2030 Agenda for Sustainable Development (2017), p 93–94
4. World Economic Forum (2010).Everybody's business: strengthening international cooperation in a more interdependent world - report of the global redesign initiative. Geneva. Available at: http://www3.weforum.org/docs/WEF_GRI_EverybodysBusiness_Report_2010.pdf. (Accessed: September 23, 2020).
5. Global Policy. (2021). Global Civil Society Report on the 2030 Agenda and the SDGs. Spotlight on Sustainable Development 2021 Demanding justice beyond rhetoric Time to overcome contradictions and hypocrisy in the COVID-19 crisis. Available at: https://www.globalpolicy.org/sites/default/files/download/_Spotlight_2021_web_gesamt_c.pdf (Accessed: September 23, 2022).
6. Banco E, et al. (2022). How Bill Gates and partners used their clout to control the global Covid response — with little oversight. 14 September 2022. Available at: https://www.politico.com/news/2022/09/14/global-covid-pandemic-response-bill-gates-partners-00053969 (Accessed: September 23, 2022)
7. Suzman, M. (2021). Why we focus on vaccine equity. February 26, 2021. Bill & Melinda Gates Foundation. https://www.gatesfoundation.org/ideas/articles/coronavirus-vaccine-equitable-access
8. Cheney, C. (2021).Gates Foundation reverses course on COVID-19 vaccine patents. May 7, 2021. Available at: https://www.devex.com/news/gates-foundation-reverses-course-on-covid-19-vaccine-patents-99810#.YJUeByidUUw.twitter (Accessed: September 23, 2022).
9. The Expose. (2021). INVESTIGATION – Bill Gates has major shares in both Pfizer & BioNTech, and an FOI has revealed he is the primary funder of the MHRA. Available at: https://expose-news.com/2021/08/20/investigation-bill-gates-has-major-shares-in-both-pfizer-biontech-and-an-foi-has-revealed-he-is-the-primary-funder-of-the-mhra/ (Accessed; September 23, 2022).
10. Speights, K. (2020).4 Coronavirus Vaccine Stocks the Bill & Melinda Gates Foundation Is Betting On. The Motley Fool. September 4, 2020. Available at: https://www.fool.com/investing/2020/09/24/4-coronavirus-vaccine-stocks-the-bill-melinda-gate/ (Accessed: September 22, 2022).

Glossary

1. Kemp, G. ed., (2015). Criminal Law in South Africa. Oxford University Press, Southern Africa.
2. Hutchison, D. and Pretorius, C.J. eds., (2017). The law of contract in South Africa. Oxford University Press Southern Africa.
3. Loubser, M.M., (2012). The law of delict in South Africa. Oxford University Press.

Made in the USA
Monee, IL
15 February 2023

27914526R10277